TABLE OF CONTENTS

Arthur J and the Goldcups, the Masque house band playing a Masque house party. – photo Gaby

FLIPSIDE #54

10 YEARS

This issue of Flipside is a documentary of the the history of Flipside, not a history of Punk Rock. We aren't going to define that... what we're saying is: "Listen to what the bands had to say..." Listen to the local bands throughout 10 years: from the the bands at Masque gigs (a small underground club in the early L.A. scene) to mega shows at Fenders (Long Beach based hall happening today). And listen to all the touring bands that internationally connect this growing rebellious scene phenomenon. But again, you are listening to the bands that we covered in Flipside, and we did cover only a small part of the L.A. music scene. A more complete coverage might include anything from the drunk rock era of the Zero or Frolic Rooms, the New Romantic days at the Veil all the way to the new glam scene happening at a lot of clubs such as the Scream. But like I said this is only what we covered in Flipside. And I think that what we've covered has a common spirit and enthusiasm. What started out being coverage of new music in L.A., eventually took it's own course through a maze of musical styles and attitudes, covering what appealed to us, perhaps overlooking others, but always following the trail of what we thought was the "punk rock" attitude. That attitude has changed to accommodate the times, the name has changed, the music has changed and the participants have changed. But the spirit lives on, and it's funny how that essence runs through just about every one of these interviews.

Not all the bands we have interviewed through the years have been mentioned and we hope no bands feel left out. We tried to cover the popular bands of the time, bands that had something to say, or bands that were the first to say it, bands that have lasted the test of time, or bands that we felt somehow made their place in this scene. Of course being based in L.A., this is all heavily biased towards the L.A. scene. There are bands we never got to interview that were very popular at the time, like The Clash and the Avengers, which make this fanzine an incomplete history, but remember this is only the history of Flipside not the history of the whole punk scene or underground scene. This is a fanzine and we are fans. We never tried to make a scene happen we just tried to capture it, and that is what this issue is.

On the more technical side, I should mention a few things about this issue in itself. First is something about the photographs used. If you look back at any old original copy of Flipside, you will notice that there is a great deal of difference in the quality of the photo reproductions. In no case did we try to reproduce any photos from the printed issues. That just wouldn't work. In a lot of cases we still had the original photos, and they were used. That was fine. However, most of the time we had the original layouts, but the photo halftones had long since yellowed, and were unusable. What it boils down to is, although the text is original (but edited) a lot of the photos are different. In the case of photos that we had negatives for, we often choose to use a different shot from the one originally published, just to throw some variety in for people who have kept up through the years.

This edition covers issues 1 through 50, which is roughly from the summer of 1977 to the summer of 1986. If you've noticed this is issue number 54, since it is the forth issue since the documentation in this edition stops. Those three issues were not included because the material was just too recent to re-publish so quickly, and 1 to 50 is such a nice round figure.

Besides those last 3 issues, other things missing from this issue (because of space limitations) are: Flipside's extensive letters section, where the most trivial topics take on prime time proportions, the massive classifieds ads section, record and tape reviews, as well as publication listings. These of course will continue....

This is the first issue of Flipside to be produced entirely by computer (C-128). The output was printed using an HP Laserjet printer. This alone is probably some kind of epic achievement for us, and what a better issue to bring in a new era with!

This entire issue was put together by:
Hud – Typing and all layouts
Al – Editing, typing and photo reproduction.
Joe – Typing and editing
Joy – Typing and editing
Helen – Painstaking proof reading!
Pooch – Typing

Flipside Fanzine
P.O. Box 363
Whittier, CA 90608
phone – 213-693-6971
   voice – 10am to 12pm
   data – 12am to 10 am

We'll make no predictions for the next ten years, except to say that WE will continue. (Some had their doubts after the long delay it took getting this one out, it almost became the 11 year anniversary!!). The next issues of Flipside will continually change and evolve both visually as well as content wise. We'll continue to branch out into video and tele-communications. We hope you'll stick with us...· [*]

Of course a thank you list is impossible, so thanks to everyone, you know who you are!

Rocking before the Masque, an L.A. music perspective.

By Pooch

Loren, lead singer / guitarist of the Dogs.

Think back. Before the Olympic. Before the Vex. Before the Fleetwood, Cuckoo's Nest, or even the Chinatown wars. Think back. Way back. Before **The Minutemen, 45 Grave, Circle Jerks,** and **Black Flag.** Before Milo went to high school. Before **The Germs.** Though we're all aware of the legendary 1960's L.A. scene, as well as the New Wave (used to be a good term) arrival circa 1977, the area in between, for many, becomes somewhat of a blur. While Disco reared its ugly head, killing any hope of a Reggae movement in this country, and the airwaves were filled with the likes (or dislikes, as the case may be) of **Barry Manilow, Elton John,** and **The Bee Gees,** as far as any real R n' R in this town was concerned it was submerged beneath the "El-Lay Mafia" of **The Eagles, Jackson Browne,** and various ex-members of '60's groups. In short, to paraphrase an old punk band, " What could a poor boy do?"

There were always concerts to see, (everyone played out here sometime), star-gazing at the Rainbow (a ritual still observed by some ex-F.S. staff), hangin' 'round the Sunset "Riot House" (read Pam Des Barre's book or any Zeppelin bio), go to the occasional free concert or "In Concert" taping, read Rock Scene or Circus to catch up on N.Y.'s active scene, buy records, and pick up free copies of Phonograph Record Magazine to keep abreast of R n'R world events.

Bands were forced to wing it alone if they wanted to play originals, and as there weren't many venues to showcase in, most had to play covers and throw in one of their own when the club owner wasn't aware. Several put on their own shows and backyard parties were all over. **Van Halen** did all three, playing Kiss covers at Gazzarri's and at every sleazy party that would have 'em. Oh ya, Dave was the same obnoxious self and Eddie had a heavy rep through the L.A. guitar grapevine. Those guys were everywhere!

About the only club that would accept original local acts was The Starwood and it was usually Heavy Metal (called at that time) that would fill the seats. Bands like **Quiet Riot** (with two Japanese albums on C.B.S.), **Smile, Wolfgang,** (now **Autograph**), **Pegasus, Eulogy** (F.S.'s first interview and featuring **Rusty Anderson,** who's gone on to do sessions with **the Bangles, Peter Case,** etc.), **Snow** (with **Carlos Caveza** on guitar), **Shock** (later turned New Wave with a couple of singles out), and many others drew crowds of party-hearty dudes and flash n' trash groupies, but typically no record deals.

The only bands to ink any sort of deal usually involved **Kim Fowley** in some capacity or another. This Svengali figure, who was later to re-open the Whiskey, which was featuring plays and show acts like **The Tubes, The Cycle Sluts,** and **The Mystic Knights Of The Oingo Boingo** (who went on to change to the more conventional **Oingo Boingo**),and in the process usher in the Punk movement officially, had been involved in virtually every aspect of any L.A. scene. It was only fitting that he used his influence to secure deals for his projects. At the time these included **The Quick** (whose members went on to record in many different situations, **Great Buildings, Three O' Clock, Danny Wilde,** etc.), **Venus And The Razorblades** (who included **Steven T.** and **Dyan Diamond**), **The Hollywood Stars** (legendary, "All The Kids On The Street" is still one of the best tunes released by anyone at the time), and the most well-known of the bunch, **The Runaways.** Until Kim lost control of the band, these girls were headlining arenas in Japan and getting a ton of press; and with good reason, I may add. They paved the way for female bands everywhere and **Joan Jett** has continued to rock with conviction ever since.

Of the bands who weren't Metal/Glam (way before **Poison** and **Faster Pussycat**) or Fowley-ized, perhaps the most influential ones were those associated with the Radio Free Hollywood crowd. This group of artists was integrally centered around a fanzine with a lifespan of two issues but the results are, as they say, history. Though other 'zines had either directly from it (Back Door Man), or independantly of it (Raw Power, Slash, and yes, Flipside), emerged to document the L.A. rock music scene, this newspaper (a freebie, no less) was the first to promote bands playing original material. To get interest in the scene was hard enough, and to find people to distribute a 'zine of this sort was nearly impossible, so for anyone to even attempt a project such as this had to do it clearly as a labor of love. The fact that it was written well and had critics who went on to write for major publications was an added plus.

The groups, themselves, and their ensuing offshoots read like a virtual Who's Who in the local scene. Though to list all the persons involved through the years with the bands would take a Pete Frame family tree, let's just say that **The Pop, The Dogs, The Motels, The Berlin Brats, The Imperial Dogs,** and others have definitely done their share to warrant a place securely in the annals of rock music history. The then-fledging Rhino Records released a compilation entitled "Saturday Night Pogo" which, if you can find a copy, is a good document of this scene-within-a-scene.

Radio airplay for local acts ...slim and none. KROQ on a.m. and f.m. was your best bet, and it figures that **Rodney's** show (started in '76) would be broadcast on this then progressive station. By the way, **Rodney** was writing for the previously mentioned Phonograph Record Magazine, which was edited by future Bomp founder **Greg Shaw,** and Rodney's English Disco deserves an article all to itself as it was a major place to be, and be seen.

Not many record stores would acknowledge, much less sell, independent records (even Zeds and Middle Earth were catering to the "Progressive" market) so not a lot of indies were released. However, some bands did release material on their own and if you can find records like **The Pop's** "Down On The Boulevard" e.p., or **The Nerves'** (a supergroup that consisted of future stars **Peter Case,** songwriter **Jack Lee,** and **Paul Collins** of **The Beat** , and were the first L.A. band to tour across country and Canada without a major deal) version of the future Blondie hit "Hangin' On The Telephone" then you've not only acquired some rare records, but a few good tunes to boot.

In conclusion, let me say that yes, there was a "scene" before the openings of The Masque and The Whiskey, and the people involved deserve a ton of credit for persisting in their belief in an often overlooked era of local R n'R history. I realize I have overlooked several bands (**The Ratz,** with **Nicky "Beat" Alexander** and **Doug "The Knack" Felger,** speaking of Doug, I can't leave out **The Sunset Bombers,** or **Zolar-X,**or well, you get the idea) and various other "scenesters" who are far too many to mention. To those I apologize and I hope they'll understand. When **The Pop** sang the question "Hey, do you recall the day...?,those people who bridged the 70's gap in the L.A. rock scene can look back and say "Ya, we knew it was happening. Even then. Think back... Pooch

Radio Free Hollywood. Early street rock tabloid.

FLIPSIDE NUMBER 1

"I am the anti-christ, I am an anarchist,
don't know what I want, but I know how to get it,
I wanna destroy the passerby,
Cause I wanna be anarchy"
"Anarchy In The U.K." - Sex Pistols

ISSUE: 1
DATE: August 28, 1977
FORMAT: 8 1/2x7" Xerox
PAGES: 20
PRICE: $.25
PRESS RUN 100
STAFF: Al, Lash, Tory, Pooch, X-8

- -

This first issue, put together over the summer of 1977, was inspired by boredom, and an underground music scene that was yet to explode. All five of us were veteran concert goers and club hoppers who had nothing else better to do while waiting for a good show to come up (in those days it could be weeks!). The shows that did happen were filled with a unique bunch of people-probably the biggest concentration of talent ever to be assembled as an audience: everybody had something to offer the scene. Most people were in bands, if not they did magazines, records, owned stores, did artwork etc... It was a scene that begged to be contributed to, and ripe with contributors. We had seen fanzines from England (Sniffin' Glue, Ripped and Torn) that covered their local underground, and were determined to do the same service to our scene which, at the time, lacked a real punk directed publication. (Slash not having it's first issue out at Flipsides inception, but did beat us to the presses!).All of us were friends, and somehow connected with the local music scene. X-8 and Tory were in Low Budget, who made their Hollywood debut playing over the Dils at the Whisky, Larry Lash was in a weird Quick sort of band, Pooch was in a progressive (!) band, and I was their friend, couldn't play anything, but still wanted to be involved.

So anyway, X-8 being editor of the Whittier High School newspaper, kinda led us into publication. Months went by, a lot of good ideas were exchanged, but we didn't get a lot of "copy" onto paper. The hardest thing about starting is probably actually starting. It was like, who does what, and if I do will we really publish this thing. So as a sort of last resort, "let's just do something, ANYTHING!" we

interviewed a local glam/rock band named Eulogy. Then since we couldn't figure out who got to review what record, we decided to just play the record, and then tape record our comments like an interview and that would be the review. This method worked well, in just one beer guzzling, festive session we got the record reviews done.(Reproduced here for your reading pleasure!) The next day we repeated the event and knocked out our editorial. Pooch (being the budding english major), wrote out a few concert reviews of his own, X-8 the artist designed the logo... So we dragged our typewriter to Rick's In and Out Burger, typed up all this stuff, added the local gossip, and Flipside Fanzine #1 was born.

This year had been very eventfull for the L.A. punk rock scene, a lot of bands formed that were to last for many years and a lot of people made connections that would shape the course of music history. From Plunger Pit parties to hanging out at the Starwood, you met the same people and reinforced bonds. It's amazing to think back and remember seeing DEVO open for the Weirdos, the Damned at the Starwood, Blondie at a deserted Whisky, the entire "punk scene" (with Bobby Pyn dressed in safety pins!) at what was then a big new wave gig (with the Pop, Quiet Riot, and Backstage Pass!!), or the infamous Kim Fowley Presents New Wave at

the Whisky, where the call was put out for every "new wave" band (it was not a bad connotation back then) from San Francisco to San Diego to come and play. In three nights everything from pop, to punk, metal to "hardcore" took the stage, and it all flew as "new wave". No one slammed, no one even pogoed. But you could tell that there was a punk element there. Slowly but surely this group seperated itself from the new wave music masses and emerged its own beast- the Germs, Weirdos, Dils, Zeros, Screamers, Deatbeats, Alleycats and a very few others made up the first wave. They were indeed different from the Quick, Zippers, Pop, Quiet Riot, Van Halen, Motels, Shock type of bands who opted for the more traditional rock and roll approach to the scene. In the punk scene

there was no rock star attitude, no boring old long hair, no managers, no salesmen. And also there were no record labels, no fanzines and no place to play. Right about this time the Masque opened up, and the whole punk scene came into focus. This new meeting place became the center for punk related activities and accelerated the development of the whole movement.

This was the time when the first Flipside came out, we found our niche as well, writing and reviewing became so much easier. But that's the next chapter.

- -

Konsert Reviews Issue number one

THE QUICK

August 23: Whisky: by POOCH
Both of the Quick's sets were very well paced with the emphasis on new material rather than familiar tunes from the much over looked Mondo Deco album. Garnishing 2 well-deserved encores after the second set, Steve Hufsteter & Co. treated the small but enthusiastic crowd to a rousing version of Little Honda & a very undisco like Motown medley. If you haven't caught these guys yet there's still hope, but hurry, they won't be

Early Flipside staff: Pooch (with Iggy), Larry Lash (with beer), Tory, and X-8 trying to escape. - Photo by Al

playing the Whisky for long. Saving the best for last, I'll say they're far better than most opening acts and should be head liners soon. Guitarists take note theirs is one of the better axe men I've seen in awhile.

DEVO / THE PITS

August 24: Starwood: by POOCH
What's with all this Devo-mania all of a sudden, are these guys even liked in Cleveland? Sure, their music is possibly the best synthesis of progressive and punk styles that I'll ever hear, but are they believable? Their factory worker appearance mixed with their bizarre lyrics and music, I can only describe as an aloof riddle. To quote Flip-side's own X-8: They seem the type of band

that goes home and spurts over the things they do. Are they not men? I can only tell you to catch them out and decide for yourself.

The Pits opened the show but what can I say about a band who consciously rips off the Bonzos, except they look like they're having fun and they do a good version of Little red Book.

"Boogie Boy", DEVO singer at the Starwood. These spuds transplanted from Ohio to become stars of the early L.A. scene playing with the likes of the Germs and Weirdos. - photo by Al

ALBUM REVIEWS

The Clash- (CBS Records) Side B: Career Opportunities, Cheat, Protex Blue, Police and Thieves, 48 hrs, Garageland; Side A: Janie Jones, Remote Control, I'm so Bored with the U.S.A., White Riot, What's My Name, Deny, London's Burning.

TORY: I like, I think it's got something to say.
AL: It's got nursery rhyme lyrics ... great!
TORY: Lymeric type, Career Opport- well, that's true- the one that never knocks, 60% of those jobs-sobs, lazy sods are unemployed.
SAM: I think it's a great cut.
TORY: Musically and lyrically

(I'm so Bored with the U.S.A)
X-8: A chanting song.
AL: Yeah, i sing it everyday.
POOCH: It's like running thru a mine field, and exploding battlefield with a transistor radio.
TORY: It's the one I'd sing off the Album ... that, and I'm so Bored with the U.S.A. ...
AL: It's a good single, the single is different but just as good with added sirens.
X-8: It's hard to believe that Paul Simonon can pull off those bass riffs when in December he had notes painted on his bass peck.
TORY: Yes, this is true.
AL: He was just learning bass?
TORY: Yes.
AL: The guy's hot.

(Deny)
X-8: Great song, it should be dedicated to HOLLYWOOD.
TORY: Not as energetic as the other songs.
POOCH: It's all right.
AL: Mediocre.

(London's Burning)
X-8: Good punk rocker.
AL: That's punk!!!
POOCH: The sarcasticness in their songs just blows me away!
AL: Nursery rhyme lyrics.

THE JAM "In The City" Polydor Records- Side B- In the City, Sounds From the Streets, Non-Stop Dancing, Time For Truth, Takin' My Love, Bricks and Mortar. Side A- Art School, I've Changed My address, Slow Down, I Got By In Time, Away From the Numbers, The Batman Theme.

(In The City)
TORY: I think it's a really good cut ... I think it's got, you know, it's my fave so far off the album, it's punk music, they have something to say, but I think for what they have to say and for the style of music they're playing it's kind of a little Clash, I mean, if they got something to say or scream about, they're not screaming, they're kicking back and saying it, so they must not really want to scream about it, say the Pistols would go out and scream about it, God save the Queen and go all balls out on it, these seem a little too laid back for what they have to say. You might say they're the Eagles of Punk Rock.
X-8: They're good at what they do.
POOCH: In The City sums up what they have to say on the whole album, you can listen to this cut and know what the album is about.
Lash: I got a good way to put it they're the Eagles of Punk Rock.
TORY: That's a fresh new phrase, LASH, seriously, uh, they could be harder for what they do.

THE GERMS (What Records?) Germs live/ Forming

X-8: It captures the feeling of a true live Germs concert- people whistleing, girls screaming, glass breaking.
POOCH: Just a garage band concert.
AL: I don't know .. uh ... I surely won't play it often.
POOCH: I thought it was a cheap way to get a flip side to a record.
POOCH: The germs are real punks.
AL: The only real punks.
POOCH: The only real punks in LA are Bobby Pyn and Joan Jett.
TORY: I appreciate them for being such assholes and admitting it.

(Forming)
TORY: I think this little, lousey, shitty piece of vinyl, has got to be the best thing Bomp has ever stocked in the singles section. I mean, it's the last name in raunchy. As far as singles go. I mean, it's so shitty. It's mastered lousy

Germs in their garage - Photo by Al

AL: Keep on pogoin' Bobby!
X-8: Really.

Debbie Harry (Blondie) one New York band that spent a lot of time playing every place they could in L.A. - photo by Al

Dogs bassist Mary, one of L.A.'s earliest cross-over bands, they fit right in playing at rock and roll shows or at the Masque as pictured here. - photo by Al

FLIPSIDE NUMBER 2

"I want toy tin soldiers that can push and shove
I want gunboy rovers that'll wreck this club
I'll build you up and level your heads
We'll run it my way cold men and politics dead
I'm a lexicon devil, with a battered brain,
I'm looking for the future, the world is my aim
So gimmie gimmie your hands, gimmie gimmie you mind
Gimmie gimmie this, gimmie gimmie that....
I'll get silver guns to drip old blood
Let's give this established joke a shove
We're gonna reek havoc on this rancid mill
I'm searchin' for something even if I'm killed
Empty out your pockets, you don't need their change
I'm giving you the power to rearrange
Together well run to the highest prop
Tear them down and let them drop away"
"Lexicon Devil" - Germs

ISSUE #: 2
DATE: Oct. 1977
FORMAT: Shitty offset, 7x8 1/2"
PAGES: 20
PRICE: $.25
PRESS RUN 200
STAFF: Al, Lash, Tory, Pooch, X-8
- -
Well the second issue came easy, and we moved 'up' to offset printing. The pictures came out shitty and the solid blacks all fell apart. So we were learning. Like the first issue, X-8 created the cover, and used a silkscreen by his mentor Andy Warhol. Format wise, this issue was a lot like the first- record reviews in interview style. This issues live reviews were mostly from the Masque and Whiskey, and contained interviews with the Weasels and Germs. (Both included here in edited form).

By now the punk scene is in full swing. Good punk gigs at the Whiskey and Masque every weekend make for really exciting times. Lots of new bands come out of nowhere (X, Dickies, Skulls, Controllers, Bags, Plugz, etc.) to take advantage to the new places to play. Lots of new friendships are forming, connections are being made and things are looking good.

Flipside gets it's first mail!! A letter from Rodney Bigenheimer! Along with our first record to review, Rodney's very own debut vinyl "Let's Make The Scene". Distribiution is up. Not only are we selling at gigs like the first

issue, but Zed Records took 5 copies. (This was par for other great L.A. stores: Poobas, Rhino, Moby, Lovells, Bomp Store...). But we sold most of our copies at the Licorice Pizza on the Sunset Strip. This store was an institution! Their parking lot was punk rock playground! Whenever you went to L.A. you had to check for new zines and new singles in their bins. Idealy situated across the street from the Whiskey, this was the place to go, why they closed I'll never know.

THE GERMS are: Bobby (Darby Crash) Pyn on lead vocals and writer, Pat (Rick Tragic) Smear on lead guitar, Lorna (Terry Target) Doom on bass, and Cliff Hanger on drums. Bobby met Pat while cutting acid in 7th grade. Pat turned Bobby onto Bowie and they have been friends since. After graduating (?), they decided to focus their destructive forces elsewhere. They met Lorna, who just escaped from suburbia, in a hotel, and picked up Donna Rhia on drums. At this time, they recorded their single. Since then, Donna got a mutual Get the fuck out! and they acquired Rodney's discovery, Cliff Hanger.

FLIPSIDE: How has your single been doing?
PAT: 500,000 I think.
BOBBY: Right, we almost sold 1,000, gotten great reviews though.
PAT: They did play it on the radio in Kentucky, Tennessee and...some other place...New Jersey, Yeah!
X-8: How many copies of the single did you print?
PAT: 3,000.
BOBBY: They messed up the first 1,000. we're pissed!
PAT: Yeah, the back says, This record causes ear cancer. We're gonna shoot him in the alley; never got around to that.
AL: Wasn't that your idea?
Bobby and PAT: FUCK NO!!! What do you think we are?
X-8: Gonna release another single?
BOBBY: Yeah, soon as we sign with RCA and throw Cliff out.
AL: Why don't you throw stuff on the audience anymore? We heard you were banned for it.
PAT: We're interested if they'll like us without it. The Weirdos finally talked the Whiskey into letting us play there. Everytime I go to the Starwood, they beat me up.
BOBBY: The Starwood used to book us every week...and cancel us.
AL: How many gigs have you played now?
Lorna: Six.
X-8: Now for a stupid question. What's your philosophy of life?
BOBBY: Kill it. Na,- we're all devout Signtologists...
PAT: We got a psycho on our hands.
X-8: How do you like the Masque?
BOBBY: Oh, it's very dirty. Too bad they don't pay us to play there. It was a benefit so that guy could live. Next time, we're gonna do a benefit for us, to pay our rent.
AL: What do you think about people scratching you, like at the Masque?
BOBBY: I really like it. It shows me people like us.
PAT: The only reason people come to see us is to get hurt. Oh, what about that jerk.
BOBBY: Oh, that guy in the back room. I go, Haven't you ever been to a punk concert before. He goes, Listen, I was into this before

Bobby Pyn (Darby Crash) rips his skin open with a broken cocktail glass. - photo by Al

you were born. Right, What a jerk!

BOBBY: At the Whiskey, the last ten minutes, I was sitting there and this girl was banging a gun on the side of my head. Did I walk off the stage?

X-8: You crawled off.

BOBBY: Did they really rip your shirt off?

Lorna: Yes, it was so embarrassing. I wasn't even wearing underwear.

BOBBY: I was going to rip my shirt off during the second song, and then somebody almost strangled me with it. I didn't get a chance to do it.

X-8: Do you like Godzilla?

BOBBY: Fuck no. I could never figure out if they were supposed to be funny or what. They were stabbing American colonialists. It's propaganda. Sell it to the Dils. The Dils were auditioning their drummer here, and they were telling him, You gotta stop acting like a college kid. You have to wear straight legs. And, did they tell him to be a communist? We're David Bowie's favorite band... I gave him this letter saying, Look, we're starting this band called the Germs and we're gonna be your favorite band, and he believed me. We put him on all our guest lists if he's in the country or not. We don't know if he's seen us-- probably not. I like the old gentlemen.

Market: He's rather old.

BOBBY: He's not, Iggy is older.

PAT: And Iggy is a fucking bastard. He used to be a friend out ours.

BOBBY: Last time we saw him, he acted like he didn't know us. Now he lives in Topanga with three faggots. We went to IPS, the school they threw us out of for having our own religion. We convinced about half our school that I was God and Pat was Jesus. This one girl almost had a nervous breakdown 'cause I sat there for like half and hour telling her I was God. She started screaming and there were all these bibles in the class and she started throwing them at us. She didn't come back for a week. They used to hassle me for having green hair. He'd walk around with ice cream in his coat without the wrapper.

X-8: Who sprayed Germs on that sign?

PAT: That was a cigarette ad.

BOBBY: 'Cause we cause cancer. We feel Germs cause everything. You know what's fun. You take ten hits of acid and drink a six pack of beer and go down to the Santa Monica pier. There's a bridge that goes to nowhere 'cause they're supposed to lower it for boats and you go out to the end and jump off. You can swim and it's so great 'cause it's dark. It doesn't matter if you live or die just swim and you can feel the fish nibbling at your feet...

(Bobby Pyn changed his name to Darby Crash, and died of drug complications a few years later. Lorna lives with Gary (Joan Jett and the Black Hearts) in New York, Pat Smear lives and plays in many L.A. bands, current is Ruthensmear, Cliff Hanger is lost.)

Mike Brophy - photo by Al

THE WEASELS

Interviewed Saturday Night Sept. 3 1977
Upstage at the Whisky
"We think 'Sheena Is A Punk Rocker' is the best single out right now."

Mike Brophy - lead vocals
Greg Durchlag - guitar
Richard Sakal - bass
Jim Connolly - drums

The Weasels started in Culver City in 1973 and have been off and on, mostly off. Picking up Jim on drums they started what is now the current Weasel line-up and have been on since December 1976. All the band had ever played was parties around the Venice Beach area until last July '77 when the played Kim Fowley Presents New Wave at the Whisky July 5th and 6th. Then they were called back to play the Whisky opening for the Zippers - and now a six show headlining engagement. They (the Ramones) inspired us to start playing again, because we heard them and said; Wow, look at these guys, look what they're doing, kinda what we're doing, we weren't copying, we were doing it a long time before.

FS: What do you guys call your music?

Weasels: Murder rock. Don't ever call us punks, we can play, plus we can fight better than them too. What's new wave anyway, surf music? New wave is new groups replacing the old groups.

FS: You guys sound a lot like new wave?

Weasels: It depends on your definition, we don't mind that definition, it's the punk shit which we're not - we'd rather be called - THRASHERS!

FS: Where do you get your ideas for songs?

Weasels: (Mike Brophy answers, he writes most of the songs). That's the way I am on the street... if you look it it by songs.. say "All Jacked Up" because we all get jacked up- be at a party we see Mike laying in the corner he's all jacked up. Or Beat Her With A Rake - the chick did him wrong and he took revenge to the nth power. We write all these songs just from our experiences, you know. A lot of people accuse us of being Hippies, you know you'd better think twice about Charles Manson, your hair's too long-- fuck you, I'll show you what's long... We have a song called Concrete Man, that's where we're at...

Germs: Bobby Pyn, Cliff Hanger and Lorna Doom in that infamous West L.A. garage where the first L.A. punk record was recorded. - photo by Al

IF THE IDEA OF TRASHING THIS PLACE HAS CROSSED YOUR MIND, GO SOMEWHERE ELSE THIS IS THE LAST VENUE FOR THIS MUSIC AND WE

Steve Samioff, Slash Magazine founder.

make way for progress, fuck the trees, we like concrete, fuck Oregon, we ain't no hippies, don't like rain or Big Sur!

FS: When you get into violence, do you ever hurt anyone on stage?

Mike: He (Richard) is nervous as hell when I swing that rake, tonight I had to watch. I had a metal one. I usually use this plastic one and the teeth break and fly all over– I had this iron one and I broke and iron tooth off that fucker last night–– nothing stands in my way.....

Weasels: Here's what we do at parties, and still do. People pass out, most people go poor guy, let him sleep, we go up with pentels, shoe polish—we paint him up, we shaved off this one guys eyebrow - so he shaved the other one off – he looked like the man who fell to earth. One time we painted him (Mike) all black, from head to toe with shoe polish, Al fuckin' Jolsen man, four days to get that shit off.......

FLIPSIDE NUMBER 3

"Up pop the boils of terminal cancer
Cells start to fall apart
We pray to a God who never will answer
Could this be art?
I draw a line for logic to walk on,
I think I'm pretty smart
But God has an old beret and smock on
Could this be art?"–Mumps

ISSUE #: 3
DATE: Nov. 1977
FORMAT: Xerox, 7x8 1/2"
PAGES: 20
PRICE: $.25
PRESS RUN 100
STAFF: Al, Lash, Tory, Pooch, X-8

- -

This issue was different than anything else we had done, why we did it I don't know. Each one of us designed an arty page: The cover was a photo of a blown up head by shotgun blast (quite similar to a recent Big Black record cover!), Dean Dead contributed his 'Art Toilet' of phony letters, Al contributed photos and flyers, Larry Lash has Donny and Marie humping each other, swasticas and a Santa Claus among other things, Pooch wrote poetry over a picture of a black guy picking his nose and X-8 wrote a story of self abuse pasted on a of a vet bill. We also got an extra 100 flyers from the Masque and put one in each zine. A very limited quantity went out to stores, some sold at the Masque the rest to subscribers (yes, we were getting a few – "Terry" being the first).

FLIPSIDE NUMBER 4

"Your mom laid an egg
where your dad had to jizz...
But you don't know who you are
And you don't know what this is...
You're the product of a fuck
and your mom and dad are too
It was really only luck
When it came to having you...
Why do you exist???

There's no one to tell ya, 'Cuz nobody knows
Who you are, and why you wear those clothes
Why do you exist????"
"Why Do You Exist" –Weirdos

ISSUE #: 4
DATE: Nov. 1977
FORMAT: Offset, 7x8 1/2"
PAGES: 20
PRICE: $.25
PRESS RUN: 300
STAFF: Al, Dean Ded, Larry lash, Pooch, X-8

- -

Typical Flipside- interview style reviews (a lot of them), interviews with Zippers and Weirdo Dave Trout (Bug Management wouldn't give us the whole band, it seems the Weirdos were becoming quite the hot item for interviews, so they were farming out members one at a time!). We lost Tory to art school and picked up local scenester Dean (now we have a typist!!)

The punk scene is starting to get national media attention, and things like "The Punk Rock And Fashion Show" are happeing in all the big cities. Yuck!

- -

THE PUNK ROCK FASHION SHOW

The Palladium must be cursed, everything held here turns to shit, look at the 'rock' awards and remember the 'death of glitter' (BDM) gig, it was here, and now this: Punk

Punk Rock & Fashion Show collage.

Rock and Fashion Show.
Devo, Weirdos, Biondie, Avengers Friday
Nov. 23 1977
Thanks to- California Productions

It was bound to happen, with so much media coverage of 'punk' fashion; Time, Newsweek, New West etc... well the punk fashion show was held at the Palladium, you all know the story...

Do we really need this, I mean punks very own existence was due to the fact that it was essentially an underground movement, kids could really relate to it because it was theirs and theirs alone and they made it what they wanted. Even denying that your band was a punk band was a revolt against establishing a stereotype to recognize the movement. Now how does a 'freedom of expression against commercialism' movement (shock chic) last when someone comes in to standardize it? Punk is not only safety pins and tears. And that Farrah Fawcet chic up there saying this is for you, punk is supposed to be fun, shit, has she ever seen a punk band before? Why was she dictating 'our' fashion show? ($) I wonder who the asshole was that choose the music to play between bands? Weirdos and Genesis don't mix. So there people created an event for the punks, remember destroy, punks, we can create our own events. I don't even want to remember that punk magician, isn't that the shit that destroyed radio and TV. Do we really need this? $Uncle punk thinks so$$

And then the bands played. Well Devo has done many better shows the past month at the **Starwood,** they didn't use their film or trash bags, in fact they got a little boring. "Jocko Homo" live still had that great science fiction feeling. The Weirdos were great, but they were so much better at the Slash benefit.

And pogoing, remember when pogo was to the music. Don't get me wrong, I like a good violent pogo, but there is a difference between pogo and football and at least one punk got fed up and said: This ain't pogo this is shit. People would stand there unaware of the music, just waiting for a chance to snuff out some person trying to pogo. I mean pogo isn't getting whiplashed between songs or during Look Good In Blue.

Biondie, oh Debbie you Fox, what happened to Gary? He was half the show. Blondie was kinda dry, even Sex Offender didn't have that pazaz it had months ago. Their new songs sound pretty good, but a lot of heavy metal.

The Avengers, now these guys and girl mad a lot of noise.

All in all these bands were better other times, I hope I never see another punk fashion show. How's this for a reporter type of statement; California Productions is trying to ride the new wave with an old capitalist board, anyway, I'll bet they made a lot of money charging $7.50 a punk. Oh yeah, the Avengers were the surprise band, I guess the Class couldn't swallow that much pride.

DAVE TROUT

Interviewed 9-22-77 at Dress Review in Hollywood. Dave is the Weirdo who plays bass, sings some back up vocals, and carries the Weirdos equipment in his station wagon. There's so much shit that the industry's produced. Just listen to the radio and it all sounds pretty much the same. For me and the guys in the band, it's more of a revolt against all this boring shit. Even with all the stuff that's out, the radio still does the same thing.

There's nothing fresh--nothing new. All the industry does is take a lot of money and make something real slick--over and over again. It's like they put it in a blender and whipped it up. No matter what they pull out, it all looks and sounds the same.

--- --- --- --- --- --- --- --- --- --- ---

FLIPSIDE: Are you a founder of the band?
DAVE TROUT: John, Cliff, and I, yeah.
FLIPSIDE: How long ago?
DAVE TROUT: About a year.

Dave Trout reads Flipside - photo by Al

FLIPSIDE: How many times have you played before the Orpheum?
DAVE TROUT: We did a S.I.R. thing. The Orpheum gigs were our 3rd or 4th. In fact, we did two weekends at the Orpheum without

Weirdos at the Masque - photo by Gaby

Nickey. The 3rd weekend we got Nickey.

FLIPSIDE: You played without a drummer.

DAVE TROUT: Just guitars. It worked, we had a nice solid guitar sound.

FLIPSIDE: Do you do the same songs?

DAVE TROUT: We only had about eight songs then, but we still do them.

FLIPSIDE: What makes you stick with this music, even though it's not commercially accessible?

DAVE TROUT: Oh, 'cause we like it. We don't even care if it gets commercially accepted.

FLIPSIDE: Can you see punk in general getting more commercial?

DAVE TROUT: I don't know. More commercial people are picking up on it.

FLIPSIDE: Do you think the Paladium thing, the fashion show, is going too far?

DAVE TROUT: The people that are putting it on are obviously doing it for the money.

FLIPSIDE: Do you think the industry will make you guys commercial?

DAVE TROUT: There are limitations to what we'll do. I'm sure they'd try to fuck us up. We wouldn't sign on a label unless they let us do our thing. We have to have enough control. A lot of people sign on a label and they have an album come out and the industry handles the whole thing. A lot of people work on an album and they don't know what the fuckin' music's about.

FLIPSIDE: Do you think you carry your dress to an extent that's unrealistic?

DAVE TROUT: The whole thing gets so unrealistic that it becomes real--we draw the line. Some people would rather hint at things or just be evasive. We like to be direct. Things aren't a little shitty, they are shit. We, like to come right out and say things.

FLIPSIDE: We heard you went to art school.

DAVE TROUT: Yeah, Cliff and I met there.

FLIPSIDE: Is the band influenced by that?

DAVE TROUT: Not our music so much, but a lot of times we do our ads, posters and stuff.

FLIPSIDE: What did you do at Cal Arts?

DAVE TROUT: Not much, got loaded. They gave us money to go to school, so we went. We'd go on field trips and stuff.

FLIPSIDE: Do you see your clothes as sort of an art movement?

DAVE TROUT: I'll let someone else answer.

FLIPSIDE: Are you gonna do anything special for the Paladium, like Nickey dyeing his hair?

DAVE TROUT: Well, Nickey Dyed his hair black three weeks ago. I don't think there's anything special. We're going to do what we usually do.

FLIPSIDE: Do you do something different every gig?

DAVE TROUT: Yeah, a lot of that stuff is made up ten minutes before we go on. we just got bags of shit back stage. There's a whole ritual we go through.

FLIPSIDE: Do you ever wear safety pins?

DAVE TROUT: No, Dix had a trick. He'd slip a bobby pin through his cheek like...it's an English thing.

FLIPSIDE: Yeah, kids in England hold them in their teeth so it looks like it's through the cheek--for pictures.

DAVE TROUT: They ought to use nails or railroad spikes if they really want to get into it. How about some guy with an ax stuck in his head. That would be real nice.

FLIPSIDE: Have your parents seen you?

DAVE TROUT: Not live; only photographs.

FLIPSIDE: What do they say?

DAVE TROUT: I dunno..., I guess they like us.

(Dave Trout lives with his wife and kids in the Valley. Nickey Beat is in L.A. Guns (with a major record deal), Cliff and John reform the Weirdos occasionally, and Dix plays guitar in Thelonious Monster.)

DRINKS

Cocktails	$1.75
Exotic Drinks	$2.25
Beer: Budweiser	$1.50
Lowenbrau	$1.75

WINES
Rose' Chablis Burgundy

By the Glass	$1.75
Half Carafe	$4.50
Full Carafe	$7.50

CHAMPAGNE

Dom Perignon	$50.00
Piper Heidsieck	$30.00
Sebastiani (California)	$20.00

SOFT DRINKS
All Soft Drinks $1.00

RODNEY BINGENHEIMER'S FAVORITE ..... TAB
RODNEY BINGENHEIMER II ..... ICED TEA
On the rocks, as Rodney would have it.
DANNY GOLDBERG SPECIAL CLUB SODA & LIME
The executive look for teetotalers
A & R EXECUTIVE SPECIAL ..... MILK
Straight or on the rocks a la Allan Rinde
EDMUNDS/LOWE A GO GO ..... GINGER ALE
On the rocks, great for anyone on the wagon.
THE ALICE BAG ..... PINEAPPLE JUICE
On the rocks, with a wedge of lime. A real tart
TOMATA DU PLENTY ..... TOMATO JUICE
On the rocks with a dash of Worcestershire.
SPAZZ ATTACK ..... GRAPEFRUIT JUICE
On the rocks with a cherry.
MABUHAY GARDENS SPECIAL ..... ORANGE JUICE
On the rocks, suitable for tossing at Dirk Dirksen
THE LOBOTOMY ..... GINGER & GRENADINE
Very Pleasant on the rocks, formerly the Shirley Temple.
CHERRY CHERIE ..... CHERRY COLA
A dash of grenadine with a splash of cola and a cherry on top.
THE GENERATION X ..... 7 UP
The Uncola for Your Generation
THE JOAN JETT TAKE-OFF ..... COCA-COLA
A Runaway best seller.

All prices include sales tax.
See reverse side

Whisky a Go Go
8901 Sunset Boulevard Los Angeles, California 90069

DINNERS

VAN HALEN
10 oz. grilled Delmonico steak (as you like it), salad, and french fries $3.75

ELVIS COSTELLO ATTRACTION PLATE
Fish and Chips, Three battered Icelandic fish fillets, french fries, lemon, tartar sauce $3.50

SANDWICHES

PHAST PHREDDIE BURGER
Hamburger and french fries $1.50

CHEAP TRICK-BUN E. BURGER
Cheeseburger and french fries $1.75

DICKIES-CHUCK WAGON BURGER
Cheeseburger with bacon and french fries $2.00

KIM FOWLEY'S FAVORITE
Bacon, lettuce and tomato $1.50

RAMONES DOG
Hot dog and french fries $1.00

MINK DE VILLE AT CONEY ISLAND DOG
Hot dog with mustard and sauerkraut, french fries $1.25

WEIRDOS NORMAL SANDWICH
Grilled cheese with french fries.
Even Nicky Beat can afford this one $1.00

SNACKS

KICKBOY FACE
French Fries $1.00

MUMPS COCKTAIL
Fresh fruit salad $2.00

BLACK RANDY AFRO DELITE
Mixed nuts and chips in a bowl $2.00

RUNAWAYS TOSSED GREEN A GO GO
Large green salad with lettuce, tomato and choice of dressing $1.50

All prices include sales tax.
See reverse side

Whisky a Go Go
8901 Sunset Boulevard Los Angeles, California 90069

FLIPSIDE NUMBER 5

"No one tells you nothing
Even when they think you know
But they tell you what you should be
They don't like to see you grow
Do anything you wanna do"
"Do Anything You Wanna Do" – The Rods

ISSUE #: 5
DATE: December 1977
FORMAT: 7x8 1/2", offset
PAGES: 20
PRICE: $.25
PRESS RUN: 300
STAFF: Al, Dean Ded, Larry Lash, Pooch, X-8

- -

We are doing better than ever with this issue, and with the discovery of xerox reducing machines (they were really rare in those days) we have been able to cram so much more into this issue! We also discover rub on lettering! This 'ish has three long interviews (Rodney, Backstage Pass, Spastics), and more record reviews than ever. We are also covering a lot more live reviews, have a regular letters section, a staff photographer Pete (Beat Lano) and regular cartoon contributors. The Masque, Whiskey and Starwood are in full swing and there are tons of shows to go to. Out of town bands like the Mumps and the Deadboys play the Starwood, so do the Dickies that now legendary night when Leonard broke his leg and landed that band a major recording contract.

Pooch and Rodney – photo Larry Lash

EXCLUSIVE INTERVIEW WITH
RODNEY!

We did this interview at Rodney's place. He lives in a small, cluttered Hollywood apartment with pictures plastered all over the walls of every rock personality you could imagine. The bathroom wall is covered with lots of nude chicks ages 13-26 (a real fun place to go). There are magazines and records piled in every room. I took a sixpac for me and two Tabs for Rodney. Harvey Kubernick from Melody Maker was there for awhile.

FLIPSIDE ...Pooch): Tell us about your background... Lash) Tell us about Chocolate

An entirely new crop

The Future is here

Avengers at he Masque – photo Al

Watchband.
RODNEY: I played with them one week. We were from Mountain View. They played the San Jose Fair and I played with them at that.
FLIPSIDE: Have you ever done any drugs at all?
RODNEY: No, not at all.
FLIPSIDE: What got you into Rock 'N' Roll?
RODNEY: I guess the Beach Boys, Chad and Jeremy, Sonny and Cher, people like that.
FLIPSIDE: How'd you get into New Wave? No other DJ knows what it is and you're playing it.
RODNEY: I've always been into it. I played Iggy and the New York Dolls at my club. They called it Glitter back then. I think that was the original Punk. When I did my first show in August, my first guests were the Ramones and the Sex Pistols.
FLIPSIDE: How do you get the guests on your show?
RODNEY: They're just friends of mine. I just say, Drop by, Come on Down. The whole show's done at the last minute anyway.
Harvey: I've seen times where at 6:30, he says who's gonna be on that show, and Kiss drops by, the Ramones, or Blondie calls from New Jersey, or Patti Smith from a hospital bed. It's good; it's a spontaneous show.
FLIPSIDE: How old are you?
RODNEY: Nobody knows. (singing) Secrets in the night...I'm not as old as everyone thinks I am. A lot of people think I'm older which I am not.
FLIPSIDE: How'd you come down here to meet all the people?
RODNEY: I ran away from home and got busted for curfew. I met Phil Spector. I lived with Sonny and Cher. Then I just started meeting people.
FLIPSIDE: Tell us about the English Disco?
RODNEY: Back then, a disco was a club with a DJ who played records. Not a place for negro music. It was Rock 'N' Roll. The only thing black about it was the color of the 45's. Shaun Cassidy played there. He opened for Iggy Pop, the Imperial Dogs, and the New York Dolls.
FLIPSIDE: What acts did you help break here?
RODNEY: Blondie, the Ramones, Sex Pistols, Cheap Trick, and David Bowie. I was his

publicist when he was on Mercury. I used to take him to Orange County radio stations.
FLIPSIDE: Has anyone you helped done you wrong like the Dils?
RODNEY: Yeah, I promoted them. They used to send tapes to the station. I listened and liked them. I got them booked at the Whiskey, and I wrote them up in Phonograph. They just didn't appreciate it.
FLIPSIDE: What do you think of the future of Punk Rock?
RODNEY: It will last for a while. Eventually, I think it will evolve into Power Pop. Punk is such a limited tag.
FLIPSIDE: How would you compare our scene to others?
RODNEY: I went to San Francisco last week planning on staying two or three days. I ended up spending the night and coming back to L.A. The only thing San Francisco has is good radio and a few bands. It's all happening down here. The kids are all here, the suburbs are here.
FLIPSIDE: What got you kicked off the radio?
RODNEY: Fuck and Shit. Also, I squeezed in a lot of free commercials. That's against the law.
FLIPSIDE: What were you like in high school?
RODNEY: I was weird. Teachers used to kick me out of school. I had long hair. I didn't look like everybody else.
FLIPSIDE: What other hobbies do you have?
RODNEY: Girls.
FLIPSIDE: What's your favorite age?
RODNEY: I like any age as long as they're firm and upright. As long as they're not sagging. That could be any age range.
FLIPSIDE: Have you done it Doggy Style?
RODNEY: Every style imaginable. I like Doggy Style.
FLIPSIDE: You were in Paint Your Wagon, weren't you?
RODNEY: Yeah, I was an extra running around like a beheaded chicken.
FLIPSIDE: Any particular period in Rock that you really got into?
RODNEY: I really like now, the '73-'74 era, and the early '60's. The worst time was when it died, like '68 to about '70-'71.
FLIPSIDE: What's your favorite hangout?
RODNEY: Denny's, the Whiskey, the Starwood, and the Masque. I don't get out of

RODNEY ON THE ROQ CHARTS

Below is a compilation of edited (top 10, not 20) Rodney on the Roq requests charts. These represent requests taken by Rodney Bigenheimer on his Saturday and Sunday night show on radio station KROQ in L.A. Rodney has had his show since 1976 and we feel that Rodney represents an unique cross section of the underground music scenes in L.A. By looking at the requests you can easily tell when different genres of music were hip. Punk, Rock A Billy, Ska, Pop, HC, it's all there. Rodney's chart may not represent all of the music that the Flipside staff listen too, but it is an indication of what is popular at any one time. Rodney's show continues to be popular and one of the only VERY large commercial radio station shows open to any kind of music. Here's to another 10 years of Rodney!

◆ FLIPSIDE #13
1. Yes L.A. Comp. LP
2. Any Siouxsie & The Banshees
3. Rotters "Sit On My Face Stevie Nicks"
4. Bags "We Don't Need The English"
5. Public Image Ltd. LP
6. Boomtown Rats "Rat Trap"
7. Any Ramones
8. Any Buzzcocks
9. X "Los Angeles"
10. Normal "TVOD"/"Warm Leatherette"

FLIPSIDE #14
1. "Rock and Roll Swindle" LP
2. Levi & The Rockats "Notes From The South"
3. Yes L.A. Comp. LP
4. Simpletones "California"
5. Buzzcocks "Everybody's Happy"
6. Pretenders "Stop Your Sobbing"
7. Bony M "Rasputin"
8. Any Motels
9. Any Clash
10. Rotters "Whales Buy Jap Goods"

FLIPSIDE #15
1. Any X
2. Levi & The Rockats "Room to Rock"
3. X Ray Spex "Highly Inflamable"
4. Simpletones "California"
5. Ramones "R&R High School"
6. Joan Jett "You Don't Own Me"
7. Any Gogos
8. Any Human Hands
9. Flyboys "Crayon World"
10. Any Germs

FLIPSIDE #16
1. Any Acetates
2. Any Buzzcocks
3. Any X
4. Dickies "Banana Splits"
5. Crowd "Modern Machine"
6. Pearl Harbor & The Explosions "Driving"
7. X "Johnny Hit and Run Pauline"
8. "Tooth and Nail" comp LP
9. PiL Live bootleg
10. Any Germs

FLIPSIDE #17
1. Germs "GI"
2. X "Johnny Hit and Run Pauline"
3. Selector "On My Radio"
4. Specials "Specials" LP
5. Madness "The Prince"
6. Suburban Lawns "Gidget Goes To Hell"
7. Gears "Don't Be Afraid To Pogo"
8. Black Flag "Nervous Breakdown"
9. Rodney "Little GTO"
10. Phil Seymour "Can't Hurry Love"

FLIPSIDE #18
1. Christeen "Is That All There Is"
2. Germs "My Tunnel"
3. Stupid Babys "Baby Blues and Babysitters"
4. The Klan "Cover Girls"
5. Red Cross "Siren" LP cuts
6. Suburban Lawns "Gidget Goes To Hell"
7. Any Plugz
8. Black Flag "Nervous Breakdown"
9. Angelic Upstarts "Out of Control"
10. Any X

FLIPSIDE #19
1. D-Day "Too Young To Date"
2. Germs "My Tunnel"
3. GoGos "We Got The Beat"
4. Any X
5. Eddie & The Subtitles "American Society"
6. Dead Kennedys "Holiday In Cambodia"
7. Dickies "Gigantor"
8. Wall Of Voodoo "Invisible Man"
9. Adan and The Ants "Car Trouble"
10. Any Cockney Rejects

FLIPSIDE #20
1. Dead Kennedys "Holiday In Cambodia"
2. D-Day "Too Young To Date"
3. Any X
4. Black Flag "Nervous Breakdown"
5. Eddie and the Subtitles "American Society"
6. ROTR Comp LP
7. DOA LP
8. China White "Dangerzone"
9. The Gears "Rockin At Ground Zero"
10. Any Gogos

FLIPSIDE #22
1. Circle Jerks "Group Sex"
2. ROTR Comp LP
3. Black Flag "Jealous Again"
4. Adolescents "Amoeba"
5. Germs "My Tunnel"
6. Adam & The Ants "Dirk Wears White Socks"
7. Black Flag "Nervous Breakdown"
8. Chiefs "Blues"
9. Jam "Sound Effects"
10. Mel Brooks "Springtime For Hitler"

FLIPSIDE #23
1. Adam & The Ants "Fallout"
2. Any Germs
3. Circle Jerks "Group Sex"
4. Black Flag "Jealous Again"
5. Gogos "Lust For Love"
6. Ventures "Surfin' and Spying"
7. Adolescents "Amoeba"
8. China White "Dangerzone"
9. Jam "Sound Effects"
10. Any early Ventures

FLIPSIDE #24
1. Any TSOL
2. Adolescents LP
3. Black Flag (tape w/ Keith Morris)
4. Ventures "Surfin' and Spying"
5. Venus & Unit 3 "I Don't Like Beer"
6. UXA "Immunity"
7. Any Exploited
8. Cramps "Goo Goo Muck"
9. Circle Jerks "Group Sex"
10. Girls at Our Best "Go For The Gold"

FLIPSIDE #25
1. 45 Grave "Black Cross"
2. Black Flag "Six Pack"
3. SOA "No Policy" EP
4. Wasted Youth demo tape
5. Bad Religion EP
6. TSOL "Dance With Me"
7. Modettes "Tonight"
8. Blue Cats "Teenage Party"
9. Venus & Unit 3 "I Don't Like Beer"
10. Girls At Our Best "Go For The Gold"

FLIPSIDE #27
1. Wasted Youth "Reagans In"
2. Social Distortion "Playpen"
3. Twisted Roots "Mommy's Always Busy In The Kitchen"
4. TSOL "Dance With Me"
5. Black Flag "Louie Louie"
6. Any Siouxsie
7. Any Cramps
8. Wigs "Stiff Me"
9. Red Rockers "Guns and Revolution"
10. 45 Grave "Black Cross"

FLIPSIDE #29
1. Black Flag "TV Party"
2. Any 45 Grave
3. Wasted Youth "Reagans In"
4. Salvation Army "Mind Garden"
5. "Hell Comes To Your House" Comp
6. Any Bad Religion
7. "Public Service" Comp LP
8. "Let Em Eat Jellybeans" Comp LP
9. Professionals LP
10. Any Agent Orange

FLIPSIDE #30
1. Black Flag "TV Party"
2. Agent Orange "Living in Darkness"
3. 45 Grave "Evil/Black Cross"
4. Abrassive Wheels "Vicious Circle"
5. Christian Death "Theatre of Pain"
6. Toni Basil "Mickey"
7. Levi & The Rockats "I Get So Excited"
8. Punkenstein "No School"
9. Salvation Army "Mind Gardens"
10. "Hell Comes To Your House" Comp

FLIPSIDE #31
1. Toni Basil "Mickey"
2. Black Flag "TV Party"
3. Tuff Muffin "Beach Rebellion"
4. Social Distortion "Under My Thumb"
5. Dream Syndicate "When You Smile"
6. Salvation Army LP
7. Bad Religion "How Could Hell Be Any Worse"
8. Gail Welch "Day Of Age"
9. Any old TSOL
10. Any 45 Grave

FLIPSIDE #32
1. Mr. Epp & The Calculations "Mohawk Man"
2. Any Jam
3. CH3 "I Got A Gun"
4. Untouchables "Dance Beat"
5. CH3 "You Make Me Feel Cheap"
6. The Jetz "Point Of View" EP
7. Toni Basil "Mickey"
8. Red Cross "Born Innocent"
9. Youth Gone Mad "Okie Dogs"
10. Agent Orange "Pipeline"

FLIPSIDE #34
1. Inflatable Boy Clams "My Skeleton"
2. CH3 "Fear of Life"
3. Bangs "Getting Out Of Hand"
4. Stray Cats "Stray Cat Strut"
5. Agent Orange "Pipeline"
6. No Crisis "She's Into The Scene"
7. Tuff Muffin "Beach Rebellion"
8. Mr. Epp and the Calculations "Mohawk Man"
9. MDC "John Wayne Was A Nazi"
10. Dead Kennedys "Bleed For Me"

FLIPSIDE #36
1. Vandals "Urban Struggle"
2. Untouchables "Dance Beat"
3. Urban Guerillas "Asylum" tape
4. Inflatable Boy Clams "I'm Sorry"
5. The Cards "Maybe Tomorrow"
6. Any Rudimentary Peni
7. The Hated ep
8. Musical Youth "Pass The Dutchie"
9. The Last "Up In The Air"
10. The Castaways "Dream Market"

FLIPSIDE #37
1. Angel & The Reruns "Buffy Come Back"
2. Vandals "Urban Struggle"
3. Dead Kennedys "Terminal Preppie"
4. Unit 3 & Venus "Pajama Party"
5. The Adicts "Sound of Music"
6. Madness "Our House"
7. Tutu Band "Sex World"
8. The Polecats "Make A Circuit"
9. 3 O'Clock "Baroque Hoedown"
10. Electric Peace "Kill For Your Love"

FLIPSIDE #38
1. Angel and the Reruns "Buffy Come Back"
2. Donnie Barren "I Love My Cats Meow"
3. 3 O'Clock "Sorry" / "I Feel A Whole Lot Better"
4. Nina Hagen "Born in 666"
5. GBH "Catch 23"
6. A-Heads "Dying Man"
7. Bangles "I Want You"
8. Venus & Unit 3 "Pajama Party"
9. Circle Jerks "Jerks On 45"
10. Tracie "House The Jack Built"

FLIPSIDE #39
1. Suicidal Tendencies "Institutionalized"
2. PiL "This Is Not A Love Song"
3. Nena "99 Red Balloons"
4. Decry "Falling"
5. DI "Richard Hung Himself"
6. Aggression "Body Count"
7. GBH "Catch 23"
8. James Bond and thre Undercover Men "Spy Movies"
9. Any Cathedral of Tears
10. Yard Trauma "Some People"

FLIPSIDE #40
1. Youth Brigade "Cure"
2. Social Distortion "Mommys Little Monster"
3. Any Suicidal Tendencies
4. Circle One LP
5. Black Outs "No More"
6. Hari Kari "The Blade"
7. Marsupials "Don't Gibe Up"
8. Veril Sin "Lina"
9. Truth "Beat Generation"
10. Peter and the Testtube Babies "Jinx"

FLIPSIDE #41
1. Suicidal Tendencies "I Won't Fall In Love Again Today"
2. GBH "Forbidden Zone"
3. 3 O'Clock "Jet Fighter"
4. Any Youth Brigade
5. Stukas Over Bedrock "Life Like Yogi"
6. Smiths "What Difference"
7. Marsupials "Going All The Way"
8. Any Seeds
9. Long Ryders "10650"
10. Pandoras "It's About Time"

FLIPSIDE #42
1. Calamites LP
2. Pandoras "It's About Time"
3. Dolly Mixture "Spend Your Wishes"
4. Any Monkees
5. Sandy Shaw & The Smiths "Hand In Glove"
6. Hoodoo Gurus "Let's All Turn On"
7. Abrassive Wheels "19"
8. Clay Allison "Fell From The Sun"
9. Blood On The Saddle EP
10. Any Seeds

FLIPSIDE #43
1. Pandoras "It's About Time"
2. Husker Du "Whatever"
3. Plan 9 "I Like Girls"
4. Bangles "Tell Me"
5. LuLu "Shout"
6. Gun Club "Love Story"
7. Social Distortion "Mommy's Little Monster"
8. Youth Brigade "Where Are We Going?"
9. Salem 66 "7 Steps Down"
10. Red Guy "Within 4 Walls"

FLIPSIDE #44
1. Paula's Pandoras "You Don't Satisfy"
2. Black Flag "Slip It In"
3. Redd Kross "Blow A Kiss..."
4. Revolver "You Don't Know"
5. Minutemen "History Lesson"
6. Jasmin Minx "30 Second Set Up"
7. Grim "Saigon"
8. Vandals "Mohawk Town"
9. Echo & The Bunnymen "Angels and Devils"
10. Lear Black "Guilty"

FLIPSIDE #45
1. Strawberry Switchblade "Since Yesterday"
2. Husker Du "New Day Rising" LP
3. Paula's Pandoras "You Don't Satisfy"
4. Things "Girls In The World"
5. Any early Sex Pistols
6. Revolver "The Girl I Want"
7. Milkshakes "Green Hornet"
8. Del Monas "Peter Gun Locomotion"
9. Jet Set "Party Line"
10. On The Air "Even Try"

FLIPSIDE #46
1. Camper Van Betthoven "Take The Skinheads Bowling"
2. Suicidal Tendencies "The Boys Are Back"
3. Minor Threat "Salad Days"
4. Pharoes Kings "Platos Cave"
5. Seeds "Flower Lady"
6. Lepers "Psychedelic Boy"
7. Makin Time "I Know What You're Thinking"
8. Doggy Style "Nymphomaniac"
9. 3 O'Clock "Taking Pictures"
10. Adult Net "Insense & Peppermint"

FLIPSIDE #48
1. Jesus and the Mary Chain "Psycho Candy" LP
2. Pandoras LP
3. Flesh For Lulu "Golden Handshake Girl"
4. Any Monkees
5. Dramarama "Anything Anything"
6. Any Seeds
7. Plastic Cloud "Shadows of Your Mind"
8. Childrens Day "Message To Pretty"
9. Tell Tale Hearts EP
10. Morlocks LP

FLIPSIDE #49
1. Dramarama "Anything Anything"
2. Monkees "Gonna Buy Me A Dog"
3. Fuzzbox "Rules & Regulations"
4. Belinda "I Need A Disguise"
5. Biff Bang Pow "Love Goes Out Of Fashion"
6. Cramps "Get Off The Road"
7. Cannabels "To Much To Dream"
8. Any Gene Loves Jezebel
9. TSOL "Revenge"
10. Any Flesh For Lulu

FLIPSIDE #50
1. Mr. T Experience "Danny Partridge"
2. Shower Scene From Psycho "She"
3. Monkkees "99 Pounds"
4. Dramarama "Scenario"
5. Ramones "Somebody Put Something In My Drink"
6. Monkees "Then & Now" CD
7. Jesus & The Mary Chain "Some Candy Talking"
8. Sonic Youth "Bubble Gum"
9. Del Mones "Dr. Goldfoot"
10. Ghost Dance "Heart Full of Soul"

Hollywood much.

FLIPSIDE: Any bad rumors you want to end?
RODNEY: (yelling) I'M NOT 45!!! I'm not 4'11. I don't just go out with 12 year old girls. I go out with all ages, beautiful girls. I'm not gay like the callers say on my show. My disco was not a gay hang out. I'm not rich!
FLIPSIDE: Have you ever had any threats on your life?
RODNEY: I've had more threats on my life than Charles Manson ever dreamed of; more than the President. I get bombs, guns, and knives. I can't go to a show without getting at least ten threats.
FLIPSIDE: How come?
RODNEY: I don't know. If they don't like my show, they could watch the Hardy Boys. They're on at the same time.
FLIPSIDE: Say something to the people who want to kill you.
RODNEY: You gotta wait your turn. It's a long line.
FLIPSIDE: What do you think of the Germs?
RODNEY: I like their sound. That's the sound everybody else is looking for, the garage sound. Their record is very well produced. I really like it.

Philomena and Kickboy (Slash), Mad Dog, Mark, Dinky hanging out at Club 88. photo by Al

FLIPSIDE: What do you thing of Parliament, the black Alice Cooper band.
RODNEY: I couldn't get into their groupies.
FLIPSIDE: What's your favorite radio station?
RODNEY: Ummmm...well, KROQ.

FLIPSIDE NUMBER 6

Black man gotta lotta problems
But they don't mind throwing a brick
White people go to school
Where they teach you how to be thick
And everybodys doing
Just what they're told to
An nobody wants to go to jail
White riot, I wanna riot, White riot, a riot of my own
All the power is in the hands
Of the people rich enough to buy it

While we walk the streets
To chicken to even try it
Are you taking over, or are you taking orders?
Are you walking backwards, or are you walking forwards?
"White Riot" – The Clash

ISSUE #: 6
DATE: January 1978
FORMAT: 7x8 1/2
PAGES: 20
PRICE: $.25
PRESS RUN: 400
STAFF: Al, Dean Ded, Larry Lash, X-8, Pooch

Continuing along the lines of last issue, the print gets smaller and we cram even more into this one, our biggest issue yet. Three interviews, all with reduced type. Along with staff photographer Pete, a local girl Gaby also starts to contribute photos, so we are moving up in that field as well. Tons of record reviews, live reviews and local news (with Trudie Plunger contributing the hot gossip). Bags and Germs go to S.F., Nuns come to L.A....and the big news: the Masque is closed by the Fire Marshall! Bummer. A benefit is planned to try to raise enough money to make renovations to bring it up to code. In somewhat lesser local importance, the Sex Pistols break up in San Francisco.

Zeros photo by Al

MESSAGE FROM THE UNDERWORLD....

Early gossip pages

THE SKULLS INTERVIEW--TAKE THREE AT THE MASQUE (3RD FLOOR)--1/10/78

FLIPSIDE: Do you really like this kind of beer?
MORBID: It's the only stuff we drink. It's blunt, real blunt.
GUN: You're not beating around the bush with this. It's actually got alcohol in it.
BONES: Two cans and you're gone.
FLIPSIDE: Do you think L.A. punk is blossoming right not or is it full bloom?
BONES: It's still a seed.
GREY: As far as the vast majority of suburban kids are concerned, it's still a seed. It hasn't reached Orange County or the far reaches of L.A. Punks now are city punks. It hasn't reached suburbia.
FLIPSIDE: What would be the ultimate TV show?
GREY: The SKULLS done as The Monkeys show was...perhaps a bit more real.
GUN: Yeah, we'd drink beer and actually fuck women. You'd see me get parking tickets and get into real fights. I'd have dirty socks on...
MORBID: A bunch of violence and stuff like that.
BONES: We'd be wanted by the F.B.I. Effrim Zimbilist Jr. would be trying to find where the hell we were staying...Running out on our dinner tabs at exclusive restaurants like McDonalds.
FLIPSIDE: Now you do Velvet Underground songs.
BONES: Songs?, one song.
FLIPSIDE: Is it different from the other SKULLS songs?
GREY: Yah, it sounds a bit different from the usual SKULLS. A bit slower.
BONES: No. We have our own sound. If we were on the radio, you could go, Hey, there's The SKULLS. It's his guitar sound and his drumbeat too...
FLIPSIDE: What's your favorite lyrics?
BONES: No planned destiny for the bullets of the sniper.
GREY: Wrap that crowbar around your head 'cause the only good baby is one that's dead.
FLIPSIDE: Do you have jobs?
BONES: Yeah, at Supply Sergeants just below the lights.
FLIPSIDE: You sell terrorist masks?
BONES: Yeah, I sell a lot of guns. That's my specialty, guns, 'cause I don't know a lot about them.

FLIPSIDE: What's a Sten Gun?
GUN: It's a machine gun made for the paratroopers. It's small compared to the ones the Americans had; very compact, but has a very powerful punch. That's why they call me Sten Gun.
FLIPSIDE: Who gave you your conehead haircut?
MORBID: I don't know. It was a mistake. I woke up and there it was. I am a real conehead.
GUN: It's obvious we don't dress up to look like anyone, nobody here does. The fashion show is over. We all have a voice in what we play. This is our sound. We haven't borrowed it. People can't compare us to the Ramones 'cause we're 500 times faster...You don't have to drop a thousand tabs of acid to see us play; you don't have to be drugged out to get into it.
BONES: MORBID's got his own star on Hollywood Blvd.
MORBID: It's right next to Red Skull-ton; it's homemade.
FLIPSIDE: What's Kill Me about?
BONES: It's about somebody that's bored, like the lyrics go...
GUN: Not necessarily with a gun or a knife, just the aspect of boredom. The T.V. set can

kill you if you get into the belief that everybody brushes their teeth once and has four meals a day.
BONES: Victim is a warning. A new song, We Gotta Run the City, is how young kids gotta take over all the old cronies.
GUN: Kids are really smart now 'cause they're not relying on this fucking poetry that was written years ago. They're not being influenced by alcoholic poets or something like that. The music of today is really down to earth.

Bags Johnny and Alice. photo by Al

BAGS

Alice (Douche Bag) : lead vocals, front person, and energy
Pat (Trash Bag) : Bass, sex symbol
Rickey (Gag Bag) : drums, solid back beat
Johnny (Doggie Bag): guitar, sex symbol
Craig (Biz Bag): Rhythum guitar, pseudo intellectual.
Craig's personal history: Craig used to play with a certain female singer in a band called the Cars. The Cars broke up and he

Skulls at the Masque: L to R – Chas, Billy, Marc, and Sten Gun – photo by Al

played in a band with Johnny and Rickey called the Invaders. Then, they broke up just before the Slash benefit. He also played in Mutards with Trash Bag and Dennis, but Dennis couldn't play drums anymore. So, he got the Bags back together.

Alice came from an all girl band called Fem Fatale, but only played in their garage. Then, the first Bags with Trash Bag, Janet, Gaza, etc. And, now the Bags!

FLIPSIDE: Who influences your music?
ALICE: Current events, Time magazine, everything. We read the newspaper. We're that type of band.
FLIPSIDE: You read the headlines because it's in bold print.
CRAIG: We get half our songs from the headlines, like Amy Carter wanting a chainsaw 'cause she wanted to see how it worked.
ALICE: Poseur's about Cherie Currie.
CRAIG: No. It's about everything. T.V. Killer's about the guy who died because he watched too much Kojak.
PAT: Bag Bondage is about...
Johnny: It means something different to everybody.
FLIPSIDE: Do you think L.A. is copying England?
Johnny: I think England is total suck of L.A. It was all created here with Jim Morrison. America's what it's all about in punk music.
CRAIG: How can we copy England? We don't see any English bands or any English people. We don't even know what they look like... I met Margo Hemmingway.
PAT: Whooppeee
CRAIG: I licked her **rosy red rectum.**
ALICE: He used to write prono books.
PAT: Yeah, he actually did. Watch, recite some of it...
CRAIG: He shoved his atomic love tool into her quivering quim.
FLIPSIDE: Didn't the Germs say that?
CRAIG: Actually, we're the Germs in disquise. We hate the Germs, we love them...Bobby is a lyrical penis, no...Johnny: He's a lyrical genius...Let's mention our new songs.
FLIPSIDE: Let me guess, We got the Neutron Bomb.

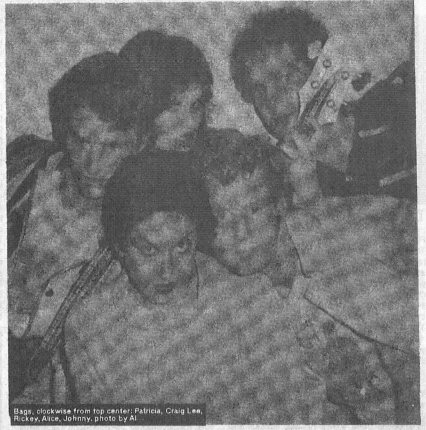

Bags, clockwise from top center: Patricia, Craig Lee, Rickey, Alice, Johnny. photo by Al

Johnny: No, it's called What Generation.
Nickey Beat: Are you guys valid?
ALICE: Yeah, 'cause we say we are. We're as pretentious as the Weirdos.
PAT: We're serious, very serious.
FLIPSIDE: What do you think of L.A. clique, the L.A. fishbowl?
CRAIG: I'm drowning in it. I thought everybody was dedicated when I got into the movement. Now I find they're all flakes...
FLIPSIDE: Tell us about Cal Arts.
CRAIG: Cal Arts is a total joke, even if every punk band came from there.
ALICE: I don't care where they come from. Everybody has different backgrounds, a different way of expressing things. If you're more educated, you're able to express your feelings better. The thing is what's felt, is important; not how educated you are or how well you play. But, if you can play better, it does help. You can't say that if the Germs played better, they'd be better 'cause they've got the feeling...
FLIPSIDE: Is their punk rock in L.A.? Or is it something different?
PAT: There are hardcore bands.
FLIPSIDE: Are the Weirdos punk rock?
Nickey: It's new music. It has nothing to do with old rock. We're plastic rock.
CRAIG: Cataloging a group is destructive. You have to live up to rigid codes, and I think we're all beyond that.
FLIPSIDE: Glad you said that. Now, would you fuck a seven foot frog?
CRAIG: Listen, my frog at home is gonna be pissed when I tell him.
FLIPSIDE: Why are you called Trash Bag? Did your mother name you that?
PAT: Yeah, she used to stop me at the door and wouldn't let me out without a bag.

FLIPSIDE: What about your bags?
RICKEY: The ones we're gonna wear next time.
CRAIG: We'll wear them when it's not important. Bags a good name 'cause it's a common denominator. It's an everyday object and it has a million different meanings.
FLIPSIDE: Patricia, is it true Fowley wanted you in the Runaways?
PAT: Yes, but he said I was too much of a lady. So, I couldn't be in it.
ALICE: He told me I was the ugliest girl in the world.

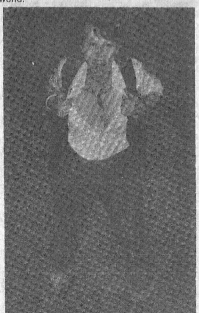

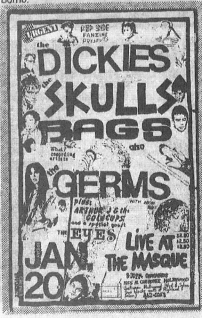

Danny Benair – photo Pete Landswick

THE QUICK

FLIPSIDE: Tell us about your new record.
The Quick: The thing being played on the radio is our fan club single. We made it available to members only 'cause we didn't want to put out an independent label (Frontier's first release).
FLIPSIDE: I noticed that you guys are changing your style.
The Quick: Yeah. The first album is neat for that type of material. Unfortunately, you can't sell records that way. We've been slowly, but surely, moving on. A lot of people said the first album sounded like Sparks. We've been trying to live that down. We're moving now to what we've always wanted. We wanted Danny Wilde to play guitar. He's a good guitarist. He used to be in a Bowie band where he was Bowie and Mich Ronson both. It's a waste not to have him play.
FLIPSIDE: How come you didn't get a lot of promotion on your first album?
The Quick: 'Cause Mercury stinks! They'll sign about fifty acts and throw the records out into the market. If one happens to click, they'll back it. Even when they do, they don't know how to do it right. A record company doesn't want to hold onto you unless you're selling a certain amount of records. You gotta move up and be a feasible thing to do that whole mass marketing. You have to think of yourself as a product. That means getting a top 40 single here and there. I'm not compromising. I'm not letting the record companies dictate what our thing should be. But, I'm now trying to use that as a form to work in.
FLIPSIDE: How do you think the L.A. scene has progressed in the last year and a half?
The Quick: There is no scene. I sit around and watch all these boring bands and it's really sad. You're in the limelight for a week and then you're nothing. I wish L.A. was better.
FLIPSIDE: What is your ideal scene?
The Quick: England. If there were other bands like Gereration X and the Pistols over here, it might mean something. We have to settle for the Dils, who are trying to be the Clash, and about forty other bands, who are trying to be Squeez or Penetration or something even lower. Oklahoma's got a better scene than we do.
FLIPSIDE: How come Danny threw a glass at the Zeros the other night?It was a war. The first day of our sound check we put some ads up. The Zeros childishly put their ads over ours. They said, There, and mimicked us and gave bullshit. They gave Danny's girlfriend some crap and he was fed up with it.

He's small, but pretty cocky. He'll punch someone and take a chance. He doesn't care.
FLIPSIDE: We've talked to Danny. He's pretty nice if you are.
The Quick: Yeah, It was just a stupid war. In six months time the Zeros will be wishing they had some place to play. They're followers of a scene; not leaders.
The Quick: About three or four years ago I started teaching some kid (Stan Lee) who sold drugs, how to play guitar. I don't know why. He was just a mess. I taught him to play in a robot-type fashion. He could play rock and would jam with a guy who eventually became the lead singer in Quiet Riot. I've also been involved with this friend of mine, Leonard Phillips. He's a really brilliant kid, really funny, incredible keyboard player. I tried to do stuff with him, but he's really unstable. He'd have nervous breakdowns and stuff. He wouldn't show up for rehearsals, so we couldn't work anything out. Stan Lee wanted to put together a band and do a tape. He was gonna spend some of his dope profits to do it. I told, him that he didn't have enough brains to make it in the real rock era. It's just too competitive. Finally, I talked him and Leonard into doing this thing. It wasn't long before they got a show together. Now the Dickies are the hottest local band that's happening at the moment.
The Quick: Some people have a dog to kick around. Those that don't; the only dog they can kick is the Quick. That's what they're doing right now. Obviously, the Quick meant a lot to these people at one time. That's why it's so easy to be hostile. It's a shame. But, we will get through it and so will they. We still have the same drummer, bass, guitar and keyboard player. They still have the same voices. It's not Zombie or Sparks b-sides that our inspiration is coming from. I'm not listening to that now. It's Elvis Presley, Eddie Cochran, and Bobby Fuller. It doesn't come out like that though. I don't know, we've got this Sparks mentality. It's still got a lot of Quick sound. Anyway, if were gonna get our show on the road next week, we gotta get out to rehearsh today...

FLIPSIDE NUMBER 7

"We are the leaders of tomorrow
We are the ones who have no fun, We want control we want the power
We're not gonna stop until it comes

We are not Jesus Christ
We are not fascist pigs
We are not capitalist industrialists
We are not communist
We are the one"
"We Are The One"– Avengers

ISSUE #: 7
DATE: March 1978
FORMAT: 8 1/2x11" Offset
PAGES: 16
PRICE: $.50
PRESS RUN: 400
STAFF: Al, Dean Ded, Larry Lash, Pooch, X-8
- -

In a historic move Flipside changes format and price. We change to standard magazine size, reduce the number of pages and raise the price to 50 cents. Like usual, this issue is crammed with photos, reviews, interviews with Zeros and F-Word and an article Gaby wrote while her, Terry Bag Dad, Mary Rat and Helen Killer chased the Sex Pistols around the country. We also print our first fanzine list. The Masque benefit happened (two nights at the Elks Lodge with every L.A. punk playing)– and from now on Brendan is to be plagued with the old "Where's the benefit money?".

Sid Vicious – photo by Gaby

The Sex Pistols Meet The "L.A. Hippies"

The Sex Pistols are backstage– Their Dallas concert is over– The rednecks have all gone home–
Now is the time for the backstage party, but the only party going on is in my car? Sid Vicious has decided to come out and drink with us, but his security is afraid he'll run off. Seems he has a habit of running away and not showing up for gigs, they certainly won't want to loose him in Dallas. (where?).
Almost all of the gin is gone, looking at Sid, Lamarr and Helen, you see where it all went. They are laying in the back of the car, roadies run around like decapitated chickens threatening to arrest us 'less we give them back their precious sack of bones. But Sid refuses to leave. Finally a security tells us where the group is staying. The entire floor of the Ramada Inn!!! We try to convince the now incoherent Pistol to continue the party at the

hotel. So he's getting cold anyways, but then Noel, his body guard (a real fucking bastard) pulls him out of the car. Sid trys to stand up but instead spins around and falls. Noel just lets him fall and Sid crashes to the floor- his skull contacting damp steamy Texas parking lot. Lamarr helps him to his feet and he leaves with Helen for the graflitti covered bus (how'd that happen???). Then Dad, Mary Lamarr and myself follow in our car to the sterility of the Ramada Inn. Strange looks from the bellhops- been so long since I've slept... fuck. The signal is given at Sids door. But oh shit, Noel opens it... He hates us so much right away for no reason he starts picking on Lamarr. She leaves to talk to Johnny Rotten. So Noel starts punching at Dad, hasseling everyone, he won't let us see Sid Vicious. But Dad is really cool, he stares the wimp down. Mary and I get bored and leave, but before we do, Mary sees an ice machine. With a maddened glint in her eye she picks up a whole bucket of ice and slams it at Noel. It melts all over the hallway. Noel the wimp, with his eyes bugging like old strobe lights at a Van Halen concert (last

Paul Cook - photo by Gaby

Steve Jones meets Paula - photo by Cindy

Sid poses for Gabys lens - photo by Gaby

Johnny Rotten in his new suit, dodges beer cans thrown by the rednecks in Texas - photo by Gaby

month they were hippies) comes roaring at us. An elevator swallows Mary and I turn a corner where a tall blonde man opens a door, which I run into. There laying on the bed, is the very symbol of our life - Johnny Rotten. In the flesh. The entire entourage is there in fact. Johnny, Malcolm McLaren, Bob Gruen (a photographer), Rory Johnston (a publisist) and some friendly guy nobody knew. Malcolm says come along to dinner. Everyone's leading up to the top floor to get something to eat. Mary is spit out of the elevator and joins us. But the Starlight lounge is closed. So the crowd sinks down to the carport, where a limo is waiting... well actually an old yellow beaverwood steal-a-car. Bob Gruen who drove got really lost. He didn't have his drivers license but he played it cool. Jumping out of the car, Bob walked over and asked "How do you get to the Fairmont Hotel the fastest? I've got a whole car load of hungary journalists?" (Would you tell a redneck cop you had a carload of hungary Sex Pistols). The rain on that seamy Texas night had slowed to a steady drizzle, kinda like a Swiss American hotel shower fixture when it's turned off. Johnny Rotten was really mad when we finally got to the Fairmont but his anger turned to pleasure when he say the luxurious surroundings we were in. When the menus came, there was so much delicacies it was hard to choose. John settled it by ordering the onion soup (his favorite) crab legs, and steamed crab. Since he couldn't decide between the Lowenbrau and the Heiniken... he had both. Johnny took one look at the crab legs though, and pushed it away. He finally took a little nibble but denounced it as being frozen crap. The creamed crab with chives on avocado AND on salad was really good, but after playing with the cherry tomatoes John decided he couldn't be bothered with the food anymore. In Texas your lemons come wrapped in stuff to keep the seeds off your fish... Well Mary thought it might be a present so I started unwrapping it. Johnny comes on like a big know it all and laughs saying "where have you been". I'll bet Johnny never saw one either.
Talk turned to the tour once again. A single is getting released "Belsens A Gas" but you KNEW that, and Johnny was really excited about it. Possibly from the San Francisco

doesn't start treating Johnny with more respect it won't happen. Nothing will. Johnny is a smart man who knows what's in store for him if he gets along. But problems exist. Johnny has to fly second class, while Malcolm flies first. Johnny's the star... he's why Malcolm has his job still. But Johnny's getting off on his position. While Malcolm supplies his clothes, Johnny says "Sure, but I have the good sense to put them together". When he's done wearing the clothes he throws them away. Tells Malcolm he needs a new suit. Okay what color. Johnny looks at Malcolms red scarf and says "Any color but red, I hate red"!!!" The waiters glare at us. We get the message and leave. The dinner cost $150 dollars. First the men try to stick Warner Brothers with the tab. Then Johnny almost has to pay. They know he has money cause during dinner he pulled it out of his pockets, straightened it out and started counting it. Everyone laughed and called him tacky but he didn't care. Tricky doors, Johnny, Rory, Mary and I spend 15 minutes trying to find a door to the street level. Miles and miles of corridors. Finally out to find Bob Gruen has left us stranded. A taxi takes us home, and back to Johnny's room. Since the top dogs have left, we spend the rest of the morning talking, then Johnny promises to put us on the guest list for the Winterland date and party and we leave him till whenever...Johnny claimed during an argument that he started the whole punk movement. Radical, huh? But off stage he's kind and gentle and aware of who he is and how to USE IT.
– Gabriela

Steve Jones and Larry Lash at the Masque - photo by Gaby

Johnny and Steve live in San Francisco

Robert, Hector and Javier – photo by Al

THE ZEROS

ELKS LODGE--FEBRUARY 25, 1978
Hector Penalosa--Bass, vocals
Javier Escovedo--Lead guitar, vocals
Robert Lopez --guitar, vocals
Baba Chenelle --Drums

The Zeros have been one of the first bands in the Los Angeles area to be called new wave this and that etc... The Zeros have been called everything from lowriders to closet surfers. Their first gig in L.A. was at the infamous Orpheum with the Weirdos, Nerves, and Zippers (4/16/77). They all possess originality. Hector Penalosa carries his priest-cum-junkie look. Baba plays second string football in school and steps in mud puddles. Robert sets styles in the vein of Question Mark and the Mysterians. Javier Escovedo possesses one of the best punk names around paralleling Captain Sensible, Sid Vicious, and Iggy Pop! Downstairs Black Randy was playing and it started getting real crowed upstairs...

FLIPSIDE: Any of you ever been cholos before?
HECTOR: We all were.
ROBERT: No, we weren't.
JAVIER: Speak for yourself.
HECTOR: Just lowriders.
ROBERT: No, lowriders are different than what we were. Lowriders are the same as blacks because they like to disco dance and stuff
HECTOR: Because they like Disco and Soul and all that shit.
ROBERT: We say we're Mexicans, but not lowriders.
FLIPSIDE: How many times have you played in T.J.?
JAVIER: We haven't played in T.J., it was in Rosarita.
FLIPSIDE: All of you played?
ROBERT: Me and Javier once, and then the whole Zeros.
FLIPSIDE: What was the band called?
ROBERT: We didn't announce a name, but the drums said, El Final--The End.
FLIPSIDE: Do you think of yourself as being Power Pop?
JAVIER: Oh shit! Hell no.
FLIPSIDE: Have you heard the English Zeros?
HECTOR: Yeah, I have their single.
ROBERT: They'll never make it.
FLIPSIDE: How did you get your name?
JAVIER: We picked it from a list.

Rich: Why don't you call yourself the Beaners?
JAVIER: Why don't you call yourself S-Word?
FLIPSIDE: What did you have in mind when you started the Zeros.
JAVIER: We didn't say anything, this is the only way it could have happened.
ROBERT: We just got started and this is how it ended up.
JAVIER: We were a lot more punk rock as the Main Street Brats.
FLIPSIDE: What groups do you like to play with?
ROBERT: The Dils.
JAVIER: 'Cause they lend us their amps. We don't have any amps, we just have stuff to practice on. It's not loud enough.
FLIPSIDE: What was the worst band you played with?
ROBERT: The Quick.
FLIPSIDE: What happened at the Whiskey?
ROBERT: They tried to get friendly with me, but I wouldn't. So, they threw glasses. They did stupid things like running through our dressing room and throwing an album cover autographed Danny Gonzalez and Ian Ramierez...
FLIPSIDE: How'd you make him throw the glass?
ROBERT: Me and X-8 were going Wonderama (waving hands over head), that's all. We didn't do it to their girlfriends or anyone associated with them.
Someone said we put posters over theirs.
JAVIER: I did. I put posters over theirs.
FLIPSIDE: What's the names of the songs you sing?
HECTOR: Nothing to do and Forget it.
FLIPSIDE: Are you going to keep doing that?
ROBERT: When we get three mikes.
JAVIER: There were three last night.
ROBERT: Then it already happened.
JAVIER: See, he writes his songs, he writes his, and I write my own. We all sing our own...
FLIPSIDE: What about Baba?
ROBERT: Basketball.
JAVIER: It was funny playing out here last night (Masque benefit). It seems that the people don't care what you're doing. They just wanna push people around and jump up and down. You could put anybody up there and they'd just be jumping around. They don't care about the music or who's playing or anything...

Rich and Dim Wanker of F-Word – photo by Al

F–Word
INTERVIEWD AT ELKS LODGE

F-Word are a bunch of rowdy punks from West Covina, who are rapidly rising to the top of the heap in L.A.'s growing punk arena. They have been declared the only worthwhile opening act, but don't want to open anymore. The F in F-Word (they say), stands for friendship, flowers, family, but we all know it stands for firetruck.

Rich--lead vocals
Steve--bass
Dim--guitar
Chris--drums
Also making guest appearances--
Dumb Girl--Dawn Werth
Van Flea--**Craig Bag**

Van Flea: Are you a political band?
FWORD: Just like the Dils.
Van Flea: Are you homos?
FWORD: Come on **FUCKER**, ask us some questions.
FLIPSIDE: Who's your favorite groupie?
FWORD: Paula, from the Stripes.
FLIPSIDE: Everybody knows your influences are Iggy, Stones, and N.Y.D...
FWORD: Right!
Van Flea: Are you going to be the next Iggy, Rich?
FWORD: Are you going to be the next...
FLIPSIDE: How do you do the Nihl?
FWORD: You destroy. It's what **Black** Randy's gonna do to the Flipsiders.
FLIPSIDE: What's your single on Dangerhouse?
FWORD: Government Official and Do the Nihl. We can't do Hillside Strangler 'cause the fuckin' Hollywood Squares did it already. Their version stinks.
Van Flea: Who gets the girls after the show?
FWORD: Me, him, me (Dim). I get the love letters. (He reads a genuine love letter he got from someone he knows.)
FLIPSIDE: Didn't Slash just interview you guys?
FWORD: Yeah, it was better than this.
DG: What do you plan to do in the future?
FWORD: We're gonna be rock stars and live in big houses and drive black Trans-Ams with F-Word 1 and F-Word 2 on the license plates.
FLIPSIDE: How many times have you played?
FWORD: Thirteen times. We played the Masque a couple of weeks and the Whiskey on two weekends.
Van Flea: Does sex and violence enter into your stage attitude?
Rich : Yeah.
Dim: I just hate when that blonde bitch from the Stripes grabs my balls.
FLIPSIDE: You hate it?
Dim: She grabs them, not massages them.
DG: Is she a big groupie in Orange County?
Dim: Yeah, she goes to the Marque West...Did you hear what we did to Lash?
FLIPSIDE: Yeah, in a car, etc...
DG: He'll fuck anybody.
FLIPSIDE: Where is X-8?
DG: Downstairs fuckin' Amber...You better print that!!
FWORD: Shut up you dumb girl, shut your mouth.
FLIPSIDE: Seriously, what's your motivation for being political?
Rich: There is a bunch of shit going on, read the **Slash** interview because I don't want to go into that again.

Van Flea: Do you get any negative feedback for doing the Hillside Strangler song?
Rich: Yeah, some chick said her friend was killed by the Strangler and was real pissed off.
FLIPSIDE: Are you pretending to be the Strangler?
Rich: It's just what I think the Strangler thought, why he does what he does. I put myself in his place and wrote the lyrics.
Van Flea: What about Eat your Dinner?
Dim: Don't you remember when you were

eight and your dad would say, Clean your plate! There are people starving in India, you know,? I'd say, Fine, send it to India.
Van Flea: How'd you like playing with the Screamers?
Rich: It was pretty good. Better than playing with the Quick.
FLIPSIDE: What makes you jump into the audience?
Dim: He likes to copy Bobby Pyn.
FLIPSIDE: Are you into nihlism?
Rich: Yeah!!
(A round glass ball smashes against the wall and essentially ends the interview.)
(This interview was possibly Craig Lee's first interview)
(Paula in this interview is Paula from the PANDORA's)

become the Gears). We also start to get international correspondance. One letter in particular is from a kid in Pennsylvania, John Angola, who I correspond with eventually ends up as a staff member. We are also getting legit ads, the Music Plus chain decides to advertise their punk selection in Flipside and also distributes us through-out their chain!

THE SREAMERS

(Interview at Wilton Hilton in Hollywood, with Larry Lash, Gabriella and Al

---

FLIPSIDE Ever see the movie "A Boy And His Dog"?
KK: I wanted to see it, Mr. Kimble from Green Acres wasn't.
FLIPSIDE: What did you think of the Screamers in it?
Tomata: I didn't see it.
FLIPSIDE: What's the idea behind your band?
KK: A boy and his dog...
FLIPSIDE: If you guys were chinese would you change your name to the "Yellers"? (Dead silence). Oh, you don't think that's funny... How much thought is put into your band?
Tomata: We're constantly putting thought into our music and it shows in our displays and style. It's a constant work effort. The idea behind the band is progressing, you know. Ummm what we're doing now isn't what we'll always be doing. We like to think that we'll be constantly changing. In a year from now I would not want to be doing the same music, words and things, it's hard to tell. Some People say we are trendy. I like to see us grow like everything else around us. I wouldn't like to be universally liked or universally disliked. No middle crowd.
FLIPSIDE: How many of you went to art school? And took jazz dancing? I heard Gear was a dancer and you, Tomata, look like one on stage.
Tomata: Gears a dancer, but I've never been on. Yet. I'm unconscious of those moves.
Gear: I was with the Royal Ballet. I'm not a jazz dancer.
KK: I studied dirt in school, at an agricultural and mining school in Oklahoma.
FLIPSIDE: So Tomata, what town did you grow up in?
Tomata: New York.
FLIPSIDE: When did you move to L.A.?
Tomata: About a year ago.
FLIPSIDE: When you went to High School, did you go to Montebello or Garfield High?
Tomata:..... I don't want to answer?!....
KK: Oh come on, you went to school somewhere, you were born, you had a mother, you did grow up...
Tomata: I went to Montebello.
FLIPSIDE: How were your roller skates?
Tomata: I went there too. (T-Bird Roller Rink).
FLIPSIDE: Where you a cholo?
Tomata: I was more a beaner.
FLIPSIDE: When did you go to New York?
Tomata: When I ran away from home. I was born there, then we moved out here and I ran away and went back to N.Y. when I was 17.
FLIPSIDE: Why don't you guys make a record?
Tomata: Who wants to make a record?
FLIPSIDE: Ok, we want to clear the air, because your name (Gear) has been dropped in every coffee house after 3am. What's the story on you and Amber?
Gear: Well, she said she wanted to pay for

FLIPSIDE NUMBER 8

LOS ANGELES 50¢
FLIP SIDE
VALLEY CATS
CONTROLLERS
DEADBEATS
DICKIES
EYES
T-WORD
GERMS
PLUGZ
SHOCK
STEVEN T.
SKULLS
WEASELS
WEIRDOS
ZEROS
MORE!
ALL OF THE UNUSUAL NOOZE AND STUFF WITH INTERVIEWS WITH Screamers Needles & Pins

I've been screaming loud but ain't been heard sometimes I wonder if it's worth the words,I've been misunderstood for too long...Ahhh... C'mon now! "Misunderstood" by The Saints

ISSUE #: 8
DATE: May 1978
FORMAT: 8 1/2x11" Offset
PAGES: 16
PRICE: $.50
PRESS RUN: 500
STAFF: Al, Dean Ded, Lash, Gaby, Pete, X-8

We start to settle into our new "larger format", This issue features the Screamers, Needles and Pins and the L.A. Shakers (who later

VERBAL ASSAULT

TRIAL

Le MASQUE (PRUTY DUSK DON CREVUS)

AUG. 28	NEEDLES & PINS
SEPT. 4	ALLEY CATS, SKULLS, GERMS, NEEDLES & PINS
SEPT. 10	BAGS, EYES, SPASTICS
C L O S E D	
OCT. 15	DILS, ZEROS, CONTROLLERS, PUNCHES
OCT. 22	DEADBEATS, DICKIES, MODEL CITIZENS, SPASTICS
OCT. 28	BACKSTAGE PASS, NEEDLES & PINS, ROCHELLE PHAEGH
OCT. 29	ALLEY CATS, SHOCK, EYES, CARS
OCT. 31	SKULLS, CONTROLLERS, DEATH BY DEATH
NOV. 5	DICKIES, ZEROS, GODS, CLONES
NOV. 6	DICKIES, ZEROS, GODS, CLONES
NOV. 12	DEADBEATS, X, MODEL CITIZENS, RIPPER
NOV. 19	EDDIE DETROIT & HIS NEW PERMANANT WAVE BAND, DOGS, SKULLS, CONTROLLERS, RUBBER CITY REBELS, MODEL CITIZENS, EYES
NOV. 23	GERMS, EYES, WAXX, SKULLS, NAUGHTY WOMEN
NOV. 25	NERVES, AVENGERS, SHOCK, F-WORD, ZEROS
NOV. 26	NERVES, AVENGERS, SHOCK, F-WORD, ZEROS
DEC. 3	GERMS, HITMAKERS, CONTROLLERS
DEC. 4	ARTHUR J AND THE GOLDCUPS, HOMOSEXUALS, BEST, INVADERS
DEC. 9	ALLEY CATS, WILDCATS, F-WORD
DEC. 10	ALLEY CATS, F-WORD, LYAN HYNTHAN
DEC. 16	WEIRDOS, SCREAMERS, SKULLS
DEC. 17	WEIRDOS, SCREAMERS, DEADBEATS, BAGS, PLUGS
DEC. 21	DICKIES, NUNS, EYES, FLESH EATERS, PLASTIKEATERS
DEC. 23	FLESHEATERS
DEC. 28	BLOW-UP, DODOETTS, SOUTH PASADENA FREE MUSIC ENSEMBLE
DEC. 31	WEIRDOS, BLACK RANDY & THE METRO SQUAD, ARTHUR J & THE GOLDCUPS, CONTROLLERS
JAN. 4	TWITS, SUNSET BOMBERS
JAN. 6	DILS, AVENGERS, F-WORD, LIARS
JAN. 7	DILS, AVENGERS, F-WORD, LAST
JAN. 11	BAGS, SHAKERS, F-WORD
JAN. 14	BLOW-UP, SHAKERS, NERVES, PLUGS, FABULONS
JAN. 17	SKULLS, DICKIES, NERVES, SHAKERS, RANDENS, RIPPER
C L O S E D	
JAN. 20	DICKIES, SKULLS, BAGS, GERMS, EYES, ARTHUR J & THE GOLDCUPS (CANCELED)(FLIP SIDE BENEFIT)
FEB. ?	WEIRDOS (VIDEO SPECIAL)

MAY — CONTROLLERS — BESTEREAS
JUNE — GO GOS — BAGS — RHINO 39 — PLUGS — PUBLIC REHERSALS AND PARTYS

DO YOU REMEMBER
THE
SATURDAY GIGS?

me to go to S.F. so we flew up and came back, that's it.

FLIPSIDE: Then all the stuff about you being a good fuck isn't true?

Gear: Well, it may be true, but I haven't had any intimate engagements with her.

FLIPSIDE: Well that's the big rumor... do any of you have jobs? (They keep shooting 'should we tell him' glances back and forth)?

Gear: None of us have jobs.

FLIPSIDE: Then what do you live off of?

Tomata: Street corners.

FLIPSIDE: (to Gear) How much writing do you do for the band?

Gear: We all work on the words and music. We steal stuff... We do a Germs song.

FLIPSIDE: How long have you been playing keyboards?

Gear: Two years. I originally played piano for the Tupperwares. They went through several personal changes. Tomata and I were always the same ones towards the end. We just had a synthesizer and rhythm generator and a bass. We try to get someone who knows us to do the sound, otherwise our sound gets destroyed. In the Germs song, we do use the rhythm generator to sound like Lorna Doom, Bobby Pyn and whoever else is the drummer for that week. When we heard "Sex Boy", we were so amazed because it portrayed Gear and Tomata so well. He really is a prophet, Bobby Pyn.

FLIPSIDE: How'd you guys like Devo?

KK: They're just like any other band. If you see 'em too much it wears thin.

FLIPSIDE NUMBER 9

"Let me touch the tips of inculcated desire
And brush the fettered veil away
Shutdown in the depths I lay...
If you want nothing then I've got nothing
I'm your annihilation man
Lemme get control
I've got your minds now I want your soul
Lemme get control
I've got your minds now I want control

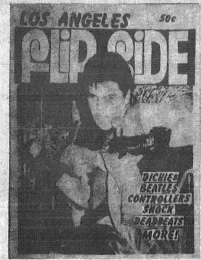

I need control
If you want something then I've got something
I'm your annihilation man....
Shutdown........."
"Shutdown (Annihilation Man)" - Germs (Official GI version)

ISSUE #: 9
DATE: August 1978
FORMAT: 8 1/2x11" Offset
PAGES: 16
PRICE: $.50
PRESS RUN: 500
STAFF: Al, Pooch, X-8, Pete, Gaby
- -
Because Dean Ded and Larry Lash aren't into magazine production so much anymore, we lower their rank to 'contributor'. This issues layout style is a brainstorm of X-8 who decides that sections are boring, thus we mixed reviews, news, interviews, pictures on each page and gave the zine an over all college look. A long time in the making, this issue contains: The Jam, Deadbeats,

Tomata Du Plenty – photos by Al

Screamers: Baby Face, Tomata, Gear - photo by Gaby

The DICKIES SUMMER VACATION

THE DICKIES ARE: STAN - GUITAR, CHUCK - KEYBORDS/GUITAR, BILLY - BASS, KARLOS - DRUMS AND LEONARD ON VOCALS AND ON PROPS

LEONARD AND STAN SHOW DISPLEASURE WITH ENGLISH PROMOTION, POSTER READS "DICKIESHIT SINGLE DOGGIE DO-

WHERE THEY WENT, AS FAR AS STAN AND LEONARD COULD REMEMBER

June 22 — the Rock Garden
June 23 — Hope and Anchor
June 28 — Nashville Rooms
June 29 — Dingwalls
then off up north:
Leeds- Roots F-Club
Retford- Porterhouse
Birmingham- Barberellas
Sheffeld- Limit Club
Edinbourgh (Scotland)- Tiffinies
Liverpool- Eriks
couldn't remember oth
then back to London
Hope and Anchor
Lycium
Music Machine

Controllers, Dickies and Shock. Although the Whiskey and Starwood are still happening, the new happening punk club is in the Valley (of all places). An old biker bar called on Rock Corporation hosts weekend punk shows and has every act in L.A. play there - including the official debut of the Go Gos. Responsible for pioneering this venue is none other than Robbie Fields (Posh Boy), who also just released the very first punk LP from L.A.; F-Words "Like It Or Not" (who also do a version of the L.A. punk anthem "Shutdown").

Controllers Kid Spike, Johnny Stingray and Maddog - photo by Al

THE CONTROLLERS

This interview was done in the **Licorice Pizza** parking lot (L.A. punk park) on Aug. 11 with the Controllers:
Kid Spike (guitar), Johnny Stingray (bass) and Mad Dog (drums). Also present were friends Mary Rat and Gary and his girlfriend.

- -

FS: So how do you like being a three piece?
KS: It's fun, it's easier.
JS: It's a lot better, we don't have to argue any more, with three of us we can always out vote the other one.
KS: It's easier to get a tight sound with three instruments. Everybody likes us the way we sound because we got a real drummer now, not one that just hit the cymbals all the time, plus she's black and everybody thought we were a racist band before.
FS: In other words you releaved the pressure by getting yourselves a token negro?
KS: That's right, that's right!!!
MD: I'm token everything, I'm black, female, Mad Dog...
KS: But she sure can drum!!
FS: Have you recorded with her?
KS: Yeah, the Siamese record, "Do The Uganda" and "Slow Boys", it'll be out next week.
FS: When did you guys move here from Michigan?
KS: About 2 years ago.
JS: About 4 years ago.
FS: Were the Dogs from your area?
JS: Yeah, they're from my home town. I never knew them but I saw them back there, we just met them out here.

FS: Do you have a Michigan sound?
KS: We sort of try to have a Michigan sound because we like hard rock, that's all there is.
JS: Like MC5 or Stooges, MC5 were dull on the whole, but they had a couple of good songs.
JS: Kid Spikes main influence is Mad Magazine!
FS: So is ours!!!
KS: I've got Alfred E. Neuman taped to my guitar.
FS: Do you guys ever stuff your pants with socks?
KS: We don't have to!
MD: I do!!!
FS: What do you think of the black Controllers?
JS: We're gonna wait till they sue us, then were gonna change our name to the Dickies! Well call ourselves the Scales because we're all Libras.
FS: Do you get any pressure from being in a punk band Mad Dog?
MD: From my family, no, they like them, they've met them.
FS: From friends?
MD: No. All of my friends are punks. I don't have any other friends.
FS: Where do you come from?
MD: Los Angeles.
JS: Compton!
MD: Shut up! You mid-western honkey!
FS: How'd you audition Mad Dog?
MD: Me and Stingray fell in love at the Masque benefit. We kept saying: "Oh Stingray, eggamuf'n" and :"Oh Mad Dog, eggamuf'n".
KS: That's how we auditioned her, we told her to say "Egg McMuffin".
MD: And I said "Eggamuf'n".
KS: And we said "You're in".

THE DEADBEATS

This is the typical Flipside story, plan an interview and something always fucks up. This time the Deadbeats split in two. We first saw the Deadbeats at Kim Fowleys new wave show last summer when they were the Whores. Later a personnel shift occurred where they acquired Geza, who

Pat Daleney and Omo Deo Deadbeats - photo Al

had just left the Bags, and the name of the band was changed to the Deadbeats.

The Deadbeats playing many bizzare gigs at the Masque. Back then we thought they we only playing the "Batman Theme" over and over, but as we saw them again and again the music suddenly became clear and swept off of our feet. Then we knew what dead beat music was. They then became one of our favorite bands, we followed them, we wrote about them, we put them on our cover. But before we got the ultimate privilege of interviewing them, they split apart, but we are still going to write this page on them and their modification.

For those of you who don't know what Deadbeat music was (and will continue to be, without Pat and Geza), it has been described as: "punk jazz", "progressive power rock", "polyrhythmic, high percussive and entertains humorous flirtations with the bizzare and avant-garde", "a mixed media vaudeville troupe", "a travelling dada medicine show", (all from Slash). You can listen to the record (on Dangerhouse) but you MUST see them live. So anyway, we talked to them, here's what they said:
Shawn: Well for publicity reasons and a lot of things have happened - we can't play the Mabuhay at the present because of Geza... we're going towards the same direction but a little different.
Scott: We've got a replacement sax, and we're looking for a violin player instead of a guitar layer. Geza left because there was a disatisfaction at the musical end of things...
Geza: (Summary of conversation) Geza felt he was ousted because of his aggressive

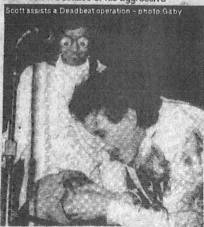

Scott assists a Deadbeat operation - photo Gaby

personality. He was taking too much control in the band. He was responsible for their 'rock' sound and was happy with the way the band was. Also, as we all know, Geza was quite a coo coo off stage and his antics got them canned from the Mabuhay. Other things like a naked appearance at a Bags gig, he feels, was upsetting the image Scott wanted for his band. Geza says Pat quit because he felt Geza was unjustifiably thrown out. He will continue in a band where he will sing and play guitar.

Pat: It's a complicated story. But he did tell us he quite for heath reasons. "I'm dying of terminal cancer".

Omo Deo: No phone number.

THE JAM

Exclusive Jam interview for Flipside done by our English correspondant Gary Crowley and Karl Eldrige from the Modern World Fanzine.

- -

FS: Well first of all, how did the first American tour go?

Paul Weller: Well ok, like we got mixed reactions but on the whole it went alright. The tour was the only one we could get into at the time you see, so we were playing to real heavy metal fans. You know like Blue Oyster Cult are like a real heavy metal band so we were playing to an entirely difference audience than usual. But we slogged on and came out pretty good, but I didn't give a shit whether or not they disliked really.

FS:Seeing the Jam before you went off o the U.S. showed that since early '77 you've really changed, like the set is so much better paced now and you are starting to drop the black suits a bit, has that been planned or anything?

PW:No it ain't, but we're just progressing you know. It's just that you've got to pace the songs out a bit, cause you can't do fast ones all the time, but then again we ain't planned to write a few slow ones neither, it just comes like that.

FS: What about the "Modern World" LP, why didn't that do as well as it should have?

PW: Well I don't know. There's a lot of reasons but I think there should have been much more fucking publicity, and more radio plays you know. Like when we released it, we thought it would easily be a top 10 album but for some reason it weren't.

FS: The production on the album wasn't all that good, have you thought of producing it yourselves?

PW: Yeah, looking back now the production was terrible in places, it sorta sounded empty. But I don't know, perhaps when we do the next single we might try producing ourselves.

FS: What do you think of Power Pop and all that?

PW: Oh I think its a load of fucking crap, you know? I think the Pleasers are shit, they're just a bunch of revivalists in it for the brew. But it's just been made up by the press and they killed it even before it got going. As for the Rich Kids, they must be the worlds first bionic band, there a bloody business not a band. Maybe they'll get better but I don't rekon them much.

FS: Have you seen any new bands that you like?

PW: Well no I ain't. I just like bands who try really hard and who are good you know. Groups like the Jolt, the Boys, Sham 69 are bands I like.

FS:You're often called by your critics as arrogant and naive and some people say you've changed. How do you answer those?

PW: Well I just think that's a load of shit, most journalists are cunts, the only person who

knows me is me. How they recon I've changed after two interviews is a load of fucking shit. As far as arrogant, well we always stuck by what we said and we try to be as honest as we can. If honesty is arrogance, then I'm arrogant but I don't think it is.

FS:What's gonna be the future of the Jam and the new wave scene?

PW: I don't know, but we ain't got it planned out or anything you know, we just want to get better and appeal to more kids. But I don't think new wave is gonna be a big scene anymore, I think people are gonna watch individual bands progress and see what direction they take. All I hope is that we're going in the right direction, I think we are.

FLIPSIDE NUMBER 10

"Adolescent you look so young
You look like fire
You look like a gun
Your mommy and daddy want to keep you at home
They want to keep you, Oh so ready.
I see you running with a gun in your hand
Your dream of becoming a man
You stole the car and your went to L.A.
Now you're hanging at the Atomic Cafe.
Adolescent you look like us
We all look the same, part of a game
We're all running and we got to get out
But we don't even know what the scenes about
"Adolescent" - The Plugz

ISSUE #: 10
DATE: November 1978
FORMAT: 8 1/2x11" Offset
PAGES: 16
PRICE: $.50
PRESS RUN: 400
STAFF: Al and X-8

- -

Our first issue after the long summer, it took a long time to come out and we lost some of our staff. Pooch is involved with his new band (Blow Up) and school, Lash is off who knows where, Pete is still contributing photos, but now that I bought Pete's old camera I take them myself. Angola becomes more than a regular contributor and coins our motto "Be more than a witness", something he used with his band The Shut-Ins. The L.A. scene has had it's taste of Madame Wongs, that didn't fly, but a new club in West L.A. called Club 88 is turning out to be a wonderful place to hang out. The other notable hangout at this time is

the Canterbury Apartments in Hollywood, up the street from the Masque, most Hollywood bands and people now live there, with rehersal space in the basement and parties just about every night, it is an ideal hangout.

Tito Lariva punk rocker - photo Al

LAS PLOGAS

Were interviewed by X-8 (who was drunk) and Al at a Warehouse No Mag party on Oct. 15, 1978 just before X. Michael Gira from No Mag was also present.

- -

X-8: How come you don't have black lips?

Tito: Cause I don't get buttfucked anymore, my assholes reserved for one person, my shit.

Al: When did you get your first guitar?

Tito: Dec. 25 19... lets see... 19... 72

Al: Have you been playing ever since?

Tito: Yeah.

Al: When did you get your first bass?

Barry: A year ago.

Tito: Yeah, Barry just started playing bass.

Al: When did you get your first drum kit?

Charlie: About a year and a half ago...

Janet He used to play 'Tie A Yellow Ribbon Around The Old Oak Tree' when he was nine years old.

X-8: Why do they call you "Tito"?

Tito: It means junior, short for Umbertito.

X-8: What are you guys, political or musical?

Barry: What's the point in saying if your music doesn't say it? If your music doesn't say it then the rest is just bullshit.

Tito: Yeah, if your music doesn't say it and that includes the lyrics, political in what sense? Like the Dils?

Barry: No I don't think we are political in comparison to the whole S.F. or London scene because it's hard to be political in L.A. Who gives a fuck?

Michael: I give a fuck man!

Tito: We don't try to be anything we just reflect who we are, and if something is happening within us politically then you know, it comes out in our music. If it's humorous then the music is humorous, and if it's gross then the music is gross.

Al: Is L.A. healthy for punk rock?

Barry: It's getting there real fast.

Tito: It's good because you can feed off of everything, like a good place to be a leach!

Charlie: A lot of bullshit though.

Tito: Oh everywhere you go.

Al: Will it pick up?

Tito: It already has compared to a year ago, your audience has increased, doubled at least.

Al: Is only double in a year good?

Michael: Without record company support.

X was interviewed at the No mag. party by Al and X-8 on October 15, 1978

Don Bonebrake (drums): cunts, cocks, cunts, cocks, cunts, cocks, cunts... AL: is that what you thought of your review? Billy Zoom (gaitar): whats this about an Elvis Costello rip off? Al: forget it, that guy is no longer with flipside. John Doe (bass): why did he say that, has he ever heard us? Al: yeah the single. X-8: are you moving to N.Y.? JD: no, we're not moving to NY, we're going there to play CBGB and some other places...Xene: I don't know where you get your information, but everything you always say about us is always wrong. X-8: yeah, we even gave you a bad review. Xene: no, that might not be wrong but some of the other things. DB: calling us a bunch of hippies from venice, you decided to.. Al: isn't that the truth? JD: of corse not, I come from Baltimore, I lived in Venice for about a year! X-8: are you a political poetry band? Xene: naw, were not political at all and John andI are both excellent writters. Al: tell us why your so excellent. JD: because we avoid being polite. AL: did you used to write poetry? Xene: no, you can call it poetry if you want but if you don't know the meaning of it...Al: define 'of good records. X-8: are you in it for money it? Xene: I can't define it, its hard to explain or style? BZ: money you fucking asshole!! JD: to somebody why we write well but we write real I'm in it so I don't have to have a regular well and I think people would be supportive of job, once it gets beyond that I'll make that considering what you have to pick from, if up my mind. Al: do you make any money you read the lines in any popular album you see now? JD: fuck no, I have a regular lines like 'sink or swim' or 'do or die' or job... X-8: stop! everybodys bored 'drowning in a sea of love' well thats bad wr- with this interview right. BZ: itting, things like vague things, cliche things no not with the inerview, I'm Al: your lyrics arn't vague? Xene: no I don't bored with you. X-8: say why think so. X-8: then why put Tomata in the song? your bored, agression, ca JD: thats a spacific person, if you want to get mon! JD: agression at into lyrics which isn't the hudge section of what? you, the tape the band. X-8: what is the hudge section of the recorder the empty band? JD: we're a rock&roll band.... any song or beers? I mean agr- poem thats good is about a particular time or a .ession comes particular instance, you know like someone ac- when somebodys osting you on the bus, somebody gives you shit pushing, ri- on the street, if you go beyond that like'my ght? X-8: life is an open book' or 'lifes been good to me I'm push- so far' ble bla bla then you try to go beyond ing!! what you can see and its week or vague... Al: JD: well, how is your single doing? JD: its out ha sold all Dangerhouse singles so far. X-8: you were hyped in the LA Times, what are your pre- ceptions now? JD: the same, unfortunatly theLA Times doesn't mean shit, not from our stand- point, its nice to read it, but it doesn't make any difference whsse we play. People at the Whisky don't read the LA Times, you don't get in the times and then get better booking. Al: what have you been doing to promote your sin- gle? JD: just playing...one thing that Danger- house missed that their picking up on now is this poster we had done by a friend of mine in Baltimore, its like 24"x18", they didn't have money to put it out with the single so what I hear is that they're gonna put it out now. X-8: do you want to say something to your fans? BZ: we're not so distabt from our fans that we have to go thru flipside to say hi to them. X-8: but the closet punks who don't go see you? BZ: all I can say is thanks for buying the single andtoo bad about the rest. DB: come with me thru a 24 hour magic carpet ride of my life and then you'll understand our band better. JD: thats what we want people to realize, they don't have to go thru rod stewert or that other guy bob segar, they don't have to live thru them they can do it all themselves. DB: I think all the girls should think abot me from midnight to 6 in the morning and send the vibes to north hollywood thatswhere I live. JD: I think success and all that stuff is fine, but I'm not going to let it go to my head. Al: do you try to put reggae into you music? JD: no. Al: youlike reggae music? BZ: yes. JD: I love the way they have the bass, reggae is like you really have to get involved in it, everybody who says reggae is like the thing to them or is their biggest interest is just bullshit, because they're just patronizing black music because its the cool- est thing... BZ: because they have the best grass. X-8: com'on Xene say something. Xene: I could say things about Jews but I don't want to. X-8: talk about Jews, paleeze.BZ: talk about r&r thats the point is'nt it. X-8: basically, who knows?..what do you guys like? BZ: rock and roll. X-8: thats it? BZ: and girls except for exene maybe Al: may be? BZ: don't want to cramp her style, I like cars. Al: do you like fast cars? BZ: I like very

fast cars, I have a 1953 Hudson Hornet, an goes real fast... its the coolest car there X-8: talk about sex: JD: ok, most of our song deal with sex and oviously we dont get enough it. X-8: what about your exene? Xene: I could ca less about anything at this time, including that BZ: how come the big thing in FS interviews is all this bullshit and not the music? X-8: cause you can listen to the music yourself. JD: well we like to live our own personal lives, basic- ally I think people can learn from us. X-8: are you trying to hide your private lives? JD: I wouldn't want everybody in the world coming over my house no. BZ: are you gonna edit alot of this? X-8: who knows.Xene: who was the guy you got rid of? Al: the guy who said you rip= ped off Elvis Costello. Xene: I'm glad you got rid of him cause I don't think most of us like Elvis Costello,BZ: he's also english and for- eigners can't play rock and roll and we dont like english bands. Al: oh yeah! well... X-8: would you want to be on AM radio? BZ: I would love for AM radio to change its format and play lots of our records.AL: then it wouldn't be AM radio. BZ: sure it would, if its amplitude mod- ulation and not frequency modulation them its AM radio. I'd love to have AM radio play lots

is alot more feeling than people are expressing in songs, I don't like the mald that you have to have an agressive or pissed off feeling in all your songs, theres more range...AL: no not like that. BZ: have you heard us? Al: 6 or 7 times. BZ: do you like the song live? AL: sometimes its great, sometimes not so good, its where you stand you get the guitars right and not all bass oh... who plays bass? BZ: you do an interview and you dan't know who plays bass. AL: I could've guessed. BZ: be sure and put that in the inter- view. X-8: all I want to know is your main con- cept of the band. BZ: were an american R&R bamd. Xene: I think we can change the whole face of music, the band that made record companies eat shit. AL: your no different, Adult Books won't change anything. Xene: I wish you'd get off the record, thats one thing, being a band and that is different. Al: then how will you change things? X-8: Anger! JD: LOOK!! I'm not going to get angry at you, because oviously your cool enough to be doing FS and be on the scene and the other bullshit, I'mnot gonna ake my anger out on you when its the people out in stwood, thats the problem, people take anger out people who are supposed to be their 'brother, they should be out bombing the goddamn rest s in westwood &verly hills botiques.

junior hi and some- body says me- et me after sc- hool, 3 hours la- ter your supposed to conjure up all this animosity, pissed off feelings...X-8; just talk. JD: ha? DB: who's gonna be on your cover? Al: oh....... exene! BZ: you dant have to make up for comparing us to EC. AL: I wouldn't make up for that,if Isaid that I wouldn't regret it, I just don't like the single, the lyrics were good when I read them but when you play it its too slaw or something. JD: there

Al: You could have Dangerhouse support.
Michael: They don't have any fucking money man!
Tito: Nobody has any money.

Al: You could promote yourselves (arguement over the price of advertising, flyers...)
Tito: We don't want to do a single on Dangerhouse because of all the shit that goes on. They don't promote their bands. We didn't want to do it on our own label because we didn't want to go through all of the trouble. We thought Slash was a good idea because it would be better than no distribution plus they could handle mailing it out and we seem to think that Slash has a lot of readers that would appeal to our music. We're doing really well, but compared to national, it's peanuts...
X-8: Why did you play at Madame Wongs?
Tito: I met this guy at the Atomic Cafe and he said he was trying to open a club and I said we'd play there.
Al: That place sucks.
Michael: They have a good sound.
Al: Sure if you want to sit and listen.
MICHAEL They said they'd move the chairs.
Tito: Tito, listen I talked to Paul, the first bands are going to be light, we are the first punk band booked to play there. I told the guy to move the if he wanted to, just like the Troubador, we told Doug Weston to move the tables, he didn't and they destroyed the club.
X-8: Are the Plugz gonna be around in 2 years?
Tito: If you guys are around in 2 years then we will too.
X-8: You're depending on us!!?
Tito: No, all I'm saying is if you guys are around in two years then we definitely will. If Flipside can make it for two years we definitely can.
X-8: Wow, that's pretty low misdemeoor for me.

(Michael Gira is now in the Swans, the Plugz it least Tito and Charlie) are the Cruzados with a major recording contract. The e.p. "Movi/"Lets Go"/Mindless Contentment" was the first record released by Slash).

BRENDAN ON THE MASQUE RE-OPNING

Al: When will the Masque re-open?
Brendan: The Masque will re-ope mid to late November... it depends on how extensive the remodeling must be... I'm trying to keep it as similar to the original model as possible, not for a nostelgia thing of last year, which could never be repeated, nor would I attempt to just open up and think things would be like last year. I will be all legal, it will no longer be an underground club.
Al: We heard that you trashed the Masque the other night, all by yourself?
Brendan: Kind of. The thing I had people beaten up for in the last 2 mons. I did it on a combination of barbituates and alcohol, something I don't usually ml I didn't really trash it, I got all this paint, re's no rational explanation, it happened last day, threw it all over the walls... The Masque has been through 3 distinct phases errys, pre-Jerrys and post-Jerrys... so the graffitti must be erased and new graffitti Someone tried to kick the door in, it was young Steven McGuire, when the security rep ed it to me, I went right over to the Cante ry, knocked on the door, was let in, t straight into the bedroom and very cr y and savagely rather

Plugz: Charlie, Tito and Barry at UCLA - photo by Al

than using my hands just started kicking as hard as I could on his head and sholders, no such violence had I done in years, after about the 7th blow when the young man was screaming... my foot hurt for the rest of the day. After the savage beating, which I actually regreted, he came down tot he Masque in despair and distress and tried to make amends.

Brendan Mullen and Dinky - photo by Al

FLIPSIDE NUMBER 11

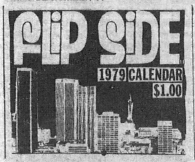

"Some people think little girls should be seen and not heard
I say OH BONDAGE UP YOURS!
Bind me, tie me, chain me to a wall
I wanna be a slave for you all
Oh bondage up yours,

Oh bondage no more......
Chain store, chain smoke
I consume you all
Chain gang, chain mail
I don't think at all
Oh bondage up yours......
Bash me, crash me
Beat me till I fall
I wanna be a victim for you all
Oh bondage up yours......."
"Oh Bondage, Up Yours" X-Ray Spex

ISSUE #: 11
DATE: November 1979
FORMAT: 7 1/2x5", offset
PAGES: 28
PRICE: $1.00
PRESS RUN: 500
STAFF: Al, X-8, Gerard, Gerber
- -
Like issue number 3, this issue was a bit of a

Alice and Pat Bag from the Flipside Calendar center fold.

X: John Doe, Exene, Billy Zoom and Don Bonebreak at the Elks Lodge Masque Benefit. – photo by Al

departure for us, this issue being a 1979 Calendar. Each month featured a different band: Germs for January, Dickies, Weirdos, Zeros, Middle Class, Plugz, Controllers, Screamers, Zippers, Bags, Alleycats, and X. Plus almost every day had a picture of somebody's face in the hole! There were birthdays and other useful info as well. Plus, Pat Bag's face was cryptically hidden on every page in the calendar! Not to mention her and Alice shared the center spred poster! What a concept!!

FLIPSIDE NUMBER 12

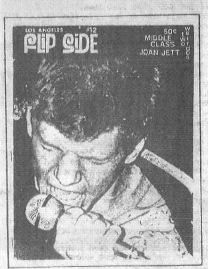

"I wanna war
between the rich and the poor
I wanna fight,
When I know what I'm fighting for
In a class war, clar war...."
"Class War" – Dils

ISSUE #: 12
DATE: January 1979
FORMAT: 8 1/2x11, offset
PAGES: 16
PRICE: $.50
PRESS RUN: 500
STAFF: Al, X-8, Angola

- - - - - - - - - - - - - - - - - -

Big changes in the scene. Our staff for one is abbreviated, the zine gets a bit stuffy when there is a lull in the live action – the dichotomy between punk and rock widens, and punks are finding less and less places with welcome mats. Skulls gig at the Cuckoos Nest gets trashed (a first for O.C.), Plugz at Troubador gets trashed, Bags at Wongs gets trashed, riot squad shows up at the Weirdos/Dils gig at Club Azteca (a first for L.A.)... The scene goes into a sort of waiting period. The old Masque is still open, for party purposes, but a new Masque is starting. This place (on the corner of Santa Monica and Vine) shows promise, but Brendan tells us that the landlord is greedy and keeps uping his rent. Steve Samioff, who created and owned Slash, the long time L.A. punk magazine, sells it off, and goes into a more art oriented direction (with his new publication Stuff). Slash Mag goes into a tail spin and the zine dies. Slash continues as a record label, but has nothing to do with the punk scene. And of course the Sex Pistols are back in the news, Sid getting all the credit this time... Orange County is

starting to show it's face, the Middle Class are firmly established as the fastest and hardest band around, and there is lots of news about other bands from O.C. that are becoming quite popular in their own party circuit. Last but not least, Rodney's Top 20 Requests is added to Flipside as a regular feature. Rodney used to do a chart in some big weekly tabloid that used to be distributed around L.A., since it folded, we gave Rodney's Chart a new home. Rodney has been instrumental in introducing new music to the masses, and listening to Rodney's show is not only mandatory, it is ritual.

MIDDLE CLASS
The Middle Class were interviewed on Dec. 16 at the Atlas house in Santa Ana by Al, Alice and Gerard.

- - - - - - - - - - - - - - - - - -

AL: Do you have problems getting gigs because you ive out here in Orange County kinda isolated?
MIKE A. Yeah, we used to have a lot of problems, and we still do, people don't remember us.
MIKE P.: If we're not hanging out when they're figuring out gigs, the spur of the moment stuff, we usually get left out.
MIKE A.: That's wha Rick (Jaffe) is for.
AL: Where was your irst gig?
Jeff: Larchmont Hall ith Bags and Germs.
MIKE A.: They don't member though.
ALICE: Yes I do! Eve though I didn't see you.
AL: How many times have ou played O.C.?
MIKE A: Just once.
AL: What are you really upet with?
MIKE A: "We want to be he band to make

JOAN JETT

JOAN JETT INTERVIEWED BY AL, X-8, GERARD ON DEC. 14 AT POWER BURGER WITH STAN LEE, LISA, CARLOS, KEN AND WHO EVER ELSE WALKED BY.

X-8: oh you got a new bass player.

Joan: Yeah, her names Lorie McAlister and shes 21, shes played bass for a long time and shes really good, we've rehersed with her for about ...this was our fifth day today- we got three days left then tuesday we go to San Francisco for two days and Palo Alto for a gig then Santa Cruz then back here to the Whisky, UCI and then the Golden Bear.

AL: where's Vicki Blue?

Joan: she's sick, I'm serious I swear to god, I don't want to tell you what but she's sick which made her unable to go en tour, she got too flipped out, I mean not mentally sick, physically...

AL: no hard feelings?

Joan: oh no. I stillcall her and talk to her all the time, I'm supposed to go to New Orleans with her in febuary or something.

AL: Why'd you dothat Slade song on the album?

Joan: cause I liked it I suggested it and just everyone liked it. I like it cause thats the kind of stuff I grew up with, Glitter stuff and Rodney's, it's a great title.

X-8: no more conection with Kim Fowley?

Joan: oh no , not at all.

X-8: we shouldn't go into that, he might kill us, tell us about your audience?

Joan: any audience to tell the truth, we havent even played in front of an audience in 6 months since europe, except for some dumb celebraty thing we did in Centuary City. Have you ever heard of Harold Robins? Well his wife threw this big homecoming thing for him and we played. It was a previewing of Annie and they wanted a band to play and Toby our manager got us the gig. Steve Jones was in town and we were doing a song he wrote 'Black Leather' so the last song of the set he got up and jamed with us, you name it, Za Za Gabor, they were all there, Jacqeline Bisset all these hudge fuckers were there and they were pluging their ears and by the end of the set they were all walking out it was really great, really fun. There was a review of the party in the LA times but it only talked about us.

Stan: Suzanne Sommers was there wasn't she?

Joan: Yeah, we got our picture taken with her, what a jerk that bitch is!

Stan: hey, leave her alone!

Joan: she's a jerk!!

Stan: I'd like to see her.

Joan: Oh, fuck you, horney bastard.

Stan: well I like girls.

Joan: not this one not if you got to meet her.

X-8: does she have a good ass?

Joan: how could you tell?

Stan: I just saw her in playboy and it had her tits in it!

Joan: she's so movie starish, phony smile....

X-8: I hear you audience is gitting lesbian?

Joan: I don't know It's hard for me to see out there sometimes plus sometimes I'm not really thinking about it, but I saw alot of guys out there. Yeah, I heard something about that - 'Runaways dyke audience'. And some people going 'Hey Sandy, what a fox!', but I don't think thats the majority of our audience thought I don't care if they're..anybody, I don't give a shit if there transexual or bisexual, gay I don't care just so long as they like it and enjoy it.

X-8: whats your own personal closet habits?

Joan: What?

X-8: Your private pleasures?

Joan: well if there private they're gonna stay that way....I buy every dirty magazine in the world. I like to read them. I do. You know how wifes go 'Why are you reading that?' , 'Well, honey the articles are good', well its true alot of the magazines have really good articles. I always buy Hustler cause they're taste less. Oui...

X-8: You check out the girls?

Joan: WEll what the hell are you supposed to do close your eyes!

X-8: what bands do you like now?

Joan: besides the old Sex Pistols, Siouxie and the Banshees, thats my new favorite, the albms really really fuckin good, the best I've heard in years besides the Pistols album.

AL: what do the other Runaways like?

Joan: I like more punk than the rest of them, I mean see, I'm really narrow minded about music, I like one kind, ya know? I like Rock and Roll, Chuck Berry but I don't have any of his records....Lita likes Ritchie Blackmores Rainbow and the older stuff, Deep Purple, Led Zeppelin the new bass player is a Zeppelin freak but Lita loves the Sex Pistols and the Clash, I love the Clash too.

Stan: you got a new roadie I hear?

Joan: who? Stan: Ken,...the stripper.

Joan: I heard about that, he gave me a big speech about that....

AL: where isyour strongest following at?

Joan: All of Europe is a really good market, better than here,States is so jaded, they've seen everybody here, everybody you could imagine. Record companys here are a lot more efficient and choosy in what they pick, they went something that sells, the same reason the American phone system is so much better here, they settle for second best over in Europe where as here its really particular. In Europe your already presented as a pop star, your already in the magazines, big color pictures, they really build you up. Our label over there gives us a lot of support. In the States our best areas are the midwest, Texas and Ohio, We got the best reaction from like Hunnington Beach, I mean they go crazy. Certain areas go for certain things, the Whiskys always been good...

Stan: Hey, its Darby on the streets,.& Helen.

Joan: where I wanna talk..

X-8: Yell! go get him.

Stan: mewww,.. I can't express myself.

Joan: why are you loaded?

Stan: yeah, on Marijuana.

AL: how was the Lycium gig with the Dickies?

Joan: really good, didn't you think that was really great.

Stan: Yeah! our first big place.

Joan: I felt good cause we were playing with another american band cause alot of the english people try to like'take the piss out of the yankees', like I heard Ken, well he sathe Clash and he was backstage just sitting and the Clash started talking to him and they go 'Oh, your american' and the girl next to him goes, 'Yeah thats why he doesn't have anything to say', like big competation.

Stan: he got an autograph so he was happy, They (Clash) signed his passport, he was happier than a pig in shit!

Joan: Sid Vicious is a hero, thats my statement, I think has a hero, especially if he gits off this he'll be the biggest hero.

AL: Do you think he killed her?

Joan: I don't, I really don't.

X-8: Stan, ask her some questions.

Stan: you want me to inerview her now?

AL: Yeah...whats different in europe?

Stan: Cheeseburgers are good here, theres Tacos and theres Soap Operas.

AL: You said that last time.

Stan: Well this is her interview Imjust sitting here on marijuana answering your questions.

Joan: Your mother will read this.

X-8: When you started were you tryong to push the female type deals, like when you posed for surfer pictures in Cream?

Joan: I wasn't,why do you think I wore a wet suit, I hate that sex ass stuff.

AL: At the Golden West you got really upset when Lita brought out that Penis squirtgun.

Joan: Its stupid, its unnecessary, I never liked it from the beginning the cor-set and all that crap.

Lisa: Why did you dye your hair black?

Joan: thats my room mate I've known for many many years, oh my hair because one of the Tubes said hey you ought to dye your hair black, like jett black.

X-8: how'd you like the party at the tropicana?

Joan: oh, were you guys there?

X-8: Yeah.

Joan: that's how I liked it, I was fucked up out of my head........closing words- Merry Christmas and a Happy New Year....Live hard die young and leave a good looking corpse. no...I already said that somewhere else.

Joan Jett at the Whisky - photo Pete L.

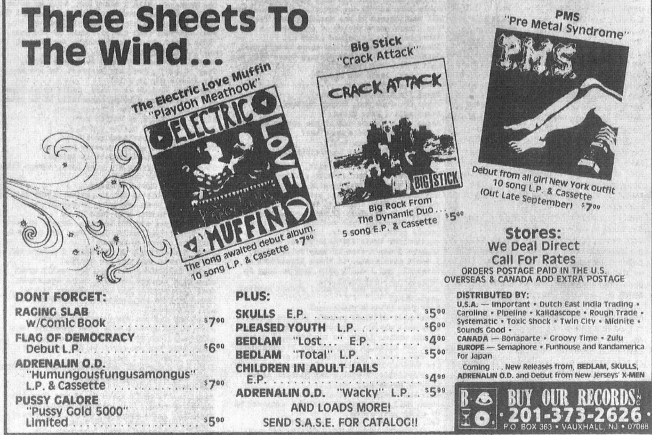

Middle Class: Mike P., Jeff A. and Mike A – photo by Al

record companies eat shit!"

ALICE: What do you think about opening for the**Gogos** when you guys have been around longer?

MIKE P: We're just easy marks.

Jeff: We wouldn't have agreed to it at first and then Randy said "Oh yeah, the Gogos are headlining". So I guess we should have said we refuse to do it unless we headline cause we agreed to it under different circumstances.

MIKE P: And its supposed to be 'billing doesn't matter' right?

ALICE: No, everybody likes to say that, but it's not true.

AL: Do you call yourselves a punk band?

Jeff: For want of something else to call us.

MIKE P: When the movement started... when we started playing, we called ourselves a punk band before anybody else did. That's the style we were playing and that's what we wanted to play, there is a certain amount of anger in the music, but it's kind of directionless. We're not at any one person, we're not mad a fascists or communists or anything like that, we're just generally mad. Kind of frustrated, but there's nothing we attack outright.

AL: Where did you develop your vocal style?

Jeff: I just happend, when they started the band there was nothing else left to do but sing. Mike was gonna sing but I couldn't lay bass... They hated my singing at first cause Mike was singing melodically, and I can't dot that, there's no way my voice can sustain notes like that.

MIKE A: So **Jeff** brought out the auctioneer style of vocals.

Jeff: I just stuff in as many words as I can.

AL: What about a political stance?

Jeff: We don't have a political stance like "We are marxists and anybody who isn't gets a bullet in the head". We are not Nazis, or trying to shock people, but we are political in the sense that we are against certain things.

MIKE P: Like living and having to grow up in Orange County, having to work.

Mike: We're like vague, we don't like things, but we don't have any answers.

AL: Why didn't you continue college?

Jeff: It's a waste of time, I went to 2 1/2 years of college before I stopped fooling myself like I was doing something there.

AL: So what do you plan to do?

MIKE P: I going to keep doing what I'm doing and put off any major decisions as long as possible. Hopefully the band will do something, if not I'll have to figure out

something else. It's frightening to think that I'm going to be a plumber in 10 years and be miserable for the rest of my life, so I fool myself into thinking **"Well, Middle Class is going to make it someday"**.

Jeff: If I wasn't in the band, I'd be doing the same thing, working at 7-11 to support myself or writing novels, right now this is the best chance of actually doing anything worthwhile.

(Bruce and Mike A. are currently in Cambridge Apostles, with Alice and Mike P. has his own band Pluto Gang)

FLIPSIDE NUMBER 13

"I don't care what you say
I'm going away and I'm gonna stay
I don't care what you do
You can press my trousers and polish my shoes
I'm in love with Squeaky Fraum
I'd like to take her to my high school prom
I quit my job at Lockheed
My girl said that's what I need
I'm ok, you're ok.....
I ran into Kim Fowley
He told me go back to the valley
I went into the Starwood
Everybody there told it it should have been good
I'm ok, you're ok.....
I ran into Tomata
He was over infantigo
He told me where to go
And he also told me on the way to the show

I'm ok, you're ok....."
"I'm Ok, You're Ok" – the Dickies

ISSUE #: 13
DATE: January 1979
FORMAT: 8 1/2x11, offset
PAGES: 24
PRICE: $.75
PRESS RUN: 500
STAFF: Al, X-8, Angola
- -

As Flipside increases it's distribution, we find that distributors want 50% of our cover price. This causes problems so we raise the cover price to 75 cents, but increase the number of pages to 24. It seems to be a good trade off. We seem to be getting a lot of people interested in promoting their scene through Flipside. At first, we just encouraged these people to do their own fanzines, but some already did. So we started printing correspondant contributions (scene articles) and more issue to issue scene updates (scene reports).

Well the 'other Masque' is having an amazing winter. Quite a few 'bigger' bands played here, compared to the the original Masque (Cramps, Dead Boys, Dead Kennedys etc). The scene, at least the part of it centered around the Masque is as happening as ever. Flipside gets a lot of new contributors that certainly help keep the enthusiasm rolling: Jill (who's party pad happends to be across from the Whisky), Paul, Nate and Lois (who all live in Whittier), and some girl named Hud who keeps threatening to help out. Gerber picks up the gosssip collumn....

Black Randy and his dog – photo by Al

Other Masque punks Michele and Barb – photo by Al

GO-GOS

Gogos: Jane, Elissa, Belinda, Margo and Charlotte at Club 88 - photo by Al

THE GO-GO'S WERE INTERVIEWED MONDAY JAN 22 1979 AT THEIR REHEARSAL ROOM IN THE REAL MASQUE. INTERVIEWED BY AL AND X-8.

X-8: WHAT ARE YOUR FAVORITE BRAND NAMES?
CHARGO: WHAT OUR FAVORITE BRAND NAMES ARE?!
X-8: YEAH.
JANE: OF WHAT?!
X-8: I DON'T KNOW.
CHARGO: GENERAL MILLS!
MARGO: I CAN TELL YOU MY LEAST FAVORITE...
AL: OK
MARGO: FIORUCCI'S -!!! YECCHHH!!
MANAGER: THEY WOULDN'T BE BAD IF THEY WOULD VOLUNTEER TO BACK US UP AND SUPPLY ALL THE FASHIONS....
JANE: WHO WANTS TO WEAR THE FUCKING SHIT WITH THEIR NAME SCRAWLED ALL OVER THE FRONT AND BACK OF IT???
MARGO: OHH - STRIKE THE OBSCENITIES....
AL: UHH, DO WANT TO BE ON BOMP OR SOMETHING?
CHARGO: WE'RE TRYING TO BE LIKE DORIS DAY AND EVERYTIME WE MESS UP...
MARGO: AND I DIDN'T DANCE ON THEIR JEAN TABLES.....
MANAGER: BULLSHIT - YOU WEEEE~
MARGO: I DIDN'T!!
X-8: WHEN YOU FIRST STARTED THE BAND, WHAT DID YOU WANT OUT OF IT?
CHARGO: OH!! - DON'T TELL HIM THAT!!!
JANE: I WANTED TO THROW UP ON STAGE, RIP MY CLOTHES OFF AND DYE MY HAIR.
MARGO: SPIT AT VALLEY GIRLS...
CHARGO: WE HATE VALLEY GIRLS...
AL: HOW MANY OF YOU COME FROM THE VALLEY?
MANAGER: HALF OF THEM, YOU LOVE TO DETEST A PART OF YOU THAT STILL LINGERS...
AL: WHAT MAKES YOU DIFFERENT FROM OTHER GIRL BANDS?
MANAGER: THEY DO ROCK AND ROLL, THEY'RE NOT A GIRL BAND, THEY JUST HAPPEN TO BE FEMALES.
BELINDA: WE DON'T LIKE TO BE CONSIDERED A GIRL BAND...
X-8: WELL WHEN YOU GOT YOURSELVES TOGETHER AS GIRLS~...
JANE: THATS BECAUSE THEY ALREADY HAD 3 GIRLS AND THEY THOUGHT "WE MIGHT AS WELL FIND 2 MORE...
AL: WHO STARTED IT?
JANE: MARGO AND ELISSA. MARGO STARTED IT AND GOT ELISSA AND THEN BELINDA..
MANAGER: BESIDES, IT'S EASY TO DO A JAPANESE TOUR WITH ALL GIRLS, AND BRIGHT COLORS.
AL: BUT YOU WERE BLONDE HAIR!
BELINDA: MY HAIR WAS BLONDE BEFORE
JANE: YEAH, MINE WAS BLONDE.
BELINDA: WE CHANGE EVERY MONTH!
X-8: WHAT ARE YOUR FAVORITE COLORS?
JANE: WHITE!
MANAGER: BLACK!~ ~ER, UH, THAT'S A STUPID QUESTION... LOOK AT THE CLOTHES THEY HAVE ON!!
AL: BUT WE'RE A BLACK AND WHITE MAGAZINE...
MANAGER: AS LONG AS IT'S FLOURESCENT, IT DOESN'T MATTER.
AL: IS THAT THE GO-GO'S THEME?
BELINDA: BRIGHT COLORS.
MANAGER: BRIGHT CONCEPTS PERIOD.
BELINDA: WELL, WE LIKE DAY-GLO. THAT'S WHY WE WEAR IT, IT'S THE WHOLE MOD THING, MOD BRIGHT COLORS
CHARGO: I USED TO HAVE ORIGINAL MOD CLOTHES THAT I SHOULD HAVE KEPT. I JUST THREW THEM AWAY...
X-8: ARE YOU A PUNK ROCK BAND?
JANE: BORDERLINE.
CHARGO: YEAH, UH~ CERTAIN SOUNDS THE BAND HAS~ YEAH.
JANE: MORE POP.
MANAGER: THEY'RE NOT A PUNK BAND, THEY'RE A YOUNG BAND AND MOST ANY GROUP THAT APPEALS TO KIDS IS A PUNK BAND NOW~ PHHHT... IF ITS GOT ENERGY AND POWER AND OLD PEOPLE DON'T LIKE IT - ITS PUNK!!
CHARGO: WHO ARE THEY INTERVIEWING ANYWAY? THE BAND OR THE MANAGER???
AL: HEY - WHO IS SHE ANYWAY???
MARGO: KITTRA
X-8: WHO???
CHARGO: K-I-DOUBLE T-R-A
X-8: OHH.... HEY (MARGO) 'MEMBER THOSE QUESTIONS YOU ASKED US FOR NEW WEST?

MARGO: OHH - NOT THOSE! - DO YOU THINK THERE'S A FUTURE FOR FANZINES?
X-8: YEAH. DO YOU THINK THERE'S A FUTURE FOR PUNK BANDS IN L.A.?
JANE: I DON'T THINK SO, NOT HARD CORE PUNK BANDS.
CHARGO: I THINK IT STARTED AS SOMETHING
BELINDA: IT'S DEFINATELY MADE A CHANGE, I MEAN LOOK AT THE GUYS WHO THEY PLAY AT THE RAINBOW...
JANE: YEAH, AND OLIVIA NEWTON-JOHN AND TANYA TUCKER ALL DRESSED UP IN BLACK LEATHER AND EVERYTHING, IT'S DEFINATELY HAD ITS IMPACT BUT I THINK PUNK WAS JUST THAT, SOMETHING JUST~
KITTRA - CRASHING THE SCENE
JANE: YEAH. OR JUST PUTTING SOME KIND OF BARRIER BETWEEN THEN AND NOW - BECAUSE NOW YOU CAN'T GET AWAY WITH THE MUSIC - WELL MAYBE YOU CAN - BOSTON'S REAL POPULAR.
AL: WHAT ABOUT CROMUN SAYING THERE'S NO FUTURE FOR LOCAL BANDS?
BELINDA: WELL, THE RECORD COMPANIES A-ROUND HERE ARE TOO AFRAID TO TAKE ANY CHANCES, THEY PLAY IT SAFE BY SIGNING ALL THESE ASS BANDS.
JANE: IF WE EVEN MAKE IT, I DON'T THINK IT WILL BE IN THIS TOWN, WE'LL HAVE TO GO OTHER PLACES~
CHARGO: I WANT TO GO TO JAPAN.
X-8: HAVE THEY HAD ANY "NEW WAVE" BANDS?
JANE: NEW WAVE!!! I HATE THAT WORD!!!! I HATE ALL THOSE FUCKING LABELS!!!
KITTRA: I HATE NEW WAVE!!!!! I HATE PUNK!! I HATE ROCK AND ROLL EVEN!!!
JANE: WE'RE THE GO-GO'S AND WE DON'T FIT INTO ANY CATAGORY.
AL: STAN LEE (DICKIES) CALLED YOU THE NEXT BEATLES...
KITTRA: I CAN SEE THAT EASILY...(TOSSES HER HEAD)
BELINDA: NOOOO!!!
KITTRA: I CAN!! CAUSE YOU HAVE VISUAL IMPACT AND THE BEATLES WITH LONG HAIR AND LITTLE SUITS HAD VISUAL IMPACT.
JANE: THEY WERE SO FUCKING CUTE.
KITTRA: THEY HAD THE IMPACT AND YOU HAVE THE MELODY (SHE JUST RATTLES ON AND ON...)
BELINDA: STAN CALLS ME JOHN LENNON. HA!
AL: WOULD BEATLE WOULD YOU BE? I MEAN WHAT BEATLE WOULD YOU BE?
JANE: I'M GEORGE HARRISON. MY TEETH ARE ROTTEN.
CHARGO: I'LL BE RINGO - NOOO!!
MARGO: I WANNA BE PAUL CAUSE I WAS LEFT-HANDED AT FIRST!!
CHARGO: NO - I'LL BE PETE BEST...
AL: WEREN'T YOU RECORDING A WHILE BACK?
BELINDA: THAT WAS JUST FOR US. WE DID ONE SONG CAUSE THAT'S ALL WE GOT THROUGH - "FASHION SEEKERS"
JANE: WE'RE GONNA RECORD IT FOR KINNEY'S SHOES - "FASHION SNEAKERS" HA HA HA!!!
BELINDA: OH!!! JANE AND I KNOW WHAT WE'RE GONNA GET IF WE EVER GET MONEY...
JANE - YEAH, WE'RE GONNA GET MOTORCYCLES!! AND BE THE YOUNG CYCLE GIRLS - AND DRIVE ACROSS COUNTRY AND MEET JUNKIES AND GET OUR HEADS BLOWN OFF AT THE END OF THE MOVIE.
KITTRA: OH GOD. YOU LIKE, I MEAN, YOU LOOK LIKE DEBBIE BOONE AND YOU'RE GONNA

BE ON THE BACK OF A BIG HARLEY-
BELINDA: NO! WE'RE GONNA BE ON THE FRONT
JANE: JUST LIKE THE MOVIE, AND WE'LL HAVE PRETTY COLORED MOTORCYCLES WITH MATCH-ING HELMETS AND JACKETS.
X-8: UHH... OK.. WHAT'S THE CIRCUMSISION OF THE EARTH?
GO-GO's: HA! HA! (HYSTERICS)
X-8: WOULD-YU WHAT GUYS HAVE YOU DONE LATELY?
GO-GO's: HA! HA! (HYSTERICS)
X-8: NO... I MEAN WHAT GIGS HAVE YOU PLAYED OUT OF L.A.?
JANE: MONROVIA MONGOLIA...
BELINDA: THE GUYS WERE YELLING "TAKE OFF YOUR CLOTHES!!"
JANE: YEAH, AND THE GIRLS ARE CLUTCHING THEIR BOYFRIENDS "OHH DON'T TOUCH OUR BOYS" HA HA HA.
MARGO: AND SPITTING.
AL: DOESN'T YOUR DRUMMER LIKE YOU?
JANE: SHE DOESN'T SPEAK ENGLISH, ONLY ITALIAN!
AL: HOW LONG HAVE YOU BEEN PLAYING DRUM
ELISSA: WELL, I STARTED PLAYING WHEN TH GROUP GOT TOGETHER, BUT BEFORE THAT A-BOUT TEN YEARS FOR JUST DIFFERENT THIN
KITTRA: REALLY!?!
BELINDA: YEAH - BEATING OFF.
ELISSA: YEAH JUST BEAT OFF ALL THE TIME.
AL: HAVE YOU BEEN IN ANOTHER BAND BEFORE?
CHARGO: UGH. I'LL TELL YOU ABOUT ONE BAND NOT THE ONE EVERYONE KNOW ABOUT. (EYES) MANUEL AND THE GARDENERS. IT WAS SUCH A GOOD BAND. I PLAYED KEYBOARDS AND WE PLAYED AT WEE AND ALL OVER.
AL: WHAT ABOUT THE EYES?
CHARGO: JOE AND ME, WE WERE IN LOVE TOO MUCH. WE WERE JUST TOO GOOD OF FRIENDS AND WE DIDN'T WANT THE BAND TO GET IN THE WAY - THATS MY STORY, SO I LEFT.
JANE: I WAS IN A CHURCH BAND WHEN I WAS 13. LEAD VOCALS. "JESUS IS JUST AL-RIGHT WITH ME!"
MARGO: I PLAYED TRUMPET IN JR. HI SCHOOL.
X-8: WHAT DO YOU WANT TO BE WHEN YOU GROW UP?
BELINDA: I JUST GOT FIRED FROM MY JOB.
AL: HOW COME?
BELINDA: THEY DIDN'T LIKE HOW I DRESSED.
JANE: THEY DON'T LIKE IT ~ NA NA NA NA
BELINDA: I WENT TO WORK WITH PURPLE HAIR THAT STARTED IT, THEY'RE REALLY CONSERV ATIVE AND I WAS SUPPOSED TO BE A MIND-LESS DRONE, AND GET COFFEE FOR ALL THE BOSSES AND SHIT LIKE THAT.
CHARGO: I'M A DRONE. I WORK AT A HOSPITAL
JANE: I'M A NOTHING. I SLEEP 14 HOURS A DAY. ITS GROSS MAN - I'M A ZOMBIE.
X-8: DO YOU HAVE - LIKE, UH, PROBLEMS?
CHARGO: YOU CAN IMAGINE. 5 GIRLS. 5 TIMES AT MONTH AT DIFFERENT TIMES - NOT NEC-ESSARILY.
BELINDA: IT WAS MY TURN LAST NIGHT.
CHARGO: I JUST FINISHED MINE.
MARGO: I JUST STARTED!
CHARGO: WHEN DID YOU START? WHAT KIND OF TAMPON DO YOU USE?" "HEE HAW"
MARGO: "I'M STARTING NEXT WEEK - I HOPE"
JANE: WE ALL HOPE. HA HA HA
BELINDA: WE ALL HOPE!

Belinda Vocals

Chargo Ld Guitar

Jane Guitar

Margo Bass

Elissa Drums

Dils Tony and Chip at the Other Masque – photo by Al

DILS

This Dils were interviewed on Jan 6th at the Original Masque by Al, X-8, Gerard, Rables and assorted punks.

X-8 You've been credited with saying that all rock bands are equal and as such should be paid equal.

Chip: Wait, that's no what the Dils said, that's from an article by Robert Hilburn, he said that about us, he said because we gave all the bands equal money that night at the May Day gig, he said something about how we think all bands are equal, but we think we are more equal because we played the full hour.

X-8 The image the Dils have in L.A. is that you're always pissed off with us because of our lifestyle, if L.A. angers you, why do you bother to play here?

Tony: I'm not pissed off at L.A. The lifestyle here is the same as in S.F., for the punks in Seattle or the punks in Portland, there's no difference. I get pissed off everytime we come down here, but I get pissed off everytime we go out of town. You go and do a show and there's no promotion, the sound check is suppose to be at 6 and it's at 7:30. I'm not angry with the punks here or the lifestyle or anything.

X-8 You've been bad rapping Brendan in the press, if Brendan didn't operate in a capitalistic way do you think he could stay in business?

Tony: I wish Brendan did act in a good capitalistic way, because then he would've promoted the show, he would have invested his money properly and wisely and he could be making a killing off this scene. He's not making a killing, he's always bitching how he's losing money. He's a capitalist and a businessman. So why doesn't he act like a good capitalist businessman. I personally don't like promoters, there a foul breed, just like most people in show biz, it really stinks, and this is show biz.

AL: What about that Cheech and Chong movie?

Tony: You want to hear the background. That's the very first time we ever played in front of anybody, it was like a week after we met the infamous Peter Urban and he had our phone number and he heard they were gonna be filming punk bands at the Roxy, if we did it

we could say we played the Roxy.

Chip: You know the Germs and a couple of other local bands tried out for that movie...

Tony: We thought for sure they'd cut us out cause we stopped and they told us not to stop at all. It was good pay though.

X-8 You resent it now though?

Tony: I won't go see it.

Chip: It's kind of embarrassing.

AL: What's this about you saying it's stupid to come up and tell a band you liked the set?

Tony: I didn't mean for people who enjoy a band to express themselves because that makes me feel really good when it happens, but you know bands that have a circle of friends who know them and they could suck shit, but their friends tell them they're great. So when you don't get any other kind of opinion but that it's like this circle of yes men.

AL: Don't you have fans like that?

Tony: Yeah we do, but we also have people like Flipside who have been going like this (elbow nudges) ever since we started and you go No who ask people about our politics and there's plenty of things like that that we look at TOO along with the people going 'Yeah, you're great'.

AL: Do you think you pick up more slag than most bands because of what you stand for?

Tony: Yeah, for what people think we stand for. I definitely think thats true.

Punk: What are your politics?

Tony: I'm a Communist, **Chip** and **JOHN** aren't. We write about what we want to write about, but shit – we play two love songs, cause we've been in love, and a song about a car...

AL: (to Chip) What do think of Communism?

Chip: I'm not motivated to be a Communist or a Democrat or a Capitalist or anything. I just write songs and play guitar.

AL: What about you John?

JOHN: Rock and roll!

Tony: And that's the Dils, see, and people can't get beyond something Peter will say or I'll say.

AL: Is Peter a Communist?

Tony: Yeah. They think that we're all alike, that we have our little red books on the table and we go, Ok lets write a song about, uh ... "Agricultural Communes For The Revolution" or some shit like that and it's bullshit. I'm the only communist in the band, and I'm only one third of the band, and two thirds of the songs

that I write have nothing to do with politics. People wouldn't have ever know we were political if Chip hadn't worn that hammer and sickle t-shirt on stage. People didn't hear what we were saying, they just saw the hammer and sickle.

AL: Why were YOU wearing the t-shirt?

Chip: Looked cool. It's just as shocking as having a beaver or a swastica, especially a hammer and sickle, that really pisses a lot of people off.

AL: What happend with John quitting awhile back?

JOHN: Joining the band I admired most in the whole scene took a lot to cope with and after awhile I just had to sit down and think about it.

Tony: We've broken up a couple of times, and it's always been the same reason, because of too much... um, just TOO MUCH.

(Tony and Chip are currently in Rank and File)

FLIPSIDE NUMBER 14

"Yes that's right, punk is dead/it's just another cheap product for the consumers head/bubble-gum rock on plastic transistors/schoolboy sedition backed by big time promoters/CBS promotes the Clash/but it ain't for revolution, it's just for cash/punk became a fashion like hippie used to be/and it ain't got a thing to do with you and me/movements are systems and systems kill/movements are expressions of the public will/punk became a movement because we all felt lost/but the leaders sold out now we all pay the cost/punk narcissism was a social napalm/steve jones started doing real harm/preaching revolution, anarchy and change/as he sucked from the system that had given him his name/well I'm tired of looking through shit stained glass/tired of staring up a superstars arse/I've got an arse and crap and a name/I'm just waiting for my 15 minutes fame/Steve Jones you're napalm/if you're so pretty vacant why do you smarm?/Pattie Smith. you're napalm/you write with your hand but it's Rimbaud's arm/And me, yes, I, do I want to burn?/Is there something I can learn?/Do I need a businessman to promote my angle?/Can I resist the carrots that fame and fortune angle?/I see the velvet zippers in their bondage gear/the social-elite with safety pins in their ear/I watch and understand that it don't mean a thing/the scorpions night attack, but the system stole the sting/PUNK IS DEAD"

"Punk Is Dead"-the Crass

ISSUE #: 14
DATE: April 1979
FORMAT: 8 1/2x11, offset

PRESS RUN: 700
STAFF: Al, Nate, Jill, Paul Problem, Lois,
Angola, Gerard and X-8
- - - - - - - - - - - - - - - - - - - -

Big things happening in the scene: the big Elks Lodge Riot causes a strong reaction from the punk community. At the same time the punk community looses the last club of its 'own', the Other Masque. Besides moving in ups and downs, the scene is also moving sideways- on one side you have a big influx of kids from the suburbs (especially the beach cities, such as Huntington Beach and Long Beach - the later with Rhino 39) infiltrating the punk ranks, on the other side you have the trends, the current one being a big rock-a-billy revival (especially since Levi and the Rockats hit town) taking from the ranks of what we all thought were punks. Me, in the face of the Elks Lodge affair and the release of the first vinyl from Crass, I'm looking towards a stronger punk attitude. In any case the scene is definitly in for some changes.

RHINO 39

Rhino 39 was interviewed on March 20 at the now famous Rhino Hdstrs in Long Beach. Flip was Al, Paul Problem, Lois and Nate.
- - - - - - - - - - - - - - - - - - - -

PAUL: Are there punk/ surfer fights at Milikan High School?
MARK: Yeah, but not with surfers, with jocks...
TIM: A lot of verbal...
PAUL: Do they get girls too?
DAVE: They don't care, it's free for all, lesbian action in the bathroom, it's the best. The whole school is generally homosexual except for the punk rockers and they want us...
NATE: To give them head?
DAVE: No we have sexual standards that we have to hold to...
PAUL: Do you have a lot in your fan club?
DAVE: Ask Sandy, she's the president, she has really ingenious marketing techniques, like she had flyers and buttons for the fan club...
TIM: Oh, don't say that Dave!!
Larry Lets forget that.
DAVE: That was at the No Mag benefit but I guess we won't elaborate.
AL: Wasn't she puking on the sidewalk that day?
DAVE: Isn't that interesting, she just passes out like - poof- falls on the floor and ... it got the job done. But no, Sandy did pay for it.
PAUL: Do you make any money?
MARK: We make about enough to pay for this studio.
DAVE: And this is Machine Shop Apartments, Tabb named them.
AL: What's gonna be on your single?
Linda (manager): It's a two sided A side, "Xerox", "No Compromise" and "Night In Watts" on the B side.
AL: DAVE, I remember when you used to come to Hollywood with curly hair and your camera...
DAVE: It's still curly, this is just a wig.
MARK: Dave would come to school "I've discovered the new thing!".
DAVE: I'd get up on a bench at lunch and try to tell everyone.
Larry: Yeah, about DEVO!!!
AL: And they flipped you off and threw beer?
LOIS: At school?
DAVE: "Punk rock sucks!" (jock voice)
MARK: "Fuckin' punkers!" (surfer voice)
Larry: "Love peace and Jimi Hendrix"

MASQUE

Rhino 39: Larry, Dave, Tim and Mark - photo by Al

DAVE: "Sid is dead" (jock voice again) The best thing is this one guy who walks around with long hair and a Grateful Dead t-shirt like "I'm so proud", wait, let's give names, Rob Whitticker, Tim Bennet are homosexuals.
PAUL: What did they say when Sid died?
TIM: They'd come up to me and say: "Sids dead and I'm glad motherfucker!".
PAUL: What grades do you get Dave?
DAVE: I get A's and B's.
AL: We decided you are all pseudo-intellectuals.
DAVE: Either you are intellectual or you're not.
AL: Or you aren't but you can fake it...
PAUL: What happend when Sandy got beat up?

DAVE: It wasn't people getting beat up, it was like they were sitting out at lunch and I came back from my house and I was gonna talk to Sandy and Cathy and the other girls sitting at this bench and I see this big crowd around them. EVERYONE at lunch was around them going "Punk rock, punk rock!!!" So we spent the rest of the day in the Administration office talking about "maybe we could tone down the way you dress, maybe you could get some OP's, we could start a fund and get you some."
AL: Is Rhino a V.D.?
DAVE: It could be.
AL: Why do you like punk rock?
TIM: Because it's not stupid, it's not mindless.

AL: What about you Dave?
DAVE: I just all of a sudden felt that I've been fooled and was just caught up in what everybody else was caught up in.
NATE: You were a homosexual?
DAVE: Yeah, I was a homosexual like everyone else at school, and then I discovered heterosexuality.

ELKS LODGE
SECRET MESSAGES FROM THE GEZA X SPYLINE
213-464-0070

I don't want to harp on St. Patricks Day, we already know plenty about that... but let's begin with the obvious. On March 17, 1979 **The Police rioted.** Nearly every news report that I've seen so far says that "between 40 and 60" riot squadders "broke up" a rock event that was "getting out of control". We all know differently: "Between 200 and 300" police maniacs "broke into" a PUNK event and "went completely out of their minds". And the news media knows differently, too. I spoke with Ken Freed of the L.A. Times Sunday morning, before his slimy kiss-ass article came out on Monday. He says: "Oh I've had about 150 calls already." He was taking notes- I could hear him typing. "Ok, I'll use your stuff in my article". Is what he finished with. He told several others the same thing-- so why the lame article? The same happened with Scott Harris at CBS. And the Examiner completely misquoted photographer Ann Suma. She is quoted as saying **line for line** the police report (as if anyone even believes that hunk of shit). The sad truth is that the media glossed over it **NOT** because it wasn't a good story, **NOT** because they weren't interested or sympathetic but because they were **told** (in no uncertain terms) to play it down. I have it on good authority-- straight from the source, in fact, that several newspeople and radio people who were on our side and did help us were threatened with their jobs if they breathed another word about it. But some conscientious people stuck to their guns and got some of the story out. They are heros and deserved to be praised for their courage: Rodney, Dusty and Barry from KROQ... KNX Newsradio... KHJ Radio (of all people)... Bob Hilburn and Kristine McKenna from the Times... Chris Morris from the Reader... and last but not least Dave Street (visiting from New York) who was incredibly helpful here at spyline. He's taking the story back to N.Y. The world will soon point an accusing finger at the LAPD but why why why is it so fucking difficult to get the real truth out? Well if, as Paul Roessler says "You're still living in a pre-Watergate fog".. I'll spell it out for you: There is a **truely vast** conspiracy going on, involving the White House, the C.I.A., the news media, disco, the excise tax on alcohol, tax loopholes for record companies, the oil companies and their sucking babies (gasoline, drugs, phonograph records. Anything that's made of petroleum.), local police, and YES, (he must be kidding), PUNK ROCK. To go into detail here would be impossible-- it's just too much of a monster, but let me encapsulate it real quick: Jimmy Carter got the dingaling notion that punk rock (as in England was a **major threat** to the cow-like complacency and submissiveness of the American public. (Us, a terror?) Yes kids, they were scared **shitless** of you and you didn't even know it. You see they have this hoax they call "the Energy Crisis" which they've spent billions of dollars

The police claims of punk vandalism and riot are completely without evidence to back them up.

Did The Police Riot?

THE FRACAS BETWEEN squadrons of helmeted L.A.P.D. troops and punk rock enthu - siasts at the Elk's Club last Saturday night has brought back memories of the '60s, when it was standard practice for then police chief Ed Davis' boys to smash hippie heads just for showing up at an event. The curious question is what provoked the police to attack the concertgoers and bring on themselves the old charges of "police riot."

numbers and why? The best answer seems to be standing by? The cops are assuming the worst that the cops are assuming the worst about punkers an do about it.

Police and Fans Disagree on Raid at Rock Sho...

Concertgoers Out... but LAPD Def... justify their action... however. I am terrified ... disgusted by the stupidity, violence and ignorance of the police. I am appalled by the enormity of this meaningless or... bloodletting. It seems almost ... were years after... cops were ... ism eleven Demo... Chicago "riot squad" seems to be ... is clear that ... the worst ... that police ... h youth is still in force. ...car that the kids will always ...e losers, and there is little that we ... do about it.

The whole thing makes me fucking sick. I only hope that it doesn't happen again. The next time, it'll be different. The next time, they'll have to take *me* to jail.

A New Wave of Police Brutality

Why a riot squed on duty?

The Elks Lodge News Conference: Jeff Atta (Middle Class) and Dorothy with fresh head stiches tell Channel 2 News what happened. - photo by Al

promoting and which American people are buying hook, line and shortage. **Unless a bunch of brats start asking embarrassing questions...** "Why are albums going up exactly a dollar a year when they sound so phony?"... "Why is gas going up ten cents a month, when they are stockpiling oil in offshore tankers?"... "Why did they suddenly remove the excise tax on alcohol? That's like spending tax money to lower the price of booze?" Listen; most Americans don't believe in their leaders anymore, not really. Did you know that there was a less than 15% turnout for the last local election? Do you know how **low** that is? In a weird way, it's great news? It means that Americans are sick to death of their dishonest government. But still they swallow the big lie. As long as they see it on T.V. and as long as they have to wait in line for gas: "Raise the goddamn price, just don't make me wait around for it- #$%&' *PLEASE?*". In other words you don't have to **like** the system, just don't complain... no even maybe. Or we'll kill you. Why such a big deal? **Because** if the public gets wise, it could fuck up the corporate profit (16% **higher** than last year, while we suffer through imaginary shortages). And **everyone** including you, me, the cops, the President, news editors, record executives, absolutely everyone lives only to serve and worship at the altar of the really powerful corporations-- the oil companies and their fantastically intricate propaganda machine. So here's what happened:

Carter had a meeting about a year ago with all the record companies and acting on orders from god-knows-where **ordered** them to put the lid on punk rock. The labels, who had been signing any act that looked even remotely punk, suddenly dropped 'em like a hot potato. And solemnly declared the whole shebang to be "commercially unmarketable". So the all powerful record industry (let's face it) can **hype** and sell any crap it chooses to, unanimously decides the **biggest news item in years** is unmarketable! Ha ha ha ah ah ha. Very very funny. Then it went gold. Then it went platinum. Despite the suppression, despite the disfavor. Now they were really sweating... "What do we do. We can't just ignore this much money, can we? This could be **bigger** than disco." (Disco only

accounts for a measly and insignificant 7% of record sales. Figure **THAT** out!) So exactly two months ago all the major labels had another meeting and quietly agreed to **start signing** and promoting (guess what?) new wave and punk rock acts. I'll just bet that Carter calls the mayors of a few key cities: "Well the record companies won't play ball anymore, so you'd better get the cops on these kids..." **And exactly two months ago the police started raiding punk rock shows!** You'll know if I'm crazy or not if somebody suddenly starts busting the record companies for anti-trust violations. After letting them get away with it for years, "You've been naughty record companies, so you're gonna get a spanking."

Now for the good news:
On Sunday, March 18, 1979 at about 12:00 noon the phone started ringing and didn't stop. **Everyone** had information about the Elks Hall incident. Rational, sane, organized information. When we figured out what was happening, and amazed Dave Street, Terry James (Bag Dad), and myself started a 24 hour information Spyline at 464-0070. We called all the news services but found out that hundreds of other people had called-- with the same exact story!! In fact what happened that week maybe completely without historical precedent.. the first glimpse of (dare I say it) **MASS TELEPATHY**. We should really be proud of ourselves. Hundreds of young people, spontaneously and independently, initiated a leaderless and unplanned moral outcry. It may also be the first time that an obviously political situation generated a **non-political** reaction. Instead of wasting our time on endless political theorizing, we made it a **moral** issue and told the whole world about it. Absolutely awesome! As a result, the public is on our side. I had always figured that his L.A. scene had some hidden magic, that we all shared some secret knowledge but we were deliberately staying in disguise-- acting like dumb shits to preserve that feeling and fool the rest of the world. Until the shit hit the fan. Until innocent people- **our friends** were hurt. And we all decided we had to put a stop to it **NOW** before they think they can get away with it again. The LAPD are too well know for their sadism and cruelty. We are not going to just

"forget" that this happened. We intend to file a civil suit, if we can. So if you have photos or were beaten or have important information, call the spy-line. We are raising such a fucking stink (P.U.) that we **CAN** win. We're telepathic, intelligent, rational, and **damn** sneaky! Keep up the good work.
GEZA X

The very first Flipside Record release. A 3 song ep by 'M'. A very limited edition to say the least.

HUNTINGTON BEACH

By Noelle
Huntington Beach (HB), here there is a new variety of people, a fast emerging group of kids. These impressionable people started as a small clique and is now a group larger than any other. The followed older friends who were involved with the beginnings of punk. There wasn't much here: no clubs, no bands, just magazines, radio and records. The older people were slow to catch on but the few who were labeled as punk were hit the hardest by all the stuck up assholes at school, but they didn't change. Then they grew and grew and within a year there was a band: the **New**, which later became the **Crowd**. At last a band for people to identify with, to draw them into L.A. into a new scene. Then it became real 'in' to be punk and it is mostly all surfer guys because the other groups at school had gone disco or something. High School became a warground. The school vs. the punks. Well the punks rule there now and the Crowd has lasted 10 months. After them came **Isolation** (now the **Klan**), then other bands of which some lasted and some didn't. Now we have the **Klan**, **Crowd**, **Press**, **Presidents**, and **Outsiders** to name a few. I never thought that in 2 years this would happen, and now it's really happening in Huntington Beach and so what if we live by the beach!!
CROWD
Tracy: L.A. people say they don't like us because we're from the beach, and our music isn't heavy metal but I think it's because we're good.
Jim Trash: I was born...
Tracy: On a surfboard!!!
Jim Trash: That's right! Surfs up. We all surf

but Jim K.

Tracy: We've been surfing all our lives. We wanna have beach parties like Frankie and Annette!

KLAN

Noise: We have nothing to do with the KKK, it's our own klan...

Jeff: He's trying to be a fascist, he's reading "the Rise And Fall of the 3rd Reich".

Jeff: We're not into heavy politics.

FS: Why do you like nazism?

Noise: It gives me lots to think and write about.

Jeff: Material for the mind.

The Crowd in natural surroundings – photo Noelle

MAU MAUS

The Mau Maus were interviewed on March 30th on the roof of their Hollywood 'studio' by Al, Nate and Gerard.

- -

(The Maumaus first played October 31st and since have played few, but great gigs. Two members of the band were in the Berlin Brats, a very popular band of 3 years ago- who were also in the Cheech and Chong movie.

AL: What does Mau Mau mean?

ROD:: Oh come on, don't you know anything, look it up in the Encyclopedia!!

AL: Is it like the Cramps song "Papa ooo mau mau"?

RICK: Eeeeeooooggghhh!!

ROD: It's an African tribe that eats people.

NATE: What bands do you hate?

RICK: The Dils, ... Screamers, everyone else.

NATE: Why do you hate the Dils?

RICK: Pretentious political crap that's way.

NATE: What's your favorite band?

RICK: Mau Maus, I can tell we're gonna get far.

AL: What happened to the Berlin Brats?

RICK: We're not gonna talk about the Brats.

ROD: Fuck the Berlin Brats.

NATE: Did you ever get paid...

AL: ...for the Cheech and Chong movie?

RICK: We never got paid for that, in fact I told off Lou Adler and got thrown off the set.

AL: How many gigs have you played?

RICK: Four.

ROD: That many!!

AL: Do people say you look like Johnny Rotten?

RICK: Do people tell me! Well sometimes, I'm sure my mother would say that. I don't know that many people that would say something that pretentious.

NATE: Remember when you puked on stage at the Masque...

RICK:: No. I puke in private. Not on stage.

AL: What do you think of glitter rock?

RICK:: What glitter rock? The Screamers?

AL: The Berlin Brats.

EARL: Glitter rock? Oh no no no...

RICK:: You've got your nerve.

AL: People scream "Glitter rock star" when you guys play.

EARL: Glitter, no way. Where have you been?

AL: You seem kinda defensive to that?

EARL: Well I've never heard it before.

RICK:: I've never heard it either, that's not

what the baseball bat was all about, that's because the guy in Fear thought he was smart, it was because I was calling him a hippie...

NATE: Were you ever a hippie?

RICK: I was never a hippie! NEVER!!! Never. I was never a hippie. Anyone who calls me a **fuckin' hippie or a jew** is in trouble. We're definitely anti-religion, anti-god, anti-jesus which is anti-art because art is just an

imitation of religion anyway.

ROD: All we live for is the Madi Gras...

RICK: ...the festival in South America and the Hollywood Santa Clause Parade!!!

AL: And your influences?

I sing like, no, I started stuff like anything, blues or the Rolling Stones or stuff. I wouldn't say that is a total influence, I simply sing like an American. I don't sing like anyone else, the people from Britain have been ripping us off for fuckin' years so if they say we are ripping them off, that's their problem. They just don't know what an American voice is like. I got certain black tendencies, I got certain Mick Jagger tendencies and certain tendencies that come from American variables. I could be like Johnny Rotten and be a real cunt and pretend like I don't like anybody and then go and rip them all off, but that's not my intention because I don't really care, ya know? You sing along with a record first to discover that you have a voice to begin with, otherwise you'd be a **FUCKING** idiot. I have my influences and I don't give a shit.

AL: So what's a Mau Mau?

RICK: I'M sure you want some great extention, uh, explanation, but we were just at the Masque and thought it up and it turns out there is a black militant group in S.F. that got $900,000 out of the government.

ROD: And there's this street gang in Brooklyn that go around with baseball bats, and they go around knocking heads in "mau mau mau".

RICK: You can say what you want about the **FUCKING** name, all we do is **fuckin'** play and **fuckin'** play what we want.

FLIPSIDE NUMBER 15

"She, had to leave
Los Angeles
All her boys wore out in black
and her toys had too
She had started to hate
every nigger and jew
every mexican that gave her a lot of shit
every homosexual
and the idle rich
She, couldn't leave
Los Angeles

Mau Maus Rick Wilder and Greg – photo by Al

"She found it hard to say goodbye
to her own best friend
She bought a clock on Hollywood Blvd the day she left
It felt sad
She had to get out"
"Los Angeles" - X

ISSUE #: 15
DATE: July 1979
FORMAT: 8 1/2x11, offset
PAGES: 24
PRICE: $.75
PRESS RUN: 800
STAFF: Al, Jill, Paul, Angola

With this issue Flipside looks different. For one thing Jill is typing everything, and with an electric typewriter it looks a lot cleaner. We are also using her Hollywood apartment as an office and doing a lot of paste up there. Hud is doing a lot of 'art direction', as well as writing a story on the original mod scene in England along with it's music ('Blue Beat', or 'ska'), Paul Problem is supplying us with all the best gossipy type news, reviews and interviews. The scene is divided up between going to the Whisky for the likes of the Screamers or Dickies, or Club 88 for X, Controllers or Plugz type punk action. Right about this time the Hong Kong Cafe opens, which will become the main focus of the scene in the months to come. This second floor venue provides a regular outlet for all kinds of bands and a unique place for social interaction (situated in the courtyard of a Chinatown shopping complex- across the way from Madame Wongs 'rock' club no less).

CRASS

Dear Al,
Small Wonder passed your letter on to us. I've inclosed this letter inside **International Anthem** (a magazine we produce) which has the words to Asylum on the back cover. No, it wasn't a publicity stunt, we seriously considered abandoning the record when the pressers at a Southern Irish plant refused to allow Asylum, but we decided to go ahead with it, making Asylum available from us on tape or word form. I feel it's too important a statement to be used for publicity purposes, and seeing as we're not interested in making money and selling ourselves, it wouldn't make any sense anyway. Over the last couple of

months we've managed to put Asylum out on a single ourselves with another track by Eve Libertine on the other side. It should be out soon, we have to print the cover yet. If all goes well and you want a copy and can't get hold of one in California, write to Small Wonder for one. I think you will get more of an idea of what we're about from reading or hearing Asylum.

If we had any photographs, I'd send one, but unfortunately we haven't any. I don't know exactly what kind of information you want but I'll tell you how it started and why we do it. All of us have been involved in other things at other times, but punk seems to be the best way of making the kind of statements we want to make NOW. The band has been together for one and a half years, growing out of an open house (a house in the country which aggravates certain people who rekon that you must live in the city to be a punk. That you must be working class etc... more prejudice!!) where we live together. The band is an extention of the way we live, so the band evolved out of our lifestyle rather than the band being the mainstay. It's one of quite a number of activities and involvements.

I think our attitude is manifested in the way the commercial press do their best to ignore us or indictively criticize what we do. Fanzines are all supportive, the commercial press recently slagged them off too.

I hope that what I've said plus the record and the newspaper will give you enough. If I went into such things as how we dress etc.. I would end up writing a book. All I can say is that we carefully consider each detail, make no compromises on any issue from bouncers at our gigs (we don't have them if we are organizing it at all) to the importance of being available to the audience during gigs. We don't preach a "way", we leave each person to find their own.
Yours,
Joy de Vivre (Virginia Creeper) CRASS

Plugz FS backcover ad featuring the lyrics to their modified "La Bamba"

GERMS

This was going to be a Germs interview, but that's really impossible. Probably as impossible as capturing the Germs on vinyl, but we will soon see about that. We tried a few times to interview them in the traditional sense, but we failed. Actually for you older

punkers, we did interview the Germs almost two years ago in the second Flipside. But things have changed since then: Bobby Pyn is now Darby Crash, Pat Smear is now Pats, and the new (new?) drummer is Don, they have two singles cut, one album cut, song on Yes L.A., and have their own album in the works. And the Germs are still going strong, uncompromising and as Kickboy (ex-Germs manager) has realized, the Germs are: "a bizarre, strangely threatening subversive cult spreading far beyond their musical frame of reference." Far beyond the limits of the band, Germs are spreading, Germs are the spirit of punk rock.

So what we give you is a Germs update, a half assed interview, a picture and some quotes- not a free plug for the Germs, but rather our endorsement.

- - - - - - - - - - - - - - - - - - - -

DARBY: Do you wanna buy Sids bass peg?
AL: Yeah. Sure.... How much?
DARBY: 250 dollars.
AL: Ok, I'll write a check!
DARBY: Helen has the whole bass, Sid busted it over Nancy's head. It's a pretty good souvenir.
AL: What about the Slash Records album?
Don: No one else would...
DARBY: They keep printing that we're unsignable.
Don: To sing the unsignable, make them real champions of the underdog.
AL: How many songs on it?
Pat: 15 songs, 15 minutes a side.
Don: 14 songs!!
Pat: Quantity, not quality.
DARBY: We're not the Screamers, charge $6.50 for 15 minutes, we know we're not worth that much.
Don: Shit, we're barely worth what you're paying and you got in for free!
Pat: Ask us about bands?
DARBY: I only like X.
Don: John punched Gary in the face at UCLA.
Pat: Did you see me kick that photographer? I kicked him off the stage, and he stood up so I kicked him in the head.
AL: How do you like the way your reputation is getting?
Don: Bee-utiful.
DARBY: Rather nice, isn't it?
Don: It's made the world a real beauty with us.
DARBY: It just proves they're all assholes.
Rosetta: "Don't let the Germs come to my party, they'll wreck it maaannnn!".
(Germs leave for soundcheck).
AL: Where did you meet the Germs Helen?
Helen: Two years ago, Plunger Pit.
AL: Is that really Sids bass peg?
Helen: Yeah, I got Sids bass in my car. When I was staying there, he hit Nancy over the

Germs with Helen and Rosetta - photo by Al

head, and he missed and hit the wall and it cracked and ended up breaking, so he gave it to me. The first one he got. The one he stole from Paul Simonon, a real bitchin' history bass.

AL: So why did Sid end up dying?
Helen: Why? He couldn't stay alive with Nancy dead. They were in love with each other, true love always dies.
AL: Sid didn't kill Nancy.
Helen: NO!!! Some nigger she ripped off that night killed her, it was his girlfriend who was in love with Sid, he was really jealous because of them two, but they split town and they never found them. When Sid died they just said what the point in looking? We can just say he did it.
AL: How long did you stay with Sid?
Helen: Two months in England.... You gotta admit, those early Germs gigs were fun, all the trash and blood and cliche punk, which no punks even did.

Germs at the Other Masque - photo by Al

Roxanne, Stiv Bators, Gerber, Helen Killer posing for photos. - photo by Al

GENERATION X

(The Teds, the Rockers, the Mods, the Hipples and now the Punks–each generation has a form of teenage rebellion.)

In 1964 the Rockers still into Elvis the Mods (usually younger than the Rockers) say the Mersey Sound is out (the beatles art to lame), the Blue Beat's driving monotonous rhythm has been made popular by the Jamaican contingents now popular by the Jamamicsan contingents now in Britian. The current dances are the Block and the Bang. The Block is a shake rocking sideways with a rotary hip movement and the top of the body bent forward in a sideway crab movement (strictly British.)

The US was starting the Surf, Swim, Monkey and Huggy-Bug. Guys dressed in Ivy League style suits, trousers with regulation 17 inch hems, round-toed boots (imitation crocodile or phython), hair high, puffed up on the sides and back, wear shift-style dresses with round collars, o lipstick, hardly any make-up. Of course, when they'd go dancing, the girls would dress in stretch slacks, black and white tweed coats with yellow collars and cuffs. Fitted 1930's shoulders. (This is only to mention a few of the styles, they created a lot of their own fashions.)

Being influenced by drinking, smoking and Purple Hearts. the Mods were also into CND (Campaign for Nuclear Disarmament.) So every generation has its own problems- SO WHAT?

The Blue beat music has been around, brought by Jamaicans, but was captured by the Mods. Ziggy Jackson, head of Blue Beat Label Records, made it popular. Prince Buster, having a hit ("Madness") selling 15,000 records, was top of the Blue Beat top twenty.

Then most of the record shops started selling Blue Beat records finally they caught on!

So, that's kind of the way it was. if you're interested in finding a record- Good Luck! Not you kids in the U.K. - you send your to me!!!]

Yes, that's right- Mod is back! If interested for more info, or if you have more info, write to HUD in care of FLIPSIDE.
(Info taken from the book, Generation X)

FLIPSIDE NUMBER 16

"Sittin' here like a loaded gun
I'm ready to go off
I got nothing to do but shoot my mouth off
So gimmie gimmie gimmie
Gimmie some more
Gimmie gimmie gimmie
Don't ask what for
You know the world's got problems
I've got problems of my own
but they aren't the kind that can't be fixed
With an atom bomb
You know I gotta go out
and get something for my head
if I keep doing this
I'm gonna end up dead"
"Gimmie Gimmie" - Black Flag

ISSUE #: 16
DATE: October 1979
FORMAT: 8 1/2x11, offset
PAGES: 24
PRICE: $.75
PRESS RUN: 1000
STAFF: Al, Paul Problem, Jill

This issue continues on pretty much the same lines as the last one. The scene continues to grow as more new, young kids read about the free for all violence at punk shows (care of L.A. Times etc al) and turn up for shows. They intimidate and actually start to replace the old hardcores. An old sort of inside joke about the availability of punk show tickets at Ticketron becomes a reality.

"They said they only wanted well behaved boys, do they think guitars and microphones are just fucking toys?" Talking revolution like processed food or I guess it was just for fun - punk becomes respectable...
Hi. It's been two years now since the first Flipside hit the stands, and boy have things changed. If you've followed Flipside at all you know that we have changed size, staff and printers. We went from a xerox rag selling in a few stores to our own modest goal of selling over 1000 each issue. We went from local to national (over a dozen states and 4 countries). We have come a long way but then again, so has our music scene. When we started we covered almost any rock show, now we only cover punk and that's getting too much to cover. L.A. must be the punk rockers dream

city. In the last month there has been a punk show someplace everynight, mostly at the punk club, Hong Kong Cafe, but also at the Troubador, Blackies, Kings Palace, Bla Bla Cafe, Club 88 and even the Whiskey. New places are also opening like the Londoner, Mars Studios, and the Culver City Arena, not to mention Gazarris. What more could you ask for? Well, it's just not the same, punk rock is respectable now. When it's safe for a Jock to take his Farrah date to a punk show, then something is wrong. It's kinda fucked to look back at the 'good old days' (anniversaries do that to you), but remember parties at the

FLIPSIDE 10 YEAR ANNIVERSARY, PAGE 44

Masque with he Skulls or the Deadbeats (the bands I miss the most)? Actually, before I get carried away, there still is some good old sleeze punk rock around, but you gotta head for the suburbs. The Church is one of the best places to see and feel punk rock, or else there's those one off gigs that we go all out to trash the hall (remember Larchmont, Lazarios etc...) What I'm trying to say is that you just don't feel like you can get as drunk at Hong Kong as you could at the Masques or even Licorice Pizza parking lot, right? I remember Steve Samioff (Flipsides "dad" figure) telling us how nice it would be if L.A. had a regular club circuit for bands to play. Hey it's nice, the bands are happy and make a lot of money, but what about us fan-atics? The whole thing is figured out down to the dollar, tomorrow there <u>will</u> be another gig, the bouncers <u>will</u> stop you from going wild, and they <u>will</u> stop you from drinking underage. It's no longer a party event atmosphere. No more spontaneity. What can you do? It took two years to build, all the trial and error was fun, the process of getting totaled and making friends was fun and the constant search for that next gig was fun. Watching telephone poles for flyers of the next punk show was a lot more exciting than picking up the L.A. Weekly and planning your next month of daily punk shows. But it's all here, it was unavoidable. And all the bands appear to be getting so big. what about the punk signings? They haven't come. Record companies claim they're going broke because of the price of vinyl, yet put out 12 inch disco singles. The whole situation is confusing and/or depressing. It's still wholesome fun though, the more the merrier, right? Well did you get a ticket for New Wave 1980 yet?

Hong Kong Cafe with Kickboy Face and Steve Stiff (fanzine types) hanging out. – photo by Al

DAMNED

--- --- --- --- --- --- --- --- --- --- ---

Paul: What was that fight about?
Dave: The American audiences.
Paul: Do you normally play for $6?
Dave: No, I don't have any control. I like to keep it down.
Paul: What was the difference between the first band and the second?
Dave: A lot of conflict in the first band was with Brian, not enough diplomacy in regards to writing songs. Brian wrote a lot of good songs, but wouldn't accept anybody elses... After we broke up everybody went their own way. Rat formed the White Cats. Captain formed a band called King, with all keyboards, completely different than us, and I was

The Damned: Captain, Dave, Alge at the Cuckoos Nest – photo by Al

working with a group called Doctors of Madness. None of these ventures worked very well, and we realized we worked best together. You've got to realize that one a good night we were some of the best musicians around. So Captain and Rat got back together and they got me and we played around as the Doomed. It went so well we found ourselves new material and it carried on for there. We got ourselves a permanent bass player, **Alge, ex-Saints.**
Paul: What were the White Cats about? Weren't they anti-punk, or what was the theme?
Dave: It wasn't any of that. People wanted just to have a go at Rat Scabies, cause he was the only real character in the band. When you looked at the White Cats, all you could see was Scabies.
Paul: Did Brian James want back into the band after you reformed?
Dave: No, Captain is now the guitarist.
Paul: What's the new stuff like?
Dave: It still retains the raw energy, but its got some subtleties in there and clever playing. This band has got massive scope. People think it's 1-2, 1-2, but it's not. The single got to #20, sold faster than the Beatles with only one play per week.
Paul: Do you want to do experimental music?
Dave: We do. We do things on our own and exchange ideas. Captain does the weirdest stuff.
Paul: Do you ever follow the Dracula theme in your music?
Dave: Not really, but I have a tendency to fall into the Gothic horror theme.
Paul: Do you study that period?
Dave: Yes, I do.
Paul: Do you visit old castles and check 'em out?
Dave: I refuse to answer!
Paul: Ever been to a Black Mass?
Dave: I wouldn't have it any other way!
Paul: What did you do before the Damned?
Dave: I was a grave digger.
Paul: Are you friends with the Bromley set, or don't they associate with you?
Dave: We have a hate relationship.

Paul: Do you have a large following?
Dave: In England we do, yeah, a massive following. We seem to attract all the nut cases, murderers and the lot.
Paul: What do you think of the scene in the U.S.?
Dave: Two and a half years ago it was just taking off and it surprised me with it's quiet state. I thought it would have been much bigger. In England there are punks everywhere, but here you can drive all day and not see one.
Paul: You've been accused of being abusive?
Dave: The best time for this band to perform is when the audience is very receptive, went they can enjoy themselves and let go and listen, then this band can be phenomenal.

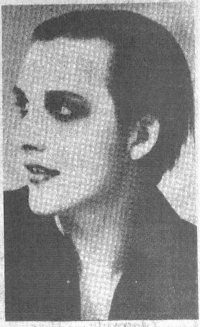

Dave Vanian – photo by Al

Balinda Gogo with Flipside sticker! – photo by Al

FLIPSIDE NUMBER 17

"I show my natural emotions
you make me feel I'm dirt
and I'm hurt, but if I start
a commotion
I'll only end of losing you
and that's worse
Ever fall in love with someone
ever fallen in love, in love
with someone, ever fall in love
with someone you shouldn't of
fallen in love with"
'Love Bites' –" Ever fallen in love"
– Buzzcocks

ISSUE #: 17
DATE: December 1979
FORMAT: 8 1/2 by 11, offset
PAGES: 24
PRICE: $.75
PRESS RUN: 1000
STAFF: Al, Hud, Paul Problem
Dee, Hilda and Gerber.(X-8 did
nothing)

Transitional, is the word describing the Punk scene during this period, and the issue was

printed at a Sir Speedy printer on blue paper which coincided with the time. Hang outs from Blackies in Santa Monica to the Church in Redondo Beach were where the bands and fans were going. D and Hilda started to contribute (DOA and Red Cross) and X-8 kinda stared to drift. Agent Orange were happening and though Ron from Red Cross was singing for Black Flag, Keith Morris could still hold a 6 pack of beer down his pants with out any problems.

RED CROSS

Red Cross were interviewed 10/1/79 at the Church by Dee
Red Cross are a young band from Hawthrone who play very fast and energetic punk.
Jeff-16, Vocals
Steve-12, Bass
Greg-18, Guitar
Ron-19, Drums

— — — — — — — — — — — — — — — — — —

FLIPSIDE: You were originally called the Tourists, why did you change your name?
Steve: It's pretty obvious, the name sucked!
FLIPSIDE: Why did you call yourselves the Tourists in the first place?
JEFF: We're from Hawthrone!
RON: I wouldn't have joined the band under that name in the first place.
Jeff/Steve: Well you did!
JEFF: Good names are hard to come by. Everyones used them up.
GREG: Black Flag got us going.
JEFF: The Last and Black Flag.
FLIPSIDE: Are you going to let your parents see you play?
Steve: No!
JEFF: No, not till we play the Forum.
GREG: My mom and step dad saw us play. They thought we were great.
Steve: Yeah, and he made them pay us. You know what happened, my mom heard our tape on Rodney the other night and she said: "The language you use!".
GREG: Rodney thinks Jeff is the new Rik L Rik!
JEFF: I'm sure it's a compliment.
FLIPSIDE: Do people try to manipulate you, especially because you're young?
JEFF: Not so far.
GREG: Kim Fowley hasn't come up to us yet.
Steve: And FUCK, I don't want him to.
FLIPSIDE: You've played live less than half a dozen times, and people are praising you, what do you think the reason for that is?

JEFF: Are they!! I love it!
Steve: I hope it's not because of our ages, but I think that's what it is.
GREG: But maybe we're good, I don't know.
DEZ: All the surf, beach energy.
JEFF: We're not a surf band, we're anti-surf.
DEZ: No, you guys are hardcore.
FLIPSIDE: Are you going to keep the 3 girl singers in the band to do "Mystery Girls"?
JEFF: That's an occasional, once in a while, just for fun thing. Ella is going solo. Mary Rat is a deadbeat.
FLIPSIDE: Who writes your material?
JEFF: Gregs done a couple of things, me and Steve have done most of it. Ron and Dez did one song.
FLIPSIDE: Is Steve the only one who works?
Steve: I'm quitting my daily paper route at the end of the month and that's how we got our first tape and certain members of this group still haven't paid me back.
GREG: I paid for the demo tape, well, my mom paid for it.
JEFF: I just wanna say, **Penelope Houston** is God.

THE CHURCH

So what's all this fuss about this place somewhere in the South Bay called the Church? Wheat's the big deal when a few kids find a place for bands to rehearse? And, didn't it happen all before? Yes and no, ya see the Church is very much like the original Masque but is still very different. For one thing, it is very underground. Why? **Ron**(a punk who lives in the Church, drummed with **Red Cross** and sings for **Black Flag** AND 'owns' the room the bands play in) tells us that's it's the only way it will work. The hippies are stupid, they have parties upstairs and get busted, we've had a lot of parties downstairs and never got busted." The Church, or **Creative Craft Center**, is a home for more than just punk rockers, as you guessed,

Red Cross: Steve, Jeff and Greg, at Kings Palace – photo by Al

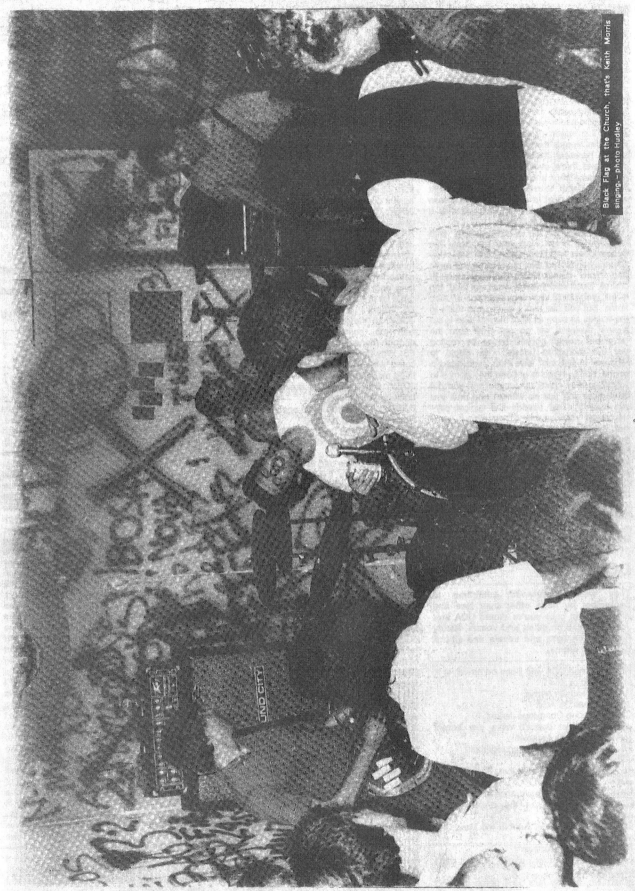

Black Flag at the Church, that's Keith Morris singing.—photo Hudley

hippies live there too, they hate each other "The hippies hate us more" Rontells us, but they do get along. They kids that live here are also very different than the early Masque crowd, there's no art damage, no rich kid poseurs and no money hungry jerks, in fact the place hardly exists.

One night the kids there wanted to throw a party, but no one could play, even the Germs had better things to do. Unfortunately the hippies had a party the same night, so the punks just stayed downstairs. And **Ron** was right, the hippies hated the punks more and started hasseling them. Eventually the police came and threw everyone out, but later the punks came back and had a great party with **Ron** and **Keith Morris** being the DJ's. That may not even exist to a lot of you but it sure beats the hell out of any SM Civic show or a lot of the Hong Kong stuff lately.

Ron lives at the Church along with members of **Black Flag**, and the Last. The **Descendents** and **Red Cross** are two other Church bands and they plan on having more and more parties there, underground of course. Slash said that this won't last long, but it will, you can't kick someone out of their home. But you can tear it down, and that's in the books, as soon as all of the red tape is cut a new business will go up. Until then the developer makes pocket money by renting out the rooms to 'artists'. "It's illegal to rehearse in this city" says Ron, "you need a permit, but if you go to get one they deny it to you, then they check up on you and you get busted, so you just do without one until you get busted". That sounds like typical city-depresses-youth-activity to me. But it won't stop the Church. Where the Masque strived to be legitimate to stay open and beat the fire laws, the Church waits out it's fate. We all know it's coming. As the Masque rocked an partied waiting for the day it would open, the Church rocks and parties waiting for the day that they will smash those stained glass windows and we'll watch as the bulldozers tear it down.

(Sure enough the 'dozers tore the place down, but not after a lot of great gig/parties).

DOA

They were interviewed sometime in September by none other than Dee and Hilda. Just in case you're stupid DOA are: Joey Shithead on guitar and vocals, Randy Rampage on bass and vocals and Chuck Biscuits on drums.

FS: I assumed DOA was Dead on arrival, is it, or is it Dead or alive?
RANDY: Dead On Arrival.
JOEY: Dopes On Acid.
CHUCK: Dumb Obnoxious Jerks.
JOEY: No, that doesn't make any sense, Dumb, Obnoxious Assholes!
FS: How long have you been together?
JOEY: Year and a half.
FS: Are you all original members?
JOEY: Yeah.
RANDY: We used to have another guitarist, a couple of them, we're the original three members.
CHUCK: We had Brad Kent in the band, the old Avengers guitarist.
FS: Where's your manager?
RANDY: He's a fuckin' hippie, so we don't take him with us.
JOEY: No, actually he's back home booking

gigs.
RANDY: Yeah, booking gigs for other bands.
FS: Chuck, you're from Long Beach, right?
CHUCK: I was born in harbor city, Long Beach, I was born there.
FS: How did you happen to meet Chuck?
CHUCK:... I lived in Vancouver for 10 years.
JOEY: And I knew his brother for a long time, I can remember when Chuck was like a real fucking rat, threw rocks threw the window...
FS: What are the two singles you have out?
JOEY: Prisoner/13 - the other is an ep recorded over a year ago, that's Disco Sucks/ Nazi Training Camp/ Woke Up Screaming/ Law of Police. Which is dedicated to the RCMP.
FS: What's the song called thats like as slow as you come to doing a slow song?
JOEY: Jamacian Joke, that's going to be our new single.
RANDY: With WWIII.
JOEY: So like the songs are really quite different, ya know, both songs are like 4-5 minutes long. That's a real weird thing for us - cause we've never had a song over 3 minutes long and like this single is a lot different, it's got a lot of textures.
FS: Where's your wife Joey?
JOEY: In Vancouver, sometimes she comes with me, sometimes we just don't have enough money.
FS: Why doesn't your manager pay for her to come with you, I thought that that was one thing managers were for?
JOEY: Our manager is like, "Boys, here's a buck for your to spend."
RANDY: "What! You guys spent $3 on beer!? No more beer for a week!"
FS: What did you hear about the Elks Lodge?
JOEY: Yeah, I heard about that big police fiasco.
FS: Are the police bad in Vancouver?
JOEY: Yeah, it's the same thing, there's a fucking constant police harrasment, yeah, the people saying "The RCMP and Vancouver Police are fucking bullshit". Well the cops say: "We'd better teach these guys a lesson". Especially this new club now, called the Smiling Buddah, half a block from the cop shop, there's only one cop shop, right? This one big building called the 'Public Safety Building'. Like every week or two they'll come down and kick people around, arrest them...
RANDY: Drag people out.
FS: Harrassed because of the way you look?
JOEY: Not really.
CHUCK: I get hasseled a lot!
JOEY: Well, it's different, Chuck will get hasseled, but I won't, that primarily because of the size difference.
CHUCK: They yell all sorts of stuff: "Punk rock faggot!"
FS: What are your political views?
CHUCK: I hate jerks, I just hate assholes, nothing political.
JOEY: I wouldn't call myself political, but I think that there are certain things that need to be said or something done about them. Cause I think like we're really moving swiftly into really conservative times, where like the police, are becoming more powerful, the government is clamping down on everything, ya know? And that's sorta what I'm reacting against. The fucking police have absolute control in Canada, but I think L.A. is one of the worst places with police I've seen, like S.F. or N.Y. isn't so bad.
CHUCK: They have worse things to worry about in N.Y.
FS: What was it like to play in N.Y.?

CHUCK: We went to Hurrahs and like Joe was running around in circles and he pushed over this woman and she was going to charge him with assault.
JOEY: It started out, like when the Dils were playing everyone was out on the dance floor and in about 5 minutes Randy, Chuck, myself, Jello Biafra and some other people from the west coast just had the dance floor cleared, and so we decided it wasn't enough and so we terrorized the fringes.
RANDY: I was running around kicking drinks outta peoples hands and pushing them onto the floor and all of a sudden there's like 5 bouncers around me.
JOEY: So the next day they said you're fucking lucky we didn't cancel your gig for tonight. People in N.Y. are weird, sorta like "We've seen it all, we're everything". But still there's some good people too. They're not all idiots, but there's a pretty high percentage of them. Actually of all of the places I've seen, the west coast is the only place where you really get people flying around and pogoing. The east coast is kinda mild.
FS: Well, what else do you guys do? Can you live on what you make playing?
RANDY: I just do lots of drugs, I'm a drug fiend.
JOEY: I like loud fucking music!!!!!

THE FLIPSIDE BENEFIT!!!
Sept. 20 1979 Hong Kong Cafe
Bags, Extremes, GoGos, Fear and Gears
By Al

Well it finally happened, but summer was already over. The story: the Gears opened, but only because Catholic Discipline could not. This was the first time I'd seen 'em with Kid Spike (ex-Controllers) on lead guitar and they were hot. They played some Controller tunes and mostly Gears faves we all know, like "Let's Go To The Beach" A fast and fun set from a band that will be with us for some time. Fear were next and there was an entire film crew there to video tape it, oh boy. It took a long time but finally Fear delivered their raunchy-raw set, rumors that Fear were going new wave must be a joke. This issue is supposed to have a good time/ new energy theme running through it, so I won't mention all of the problems with this show, just the good parts. And next were the surprise band, Go Gos! Their first local show in awhile and it shows the girls were practicing, an excellent set even if Belinda was drunk off her ass. The Bags also turned in a fine performances (I know it was our show, give them a good review) but no, the Bags were more loose tonight, maybe because this show was supposed to be an easy, informal event. I don't know... but Alice hasn't been that wild in awhile. Craig was funny, played a whole song with a clothes pin across his strings and didn't even know it, ha. The Extremes deserve Flipsides biggest thanks, they were the first to volunteer to do the show, Maicol said he'd do it if he had to do it solo, and they came in wearing custom made 'Flipside' t-shirts too!! The were also good guys and took the spot of going on last, to which many people missed a very inspiring set. The new keyboard man is very good and complements the whole Extreme sound very well. The whole set was an experience in newer mood music that seems to be finding a place in this town. All in all a good set from a talented band. Thanks Extremes... and thanks to the rest of you too, especially Barry and Kim and the Hong Kong staff.

FLIPSIDE NUMBER 18

"I've found my priority, I'll drop out of society,
confrontation with the facts,
I'm tearing up my income tax!
I'm white and middle class,
Life sucks me dry.
And my reply –
Shove it up your ass!
I'm the silent majority, excluded from your charity,
martyr me with all the rest,
Kill me with sterile success"
– 'I'm White and Middle Class' by The Urinals

ISSUE: 18
DATE: 5/80
FORMATE: 8 1/2 by 11

PAGES: 24
PRICE: $.75
PRESS RUN: 1000
STAFF: AL, PAUL, HUD.

Hey, this was the first issue to be printed on a Rotary Offsett Printing Machine, hum.. hum.. that means we went full on News Print!!! Gerber said that this was our most boring issue but I say it had some good stuff. This issue was the kind you could roll up and put in your back pocket. Chuck via Black Flag had the 1st mohawk in town....before Darby even and this is around the time the Circle Jerks were formed!! The Fleetwood in Redondo Beach is starting up and old jocks Like Jack (from- Vicious Circle – then- TSOL) burn their jock straps and become punk rockers full color. This is a time of violence and the movie 'Decline of Western Civilization' highlights this period of the punk scene in the worst and most ignorant, superficail and exploited way..

TWO TONE

MADNESS

(This interview was done for us by Rodney Bigenheimer on his radio show Sunday March 16.)
RODNEY: Tell us about these new dances...
MADNESS: We're emulating L.A. dances, they've got some pretty good ones, like the Worm. We're worming it up, doing the 'Crawl on the floor'.
RODNEY: What is Madness all about for our listeners?
MADNESS: We're about "ha ha ha".
RODNEY: We had the Specials in here a few

weeks ago and they were very serious.
MADNESS: Wa....
RODNEY: Their whole attitude about...
MADNESS: The Specials... we're different from each other, they're serious but we're funny, they're older than us, we're younger.
RODNEY: You were in different groups, you were Morris and the Invaders.
MADNESS: Same group different name. A group came along called the Invaders, so we picked the name of one of our songs, one of our songs was Madness, how appropriate! Like Prince Busters old hit.
RODNEY: Someone has actually found **Prince Buster** down in Florida and are booking him!
MADNESS: We heard from a magazine, the Observer in England, that they've been talking to him but he's not really interested.
RODNEY: The Specials have a Two Tone man, Walter Japscott, what's the name of yours?
MADNESS: Chas Smash!! Ha ha, the nutty man, no, we haven't got a cutsey name for him.
RODNEY: The Beat (UK) have got one also.
MADNESS: The Beat one is taken for a photo of a girl dancing to Prince Buster.
RODNEY: Well the Gogos are getting ready to go on, they're incredible!
MADNESS: They've improved a lot since we last saw them, they're coming on tour with us in England, that's an interesting tidbit.

SPECIALS

Interviewed at the Whisky just before the start of 8 sold out shows and after a very successful autograph session at the Licorice Pizza, on February 8, 1980 by Hud, Pete, Al, and Jill.

SPECIALS

MADNESS

Photos by Pete

HUD: What do you think of America, the U.S.A, uh, California?
LYNVAL: I like California. I think it's great, the weather is what I like ya know.
HUD: How long have you been here?
LYNVAL: 3 days.
HUD: What do you think of all this decoration? (the Whiskey painted in black and white two tone checkers)?
PETE: All the hype!
LYNVAL: It's not hype because we're playing real music, we don't need a lot of this because the music speaks for itself.
AL: Did you know it would be like this?
LYNVAL: NO! I passed by here a couple of nights ago and it was alright, and suddenly, WOW!
HUD: What do you think (to Terry)?
TERRY: (Has a Specials balloon in his mouth, just shrugs his shoulders and looks up at the paint, about 10 minutes earlier when He and Jerry arrived they were easily overheard saying "Look at it, we don't want this!").
AL: How long have you been together?
JERRY: 2 1/2 years.
HUD: Mods are a big thing over in England now.
JERRY: Bigger than punk definitely.
AL: Are you a mod band?
JERRY: No, the mods consider us their band, the mods came after us.
AL: Did you think of bringing the "Two Tone" tour here?
JERRY: Too expensive!! There's three bands, like Madness...
LYNVAL: 40 odd people, and 40 is a lot.
JERRY: ...the Selector and the Specials and thats a lot.
TERRY: If the Two Tone bands were all trios, but we're not, we have 9 ourselves.
AL: You were over there signing autographs, what do you think of that?
TERRY: People want to see us and bring their records to get signed, so it's alright.
AL: Do you do that in England?
LYNVAL: Oh yeah.
AL: Jerry called Rodney from Germany and gave the impression that he started the Two Tone label?
LYNVAL: No, all the Two Tone thing is, is some of us in the band... the band started off with me, Jerry and Horace the bass player, later on it got bigger, 7 members and now 9 with the brass we use on the road.

JILL: Wait, I get to put my 2 cents in. I saw you guys play in Birmingham opening for the Clash in July 78, I thought these guys are great, but they'll never make it with 8 people in the group, you were the Coventry Specials then and I didn't connect that this is the same band playing the Whiskey. Big stars and all.
LYNVAL: It's like... I don't look at us as big stars as such, we just came like everyone else you know...
JILL: Getting the Whiskey painted for your band is pretty big stars... when I saw you in England you mixed...
LYNVAL: Yeah, a lot of bands do straight punk, straight rock, whatever, we thought stick it all together and be different from the rest of them, and that's what we've done. I'm quite pleased to be here, I thought I'd never get to America you know.
AL: Is there a music scene in Coventry?
LYNVAL: There's loads of bands there, it's only a small town but like us and the Selector, my best friends, the 4 bands from Coventry are like a family. We've played together in the same bands, we've chopped and changed. We got a label together like what the early Motown sounded like, and we intend to keep Two Tone that way. We have Madness (from London), the Beat (from Birmingham), and the Selector. In England it's Two Tone, in America Chrysalis. But soon to be Two Tone world wide, cause we've had 7 hit singles: Specials 3, Selector 2, Madness 1 and Beat 1. If we have so many hit singles we could renegotiate the deals for everything to be on Two Tone.
AL: Who does the art work, like the little guy who is on all of the records?
LYNVAL: Jerry drew that.
AL: Does he have a name?
LYNVAL: We call him Stan or Walt or anything really.

URINALS

The Urinals were interviewed at the Hong Kong Cafe March 22, 1980 by Hud, Pete, X-8 and Al.

JOHN: We're glad you're still around, we

though you folded.
Al: No, we never folded, just a long time between issues.
FLIPSIDE: Do you all go to UCLA?
KJEHL: We did, but I graduated.
FLIPSIDE: What do you have degrees in?
JOHN: Motion pictures.
X-8: Wow, that's your influence, ATV?
JOHN: I don't know about ATV, I listen to Wire.
JOHN: Early Dils.
KJEHL: Yeah early Dils, the singles!
JOHN: Wire, Philip Glass.
Keven: Buzzcocks.
X-8: When you play, are you in street level or art level?
JOHN: Sometimes we're street level, tonight we're street level because we're sloppy, but sometimes we imagine we are artists which is probably totally wrong but...
FLIPSIDE: Who writes your songs?
KJEHL: John writes most of them.
Keven: But we've all come up with stuff lately.
Cathy: I wrote "Ack Ack Ack Ack"!(Cathy is a 'roadie')
X-8: Why did you get together in the first place?
JOHN: To make noise. It was a joke when we first started, none of us knew our instruments.
FLIPSIDE: Just like Wire!
JOHN: Like Wire, but we thought, wow two notes and we have a song. "Ack Ack" was one note but Kjehl added a second one and sort of ruined it.
KJEHL: Sorry, well..... We originally had one guy on acoustic guitar John singing and 10 or 11 other people singing.
JOHN: Kevin and I are self taught (hic) we bought our instruments and learned how not to play them all by ourselves and then Kjehl bought a guitar (hic – John is drunk).
X-8: Do people take you seriously?
KJEHL: No, no one could take us seriously.
JOHN: Someone called us "Post apocalyptic doom".
Cathy: The Communist Workers Party is really hot on us.
Keven: We put up a flyer for a show, and I drew a picture of Rat Scabies and I wrote Bob Avakian and put an arrow pointing to rat that

Urinals: John, Kevin & Kjehl at Blackies – photo by Al

Jack, Vicious Circle, the band that still has rumors going. At the Fleetwood – photo Al said "Hands off Bob Avakian", Revolutionary Dooms Day 1980. And this guy thought we were communists. They came up and said, "We have this poster, are you real serious?". We said we thought it was funny.

FLIPSIDE: Do you have political affiliation?

KJEHL: No, we are not political.

JOHN: We have solcialogical affiliation but no political affiliation because if you believe in any sort of dogma then you're being led, and we don't want to be led.

FLIPSIDE: Do you guys work?

JOHN: I work in a bookstore, can't you tell, I have glasses!

X-8: Why do you market your band for guys?

KJEHL: What are you talking about?

X-8: Urinals! Girls can't relate to that!

JOHN: We got all sorts of romantic songs. Look. (Seriously) A urinal is a real functional and clean device that's always there when you need it, we're not trying to be sexist at all!!

X-8: Do you think you look like a college student gone wild?

JOHN: Sometimes I worry about that, yeah.

FLIPSIDE: People think you're a surf band, did you ever surf with Greg Shaw?

JOHN: We used to hang out, we do hang out with surf people. The first people to recognize use were the people at the church, we sort of fell in with them.

FLIPSIDE: You don't plan on breaking up do you?

JOHN: Oh no. I'd like to keep it the three of us because Kevin and I are regressive and Kjehl is progressive, so the two things are just sort of...

(The Urinals changed their name to 100 Flowers a few years later and eventually broke up. John and Kevin are now in Radwaste, Cathey and John got Married too)

FLIPSIDE NUMBER 19

I've got the world up my ass and I'm gonna move fast/ Gonna be the first, won't be the last/ I've got the world up my ass/ Society is burning me up/ take a bite then spit it out/ Take their rules, rip 'em up/ tear them down, twisted mind withered brain/ You know I'll go insane/ I just tell them to get back/ When they tell me how to act "World Up My Ass" Circle Jerks

ISSUE #: 19
DATE: August 1980
FORMAT: 8 1/2x11, Rotary web offset
PAGES: 32
PRICE: $.75
PRESS RUN: 1500
STAFF: Al and Hud

Adam and his Ants hang out with Rodney and read Flipside at the Starwood - photo Robert Hill

----

This issue continues in the whole slump. Our big staff from a few issues ago is gone. People are bummed at the new kids, the new bands the new ways. What started as a real unique burst of energy from the Beach area (you know the day-glo sweaters, and weird dances the HB's did), is slowly turning into adolescent male violence. The older people who managed to hang on are abandoning ship for other things (such as Adam and the Ants). The scene no longer seems to be attractive to the more creative, artistic (and pacifist) people, but if appealing more to the stupid jock type thugs or just kids out for a joy ride. The Fleetwood is just starting up and it is ugly. There are lots and lots of fights (like at least one every song!). It's real depressing – however, there is always an alternative: bands like 45 Grave, Urinals, Descendents, BPeople etc... are doing punk rock without the violence, but they have hardly any place to play. Because they are associated with the bad side of 'punk' they are blacklisted too. Worse yet, the clubs are starting to bring back - you guessed it, metal bands!

Jayne County - photo by Al

JAYNE COUNTY
June 24, 1:30, Tropicana Hotel, Rm. 5 Hollywood

Jayne County- Vocals, Sammy Minnelli- Drums, Jerry Gora-, Joe Provede- Keyboards, Chris Garl-Bass.

X-8: Jayne writes all the songs and stuff, how do you guys like being the back-up band?

Sammy: We work together, we arrange the songs.

Hud: Do you have a name for yourself?

Joe: In Canada, they booked us as the Electric Chairs, Jayne wanted to call us the Caucasions.

X-8: What did you think of the crowd at the Starwood?

Chris: The crowd there is really into their music and they won't accept anything that's half done. I kinda like that reaction from the crowd.

X-8: What do you think of Jayne throwing her feminity all over the stage?

Joe: It's great, Jaynes totally different on stage. Jayne gets a lot of energy from the audience. At the Starwood she was doing things we weren't ready for!!!

(interview goes to the backroom at the Troubador)

X-8: There's been a lot of talk about a glitter thing coming back, what do you think?

Jayne: Oh, I don't think you can say glitter. I think you can say people are now ready to see something a little more flashy. I don't think we're gonna see David Bowie/Ziggy Stardust wings again, but we're gonna see a little more glamour.

X-8: How's the tour doing?

Jayne: We've had some really great gigs and some shitty ones. The Starwood was great, it was incredible! I think we should have come in and played the Starwood and left instead of sticking around. I mean we don't even know how we are going to pay our hotel bill, literally! In Canada I actually had to go our on the streets and turn tricks....

X-8: To pay the hotel bill!

Jayne: Uh, no. I had to buy new clothes, we're just running short of money. Hopefully I'll never have to go to Canada again. I think the Russians can handle it (laughs).

X-8: What do you see in the future of rock and roll in America?

Jayne: Hard times. Because the minute a really good rock and roll band begins to make it, their record companys real bland and they make them real bland. I think the best rock and roll bands will remian in the clubs, because the moment millions of people are buying their records they become bland. Just because the majority of people have a bland attitude!

X-8: Ok, this might be a kinda personal question, but do think that changing your name from Wayne to Jayne will hurt you as far as effecting audiences?

Jayne: Uh, maybe for the time being. But it

had to be done, you know? I don't think of myself as Wayne, I think of myself as Jayne. That's tough shit, because I had to do what I personally had to do.

Subhumans and Samoans: Greg Turner, Metal Mike, Wimpy, Hud, Gerry and Jim

Wimpy and Gerry – photo by Al

SUBHUMANS

AL: What's the scene like in Vancouver?
GERRY: The biggest other than us is DOA. They reformed, it's the old line-up with Randy and Chuck.
MIKE: One of you guys was in one of the original Vancouver bands in 1977?
WIMPY: Yeah, I used to play bass in a band called the Skulls. I heard there was an L.A. band called the Skulls, we both came up with the same name and neither band had heard of each other. It was the third punk band I had ever heard of...
MIKE: Who was the DOA guy?
WIMPY: Shithead, he used to sing totally, no guitar. The Dishrags were formed before the Skulls, so they are the oldest band in Vancouver still going.
HUD: Where do you play?
WIMPY: We usually scam up halls, we play lots of high schools...
GERRY: We don't play "Fuck You" and stuff like that, but we got to get to the young people and start them off and they can take the ball from there and do whatever they want. That's where a lot of them new bands are coming from.
MIKE: What about 'fuck' bands?
GERRY: Me and Wimpy have quite opposite views on fuck bands.
WIMPY: He hates fuck bands, I play in 'Rude Norton', biggest fuck band in Vancouver. A fuck band is like somebody plays an instrument they don't play...
GERRY: ...and do covers, old covers, or silly stuff like 'Gilligans Island'.......

THE CROWD

AL: Tell us about HB?
Tracy: Sun tan city, a lot of people fighting each other..
AL: Why?
JIM K: I don't know why. I wish I knew.
Tracy: Spray paint capitol...
JIM K: But there's a lot of bands... A lot of nice girls Tracy says, that's the main attribute to HB, the girls, the weather's been terrible!
Tracy: The seaweed at Brookhurst St.
JIM K: Yeah, the seaweeds been terrible, a lot of debris in the water.
Tracy: We're gonna make beach movies again.

JIM K: "Beach Blanket Bong Out"!
AL: Why are HB's so violent?
Jim T: Cause they're young and have a lot of energy.
Tracy: Cause the red tide is in.
Gerber: It's hereditary.
Tracy: Because they all idolize Sid Vicious and he's so radical. There's nothing better to do, save up your money and get a Sirocco... we're just burnt because we live by the beach.. damn seagulls!!!
Hud: Say anything you want to say.
Jim K: We have a new drummer named Denny Drum and he's real good, he used to be in the Flyboys. We want a cover story!

FLIPSIDE NUMBER 20

"Dead, like a piece of old wax
Non-existing and all burned out
Thrown away and broken, unwanted and unloved
It takes all things to be like wax
Useless and unwanted, a cruel way to end
But it's essential to the way of life
Just like a piece of wax, molded and hardened
lit and extinguished with a blow, nothing but wax
Existing for the benefit of being blown out, blown out
Bent and lame, how unfortunate for me
I am just the same, a glob, a thing
How depressing for me to see someone as a piece of
wax, nothing left, no feelings

Crowd: Jim Trash, Jim Kaa, and Tracy show Gerber a good time at the Starwood – photo by Al

Some band you'll probably never see again: Keith Morris on drums, Ron Reyes vocals and Chuck Dukowski on bass, guitar? – photo by a!

Waiting to die, twisted and melted
Look into the flame
Extinguish my life, melt the wax, no flame, no warmth, no innocence
Hey it's my life, melt the wax, no flame, no light, no reflection
Waiting to die, just old wax, old wax....."
"Wax" – 45 Grave

ISSUE #: 20
DATE: October 1980
FORMAT: 8 1/2x11, Rotary web offset
PAGES: 32
PRICE: $.75
PRESS RUN: 2000
STAFF: Al and Hud

- -

This is the first issue with Flipside Punk poll results (taken last issue). This turns out to be a regular yearly feature. Well the punk scene is where you find it, and we certainly are finding it. New bands (like the Adolescents, Eddie and the Subtitles, Detours, Agent Orange, and Social Distortion) are popping up with a good attitude and great sound. The parties in our local neighborhood (Fullerton, Placentia, Whittier) are happening (for once) and we forget about the violence at the bigger shows. Orange County even has a big punk festival, put on by Eddie at La Vida Hot Springs, it lasted all day until the cops broke it

up. The staff has perked up with Michele and Helen becoming stronger contributors, and Pete getting back into heavy photography now that he has a new darkroom!

Eddie And The Subtitles
--- ---- --- ---- --- ---- --- ---- --- ---- --

Here's the scene: We're backstage at the Starwood, the Muntants are downstairs, the Eddie Empire is backstage living it up in full Eddie tradition and I'm just drunk enough to be sleepy and want to get his interview over with, my first brilliant questions are lost in the sound mix of a dozen drunk people all joking of the idea of an interview here! But X-8 having a bigger mouth than mine, manages to break through the sound barrier:
X-8: HEY! Eddie talk about you life for 5 seconds.
Eddie: Been too long.
Dinky: How's you band, Eddie?
Eddie: Been too long.

Dinky: How's your sex life?
Eddie: Been too long.
Dinky: We heard you quit drinking.
Eddie (with beer): I'm not. I stopped.

X-8: What were you like as a boy?
Eddie: Like him (Tony Adolescent).
Eddie is one of the original O.C. musicians. Although he's been know to say that O.C. is a **"mindless, sexless, funless monster that should be permanently shut down"** he supports the scene fully. He manages Middle Class and the Ads, loves Social Distortion. He even organized an O.C. punk festival at La Vida Hot Springs...
Brendan: What happened at La Vida Eddie?
Eddie: I don't know, I wasn't there...
Mike Patton: Weren't you arrested?
Eddie: I got arrested. 2 counts of murder and drugs.
X-8: Do you wanna be a rock star?
Eddie: Too much pressure
AL: What do you call your music?
Eddie: Heavy metal punk fusion.
AL: How do you like playing heavy metal punk fusion?
Matt Simon: As long as I get free drugs.
AL: Where does everybody get the drugs!!!?
Mike: Where DOES Eddie get the drugs?
Eddie: I don't take drugs. I never did.
Brendan: What about Pop Eddie?
Eddie: That has nothing to do with the Subtitles, it's me Geza X, Nickey Beat and Bobby Pain. We're just called Eddie... The songs I write are pop songs, Mike writes the Subtitles songs – I wrote "American Society". The Subtitles songs are like depressing and the Eddie pop songs are more like happy pop songs. The difference is like black and white.
Brendan: Who started the 'fuck you Eddie' fan club?
Eddie: Mike Patton.
Mike: It seemed appropriate, we were listening to this tape and all these people were going **"Fuck you Eddie"**.
AL: What about the Eddie Empire?
Eddie: Doesn't exist!
Brendan: It's real : No Label records, Iron Lung, the Subtitles, Eddie, the Adolescents, Middle Class...
AL: How do you do it Eddie?
Eddie: 5 minutes on the telephone.

Eddie Subtitle – photo by Al

IDEAWAY SEPT. 19, 1980

Wow!! What a great place thi[s]
[sh]ould be!!! Isolated, scummy!!!! Tonight all
[kind]s of bands are supposed to play including
[Blac]k Flag and the Circle Jerks!!! But.........
[But] management fucked it up. First off they
[ha]d 300! punks waiting outside while the first
[ban]d played!!! So the kids had to break the door
[dow]n to get in. Inside was great. Like this....

The Stains were on, played too long
and really got the crowd going.

(2) Mad Society were next, a new 'young' band who were actually
good and even tried to stop some of the fighs and distruction.

(3) But the people got bored and being locked in a crowded room decided
to break the walls down.

(4) And they did........

(7) You see— it was very hot inside
and they didn't sell any beer
only sticky sweet cokes and you
couldn't even go out side to get
a drink or get air. Well, they
said you could go out but then
how would you get in thru a
crowd of punks — still waiting
to get in!!! And they didn't
honor their stamp anyways! Really fucked. AND from 9 to 1AM
only TWO bands played!!! Would
you get restless? Well the big
door that got the car rammed thru
got reopened and we escaped.....

(6) They even broke the door down to get out.

[T]he place was a disaster and the
promoters said it was over.

(8) But only to find the police riot squad waiting....

(10) This could have been a great club, but the kids wrecked it! NO
WAY, it was not entirely the kids fault!!! There are alot of clubs
around here that think they can stuff everyone in a room and make
them pay for it, well, this was hotter than the CooCoo's nest, and
I was glad to see that the punks did not put up with it. People
should also be entitled to go in and out freely (with a hand stamp)
so they don't have to pay the clubs rediculous prices for a beer.
You paid your money for a good time, clubs should realize that.

(9) And they chased everyone home......

FLIPSIDE 10 YEAR ANNIVERSARY 56

SOCIAL DISTORTION

On our way to the liquor store we ran into Social Distortion, so me (Al), Hud, X-8, Pete, Chris, Val, Mike and Dennis, beers in hand, went into the Starwood alley for this interview.

- -

MIKE: The original Social Distortion started about 2 years ago. You know the Adolescents, well two of them were with me then. We broke up because they didn't think Dennis was good enough. So we quit, waited around a year to find a drummer, and we found John from Garden Grove...

Skatepark, Gerbers reception was our first gig without a lead singer. We practiced three weeks with this lead singer (Dee Dee) and then we went to that party and Tony Adolescent said "You guys should play, there's a lot of bands playing". But we said our lead singers not here, but we got our drums and we started playing and we sounded better than 4 weeks of practice!!!

X-8: Who do you wanna sound like?

DENNIS: We don't want to sound like anyone else, we want to sound like us!

MIKE: We stress anti-violence, anti-racist and pro-creativeness.

AL: What are your songs about?

MIKE: We have a song called '1945', Hiroshima, a theme song 'Social Distortion'... like 2 years ago we had a singer, I wrote the guitar riffs and the singer and drummer would write the songs, but the songs did't mean anything!! They wrote a song about an Amoeba!!! A fuckin' stupid little cell! They still have that song.

AL: When did you start coming to Hollywood?

DENNIS: When we saw the Avengers at the Masque, I was 16, had long hair...

X-8: Yeah, and Gerber cut your hair and said you looked like Shawn Cassidy!

MIKE: I live in lowrider territory. I used to have my own apartment called the Black Hole where all these punks used to lurk. It was one bedroom but sometimes we'd have 50 punks packed in there, cops never came back then. We have a song about it called "Playpen" all the punks from O.C. would come there, but no beach punks ever, they didn't even know about it. We want to be excluded from the beach punks.... Yeah the main goal was to like get O.C. happening and then the beach had to ruin it. The L.A. Times, fuck &%$#&#. I've read so many articles, they interview these people like in H.B., they interviewed Gidget and all these chicks and Pat, Pat had multiple slash marks and they ask her why and she says "Cause it's fun", you know!! They had all these air heads going! Why don't they get someone with some background or knowledge, that it means something to, so the public doesn't think we're a bunch of degenerates no worse than lowriders or whatever.

CIRCLE JERKS

- -

Interviewed October 9th at Keith Morris' house.

Keith-Singer, Lucky-Drums, Rodger-Bass, Greg-Guitar.

Al: How'd you get on Frontier Records?

Greg: Thru Posh Boy, Lisa Fancher wanted to do the Crowd, but Posh Boy said "I'll give you the Circle Jerks, so I can go after the Crowd, I want money".

Keith: Hey, Lisa would have taken the Crowd

Social Distortion: Dennis, Mike, Carrot – photo by Al

Circle Jerks: Greg, Lucky, Keith, Roger – photo by Al

over us, they're a more popular sounding band.

Al: Keith, are you an artist?

Keith: Yeah, see my X poster (Points to a painting with paint all over it, it used to be pictures of Xene, Bill and Don).

Lucky: He's been working on it all summer.

Al: What are you pissed off about?

Greg: Cause the world sucks.

Al: You live in a nice neighborhood!

X-8: We tried to find a burger stand but there's only fried chicken around here.

Keith: Yeah, and I hope you break out in a real fuckin' bad case of acne!!!

Hud: What's wrong with acne?

Lucky: Works for Axxel! Oh, Greg said that, let's talk about November 4th, who's gonna be president?

Hud: Who cares!

Lucky: Who cares! That's the typical punk attitude, we don't stand for that apathy, I care.

X-8: Aren't you a typical punk?

Al: Who are you voting for?

Lucky: I'll have to make a defensive vote for Carter, although I'd like to vote for Jon Anderson I feel it would be a wasted vote.

X-8: Keith, if you had a week to live, what would you do?

Keith: The first thing I'd do is take my old mans truck, and I'd smash everything in my way! I'd pull into the left lane, I'd pull into the right, I'd weave (Keith simulates his dream) I'd make every car going in either direction crash into each other, then I'd have those people get out of their cars and I'd say (Keith gets up and shouts) BUTTFUCKERS!!!

Lucky: In other words, you'd spend your week in jail!

Keith: I'd run from the cops, cause I've only got a week.

X-8: What would you do Greg?

Lucky: Fuck Charlene!

Greg: Uhhhhh.....

Keith: That's better than his answer!

Greg: I'm still thinking!

Keith: He's still thinking, he doesn't know what he'd do. I'd go down to Zed if I had one day to live, and to Bomp and to fuckin' Rhino and I'd tell them "YOU'RE ALL FUCKED!!!" Then I'd turn my car sideways on the freeway and I'd climb to the top and fuckin' start flippin' them off. In the meantime I'd bought like 7 or 8 cases of beer, hey this is my last day man...

Greg: What about sex?

Keith: A lot of girls I'd ask for sex wouldn't give it to me so I'd rape 'em.

X-8: Being the pinnacle of the punk rock scene, do you have girls crawling all over you?

Keith: Well that's a strange story, cause I've got a squid for a penis, it used to be a big pink errect thing, but now it's white and glowing and goes BLIP BLIP BLIPPPPP.

Al: They threw you out of Black Flag....

Keith: THEY DID NOT THROW ME OUT OF BLACK FLAG! (Keith is yelling). Let's talk about something else! AND DO NOT bring up Red Cross shit, cause that's all fuckin' crap.

Roger: I've got one fuckin' thing to say, I've been playing guitar for 15 years, I went to college and I can play classical music, I can play Mozarts 5th with my dick tied around the fretboard - but I'd rather play "World Up My Ass" or "Deny Everything" which is a great song that I wrote. I can play in my sleep but this is the most energetic statement oriented band I've ever been in, including 47 cover

western...

Al: Where did you find him?

Greg: Keith and I both quit bands, and Keith said fuck those guys, lets start our own band!

Keith: Then I found fuckin' Roger and he had a bottle of wine bigger than any other- bigger than all those other assholes....

THE WEIRDOS

The Weirdos (Cliff and John) were interviewed by Al, X-8, Pete and Hud on October 1st. at Cliffs pad.

X-8: What do you want from the Weirdos?

John: Money.

Cliff: Not not in a greedy sense, but enough to do our art, we are real creative and we want to do our things.

John: We want to be in control of everything, if someone wants to give us a million bucks for that great, until then...

Cliff: How many bands have gotten signed? There have been a lot of bands, but not from the original L.A. punk scene, they're just new wave bands that formed after it all happened.

John: Gary Myrick and the Oingos...

X-8: The whole Madame Wongs scene.

Al: Yeah, but they put out albums that flop.

John: Everybody thinks that signing to a major label is... the pot at the end of the rainbow, I'd rather be on a small label and be in control than be forgotten.

Al: You guys are letting small punk bands open for you now.

John: We like the action, that's what the Weirdos were always about.

X-8: At first it seemed the Weirdos wanted to attract a certain amount of glamour with punk rock...

John: ....sure....

Cliff: Too bad you couldn't get the look on his face when he said that!!!

Al: You guys don't wear garbage anymore.

John: Oh, we're about to break thru into a different realm, we've got it all figured out but it's top secret.

Al: Oh, you're a preconcieved band!

John: No, it's not that formula, you say we don't wear our shit anymore, well it's gonna be a new kind of shit! You don't want to see the same old thing.

Al: Like the flag.

Cliff: Yeah, everything represents a point in time, things get old fast.

Weirdos Cliff Roman and John Denny - photo Pete

Al: So why release old songs.

John: We figured those two deserve to get out, it's two songs form 1977 updated, but we have about 40 others. We were ahead of our time but now it's right on time.

X-8: Do you think the new stuff is more accessible?

Cliff: Yeah it probably is....

Hud: What's the idea behind the name 'Action Design'?

John: I wanted something with action in the it and Cliff wanted something with design in it so I said 'How about Action Design'? Dix named Who What Where When Why.

X-8: With the recent explosion in suburban 'new wave', all the kids listen to X or the B-52's rather than Van Halen, is that better for the Weirdos?

John: Yeah.

Al: All that question for a 'Yeah'! It seems like you guys have been at this point before, right after 'Who What...' you lost your band and it was just the three...

John: (Snapping his fingers) Snap the angry snap three snap snap snap, it wasn't really cooking at snap that time, snap snap, people were coming to our shows, snap snap and thinking they were snap superior snap...

X-8: The old Hollywood crowd right.

John: Snap yeah, snap with their snap hands on their hips snap trying to see who was wearing what snap, with the HB's we were snap down at the Cuckoos Nest snap about a year ago and that's what snap the Weirdos are about, action snap snap cutting loose. Our intent snap was action snap snap snap...

Hud: Gut feelings.

John: Right snap, that's what the HB want, they wanna shake loud fast, they want snap action.

Hud: What about the violence?

John: Well I don't like people getting beat up but it depends on the situation. We played a show at the Fleetwood and these jock and football players were attacking anyone with short hair, and there was retaliation after that.

X-8: Cliff, what would be your utopia, the perfect setting for the Weirdos?

John: Eternal ejaculation.

Cliff: Thanks Cliff!!!

John: No, that was my quote.

X-8: Who what where when why?

Cliff: That's a good question, let me think about it...

ADOLESCENTS

Steve: When I was in Agent Orange, Tony was always at our shows, diving off the stage and just amazing us. This skinny kid diving off the stage. We look so good together, we're such a clash, we just had to be in a band.

Tony: They still laugh at me **"Look at that skinny kid"**, but they see us and a lot of things change.

Casey: (Slash marks on arm): I got bummed because I made a mistake, I didn't do it for nothing, that's dumb!

Steve: The first time we played a party with **Agent Orange** and **Social Distortion**, we threw Eddie and Mike Patton out because they didn't have invites, we didn't know who they were.

Casey: Then they saw us and said "God, the Adolescents are young, good kids".

Steve: Tony's house was a good place to practice until Tony broke out the windows... if we bring money home and wave it in our parents face, they don't care if we play, but if we don't they mind.

Casey: Rikk and Steve write most of the songs, but we all write a few.

Steve: Rikk was in the Slashers and they stole "Creatures" from us, and the song "Breakdown" Mike (Agent Orange) kinda took, it was my song 'cept for the words.

Tony: I don't fry no more, swear to God!... I use to be I'd get beat up in school and shit and everybody hated me, now all of a sudden these people are being real nice, I don't understand it at all, it's hard not to let your head explode!

Frank: My old band (Social Distortion) played our school and nobody came, they all hated us, but now they beg us to play – NO WAY!!!

Casey: Should we hate the people that hated us then, that like us now????

Steve: Casey sucks.

FLIPSIDE NUMBER 21

"They can make things worse for me
Sometimes I'd rather die
They can tell me lots of things
But I can see eye to eye
I know they know the way I think
I know they always will
But someday I'm gonna change my mind
Sometimes I'd rather kill....
Bloodstains... Speed kills... fast cars... cheap thrills...
Rich girls... fine line... I've lost my sense... I've lost control... I've lost my mind...."

Adolescents at the Fleetwood – photo by Al

Things seem so much different now
The scene has died away
I haven't got a steady job
And I got no place to stay
Well it's a futuristic modern world
But things arn't what they seem
Someday you'd better wake up
From this stupid fantasy"
"Bloodstains" – Agent Orange

ISSUE #: 21
DATE: December 1980
FORMAT: 8 1/2x11, Rotary web offset
PAGES: 16
PRICE: Free with ROTR Vol. 1
PRESS RUN: ?
STAFF: Al, Hud, and Pete

- -

This was another unique issue for us, what we did was put together an insert for the Rodney On The Roq compilation LP, in the form of a Flipside. The issue contained reprints and make shift articles on the bands included on the record. One side was mostly punk stuff, the other side more pop oriented stuff. The stuff was compiled by Rodney Bigenhelmer (from his KROQ radio show requests) and put out by Posh Boy.

AGENT ORANGE

Al: What the story behind "Bloodstains"?
Mike Rikk Agnew, one of the guitar players for the Adolescents, well a long time ago he was in an experimental band called the Mertzes, and I just met him and he was saying he was gonna do an Orange County album. At the time I didn't realize that it probably wouldn't happen, but he said if we had an original song we could be on it. So we got all excited and wrote the song- cause it was our only original, our first song I guess.
Al: What stuff did you play?
Mike Oh we had some original stuff, but mostly covers and old surf music.
Al: You're really influenced by that?
Mike Well... yeah!
Al: How big is your collection?
Mike It's not real big, there's not a lot of really good stuff, the best is the Lively Ones, they're the best surf band given to mankind! And they're from Orange County. My cousin used to be their guitar player, and I've got Dick Dale and all the typical stuff too...
Al: What's your attitude towards the new punk scene?

Mike Well like... what generation is this for punks? Think of the ones that are out there... it's gotta be third or fourth generation, it's changed so much from the original idea. They look and act so different. It's not what it started out to be, it's changed too much. The violence aspect has definitely gotten out of hand, it's just, we can't tolerate people beating the hell out of each other, I mean all the time, at every show. So we end up playing with terrible bands like the Chills, it's not fun, but at least we get away from the same old crowd. It's easy to have a crowd full of spike heads cause anything you do will make them dance, you get a reaction from anything you do. We've seen a lot of really bad bands, but people seem to like them. Then there's another crowd, there's a lot of people out there besides punks, we try to draw from a different crowd. The whole punk scene seems a little limited lately because it's not growing much anymore, it seems to be the same people over and over and the same problems and the same troubles over and over. We didn't want to play at the Fleetwood because of the fights... after awhile the whole violence aspect and the trouble get boring, it gets to the point where the people aren't interested in the music anymore, they just go out and break things. These people have disappointed us.
Al: Do you consider yourselves a punk band?
Mike We never were. No way can you consider us punk, we're way too young for that. None of us were around for the things that happened originally - none of us had ever seen the Masque, ever, or any of the good bands that started it out. We don't even know what it's about. A lot of people out there don't either, but they're getting away with it- this isn't the first generation. Here we are a bunch of kids in Orange County going to school and stuff calling ourselves punks, what are we gonna do? How are we gonna prove it? I don't know, maybe like Mike Ness, there's a few that are actually punks. If we called ourselves punks people would laugh at us, then again we walk down the street and people yell at us: Why are they calling me a punk? My hair doesn't stick up and I got my jacket at Brea Mall!!! There's no middle ground, either you're very normal or a punk or new wave whatever that is. There's gotta be an alternative, there had got to be something besides just punk and just rock and roll.

Early Agent Orange

FLIPSIDE NUMBER 22

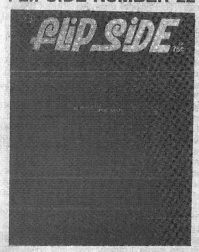

"It feels so good to say what I want
It feels so good to break down the walls
You see the disgust in their eyes
and I'm gonna go wild
Spray paint the walls
There isn't room for someone like me
My life is their disease
Spray paint the walls"
"Spray Paint the Walls" Black Flag

ISSUE #: 22
DATE: December 1980
FORMAT: 8 1/2x11 rotary web offset
PAGES: 32
PRICE: $.75
PRESS RUN: 2000
STAFF: Al, Hud and Pete

– –

This issue was our famous all black cover Darby Crash memorial issue, because it was then that Darby died. I guess this is as good a point as any to say that punk it had been know, was also dead. The 'punk' of 1980 was a different beast than it was in 1977, even as today it is so different we have to call it something different (like 'hardcore'). So the scene and audience become polarized, there are bands who just won't play at the Fleetwood, just as there are bands who CANNOT play at Madame Wongs. Flipside's direction seems to have stayed with the loud, fast rules philosophy, even as the audience

went from bad to worse. Then again we always felt that we could out live the trouble makers just as the trouble makers themselves were to quickly out grow the punk scene (and quite predictably went back to the discos or football fields). Unfortunately some exploiters (such as in the 'Decline'), choose to glorify the ugliness of this scene, and thus spread the rot that is the suburban jock plaque to other scenes. Nevertheless, there are still decent shows, more of an 'underground' to the now above ground punk scene. And that's the inspiration that led us through these bleek times.

BLACK FLAG

– –

Black Flag were interviewed on November 27 at their 'business' home in Torrance. The business is SST Electronics, based around Greg's invention of an antenna tuner. The entire band lives and practices here, which is surprising since the place is small and cluttered with poster art work, magazines, electronic gear and the bands equipment and personal stuff. This place is only one is a long series of homes for them: they started at the infamous Church in Hermosa Beach, moved to the Hermosa Strand, a place called the 'Worm Hole', where minors hung out and thus attracted the police and eventual running out of town by the city council. The new place was in Redondo for awhile, but it was expensive, so back to the Church, only to get evicted, which gave good reason to have a demolition party, and now they are in Torrance.
Black Flag have toured this country extensively, the latest being the December 'Creepy Crawl' tour.

Al: Tell us about the name Black Flag, you didn't get it off the bug spray.
Chuck: Originally we were Panic...
Hud: Like Panic fanzine...
Chuck: That's why it stopped, too many Panics. Panic break out, Panic cut loose, Panic desperation - Black Flag, pretty much the same angle but a little deeper concept. Same basic idea, it was Ray's (Greg's brother) idea originally, they both floated around at the same time, even at the time of Panic we wanted another band called Black Flag which would be more of a threatening

thing. The name has the connotation of anarchy, negation and all that.
Dave: Opposite of white flag, which is surrender, you're taken over...
Greg: No.
Chuck: Kicking things over.
Greg: "Our ambition is to be the number one punk band", that's what a lot of bands think unfortunately. We're not taking over anything.
Chuck: Anything established too long is sick. There's no formula to anything we do. Our songs have no formula to it, there's always a certain intensity to it and all that but it's not formulized. Each one is an approach to a seperate emotion.
Greg: That's what created problems in our band with personal changes, people haven't wanted to change at all. We're not satisfied with recycling the same material.
Chuck: It's easy to get somewhere by pushing a formula, like Elton John or somebody.. you keep putting out those same formula records and you get famous. You don't get famous by hitting people over the head with something new.
Greg: Like our band, the personal changes have been for the better because now I feel like everybody doesn't care about a music career. You'd be surprised the people who think that way. Even if they are a punk band, their main thing is to get signed to a major label or something like that.
Chuck: They're aiming what they do at that, not that they're aiming to get something out, they're aiming #1 to get a record contract, #2 to fuck 1000 girls #3 ya know? I mean, however crass you want to be about it, those would be fringe benefits. A major label is a way of distributing what you want, if they can be used by you and everything else that comes along the way is like eating hamburgers. Those things become peoples goals, not something outside of it.
Here's the angle, I would much rather make my compromise going to work and come home and do something that's really me, a real outlet, than to go to work all the time and always be making compromises. You actually get some gratification.
Al: Why compromise at all...
Greg: The point is not making money or not, it's the motivation behind it.
Al: What's your motivation?
Chuck: He needs it.
Greg: Basically it's something that's turned out that way, I used to write songs by myself, I never thought I'd get a band together. I couldn't find people that wanted to play what I wanted but I still wrote songs. The motivation is to express something. We do want to get our material out as widely as possible, but we don't want to change to do that.... what we try to do is create a situation that opens peoples minds up to something new and possibilities of something different.
Al: Do you think they get the message?
Greg: There isn't any message.
Al: I mean the way they react to your band.
Greg: A lot of them, yeah, it works. It works for me.
Chuck: I get what I want out there. I know an awful lot of people get the same way. Real direct physical release, you get out, you go nuts and it's tied into things that are personally meaningful, like "Nervous Breakdown", you get out there because you got tension that's grinding away, and if you don't kick the door off the bedroom or something... After it's better you feel a lot better.
Al: What about people smashing up the hall,

Black Flag: Greg, Dez and Chuck at the Vex – photo by Al

if that's how they have to get it out.

Dez: They usually do that after they hear that our concert has been cancelled.

Greg: People ask us, why don't you get up there, you've got authority..

Chuck: We've go NO authority!!

Greg: We don't want to get on stage and be authority figures and tell people what to do, we feel that that's wrong. We want to get up on stage and create an atmosphere where people can think for themselves. They're not always gonna do the right things.

Al: Explain Creepy Crawl?

Dez: An exercise in fear, give somebody the shakes. Say a punk with chains walks into a liquor store and...   ♦

Chuck: And the little Oriental guy starts shaking and goes "Oh fuck, they're gonna do something, I know it".

Greg: Fear of the unknown.

Hud: You got that from Manson.

Greg: Yeah.

Hud: Do you idolize Manson or something?

Greg: No, but we feel a certain affinity for him.

Chuck: There's a lot of things that are mutual, the whole motivation behind the Sharon Tate murders.

Greg: In a way Manson was a lot stronger than us in certain respects, he wanted to murder, tried to murder Dennis Wilson of the Beach Boys for stealing his song and instead he got Sharon Tate. We're not quite that severe!!!

Chuck: Manson and his family used to go into a middle class home and walk into the room and the family would be watching TV and they'd march around and they'd call that a crawl.

Hud: Creepy crawls, but I thought he did that at night?

Greg: Yeah.

Al: And you're gonna creepy crawl the whole country?

Greg: Yeah.

FLIPSIDE NUMBER 23

"Why are scientists in the lab
Looking through the microscope
Tosses little glass slides, they never lie
How can this small mind cope?
I've never seen anything like it before
This amoeba has a mind of it's own
But don't turn your back you stupid science world
Watch this amoeba split into a clone
Amoeba – amoeba
Amoeba – amoeba
A one celled creature, a one celled thing

It hardly knows it's alive
No legs, no arms, no eyes
It sees, its thinks, it grows
Its......... Amoeba....
"Amoeba" – Adolescents

"Flying over Hiroshima, 1945
City looks so small from way up here
I wonder who'll survive?
Atom bomb, TNT, new disease, poor city...
A blinding flash, hotter than the sun
Dead bodies lie across the path
Radiation colors the air, finishing one by one...
"1945" – Social Distortion

ISSUE #: 23
DATE: March 1981
FORMAT: 8 1/2x11, rotary web offset, color cover/ insides
PAGES: 40
PRICE: $1.00
PRESS RUN: 1600
STAFF: Al and Hud

- -

This issue marked another change in the Flipside look. This is our first issue with two colors of ink!! This issue also had color ink on the inside pages, not just on the cover. Of course to go along with this we had to raise the cover price to $1.00, but we did add an extra 8 pages. Flipside is finally looking a feeling (thickness) like a 'real' magazine. We are even getting distribution thru magazine distributors now, which really helps. Staff wise we are picking up a lot of contribution help from local friends again: people like Helen, X-8 (again), Gerard, Carl Marks, Pooch is starting to do a few record reviews, Steve Masi, Pete's pumping out more photos, Michele is covering O.C. really well, Robert

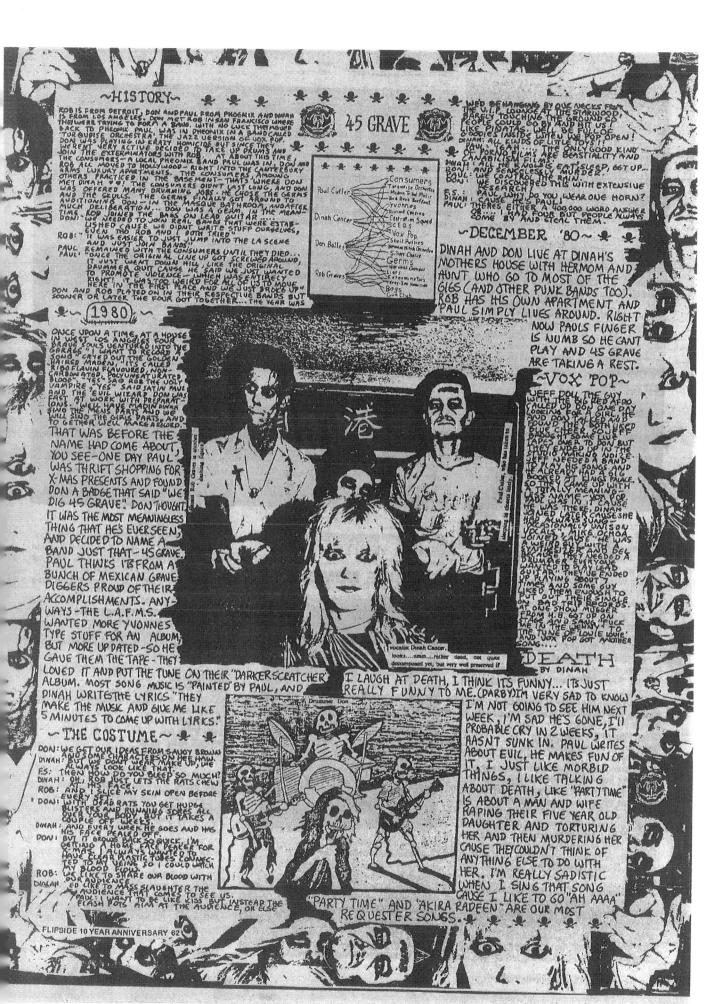

~HISTORY~

✠ ✠ ✠ ✠ ✠ ✠ ✠ ✠ ✠

45 GRAVE

ROB IS FROM DETROIT, DON AND PAUL FROM PHOENIX AND DINAH IS FROM LOS ANGELES. DON MET ROB IN SAN FRANCISCO WHERE THEY WERE TRYING TO FORM A BAND, WITH NO LUCK THEY MOVED BACK TO PHEONIX. PAUL WAS IN PHEONIX IN A BAND CALLED "TURQUISE ORCHESTRA", THE JAZZ VERSION OF BOX POP. DON WAS PLAYING IN KRAZY HOMICIDE BUT SINCE THEY WEREN'T VERY ACTIVE DECIDED TO TAKE UP DRUMS AND JOIN THE EXTERMINATORS WITH ROB. AT ABOUT THIS TIME THE CONSUMERS—A LOCAL PHEONIX BAND AND PAUL WAS IN. DON AND ROB ALL MOVED TO HOLLYWOOD—RIGHT INTO THE CONSUMERS ARMS LUXURY APARTMENTS. THE CONSUMERS AMONG OTHERS PRACTICED IN THE BASEMENT—THAT'S WHERE DON MET DINAH '99. THE CONSUMERS DIDN'T LAST LONG, AND DON WAS OFFERED MANY DRUMMING JOBS. HE CHOSE THE GERMS AND THE SKULLS. THE GERMS FINALLY GOT AROUND TO AUDITIONING DON IN AN MASQUE BATHROOM, AND AFTER MUCH DELIBERATION... DON WAS A GERM IN THE MEAN-TIME. ROB JOINED THE BAGS ON LEAD GUITAR.
DON: WE NEEDED TO JOIN REAL BANDS THAT WERE ESTAB-LISHED CAUSE WE DIDN'T WRITE STUFF OURSELVES, EVEN THEN ROB AND I BOTH TRIED.
ROB: IT WAS EASIER TO JUST JUMP INTO THE LA SCENE AND JUST JOIN BANDS.
PAUL: REMAINED WITH THE CONSUMERS UNTIL THEY DIED... ONCE THE ORIGINAL LINE UP GOT SCREWED AROUND, IT JUST WENT DOWN HILL, LIKE THE ORIGINAL DRUMMER QUIT CAUSE HE SAID WE JUST WANTED TO PROMOTE VIOLENCE—WHICH WAS ENTIRELY RIGHT! IT WAS TOO WEIRD FOR ALL OF US TO MOVE HERE IN THE FIRST PLACE AND WE JUST BROKE UP.
DON AND ROB PLAYED ON IN THEIR RESPECTIVE BANDS BUT SOONER OR LATER THE FOUR GOT TOGETHER... THE YEAR WAS

~ ☠ **1980** ~

ONCE UPON A TIME, AT A HOUSE IN WEST LOS ANGELES FOUR BRAVE SOULS VENTURED INTO THE GARAGE. I WANT TO RECORD A SANG CRIED OUT THE GOLDEN HAIRED MAIDEN, IT'S ALL RIBO FLAVIN FLAVOURED, NON-CARBONATED, POLYUNSATURATED BLOOD. YES, SAID ROB THE UGLY VAMPIRE, YES, SAID SATIN PAUL THE EVIL WIZARD, DON WAS FAST AT WORK WITH PREPARAT-IONS. WE WILL HAVE CARDBOARD SO THE MEN'S PARTS AND WE WILL SING THE GIRLS PARTS, AND TO GETHER WE WILL MAKE A RECORD.

THAT WAS BEFORE THE NAME HAD COME ABOUT, YOU SEE—ONE DAY PAUL WAS THRIFT SHOPPING FOR X-MAS PRESENTS AND FOUND DON A BADGE THAT SAID "WE DIG 45 GRAVE". DON THOUGHT IT WAS THE MOST MEANINGLESS THING THAT HE'S EVER SEEN, AND DECIDED TO NAME A BAND JUST THAT—45 GRAVE. PAUL THINKS IT'S FROM A BUNCH OF MEXICAN GRAVE-DIGGERS PROUD OF THEIR ACCOMPLISHMENTS. ANY-WAYS—THE L.A.F.M.S. WANTED MORE YVONNES TYPE STUFF FOR AN ALBUM, BUT MORE UP DATED—SO HE GAVE THEM THE TAPE—THEY LOVED IT AND PUT THE TUNE ON THEIR "DARKER SCRATCHER" ALBUM. MOST SONG MUSIC IS "PAINTED" BY PAUL, AND DINAH WRITES THE LYRICS "THEY MAKE THE MUSIC AND GIVE ME LIKE 5 MINUTES TO COME UP WITH LYRICS."

~ THE COSTUME ~ ☠ ☠

DON: WE GET OUR IDEAS FROM SAVOY BROWN AND SOME CHARACTERS ON HEE HAW.
DINAH: BUT WE DON'T WEAR MAKE UP, WE ALWAYS LOOK LIKE THAT.
F.S.: THEN HOW DO YOU BLEED SO MUCH?
DINAH: OH, ROB JUST LETS THE RATS CHEW ON HIS FACE.
ROB: AND I SLICE MY SKIN OPEN BEFORE EVERY GIG.
DON: WITH DEAD RATS YOU GET HUGE BLISTERS AND RUNNING SORES ALL OVER YOUR BODY BUT IT TAKES A COUPLE OF WEEKS.
DINAH: AND EVERY WEEK HE GOES AND HAS HIS FACE PEELED OFF.
DON: BUT IT GROWS BACK SO QUICK. I'M GETTING A HOME FACE PEELER FOR X-MAS. I ALWAYS WANTED TO HAVE CLEAR PLASTIC TUBES CONNEC-TED TO MY VEINS SO I COULD WATCH MY BLOOD FLOW.
ROB: WE LIKE TO SHARE OUR BLOOD WITH OUR AUDIENCE.
DINAH: ED LIKE TO MASS SLAUGHTER THE AUDIENCE THAT COME TO SEE US.
PAUL: I WANT TO BE LIKE KISS BUT INSTEAD OF FLASH POTS AIM AT THE AUDIENCE, OR ELSE.

WE'D BE HANGING BY OUR NECKS FROM THE V.I.P. LOUNGE AT THE STARWOOD. PEOPLE COULD GO BY AND HIT US LIKE PINATAS. WE'LL BE FULL OF GOODIES INSIDE WHEN WE POP OPEN!
PAUL: YEAH THE ONLY GOOD KIND OF PORNO FILMS ARE BESTIALITY AND CANABILISM FILMS.
DINAH: ALL THE BANDS IS EAT, SLEEP, GET UP...
DON: AND SENSELESSLY MURDER.
DON: WE CONTROL THE RAIN.
DINAH: WE DISCOVERED THIS WITH EXTENSIVE RESEARCH.
F.S.: PAUL, WHY DO YOU WEAR ONE HORN?
DINAH: CAUSE HE'S PAUL.
PAUL: THERE'S EITHER A 400,000 WORD ANSWER OR I HAD FOUR BUT PEOPLE ALWAYS COME BY AND STEAL THEM.

~DECEMBER '80~ ☠ ☠

DINAH AND DON LIVE AT DINAH'S MOTHERS HOUSE WITH HER MOM AND AUNT WHO GO TO MOST OF THE GIGS (AND OTHER PUNK BANDS TOO). ROB HAS HIS OWN APARTMENT AND PAUL SIMPLY LIVES AROUND. RIGHT NOW PAULS FINGER IS NUMB SO HE CANT PLAY AND 45 GRAVE ARE TAKING A REST.

~VOX POP~

JEFF DOLL THE GUY WITH THE BIG RED AFRO CALLED UP DON ONE DAY LOOKING FOR A GIRL. HE FOUND THEY BOTH LIKED BLUE CHEER. SO JEFF BROUGHT SOME BLUE TAPES OVER TO DON BUT THEY ENDED UP IN THE STUDIO MAKING NOISE. JEFF NEEDED A BAND TO PLAY HIS SONGS AND HE ALREADY HAD A GIG SOONED AT KING'S PALACE, SO THEY ALL CAME UP WITH A LESS NAMELESS NAME. VOX POP DADE WAS IN. VOX POP HE WAS THERE. DINAH JOINED LATER CAUSE SHE HAD ALWAYS SUNG OCCASIONALLY UNISON VOCALS. I LIKE OCHOA JOINED CAUSE HE WAS A WEIRD GUY WITH SYNTHESIZER AND BEL. WHEN THEY NEEDED A DRUMMER EVERYONE WANTED TO PLAY LEAD GUITAR. THEY UP ENDED UP PLAYING ABOUT 4 TIMES AND SOME GUY LIKED THEM ENOUGH TO PUT OUT THEIR SINGLE ON A BAND TRIP RECORDS. AT ONE SHOW MUGGER FROM H.B. GOT UP ON STAGE AND SANG FUCK ME IN THE JEMMY TO THE TUNE OF LOUIE LOUIE AND VOX POP GOT ANOTHER SONG...

DEATH
BY DINAH

I LAUGH AT DEATH, I THINK ITS FUNNY... ITS JUST REALLY FUNNY TO ME. (DARBY) IM VERY SAD TO KNOW I'M NOT GOING TO SEE HIM NEXT WEEK, I'M SAD HE'S GONE, I'LL PROBABLE CRY IN 2 WEEKS, IT HASN'T SUNK IN. PAUL WRITES ABOUT EVIL, HE MAKES FUN OF IT, I JUST LIKE MORBID THINGS, I LIKE TALKING ABOUT DEATH, LIKE "PARTYTIME" IS ABOUT A MAN AND WIFE RAPING THEIR FIVE YEAR OLD DAUGHTER AND TORTURING HER AND THEN MURDERING HER CAUSE THEY COULDN'T THINK OF ANYTHING ELSE TO DO WITH HER. I'M REALLY SADISTIC WHEN I SING THAT SONG CAUSE I LIKE TO GO "AH AAAA". "PARTY TIME" AND "AKIRA RADFEN" ARE OUR MOST REQUESTER SONGS. ☠ ☠ ☠

vocalist Dinah Cancer, looks... umm... rather dead, not quite decomposed yet, but very well preserved if

guitarist Rob Graves a another dashing figure

Paul Cutler, who has taken to dropping in clowns lately

Drummer Don

FLIPSIDE 10 YEAR ANNIVERSARY 62

Consumers
Turquoise Orchestra
Modern Tribal Music
Bad Brock Buffant
Paul Cutler
Yvonnes
Distant Cousins
Castration Squad
SEEDS
Dinah Cancer
Vox Pop
Skull Pushes
Don Bolles
Human Hitch Orchestra
Silver Chalice
Germs
Liars
Rob Graves
Exterminators
New Wave Gender
Easy-Zen New Code
Bags
Gun Club

Tom, Paul Cutler and David Wiley – photo by Al

Hill and Ed Colver are contributing lots of photos and Dave Damage is starting to get involved with interviewing.

What's happening on the scene? Well the violence is still happening (if you have long hair, you get beat, no two ways about it), the Starwood is happening, more and more skateboard kids (Dogtown) are getting into punk rock, Black Flag are happening and making headlines with a rash of mini-riots at what seems like every show they do, and the Ventures are back! They debuted at the Starwood (first gig in the US in 10 years) and gave the scene a needed jolt of good times, as well as fresh air!

BPEOPLE

The BPEOPLE were interviewed by Al and Dave at the Starwood on Feb. 24, 1981

Al: You started as the Little Cripples and then the Strict Ids, what happened to that?

Alex: We lost the singer, he left.

Fred: Or who was in 'intense personality conflict'. He went to New York, he's in the Swans, (Mike Gira)

Alex: He used to be in Circus Mort but not no more.

Dave: What does BPeople mean?

Alex: Nothing (Shouting) RANDOM

Fred: We won't tell you now, later.

Dave: I had a dream the other night, I thought it ment B Movies, B People or sub-people...

Fred: That's a good idea, if it had B Monster movies it'd be fine because B Monster movies are like the greatest thing ever.

Al: A lot of people think it means Boat People.

Alex: They're wrong about insects too. B means nothing, as most bands names mean nothing, what does X mean? What does Plugz mean? Think about it for a minute... stupid name...

Al: You started playing with punk bands, now you're playing with like Human Sexual Response...

Alex: We had no choice over that, we need to play. We like to play.

Fred: What's a punk band? The Circle Jerks? What do you define as a punk band? We get harrassed and shit when we play with punk bands, because some of the audience doesn't like us intensely... So it's not like, uh, we're not that aggressive to want to beat people up, we would rather run the other way, who cares about them, they're only about 500 strong. But I like the Circle Jerks, they're one of the best bands in L.A.

Alex: Yeah, Keith is great.

Fred: But when their friends want to beat us up, we don't want to play.

Alex: We're anti-violence, you can quote us on that... I saw a fuckin' Black Flag show and there were so many fist fights I had to leave, it was nauseating. Violence is ridiculous, any bands that promote violence do not need to play.

Al: What do you think about being called 'Art Damage'?

Pat: Art Damage???? I don't know, I think it's just something you say when you don't like the music.

Tom: You could turn around and say 'Punk damage'. I think Black Flag is as artistic as we are.

Al: Who are your favorite musicians?

Pat: People I know like, Monitor, those people, Victory Acres, 45 Grave are pretty much my favorite bands.

Dave: The saxophone is mixed down...

Pat: Yeah I know, that always seems to be a problem. I try to play as loud as I can but sometimes it just doesn't come thru - I like to play the sax so it doesn't sound like a sax.

CHINA WHITE

After my first attempt of doing this interview and passing out as my friends drove me to their studio, I decided to try it again at the Nest. Couldn't get it done there either. This was the final attempt. I drove down from Fullerton with Steve (Adolescents) and Sparkey (Fullerton Bro) wondering if we would get the whole band. Anyway, it was done at Marks house...

Mark (18) - vocals

Frank (18) - guitar
James (18) - bass
Vince (20) - drums

Michele: How did you come up with the name China White?

Frank: We're always talking about heroin so I decided China White while we were nailing up padding in our garage.

Steve: Were you guys all original members?

Frank: Just us four.

Sparkey: What do you think of all the violence?

Frank: I was into it, I used to watch it playing in my old band.

Steve: What bands were you guys in?

Frank: I was in the Outsiders and so was Mark. I was also in Anti-Fascist.

Sparkey: What do you think of the violence?

Frank: They should do what they want...

Sparkey: You don't care if the music...

Frank: It brings OUT the violence.

Steve: What bands are your influences?

Frank: The Damned.

Mark: Stiff Little Fingers.

Michele: Well you guys are more sophisticated than your average punk band..

Frank: I'm the guitar player and I don't like to be boring! That's how I like to play. I have old influences too you know.

Sparkey: What do you guys think of punk in HB?

Mark: It's not as crazy as it used to be...

Frank: It's a gossip scene. It's a joke. I've been playing in front of these people for as long as I've been playing. It's ok, but I want to go around and check out every place.

Steve: Do you guys ever get beat up?

Frank: No, we're the ones that could fuckin'...

Mike: Fuckin' hell, are you kidding! People just leave us alone.

Steve: You fuck people up?

Frank: Sometimes. You know, a long time ago, there was day-glo, that bullshit. Then there was the black leather band - that was us! There was nothing else besides assholes.

Sparkey: What do you think of all the violence?

James: I think it's bitchen! You know the guys that get beat up are back next week beating on other people. It's just an endless circle, you could call it a Vicious Circle (laughs). Fuck, of course I've got my head beat, that's just the way it goes.

Sparkey: Do you think you are developing a following outside of HB?

James: Yeah, it seems like no one from HB goes to see us anymore. More people from L.A.- you see HB people don't like to travel.

Someone: What do you think of chains, boots and bandanas?

James: In Huntington people are afraid to wear them because they might have to back it up... We'll play a house, you know, if we can destroy it.

Michele: What about that house, Robins house...

James: It was after we played the Fleetwood and our friends just shreaded the place! That was our China White party. She kept saying don't do it, so of course they're gonna rip the place apart... they swung on the chandeliers and broke them off the ceiling...

Michele: (An expensive tract house was demolished, there were holes in the walls and spray paint all over...)

James: No windows were left! Water was all over. She was running around going "Don't break the windows!" We're just the fucked people man!

BPeople: Pat, Fred, Alex and friend – photo Al

Christian Death: Jay, George, Rozz and James - photo by Bill

CHRISTIAN DEATH

Christian Death were interviewed Sat. December 27th in Pomona - 2 days after Christmas.

- -

Dave: Why did you choose the name Christian Death? Do you have anything against religion?
CD: Because it's the only insulting thing now.
Hud: You don't believe in God?
CD: We believe in God, we just don't believe in religion, God is not religion... I don't believe in God... God is in your mind.
Dave: What about Jesus?
CD: Because Jesus is a fascist religion. It's saying you have to like do this and do this unless you won't go to heaven.
Dave: Do you ever go to church?
CD: I've never been to church in my life.
Dave: So why did you choose that name?
CD: Because I've heard, I've been preached to by Christians.
Al: So how long have you been into this?
CD: I've been into it since about 77, and all these guys used to drive by and go "Fuck you, punk sucks!", now you see them out here with their Klu Klux Klans and their bandanas, now it's just like I'm not a true punk because I don't go to every Black Flag concert.
Al: They are playing tonight.
CD: I only like to listen to Castration Squad and 45 Grave, but I get shit, I swear it, because these guys go "You're not punk", but back then they were driving around with long hair. These people, the ones here tonight (Circle Jerks gig) are just followers. One skateboarder turned punk, then half of these people that are here. They don't really care, they don't know a thing about it. They're the type that walk around with a swastica pinned right next to an Anarchy badge... They'll go beat up hippies and they don't understand that hippies did more for society, real hippies - they don't understand that hippies were doing the same thing we're doing now, now the word hippie means O.P. shorts, that's the KMET people, but real hippies, I don't mind real hippies because they've got political attitudes and stuff.
Dave: What did the Red Brigade say?
CD: They tried to cut us down by writing a song called "You're So Morbid".
Dave: I think that's good because I hate Christianity, I used to be a christian when I was 8 years old.
CD: But a lot of the stuff we're talking about

people misunderstand. We're trying to get out of the church age and wait for the revelation.
Dave: Right, it's good to say fuck you to Christianity.
CD: It's not really that too much, we just don't like these guys who call themselves preachers, they are on TV and they tell everyone so send in their donations, and you look on their hands and they have these diamond rings, and three mansions and all these cars and they're trying to preach stuff out of the book, they make up stuff....

THE VENTURES

- -

The Ventures were interviewed on March 6, 1981 at Don Wilson's house. Present from Flipside were Al, Hud and Pooch. Don, Mel and Leisha: represent the Ventures.

As you probably know the Ventures are one of the oldest and most renowned rock band in history. They were formed by rhythm guitarist Don Wilson and bassist Bob Bogle in 1958. In a short time they were playing around the Seattle area. The hooked up with lead guitarist Nole 'Nokie' Edwards in the summer of 1959 and recorded "Walk Don't Run" which was released on the Blue Horizon label. That song went on to become a million selling number one hit. Mel Taylor joined in on drums at about that time and the four (except for Jerry McGee replacing Nokie in 1967 for a few years) have been together ever since. The Ventures have been around and have been active all these years. Mostly recording and playing in Japan and Europe. They have over 150 albums out in Japan which range from classical to psychedelic, and have about 78 domestic releases. The best sellers are: "Telstar", "Golden Greats" and "Surfing". The Ventures are into their 21st year recording and say they can do it till they're 60.
Flipside: Why haven't you played the U.S. in over 10 years?
Mel: Things were so good for us in Japan, even though we were recording domestically as well. We did some albums here but the push wasn't exactly 100%. It was the same record company over there, but there's nothing bigger than the Ventures in Japan (the biggest selling act in Japan's history - over 20 million sold).
Flipside: Did you live there?
Mel: Well, half the time..
Leisha: In hotels.
Don: In one year we did 108 concerts in 78 days without a day off.

Leisha:: I had it easy when I was there, we did like 100 days and we had 3 days off.
Mel: We did like 3 shows a day, when we did only one it was like a day off.
Flipside: What kind of places did you play?
Mel: 3 to 10,000 seat concert halls, no schools, because we always went there in summer when the kids were out. They really love instrumental music.
Leisha:: The Ventures brought the electric guitar to Japan!
Mel: Exactly!
Don: The first tour was in '61 I think we were unknown then, but when we came back in 1965 there were 20,000 kids at the airport, we thought the president was behind us but then they held up the "WELCOME VENTURES" sign!
Flipside: How did you end up with 150 albums out in just 20 years?
Mel: They way it worked in the early days is we'd all listen to he radio, all different stations, and like the Telstar album, which was gold twice for us, was originally scheduled to be called "Hits Of The 60's"... Don came in and said "I just heard a song called "Telstar" on the radio" and we listened to it and recorded it, and that's what the album became.
Don: Basically we stick to current hits, with our instrumental adaptation, with some of our own material, like about 4 or 5 originals on an album.
Flipside: Was "Hawaii 50" or "Pipeline" originals?
Don: Actually "Pipeline" was done by the Surfaris, but they sold 50,000 of theirs and we sold 500,000 of ours. Who's hit is it?
Mel: Same thing with "Telstar" and "Lonely Bull", which was Herb Alpert, we orbited his album, which was a hit, and sold a million. Matt Stevens did "Hawaii 50".
Flipside: what has helped your resurgence?
Mel: Rodney Bigenheimer!!! Rodney told me one night he was having problems getting the kids to dance at the Starwood, so he put on "Walk Don't Run" and the dance floor filled up. He was playing our stuff on KROQ and he was getting requests for Ventures records.
Flipside: How did you like that first show at the Starwood after 10 years?
Don: Oh, we really enjoyed it!!
Flipside: What'd ya think of the kids jumping around and stuff?
Don: It was certainly a new experience, we were warned about that (slamming).
Mel: We were doing our thing, and they might as well be doing theirs, and they were!
Flipside: How did the Gogos get together with you guys that night?
Mel: Thru Rodney.. and the Gogos wrote "Surfing and Spying" which is the new single, with "Showdown At Newport", an original, on the other side.
Flipside: Didn't you think about making a comeback after 10 years anyway...
Mel: Again, it gets back to who likes you, if we'd tried this 4 years ago in the middle of the disco era, they would have thrown us out, or throw tomatoes at us.
Don: In the cans!!!
Flipside: If it picks up will you do a U.S. tour?
Mel: We're doing one anyways! It's a lot of fun now, we're doing what we like to do and the kids are getting off on it, we don't have to pretend to be what we're not, we're doing what we know how to do and they like it and only because it's gone back to the roots. It's come back to something you can understand, you don't have to do a 28 piece session to get a hit record today. With disco you had to have

The Ventures with David Roth, Rodney etc... after the Starwood gig. - photo Al

that or you weren't in the ball park.
Don: We've had a lot of people in the business that are hot tell us that they learned to play off our records: Stephen Stills, Ted Nugent, Al Stewart, Peter Frampton, the B52's...
Flipside: Did you guys ever surf?
Mel: Everyone asks us and all the surf bands that, I'd say 70% of the surf music players don't surf or never have. I got a surfboard once and fell off and never got on again.
Flipside: What do you think of the label 'Surf Music'?
Don: The "Surfing" album was one of our biggest and people put us in that category, but we've never really liked it, we've always played soft.. tasty rock that's wild, but now surfing, new wave, rock, it's all balanced in and hard to classify.
Flipside: When did that label come about?
Mel: It started in 1963, it's just like the disco era, it just landed on it, the music was always there. We were doing the instrumental big guitar sound 2 or 3 years prior to the surfing sound, and then we did the "Surfing" album and got pegged a 'Surf' band. We have an album which is called "Joy", which is Bach, Beethoven and Mozart, ya know, come on. Sometimes the industry dictates what you do, but if something happend to you because you are already there...
Don: We can play anything, we have 78 albums, you can't play the same thing on 78 albums. What we're trying to do is stay in the solid surf rock beat and try to appeal to that audience.
Mel: The stuff we do the best is what the audience is getting off on.
Flipside: What about the"Play Guitar With the Ventures" albums?
Mel: That might come again because of the new wave kids, we keep getting comments like "We learned to play off the "Surfing" album etc", and I think this is happening all over again. Ventures albums are easy to understand, kids can go: "Hey, I can play that!". After Rodney had been playing us on his show, we had people going into Poobas Records and saying: "Do you have that new punk band from England, the Ventures?".

CRASS, THE ARTICLE

Crass are a group of people who live together in a farm house in the country side of Essex, England. There are about a

dozen people involved in the band that started around 3 years ago. The are also involved in other activities like film, a record label and a newspaper. The record label is being very successful and have had a record "Bloody Revolutions" in the English charts, however it's place in the charts remained blank for over a week (remember 'Anarchy in the U.K.). They will be the first to tell you that they are a political band, but they don't affiliate with any political groups – not left wing, not right wing, not even RAR. A U.S. tour is not likely, however the band did play in New York in 1978, and many of our correspondents were impressed.
The following bits of information were taken from fanzines, mainly Toxic Graffitti, Kill Your Pet Puppy, In The City and Jamming.

ANARCHY
"Anarchy is the only form of political thought that does not seek to control the individual through force. Right and Left wing politics are concerned with the control of people through the use of power, State Control. Under both left and right wing governments people are secondary to the state, they are seen merely as machinery of that state and they are expected to live, and if need be, die for that state. Anarchy is the rejection of that State control and represents a demand by the individual to live a life of personal choice, not one of political manipulation. Anarchy is the first step towards a life of PERSONAL RESPONSIBILITY. By refusing to be controlled you are taking your OWN life into your OWN hands, and that is, rather than the popular idea of anarchy as chaos, the start of personal order. A state of anarchy is an internal state, a attitude of mind, NOT A FORM OF GOVERNMENT. The state of anarchy is where individuals live with other individuals in trust and with respect and not a chaotic bedlam where everyone is out for themselves. It is because of that sense of responsibility that very few anarchist advocate violent revolution, the people that do are usually Marxists. Anarchy and peace are one of the same thing... on a social level maybe just a dream, BUT ON A PERSONAL LEVEL IT CAN BE A REALITY. Anarchy and peace are internal personal facts, decisions in YOUR own head to live YOUR own life. If you're not looking for an answer, you are part of the problem"

PACIFISM
"There is no contradiction between anarchy

and pacifism. Pacifism is not passivity, to me it represents a deep repulsion at the taking of life, for that reason I am also a vegetarian, as are all the band. The idea that pacifism is passivity is as naive as the idea of anarchy being chaos, anarchy is the politic of the free mind. I could not stand by as the gas tap turns, nor will I permit myself to be abused physically or verbally by another, exactly what I would do would be determined by the situation itself, not by some preconceived notion of how I 'ought' to act. There are occasions when I feel capable of defending myself from attack, others when I feel afraid and nervous, I am not able to predetermine my response to things. As a pacifist I stand against organized militarianism, believing that the use of power to control people is a violation of human dignity, if I were to find myself in a position where that power threatened to directly violate me, I would stand against in in whatever way was necessary to prevent it, in that situation I do not rule out the possibility of force. As an anarchist I stand against ALL authority (it would seem to me on this level that an anarchist almost by nature is a pacifist) and in doing I must also recognize that I stand against authority imposed from outside, I have no right to impose on others MY authority... On the occasions that violence has broken out at our gigs; one or other or all of the band has intervened. It is vary rarely that any of the audience has offered help. I would stress that it is not for us to tell people what to do, or to expect anything, **BUT WE CAN HOPE.**"

CASTRATION SQUAD

The Castration squad were interviewed in January at the Starwood. Present were Tiffany, Shannon, Alice and Tracy, Mary went home (sick). Also present were Al, Pete, Gerard and X-8.

Al: How are you going to repair men?
Shannon: Wanna find out!!!
Al: Uh ... Nooooo.
X-8: What does Castration Squad symbolize, do you mean it literally?
Shannon: It's not just a name for a band, it's a concept, we wrote the Manifesto to avoid questions like "what does it mean?" We're not just feminists– we're against morons, guys or girls...
Tiffany: We want to castrate girls too, were talking about fixing people, jerks...
Shannon: There's alot of unintelligent people that do need to be repaired not just men. We don't think we have to call ourselves feminists so people will treat us equally– because we are equal anyways, as a matter of fact, we're above most people.
X-8: You're very strong about your opinions, why do you...
Shannon: I want to save the world from distruction...
X-8: Are you a humanitarian then?
Shannon: Yes, that's good enough for a yes and we are all interested in politics and all want to go into that in later years...
Tracy: No, I don't...
Shannon: Tiffany and Alice and me are going to over-throw the government.
X-8: What would you do if you were president?
Shannon: Ok, I wouldn't be president because the president has no control and doesn't make enough money, but what your saying is if I were in control. Alot of things

CHRIS STAMEY

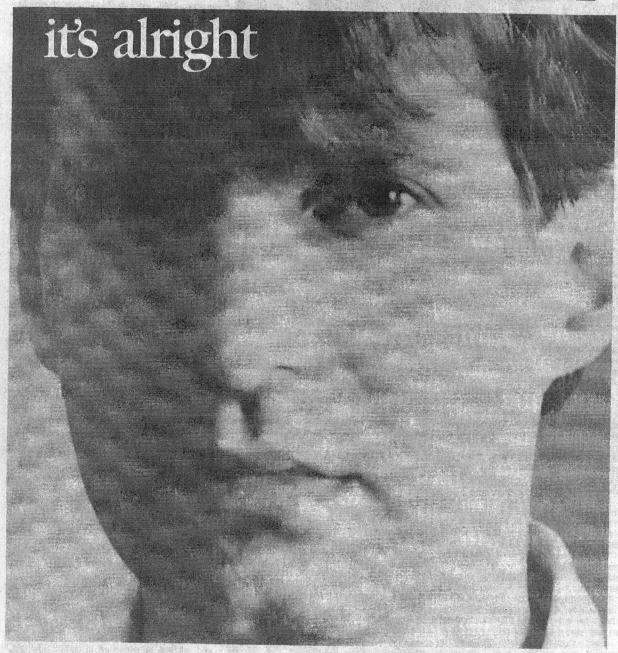

it's alright

Between Love and Heartbreak Lies a Lifetime. And a Record.
A Record everyone always hoped Chris Stamey would make. Now he has. And it's on a major label,
but you're allowed to like it anyway.

 A&M
RECORDS

OH YEAH NOW

UST YOUR AVERAGE DAY WITH

WENDY O AND THE PLASMATICS

THE IDEA WAS TO SPENSER A PLASMATICS LOOK A-LIKE CONTEST. ANYONE THAT WANTED TO COULD SIGN UP TO APPEAR ON NBC'S "FRIDAY" SHOW WITH THE BAND AND BE JUDGED BY KROQ'S INSANE DARELL WAYNE WHO WAS HOSTING THE EVENT (WITH RODEY THE ROQ PROVIDING SILENT ASSISIANCE) AT THE LICORICE PIZZA ON SUNSIT BLVD. IN HOLLYWOOD. NO ONE SHOWED UP LOOKING LIKE ANYONE IN THE PLASMATICS, BUT SINCE EVERYONE KNOWS THE BAND IS ONE OF THE MOST OUTRAGEOUS ACTS IN CAPIVITY, THE PRESS AND THE GAWERS WERE THERE KNEE DEEP WAITING FOR SOMETHING CRAZY TO HAPPEN. ALL THIS MEDIA COURTING IS TYPICAL OF THE PLASMATICS. THEY HAVE VERY LITTLE TO OFFER MUSICALLY (OH YEAH—ED.) BUT THEY DO PUT ON AS INTERESTING SHOW. WHEN THEY WERE AT THE WHISKY LA LAST OCT. WENDY O WILLIAMS (WOW FOR SHORT), THE

LEAD SINGER AND CENTER OF ATTENTION, FIRED OFF SHOTGUNS, LET LOOSE LIVE CHICKENS, THREW FLOWERS AND DIRT AT THE AUDIENCE, JERKED OFF MICROPHONES, SLEDGEHAMMERED TV'S AND FOR THE GRAND FINALE, CUT A GUITAR IN HALF WITH A CHAINSAW—DRESSED ONLY IN SHORTS & EVAPORATING WHIPPED CREAM. NOT THE KIND OF THING YOU'D WANT TO SEE EVERY NIGHT, BUT PRETTY INTERESTING AS A ONE SHOT. THE PLASMATICS ARRIVED RIGHT ON TIME. AFTER SHAKING HANDS WITH THE DJ'S WINDY O GOT UP ON THE BOXES THAT HAD BEEN LAID OUT IN FRONT OF A WALL PLASTERED WITH PLASMATICS POSTERS AND DID WHAT WAS, EXPECTED OF HER, "ALL THE RECORDS

IN THIS STORE ARE FUCKE" SHE SCREAMED, DISCO SUCKS!, WHAT WE NEED IS GOOD RAUNCHY ROCK AND ROLL, AND THE ONLY PLACE YOU'RE GOONA FIND IT IS ON OUR ALBUM! BUY IT!" AFTER A LITTLE MORE RANTING IN THIS VEIN WINDY SEEMED TO RUN OUT OF MATERIAL. SHE LEANED OVER TO ONE OF THE BAND MEMBERS AND ASKED HIM WHAT SHE OUGHT TO DO NOW. SHE WAS RESCUED BY SOMEONE IN THE AUDIENCE YELLING "SHOW US YOUR TITS". THIS HAS TO HAVE COME FROM A FELLOW WHO TOTALLY LACKED IMAGINATION. WINDY WAS WEARING A T SHIRT CUT OFF JUST BELOW HER BREASTS THAT FIT HER LIKE ANOTHER SKIN. HER NIPPLES WERE JUST XPLODING THRU THE THING. BUT WINDY ISN'T ONE TO IGNOR A CHALLENGE "I'LL SHOW YOU MY TITS IF SOMEBODY SHOWS ME THEIR COCK" SHE SAID. A VOLUNTEER MAKE HIS WAY UNSTEADTLY TO THE BOXES WHERE WENDY WAS STANDING. THIS GUT WAS SO WASTED IT WAS A WONDER HE COULD STAND UP LET ALONE WALK AND BREATHE. HE MANAGED TO CLIMB UP ON THE BOXES BUT JUST COULDN'T DEAL WITH WNZIPPING HIS PANTS. THE CROWD CHEERED THIS STRUGGLING WNFORTUNATE ON WHILE WENDY WATCHED THE PROCEEDINGS IMPASSIVELY. OUR MAN FINALLY MANAGED TO GRT HIS PANTS UNDOME, WHIPPED HIS SHORTS DOWN AROUND HIS ANKLES, AND WHEN HIS PANTS WENT DOWN HE STARTED TO JERK OFF. THE RESULTS WERE PRETTY DISAPPOINTING. HE COULD'NT GET IT UP AT ALL. BUT WHAT THE HELL, HE DID MAKE THE EFFORT, WENDY O KEPT HER PART OF THE BARGIN AND WHEN HIS PANTS WENT DOWN HER SHIRT WENT UP. EVEN IN 1981, THE SIGHT OF A WOMAN STANDING WITH HER TITS HANGING OUT WHILE A GUY JERKS OFF IN FRONT OF HER IN A RECORD STORE ON SUNSET VLVD. IS PRETTY RIVETING. THE CROWD STARTED TO PANT HEVILY AND SURGED FORWARD. BUT WINDY AND THE BAND NIPPED THE BUILDING RIOT IN THE BUD BY HER PULLING THE T SHIRT DOWN AND HER PATIENTLY STARTING TO SIGN AUTOGRAPHS. I SUPPOSE IT ALL WORKED OUT IN THE END. THE PLASMATICS GOT SOME FREE ADVERTISING FOR THEIR NEW ALBUM AND APPEARANCE ON "FRIDAY". LICORICE PIZZA SOLD ALOT OF RECORDS, AND THE AUDIENCE GOT TO SEE WENDY O'S TITS. A COUPLE OF PEOPLE EVEN SIGNED UP FOR THE LOOK ALIKE CONTEST.

TOM ZIMMERMAN

PUNK NIGHT IN SAN PEDRO   One friday night Saccharine Trust threw a big party in what must have been an old movie theater....

THE MINUTEMEN opened - played great 'minute songs' with lottsa power

SACCHARINE TRUST were next, much better tonight than other times , the singer was really wild - sliding on his knees and pouring beer on his head

PEER GROUP played a fast set of yer typical P rock

Dez

With Jeff McDonald on drums, SEXUALLY FRUSTRATED played a short inspiring set in here somewhere

MOOD OF DEFIANCE with a great girl singer, got the whole place going, they were really rad - even burned a flag

TOXIC SHOCK were a bit slower - but really good - filling a gap for that kind of 'Fall' music in L.A.

RED CROSS did their first reformed gig - a three piece sounding more like the Velvets (even did a V.U. song!!)

THE STAINS were totally wild and full of energy in the late hour
ELLA AND THE BLACKS came out of nowhere to play

THE DISPOSALS were like a drone - I think the P.A. had aproblem by now - so did the crowd

and BLACK FLAG didn't play afterall. Good night.

Punk day at Disneyland was great, everyone was there, except for people who came too late (like the Cramps) who got refused enterance at the gate.

Brian came with Terry and Craig etc... the other Cramps didn't make it.

NIGHTTIME ENTERTAINMENT

MAIN STREET ELECTRICAL PARADE
Main Street, U.S.A. (See map for parade route.) 8:50 & 11:00 PM

FANTASY IN THE SKY FIREWORKS
9:30 PM

FRANKIE AVALON
River Stage, Frontierland
8:30 & 10:30 PM

JAN & DEAN
Space Stage, Tomorrowland
8:15, 10:00 & 11:15 PM

THE VENTURES
Space Stage, Tomorrowland
7:30, 9:30 & 10:45 PM

THE ASSOCIATION
Tomorrowland Terrace
7:30, 9:00 & 10:30 PM

THE SURFARIS
Plaza Gardens, Main Street, U.S.A.
For dancing: 7:30, 8:30, 9:45 & 10:30 PM

Disneyland.

Craig, Rob and Elissa raced Alice, Mary and Lois on the Tea Cups, who won?

Hud, Pooch and Pete kept eating.

Al & Hud on the Mine Train ride.

THE SURFARIS

Mel Taylor (Ventures) calling Rodney's show.

THE ASSOCIATION

Mods from San Diego

The VENTURES played to about 2000 people, some punks got on stage to dance but were thrown out.

Paul, Rob and Mary of 45 Grave Alice, Craig and Elissa of the Boneheads

Rob's first time to Disneyland, "He even smiled"

Terry Gun Club and Brad

Paul liked the Electric Parade. Craig didn't.

Castration Squad; Tracy, Shannon, Tiffany and Mary at the Starwood. - photo Al

would change ok, a lot of things would not be allowed: Vivisection would not be allowed, I'm not going to go into that, child abuse would not be allowed, pornography would not be allowed...

Al: But.. you were in a porno mag..

Shannon: Not by any choice of our own. They said we were in a tasteful nude magazine. I see nothing wrong with tasteful nudity.

X-8: What's the difference between pornography and tasteful nudity?

Shannon: Open one of those magazines and you'll see. I don't like sex being exploited. Alot of those mags make it really vile and nobody wants to do it anymore- ok, I won't say I'd stop pornography, I'm giving you generalization because my views could go on all night... Rape would not be allowed...

Tracy: You can't stop things like that.

Shannon: Yes you can! This country has to be socialist. If you have Socialism things are more in control.

Al: What about religion?

Shannon: I've very religious. I'm non-denominational, I was born a catholic but the Bible was just written by bigots. The Bible was just written by a group of people like us, so a lot of it doesn't make any sense, a lot of it is ridiculous. Like it says Eve ate the forbidden fruit and women are cursed forever, that's how ridiculous. You can't get a tattoo, that's sin! There were morals of the people who wrote it, I have my own religious beliefs.

Al: Does it have to do with Jesus?

Shannon: of course it has to do with Jesus!! I believe in God if that's what you're asking. Religion something you have to discuss in depth, I could talk about it for hours. All I will say is all of us here have our own seperate views on it, everyone should make their own Bible, so long as they believe and pray. God takes care of me everyday.

Alice: I don't believe in organized religion.

Tiffany: Organized religion makes rules that are really hard to live up to and morals are really a matter of choice, if somebody wants to have no morals...

Alice: I definitely agree with you.

X-8: What got you together?

Shannon: It was our beliefs that got us together, first with Tiffany and I. We don't have the same musical interests, that's why we have so many different styles of songs- we all take turns writing alot.

X-8: Do you argue alot?

Shannon: No.

Tiffany/ Alice/ Tracy: Cough, gag...

Shannon: We don't argue about music!

X-8: Is the band a vehicle for your messages?

Shannon: No, the band is entertainment, not like the Dils or anything, you can't really do anything political by getting up on stage and playing music, but it is also a stepping stone, maybe I'm agreeing with you, to give people the idea what I want and mean for later on.

X-8: Are you a punk band?

Shannon: I can't say that our music is typical punk rock, it has more eerie qualities to it.

Alice: It doesn't have a label for it, but compared to hard rock or new wave then it's punk rock..

Tiffany: We do a variety of music!

Shannon: We do alot of theatrics, me and Mary go into alot of theatrics, like the clunky wooden cross we lug on stage- that's what the Herald Examiner said, and we throw bats out of a baby coffin. But our music is changing, and I'm glad the punk scene has survived and will continue to survive and wasn't just a fad.

Alice: But now it's got to do more than just survive, it's got to work to change and stand for something.

Shannon: That's what we are doing, not just getting up there and playing anarchy songs, anarchy is ridiculous ; a lawless community- there's always a leader, it doesn't make any sense to go around screaming anarchy, Socialism, this country should be socialist.

Al: But all these new punks go around screaming Anarchy, do you think they know what they are screaming about?

Alice: probably not.

Shannon: Three years ago we were screaming anarchy too, it was fun, there's nothing bad about it.

Mary Sims/ Dinah Cancer - photo Al

FLIPSIDE NUMBER 24

"Abolish government
It's nothing to me
Forget about God
He's nothing here to see
We live by a system
A perfect mold
People perfect people who are poor and old
Lives are spent on the ladder of success
Working for nothing in this worthless mess
Presidents a names, president is a label
The highest man on the government table...
America...
Land of the free...
Free to the power of the people in uniform!
People are so blind they just can't see
Send your son through bootcamp
Send him off to war
If he comes back he'll be dead and nothing more
A strugle for land, for country, for freedom
A lot of mindless people look for someone to lead them"
"Abolish Government" - True Sounds of Liberty

ISSUE #: 24
DATE: May 1981
FORMAT: 8 1/2x11 rotary web offset, with two color cover and inside pages
PAGES: 48
PRICE: $1.00
PRESS RUN: 2200
STAFF: Hud, Helen, Pete, Pooch, Michele, Steve and Al

- -

More big changes with this issue: first off a new typewriter system that right justifies!! Secondly, more pages (on better quality paper) and more color. Same price. I guess this increase was due partially to a very successful benefit held at the Vex (3rd location) with the Circle Jerks, Adolescents, Crowd and Societys Victims.

As the Hong Kong slowly phased it's self out after a very memorable scene accelerating history (and the Fleetwood, Cuckoos Nest, Whiskey, and Starwood are also in a low punk profile period), the Vex, a multi-location club (usually in or around East L.A.) welcomely opened it's doors. Joe Vex kept the door price reasonable and the band energy high. Catering mostly to punk bands, the Vex sits alongside the Masques, Whiskey, Starwood, Rock Corp., Fleetwood, Club 88 and Hong Kong Cafe as a definite era of punk evolution in L.A.

UK Decay at the Vex   photo Al

U.K. DECAY
- -

After a lot of foul ups U.K. Decay arrived in L.A. with borrowed equipment (c/o Dead Kennedys), a borrowed bass player (Creeton Chaos c/o Social Unrest) and a last minute, U.S. debut gig, unadvertised at the Vex. This interview took place at the Vex in April by Al, Hud and Helen.

Helen: Have you had any Mexican food?
Abbo: No absolutely none, not enough time, we were warned not to wander out side of the club, it's supposed to be real violent out there.
Helen: Who do you feel are your influences?
Abbo: We were into the 76, 77, 78 scene, our musical influences aren't that strong but we have the basic ideas from that time from just going to gigs and stuff around England.
Hud: Do you have a big following?
Abbo: Yeah, especially in and around London, where were from basically.
Helen: Is your music political?
Abbo: Uh, well yeah some of it, the early stuff is real political, "For My Country" was a sort of anti-nationalist thing, pacifist. Our lyrics are now sort of based on death and sex, mystical, gothic is how we describe it in England, the new single is about violation or privacy, unexpected guest in the house, surreal...
Al: How is the audience for you and the bands you play with?
Abbo: Well Crass have a very heavy punk audience, Killing Joke is slightly more sophisticated, a lot of poseurs you might say - can't really tell what kind of audience us and Killing Joke draw, it's a mix between hardcore punks, normal punks, straights, hippies, trendy punks... In London there's still a really good punk scene, there's a lot of places that are really tuned in, other places it's dead.
Al: Do you align yourselves with the more pacifist followers?
Abbo: Yeah, we used to be very pacifistic, but now only in our views on war and stuff, it's basically impracticle to be a pacifist - you've got to get off your ass and do something about it.... We can't even play in our hometown because we are associated with punk, smaller bands get away with it if they keep it low key, we try to, but in London there's always a place to play, if one place closes down there's always another place opening up.
Al: There's a lot of punk factions...
Abbo: Oh yeah, there's the Spandau Ballet/ Stray Cats type of bands, Adam and the Ants, there's us, Theatre of Hate, Wasted Youth (not L.A.'s) bands on a different level, then there's the Cockney Rejects, Sham, Upstarts.,
Spon: Football, Oi Oi bands...
Abbo: Totally three factions that don't mix. Over here we've been playing with the hardcore punk bands which is strange.
Hud: Do you live with your families?
Abbo: Well I do, but the others don't, they used to live in a shop but the shop got closed down and now they live around.
Spon: I live here at the moment.
Abbo: We've done a lot of touring at the moment so we don't require that sort of thing, I go home 2 or 3 times a week to get a nice dinner from mummy.
Helen: What do the U.K. bands think of Adam and the Ants?
Abbo: They've disowned them... sold out is a common term... by signing to CBS. But he has broken down a lot of barriers, 6 year old kids to 60 year old grannies wear Adam badges. I think it's helped us and Crass get into the charts.

SOCIAL UNREST
- -

Social Unrest were interviewed in April at the Vex by Al and Robert Hill.

Flipside: So what are you doing down here? (Hardly anyone at the gig)
Social Unrest: Good question!!!
Flipside: You're from Hayward? (a suburb 40 miles south of San Francisco).
Social Unrest: Yeah, we're not ashamed to say we're from Hayward, totally fucking suburban place. The city scene has practically dried out, we're trying to start something new, get it going in the suburbs. Just like what happened here in Orange County. The suburbs aren't big but they're full of a bunch of wreckless people who don't know about punk rock cause they don't do to the city. Bands like us have to bring it to them. Friscos dead and over with, it started there with just a few punks, but now there's a lot and it's spreading all over.

There's a lot of hardcore, but now days they judge you from like Black Flag - "Oh, are they like Black Flag?" or "Are they as good as Black Flag?", if you play Black Flag level they'll love you, anything less than that forget it!. We've been playing 60 miles per hour since we started, it's what gets us off. If we were located in L.A. instead of San Francisco we'd probably be twice as far as we are now. We started when hardly nobody had heard of Black Flag, we're not a bandwagon band.

A lot of people say we should change, that we've been playing the same stuff we played a year ago, but that's generally what they people want, they want fuckin' fast music. If we change too much we'd become a fuckin' art band and sell out!

Every song we have is like a new topic, one song attacks the court system - cause it sucks, the next attacks the government - cause it sucks... "Making Room For Youth" talks about how the last generation really fucked things up for this generation - there's no place to go, there's gonna be a war pretty

Social Unrest, Vex bathroom – photo R. Hill

soon and we're the ones that are gonna get drafted, we're the ones that get blown away. We're political, but that's just like any other punk band, the only difference is that we're from Hayward.

CHEIFS

The Cheifs were interviewed at their pad by Steve Massel

Steve: So who thought of the name 'Cheifs'?
Jerry: It's from an old expression... "Cheif Out!"
Bob: Cheif Out, it means like to be top dog. I heard Roger of the Circle Jerks thought of it.
George: Rogers cool.
Steve: Did you guys play any gigs where the Decline was filmed?
George: Yeah we played a couple.
Steve: (To Eugene) Did you get any money for being in that?
Eugene: No, I didn't get shit, I heard there was free beer so I went down there and I said what I wanted to. What I said in that movie is not even what I think now.
Bob: Yeah in front of the theater last night they were selling Eugene buttons!
Keith: A picture of a duck with ears!! (Laughter)
Bob: Yeah, that's why Eugene won't shave his bald head, people might come up and stroke his head! Ha ha haaaa.
Bob: Me, Rabit, Eugene and Kurt are in another band called the Wayward Kanes. Wayward meaning going away from what is right, Kanes means murder.

Steve: How come they didn't film any other band for the movie?
Jerry: Well they took the bands that were cranking at the time. But we've been on ON TV. One of our very first gigs, at Blackies was filmed. They stuck the camera in everybodys face.
Steve: You guys played with Darby?
George: Yeah, he's our creative consultant.
Jerry: His name is on our record.
George: We got bombed with him, he really produced our record in a technical way.
Bob: I knew Darby from Hollywood, he used to come over to shoot his coke.
George: He was never straight. Our number 1 priority is to record a 4 song demo and have Rodney play it.
Steve: What about Posh Boy?
Jerry: Posh Boy told us: "Anytime you want to go into the studio, tell me." and I told him we're not that desperate yet! Posh Boy sucks.
Bob: Big dicks, only big dicks.
Jerry: That's what it says on his records PBS– Posh Boy Sucks!!
Steve: Were you guys in any other bands before?
Jerry: Me and Rabbit were in the Simpletones when they first started.
Bob: I was in a band in Portland called the Rubbers. We were put on a live compilation album, which is a piece of shit and if I find anybody with it I'll break it.
Jerry: Lets talk about music.
Steve: Ok, what kind of music do you play?
Jerry: Creedence Clearwater Revival!! (everyone laughs!) I think they're bad!

Cheifs – photo Ed Colver

Bob: I think they're bad too – bad suck bad.

LEAVING TRAINS

The Leaving Trains were interviewed at 10am in April at L.A. Studios by Hud, Pete and Al.
Al: What's so important you wanted to say?
James: Did you bring any beer?
Al: We just got up!!!
James: Told you they'd say that!
Al: What's the Leaving Trains about?
James: There's an answer to that.. we just make big blues noise to scare away death.
Al: Huh??!
James: What that means is... sometimes when I'm feeling really bad, the only thing that helps... is playing our type of music which I consider blues. That's an answer of sorts.
Al: Are you guys backup musicians for James?
Manfred: No. I come up with inspiring music that he has to put lyrics to.
Hud: You've been together how long?
Manfred: Half a year.
James: No not really, we're not part of any scene really, it's not really our choice– we wouldn't want to be part of any scene that includes the Circle Jerks. They do good covers but they steal from the scene in more ways than one.... We'd be pretty stupid if we believed we'd make a lot of money, even the Circle Jerks would if they believed that, I mean one is gonna be a lawyer. I wish the scene would start over, burn it down and start over. I guess it's naive to expect to get anything from it, but I should believe in something. We aren't in a position to prove it yet but it seems inevitable: X, the Circle Jerks, everybody – maybe we won't avoid it. Right now we're as underground as you can get, we don't play in front of a lot of people who have read about us.
Al: That's not your choice.
James: We'd like everyone to hear us, but don't expect to become a trend or want to. (We start to talk about their music)
Hillary: Slow painful suicide music.
James: Yeah.
Manfred: Not all songs have omnipresent death themes, we have more cheerful stuff.
James: A lot of our songs are about death because to me it's a very scary thing. Last year was a really bad year for me. I'm still alive but... I think music should have passion, I guess it's easy talking about it but singing is a way of purging your feelings or at least feeling less alone when you hear a wall of noise behind you – it just keeps death away a little longer. That's the closest I come to hope, that's what our music is to me.
Hud: Do you all agree?
Manfred: Pretty much, I just sing through my guitar...
James: I like chaotic things and anarchy but there's nothing anarchic about putting your arms around another punk and pushing him back and forth – it's a game, I'm really sick of games. If they are gonna wreck, why don't they plan what they're gonna wreck. They plan so much about how they're gonna dress....

TSOL

True Sounds of Liberty were interviewed by Al, Hud and Pete at their studio in Long Beach in May 1981. These guys are athletic in such

Leaving Trains: James, Tom, Manfred and Hillary –
photo by Al

things as surfing, golf, swimming and tattoos.
The band is very cooperative and seem to
have their shit together.

Pete: How come you all have tattoos?

Jack: I don't!!

Mike: I can't afford it. Jack wouldn't ruin his
body with anything, let alone a tattoo. I
change my mind too much. I had TSOL
tattooed right here (arm) but had it covered
up when the band was shaky.

Jack: I had a dream of these guys holding me
down and giving me tattoos.

Ron: I wanna get one like the big dragon that
Todd has..

Jack: Fuck, I'm schiz, so I...

Ron: That's why you aren't playing the
Starwood, there ain't no fuckin'...

Jack: YOU WEREN'T THERE! MAN. I'll play it
I'm gonna wear a bullet proof vest and a riot
helmet.

Mike: He thinks someone is gonna bring a
gun to the Starwood and shoot him.

Ron: There's this big rumor that all of these
people are after us because of Jack.

Al: Why don't they like you?

Jack: It started like when we got together we
had the idea like we're not gonna cause any
trouble...

Mike: Give the people good ideas, you know,
fight for a worthy cause...

Jack: It's been really good, there haven't been
any fights at our shows, and then this one
guys who gets drunk and shit and his ugly
bitch he calls a girlfriend, she goes around
telling people we'll beat them up. If she
bumps into people she tells them "TSOL will
kick your ass" and shit like that.

Mike: Not only her, but kids who like our
band and get into fights and if they win or lose
they emphasize our name 'TSOL' (with fist in
the air), and plus Devonshire Downs too –
that day me and Ron went to thrift stores and
bought some suits and our hair was all down,
it's pretty long for the punk scene these days,
and Jack was wearing a blue boy outfit, and
all these little skinheads were bummed.

Al: What happened to Vicious Circle?

Mike: It died!

Jack: Cut that out!

Mike: That's what all these kids with their new
haircuts are trying to bring back, half of them
weren't even there!

Jack: I had a skinhead back then causing
trouble and shit...

Mike: And so they burn us and were trying to
do something a little different. In a year or 6
months what will they have? These kids don't
understand, back in the Fleetwood days we
were involved in some... just... the worst gang
fights, and usually we came out on top, but

we just got sick of it. Fights where people got
knifed and stuff and it's just foolish: "That guy
called me a name so I'll kill him", not very
smart ya know?

Pete: What are your influences?

Ron: Todd's big influence is Judas Priest and
Rush, cause they're really good drummers
(their names were written on the walls behind
the drum set)...

Mike: It varies a lot...

Al: How come you paint your face?

Hud: You like the Damned, right?

Jack: Yeaha, the new Damned are better.

Al: Why don't the rest of you paint up?

Mike: We used to, white usually...

Ron: When my hair was red, I used to do my
face grey all the time.

Mike: The original thing was one night a
bunch of our friends went to the Cuckoos
Next with all white faces and got on a big fight
and got banned from the club.

Ron: Jerry Roach said "No more white faces".

Mike: So, uh, he called up and asked us to
play so we called everyone and told them
"Wear a white face".

Jack: One night I was drinking beer and I got
really scared cause the cops came and I
looked really fucked – I was wearing a little
dress and eyelashes and shit and the cops
go: "They're gonna love you at county,
fucker". And I go Oh shit. So when he turned
his back, I ran! and they were chasing me.
The bouncers caught me and the deal Jerry

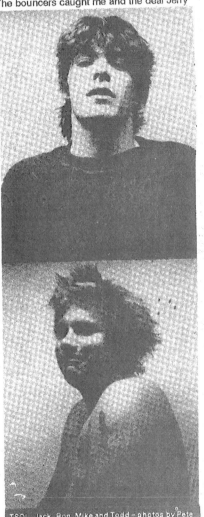

TSOL: Jack, Ron, Mike and Todd - photos by Pete

Roach made was "I'll tell them to let you go if you tell the white faces to never come back" and i'm going "I'll tell them". They got me anyways...

Al: Who came up with your name?

Mike: Ron and my roomate used to sit around in the middle of the night and they were fucked up and would call those church shows where you call up and repent your sins, and they'd call up and say "You fucking liars!".

Ron: They'd talk to you for hours and they had the "Sounds of Liberty" church choir on the show...

Mike: We were all bummed cause the words to all of their songs were lies, so we said we should make a band and call it "The TRUE Sounds Of Liberty", and we all had skinheads then and listened to Crass and took too many drugs and they name kept coming up so we finally took it.

Al: And that's the theme of the band?

Jack: Used to be, we used to be real political.

Ron: All propaganda!!

Mike: We got around a lot by that, we did a lot of advertising, wrote it everywhere.

Ron: Now we're more advanced.

Jack: If you call fucking dead people advanced!

CRASS

This interview with Crass is a continuation from what was printed in issue #23. Steve Ignorant and G responded to this mail interview that was sent some months ago.

Flipside: Did you go to schools, are you artists?

Crass: What is an artist?

Flipside: How many "Feeding of the 500" were sold?

Crass: About 50,000 "Feedings" were sold (we've reissued it as a second sitting on Crass records since Small Wonder didn't want to do it anymore). The record Company is doing well although there are times when we have to scrimp and scrape.

Flipside: Explain: love, anarchy and peace?

Crass: Anarchy does not mean chaos and disorder like o many people are quick to say it is, it's respect for ones self and others as human beings. So peace goes hand in hand with anarchy (I'm writing it very short here) and out of that must come love.

Flipside: What do you think of hippies? Were any of the band once or now considered hippies?

Crass: I try to see people as people and not as labels eg: hippies, skinhead, mod, punk etc. I think most people are alright.

Al: Where did G or whoever does all of the art work become skilled?

G: Yes I did go to art school and like all such places it teaches fuck all. They're institutions to be used by you not you used by them. It gives you space and time.

Flipside: How did you manage to play in New York? Any plans on returning?

G: I lived in New York for awhile, new some contacts and fixed up some places as none of us wanted to deal with the usual clubs. We fixed up places like the Puerto Rican center and the original 57 Club, consequently the whole thing was an experience and one we won't repeat.

Al: Does violence occur at your gigs? How do the kids respond?

Crass: We got some fights at gigs but only had a couple stopped because of it. Normally we can control it. People respond in different ways, some fight, some run, some people

seem more able to handle a situation like that more than others.

Flipside: As perfect as anarchy sounds in ink, in reality some people are pigs. How do you propose to stop them from screwing it up? It seems that complete trust is a key, but we know a lot of people are not trustworthy.

Crass: Its like, although you may offer someone trust and respect, it doesn't mean that they will give it back. Obviously a state of anarchy will never spring up overnight so it's more individuals, in different places living in anarchic situations. Of course people will try to fuck it up, and that's the establishment, police, government, army etc... Quite a battle. All I can do is keep trying.

Flipside: Have you had any offers from major record companies? How does the band support itself?

Crass: We had an offer from Polydor the day after Small Wonder got in touch with us about doing a record, they offered us a 7 year contract with 250,000 pounds and 23000 cash cash across the table. We didn't take it because all they wanted us for was our "rebel rousing stance". We are now is a position where we don't have to go out and pick bloody potatoes or decorate someones house anymore. We get 280 between 9 of us each week and we just about manage. Most of the finance, in fact, all comes from "Stations of the Crass", which is the only record we get a little profit from. All the rest of the other records goes on other stuff like magazines, more records and that.

Flipside: What exactly is ment by your Crass symbol?

Crass: Many people ask us about the symbol, basically it is a mixture of symbols of oppression. The church, the state the family, into which a serpent is curled, the serpent will devour itself eating itself, eating its own tail, evil destroys evil, power corrupts, power destroys itself. Please don't imagine that we are pleased about the commercialization of the Crass, the t-shirts, armbands etc. We have nothing to do with that. We still give away badges and believe that it's better to do things yourself. Making stencils is really easy and if you use car spray paint you can decorate your own cars with your own design. Punk is ment to be about doing it your own way. Give the merchants a big V sign.

KOMMUNITY FK

One afternoon Pete & I interviewed Pat & CeCe from Kommunity FK in the likes of a British pub perched near Santa Monica beaches. Feeling that the band brings a new sound as a reaction to music missing in the L.A. scene, the members of Kommunity take a pride in being the first to bring us this musical movement. They are highly critical, opinionated, eager, and I like them a lot.

Pete: How did you come up with that name?

CeCe: This town is fucked, and that's where the name came from.

Pete: The "community"?

Patrick: Yeah. It's a protest, because for some reason, people have been trying to keep us from coming up from the street...and from doing something where we can change things locally...and hopefully take it beyond.

Helen: To mean you don't get any cooporation?

Patrick: No. None at all.

CeCe: We just met Matt (drummer) last month (January). And Pat & I have been

CeCe and Patrick – photo by Pete

together and working at this for about a year. Pat was kicked out of about 20 bands.

Patrick: I've played in tons of bands locally. And some people wouldn't want me. (pause...chatter...naming of names).

Pete: So how do you like playing in L.A.?

CeCe: Great. We need the money.

Cheeky Pete: Are you making any money?

Patrick & CeCe: No!

Helen: Is there any kind of philosophy behind your music?

Patrick: Just to do what we feel.. We strive to be a magical eminence..or element...that sounds stupid when I say it.

CeCe: We're not going to make a million bucks.

Patrick: We're happy with what we are playing. We are into a spontaneous music where anything can happen...with a basic structure.

Helen: Are you jazz influenced?

CeCe: Sure we are...deep inside of me, I don't play like jazz music. There's a lot of great jazz people that have inspired me at some point in my life but I don't want to play like that shit.

Helen: Then, are you "musician's musicians"?

Pete: Do you practice a lot?

CeCe: I just started playing bass about a year and a half ago.

Helen: Do you think uour audience will be interested musicians or a cult type following?

Patrick: Right now we have an "anti-cult"! People don't realize yet that things are changing.

CeCe: We're new blood for the vampires to suck on.

Helen: When I first saw you perform I was impressed that you didn't play just one kind of music...weren't just another assault band. You can do quiet stuff and Patrick can really sing.

CeCe: He can talk. He can so a lot of things! Ha ha ha ha...

Helen: Do you concentrate on lyrics very much?

CeCe: As much as everything else. It's all important. We're just into doing our own shit.

Patrick: Look,...why do punks have to be entertained by Fear flogging a dead horse, as it were. They are afraid to accept us. God knows why.

CeCe: Because it's not on vinyl. It's not on

the media.

Patrick: We do everything ourselves. We have a shitty publicity machine because we don't have anyone we pay.

Helen: What do you think about all of the bands coming in from other towns and relocating?

CeCe: They think the industry is here. But not all the creative musicians that each individual is looking for are here. L.A. is just straggling along and it's easier than trying to make it in New York. And if you can't get to Europe you've got to do what you can. It's not happening here creatively. It just happens to be where they grind out the vinyl. I mean, what bands have come out of here? Maybe the Germs and the Doors. Who else has come from L.A.? Nobody.

Pete: Where do you guys live?

CeCe: Hollywood...it's my hometown.

Patrick: I want to split. I want to get out of here. But I want to leave my mark first. Right now in Hollywood...in the "social world".

CeCe: ...the community...

Patrick: ...it sucks. We are angry because it has taken so long to catch on. I don't feel like I am in the past. I think there will be other bands like us soon.

Helen: You ARE very different. What are your influences?

CeCe: Joy Division. We discovered Joy Division after we had been making music, and when we heard them, this is not meant to sound egotistical, we said "Wow, that sounds like us!". And we thought we were on the right track. And we thought if people are accepting them, they'll accept us. They were an eye in a fucking storm .

Patrick: Velvet Underground.

CeCe: We know what's good. There's a lot of good American music.

Helen: Are you religiously inclined?

Patrick: You mean, was I raised Catholic? I went to catholic school half of my life.

CeCe: I wasn't.

Patrick: I'm not an artsy-fartsy bastard. Why can't people accept the fact that I can create? I'm inspired by the elements and things beyond this stupid planet.

Helen: Do you think record companies and standard audiences are really concerned about YOU being creative?

Patrick: Look. Those are the people I care about. And I know they are there. I don't want to live in an etherworld where I'm the only guy who is like that. Our time is now. All signs point to us. There is no one out like us.

Helen: Do you see yourselves as The Answer?

CeCe: To my own fucking problem,-yes, but I don't know what I'm going to do for anybody else.

Patrick: It's like it's our hobby.

Helen: Do you think that some punks are rednecks in their own way?

Patrick: Sure. The man is the guy. Rape the girl. The blonde, blue-eyed male audience. I love the energy, but why can't we have the rage in a positive way? Why can't we have it towards a powerful situation? They are expending a lot of energy with no goal in mind. You can still have chaotic positive power. They are repeating their parents...no mind of their own. With that many people

behind the punk attitude, you would think they would change things. All the kids on the street corners- what if they had a REASON?

Boy George - photo Tom Jamison

Rob and Gerber at their reception - photo by Al

Jim Trash - photos by A

DOCTORS MOB

"SOPHOMORE SLUMP"
THEY'LL OPERATE ON YOUR EARS
LP, CD, & CASSETTE AVAILABLE NOW ON *Relativity*

88561-8149-1/88561-8149-2/88561-8149-4

FLIPSIDE NUMBER 25

"You say there's talk of revolution
So what's new?
You say there's fighting in the air...
You think that I've got solutions
But do you really think that's fair?
Try to take control of it
Cause what you see is what you get
Try to take control of it
And not me
Don't want to be nobody's hero...."
"Nobody's Hero" – Stiff Little Fingers

ISSUE #: 25
DATE: August 1981
FORMAT: 8 1/2x11, rotary web offset with 2 color cover and insides
PAGES: 48
PRICE: $1.00
PRESS RUN: 2200
STAFF: Al, Hud, Pooch, Michele and Helen

4 year anniversary issue, nice and thick with good paper and lots to talk about. One immediately interesting thing about this issue are the scene reports: the country is exploding with punk rock activity! Here are some examples of what these scene reports covered: **North Carolina:** Many small clubs and lots of influential fanzines (Fred Mills Biohazard, Butch Modern's Modern World, Blind Boys Gazette etc...), in **Washington DC** local happening bands include: S.O.A. (with Henry Garfield), Minor Threat, Government Issue and the Bad Brains! In **Texas** the scene is alive with the likes of the Big Boys, Really Red, Hates, AK47, the Dicks and the Stains (who later changed their named to MDC). In **Minnisota** a big noise is being made by a band weirdly named Husker Du, who are threatening to release a record very shortly! **Toronto** is on the down with two clubs closing (the Horseshoe and the Edge) but the Viletones are still around. So punk rock is now a national disease.
In L.A. things are up and down. The Vex closes in East L.A. but reopens at a new location (for a short time) in downtown L.A. and hosts some killer shows including the Slits. The Screamers, rather Tomata tries a come back at the Whiskey with his Palace of Variety and sort of bombs. Meanwhile punks shows are sporadic at the Whiskey and the Starwood in not happening. The downtown L.A. art and music scene is finally coming of it's own with Al's Bar and the Brave Dog (as well as the Atomic Cafe of course), and many

John Lydon – photo by Al

good punk shows are happening here. Many night are spent in drunken stupor in the alleys around Al's. And on the other side of the coin, the big time punk/hardcore thing is starting to happen with massive shows at the Florantine Gardens, where high ticket prices are paid to enter a massive hall that sounds bad, has no atmosphere and is conducive to a bad time.

JOHN LYDON

John Lydon was interviewed one hot afternoon in June at the Sunset Marquee in Hollywood.
There has always been something about this man that has attracted so much attention. I can remember back in 1977 listening to Rodney say on his radio show: "We've got something special tonight, it's the first single from the Sex Pistols". I didn't know what to expect, we had been hearing so much about this band, now we were finally going to get to hear them. Well as usual I wasn't paying very much attention, but when I heard the opening chords to "Anarchy In The U.K." I didn't have to be told it was the Pistols, I knew it was them. I knew by the singer. This guy was angry. Then there was "God Save The Queen", who could pull of a line like "We mean it man"? You all know the rest. John continues to be the only member of that band doing anything original, he was the one that would continue to keep the world guessing.
Al: What are you doing here in California?
John: Being fuckin' bored!
Al: Hmmmmm, I guess you can't go out?
John: You have so many fans, won't people mob you?
John: Too fuckin' hot to get mobbed here... everythings done like 40 times slower.
Pooch: How's the new record doing?
John: Yeah, it went straight in at #12, fuckin' gave me a heart attack I'll tell you! Cause I thought it would go nowhere fast.
Al: Why did you think that?
John: Well, we handed it in last November and the record company has absolutely no faith in it at all. They had pressed the

minimum amount and it's just fuckin' sold like no ones business. You don't normally expect stuff that's off the wall or different to be consumed so quickly, it made me feel very happy about society. I suppose it's because people are just so fuckin' bored with fuckin' normal... anything – just to get away from it.
Pooch: Did you do it...
John: I did it because I like making records.
Pooch: Are you under pressure to do things differently?
John: No. If I like it that's that. Fuck off, what do you think I am, some kind of "conceptual artist"!? "I've got to be weird, I've got to ruin this tune." Bullocks to that, I'll leave that up to Eno.
Al: Who does your song writing? You never...
John: I've got a question to that – how can you write a song?
Al: Ok, who write your lyrics then?
John: I write the words, I have to I'm singing them or yelling them.
Al: Do you have a part in the music?
John: That's done between us, like whoever is doing whatever or bla bla sounds the best, that's what will be used.
Pooch: You must have a lot of unused studio tape?
John: Funny enough, no, we use practically everything. Things are usually done in one take and then worked on from that – no rehearsals. We never rehearse... well we did once for 15 minutes (laughs) I'm not joking!
Pooch: You guys have a good feeling between you...
John: (Nodding) It works. It works fine.
Al: What happened to Wobble?
John: He got interested in jazz/funk and that's where he wanted to go, and to me that's too fucking limiting by far – you know pseudo-Miles Davis, I'm not interested, I mean that stuff's been done to death, I don't need to carry it on.
Al: Will you be doing any more gigs... tours?
John: Tours, no that's awful!
Al: Sporadic shows?
John: Yeah. We need a lot of equipment first. We've built a recording studio and a video studio, when we get the equipment... we have the films and stuff, it's just the money...
Al: And that's why you're out here.

Public Image Ltd – photo by Robert Hill

John: I'm on the beg, right, "All donations accepted, I need your money, it will be worth it all in the end." We've got a lot of video stuff, film we haven't ever shown yet. The Ritz gig was about the closest we've come to showing a lot of our stuff, but the audience wouldn't have it so fuck them, they don't know what they missed, ha ha.

Al: That may have gone over better here...

John: I doubt that! The Olympic gig, that was a piss off! Too many people bummed out of their brains, too fuckin' thuggy, too much into like smacking each other up for no real reason, just like "I'm dumb and I'm proud of it". I don't like that at all. There's nothing clever about being an asshole. They're no better than fuckin' headbanging hippies.

Al: You don't like the spitting.

John: No. It's bullshit. It's what they've read in the papers or seen in the movies.

Pooch: Do you feel you are getting through to the audience, are they learning anything?

John: I hope so, I mean that's the whole fucking point, but if I'm not that's too bad cause I'm still very very happy doing what I'm doing, and I'll continue to amuse myself for many years yet. I will not go away!

Al: Do you get a lot of feedback, fan-mail?

John: Yeah, it's all fuckin' looney. All lunatics.

Al: Doesn't that make you wonder about your audience?

John: Yeah, if you question yourself. I've had too many fucking marriage proposals, right. You end up banging your fucking head "Aaarrrrgggghhhh!!" Don't they fucking understand? "Oh, you're so handsome and adorable!" and I know I'm an ugly cunt!!! And if I know that, I'm damn sure they should be aware of that. What the fuck does it matter what I look like anyway?

Al: What is your natural hair color?

John: I don't really know, ha, I've dyed it so many fucking times, it could be anything. If you use dye long enough you don't have natural hair color anymore.

Pooch: Did you ever think you'd be a public figure like...

John: If you mean better than the rest...

Pooch: No...

John: Put it this way, when I was at school I loathed it. The way they would always accept

what's being told them blindly, so I've always been against that sort of shit, I've always questioned everything that's been told to me, till I find out the truth behind it.

Pooch: Does that cause problems with Warners?

John: Yeah, caused problems for me, cause like at school you notice kids that do that get treated real bad by the rest of the class, you're not liked trying to be too smart for them... wankers. Yes I had it tough (laughs). I didn't though – I had it so easy it was a joke, I just never went!

Pooch: Would you ever move out here?

John: No. Not for ever, no. We're here because there's more facilities here. We can get access to cable TV real easy here. Yes you'll be seeing us on tele real soon, folks, our very own programs, you can't do that in England.

Al: What do you have in store for the future, have you changed the goals of your company?

John: No, I just don't want to make records forever and ever and let that be the only thing. I like making music, it entertains me, and hopefully it entertains others. But there's more in my brain than just that. If I get the chance to use it in other ways I will, I think that's only fair.

Al: How long does it take you to put words down to your songs?

John: Some songs take months, some only 10 seconds. "Under the House", that's about a real actual haunting. I'd fucking watch this fucking beast running around for several nights, fucking frightening the living daylights out of me.

Al: Where's that?

John: This studio that Virgin owns, it's spooked. We were scheduled to record but we did nothing.

Pooch: I heard that's a nice place?

John: Well I saw things these stoned out hippies don't bother to notice. I've either got a very good imagination or I'm psychically in tune..... Our position with Virgin is very clear, soon as they try to dictate we cease to function. I'd rather cease to function than be dictated to by any of those cunts.

Al: What do you do all day... watch TV?

John: TV is one of my hobbies, yeah , I like to absorb all of that crap, I think it's fascinating.

Al: What's your favorite show?

John: Mary Hartman... I like to see what it's function is, what it's purpose is, how bad the commercials are.

(Stacy, a part of PIL, walks up)

Stacy: Oh, you've got a sunburn!

John: Naw, I've just been scratching.

Al: You've got enough cigarette burns on your arms.

Stacy: Memories.

John: They're still with me, some of my best friends have been up my arm.

Al: Have you tried the pool?

John: (Looking surprised and puzzled) Naw...

Al: Can you swim?

John: Yeah, I just don't want to - the fucking water is heated. It's nauseous, it's not refreshing. Where'd we go today, up in the hills, the Hollywood sign. We could see all of L.A., it was sickening, you could see no further than that! (Arm gesture)

Al: It's a bit smoggy, you'll get used to it. Have you been to Mexico?

John: Yeah, I loved it!!! We went all over Baja, we had a recreation vehical,an RV with 6 beds, fucking excellent hotel. It was hot down there, but it's natural heat, there's no air conditioning, you can take it. It's a real pleasure.

Al: Where did you go down there?

John: I Dos Equissed about! (Laughs) Fuckin' excellent place. No one for a hundred miles in any direction. Deathly stillness, fucking loved it.... I was on the beach one day and there were loads of American tourists in their dune buggies zooming by going: "Oh look, thinks he's Johnny Rotten!" Little did they know! (Laughs) That's good fun, getting accused of imitating yourself.

Al: Did you ever think that you'd be that kind of a 'rockstar'?

John: Oh yeah, all my life. I read it in the stars! It's a pain in the ass right, when you want to go out and enjoy yourselves. I want to go see Dennis Brown tonight but fuck knows what will happen. I hate when people keep pointing at you and fucking bothering you. If you tell them to fuck off they just think you're a snot nosed super star cunt. I can't spend my entire life talking to every cunt, it's not fair, I have my life too.

Pooch: There's good and bad that goes with that, you could have stopped it before it got out of hand.

John: I thought I did, it was out of hand before.

Al: Do you think people will accept anything you do?

John: The exact opposite. They'll be more critical. There's a lot of bullshit that's recorded these days and it is accepted blindly...

Pooch: Like all the new Pistols stuff?

John: That's all disgusting - it's like death cult. I thought if I had nothing more to do with that lot, all that would cease to function, but if anything, I've mad it more profitable by finishing it.

SLF's Ali and Henry -photo by Pete

STIFF LITTLE FINGERS
- - - - - - - - - - - - - - - - - - - -

We did this interview with Jake Burns, Henry Cluney and Gordon Ogilvie (manager and co-writer) at Chrysalis Records. Asking questions were Al, Hud and Pooch.....

Pooch: Coming from Belfast, Northern Ireland, I kinda thought you guys would write something maybe about hunger strikers and stuff like that?

Jake: It's too much of a ridiculously complex issue. People take things wrong anyway. There were so many different opinions in the band regarding these matters that it's too much of an issue basically.

Hud: What was it like playing with DOA and the Adolescents?

Jake: I never heard them. I caught the end of the Adolescents, thought they were ridiculous. Played with DOA for two nights and still haven't bloody seem them!

Gordon: I saw them in San Francisco and I was disappointed a bit, principaly because they can obviously play, they were in tune, that was a refreshing contrast to the Dead Kennedys that I saw the week before. I just felt a bit disappointed that is was so like 3 years out of date and stuff and not doing

anything new. Which is something I've always been hot on. If you're going to do something you might as well do something different.

Pooch: Do you like L.A. at all?

Gordon: I don't, but I don't think I've seen it in the right way, horrible.

Al: Last time you were here you got pissed with people who were wearing swastikas.

Jake: Yeah, I haven't seen any of those this time, I've just seen them beating each other up, which is equally as bloody stupid, really it's fuckin' silly. But I mean again, if you're battling against people who wish is was like 3 or 4 years ago, then it's what you've got to expect, cause thats what people were doing 3 or 4 years ago.

Gordon: This is what they do. But they never did that even in 1978 - slam dancing. But as for people launching themselves off 6 foot

high stages on top of other people, it's wrong, because somebody could get very hurt.

Hud: On your latest album ('Nobodys Heroes') you have a variety of different types of music and styles, it's kind of confusing, what direction are you going?

Jake: We don't know the direction we're going in!!

Gordon: All directions at once mostly.

Jake: I don't think we're confused. I think basically we're just gonna carry on doing what we're doing, which is writing songs which make us want to jump about.

Hud: Are you guys anti-punk? You liked it at first, now you seem to not like it, like it has past, it happened.

Jake: Well I wouldn't say that, I mean we still listen to the records we bought then. But it's like saying whenever the punk rock thing came along, up until then, say the people that didn't like heavy metal, don't like it anymore. It's stupid to say "we hate all of it". Obviously we still like the records that we bought then, but I just don't see the point in it, it's like any musical thing, whenever it's new it's exciting and interesting. There's not point in just churning out the same thing. You've got to build on it, you've got to change, otherwise you become stagnant. To me bands like DOA or the Dead Kennedys are just as boring as bands like Led Zeppelin.

Pooch: Do you listen to a lot of reggae?

Jake: Quite a bit yeah. Even there you've got to watch, because a lot of it just becomes churn out, the same old formulas. I mean you get ten thousand songs about how hard it is to be a rasta in todays world.

Pooch: What have you found new and interesting?

Jake: Well my actual fave band in the entire world has become a bit of a personal crusade over the last year and a half whatever are U2.

Pooch: You must be friends with them?

Jake: Yeah, known them for a long time.

Gordon: I've got a lot of time for the Jam. I think they're now a great band. I think Weller really is a real artist and I do like the way there is a certain Jam style. They're a great band and will be regarded as such.

Pooch: Do you guys record everything you write?

Jake: We have to we just don't write enough, that's all. We still only manage an album a year. We're just lazy.

Gordon: It's partly a sort of a philosophy, we've always believed there's no point in making it into work. So to some extent we do the minimum I suppose.

Jake: There's also just no point in writing songs for the make of it, I mean anybody can just sit there with a handfull of chords and stick them together and make noise

Gordon: It's like when we travel abroad, like we are here, we try to have some days that we can actually go see places and meet people. There's no point in coming to America and seeing the inside of a hotel room.

Al: Do you like playing those big places?

Jake: It's a lot easier to play a big place-another problem is that when we play here the act doesn't belong with the stage, we paced a set for those big places. You've got the power to project that sort of length and then suddenly come into that small club and you can't swing the guitar around without hitting Ali in the head, or I can't jump in the air without kicking somebody in the front row in the teeth or hit my head on the ceiling. You're suddenly constricted and it's really weird to get used to play in a small confinement again.

Pooch: Do you care about your fans?

Jake: As much as I think it's possible, yeah, If it wasn't for them we wouldn't be here. We feel responsible for them when we are playing - which is why we got Wally with us (own personal bouncer), so they don't get beaten up by the average idiot club bouncer. I think we try to do as much for them as we possibly can. We make sure that we talk to anybody that wants to talk to us after a show.

Gordon: Treat them like people, I mean if you say to a kid "Look, it's been nice talking to you, but I've been up for 24 hours and I've got to go now", he's gonna say "Sure", but if you say "Go away kid!", he's gonna go off and tell his parents what a nasty bastard Henry Cluney is!! (laughter)

Al: Did you think you'd get this far?

Jake: No. (pause)

Gordon: It gets a bit scary actually. I remember going to places like Halifax, nobody goes to Halifax, it's up in the hills - it's almost a foreign country and we turn up there and 300 kids are singing our song word for word and you think "What have I done!?", Then you start thinking about the sort of responsibility I have now, it's scary. That was crazy that tour. That was the tour in which the first album sort of went smashing into the charts - it charted at number 14 and we were playing at places

SLF's Jake and Ali, Florentine Gardens – photo Pete

that were like 400 or 500 at best.

Jake: A top 20 album, we had like twice as many people outside the gigs as inside. I had my 21st birthday the day I heard that we'd gone into the charts. I was sober that night, I didn't have a drink all night.

Al: Do you think people are listening to you lyrics?

Jake: Yeaha, I think so, they really have to don't they?

Al: What about in America?

Jake: ...I suppose so. It's a bit difficult because obviously, especially around here, there's a lot of people that have a lot of money. They can't be serious. I don't know that the lyrics can have as much clout then, as they would in London.

Pooch: Do you get saddled with the political image?

Jake: Yeah to an extent. I think that's dying now, thank God.

Al: But you still have something to say...

Jake: Yeah, we always have had but I don't think we were ever political.

Gordon: It's more personal satisfaction.

Hud: Why the name Stiff Little Fingers?

Jake: Stole it from an album track by the Vibrators..

Al: What about Ridgid Digits?

Jake: That was a guy called Ian Duncan who did a really early review of us, he called us that.

Gordon: We go: "That's good, we'll steal that!"

Al: What is it like in Belfast, we get the impression that bombs are blowing up everywhere? (Henry is the only one that still lives in Ireland).

Henry: Ah well, it happends, you get used to it,

Hud: What religion are you?

Jake: We never tell that to anybody.

Henry: It gets us into trouble back home.

Jake: Or at least it could get our parents into trouble.

Gordon: To us as people it isn't significant anyway. I don't think any of us even goes to Church.

Pooch: I didn't know if you could walk down

the street safely.

Jake: You just have to know where not to go. It's like nobody in New York would walk through Harlem if they would know you are a stranger, very similar. You don't walk down the streets with hails of bullets flying over your head.

Gordon: I've never even seen a gun fired.

Jake: It's very directed, there's not so much indiscriminate violence.

Pooch: What are the differences in the groupies over here and over there?

Jake: I haven't a clue! You've got exactly the wrong people in the room.

Hud: You guys are married?

Jake: I've been with the same girl for the last 3 years, so that's why you've got the wrong two, the other two, Ali and Jim, yeah!!!

BAD RELIGION

Al: Do you live with your parents?

Greg: Heck yeah! You're in my mom's house right now!

Al: Does she like the band?

Greg: Yep, she's at all the gigs.

Brett: She doesn't mind it, but she gets pissed at us sometimes for walking through the house and drinking all the milk.

Al: How did you come up with your name?

Jay B: We don't like religion.

Brett: It's a good way to tell everyone to fuck off and they have no idea why you're doing it because they're so stupid. All the other ways you've got to pay for it somehow. This way everybody respects you for it.

Jay Z: I was healed last night. These Jesus guys came up to me and one said that he had a feeling I have back problems and that one leg was longer than the other. I said, Yeah, I do have back trouble once in a while. so, he brought me to this bench, took off my shoes, and held my feet together. This foot is a little bit longer than the other. So, he grabs my feet and says, In the name of Jesus Christ, make this foot grow! And it grew right in front of my eyes! They were exactly even. I don't believe it was Jesus. I was a good trick, whatever it was.

Brett: And that's really unique because you just heard an atheist say Swear to God!

Michelle: Do you think the police know about you?

Jay Z: I don't think they even know.

Greg: No, here's what they told me when I got arrested: Here we have a small community and you guys don't fit in around here. You fit in Hollywood because there's no community in Hollywood. This is a definite community and we cannot allow it around here.

Al: And you have a record out. Cut your own record?

Greg: A new 6 song E.P. It's selling real well all over the place.

Brett: It's released on Epitaph records, we just made it up. We weren't all that happy with the sound on it. The studio really fucked us over. The mix isn't that good. The voice sounds like it's underwater or something.

Jay Z: We owe that to Real Life studios in Agura; don't anyone go there.

Al: Do you do all your own distributing?

Greg: Recently JEM bought 300 of them. But, we distribute mostly in L.A.
They said they're distributing up and down the coast.

Al: So, are you going to S.F. or someplace?

Jay Z: In August, we'll probably go to Frisco for four or five days.

Brett: Frisco's weird too. Either you see some old, deformed, Chinese, homosexual, or black. Plus...Well, maybe it has to do with everytime I've been there was on Acid. (laughs)

Bad Religion – photo by Pete

Dianne Chi Alleycat – photo Hudley

FLIPSIDE NUMBER 26

"Down by the housing projects
The senator came in his limosine
His soldiers passed out buttons

Hollywood/Fullerton crew: Trudie, Bruce Atta, Mary Sims, Mike Atta, Connie, Becky, Loren, Jeff Atta, Dorothy and Mary Rat – photo by Al

His daughter wore tight blue jeans
Their faces were clean and shiny
Everybody danced cheek to cheek
You danced with a dude named Tiny
I danced with a ceramic freak
Too much junk, too much junk.....
We used to walk down the boulevard
We used to float in neon soup
I kissed you eyes in the shadows
We sparkled on down the loop
Now you've joined the revolution
And you say you're having a real good time
Well I spend my time shooting up television
And I guess I'm doing just fine
Too much junk, too much junk....."
"Too Much Junk" – The Alleycats

ISSUE #: 26
DATE: September 1981
FORMAT: 8 1/2x11, rotary web offset with 2 color cover and insides
PAGES: 48
PRICE: $1.00
PRESS RUN: 2400

This issue was another special edition for us, this being our "Greatest Hits Vol. 1", in fact it was a lot like this issue, except that it only covered the first 16 issues. A lot of people were into reading and seeing what those old issues and interviews were like, so this was a simple compilation, not many interviews were re-typed (as is the case with this issue). Here are two interviews from that issue, the Alleycats in full and an edited 999....

999

---

999 were interviewed on April 10 at the Woodsound in Arcadia by Jill and Paul.
Paul: What are some of you new songs...
Guy: 'Inside Slot', 'Oiler'...
Paul: Will you do a live single?
Nick: What we've been trying to do is get a lot of bands that, like Ultravox, Police, that are playing the clubs and put together a live compilation album, and hopefully at a really cheap price. If not we would like to sway A&M to sort of put out songs by all of those bands as sort of a compilation album, that was mine and Ian Copeland's idea.

Paul: How did the song 'Homicide' come about?
Nick: That's funny because I wrote that with America in mind. Homicide is an Americana term, in England it's just murder, over here you've got homicide squads, homicide this and that, so I wanted to write it in an American sort of way.
Paul: When was it written?
Nick: End of last year, September.
Paul: What do you think of Sid Vicious?
Nick: I think it's really sad you know. I think he's a victim of circumstance. It was exploited by everyone and they have caused that blokes death. No doubt about it. That's the stinking shitty thing about those English newspapers.
Paul: What will your next record be?
Nick: Oh, we've written a lot of songs, when we get to London we'll start demo tapes. There's an album coming out in America that is basically 'Seperates' but will be called 'High Energy Plant' and will have a different cover.
Paul: What was the best U.S. gig?
Guy: It's hard to say, it's hard to judge that way.
Nick: We've enjoyed a lot of different shows for a lot of different reasons but on a whole it's been pretty good.
Paul: What about the Whisky?
Guy: Oh great, really good gig.
Jill: Did Forrest ask you to calm the crowd?
Guy: You know he did, the manager said: "Can you try to keep it down a bit, don't play so hard and get so excited".
Eddie: Cause they were dancing so much!
Paul: What about the Cuckoos Nest?
Guy: Great audience.
Paul: Why did you play 'Homicide' twice?
Nick: Well we really didn't have any other songs rehersed, sometimes when we first started out, to get our songs known we'd play them 3 or 4 times!!
Paul: Are you into bright colors in your clothes?
John: Yeah, we're trying to get our own...
Paul: Image?
John: No, like on stage it's good to wear bright clothes, attracts attention.
Paul: Do you like day glo?
John: Yeah, I don't mind.
Nick: No, day glo sort of, but bright colors. I'm

RANDY STODOLA was interviewed on Jan. 6 by Al in Lewits. Randy's band the Alleycats (Dianne Chai on bass and vocals, John McCarthy on drums and Randy on guitar and vocals)have been on the scene for about 5 years, surfacing before the punk explosion in the summer of 1977.
AL: What have you been doing since, say the single from Dangerhouse?
Randy: Oh, that was over a year ago, that was in march, it would take a long time to tell all th t happend...
AL: Well, have you recorded since?
Randy: Yeah, we have a song on that compilation album they got.
AL: Did you like that?
Randy: Yeah, it sounds pretty good---we don't have a record played so, wh..the only time we hear it is at someone's elses house, everyone has a different system but it sounds pretty good, seems they get better fidelity on 33, I dón't know why that is.
AL: Are you satisfied with Dangerhouse?
Randy: Oh, they're ok, Well see with Dangerhouse we work out our problems with them and not go thru alot of intermidiaries which alot of other people seem to do, It's not to say we've had fewer problems, sometimes these people are a little maieve, they're doing a recording in a $15 dollar a hour studio and they gotta realise there's gonna be problems, and they're working with a record company that's just started, the bands just started.. I think alot of complaints the people have is just based on that.
AL: Have you been doing more recording?
Randy: We do alot of recording, we have a 4 track recorder and we have a friend that has a, I guess you'd call it a studio, it's a room he built for recording, we just record there.
AL: You've been playing all over...
Randy: Yeah, we played out at U.C. Irvine, at Squeeze out in Riverside, U.C. San Diego, Berkley were playing in San Pedro on the 17 th I think and we'll go back to San Diego as soon as the guy gets the permit worked out. Alot of bands seem like they only want to play in hollywood and we have a little different attitude--see, they want to play Hollywood cause they want to get a record contract right away and they think that's the place to play, nobody else matters....
AL: It's easier to get a gig in Hollywood,
Randy: It's hard to say, I don't NN know if you make that much money playing Hollywood, for me part of it is economics, we survive at a low poverty level off the money we make playing so we gotta play as much as we can without boring people by playing the same people over and ever again, so the more places we play and the more we spread out

FLIPSIDE 10 YEAR ANNIVERSARY, PAGE 82

geographically the more we can play without boreing people and I think we probably bore people quick, ya know? I like to think we play for people that haven't seen us before - that would be the best time to see us.
AL: Does the set change all the time?
Randy: Yeah, we try and write a new song everytime we play, were not changing in that alot of the songs we do we've done for a long time like the song on the Dangerhouse album we started doing 2½ - 3 years ago 'Too Much Junk' In fact, we did that for a high school dance once, that was one of the songs we did, The Alleycats started I guess 5 years ago. We had a different drummer and before that I was in a band called the Hubcaps. And when I started playing withDianne we changed our name cause the Hubcaps--everybody wanted us to play for 50's dances, and we weren't a 50's band.
AL: when your booked now do you tell them your a 'Punk rock band'?
Randy: See I don't know that weare, I guess Punkrock is defined more by the audience, in that way we are cause most of our audience at least in Hollywood and in San Francisco are people into punk. I thaink we are different that most cause most punk bands said ' 'Look, let's start playing punk rock' and start a punk rock band where as we us a band and got a punk rock audience...alot of people into punk think we're not. People who don't like punk think what we are. I guess it just depends on your point of reference.
AL: You don't mind being on the Punk album?
Randy: No, no I don't, I see people like Dave saying punk rock is stupid, but I don't think that. It's just that alot of bands try to exploit punk rock, like the Dictators, they're not punk but they say they're punk, but they're not and I don't want to be in the position of a band trying to do that.
AL: Of the places you've played how does it compare to Los Angeles or Hollywood?
Randy: Well I think Hollywood and San Francisco audiences are more open to things....
AL: Do you think the S.F. scene is getting as good as everyone thinks?
Randy: Well part of it is that the grass is always greener on the other side, because,.. maybe....we do ok down here and more bands could if they were interested in breaking out But one advantage S.F. has is people don't live 20 million miles away from everywhere else, that's the problem here, everybody's spread out, so if your doing something it's hard to publicise it and also it's hard for prople to get there. Like when we played Moose Lodge in Redondo alot of people there were 13, 14, 15, 16 who live in that area who don't have a car who can't get to Hollywood all of the time or hardly any time, but they like to see things besides the same Heavey Metal cover bands and what ever else. And I was surprised as many local people showed up. Everywhere we play there's bands ...people say there in bands--we played Riverside and people said they were in the Reactors or something, everywhere we go there's a budding punk rock bands with no place to play,...because first: they dón't live close to Hollywood and secondly they don't have the connections.
AL: What about that Richard Cromlin artical?
Randy: Yeah, I never met Richard Cromlin but he calledme on the phone, he seems like a nice guy, he was asking me about the record scene and I told him we haven't had any contact with major labels so we don't know. Some of the quests were a little out of context, I wasn't sure he was gonna write an artical. I told him what helps us was when they write articles about us it helps us obviously but I was surprised to come home (from S.F.) and people tell me I was in the Calendar section.
AL: What about 'chances look grim for local bands'?
Randy: I don't know that may be true...w.see that depends on the bands reason for playing, if there only reason is to get a million dollar record contract maybe the chances are grim, I don't know...if they have other reasons for playing then it isn't grim, certainly there's alot more places to play and a lot bigger audience than ever before locally.
AL: Are you kinda satisfied?
Randy: Your never satisfied, because every

Randy Stodola ~

Alleycats

month when we pay the rent we have like $4 left, so I guess you always want to make some more....
AL: I mean, your not especially looking for that million dollar contract right away...
Randy: No. It would be good, but...it eliminates alot of bands that thought it was faddish or they were gonna get rich or this and that. Funny thing is people would say our songs are too simple or too fast, and then Punk started and people said we were too complicated,..now...it think it's starting to swing back, but I'm not for complication for complications sake, I don't think our songs are that complicated,.... We seem to be more successful as time goes on, maybe just because we're surviving, we sorta just go up the eschelon, after awhile they give up and as a band gives up at the top we go up another step.............

always changing my mind.

Guy: You just want to look bright on stage.

Paul: Do you have a lot of groupies?

Guy: Yeah well we haven't had a lot ourselves but there are a lot about, there are a lot in America.

Paul: Does your manager keep girls away from you?

Guy: Well see when we come off stage we need time to relax so he keeps them away but he doesn't tell us what to do, but we don't sort of get into that really, you know?

Paul: Did he tell you stories about VD?

Guy: He's made jokes about it, everyone does.

Paul: What are differences between the audiences here and in England?

Nick: Not much really, basically a difference in money- small money over here, it's easier to live and get a job over here, easier to get a place to live, it's bigger, it's nice you don't have the same pressures England's got. But there are a lot of things very very wrong with American society, and everywhere go. But what is good is that the kids are doing something about it, they come in together to music, it's a way out but ti's also a bad thing, ya know?

Paul: They say the kids in the U.S. have nothing to rebel against.

Nick: That's rubbish!

Paul: Did you hear about the Police riot at Elks Lodge?

Nick: When that happends that's an infringement on human rights, on your personal privacy, on your right to be a human being because when you're doing that you're being segregrated from the rest of society because of the music you like and the way you dress, and that wrong! There's an awful more of that in America, so in actual fact you've got a lot more to rebel about in those sort of terms.

Paul: In England did the scene start around the lack of jobs?

Nick: That's not true. Not strictly true. There are a lot of different reasons. You've probably got your own reasons, you may identify with this, it makes you feel better, it means something to you. It's just how you feel, how you want to look, what you want to do, how good you want to be, how you want to get your aggressiveness out without hitting someone around the head, how you want to form your own life in the future, freedom you want to impose, how free you want people to be around you... See, the thing about new wave, it doesn't offend people on a level of obsenity or something, it offends them right through politically, and everything, and every aspect of everything.

FLIPSIDE NUMBER 27

"Punk ain't no religious cult
Punk means thinking for yourself
You ain't hardcores cause you spike your hair
When a jock still lives inside your head
Nazi punks, nazi punks, nazi punks
FUCK OFF
If you've come to fight, get out of here
You ain't no better than the bouncers
We ain't trying to be the police
When you ape the cops it ain't anarchy
Ten guys jump one, what a man
You fight each other, police state wins
Stab your backs when you trash our halls
Trash a bank if you've got the balls
I You still think swasticas look cool
The real nazis run your schools

999 at the Nest – photo Al

They're coaches, businessmen and cops
In a real fourth reich you'll be the first to go
You'll be the first to go....
Unless you think."
"Nazi Punks Fuck Off" – The Dead Kennedys

$1.00

DATE: October 1981
FORMAT: 8 1/2x11, rotary web offset with glossy 2 color cover and insides
PAGES: 52
PRICE: $1.00
PRESS RUN: 2600
STAFF: Al, Hud, Helen, Pooch, Michele, Robert Hill

- -

Another and perhaps the biggest physical change for Flipside - we go glossy cover! If you have them, you know that the last few issues with the two color covers were nice, but... but the colors sucked. You can't print big solids on newsprint. So we went to professionally printed glossy paper bound to our usual newsprint insides. The results: it looks great, the red (on this ish) is red, and now newstand distributors are taking Flipside, which made this issue sell out really fast.

The scene is sort of in limbo with the Vex's new location closing and there is nothing yet to replace it. Hall shows (including Florentine, Centrex, Bards Apollo, L.A. Press Club, Devonshire Downs and the start of Perkins Palace) seem to dominate, but the Whisky is still squeaking in a occasional show of interest.

KEITH LEVENE

- -

By Bill Bartell and Darby Crash, 6 months late because it was first submitted to Creem, but here it is!!)

If it can be said that John Lydon is the Public in PiL, then the Image and it's limitations is in the brainchild of Keith Levene. As guitarist of Public Image Ltd., and as I see it, the true genius behind the band, Levene is often overlooked in the presence of one John Lydon, and the public is missing a great deal. L.A. and in spite of the absence of a reception party, Keith was still in a talkative omniscent mood in regards to 'his' band, and the manuscript that follows is an account of the interview.

Bill: What did you think of the L.A. crowd?

Keith: I was really surprised, I dunno, they just annoy me. They were like pseudo-skinheads, gobbing all the time, it just didn't mean anything to me.

Bill: Do you think that most of the audience was living a Pistols fantasy?

Keith: I think that like a third of them were, and because of that they really limited what the band could do, they just blew it for themselves.

Bill: Do you think there is hope for the audience you saw tonight?

Keith: No.

Bill: Do you classify your music at all?

Bill Bartell, Keith Levene, & metal box

Keith: I'll just say we're not a rock and roll band, I'm anti-rock and roll, rock and roll stinks to me. It was great 10 years ago, but it's got nothing to do with what is happening now. Nothing is happening anymore, it's just like, so much of nothing.

Bill: What about the new album?

Keith: Well, I want to do an album here, release an album out there (waves hand towards Los Angeles). It won't be a Public Image album, well it will be, but it will just be me and John on it.

Bill: Do you think the band would be receiving as much attention as it is had John not been in the Sex Pistols and you in the Clash?

Darby: You were in the Clash?

Keith: That thing with John cancels itself out, as popular as with the Sex Pistols, it also has bad points to fuck it up, like the audience tonight, it's not really that important at all. We could have made it within, say, six months as some mega-band, and done Sex Pistols things, but we didn't and it's taking time. Our ideas are so different anyway. You see we're Public Image Limited, we're a limited company, we're a company not a group, we've got a company over here, we are incorporated. And it's all part of PiL, and PiL is a company, a group of people like Jeanette who is in the band. We're individuals and we've got creative output, and this (tapping my Metal Box) is what we're doing at the moment. We're just trying to use all the companies positively. When we Do do gigs, we're not necessarily out there to give people a good time, I just do whatever happens, at the time is has to be spontaneous.

Bill: Like John bringing the kids on the stage tonight?

Keith: Yeah, he's done that once or twice before, but it isn't planned or anything.

Bill: So what influences do you have, do you like Can, Faust and those kinds of things?

Keith: I like Can, but nothing influences me, it's coincidental. I like Eno, I used to like Bowie a lot, I liked Roxy Music. I think Eno is one of the most important people on the

scene, but I think he might blow it by mistake though.

Bill: What do you think of the turn the Clash have taken since you left?

Keith: I think they're pathetic wankers and have been since I quit.

Darby: Why did you leave?

Keith: It was either Mick or me, so I let Mick stay because I didn't want to be with them.

Bill: Did you like the music of the Sex Pistols?

Keith: I thought the Pistols were great.

Bill: You used to do some Pistols material like Belsen" and "Problems" didn't you?

Keith: "Belsen" was my song, I wrote that with Sid and John, that's a Public Image song. We didn't do it tonight because we didn't want to. We did "Religion" tonight and we haven't done that before on the whole tour, and we did "Home Is Where The Heart Is" and we haven't done that one ever.

Bill: So does you comapany have any movie or video projects coming up?

Keith: Yeaha, a load of video ideas running around, but the thing about video is that it is changing from tapes to disks. It interests me, not like a band performing on disk, but that people have the opportunity to make short movies, with their music included.

Bill: Do you want to be a superstar?

Keith: No. I'm not trying to be a superstar, I don't know what I really want... I don't like doing gigs because it is format rock and roll. There is no way you can do heavy gigging and say you are genuinely giving it your all. We never wanted to do a tour because it obviously destroys bands, I'm not trying to be a star, I just want to see a lot of fucking things change, people being a lot more honest and a lot more creative again - to stop following. I like Eno, I like Peter Hamil and Abba. I hate the Clash. I hate the Specials.

Bill: Do you dislike Ska music in general?

Keith: No. I just don't like third rate imitations. I'm dead against anything like that. I'm against film unions, and musicians unions, any of that stuff. I'm not in any of them.

Bill: Doesn't not being in cause some problems with royalty checks?

Keith: I don't know, I've never had one, we negotiate our contracts and pay ourselves. We just blow it all. Warners works for us, and so does Virgin. Warners just doesn't realize it as much as Virgin does. The record company is supposed to release and distribute your record, they give you an advance but they're still working for you. Most bands let companies dictate to them, tell them to cut their numbers short, what to put out, that sort of thing. They wanted us to speed up "Fodderstomp" and to turn up the vocals on the "Public Image" single, we told them to fuck off.

Bill: Do you want to become a label that takes on other acts?

Keith: I'd like to be like World Enterprizes in that Bowie film "The Man Who Fell To Earth". Massive but honest, making loads of money, but not ripping people off. With people like Warners there's a lot of CIA involvement, money exchanges. I'll talk about it with the tape off if you like, but not with it on.

****

Bill: What about American alternative bands like the Residents?

Keith: I think that is all full of shit, full of influences. I like the idea of people doing things, but it would be so much better if they would look into themselves, so much easier, so much less effort. Like me, I'm into monotony. I'll tell you if I'm nicking, like I nicked "Swan Lake" but I didn't nick the idea, I just used it. The way I play guitar now, I hardly use chords, I just play, with no limitations with respect to key. Wobble is like a scaffold for me to build around. I don't play guitar really, I just use it to get sounds.

Bill: This is getting rather lengthy, do you have anything final to say?

Keith: I think L.A. is a killer city.

Darby: Bill, throw your "Metal Box" over the balcony.

BILLY IDOL / GENERATION X

By Craig Lee

Craig: How did Generation X fall apart? There was a big difference between your first album and your second "Valley of the Dolls".

Billy: We needed a new sound because I hated "Valley of the Dolls" of intensly, because there's fucking crap on it, didn't like the way we were going. I said: "Look, we're really fucking up here, we gotta play real simple", cause that was the only way we could play together. Play really simple. Tony liked the idea of playing like that, but it just didn't go anywhere. When Derwood and Mark went, it was like, you can't really look at them and think "Yeah, I really want to play with them". I'm going backwards again. Right back to the beginning. It's a change to do anything stupid I feel like doing again, rather than having to be sensible. I can do what I want.

Craig: What kind of music are you listening to now?

Billy: I'd rather listen to reggae than heavy metal because it's more interesting. Now I listen to the Cramps and Suicide. I'm listening to the Doors at the moment. I like it, it's L.A. I walk down the street, I'm a tourist, and I go "Ohhhh, that's where the Doors recorded!" I'm such a fan, such an idiot.... I had such weird views about L.A., I really didn't like it when I got here in 1978, really thought it was horrible. So I'm here for two and a half days and I form this massive opinion. I was going on about a

Craig Lee

lot of things and bringing my snobbish attitude with me - - I was thinking "You are an idiot, really!" You don't do what you really think half the time, you do things cause you get an idea and then half way through it, someone is bugging you about something. You start thinking, maybe they're right, and you go "No no no" That's why I had to get out of the group and start doing what I thought was really right, EVEN IF IT IS CRAP. Otherwise, I'm always going to be walking in a tunnelvision world.

Craig: Why did you move to New York?

Billy: I've been in New York 5 months. London is a great place, I really like it, fucking brilliant, but it's another hole in the ground. It's weird being in New York on me own, can't be safe in your own little world and that's what this whole thing is about. Me facing up to life, getting on with people, not being an asshole popstar. It's much more exciting.

CRAIG LEE

- -

Craig Lee (writer for the L.A. Times and the L.A. Weekly and x-writer for Slash not to mention former invader, Bag, Catholic Discipline and Bonehead) was interviewed in September of 1981 by Shredder from Rag in Chains and Paranoia.

Craig: When the original punks started in Hollywood, they were outsiders - they were total outsiders! It was not a safe thing to do, it wasn't part of a club. It's still not easy or safe, bouncers still beat the shit out of punks and cops harass them. But now they run in these big packs and and like I see all these groups and they're all like each other. They're not doing anything that's unique or original anymore!! Not making any statement - just following a trend. A friend of mine was saying - what's the difference between rednecks who go to a bar, drink a lot, listen to lour music and get into fights - and punks that go to a gig, get loaded and beat the shit out of each other?!! I mean what is that changing, what is that altering?

Shredder: How different was it back then?

Craig: The difference was it was like a revolution!! We were gonna change the boring old rock cliches, we were not gonna be rock heroes. There was gonna be energy again. Everybody was so passive and dull then, you know James Taylor and Carly Simon. I was like a real revolution then... This is what people wanted when things first started. Just like a lot of original Hollywood people couldn't handle it because it wasn't their scene

anymore, it was out of their control and they flipped out - but what did they expect? They say "Oh, we did that 3 years ago!" but it still means something to a lot of people, it still has that energy, it's still passionate, it's still real... bands like TSOL, it's real, ya know?

Shredder: A lot of kids get into it for three months and come out of it with an attitude that they've been at it for years.

Craig: That's always happened. What makes me laugh is I'll go out to shows and a lot of new kids don't know who I am and of course I'm older than them, and maybe they'll give me shit, or make fun of me and I'll just laugh inside: "You fool, you don't have no idea!" or they put down La De Da and say "Who is this asshole?" They don't know what I've been through. Like there was this whole period when bands could not play anywhere. There was a real struggle to keep things alive. People don't realize that when he say "Oh, X sell out, they play the Greek". They don't realize.

Shredder: Do you feel cheated when you see people abusing clubs and you worked...

Craig: It's so fucking lame!! That really bothers me. Like being in the Bags, when we played shows it was real exciting. People dancing all over, and people used to love to show how much they were into a band. I did too. There no difference between band and audience. I'd be screaming and dancing and applauding to the Controllers, then I'd get on stage and play with the Bags and they'd be screaming and applauding for us. Everybody was excited and real happy - then there was this turning point and people were out there going "Oh, I'm too cool to applaud, fuck you, I'm not here for the band, I'm here for myself" What the fuck is that? Then I'd get pissed and yell at the audience and I'd get spit on or whatever. So fucking negative. When people trash clubs they're just trashing their own scene, why are the fucking trashing the clubs they go see music in? That was bugging me. It wasn't a music scene anymore, it was hanging out and be cool for your friends and nobody was thinking about the band on stage.

Shredder: Why do you think people are afraid to play different music?

Craig: They're playing it safe, but I shouldn't speak for them, they're probably really into what they're doing, but why not find something that's your own? Like when I first met Helen (Killer), that's real funny, she had short hair on top and hair sticking up on the sides - like Sue Catwoman (famous Bromley Set scene maker in London 1976) and then I

went out to a show a couple of months ago and there was a girl looking like Helen did 4 years ago - come on!! She probably thinks she's the coolest punk on the block.

Shredder: Do you think she saw pictures?

Craig: She had to because it was exactly like them.

Shredder: She could have gone to Atilla?

Craig: Yeah, maybe. But it's not making a statement anymore, at the time it was real shocking to people, it scared them, it's not shocking now, they just go "Oh, it's a punk".

Shredder: If you live in....

Craig: If you live in suburbia it might scare them, but if you go to Okie Dogs at 2 in the morning it doesn't mean a thing! It's all running with the pack, where's the revolution in that? How are you provoking people, how are you changing people?

Shredder: What did you think of your part in "the Decline..."?

Craig: That's a SORE subject. Originally we weren't supposed to be in the movie at all because Alice - the first time we met with Penelope, Alice and her didn't hit it off. Alice didn't want to be made to look like a fool - she wanted to see the film before they used it in the movie. Penelope was insistent that not happen, she had to have total control. When anybody tries to pull total control on Alice she rebels against it. The editors of the movie kept saying "Look Penelope it's a good band, it fits in the movie". Between that time and the movie we lost our bass player, real petty... I don't know why they wanted us, cause Alice was a real strong woman performer, cause the movie already had the male macho punk sterotypes. The night we were filmed at the Fleetwood there was a big screw up. We originally set up the show with the promoters, and they said Fear and the Gears were also on the bill, so we said ok, but we want to be 3rd or 4th on the bill but not last... so the Urinals played and the Gun Club played and we were setting up there's Fears equipment up there, what the fucks going on! Fear's manager Danny Hutton, formerly of 3 Dog Night, comes up and gives us this bullshit, and here's Fear fucking us over. Fear used to open for us!! And the Gears were saying, "We're not going on either!" So Alice flipped a coin and we went on last, we almost didn't get filmed and were really pissed. Then we saw the film, they did three songs and it looked really good. Then, I don't know why, they really cut our stuff and did weird things. There's this guy who wrote "I want your body" on his arm and he's reaching out to Alice and they put that part in Fear's section!!! Another part in the middle of a song they use a clip from later on in the set, not the same song! I think Penelope really liked us, but it's obviously a Slash promo film, cause Bob Biggs, Penelopes husband, is the head of Slash records, and who has the big sections in the film: Germs and X, cause of course he felt those were the most important bands........ When I first started writing for Slash, Claude Bessey and me got along real well, I could write anything I wanted to. And so now Biggs took over ($) and he was real cold to me. I always felt there was this latent anti-semitism that runs around the scene. Biggs would make jokes like "Oh there's the jew, maybe he'll clean the toilet". Cause I wasn't cool, I didn't fit Biggs' stereotyped image of what a punk rocker should be, or Chris D's image.... It's getting harder to hangout because people are giving me shit all the time. Everybody's got their great goddamn opinion and they have to

come up to me and say the columns sucked. Write a letter, don't tell me, don't tell me at a club, I'm here to enjoy myself just like you. I happends a lot.

There are people who will say "I don't want to tell people what to do, we're not ordering people or telling them what to think" and then they're singing "Revenge". So they ARE telling people, that's such a cop out! People should be opinionated, that's what you have a brain for. That's what the whole thing was for, if they disagree then they should say what they feel. Like I went to interview Black Flag, they felt they were getting bad publicity, they wanted to clarify things, so they are telling me this stuff, which sounded ok, I like them, they're nice people and stuff. But then the music editor was pissed because they were going to every paper in town... (talk goes on to superstar punk groups, like Twisted Roots, who start our by headlining the Whisky). It's just the same rock and roll show business hype, game playing and I guess it will always exist and will never change. And I don't have to like it. The best thing is to be talented, to really say something, to really believe what you're saying and be good and clean about what you're doing.

Paul

KILLING JOKE
- -
Killing Joke were Interviewed by Al, Hud and Pooch on a hot (105) August afternoon at the Tropicana Hotel. The interview took place before their first of 5 shows a the Whisky A Go Go. Present were Youth, who was a bit stoned and quite comfortable in his patio chair, Paul who was the most talkative and later Jaz who was not in the best of moods. Geordie sat in their room and watched cartoons.

Al: Have you changed any of your opinions about America, in past interviews you've said you hated it?
Paul: I never said I hated it!
Al: Oh, it must have been Youth.
Youth: I might have said I hated it!
Paul: As he enjoys himself!
Youth: I think it was Americans I met in England that led to believe I hated it, its ok, this moment it is.
Pooch: "Follow the Leader" is getting a lot of airplay.

Paul: Yeah....
Pooch: It's also in the disco charts!
Paul: Yeah, it seems to be. Great.
Youth: Better than punk or heavy metal fucking charts.
Al: You'd rather be on disco charts?
Youth: Yeah.
Paul: A lot of people label us punk heavy metal and it isolates us so if it goes into the disco charts that's great, it's something else again.
Al: Do you think Americans can relate to your songs?
Paul: It's not quite as easy, but places like Chicago, they really understood what we were about. I think if Americans can't now, the will in the future.

Geordie

Pooch: Industrial cities..
Paul:, Yeah, the less money the more frustrated, the more the response.
Al: And so they understand the 'killing joke'.
Paul: Yeah, it's very relevent, but it won't be relevent to everybody, but it will.
Hud: Are you guys into the Occult?
Paul: Yeah.
Hud: All of you.
Paul: Oh, to varying degrees.
Youth: (Referring to the coffee shop) They threw me out twice, once cause I had no shirt, once cause I had no shoes, but it's an alright place.
Al: Yeaha, it has palm trees, is that why you do your hair like that?
Youth: Why? Like palm trees? Yeah!
Al: Jaz, does your necklace symbolize anything in particular?
Jaz: No, it's just jewelery, that's all.
Hud: Are you familiar with Theosophy?
Jaz: No.
Al: I heard you had a wizard or something open for you at some gigs?
Jaz: No.
Pooch: How do your gigs go in England?
Jaz: It's a lot different from here, I'll tell you that. People still view you as a rock and roll band here. Over there it's just like something to get your fucking emotions out. People take it a lot more seriously in Europe. It appears to me that way, that's cause they're so bored there nothing else to do.
Pooch: (to Paul) How'd the band start?
Paul: Jaz and I were playing in bands already and we met each other and we started out doing what other people wanted us to do

Youth

musically. We had a lot of things in common, and things we'd like to see changed and things we wanted to do, so we started a band.
Pooch: Is it going the way you wanted?
Paul: Yeah it is. But coming over here it's really gotten sick. It's really rock and roll really, but it's something I never imagined would happen. It's always been a very exclusive attitude amongst us – and if we did a gig it was because we wanted to do a gig. It was special, we'd give ourselves time to warm up to it. But over here it's just fucking rock and roll, it really is. It's club to club, some real seedy joints.
Al: Have you been doing one show per town?
Paul: Except for New York, we did two. And the Whisky is 2 shows the first two nights and then one. Which is bound to be interesting because we haven't done anything like that before. But, yeah, we knew what we were getting into coming over here, we knew we'd be playing small clubs, we knew we'd be playing a lot of gigs and we knew they'd be hassles... but with the schedule we've got it's really hard to come up with much enthusiasm for anything.
Pooch: When you're on stage, do you want to entertain or teach people or...

Jaz - photos Al

Paul: If it was just for entertainment, I'd give it up - I want people to be entertained, I want people to enjoy it but I want people to understand it and gain something. I don't want people to feel like they're being preached at. That's why we're using dance rhythms in songs, it can be physically enjoyable as well. We're not trying to preach anything... people seem to think that our music is pessimistic, I think it's optimistic. I find it very vocal and full of intensity. It's a release to get them physically involved in something.

ZED RECORDS

Anyone into music at all knows about record stores, especially if they are into punk music. In L.A. there are only a handfull of record stores that have been carrying punk music from the start, have been keeping up with what is happening in the scene, and have salesmen that know what it is they are selling - perhaps the biggest is Zed. Zed not only has the the most complete stock of records, they have t-shirts, badges, fanzines, punk gear, and everything else (besides they sell twice as many Flipsides as the next store!)
Interview at Zed 9/16/81
Flipside: What do you like on your pizza?
Steve: Oh, pepperoni and mushrooms....
Flipside: Really, tell us about Zed...
Marlene: June 1974...
Mike: (as if he had this rehersed): In June 1974 my brother lived in England, he moved there and he was working for Island Records. He had connections to get records cheap over there. So he sent us a bunch of boxes of records, we rented a store, go those boxes and started with them: Island promos and cutouts.
Marlene: Island is gonna be thrilled about that! Also there were New Musical Express singles, he was NME's single reviewer, so he got every single in England cause they sent it to be reviewed.
Mike: Yeah, we opened right at the time of the first Bad Company, first Sparks and first Eno albums came out. We had them a month before they came out here, we didn't know who they were but that is what got us started.
Flipside: You used to be a big progressive store.
Mike: That was the whole thing then. I used to be into record myself and I had to go all the way to Laguna Beach or to Sound Odessey in Hollywood to get them, that's a lot of driving.
Marlene: Our knowledge of music was marginal until we got the stuff form England. The we didn't know what Roxy Music was, we'd just give away all this promo stuff.
Mike: They sent all these rare records from England and we didn't know, we sold them at regular prices.
Marlene: The progressive stuff got us through, then that slowed down. The we got into bootlegs and that got us through for awhile but bootlegs went out and this new music started to carry us through...
Mike: Yeah we heard about the Sex Pistols about 6 months before they had a record out and finally we got some records in – I think the first punk record we ever had was the Germs "Forming" or maybe the Damned's first single.
Flipside: And all you had was one little punk bin.
Mike: Yeah , our little punk section!! After the singles came out we'd always get a few

and say, "Well we gotta carry it, there's not that many anyways." But it got to a point where there got to be so many that we had to decide to carry everything or just do it on the side. So we said "Lets go for it, nobody else is doing it!"
Marlene: We tried reggae, and that just does not work in America, just no interest. Our whole store went to see the Sex Pistols in San Francisco, all of us.
Mike: That was the point where we really changed from progressive to punk.
Marlene: To hardcore!!! (Laughs)
Flipside: And then you all cut your hair!
Mike, Steve: Yeah!!! (lots more laughs!)
Mike: And we took down the Genesis posters and flags.
Flipside: What kind of customers do you get?
Marlene: All kinds, we get teachers...
Mike: Cops, we get L.B.P.D. who come in and buy Wendy Williams posters and "No One Is Innocent" badges.
Marlene: And Police badges.
Mike: One guys has his uniform on and when he lifts up his pocket flaps he had "No One Is Innocent" and "Don't Fuck With Me" and they hang the Wendy poster up, the one where she's licking the end of the rifle, in the station.
Flipside: What about little kids with spiked arm bands?
Mike: Yeah a couple of times we've had parents come in waving the arm band saying "You sold this to my son!!" and it's got big spikes on it! They think it's for warfare or something. So we had to put up a sign that says you gotta be 18 to buy spiked arm bands.
Marlene: This was a temporary thing, we thought if we did it for a year it would be fun. No plans, just a hobby. Now I don't know what we'd do without it and it's still fun after 7 years.

DEAD KENNEDYS

As I walked into Biafra's house, situated in S.F.'s Mission District, I saw Microwave, roadie, right hand man, confidant and cook in the kitchen preparing chicken. I went upstairs to where Biafra was, on my way upstairs I couldn't help notice Biafra's unusually large collection of black shoes (fetish?). Biafra was a bit under the weather this day, experiencing either a post nasal drip or else a bloody nose and had wad of

kleenex shoved up his left nostril as we began the interview. Klaus Flouride bass player and Daren Peligro drummer, arrived soon after I did. Klaus had these uncommon pointy shoes on and Daren was wearing a black leather jacket among other things. -(Interview by Jill and Lisasa Turnstile)
Flipside: I know it's been asked a thousand times but it has to be asked again...
Jello: No it doesn't!
Klaus: How did we get our name?
Jello: It is to symbolize the end of the American dream and the beginning of the decline and fall of the American Empire. America is falling apart at the seams for a variety of reasons and so in order to call attention to that we call attention to what the catalyst was. Why people are so self-centered these days and they are all totally in it for themselves. This is how every single empire throughout history, when the people get too rich and stuck up and snotty. In the 1950's you see Life Magazine ads... "America, bigger, bigger, stronger everyday, fancier appliances..."
Flipside: Like own a big car?
Jello: Yeah right, and then suddenly Kennedy got killed. The glamour boy president and his gorgeous wife are no more and they are stuck with Johnson instead. The the other Kennedy brother gets killed too, thus painting the seed for a real extreme brand of cynicism that you have in this country now where nobody trusts anybody else and constantly everybody is out to rip off everybody else. I think Viet Nam and Watergate were the main cause, but the ball got rolling with the Kennedy killings. Therefore Dead Kennedys. We are also keenly aware that it is a direct kick in the balls to a religion that sprung up in this country. We have no objections to that but we figure that the name is not just to go "tee he , ha ha, lets make fun of the Kennedy family. That is totally hokey. That's why we didn't put Kennedy faces on our record covers or posters, or anything. The name goes way beyond that.
Flipside: Were you contacted by people representing the Kennedy family in regards to your name?
Jello: Not directly, there was a rumor one time when we were playing in Portland....
Flipside: Were you guys sitting around the table eating cerel or looking over the phone bill thinking "Gee, we've got to think of a name"...?

Dead Kennedys - photo Ed Colver

Jello & Ray - photo R. Hill

Jello: No, an friend of mine thought of it. He said one day "You what would be a really sick name for a band, Dead Kennedys" and I thought hmmmm. He knows we used the name and he's glad somebody used it. His band was playing Springsteen covers in Colorado bars, so Dead Kennedys wasn't appropriate for their level of thinking.

Flipside: What do you think of the kids that go to your gigs?

Klaus: One reason they wear that stuff is because the have a media idea of what they are supposed to be wearing, they also want to be shocking but arne't quite bright enough to figure out, some of them, how to be shocking originally. Most of those people that were wearing swasticas in 1977 have gone on to more better ways of shocking people that are a little more directed to the right direction. The people that come with those things on obviously aren't think about what they are doing as much as just being clones – punk clones, which is no stranger than Castro Street clones.

Jello: Needless to say, since the very nazis are real close to having a real stranglehold on this country as it is, it ain't gonna be the punks that have a field day. They are gonna be the first to go, rubbed out, gassed, shot by the police etc...

Flipside: You speak of Haig, Henkley, a lot of political things, does your audience know who they are?

Jello: A lot of them do and some of the ones that don't are sometimes motivated to find out. There is nothing wrong with sharing a bit of knowledge with people.

Flipside: Are you saying that by doing this, maybe you are encouraging them to open a newspaper, listen to the news, find out...

Jello: At the very least they have their own fucking opinion, instead of being told... going around wanting other people to tell them what to do. Notice we usually try to lay certain issues and incidents out on the table. We don't immediately substitute our own kind of tunnelvision for someone elses. That's not what we are doing at all. The idea of getting people to think for themselves, which is frowned upon is this country pretty severely, part of that means you've got to give them something to think about.

Flipside: Does your audience take you seriously?

Jello: I think you should ask them rather than us. You occassionally find people who take us

a little too seriously.

Daren: They kind of pass over the humor, they take it literally. Like "Kill the Poor" or something, they really think that we want to kill the poor.

Jello: That's not so much taking us seriously, it's not taking us seriously enough to bother to read the lyrics. One thing that's never been gone over, is where Daren came from. He's been in other S.F. bands.

Flipside: S.S.I,?

Daren: That was the first band that influenced me on the so called punk scene. I came and auditioned for them and they said "Hey, we want you to be our drummer". I just started hanging out at the Mab and I started seeing all these great bands, but at the same time I was seeing a lot of shit as well.

Flipside: Do you find it a challenge or do you ever get ugly comments on the fact that your are black and you are playing in a punk band...

Daren: Not so much in the punk scene. That was more like in the white rock and roll scene where clubs wouldn't hire you if you all didn't look the same or if there was one odd member in the band. Like if there was one fat guy or one black guy or something, they just wouldn't hire you. They would rather have a clean cut band. It's not like that so much in the punk scene. It's more open, but then there are still your basic nazi-punk assholes who yell out all kinds of shit.

Flipside: What direction are the DK's going?

Jello: East I guess.

Flipside: Over the Atlantic?

Jello: We do not plan our directions in general. We have more songs up our sleeve that is kind of in the "Holiday In Cambodia" psychodelic direction. None of the flowery Echo and the Bunnymen side of things at all.

Flipside: Was "Too Drunk to Fuck" written from past experiences?

Jello: Hm, yes, it's our token pop song. Something everybody can relate to. The part of sex your parents and church didn't dare tell you about.

Theresa: Why even the girls in my office have heard of that record.

Jello: I'm hoping that this new record will have the same kind of publicity coo that "Too Drunk To Fuck" had. It had a great publicity coo in England cause every right wing church group around came out against it. Maybe we got loads of free publicity which sold a hell of a lot of records, meaning if Jerry Falwell and his idiots pick up on the next one, they will get our message across to a lot of people. Another question is, in reply to those people crying rich rock stars simply because we put out an album that did fairly well overseas, where our money is going is into a compilation album, released in England and eventually released in America.

Flipside: What was your audience like in Europe?

Jello: Again they're real violent, but for the most part it's positive violence rather than macho violence.

Flipside: Maybe because they don't have as many jocks over there?

Jello: We're totally aware of them! That's why we have "Nazi Punks Fuck Off" as one of our songs now. I think that that is one thing that is wrecking the whole idea of slam dancing. When some asshole jock comes in who doesn't realize that it is supposed to be fun and takes it seriously and thinks in order to dance he has to clear the whole dance floor for nobody but himself. Once that is done, oh

boy I win! The whole idea that you have to fucking win at everything is one of the reasons why Americans are so mentally corrupt. Vince Lombardi damage is so deep in our generation because we are taught from all these PE teachers and other people in school that you've got to get a good grade if you are going to go anywhere and the only way you are going to get a good grade is to cheat. Therefore if you cheat you are going to win win win!!! Winning is the only thing says Vince Lombardi, and so you have this whole generation of numbskulls coming out who actually believe that winning is the only thing and anything they do or the way they behave and act is all related to winning. To me, this is the ultimate cancer of the me-generation.

WASTED YOUTH

Wasted Youth were interviewed at Dream's house 9-21-81 by Al and Hud. Brief History: Danny and Huey had a band called Wasted Youth four years ago. They practiced Jimmy Hendrix and Robin Trower in a garage and played one party with Danny drumming. The more recent Wasted Youth developed from the Runs about five months ago. Dave was their singer, but had to quit to take care of business so Danny joined again. Shawn had to quit because he kept getting hurt and Jeff joined on bass. Chet, who used to be in Red Cross, plays guitar and Allen, from the Stiffs, is the drummer (who wasn't here):

AL: What are you trying to accomplish?

DANNY: We want kids to go see shows, dance, and have fun.

CHET: In three or four years, what we're saying is gonna be heard by these kids in South Carolina, who are gonna take our information and apply it to themselves. We're saying Fuck Authority, and they're gonna be walking around thinking that.

AL: Are you purely entertainment then?

DANNY: Yeah, were anti-government, we're anti war and authority...We don't really have a message. We're just sick of being harassed by the police, officials, shitty girlfriends...

AL: Your new album's called Reagan's In.

DANNY: Yeah, Fuck Authority, Teenage Narc that's anti school cops, Unihigh Beef Rag about this girl we hate, We want Heroin, You're a Jerk, and Punk for a Day. We want to put an album out so we can get as much out as possible.

CHET: We have a lot of material. A single is too small.

AL: Do you play in other bands?

CHET: Me and Jeff are in Sherm 49.

JEFF: This black guy that toured with Funkadelic plays drums. We like hardcore funk.

CHET: We have the ability to play that; most of the stuff on the radio can't compete. We have this idea, we'll do the recordings, then look in the Recycler and get four black people. We'll write the music and they'll be on the album cover.

AL: Don't you wanna play it live?

CHET: No, we don't want to play in front of black people.

DANNY: How about what is our music influenced by? Crass, Discharge...

HUD: What about Adam and the Ants?

CHET: What's funny is Darby came back from England and told everybody how cool they were and what they wear. Everybody started

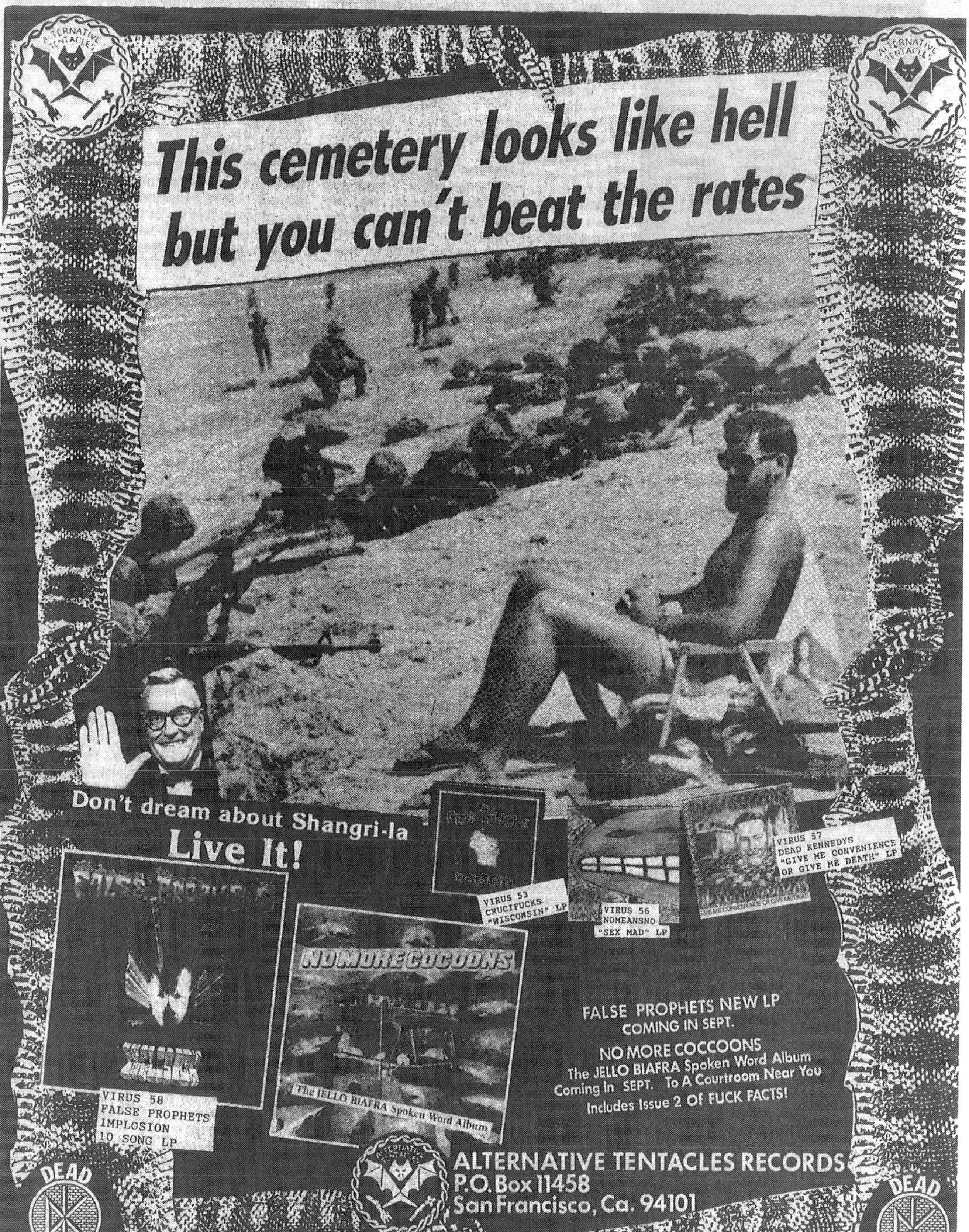

ALTERNATIVE TENTACLES
This cemetery looks like hell
but you can't beat the rates
Don't dream about Shangri-la
Live It!
VIRUS 53
CRUCIFUCKS
"WISCONSIN" LP
VIRUS 56
NOMEANSNO
"SEX MAD" LP
VIRUS 57
DEAD KENNEDYS
"GIVE ME CONVENIENCE
OR GIVE ME DEATH" LP
NO MORE COCOONS
The JELLO BIAFRA Spoken Word Album
VIRUS 58
FALSE PROPHETS
IMPLOSION
10 SONG LP
FALSE PROPHETS NEW LP
COMING IN SEPT.
NO MORE COCCOONS
The JELLO BIAFRA Spoken Word Album
Coming In SEPT. To A Courtroom Near You
Includes Issue 2 Of FUCK FACTS!
DEAD KENNEDYS
ALTERNATIVE TENTACLES RECORDS
P.O. Box 11458
San Francisco, Ca. 94101
DEAD KENNEDYS
PLEASE SEND A SELF ADDRESSED, STAMPED ENVELOPE
FOR A COMPLETE MAILORDER CATALOG, NEWSLETTER & STICKER.

Wasted Youth – photo Ed Colver

dressing pirate style. Then, Black Flag came out with the anti Ant stickers. Now, everybody doesn't like them. It's funny how people can be manipulated.

DANNY: We're sick of getting ripped off by the clubs or the clubs ripping off the kids. We like to play parties--charge fifty cents to get in so we can get twenty dollars for gas. It's keeping the kids happy, not getting uncle Jerry Roach (Cuckoos Nest) rich.

DANNY: He payed us $75 and let four people in on our guest list. My parents were standing outside and Jerry said, Fuck it. If you don't like it, you can leave. He's a sheman. He used to be a female, but he had a cock sewed on!

AL: If you don't make a million dollars as a punk band, are you going to compromise to get that record deal?

DANNY: Yeah sure, but right now we're just doing what's fun. We're doing it for the aggression--not so much the violence but the energy--the kids slamming, you're drunk, you're sweating, you're playing, the lights, the music, it's...

CHET: Let's talk about Dominant Force.

DANNY: Yeah, we're trying to start something in Hollywood. You heard of the Mercenaries and the Lads; Dominant Force will take over.

CHET: Dominent Force is an organization to try to change some things around here and talk some ideas. There are certain people, who have gotten into the scene, but think they're big chiefs.

DANNY: So everybody can unite so they won't get fucked up.

AL: Get fucked up by who? Can everybody unite?

DANNY: That would be best. but, L.A.'s too... It's like Venice hates 18th Street, Sautel hates Culver City, but they're all the same. Like punks hate punks.

AL: Aren't you supporting that by making another gang?

DANNY: Sure, but we'll try to make the strongest one.

AL: This tapes gonna end. Say something to finish up.

DANNY: Destroy power not people.

NERVOUS GENDER

Nervous Gender were interviewed at Shakeys Pizza in Little Tokyo by R. Hill.

FS: Your songs are pretty extreme, should they be taken seriously?

Gerardo: They're not extreme, they're pop songs. We follow the basic formula the Beatles set down.

FS: Who does most of the lyric writing?

Edward: Gerardo does most of the lyrics, I do some of them. The lyrics come first and we fill it up with sounds that are appropriate to the words.

FS: What are your lyrics based on, personal experiences or just fantasy?

Edward: Some are fantasies that hopefully will come across in time.

FS: How did you think your opera came out?

Gerardo: It's not an opera; it's a thing. It fell apart, the first part was good, but it was too much to do in a short amount of time.

Edward: But, a lot came out that we can use for other things. In the video, we'll have a lot more control and be able to use stronger images.

FS: Are any of your songs meant to be antagonistic towards women?

Edward: Are you talking about "Fat Cow"? It was towards a women. I generally don't react strongly towards people I don't like, so I don't write about them. That song was about one woman that I did love, but it didn't work out. So, I felt anger.

FS: When will your album be out?

Gerardo: About three weeks.

Edward: The opera, our thing, will be on it. Some of the opera really will offend and I get paranoid sometimes.

Gerardo: We're scared to shit of Christians and Jews.

FS: Do you think they will take any direct action against you?

Gerardo: I hope they burn the record. You know how they have had record burnings lately? It's sort of like, We always knew that rock was devil music, but this one isn't even trying to hide it.

FS: It's obvious you have pretty strong political views, why aren't they in your songs?

Gerardo: I sing about love, but also my frustrations about love. Take this one song Edward wrote Christian Lovers. It's about mutilating Christians and eating them. It's all because they are responsible for sexuality of any sort--be in bestiality or whatever--to be considered evil. In the Old World people didn't care. We're trying to start a pagan religion 'cause we want people to feel the same way. What people do on their own time is no sin against God.

FS: What happens to the people who don't believe your religion?

Edward: If we are successful at the brainwashing, we won't have to get rid of

Nervous Gender – photo R. Hill

I dreaded this one ... interviewing Siouxsie and the Banshees. We had arrived to meet them at Vinyl Fetish where they had scheduled an unanounced appearance for autographs and P.R. When we arrived the celebrites hadn't shown up. I felt out of the swing of things (so many people in costume / make up) until I recognized people from Anaheim, Eagle Rock, all over, my friends!! After some great gossip and seeing the cover of the 45 Grave single hot off the press, we adjourned for booze at Sloane's and a good game of Pac Man.

Upon return - there they were!! Siouxie was obviously the main draw - signing all manner of autographs, wearing quite a sleek outfit which revealed all she did and did not have from all angles.

We confirmed the interview then made another side stop at Sloane's for cheap booze and a gathering of wills. I wnated to approach the whole thing like the band were not famous - like they were a familiar ordinary L.A. band - to establish a repoire. But they were famous. They know it. And even when they turned out to be just ordinary folks - the whole thing became quite a disappointment - for them as well as us. Granted, they had been up for 22 hours and hadn't a chance to recover from a long London flight. Entering the room, Siouxie drawled, "It's time for creature features."

Also present were drummer Budgie and original guitarist Steve Severin. Steve told us that "Siouxsie and the Banshees" does not describe a singer and her back-up band, rather it should be "Siouxieandthebanshees - one name, one group of people". Steve quickly left to join John, who was asleep in another hotel room.

(I for one didn't want to fall into the rut of interviewing just the 'girl singer' as if she was most important in the band, I don't think Steve wanted that treatment either, but what did they leave us with? "He's just a drummer" says Siouxie.)

Five minutes into our dueling session, Kid Congo from the Cramps and Lydia Lunch's manager entered - it was as if we were crashing THEIR party from then on out. Replies to questions were non-committal and contradictory...

F.S.: Who are you doing your music for?
Siouxie: Ourselves primarily.
F.S.: How do you choose members of your band? (There have been a few personal changes since the original Banshees, and it seems new members are slow to gain a 'permanent' status).
Budgie: I had an audition... I had to meet them in a pub somewhere to see how many pints I could drink!

steve + John

Siouxie and Budgie

Siouxie: Don't lie Budgie.
Budgie: I was in the Slits before this band.
Siouxie: They just have to drop their pants and... (long frustrating attempt to interview, Siouxie would rather sit in the corner with Lydia's manager and snicker at our questions).
F.S.: Was it competitive in the early days (the emergence of so many bands) or was it like a spontaneous combustion?
Siouxie: Yes! That's the right word!
F.S.: Did you take things seriously?
Siouxie: Deadly seriously. Deadly seriously. It was very competitive then.
F.S.: Do you like any of the bands now?
Siouxie: No.
FS: Do you think people in England are maybe more politically active or aware?
Siouxie: I don't know, I wouldn't know, I don't care.
F.S.: How do you write the songs that you do?
Siouxie: It's a load of bollocks, really. I don't write the songs, I let the record company write, they write the lyrics they write the music, they just say "Pose for this picture".
F.S.: Did they ever reject any of your material?
Siouxie: How could they? THEY write it!
F.S.: Do you think your band has influenced alot of people?
Siouxie: I hope not.

(More helpless attempts to do the interview, with all seriousness on our part lost because of the cracks. Had a big fight with Lydia's manager over the Veil. She likes it.).
F.S.: What do you think of New Romantics? (S. and the B.'s guitar player is also in the N.R. band Visage).
Siouxie: I don't want to beat anyone up but they don't show their faces up when we play.

We got kicked out and left feeling rough housed. Then Budgie leaned over the railing and apologized that it had been such a poor interview, it hadn't gone well, we agreed. But "it was the best interview we'd had all day, at least we got a fight going, some real emotion" he commented after saying they had done at least 16 interviews earlier.

It showed. Flipside isn't Rolling Stone, so we get the meat when it is beat. So we crashed a party at Al's Bar with belly dancers and wouldn't you know... turns out I knew half of the people there and had a swell time. It's grand amongst your own. Oh yeah, Siouxie likes garlic on her pizza and Hud says Siouxie has braces. No wonder she doesn't smile! I still think the Scream is top stuff.

Nervous Gender - R. Hill

anybody.

Gerardo: We're already working on our second album. It's going to be called The American Regime and it's all about implicit fascism. The songs range from one about how great it is to be totally controlled.

FS: Depends on who is controlling.

Gerardo: If you're totally controlled it doesn't matter. Americans have this false idea of freedom. Freedom is just another word for nothing left to lose. You can lose your life, then you'll be totally free.

FS: If you don't believe in individuality.

Gerardo: It's not that I don't, but I think it should be programed into you.

FS: You want order.

Gerardo: Yeah, but to the outside world it will look like anarchy.

FS: Don't you think there will be a lot of conflict?

Gerardo: I certainly hope so. That's the difference between Marxism and Fascism. Marxism thinks there will be this world with peace and everyone will love each other. That's stupid, that can never happen because people are not equal. Some people are born to control and others to be controlled.

FS: And you're one born to control.

Gerardo: I certainly hope so. Deep down inside everyone wants to control. That's why everyone is a fascist pig. Whether they try to avoid it or not, that's something else.

FS: Is there any reason you never play with punk bands anymore?

Edward: They don't ask us. Generally most bands are paranoid to play with us no matter what they are.

Gerardo: One thing that stood in our way is that we don't have guitars. It's not my fault I can't play guitar. They see us onstage and go, Like man we don't comprehend. They must be like art rock or something. The electronic bands hate us because we don't sound like Kraftwerk or disco.

Edward: I'd like to see more unity in the scene be it art or punk, but it's just not

happening. It was going on in the beginning, but now there are so many punks—many became punks just because of the TV shows and media image.

SUBHUMANS

While the Subhumans were stranded in L.A. waiting to play the next Friday, we got a chance to do an updated interview with them. This interview was conducted on 9-21-81 by Al, Hud, and Ed Colver.

FS: Obviously you have new members.

Wimpy: Yeah, Jim decided to quit when Jerry decided to quit. Jerry wanted to persue a different line of work—he wanted to become a Jr. Forrest Warden. (The rest of the story is: Jim quit due to a lazy streak. The new drummer is Dim Wit, who was their original drummer. The new bass player is Ron, a punk from Vancouver.) So, that's the present line-up and we have big goals for the future! Our

last album has been out now for eight or ten months so we have to get some new vinyl out. We don't have any record companies backing us so we are open for offers if anybody wants to sink any money on a sure thing!!!

FS: You were just interviewed by the Revolutionary Worker. If they asked you about your politics, what would you tell them?

Wimpy: We definitely don't support communism. We don't really support democracy either—politics of this age is really too fucked up for me to understand. So, I don't worry about it too much. It just seems to be leading towards some sort of confrontation.

FS: You've had bad luck with gigs here.

Mike: Last time was at the Vex. We did get on stage, but they closed it down. Before that we played Polish...

Wimpy: Well, we didn't play Polish Hall.

Mike: Right, we were there waiting to play and then last night Bards Apollo got closed down.

Wimpy: L.A. could be a lot of fun if the police would let their grips of things go. But, when the police come by the punks feel antagonized and start throwing bottles. Then, the police say the punks are violent. So, the police go to the next show. It seems like a vicious circle. They should call a truce. It seems like if you give the police here an inch, they take a mile.

FS: Do you have other jobs?

Mike: Yeah, and we're really in quite a bind right now as a matter of fact. Money is running out; we'll be eating paper soon.

Wimpy: Hopefully, they won't fire us.

FS: What are some song themes?

Wimpy: We've got Canada's Favorite Sport, about nifty jock type people in Canada who spend all their money on souped up cars. Then, a new song America Commits Suicide about the Canadian point of view towards Ronald Reagan and the situation with the Soviets.

Mike: We're right on the firing line if anything happens.

Ron: We're the net in the tennis game!

FS: Do you think you'd go commercial like the GoGos just to make money?

Mike: I think we have a pretty clear idea of what we want to play and what we want to say. We wouldn't mind being hooked up to someone to get our records out to the general public, but we're not about to change our whole direction to accomplish that.

Subhumans - photo Ed Colver

Ron: With this scene, it's easy to be a survivor, but it's hard to stick to your guns.

Wimpy: Some of the real hardcores say that we sold out on our album. They're few and far between and live in gutters. Hardcore is the only way to go. There's no point in dropping your morals now. Things could get totally out of hand. We might as well get as many people as we can to know what's going on.

FS: Is it better than being back home shoveling fish?

Wimpy: I'd rather gut fish than go back on my morals and become a sellout commercial band!!!

Mike: Rather than become a tool of some organization, we'll quit and get straight jobs.

Ron: I may quit, but I'll never get a job.

Nickey Beat and Pat Smear – photo by Al

Black Flag as live as it gets. – photo Pete

Top Jimmy & The Rhythm Pigs – The Cathay house band.

FLIPSIDE NUMBER 28

"Burnout, can't go any farther
Burnout, I'm not getting smarter
Burnout, something once for fun
Burnout, now I can't get it done
Leave me, leave me, leave me alone
now now now
and please don't make fun of me
Burnout, get off my case
Burnout, can't you see my face
Burnout, say it with a grin
Burnout, paranoia set in".
"Burnout" – Red Cross

ISSUE #: 28
DATE: November 1981
FORMAT: 8 1/2x11, rotary web offset
PAGES: 24
PRICE: Free with ROTR 2
PRESS RUN: ?
STAFF: Al, Hud, Pooch, Pete and Robert Hill

- -

Like issue number 21, this was a special insert for the Rodney On The Roq Vol. 2 compilation album. It included edited version of interviews that had been in previous Flipsides, lyrics, photos etc. We got an amazing response from all over the world doing this insert.

FLIPSIDE NUMBER 29

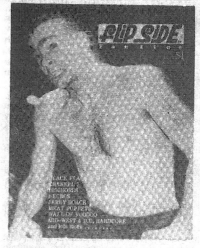

"Sing a song of violence, and listen for the sound
Of all the little soldiers who start to come around
Start with a rumor, a whisper in an ear
Suspicion don't take very long before it turns to fear

Give the chance of glory, give the chance of fame
Give the boy an enemy, give the dog a name
Keep the factions fighting, start them off at school
Keep the factions fighting so you divide and rule
Football teams are splendid and fashion just a tool
Keep the factions fighting so you divide and rule
Frightened of the humans, frightened of the stares
Frightened of the poisons, the pump into the air
Frightened of the chemicles, they spray onto the land
Frightened of the power, they hold within their hands
Frightened of bureaucracy, frightened of the law
Frightened of the government,
and who they're working for
Frightened of the children,
who won't know how to cope
With a world in rack and ruin,
with their technocratic dope
Fear can be a bum thing, a silly and a dumb thing
Fear can be the one thing, that keeps us in the dark
That's keeps us all apart"
"Fear" – by Zoundz

ISSUE #: 29
DATE: December 1981
FORMAT: 8 1/2x11, rotary web offset with 2 color cover
PAGES: 44
PRICE: $1.00
PRESS RUN: 3000
STAFF: Al, Hud, Helen, Michele, Robert Hill, and Shredder.

Pretty standard Flipside if there ever was one. Well, a few minor changes – we dropped the inside color because our printer could never get the registration right anyway. It turned out to be more trouble than the expense was worth.

As far as the scene goes, after L.A. went through a bit of a slump in club action, a place called Godzillas opens way the fuck out in Sun Valley. I proves to be a great place for small to medium sized shows. The place is being run by the BYO, so a lot of the local scene characters are doing such things as taking tickets and bouncing. This place really got things moving again....

MEAT PUPPETS

In early December the Meat Puppets drove in from Pheonix in order to record some tracks for SST and perform around town. Chris, Scott, Kelly and I (Helen) spoke to them after a rousing set at Al's Bar. The band is:
Curt Kirkwood: guitar and vocals
Cris Kirkwood: bass and vocals
Derrick Bostrom: drums
Our talk was disjointed and extremely entertaining, but don't count the interview to help figure out their perplexing and rather demanding form of music/noise.
Flipside: What's your biggest influence in music?
Curt: Mommy, my mommy made me what I am.
Derrick: My mommys heartbeat.
Flipside: What gives you more satisfaction, live performance or studio recording?
Curt: We like live performance, except I want to be able to hit people with my guitar. I like it ALL a lot. Most of the time in interviews people deal with 'like' and 'dislike' and recently I've been thinking of things in terms of 'up' or 'down'. Today when I was driving here I couldn't figure out if I was right side up or upside down and I couldn't figure out how to pull the car over, I lost all my will. My will to

Meat Puppets - photo Al

drive. My will to stear. Only my motor reflexes were working.
Flipside: How do you like Gary Gilmore?
Curt: He's dead.
Flipside: Do you think SST is aligned with Manson?
Curt: No way. The recording session was really super.
Flipside: Did you see the Manson interview with Tom Snider?
Curt: Yeah, I thought it was an accident. It was the only accident that ever happened in history.
Flipside: Is there some deep basis for your music or is it just for fun?
Curt: In a way it's deeper than we can figure. We hear it the same as you do.
Flipside: What about your vocal influences?
Curt: Almost 23 years.
Derrick: Our main influence is the desert.
Curt: The main influence on my voice is smoke. I have a natural ability to sing.
Flipside: Do you believe there is a God?
Curt: I believe there are many Gods.
Flipside: Do the cowboys hassle you in Arizona?
Curt: There's no cowboys there. I am a cowboy.
Flipside: What do you do when you're not doing music?
Curt: Well – we smoke pot, trade pornographic magazines.
Derrick: Draw pictures, read comics.
Flipside: What constitutes a good performance for you?
Derrick: Us liking it.
Cris: We came here to play the freeways. With regards to the audience, we play it with all our hearts.
Flipside: Do you have a fan following?
Curt: Just flies.
Flipside: What your favorite food.
Curt: Bee pollen.
Flipside: Who don't you like?

Curt: I can't think anymore. It's too much of a pain in the butt to think about things I don't like.

CHANNEL 3

Channel 3 are a group of young guys from Cerritos, you know they typical suburb. Perhaps the only thing most people know about them is that they are putting out lots of records with Posh Boy. The name CH3 or Channel 3 means nothing to them. Interviewed by Al and Pete.
Flipside: So what about influences?
Mike M: I like the Jam, and... the Clash.
Flipside: You still like them!
Mike M: Yeah.
Kimm: "Sandinista" is kinda far out.
Flipside: You guys do "My Generation", is that your Who influence?
Mike M: Yeah, I like them.
Flipside: Do you have any hobbies?
Kimm: Play guitar.
Flipside: Dirt bikes?
Mike M: Yeah, but they cost too much, it's unbelieveable, I used to race them.
Flipside: Any of you surf?
Kimm: Burton surfs.
Flipside: Do you consider yourselves a punk band?
Kimm: Yeah, it's the closest thing to call us.
Mike M: The thing that attracted me to punk was that you didn't have to have the limitations, I think that's the original idea, and so if you start giving punk bands certain limitations, "you can't play under a certain speed", then that's not what punk was all about.
Flipside: You guys are real professional, who typed up all of your lyrics?
Mike M: I did, I'm an English major. We are influenced by Hemingway!
Flipside: Did you write most of the lyrics?

CH3 - photo Pete L.

whole world and he doesn't take drugs either. I've seen so many people from Washington, friends, people I've grown up with, you know heroin, all the lumpy headed heroin people... People that get drunk and stupid offend me. Now like I'm not into enforcing stuff. I don't care if people drink or not, but to me it's a lot better to be alert and aggressive, rather than wasted and fucked up. That's a good chance to get your ass kicked, and to me it's just not a good time either.

Flipside: How do you like the new album ("Damaged")?

Henry: I like it, I think we played real good. We worked on it till it came out the way we wanted. Black Flag songs are... they take a lot out of you. After you do even a practice you're emotionally and physically drained. At least that's the way I am.

Flipside: Wasn't it the same with S.O.A.?

Henry: Yeah. S.O.A. was a very very intense band, that's one thing that made us different in the whole DC scene. Like Ian's band was intense, cause Ian is probably one of the best singers I've ever seen. But S.O.A. had this whole cohesive thing, everybody in the band was just doing this one big thing. I used to come a lot more unglued that a lot of people in other bands in DC. Black Flag songs I think hit a little more deeper than the songs I was doing in S.O.A., they sing home a little more, make you feel.

Flipside: When did you meet those guys?

Henry: Ummmm, last year when the came out to New York. I talked to Chuck a couple of times before they came out. They were my favorite band so Ian and I would call them just to talk to them. By the time they came out we knew them kind of, and they stayed over at Ian's house in DC. When they came out again I drove to New York to see them, of course I hung out with them and when I was at my job one night about a week later, they said "Why don't you come up to New York, get up here tomorrow and let's do it" I didn't really understand what they ment. They were just saying Dez wanted to play guitar and I thought they just wanted me to come up and jam with them because I knew all of the songs. Just to have a good time. So I went up there and they said "Here's the deal..." and we practiced and they said "It's happening, do you want to do it?" and I said "Yeah". Quit my job. Sold my apartment. Sold my car. Took off on a bus and here I am.

Flipside: Have you been out here before?

Henry: Yeah, couple of times every summer for the last 4 summers. I used to come out here just to skate. As far as bands I came out here with the Teen Idles last summer when I was roadying. I saw the Circle Jerks up in San Francisco and hung out with all those HB guys... (Greg and Spot enter after being on the phone the whole time).

Flipside: It's awful busy around here.

Greg: It's not usually this busy, but we have our label and we have this tour...

Henry: Plus we have this unbelieveably handsome guy, and like all of these people call up and say "Can I have you mail me some of Henry's dirty socks so I can touch them?", I'd like to say it right now in Flipside, I'm sick of all these groupies, thousands of them (yells out the window) "Get out of here, I told you not to come back!!" Yeah, so we have these groupies with blue uniforms, like to check us out...

Mike M: Yeah, I write all the lyrics. Basically lyrics are just like poetry, you pack the most meaning into as few a words as you can. You can read a lot of meaning into songs. I'm not really into political lyrics because I don't think you're gonna change the world, or reach that many people with it.

influences to the band?

Henry: I brought myself. My DC influences is basically me.

Flipside: I mean as far as anti-drugs, anti-alcohol...

Henry: I don't drink, I don't smoke, I don't take no drugs... I don't care what anybody

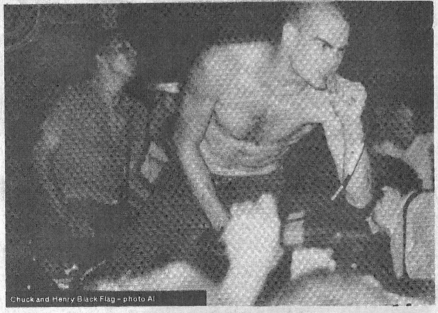

Chuck and Henry Black Flag - photo Al

BLACK FLAG - HENRY ROLLINS

Flipside: How do you like being in Black Flag Henry?

Henry: I like it fine. It's real good. I'm working out fine.

Flipside: Have you brought your DC

else does, it's not tempting at all. Never has been. I don't feel any kind of peer pressure. People can do what they want, I don't give a fuck.

Flipside: What brought on this philosophy that you and Ian share?

Henry: Yeah Ian is my best friend in the

LE FORTE FOUR

L.A.F.M.S. by Robert Hill

LIGHTBULB
TURKEY EDITION

Somewhere in Pasadena, a group of loosely-knit people have been pooling their talents and resources together in the name of artistic freedom. Know as the Los Angeles Free Music Society, these people have, withen the last 6 years, released an impressive collection of records, cassettes and magazines all on a less than shoestring budget. While the earlier releases were put together primarily for the organizers of LAFMS to get their own material out, the LAFMS has expanded to the point of their latest release "Lightbulb 4, Emergency Cassette", with contributors coming from all across the United States and even two from Germany.

The two hour long cassette, released in a limited edition of 200 copies with 150 of those going to the artists, features previously unreleased songs by Bpeople, Human Hands, 45 Grave, Phranc and the Meat Puppets plus various collaborations from regular LAFMS contributors.

Kevin Laffey: "The new cassette really changed the face of LAFMS. It's much more than a group of people in Pasadena now. It's open to anyones contribution".

Fred Nilsen: "The cassettes good because it brings in alot of different stuff, like from the Happy Squid crowd. Those people have been doing something similar for a long time now".

FS: Do you think your future releases will go in that direction, more open?

Kevin Laffey: "It might go in both directions".

Jerry Bishop: "There's a possibility of putting out more of a commercial product and at the same time put out a cass-ette that's only 200 copies".

"DARKER SKRATCHER", the most recent compilation album, is the closest LAFMS has gotten to commercial product. The 5000 copies sold is far more th than the average 200-1000 copies for previous releases.

Jerry Bishop: "There was a big demand for them (Darker Skratcher) at one point. We were only able to press 1000 copies at a time, and we got the first 1000 out and had to wait until we got money back before we could get the 2nd 1000 out and there was a demand for it. So I think we missed maybe a month or two when we could have sold a lot."

Due to the budgetary limitations, the LA FMS is often forced to produce packaging that is convenient, but also interesting and imaginative at the same time. Hnad silk-screened record sleeves, trick or treat bags stuffed with artwork, candy and pieces of tile released as a magazine coloring books; these are all common among LAFMS releases.

Although the LAFMS artists are very prolific with their recorded material, live shows have been very rare, but they have always proven to be very unpredictable. Airway, a LAFMS band that uses subliminal messages played behind a wall of noise, has had pandemonium created with audience members literally taking over the band. The Doodooettes got blackballed from virtually every venue that would let them play, after one performance in a serious jazz club in which Dennis Duck went into a violent frenzy that resulted in broken glass, damaged property (some paint peeled off the floor) and an outraged club owner.

Fred Nilsen: "We have to get ourselves in a frame of mind of playing live again. It takes acertain amount of fortitude to play and have people come up and saw what you're doing is bullshit, because they think you're just dicking around and sometimes you are, but the nature of what we do is that you try things and you go way out on a limb as far as you can go and you try things and sometimes it just floats around and sounds boring, but

the more often you try it, the more often you hit it."

Rick Potts: "Sometimes it works and sometimes it doesn't, but when it does work it's amazing. The situation is so loose that any other way you couldn't come up with that idea".

The spontaneousness of live shows is often carried through onto the records released. On the latest Le Forte Four album "Spin 'n Grin", some songs were recorded in dining rooms, at birthday parties and one using only kitchen utensils and gardening tools. "Spin 'n Grin" was compiled from tapes done over the years, and it shows the variety of material a small group of people can cover. With the success of "Darker Skratcher" and the increasing amount of interest in the LAFMS, it should be easier now more than ever before to get records and cassettes released. Currently in the works is a collaberation with sound artists in Japan. The Japanese groups do basic tracks and send them to LAFMS who will finish and relese those tracks. At the same time four LAFMS groups do basic tracks and send them to Japan to be finished and released. In addition to that, the Doodooettes are working on an album, and there willl undoubtably be more compilation albums to look forward to.....

The LAFMS has come a long way since the days when their tapes would be rejected from tape festivals due to the lack of "aeshtetic quality", and they will surely go a lot furthur. Any correspondance should be sent to:

LAFMS c/o Foundation Boo
P.O. Box 2853
Pasadena, Calif. 91105

LAFMS CATALOG

L.P.'s
1. Le Forte Four "Bikini Tennis Shoes" (1975)
2. I.D. Art #2 (1976)
3. Doodooettes "Live at the Brand"
4. Le Forte Four "Live at the Brand"
5. Blorpessette Vol I (1977-1978)
001B. Le Forte Four "Le Forte Force"
6. Airway "Live at LACE"
7. Blubkrad (1978)
8. Smegma "Five Years Wasted" (1978)
9. John Duncan "Organic" (1979)
10. Blorpessette Vol. II (1980)
11. Blorpessette Vol. II (1980)
12. Darker Skratcher (1980)
13. Le Forte Four "Spin 'n Grin" (1981)

CASSETTE ALBUMS
1. Seldom Melodic Ensemble "Godzillas Mystery Abortion" (1976)
2. Chip Chapman "Magic Beans" (1977)
3. Dennis Duck "Dennis Duck Goes Disco (1977)
4. Ju Suk Reetmeate & Dr. Id "Anode One" (1978)

LIGHTBULB MAGAZINE
1. Back to school issue
2. Halloween Issue
2 1/2. Gobble gobble issue
3. Christmas cassette
3. Lightbulb '78
4. Emergency Cassette (1981)

ID ART
1. Spiral Book 2. LP 3. Coloring Book

SINGLES
1. Airway
2. Slimy Adenoid & the Pablums "The Residents" b/w Joe Potts & Vetza "Mother - Daughter"
3. Slimy Adenoid & the Pablums "Under My Guns"

ROB, JEFFREY, TERRY + WARD

by Shredder

The GUN CLUB don't give a shit. Born and bred under the scorching suns of Dallas, El Paso and (yuk yuk) Los Angeles, rifle in hand, they arn't playing for YOU to have a good time (although you're gonna anyways). In this ever nifty world of "1 2 I fucked your mom" high speed noise, and sickly feeble populisms, British guitar disco (called post punk) and all in all music that cares, music that attempts too...whatever, and music that, worst of all, sounds like all other music, the Gun Club will scare you shitless, then spit at you, make you laugh at the evening you just had. When they scare you it won't be in the corny cheesy Boneheads and 45 Grave style, when they spit at you it will be with a lot more loogy than any so called hardcore band in L.A., when you laugh it will be with more alcoholic breath than Fear or Top Jimmy and the Rythm Pigs can supply. And what kind of music do the Gun Club play? Here's a shot at it: Lee Ving dresses up as Marc Bolan, picks up a slide guitar, and recites a Jack Kerouac quote, over and over, with Arabic music played on mosrites in the background. Of course it's confusing, the skinheads stand there trying to dance but the guitars keep starting and stopping, the art creeps don't understand the words and therefore don't <u>relate</u>, and the rockabilly Cramps fans just cannot take the thumping four beat, but everyone goes home saying they loved it,... this isn't an easy article to write.

"I was up this morning, blues walking like a man,
me and the devil walking side by side,
I'm gonna beat my woman till I'm satisfied"
Robert Johnson, blues performer of 30's & 40's

Jeffrey Lea Pierce, singer for the Gun Club, walks onto the Whisky stage on a very very sweaty uncomfortable summer night. He's kind of pudgy and a little short, I heard that they played swamp music, expecting wimpsville. What I got was revenge of the wimps, the most brutal attact on innocent instruments since...since I don't know, maybe the Munsters theme. Bassist Rob, member of 45 Grave, is the best bass player in L.A., guitarist Ward from O.C. is just a thrasher and the only person I've seen make a guitar cry and beg for mercy on stage, drummer Terry is infamous and deservedly so, singer Jeffrey besides being somewhat of a good joke teller, is the loosest, most uncaring singer since Mr. Rotten himself, only in an ever more perverse way. He says his biggest sexual fantasy or tease is to see a blond girl standing in the woods holding a rifle. A few articles on him have de-

scribed him as hateful, vicious and downright a nasty bummer. Talking to him makes the word sweet come to mind, you wouldn't know it form the lyrics:

"I'm gonna buy me a gun just as long as my arm,
and kill everyone who ever done me harm"
Even worse, some call the band rascist, but their lyrics really can be looked at in a historical sense. "Searching for Niggers down in the dark", is real, uncut lifestyle. On Saturday nights in Texas you kill minorities for thrills. Lastly they are called spooky, who can argue? I don't mean "Crabs in my left eye" spooky, that's silly. I mean "Going to the Mountain with a fire spirit, I will be cheating the whole ritual" spooky. The back of their album on Slash, called "Fire of Love" has rows of voodoo potion bottles with the names of their songs on them. I want to know how many of you big shit TSOL followers have ever been to an occult shop, or gotten a whiff of some voodoo perfume. I guess you're all too busy worrying about this political problem, and that social worry to walk through cemeteries for fun. You will see a big turn in this scene, if you haven't caught on to it already: all that bullshit caring is going to melt into pure entertainment, drunken fun, dancing and loud clubs. Gun Club, Fear, Castration Squad, Boneheads amoung others, have all displayed this lackadaisical nihilism at one time or another. It's out and out selfishness, you better get yourself in on the fun fast,before the people already in on it won't let you figure out the punch line to their very inside joke.

"We can fuck forever but you'll never get my soul"
from "Sex Beat", The Gun Club

"What I'm starting to see us acquire", says Jeffrey Lea. "is a certain amount of control over the audience which we destroy by turning into a parody of ourselves before the night is out. Sorta makes em feel left out, who cares". If you are fed up with the overbearing politics of L.A.'s so-called hardcore (TSOL, Shattered Faith, Bad Religion, etc, ad infinitum, all good bands, but let's face it, a little tiring) and you are fed up with the flock of sappy foreign bands, and you're fed up with the radio-cock-sucked newwavepopeldullo bands, and you're fed up with all that progressive psychedelic scum (Aphoticulture, die!) and you're so fed up with that you could just give two wet farts about life, grab a large bottle of vodka, you're car keys,and a wicked female, head on to the closest Gun Club performance, and put your God forsaken life back into the right perspective.

Necros: Corey, Todd, Barry and Brian.

NECROS

The Necros were interviewed October 13, 1981 after practicing. Present were Andy (ex-guitarist), Brian Pollack- guitar, Barry Hensler- vocals, Corey Rusk- bass, Todd Swalla- drums and Allison who did the interview.

Flipside: How long have the Necros been a band?
Corey: With this line-up since march.
Flipside: Do you see a time when you'll just break up? Forget the name Necros, start other bands?
Brian: Perhaps.
Todd: Yeah, in about a year.
Corey: I don't know if I'd like to last longer than that.
Barry: The Necros lasted over two years, and it's lasted as long as it has simply because there was no one else here, it was all we had. You couldn't like break up and start a band

with new people.
Corey: When it started out there were like 4 or 5 people here and that's it. We didn't know anybody in Detroit or Lansing or Ann Arbor, or anywhere, there was nobody else. It was like break up and do what?
Flipside: How do you compare yourselves with L.A. bands?
Corey: When we started, originally we hadn't heard any L.A. bands, I think we heard the first Black Flag ep.
Barry: We had the Germs LP too.
Corey: But those aren't our influences at all, and since then we've progressed and obviously we've heard plenty of L.A.'s music since then. We don't try and play like L.A. bands. Some of these songs on the new ep were like the first Necros songs. There's older demos of them that are slower, and they were written before we'd heard any L.A. music.
Barry: If it can happen in L.A. it can happen here. Like in DC it's true, those kids never

heard any Black Flag stuff and Eddie (Mashety) of the Untouchables was doing like Greg Ginn, like real atonal guitar solos and stuff. It can happen anywhere. It just happened in L.A. and they had the media.

WALL OF VOODOO

At last a Flipside interview with the fun loving Voods, taken place on the eve of an east coast tour, at a sports bar by the Masque with Hud, Al, and Pooch interviewing Stan, Joe and Chas. We launched into a myriad of pertinent topics of debatable historical significance (these guys go way back).
Al: How did you get started?
(Trying to make this concise), Mark, Bruce and Chas were in the Skulls around the start of the Masque (Oct. 77) and Joe and Stan had been living together and playing a lot of alternative styles.)
Stan: The way I found Joe was through an ad in the Recycler which said: "Drummer looking for musicians interested in Iggy Pop, John Coltrane, Sun Ra and the Ramones". Me and Joe had a trio that didn't go anyplace but in an old garage. (When the Masque started Stan formed a band called the Model Citizens, while Joe and Geza were playing in the Bags, Mark, Chas and Bruce had left th Skulls and Bruce finished a brief stint in the Weirdos. All the while Stan and Joe started to write sound track music for movies).
Stan: I put on a nice Brooks Brothers suit and went upstairs (Across from the Masque) and rented an office out under the auspices that we were going to be a small mail order company selling Sea Monkeys or something. Mark literally moved in and lived there. We were such failures at getting any of our music accepted for movies, that it kinda started turning into "well, we ought to start playing again". (Eventually Bruce joined and almost immediately they played their first job as Wall

Wall Of Voodoo in London - photo Pete L

FS: Tell us about your new record.
Greg: Well, there's 15 songs on it....
FS: Does it sound like the Gogos?
Greg: No, it sounds nothing like the Go-gos! It sounds like the Circle Jerks, some old stuff, same type of music we always play. It just sounds a little better, the quality, you can hear all of the drums! And all the other instruments.
FS: What made you do "Put A Little Love In Your Heart"?
Greg: We heard it on the radio one day and we thought it would be funny to put on the record. So we just decided to do it and made it as stupid as possible.
FS: I hear you and Keith are big Motley Crue fans.
Greg: We like Motley Crue, they're alright, you can't take them too seriously though. They're cool people too. We were practicing at this one place and they were practicing next to us and they came over and watched us and thought we were cool so....
FS: Will you ever be playing with them?
Greg: I doubt it. It would be pretty funny, we'd have a little war.
FS: Is that the direction your band is going in, heavy metal?
Greg: No, I don't know what direction we're going in, every direction.
FS: The new album sounds more varied.
Greg: Yeah, it more varied, it should be out in about a week or two.
FS: You keep saying that!
Greg: This time for sure, right after we sign on the dotted line, then everything will be happening.
FS: What do you think of the L.A. punk scene?
Greg: We have the best bands in the world in L.A.
FS: What about the audiences?
Greg: They're pretty good, not too many fights the last couple of shows I've been to. The fighting is pretty stupid most of the time, but I think it's gotten a lot better. People realize that if they fuck up then there's no place to go anymore. Everybody's getting their shit together.
FS: I hope so. Why arn't the Circle Jerks playing around anymore?
Greg: We haven't practiced in a long time. We've been working on the record getting the art work together and we haven't had time to practice or do anything. When we get the record out, then we'll practice and play, do a tour or something. Last gig we did was New Years at Godzillas, a most memorable gig. One disturbing fact about Godzillas, even more than the new bouncers outside - it's supposed to be an L.A. club, so why do they play English music inside? It's really stupid. They should support the L.A. bands first or American bands first, do everybody a favor. Buy our album, read the book, see the movie, get the t-shirt, the buttons, the stickers......
FS: The cartoons! I saw this guy on TV some religious guy that was smashing all these rock albums....
Greg: Yeah, there's this guy that plays albums backwards like "Stairway to Heaven" to see what they say...they have mentioned us a few times. They recited the words to "Live Fast Die Young", it was really funny. And then they prayed for us and all the ounk rockers.

Greg (photo J. Sargent)

the other Jerks (photos M. Probert)

Of Voodoo (with Brendan on drums) at Immaculate Heart girls school with the Eyes and Holly and the Italians. When Mark tripped and broke the stage lights they performed in the dark, and rather than admit their mistake, they called it a concept.)

Stan: That really started our lives, right there. For the first three week we didn't name ourselves. Me and Mark were mixing some tapes down and I said "Mark, is this like a wall of sound?", and he goes "No, I don't think so" and I said "Maybe a wall of voodoo" He goes "Yeah!". We finally settled on Wall of Voodoo because it was something that kind of communicated the mood that we wanted to get across.

(Soon the band finished up an Ep, with some of the sound track material inbetween, and got it distributed through Index, a subsidiary of IRS, but were eventually signed to IRS proper.)

Joe: I can remember when people were playing more or less with the same kind of spirit as the hardcore scene now but not with all of the violent overtones.

Stan: I remember when punk first started it was like a paradox because it was negative imagery actually representing something that is positive. Now there's a faction of people that will never see the paradox. They're never going to see irony in it at all. They're just going to see the "destroy, blood, guts..."

Joe: They people who don't even understand what "White Riot" was about, I mean to them the first Clash album was "Sandinista". This is not to say that there is no legitimacy to the things behind what the 'surf punk' trip is about because in a lot of ways I think it is great. The energy is really really great.

Stan: Sometimes it's more important for me not to remember all these things, to not get too jaded about it. You do too much thinking about it, too much "I've been around for this long", and that's the start of a lot of bitterness. Things like that can really keep you from going forward.

FLIPSIDE NUMBER 30

"Memories as time goes by
Memories of a age gone by
All that's left is the time that's spent
Living in a dream time,
Inbetween prancing and dancing romancing.
Ask if she knows where her mind goes
Ask if she knows where the garden grows."
"Mind Gardens" - The Salvation Army

ISSUE #: 30
DATE: March 1982
FORMAT: 8 1/2x11, rotary web offset with 2 color glossy cover
PAGES: 52
PRICE: $1.00
PRESS RUN: 4000
STAFF: Al, Hud, Helen, Pooch, R. Hill, Shredder, and Michele

Gosh, this was a strange time now that I think back... In the issue, we had record reviews and a Words of Wisdom page and Live reviews and yes the wonderful scene reports. All the stuff that made this zine so much fun back then. Godzillas and the Ritz and the Whisky a Go Go were happening places to go to! (Remember Geronomo tablets) Lots to do, the scene was strong and the bands were great esp. bands like Salvation Army .Key word was variety. No time for the movies the scene was a boiling!!

Rodney with the Bunnymen - photo Lydia

ECHO AND THE BUNNYMEN

(While sight seeing in L.A.)
Will: Look at those skaters!! He skates backwards.
Jake: I skated once down a main road.
Debra: How did you stop?
Jake: I had to grab on to a lampost or something and sitdown. But that's like good fun.
Lydia: How did you get the name...
Will: Oh, that's a silly question!
Will: 877,998,345,629 times that question has been asked.
Lydia: It's the first time asked by me...
Jake: That's weird because of every single person that asks that question, it never gets printed so nobody knows the answer.
Lydia: Well it will this time!
Will: (Sounding like a robot). Where did we get the name Echo and the Bunnymen? Answer is, one, Mac used to live with a bloke called Paul Alabach in a flat in Liverpool, me and Mac were making tapes but we didn't have a name. We got asked to play with Teardrop Explodes at Eric's in Liverpool and we needed a name quickly. We couldn't think of a name as we didn't think it was very important - Paul Alabach took out a big list of names that he was kind of thinking of cause we asked him. One of them was Echo and the Bunnymen. Up to this very day we didn't know what we were going to be called. We sort of went on and Julian Cope went on and said "Here is Echo and the Bunnymen", that was it. We picked that one that night.

THE EFFIGIES

If you have to call something the beginning, it would be a club called La Mare's for Chicago punk scene. That club quickly closed, supposedly the police set the fire that burned it down. Chicago has always been known for it's political corruption, which is very evident in getting and keeping bars open, especially with the police payoffs. This brings us to the Oz Club, which happened at a couple of locations, and is responsible for spawning the Chicago punk scene of today. Most of the hardcore from the La Mares days ended up at inner city bars like Oz, but as time went on they were replaced by a new crowd and new bands like the Subverts, Strike Under, and the Effigies. The Effigies are perhaps the biggest and most popular of these bands now. They have an album out and just completed their first tour to the West Coast. We're glad to get the band exposure and see parts of the country that we have. The record didn't seem to be distributed too well, so we were virtual unknowns this tour. This fact led to the Effigies breaking off with Autumn Records and planning their own release in the near future. As for the tour, well, here in L.A., they barely got off two gigs--both at Godzillas. The band was left with little money but a lot of experience. We interviewed the band on one particularly dull night. They all seemed to have a lot on their minds and showed that a lot of thought was going into what they do.

John: With punk, the name Effigies was sort of the way it was with the fashion and shit to to begin with. At least, that's how I like to think it was when we started out. Now, it's almost become a parody of itself with fashion nonsense.

Steve: We think of ourselves as a hardcore band, but not as a thrash band. We've got some fast songs, but we've got some slow ones too. Some have a disco rhythm behind them. Thrash music is good, but there's so many bands these days that it becomes repetitious.

Oli: We don't want to sound like the next band or every other across the country. Lyrics in punk are fifty percent of the whole thing. If you're a real punk band, then you have something to say. If you don't, you might as well going the heavy metal scene. John writes all our lyrics and, as far as I'm concerned, they have a lot to say.

John: You gotta tell people to to think for themselves--get them to wonder why Nazi punks are assholes instead of just telling them. Scenes need leaders, but Jello Biafra comes out with this big Nazi Punks Fuck Off. How many people are gonna follow what he says 'cause it's the thing to do? Bands should get right into the muck and say, Why don't you take a look at yourselves and tell me what you see. Imitation is a sincere form of flattery, but all these thrash bands are trivializing everything Black Flag is trying to do. If you really want change, put yourself up as an example and say, Look, this is what I'm doing. If you want to do it, fine, but, at least look at it. I'm not trying to knock anybody over the head, but we're here!

Oli: People said we went over really good in L.A., so why don't we move out here. That's just fine but we want to put Chicago on the

Effigies at Godzillas - photo Ed Colver

Flipside: Are you guys all friends?
Greg: We get along, we don't all hang out together. From past experience when people hang around together too long they get on each others nerves. Like this guy (Troy) is into getting high, I'm into video games and he's into just being by himself, really. We get into arguments but we work things out.
Flipside: Well if Rickey writes all of the songs, do you feel like your voice is being left out?
Greg: We were just talking about that today. I want to start doing more, up to this point Rickey carried the band. I'm gonna be more active, you'll see.
Rickey: (Rolls his eyes and grins).
John: (spiritual leader and drug guru) And you can interview Greg's new band in 6 months!
Flipside: What about the backwards guitars and drums like on the single?
Greg: Well, we can't do that live but...
Rickey: When I get into a studio I like to twist music, like clay you can mold it, most bands go in and play like the do live but if you add these things and if it goes with the music, it adds to the whole "trip" I want to convey. We mix art and pop and dance and...
Flipside: What will you call your first album?
Rickey: "Looking Thru The Walking Four O'clock".
Flipside: How about religion?
Rickey: We're devout Roman Catholics, at least I am (Rickey has a religious picture of a heart with barbed wire around it on his wall and Hud comments that it so "gross") ...but yes it is possible to be catholic and psychedelic at the same time.
(Well that ended the interview, oh we forgot to tell you why they call themselves Salvation Army. It went something like this: they were

map. So, when this tour is over, we're going back to Chicago, back to our jobs. (We talked about lots more like how the radio sucks in Chicago (it amazes me how people complain about KROQ and KNAC, Black Flag at ten in the morning, what more do you want? is their comparison), blues in Chicago, the abundance of preppie types, and about music in general. One last thing we have to say is on the Effigies manager, John Bonham. If more people had his enthusiasm, we would really have a great national scene.)

SALVATION ARMY

The Salvation started just about a year ago, it was Rickey Starts Idea. He put an ad in the Recycler and met up with John, their first guitar player. After looking a long time for a drummer they found Troy, from Rickey's old High School. The first Salvation Army gig took place in San Pedro on June 11. John, who first introduced the band to New Alliance, grew tired of the bands style and eventually left the band. They recorded the single "Mind gardens" just before he left, he was soon replaced with Greg from Youth Brigade.
Rickey: I like a lot of mid-60's stuff and I like to incorporate that in with new music and stuff.
Flipside: Do you have psychedelic "drug" influences in the lyrics and music?
Rickey: I like the surrealistic level, surrealism and certain things that make you see things, I think it's interesting, it makes you delve into things that people don't understand.
Flipside: Where did you get the name Rickey Start?
Rickey: It came out of my wall. (Everyone looks at the wall) That one! I get vibrations from that one, I kept hearing "Rickey Start", well not exactly Rickey Start but I incorporated that with... well, because it sounded a lot like that too.
Flipside: What kind of followers are you getting?
Rickey: Hopefully somebody out there! We get some of the people who don't really like some of the harder sounds.
Greg: I don't understand, like when we play and people have to get out there and slam into each other. We don't play that violent.
Rickey: We have a beat but...

Greg: They don't care about the music and don't even listen to what is being said.
Rickey: Oh, somebody came up to me at Godzillas and like I was kidding around on stage saying we were the Byrds or Chocolate Watchband, and this kid goes: "Arne't you the lead singer of the Byrds?" and he was serious. I wish, ya know. I go "No", so I guess they don't really know. People say Echo and the Bunnymen are like "new psychedelic" bands, but it doesn't sound anything like the psychedelic records I have. I like a lot of 60's punk and garage...

Salvation Army: Troy, Greg, Rickey - photo Chris

Various Bangs, Salvation Army and Romans at the Mercury Arts Center – photo Al

Flipside Presents at the Whisky...

making fun of hardcore names that sounded so violent, all the while being hard pressed to come up with a name for their first gig. Someone said "Goodwills", John didn't like that (John being the hardcore punk of the bunch), so while on the topic of Thrift Stores someone jokeingly said "Salvation Army". John liked it because it had "Army" in it, and Mike liked it because that's where he got all of his paisley shirts and Troy liked it because he wanted to get the naming ceremony over with.)

(As you know Rickey Start is really Michael Quicero, Greg is Lewis. Unfortunately this band that I liked well enough to put on our cover, soon changed members and name (to The Three O'clock), lost all the "punk" edge that I thought made them so special and became just another wimpy pop band. Too bad, now Greg has his own band "Lewis and Clark").

FEAR

Fear were interviewed by Shredder and Grant Miller.
Derf: First I want to say that we are all homosexuals. Ya know we played our first gig in Frisco, but we are from L.A. so everyone thinks we're locals there, but we're not, we're from... Frisco!
Shredder: Do you like the crowds better now or then or what?
Spit: Yes.
Shredder: What do you think of punk rock violence?
Lee: What violence?

Grant: What about the Stardust, Derf?
Derf: When, I don't remember. I guess I got my brains knocked out. Seriously, someone told me that the guy beat me up because I spit in his ear during the performance.
Shredder: How seriously do you take yer stage attitude?
Lee: Very!
Derf Not at all. As me if me and Lee agree on a lot of things.
Shredder: Do you?
Derf: What do you say Lee?
Lee: You answer first...
Derf: Yeah!
Lee: Absolutely nothing!
Grant: Do you get a lot of trouble for your stage jokes?
Lee: Sometimes, as strange as it may seem, even some skinheads think we are insulting them, and we care about that SO MUCH that

Yeah, this is Fear.

we continue to do that at every chance we get. Some people walking around with shaved heads, pretending to be whatever they think they are don't get he joke. They think we are actually personally attacking them.
Derf: Which we are!
Shredder: What was bing on TV like? (Saturday Night Live).
Lee: The guy who did the interview just kept yacking and not giving us a chance to talk. The only time we got a chance to talk was when we interupted him and then he tried to say we were subversives and anti-American, just cause we were complaining about the way things were.
Grant: Was he right?
Lee: I don't...
Derf: He was a latent homosexual...
Lee: No. Saying what you think is the American way, and not saying what you think they do in Russia, that's what this whole thing is about.
Shredder: what did you think of the Decline?
Lee: You have to understand that Penelope was trying to ensure the scenes continuance by making a movie cause at the time it was real iffy... She didn't want to make the movie so outrageous that oh you know "Well fuck, that's what it's like!? Well then Wilbur ain't getting the car friday night to watch the faggots downtown." She was trying to show that it really is just an American movement.
Shredder: But you know it isn't.
Lee: Yeah, well, yeah it is. To show you're upset is at least to show that you are not being lulled to sleep by the crapola on TV.
Derf: We try to turn most people into bigots.
Lee: No really, to show anger is to show you're thinking, and that is American.
Shredder: But it doesn't make sense when you're on stage expressing conservative ideas, with the "fag this and fag that".
Lee: Well there are radical conservative attitudes, there's a large segment of the population that's gay, and if we rake 'em a little ya know "What's he saying!". it's better than having them jerk each other off when they paid $6 to get in. We tune them out of that world they are burried in, into some other world for awhile. They start to pay attention to the band. We don't want to come on the

stage like Darby and be so fucked up that he can't see straight and not get any point across to the audience.

Shredder: Why do you think bands with more radical ideas, bands that at least say something, go up in the charts in England?

Lee: In England the situation is totally different. Everyone hates everyone. People are burning each others houses down. It's black against everyone white against everyone. This isn't anything you can tune out. Ya can't cruise down to he Country Club or Gil Turners or down Sunset and forget it all. It's real there. Here, the only thing to protest is apathy, and it abounds, it's a monster enemy. That's why REO Speedwagon is number one here and the Specials are number one there.

Shredder: What about New York?

Lee: Well New York is a jazz town. It's alright if you like saxophones. So we try to take these apathetic people and try to make them think.

Shredder: It seems like they get more and more apathetic?

Lee: Well that's true. Either we make em aware or we give them enough rope to go hang themselves. Either way, they are out of that apathetic core.

NEW ORDER

This interview was done at two seperate intervals. Neither of the members knowing it. Peter Hook was done behind Perkins and Bernard was done behind the Tropicana. It was difficult but who else by Flipside would come through for you?

Helen: Do you say it all in your music or what?

Peter: (No comment).....

Helen: At least say why? Why would you give the L.A. Times and interview and not us?

Peter: I didn't do an interview.

Helen /Debra: Well they have one!

Peter: That's news to me.

Debra: Why won't you do an interview with people that know something about the band?

Bernie (above) and Peter New Order - photos by Lydia

Peter: I am doing an interview! If people want to know, they can come to the shows.

Helen: You wouldn't sit down and do an interview?

Peter: No.

Helen: Why?

Peter: Don't want to. Bored. Why should I sit down with people that I don't know. They can just walk up to me if they want to know.

Dave: (roadie) I think you're being taped.

Peter: I know (reaches over and shuts the tape recorder off).

-- Now at the tropicana- --

Lydia: What do you do with the band?

Bernie: I'm the lead guitarist and singer.

Lydia: What's this with you not wanting to do interviews?

Bernie: We just don't! I don't see why I sould sit in front of people I don't even know and tell them about me. I feel what goes on in my personal life if my own business and no one elses.

Lydia: what about pictures?

Bernie: I just don't like taking them. None of us do.

Lydia: That's what you think! I got one of Peter and he even posed for me!

Bernie: (laughing) Yeah, and you even got one of me!

ANTI-PASTI

Anti-Pasti were interviewed by Carol Canada at Godzillas after their second nights performance. There were quite a few people in the room when the interview was being taped. Anti-Pasti are one of the top "Oi" bands from England. Their album "The Last Call" has been on the English charts since it first came out.

Flipside: What's you first impression of America?

Will: It's alright, we haven't been able to see much.

Flipside: What did you think of the fighting tonight?

Will: It's much more vicious here!

Flipside: How long have you been together?

Kevin: Me and him have been together quite a few years!

Flipside: No, seriously, as a band?

Kevin: Oh as a band, not as lovers. About 3 years.

Flipside: Did you get visas to get over here?

Will: Yes.

Flipside: How old are you?

Will: Nineteen...

Flipside: What does Anti-Pasti mean anyway?

Will: I don't know.

Flipside: A lot of people mispronounce the name and make jokes about it.

Will: What happends to Anti-Pasti is like they spell it wrong. They spell it like "Pasta".

Flipside: Anti Noodles, you're against Italian food.

Dugi: (Dugi takes the tape recorder and starts to interview Will) At least it's good we got Oi lads here now. That's what we've been wanting for years, what do you think of that?

Will: They're just wankers!

Dugi: I'm hearing a lot about these groups now, I mean like Journey and Foreigner. The just packed Madison Square gardens, two nights in a row! I mean you guys are playing here, in two nights you pull 1500 people, these other bands get ten thousand a night.

Will: We could pack it out if we wanted to!

Dugi: That's fair enough then...

RF7

RF7 were interviewed at Darbys Coffee shop in Canoga Park by Carol Canada.

Flipside: Do you feel distant from the L.A. scene being out here in the Valley?

Walt: Not at all.

Nick: Yes, we have no friends. I live in an apartment and no one wants to visit me. I have probably 5 friends.

Flipside: How do you want to be popular?

Felix: By having people hate us.

Nick: We like that thought. What if we had even longer hair, wouldn't that make them even more mad.

Felix: And we'd play even faster.

Walt: We'd play so they'd hate us but they'd love us.

Nick: But who's them, that's my question.

Flipside: Do you think when your album comes out you'll draw a bigger or different crowd?

Felix: Maybe not around here, but elsewhere.

Walt: We like the crowd we got now.

Flipside: When on stage what do you model your singing after?

Anti Pasti - photo Ed Colver

RF7 Walt, Felix, Nick & Robert

Walt: Alice Cooper! (laughter)
Felix: No. I think more like the Clash, Darby, Dez...
Flipside: Did we cover what RF7 means?
Nick: Names are stupid for bands.
Felix: We were just thinking of non-sense names, like Nerves or the Forks.
Walt: So we just labeled ourselves.
Nick: The Turtles were never Turtles, the Beatles never acted like bugs...
Walt: The best thing about it is that it means nothing. That's what our music means, nothing.
Felix: It defies catagorization.
Walt: Right, thank you.
Flipside: How come a majority of your lyrics are related to God, Satan and religion?
Nick: That's the indecision. Speed and Alcohol make people go against God.
Felix: I'd say we never really wrote songs about girls, or driving cars, or drinking beer. After playing around we saw that a lot of people were anti-God, so we changed the title of "Hey Tequilla" to "Jesus Loves You".
Flipside: Are you essentially pro-God then?
Felix: Personally I don't care.
Nick: God is like, I am really high now, and can be cool with my friends, and go against him. Or I am really alone in my dark room and want him to like me. We like to get drunk, getting drunk is really fun. I think marijuana is a plot by the government to erase millions of people. It's changed the whole American lifestyle, people are becoming too paranoid, and are afraid to be themselves. We do promote Magnum beer. How about when people snort cocaine and run around like idiots, unless you give them more. They rip off their own friends, or feel excluded just for that one or two more lines of cocaine. I'd rather drink Magnum.
Walt: That's very true, that's why I like cocaine.

CRUCIFIX

Crucifix were interviewed in February at Dreams house. Present were Chris (17) the drummer, Sothira (18) singer, Jim (older) guitar, and Matt (16) bass.
Flipside: Is this your first time down here?
Band: Yeah, our first tour anywhere outside of San Francisco.
Flipside: What did you think the audience would be like down here?

Matt: We went to a show at the Palladium and saw people beating each other up. We didn't know what to expect. We thought our audience would be like that.
Sothira: We heard all of the horror stories.
Flipside: Are they into stage diving up there?
Band: Yeah, rarely, but every once in awhile when there's a big show.
Chris: Mostly at smaller shows they thrash around a bit but that's all. They stagger around a bit.
Matt: Too much alcohol.
Flipside: At the Palladium you guys were watching or thrashing?
Band: We were watching (laughter!)
Chris: It used to be like dancing, but now it's more like killing each other.
Chris/Matt: We used to do that, dive off the stage and stuff..
Flipside: But now you're older.
Band: Yeah, wiser (laughter!)
Flipside: How did you come up with the name?
Matt: It just came out that way?
Chris: We were thinking Crucifixion or something like that, this friend of ours said, why not "Crucifix". We're not religious or sacreligious.
Flipside: What your stand on religion?
Chris: We he's (Matt) a catholic...
Matt: I went to school, but it does not mean that I am a catholic. I'm against organized religion.
Chris: He (Sothira) is a Buddist.
Sothira: I'm against all religion that turns into mass media. Like on TV that type of thing. I'm into religion as a personal thing...
Flipside: Who wrote the song "Religion Kills"?
Sothira: I did. I write all the lyrics and they write all of the music.
Flipside: You say you are "political", but not in your lyrics, how's that?
Chris: We don't want to tell people what to do, they can do what they want. Like bands like Warzone that preach on stage and use the music as a backdrop. We're music to

Skulls give a nostalgic performance at the Cathay Masque reunion party – photo Al

Crucifix: Jim, Matt, Chris, Sothira - photo Al

DATE: April 1982
FORMAT: 8 1/2x11, rotary web offset with 2 color cover
PAGES: 52
PRICE: $1.00
PRESS RUN: 4000
STAFF: Al, Hud, Pooch, Helen, Michele, Robert Hill, Tar, Shredder and Pete

- -

This is the last issue that we print scene reports in, our reasoning was that we believe fanzines should be regional, and since it was out of Flipsides ability to do a good job covering the national scene, we just decided to drop them. It was a pain in the ass: people writing bogus reports, just hyping their own band or group of friends, printing rebuttals to reports, not getting consistent, responsible, unbiased reporters – and for what? A scene of 10 people that could be better covered with their own fanzine (if they weren't so lazy to do one). Of course this thinking was quite the opposite of what others felt, and consequently another zine (Maximum Rock N Roll) sprung up to cover the "void" left by our lack of "national and world" scene coverage. It was never Flipside intention to really cover anything but L.A. (hence the old "Los Angeles" prefix to our name), I guess we just lost sight of that. It would simply take too much time and energy to go "big time" with a staff that is extremely part time and with no real profits to speak of. Ah well, I can say that it has worked for the better.

As for L.A., well Godzillas had come and gone, and with it some things were created, some destroyed. About this time L.A. got it's first taste of "skinheads" (remember Skinhead manor) and punk gangs. The gangs at the Fleetwood were not real "organized", but the reaction to those pre-gangs were the real thing- a weird combination of mexican street gang violence and English skinhead blind

listen to and have fun to.
Flipside: What are you political views then?
Band: Anarchists, anti-war...
Matt: We hate everyone, we hate everything, ha ha, I like things...
Band: Yeaha, he's a bitter art student.
Matt: I'm a wanna be.
Chris: He wants to be a biker.
Matt: Ask Jim about his business.
Flipside: So you fix guitars as a business?
Jim: ....yeah....... (silence)
Band: (Laughs). He tried out for UFO!
Jim: I don't like talking about it.
Matt: Get him drunk, he'll tell you.
Jim: It was just an audition, but shoot!
Matt: Get Sothira drunk and he'll tell you about Cambodia, in detail (Sothira tells us about living there and in England. The only reason he is in the U.S. is because the U.S. destroyed his country. His father went from a high position in Cambodia to nothing when very came over here, but they're surviving.)
Chris: We used to be an experimental band, Sothira was the singer, Matt played synthesizer, I was playing bass and we used a rhythm box.
Matt: The first time we played I spilled beer on my synthesizer and broke it.
Chris: Flipper helped us out a lot! Thanks to Will.... and Bruce... and Ted.... and **Steve**:.

FLIPSIDE NUMBER 31

"Brain invasion going on in everyone
You feel the things to make a world turn angry red
Because the next time you can't take it
Next thought murderlation
And hate is all you wanna know
Murder one inborn in every cell
It's in your blood and you can't shake it
Because you were bred to take it
Next stop annihilation
The breed the hate right in your bones
Hate is your mistress, you shall not want
You shall not want because your breed is strong
Because when they try to break you
New world desolation
And strength is all you gotta know!"
"Hate Breeders"– the Misfits

ISSUE #: 31

Red Cross: Jeff, Tracy, Steve, janet – photo Al

pride. Whatever the case, now the gangs could fight each other, and indiscriminate violence was definitely on the decline. Whatever you think about the contradictions of the very term "punk gang", there were gangs of kids in the "punk" (or was it hardcore?) scene, that had a stupid territorial and even racist pride, and did fight and cause trouble at shows. And, they are still with us today. Of course, the good side of Godzillas closing was that without a central focus, the scene was spread far and wide to a number of various smaller clubs (like the Brave Dog, Grandia Room, the Barn and yes, the Cathay De Grande!) with a more intimate atmosphere - that were not so conducive to a gang mentality. L.A. had passed it's most violent stage at the Fleetwood, but Godzillas never got quite that bad. Funny, though, our guest editorial from one Mykel Board, talks about the increased violence at gigs in New York! Written while Mykel was nursing a 20 stitch wound he recieved while watching a fight in New York.

RED CROSS

Red Cross were interviewed by Al and Hud in April at the McDonald's house in Hawthorne. They live in a run down neighborhood that is being torn down for a future freeway. Red Cross (or as they would say "Linda Blair's Cross) are trying their hardest to be L.A.'s best all girl band......

Flipside: Are you and Steve getting sex changes

Jeff: Yeah, when we can afford it. When we make as much money as the Circle Jerks.

Flipside: You want to be an all girl band?

Jeff: It's difinitely our goal.

Flipside: Do you worry about Charlies family? I mean you didn't give him credit.

Jeff: Yeah, it's a bonus cut on the album so it's not listed... on the insert it thanks Charlie for writing a hot tune. We are going to send him some records in the mail and maybe some money...

Flipside: So he won't kill you?

Steve: Well, he fucking wrote it!!!

Flipside: A lot of people still think Steve is 12.

Steve: Fuck, I'm 14, they're living in the past.

Flipside: What do you write songs about?

Steve: Linda Blair, Russ Meyers.

Jeff: We're into exploitation of all kind.

Flipside: What do your parents think of the band nowadays?

Jeff: Oh, they're real supportive. They didn't like it at first. They haven't seen us live yet.

Steve: We told them we're not going to go to work, whatever. We're not going to be welders, so you might as well support us. This is what we're gonna do, make music so...

Jeff: We got a young start and probably by the time I'm 25 I'll be a real guitarist. He got his bass when he was 11.

Janet: My parents are glad I'm in a band 'cause at least I'm doing something. I quit school and I won't get a job, and they're glad I'm in this band because of the album.

Jeff: My grandmother bought a bunch of our first record and gave them to all of our family for Christmas!

Tracy: My parents are glad I'm not sitting at home doing nothing anymore.

Flipside: What about the new punks?

Janet: I used to be real obnoxious, like hipppies' hair on fire, but now it's not the same, There's no sense of humor. It's just a bunch of dicks trying to prove they're cool. They're bummed because they missed out on punk rock. They're just macho-jocks, they've got no place in anything.

Flipside: Is this band gonna stay together?

Steve: I hope so! We have to record something for a compilation album on Bomp. It's not punk stuff.

Flipside: Are you a punk rock band?

Jeff: We're a punk rock band.

Janet: Punk rock means a lot of things.

Jeff: If it's hoodlum, vandalizing teenagers, then we are. We are as obnoxious as anybody. It's not getting into beating each other up. I would be in pain and I wouldn't like that.

Janet: They got rules, you can't be punk rock if you're not this tough...

Jeff: Rules and standardism is bullshit, trendyism is not an uncool thing anymore, people don't even know what the trends are

Flipside: Was it a trend when you started?

Jeff: No! It wasn't 'in fashion' back then. I just went to see bands I liked, I freaked out. Music was what got me into it. I dress weird because it's fun. Setting standards for yourself and others is what you try to get away from in High School and shit.

Janet: Still the only good bands are punk rock, there's assholes and they suck.

Jeff: What makes the band? The people in the band, not the people who go to see the band.

Steve: If you don't like it why should you even be playing?

Jeff: Hardcore is another term that bugs me - hardcore is dedication, you are really into what you are doing but now hardcore has these bands... people might not consider us 'hardcore' but dedication is dedication, anarchy is anarchy, why don't they stop being fascists????????

Sacc. Trust: Joe, Rob, Earl, Jack – photos Al

SACCHARINE TRUST

Saccharine Trust were interviewed in early April at the Barn before their show. Present were Joe Byza (guitar), Earl Liberty (bass), Rob Holtzman (drums), and, of course, Jack Brewer (singer). Al, Hud, and Paul did the interviewing. After a long attempt to find a quiet place, we started in a back room.

Al: What does Saccharine Trust mean, is it like the sweetner?

Joe: To me it represents Jack's personality. Saccharine the adjective; like hard to believe, over trust, whatever. A strong amount of faith in something, that's Brewer. It just came to his head one day.

Jack: The whole think started coming to me eight years ago. I wanted to ditch school because we had a test the next day. At that point I never heard about going out or anything like that. I was just fifteen and watched a lot of T.V. Before, I'd hide in alleys and stuff, but it gets hard roaming the streets for eight hours. So, I went into the trunk of our station wagon. My family went someplace and got into an accident; the car almost turned over. I don't know what happened. I just know that somehow the car got home. While I was in there I was thinking, not in the exact words, but Saccharine Trust.

Al: Do you have any big influences? I think you sound a lot like Television.

Joe: Really? It's just the tone I picked up somewhere. I don't listen to records and try to sound like someone. It's a lot more inspiration than influence.

Earl: A lot of people say we don't sound like the typical L.A. punk band...

Jack: And it hurts us so deeply...

Earl: We don't try to be different--it just comes out that way. It's from our different musical interests.

Al: It seems like you are down on some of our hardcore bands.

Joe: I think some could use some originality.

JFA at the Whisky – photo Al

Jack: I don't put them down. There's a lot of people in the world who aren't original, except they're not in bands. You have to have some sense of purpose. Getting popular and making money might be a purpose, but, it's without any mission to it.

Al: So, what's your mission?

Jack: To the best of our ability to make music that we feel is honest and original. A lot of these other bands, I question their honesty. I won't go into the spook band subject, but I don't think they're sincere. I don't like any bands with any numbers or initials in their name. You can't judge a band. One thrash band sounds is just as good as another.

Al: I think a lot of them are different and I think an initial band like TSOL has a lot of originality...

Jack: It's not a contest, or even being original, but honesty in the music is what I'm talking about.

Joe: The problem is, if you ask a question to Jack and he answers, it's each individual's opinion. It's not a group opinion.

Al: Is "Mad at the Company" from personal experiences?

Jack: Yeah, from working. I had the title first, I was mad at my boss. No matter how good you did anything, it goes on completely

unappreciated.

Al: What about,"I Am Right?"

Jack: The lyrics to that were written over a period of two years, about four years ago. It's a story of different people at that point. Different people at the same time being everyone also at the same time...

Al: How long have you been a band, that song is four years old?

Joe: Jack and I are the original members we didn't have a name for a while and people have come and gone. Like who we recorded with on "Cracks", they're in Hari Kari.

Earl: Me and Don were in a Ska band called the Jetsons awhile back. It was more or less a house party band. We did one club gig and got thrown out. Then, I met Joe and Jack at Polish Hall and Don joined the band. I used to go to their practices all the time. Back Flag offered to pay for the recording of the album, but the bass player was shakey and didn't want to do it. I was playing the bass parts on the album by the book. I had no time to put little runs or my personality into it.

Jack: He barely got his face on the cover.

Earl: It's slower than what we're like right now and there are other changes in it.

Jack: At that point I didn't know what I wanted at all. I was just doing my best trying

not to sound like Darby Crash.

JODY FOSTERS ARMY

Jody Fosters Army were cornered after their gig with the Bad Brains in March. Bam Bam (15) drums, Brian (15) sings, Michael (22) plays bass, and Don (22) is the guitarist.

Al: You used to live in H.B., right?

Don: Yeah, I still do, sort of. I just live in Phoenix to go to school.

Al: How did you all end up in Phoenix?

Don: I went to school there and stayed. It's a trap. It's too hot to get motivated to move away.

Michael: Plus retreds come apart on the freeway. It's so hot that you have to stay.

Al: Why is the record called Blatent Localism?

Bam: 'Cause I thought of it. One day I saw a bunch of guys arguing (at a skate spot). That's blatant localism at its best and that's that.

Don: Don't live here, don't skate here.

Al: What's J.F.A. about?

Don: Skateboarding and being unpretentious.

Al: Did you have a band before Hencley.

Michael: We started nineteen days after he

shot Reagan. We were called by a different name but...(All: Shut up!!!) I won't even mention it.

Dennis:(Social Distortion): It should be Jody Fosters Army.

Brian: Or Foster's Army like the beer.

Dennis: Who is Jody Foster anyway?

Michael: I don't know. I read about it in Newsweek.

Al: What inspired your name, her or Hencley?

Michael: It was kind of him, it was Hencley, yeah.

Don: It's like Gilligan's Island generation gone wild. Hinkley was wimp.

and look what he went and did. How would you like to see Bam Bam snap and turn loose on somebody? There's a lot of time bombs ticking out there. I hate Ronald Reagan!

Al: Did you send Jody a record?

Don: If she wants it to blow over, she won't say anything in public. If she sues us, we'll be in People Magazine. I'll get to share my recipies for peanut butter sandwiches. We can go to parties with Tredeau. And all she'll get is four skateboards!

Al: Who writes your songs?

Don: We got "Beach Blanket Bongout" out of the Crowd interview in Flipside. Jim Kaa's a friend of mine. H.B. was a real small scene at one time. The Flyboys, the Screwz, the Klan, and the Crowd are all from the same car wash.

Al: Who skated first?

Michael: I started eleven years ago in Kansas.

Don: I used to skate when the waves were flat and my girlfriend was on the rag. Every twenty-eight days we'd hit the Fruit Bowl for about a week.

Michael: Bam Bam and Brian have been skating for three or four years. Don and I started the band and said that you have to skate to be in J.F.A. So, we found two skaters who played well.

Brian: Hey, if you cruise the ditches in Phoenix you'll see...

Don: Home Turf with a skull in caution orange, our team colors.

BAD BRAINS

Flipside: This is your first time in L.A.?

Gary: Yeah.

Flipside: What do you think of it?

HR: We just got here five minutes ago. All we see is rain and smelling stinking air.

Flipside: How'd it go in San Francisco?

HR: It's OK, but too many faggots. They act confused. Well, that goes along with it, but mostly if they just act sensible they wouldn't be so bad. Most of them act so crazy even out in public, it disturbs me. Makes me want to go and shoot one of them.

Gary: We have an album that we're working on next, primarily East Coast and South Coast bands that will be out within two months, then the next Bad Brains 45.

Flipside: What's the album gonna be called?

Gary: We don't want to say that yet, save it for a surprise!

Flipside: Is it on Bad Brains Records?

HR: Yeah, that's what has been taking us so long to put out another record. It's because we've been setting up and waiting for the right

Bad Brains - photos Pete L.

opportunity. A couple of people have given us offers, but we don't want to compromise, because you know what happens when you sign the dotted line! So, we've just been working, saving and now we're in a position where we can put out another record.

Flipside: We heard you used to be a jazz quartet?

HR: We just screwed around with fusion for awhile. We only had one gig and that was in our basement. It was a flop.

Flipside: Did you have the same name?

HR: No, we were called Mind Power back in '77.

Flipside: Then punk came around...

HR: We found out about hardcore through a good friend called Sid Mc Cray who lives in DC. We just went over to his house one day and put on some albums--Never Mind the Bollocks, No NY, and that was it.

Flipside: Where did you get the new name?

HR: We wanted to keep something along with the mind. So, I was talking to Darell, our bass player. I was saying to him, Yeah, it's got

to be something dealing with the mind, the brain, something like that. Then, I said, It's got to be 'bad'. Then, he said, Bad Brains! After that he told me there was a song by the Ramones called Bad Brain. I said, So what. It's a bad name.**Flipside:** Do you enjoy doing reggae more than punk?

HR: No, it's the same. Reggae music is African and punk is American. When I say American, I mean more European oriented. Right now I am in this predicament. I am African in a European environment. I find myself with two likenesses. The thing with hardcore music is reaching out, searching. It's the youth saying, Boy, I can't deal with this. What can I deal with? I can't deal with that. And here comes reggae now with direction.You see, the energy that punk rock

projects, it's so hard that a lot of times the message is lost in the distraction. So, here comes Jah now with the answer. What we have to do is deal with unity, and not fighting, that's our theme or mission.**Flipside:** What makes you divide up your set between punk and reggae?

HR: You've got to ask Jah that! We did not plan it. It just happened.

Flipside: Do you try to keep it fifty-fifty?

HR: No, whatever we feel. Like one night in Boston, we played the first set in reggae and the next all rock. One night we made a gig with Peter Tosh and they wanted us to play all reggae, but we wouldn't do it. We came to the conclusion that if we were to play all reggae at Peter Tosh and then go back to rock and reggae, that's not being sincere. If we decide to become all reggae, well that's fine.

Flipside: Who writes your songs?

HR: Well, Darrel and Gary Dr. Know, the guitarist, write the music and I write a little bit. I do ninety percent of the words. I just write them, Jah get 'em.

Flipside: Is there a favorite song you do?

HR: No, Something beautiful happened in S.F. We came out and everyone was skanking and after the third song we went into a dub and man everybody just rushed the stage. That took me by surprise. If you could have seen the music take over, I ya.

Flipside: You fit all your equipment and youselves in your van?

Earl: It's work, it takes a positive mental attitude.

Flipside: PMA, I like that.

Earl: It's easy to be negative. It's hard to be positive. We got PMA from Think and Grow Rich by Napoleon Hill. Everybody in the band read that book when we were starting out. That book relates a lot to the Bible. It said, sight God, keep the faith. See what you want and keep it in your mind. God says that if you work at it, you can eventually achieve it. If it's sowing a good seed, it's positive, then you are stronger. But, if it's negative, it's not gonna work. It's gonna break up.

HR: Selassie says that until the day when the color of a man's skin means no more than the color of his eyes...

THE MISFITS

Interviewed by Al, Hud, Paul and Kori

FS: So what about your 'horror image'?

Glenn: Well mostly what we sing about is like everyday things and about survival. Like you read in the paper about some guy that kills his wife and hacks her all up, and all of the details are right there, it's fun. I've been into gore all of my life, this is my life, this is me. I'm into gore and horror and shit like that. We're serious about this, a lot of bands do it but are jokes.

FS: Like is "Skulls" from the news?

Glenn: Yeah, or like "London Dungeon", I wrote in London because I hate it so much. All the cops over there hate Americans so I wrote that in jail over there...

FS: Whatever happened to Bobby Steele?

Glenn: We booted him out. We were trying to record and he would never show up at practice. We were trying to work Doyle in anyway! So Bobby would say "Let Doyle play for me tonight", so we said fuck that, let's just get Doyle in the band and we did. I can still

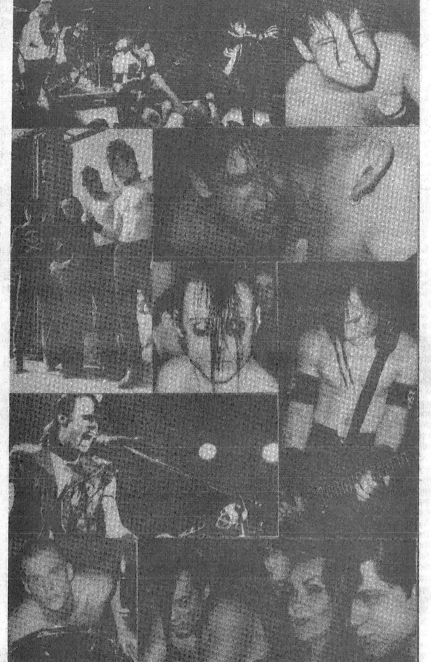

see him and his old girlfriend picking each others noses and putting it into their mouths!!! Discusting shit! I can't be into that shit! (Cringes and laughter!)

FS: But that's gore!

Glenn: You look at his girlfriend, that's gore! When you see them eating each others snot and it totally wipes you out! "Get out of here!". I mean what's a little blood compared to people eating snot! Shit!

FS: Where did you fing Googy?

Glenn: We came back from England and had no drummer. He split on us, we were gonna jump of of the Damned tour and get on with the Clash, and they already announced a surprise band – us. Then our drummer went home, he was a junkie.. his girlfriend was crying the blues "I just can't cope without you", ya know? So no more junkies in the

band. It was 4 months before we got Googy. It's his first band, same with Doyle and Jerry, it's their first bands too.

Jerry: I didn't even know any other songs, we tried to learn some Black Flag, but we don't know them, we just do our stuff.

Glenn: I've been in a few other bands.

FS: Have you ever had like Kiss or somebody ask you to open for them?

Jerry: We'd fucking blow them away!

Glenn: No, fuck that shit! We've got music behind us – I don't think we're all image, Kiss is, they're all image. We don't rely totally on image, we've got good songs. And Kiss is a different direction, it's like "Hey let's party, lets boogie" and we say "Mommy, can I go out and kill tonight!" and we just go wild. Like we can't play places with tables, cause it would be wrecked.

FS: What about future releases?

Glenn: Oh, we got an album all ready to go out, the songs are almost all worked out. We were gonna get Spot to record.

Jerry: Yeah, live with one microphone in the room. That's the way we wind up doing it anyway. We don't use any fancy studio stuff, 16 or 20 tracks, we end up using the basic live tracks we put down.

FS: And no slow songs for you guys?

Glenn: I hate any kind of dilution, ya know. Well we might do a song like, like "Halloween II" or something like that, that's the closest thing it will come to slower, but it will make up for it in sheer terror!

FS: Did you see any ghosts after your recorded in that haunted house?

Glenn: We seen like this bloody rag there, we opened the door and ARRGGGHHH!!! And there's this bloody rag with a snakehead on it, but you could walk around and hear footsteps after you stop. It was the real thing. I didn't get scared, I thought it was cool.

FS: What do you do with the skulls?

Glenn: We collect them, we have all kinds of skulls at home. Some guys gonna send us a bear skull. Anybody out there, send your skulls to the fiend club.

Jerry: And wrap them good! We take dead animals, we take anything.

Glenn: Send your mother dead, we don't care, just chop her up a little so the box ain't too big.

Jerry: Any bones, dead animals or bullets...

FS: Are you involved with any black magic?

Glenn: No...... but I read a lot.

Jerry: We do a good job of leading ourselves. If we did that kind of stuff we might get a fucked up leader and be in trouble, have some demon lead us down the road...

Glenn: I'm into exploring that stuff, getting into it and finding out about it, but not practicing it, just exploring it and understanding it.

Jerry: We don't start drawing shit, pentagrams on the walls, or eat a bug and sit in the corner for a month.

Glenn: It's just knowledge, it's good to know about everything, it's not good to close out any avenues.

FS: What do you think of L.A.'s horror bands?

Glenn: Most of them are a joke.

Jerry: They should learn from the masters!

Glenn: It's unfortunate when we come out here we hear shit like "Oh, you're ripping of these guys", "Jumping on the horror bandwagon". But we don't care, we we cared about what people thought about us, we wouldn't do this.

FLIPSIDE NUMBER 32

"They call us fascist and then they pray
To the God that mad the world their way
In whose name they kill and teach
The sermons and the laws they preach...
Violence just for kicks...
Violence does it make any sense?
Violence can you stop it?
Violence, do you want to?
Philosophy born to mind
Try to explain the problems of our lives
It can't explain away
The violence is here to stay
Say it's just our nature
We have to fight fight fight
Doesn't matter that we've been taught that might makes right."
"Violence" Youth Brigade

ISSUE #: 32
DATE: July 1982

The last Scene Reports in Flipside

FORMAT: 8 1/2x11, rotary web offset with 2 color cover
PAGES: 52
PRICE: $1.00
PRESS RUN: 4000
STAFF: Al, Hud, Pooch, Helen, Shredder, Carol Canada, Tar, Michele, Robert Hill and Pete

This issue continues along the lines of the last one (and scene reports of course). Tar's gossip collumn is getting real controversal, Carol continues to track down the strangest bands, Shredder is in the Hollywood groove and Michele reports of what is happening in the retiring HB scene. The scene in general is spread from San Pedro (Dancing Waters) to Riverside (the Ritz), to L.A. (El Senorial, Florentine, Whisky, Cathay, Lengerie etc...). Things are pretty happening, with variety and enthusiasm at a high.

YOUTH BRIGADE

Youth Brigade were interviewed on June 16 by Al and Hud. The band (from left to right above) are Adam Stern on bass and vocals, Shawn Stern on guitar and vocals, and Mark Stern on drums. The do have a younger brother in case they want to add a guitar or something. The Sterns have been 'on the scene' for a long time, playing in such bands as the Extremes. The are also heavily involved in the BYO and are dedicated to something a lot of people overlook - doing something.

Flipside What are some songs about?

Shawn: One song is called "Violence" & it's about violence and it says, well, is violence something we have to do , or are we taught to do? Is it human nature or is it something we were taught, like might makes right, power? Someone always gets into a fight when we play that song.

Flipside Do you like it that way?

Shawn: No, not necessarily. It's just kind of ironic, I guess. A lot of our songs are about unity and stuff. We don't think fighting is ever gonna stop- we'd like to see it stop, but people get drunk and act like idiots and things happen. We won't stop fighting, but I think a lot of it has to do with people growing up and being taught it's cool to fight. We're basically from animals, so I guess it's our instinct; our nature

Flipside But we're supposed to be civilized.

Shawn: That's what seperates us- civilization, but it's not necessarily true. You know what's a joke? People that walk around with stickers or buttons that say "Anarchy and Peace". It doesn't make sense. You can't have peace AND anarchy. Anarchy is like total chaos and peace is the exact opposite.

Flipside I've never heard that slant on it, but I think they can exist together...

Shawn: How can they? They're total opposites , Figure it out. Anarchy is total chaos, peace is like everything in law and order. Law and order comes from civilization, what sets man apart from animals.

Mark: We're not an anarchy band.

Shawn: But we're not a law and order band either. We're like, who the fuck cares? It's like there's a thin line, that's what's great about punk. You go to a show and there's a real thin line between order and total chaos, and that's what makes it so exciting. That's where we are. We like to be right on that thin line. That's what a lot of our songs are about. We like to explore that.

Mark: We write songs that say what we feel, and anyone else can interpret them how they

Youth Brigade at the Whisky – photo Al

want!

Flipside What do you think of bouncers?

Shawn: Bouncers are fucked!!! But unfortunately, sometimes you have to have them. Like the Palladium show (that the BYO put on) we had to hire off duty L.A.P.D. and bouncers like West security are totally fucked...There are some cool bouncers, maybe like a handfull in L.A. that have been around punk shows enough that they're not gonna hassle you because you look weird at least, and just do the job. Punks as bouncers are good, but most of them would rather watch the show and get drunk, or else they get their own power trip going...(lots more talk about good and bad bouncers).

Flipside You guys are also in the BYO.

Shawn: Yeah, but the three of us are the Youth Brigade and the BYO is something entirely different. Everybody can be in the BYO. (and you can read all about it below.....)

BETTER YOUTH ORGANIZATION

This "Interview" was conducted backstage at the Whisky in June. Many people were present including the Sterns, Eugene, Dana, Brian etc... It was impossible to tell who was saying what except that Shawn did most of the talking.

...Anybody is the BYO, anybody that comes to a show is in the BYO because by coming to a show the support it and that money goes back into the scene. The idea for the BYO came after the Elks Lodge Massacre in 1979. The idea came then but nothing really happened. Then Skinhead Manor started in the fall of 79 after Sham 69 came, and by Spring 1980 Skinhead Manor was really going good. The Fleetwood was closing down and everyone was coming here to meet and hang out. The Manor was a place where people from Huntington, Oxnard, some people from the Valley and all the Hollywood people hung out, everybody had these great ideas and we

wanted to do all these things. Like we wanted to do a bootleg radio station, we had a studio where bands played, Circle Jerks practiced there, No Crisis and Youth Brigade started there. The ideas started to happen and we put out a phamplet at the Urgh Show which was like a comic strip that Adam (Stern) drew and some stuff we wrote up. It got a good response. We made home brew there from a big grape tree out back-we made wine, we did speed, we had a coke machine stocked with beer.... But then the Manor kind of fell apart because we got too many assholes that didn't give a shit. There wasn't any money to support the ideas. That's the most important thing, you need capital. So we split. Then the place was mysteriously burned down. Somebody said: "If we can't have a Manor, nobody shall". Then the Youth Brigade started and Mark was playing drums in No Crisis, thats how we met Frank. Frank had this place (Godzillas) and we got the whole BYO working. We called up everybody and got all of the punks working there. We had a security system made up of punks from all over: Huntington, Long Beach, Valley, Oxnard, Hollywood. It worked pretty cool. We put up a headliner with bands that haven't played much. A chance for new bands, that was the whole idea, to better the scene. The main thing about Godzillas was we got the reputation and we got the capital so we could do things by ourselves, and when Frank started getting greedy, we bailed out. Then we did the Palladium show - which was a success. The BYO can and did do that on it's own. But some rag got drunk, came in on our guest list, fell off the balcony, and is sueing the Palladium, so they are holding all the money we made at that show.

We just want L.A. to know that the BYO is run by kids and is for the punk scene and all the money that goes into it goes back into the scene by putting on shows, putting out records... We help bands when they come out

here, like: Anti-Pasti, Upstarts, Effigies, Misfits, Minor Threat, Husker Du... If we could get people to do a similar thing like what we're doing all across the country, set up shows where bands can make money, set up a tour schedule, put up bands etc, it would make things a lot easier. Also any shows we do, if people think the prices are too high, they should talk to the bands and tell them not to charge us so much. These bands are getting out of control. $12 for the Clash, 2 or three bands!! It's not a gig it's a concert - concerts are for hippies, gigs are for punks!!

SIN 34

Sin 34 were interviewed June 22 at Dave's house in Santa Monica by Al and Hud. Sin 34 are Dave on drums, Julie on vocals, Phil on bass and Mike on guitar.

Hud: What are your songs about?

Julie: Ken and Barbie, everything, religion...

Dave: Not really, how many religion songs do we have?

Julie: Only one anti-religion song, well anti-TV religion, we're working on that.

Dave: Religion is such an easy target today.

Phil: Most of our songs are about personal experiences, we have a couple of joke songs, some love songs and our token political songs, but it's not like "I believe in anarchy" anti-anarchy...

Julie: Anti all those people complaining and they don't even know what they're complaining for.

Dave: People wear anarchy t-shirts and they don't even know what it is.

Al: Who writes your songs?

Dave: We all do except for Mike?

Mike: I just don't ever sit down, I'd rather, I guess, ...I don't, I just don't... ever.

Al: What do you want to do with this band?

Julie: Practice hard and get really good.

Mike: We're gonna get our set down.

Phil: We grow as a band, a lot bigger bands

Sin 34; Mike, Phil, Dave, Julie - photo Al

have been doing the same songs for so long, over and over. All the time we're doing new songs, changing our set around.

Al: Why do you do a Devo song?

Dave: Because we like it.

Julie: To burn all the punks.

Mike: That was the hardest song "Uncontrollable Urge" for us to learn. Yeah, I want to buy a synthesizer now...

Dave: We've been compared to 45 Grave!

Julie: How could we, we're hardcore!

Hud: What's hardcore?

Mike: That's when it's hard to listen to.

Dave: A lot of people call hardcore a lot of noise by a bunch of nazis but that's what I like about it because a lot of people that I hate, hate hardcore and they go against everything that it stands for so that gives me more reason to totally stand by it. As long as you're honest with yourself, no matter what you are into, then you are a good person.

Phil: What's good about our band is the lyrics, a lot of bands write totally stupid lyrics. Some of our songs are really meaningless but the majority of the songs are something we can explain intellectually. We feel good and honest that we can explain it that way.

Dave: You know it's a total head rush hearing yourself on the radio.

THE BIG BOYS

Were interviewed backstage at the Whisky June 23 right after their L.A. debut opening for X. by Al and Hud.

HUD: Hey Biscuits what's your real name?

BISCUITS: Randy

HUD: Do you like pink?

BISCUITS: (Texas accent) I love pink.

HUD: Where'd ya get the pink boots?

BISCUITS: I made 'em! They used to be shit kickers. I had to clean the cow shit off the heals before I could paint them. I didn't buy them at Rodeo Drive like everyone else.

HUD: Did you like gettin' spit on tonight?

BISCUITS: I like spit. It cheers me up. It makes me feel like everyone's an ASSHOLE with nothing better to do. If it's animalism, then go for it.

AL: Are you gay?

BISCUITS: I don't know if I want to answer that or not because it doesn't make any difference if I'm gay or not. I'm a human being and my sexual preference doesn't play into my lifestyle. It comes from my heart and I want people to look at me and say I'm a human...

HUD: Is it fun wearing pink tights and a skirt?

BISCUITS: Oh, that's a stupid question to start out with...

HUD: Well, it's a lot different than our scene. You must get a lot of shit.

BISCUITS: I get a lot of shit and I feed on it because I enjoy seeing people switch those channels in their heads and think about something else. I could get up there like everyone else with a t-shirt that says something cool on the front. I choose to do something different because it's in my heart that I feel a little art needs to happen.

AL: Where's your skirt Tim?

Tim: It's in the wash tonight.

BISCUITS: He's a different human being. Ever since I was a little kid, I've been at the other end of the world. I play on that and enjoy doing it.

AL: It's more of a statement than just conforming to what's cool with everyone.

BISCUITS: It's definitely more of a statement. We have been the KKK on stage, Africans...I've been in drag. I don't care what you think I am. I'm gonna be an entirely different person the next time you meet me, so don't classify me as a drag queen.

Tomorrow, I'll work in an oil field The next day I'll cook eggs in a restaurant. I'm a hundred people and I'm the one person you saw tonight. That's what I love. If you're behind something, that's what I love because you fucking believe in it. That's all we're here for...It's been fun for us. We've been friends ten years before this band started. This is just a small sideline.

AL: And you guys skateboard...

TIM: Yeah, we skateboard.

BISCUITS: I wrestle refrigerators and I expect somebody to invite me to wrestle theirs.

AL: Do you have a lot of skate parks in Texas?

TIM: It's mostly street skating ramps and ditches--the parks are defunct. Fuck the rules and have a good time. I got plates in my arm from a pool when I busted up, got stuck in the gutter coming down. Since the bands started we don't ride vertical as much as we used to-- a foot is about as much as we'll ride. I used to surf too. There is surf in Texas. Port Isabel is like waves in Cal.

AL: Do you surf Biscuits?

BISCUITS: Actually, I do real good on a skateboard. Look at my knees. Those black spots are ground in dirt!!!

AL: Do you skate Fred?

Fred: Not as much as the others, but I'm trying my hardest.

TIM: But Texas is really happening with bands and lots of clubs and kids--the average age is sixteen. It's really getting neat. No bullshit about bands battling each other 'cause we are all in it together. I don't care if you play something weird or bizarre. If you're sincere and trying to knock the system, great! The more bands that get to play, the more kids start bands and that's hot!

THE MINUTEMEN

The Minutemen were interviewed by Al and Pete in late June 1982. The Minutemen live in San Pedro (south of L.A.) and have been playing the scene for a few years now. They have a few singles out on their own

Big Boys at the Whisky - photo Al

BYO 001

BYO 002

BYO 002R

BYO 003

BYO 004

BYO 005

BYO 006s

BYO 007

BYO 008

BYO 009

BYO 010

BYO 011

BYO 001 — SOMEONE GOT THEIR HEAD KICKED IN — (RELEASED 1982) BYO Compilation Album. ADOLESCENTS, BAD RELIGION, SOCIAL DISTORTION, YOUTH BRIGADE, BATTALION OF SAINTS, AGRESSION, JONES, BLADES.

BYO 002 — YOUTH BRIGADE — (RELEASED 1982 — 800 COPIES ONLY! OUT OF PRINT) Sound & Fury LP/The rare underground version. Completely different from the 1983 release, already a collector's item. (NOT FOR SALE!)

BYO 002R — YOUTH BRIGADE — (RELEASED 1983) Sound & Fury LP/The classic debut album by one of L.A.'s most prolific bands. Featuring Sink With California, What Will The Revolution Change? Men In Blue, and the classic cover of Duke Of Earl.

BYO 003 — AGRESSION — (RELEASED 1983) Don't Be Mistaken LP/The debut by Oxnard's finest. High energy skate music to keep your adrenaline going. Includes Dear John Letter, Money Machine and Intense Energy.

BYO 004 — SOMETHING TO BELIEVE IN — (RELEASED 1984) BYO Compilation Album. DOA, YOUTH BRIGADE, 7 SECONDS, SNFU, CH3, KRAUT, BIG BOYS, TOURISTS, YOUTH YOUTH YOUTH, YOUNG LIONS, ZERO OPTION, STRETCHMARKS, UNWANTED, NILS.

BYO 005 — 7 SECONDS — (RELEASED 1984) The Crew LP/Reno hits the jackpot with the debut by this group of positive minded, individualistic young men. Features Young Till I Die, Trust, This Is The Angry, Not Just Boys' Fun and lots more!!!

BYO 006s — YOUTH BRIGADE — (RELEASED 1984) What Price Happiness 7" EP/This 3 song EP shows the diversity and originality that sets the brothers Stern apart. Features the title track, Who Can You Believe In and Where Are We Going. Questions that are still unanswered.

BYO 007 — STRETCH MARKS — (RELEASED 1984) What D'Ya See LP/The debut album by Canada's premier tag team. Try wrestlin' those 13 powerful songs onto your turntable!!!

BYO 008 — UNWANTED — (RELEASED 1984) Shattered Silence LP/11 hard rockin' tunes from the western plains of Canada. Their one and only album.

BYO 009 — S.N.F.U. — (RELEASED 1985) ...And No One Else Wanted To Play LP/From the wilds of Edmonton comes the demented meanderings of the hottest Canadian band of 1985. If you don't already have this 14 song debut slab o'vinyl, GET IT!! (OUT OF PRINT).

BYO 010 — 7 SECONDS — (RELEASED 1985) Walk Together Rock Together 12" EP/We didn't think it was possible but Kevin and Co. have surpassed the 'Crew' LP with seven new powerful anthems. Produced by Ian MacKaye. c

BYO 011 — UPRIGHT CITIZENS — (RELEASED 1985) Open Eyes, Open Ears, Brains, & A Mouth To Speak LP/Here is all 15 hard hitting tracks on this U.S. debut album by Germany's finest, on BYO of course. c

BYO 012 — THE BRIGADE — (RELEASED 1986) The Dividing Line LP/Youth Brigade has changed its name but the music is as powerful and poignant as ever. An album of epic proportions. Features the title track, Scream, It's A Wonderful Life, The Struggle Within, War For Peace and 4 more. c

BYO 013 — THE SMARTIES — (RELEASED 1986) Whole Bunch O' Weirdos LP/Hard driving music with humor is delivered by this self professed skate band from Germany. They do a great cover of San Francisco, and show their diversity with songs like Apocalypso, Ghost Ryderz, and Money Has Priority. c

BYO 014 — 7 SECONDS — (RELEASED 1986) New Wind LP/The second full length LP finds the band maturing and expanding their music and ideas. A great transition record and their last record on BYO as they move entirely on their own. c

BYO 015 — HUNGRY FOR WHAT — (RELEASED 1986) The Shattered Dream LP/This band from Switzerland is blowing minds with these U.S. debut 12 songs that rage with the spirit of '76 while still sounding fresh and honest. Check out the title track, Religion and Misanthrope. c

BYO 016 — JUNIOR GONE WILD — (RELEASED 1986) Less Art, More Pop LP/These daring young men from the wilds of Canada take the jangly guitars of the 60's and incorporate them into an original and modern sound. You'll be amazed by the epic God Is Not My Father, intrigue tied by Dreams and pleasantly surprised by Heather On A Bad Day, Tragedy In E, and all the other gems contained herein. c

BYO 017 — S.N.F.U. — (RELEASED 1986) If You Swear You'd Catch No Fish LP/Mr. Chi Pig's sardonic wit once again shines through the crunchy rockin' guitars of one of Canada's premier rock bands. Features Black Cloud, Where's My Legs, Better Homes And Gardens. c

BYO 018 — THE BRIGADE — (RELEASED 1986) Come Together EP/The Brigade marches on! This 6 song EP is a cohesive collection of heartfelt songs that further expound the sound developed on 'The Dividing Line'. c

BYO 019 — MAD PARADE — (RELEASED 1987) A Thousand Words LP/In a world of clones, MAD PARADE lead the way into an ever widening gap between true rock and the underground, and at the same time fill it with the powerful music long awaited and finally found. A picture is worth... c

BYO 020 — SCRAM — (RELEASED 1987) Stand Up LP/Rockin' Reggae beats combined with Motown, Ska and an 80's twist with leftist political overtones are sure to make this Philadelphia 3 piece one of the new BIG bands. Just How Much, and their cover of the classic Imagine, are sure to bring out emotions and make you STAND UP AND... c

BYO 021 — WONDERWALL — (RELEASED 1987) Blueprint LP/A new group from the guitarist of L.A.'s seminal punk bands, The FLY BOYS and CHOIR INVISIBLE. This hypnotic and twisted pop album is an electric hybrid that recalls elements of T. REXX and of 'Abby Road' in the same moment. c

BYO 022s — THE BRIGADE — (RELEASED 1987) It's a Wonderful Life B/W Remember 7" single/Through a twist of irony and a picture of paradise comes this gem, soon to be a video. And with a new B side The world never seemed so light and dark.

BYO 016

BYO 017

BYO 012

BYO 013

BYO 014

BYO 015

BYO 018

BYO 019

BYO 020

BYO 021

BYO 022s

S.G.T.H.K.I.
Compilation Cover — 4 colors on white
T001

BYO LOGO
3 colors on white
T002

YOUTH BRIGADE
Skinhead Logo — 3 colors on white
T003

YOUTH BRIGADE
Coat Of Arms — 3 colors on white
T004

YOUTH BRIGADE
Sink w/Kalifornia — 3 colors on white
T005

YOUTH BRIGADE
Silhouette Logo — 3 colors on white
T006

STRETCH MARKS
Alligator Logo — 4 colors on black
T007

7 SECONDS
Crew Album Cover — 2 colors on black
T008

S.N.F.U.
Skull Drawing — 2 colors on black
T009

7 SECONDS
Walk Together Cover — 4 colors on white
T010

UPRIGHT CITIZENS
Cover Logo — 2 colors on black
T011

THE BRIGADE
Dividing Line Cover — 4 colors on white — Heavy 100% cotton
T012

THE SMARTIES
Face Logo — 4 colors on white — Heavy 100% cotton
T013

HUNGRY FOR WHAT
Shattered Dream Cover — 2 colors on black — Heavy 100% cotton
T015

SNFU
If You Swear, You'll Catch No Fish Cover — 4 colors on white — 100% heavy cotton
T017

T-$HIRtS

P R I C E L I S T

LP's	$6.00
12" EP's	$4.50
7" EP's	$2.50
T-Shirts (Standard)	$6.00
T-Shirts (Heavy Duty)	$8.00
Posters	$2.00

All prices include UPS delivery in the Continental U.S. only.
Add $1.00 per item for Coloured Vinyl.
For 12" LP's, EP's Cassettes & T-Shirts:
  Add $1.00 per item to Canada
  Add $2.00 per item Overseas
For 7" EP's & Singles:
  Add $ .50 per item to Canada
  Add $1.00 per item Overseas
Send SASE for updates on the latest band, record, tour and political info.

POSTERS:
All Posters are Full Color On High Gloss Paper

T-SHIRTS:
T-Shirts Available in M, L, & XL Sizes. Please Specify Sizes. Give 2 Alternative Choices FOR EACH ITEM When Ordering!!!

O R D E R F O R M

Name _____

Address _____

City _____ State _____ Zip _____

ITEM NO.	QTY.	DESCRIPTION	SIZE	ITEM PRICE*	TOTAL CHARGE

TOTAL	
VINYL CHARGE	
CANADIAN & OVERSEAS SHIPPING	
GRAND TOTAL	

CHARGES PER ITEM

Minutemen: D. Boon, Mike Watt, George Hurley, in skinhead days! - photo Al

New Alliance label and also have an album out on SST. The latest Bean Spill EP should be out by now on Thermidor and the second album will be out soon titled What Makes a Man Start Fires?. The Minutemen are intelligent and like to talk, but, in the past, have been reluctant to do interviews. We finally got this one after a lot of pestering. They have developed their own unique style that definitely sets them apart. (George Hurley wasn't present).

Flipside Why do you play those minute songs?
Mike: You don't know the story?
Flipside We've read the press releases...
Mike: That's the truth. But, now we got a song that's almost three minutes long called the Anchor. It's an opus about George dreaming that he gets raped by five women then he wakes up and his girlfriend is next to him--the anchor. We're into playing longer 'cause we're in better shape now after two years. We're

forced physically, but now... We don't want people to nail us down--Minutemen: the name and the songs. And with political, well, we write political songs, but we aren't nailed to that. You really can't get too political with a song. Campaign songs are about as political as you can get. We really just talk about what's on our minds.
Flipside And you both write the songs?
Mike: And George too. We don't have a leader in our band...no leader, no laggers.
Flipside Did you guys go to college?
Mike: Yeah, I went for Electrical Engineering. George is a machinist.
Dennis: I just went for a general degree for teaching.
Flipside No political science?
Mike: I read it. What can you really do with that stuff? Politics is guns if you really get down to it. I'm addicted to newspapers. That's my problem. We all feel helpless like we're all on a big bus ride to the edge of a cliff, so, we're gonna shout.
Mike: There's two ways, there's words, but there's music. We like jamming, ya know? This feeling gets in you... Then you want to do the words too. But, words are too nailed down. Sometimes you get all ashamed six months later, shit...
Dennis: You can't revise what you write. When you do music, you can go, Oh, I'll play this part different, but, with words you can't do that.
Mike: In a way, words are good because there's no shitting around, no symbols like music. Symbols get boring sometimes because you want to just say what the fuck is on your mind.
Flipside And sometimes you can make your lyrics vague.
Mike: But we don't try to be.
Dennis: We don't want to put any nails in the cross...
Mike: Took three nails to sink Jesus... We put our words on our covers, I say, up front with it, you can't prey to words. One of the reasons people go to war is over words--they're just symbols--more than music in a way. That's why you do songs. Giving speeches would be happening, but doing songs can do more.
Flipside You guys get real excited live.
Mike: I told you that feeling is there--even in the studio, but we try to calm down. That is why we can only play a half hour or we'll have a heart attack.
Dennis: We have to pace the fast songs with the slow ones...
Mike: And the songs are short. On the record, it seems weird. We never thought of going in the studio at first, we just wanted to do them live.
Dennis: And we don't like to put breaks in there, we just jam.
Mike: Steamroller, we let each other have intros to songs so the others can be calming down. It's like a battle everytime we play.
(Talk about negative Oi bands in England. Mike, however, thinks that's all a rock and roll scam...)
Mike: It's almost rock and roll again. That's what you have to keep playing at your own little dream. We're too rough to be mersh (commerical).
Dennis: I'm march, I write march songs...
Mike: Ok, we're all individuals. I don't think I'm mersh and I don't think George is.
Dennis: Well, what's commercial? I write songs, to me that's being commercial.
Mike: I think march is more like selling things. I know rock and roll is real sacred, but you

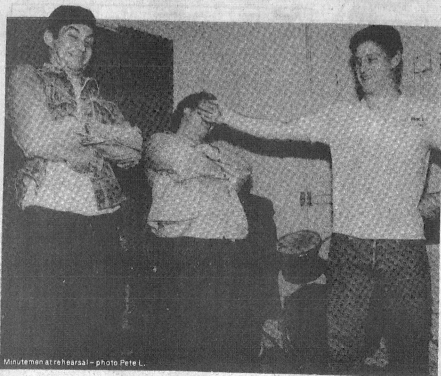

Minutemen at rehearsal - photo Pete L.

can't have it as a part of your life and not have to sell your soul to the business. Selling records and making a living is happening. but, what if it's not? Do you stop playing?

Dennis: Bands loose a lot of real gut when they don't get what they expect. They have their own reason for being in a band--we like to play and go crazy.

Mike: In a way, it's torture, in a way it's fun, it's therapy.

Gene: Well I believe we'll be around for another 5 or 6 years, Chelsea.

Al: Why do you keep that name, Chelsea?

Gene: Well why not!? The band is more important than the musicians in it! The concept of the band is more important than any one person. "Chelsea" sums up that concept - the spirit of the beginning of the whole thing, where it was born, the fashion thing and everything. It was born in Chelsea.

Gene October

CHELSEA

In late May I flew to London care of IRS Records to interview Chelsea. The band had just finished a great gig with Anti-Nowhere League, Chron-Gen and the Defects and I am backstage with manager Harry, Gene october (singer in case you didn't know) and Nick Austin (who is naked) on guitar.

Al: Is that a typical bill for you to play with a bunch of punk bands?

Gene: Yeah, they're all very heavy punk bands. That's what kind of audience we have, but mainly in England, I don't know if we attract that kind of a crowd in the States... Have you heard our new album?

Al: Yeah, it's pretty good, sounds a lot like the direction Stiff Little Fingers are going.

Gene: Well, before we were lacking a bit on the musical side, y'understand. A more lyrical sort of contact before, so having been playing with Chelsea for 5 or 6 years and having been through the whole punk thing, well I sort of discovered music. So this time I thought I'd try to catch people with the music side but add the lyrics in there.

Al: And you still seem to write about the same stuff.

Gene: Oh sure, like "Evacuate" is about C.N.D. and nuclear war - "Evacuate there is no time because we'll all be dead by the stroke of nine".

Al: How do you feel about playing to the newer punks who don't yet care about the music?

Gene: Well after all this time the pressure is on us to be capable of both - coming up with good lyrics and good music. Our audience grows all the time and they become like, uh, connoiseurs, you know what I mean? So we have to be sort of, ...good, to keep the attraction of the early punks as they grow older, as they mature. Cause their taste in music matters as well.

Al: How did you manage to keep going?

That's where Seditionaries is, where Malcolm McLaren first got the Pistols together, where I met my first manager, where the Damned met up, and the Clash. That's where all the little shops sprang up. It's like there's Greenwhich Village in New York where everyone hangs out, that's Chelsea.

Al: Do you mind being labeled as a punk band?

Gene: No, I'm not frightened of it at all. A lot of people think it's the kiss of death to be labeled that way and go out of their way to deny it. But I would say yes.

Al: Nick, how do you like working with Gene?

Nick: Oh it goes good, it goes like clockwork.

Al: Were you always a big Chelsea fan?

Nick: Oh yeah, going back to the early days, '76, '77, I'd go to all the gigs. I was 'on the scene' so to say.

Al: Do you write any of the songs?

Nick: I wrote most of the stuff on the album. Gene and I wrote a few things together and Gene wrote some of his own and I did basically the rest.

FLESHEATERS

The Flesheaters have been in existence since 1977, but with constant member changes they were often considered a side or experimental band for the flexible members, and also a chance for Chris D. to have his lyrics and ideas recorded and performed. Chris D. is well known for his cat like voice so out of curiosity I asked him if he was a cat person, he reluctantly stated that he wasn't, but had seen the movie "Cat People" 8 times. The Flesheaters were interviewed in their studio by Carol, Maw and also present was Lesa.

Edie: How did you get such a morbid name?

Chris: We were trying to think of a name a long time ago and there were a lot of different names I came up with. On of the names was

Screaming Target, which was from a reggae album, which I really wanted to use but everyone that was playing with me hated it. One of the second choices was the Flesheaters. Everybody liked that so we just went with that. Things that people have read about the band have been with the name Flesheaters, it didn't seem wise to change the name. I don't love the name but it's ok.

Carol: The first album, lyric wise, boardered along the morbid.

Chris: The "No Questions Asked" album, the name Flesheaters had a real reputation with a lot of the, it seemed to me, a lot of the beach

Chris D.

punks and skinhead kids, with that album it was a real reputation we had. But when they came to see us with the new line up, with the guys from the Blasters, I got a real sense of disappointment, because we weren't a real hardcore, slam, thrasher type of band. "No Questions Asked" was more like that in a way. It was more simple.

Robyn: Lyrics on the 1st album, I don't think there was a real connection with satanism.

Chris: It's just like I'm really obsessed with death.

Carol: Are you afraid to die or does it just intregue you?

Chris: Um, yes, it's...

Carol: How would you like to die, if you could?

Chris: If I could! (Laughs) We're immortal.

Robyn: Some kind of sacrificial death, offer ourselves to our audience.

Don: You'd better not say that Robyn.

Eddie: Is there a certain message you want to convey to the audience?

Don: Happiness, good times...

Robyn: In these times of depression, we remind people of them.

Chris: And besides there is no reason... the one thing I want to convey is that there is no reason to fear death.

Wally: Life, well that's another matter.

Chris: The one thing that we do that mystifies our audience is we don't play in one catagory. The music that we play is real loud. It's real metalic. It could be described as heavy metal, or what was in 1977 was punk. We're not like a slam type of thrasher band... There's a lot of country western influences in it, a lot of music just sounds like heavy metal, but a lot of melodies.

Robyn: For me there's a big difference in what I like to listen to and what I like to play. What we play is nothing like I've ever played before. In this band it's like something coming

Flesheaters at Al's Bar – photo Al

through the air and we sort of catch it.

Chris: And it's real intuitive. We have a real intuitive bond between us... There's a lot of influence there, but it doesn't sound like were trying to be real dilettantes.

Carol: Do you think that that attitude comes with the fact that you are older than some bands that are coming out now?

Chris: I don't want to get into ageism, but I know we listen to a lot of more different music than some of the kids that got bands now.

Don: We're influenced by a lot more different kinds of music than the average band you're refering to because we have been around a lot longer.

PAUL WELLER

Paul Weller – photo Pete L.

– THE JAM

Paul Weller was kind enough to let me interview him. It was an honor for he turned down pleanty of other interviewers all across the U.S. He's still got a lot to say and a lot to complain about and I found him extremely intelligent. If you didn't catch the Jam, too bad, they were good. At 24 years Paul Weller is going to be the man behind pop music in the years to come, sorry Shredder. By Karl Markz

Flipside Why did you like the Beat so much, yet in recent interviews you've said that "People shouldn't depend on pop music so much".

Paul: No, I just think that people don't really use pop music. The seem to place their music in one basket, and that music is pop music. It's like a lot of people agreeing with our lyrics and saying "yeah I like that" but never acting upon it, never taking it any furthur than that.

Flipside No heart and soul.

Paul: Well if you seem to agree with what a band is saying, you should act upon it. It's not enough to just walk away from it, nothing gets changed.

Flipside Do you like challenges?

Paul: I find a lot of the stuff out in England right now contrived in that, yeah all of those bands seem to hold down images, silly. It's like that bloke in Haircut 100 and Clare of Altered Images starring on "The Boy and the Girl Next Door". I see no challenge in that. Boring. I like bands that make you think and I don't think they do. They just entertain. Basically we're trying to motivate people with it.

Flipside Motivate in what way?

Paul: Getting people out of this fucking rut, the way people are in England, this "no hope" feeling. It could apply to anyone in the world or anywhere but it's really English and I see it from an English standpoint. Our country is so fucking dead, so grey, and it's got so much potential.

Flipside What do you think of the mods in Southern California?

Paul: Must get hot under the sun with those parkas on (laughter). It's ok if someone really gets into it as long as it doesn't turn into tunnel vision where you can't see anything else. That's what ahppened in England... the real modernists, the 60's modernists were really looking towards the future, the whole idea was open mindedness.

Flipside How involved are you with the Campaing For Nuclear Disarmament (CND)?

Paul: Well, don't know, I am a member. It's difficult for us cause we're hardly around.

Flipside Are you afraid it might be considered a political stance?

Paul: No, I don't really see it as being political, it's common sense, the question is: do you want to continue living or don't you? That's the politics.

Flipside Do you feel a threat of nuclear war?

Paul: Yeah. In Europe, Europeans are more prone to it, that's probably where it will be.

Flipside What do you think of the Clash?

Paul: Oh I think they're full of shit. All of their songs got that hardened image, the urban guerrilla touch and all that bollocks. Stupid. Not enough reality ya know, dressed up like a fucking urban guerrilla.

Flipside Do you see England as a major power in the world?

Paul: Naw, not really. Look at the Faulkland Islands thing, it's nothing but a fucking joke! I really can't make any statement on the whole thing. It's total madness. Most of the people in England didn't even know where the Faulkland Islands were, like me. I thought they were off the coast of Scotland, and that's the truth. And now you've got Argentine boys as well as English boys dying for a piece of land, for what?

Flipside What do you think of the U.S. missiles all across Europe?

Paul: It sickens me. I really get upset thinking Englands spending money on destruction insted of building up stuff. It's sad, the education system is crap and they can't get civilization together.

JEFF DAHL

(Powertrip, Vox Pop, Angry Samoans...)

Powertrip is based around the song writing

Vox Pop: Dinah, Don, Jeff, Paul, Gary, Michael – photo Ed Colver.

talents of Jeff Dahl, backed by Ed Danke on guitar, John Bliss on drums and Zap on bass. Jeff Dahl has also been in several other bands, most notably Vox Pop and the Angry Samoans. His self destructive performances have resulted in a shattered tailbone, four broken ribs, a broken wrist, broken toes, chipped teeth a broken nose 3 times, torn ligaments and one time Jeff bit off the tip of his tongue! Interview by R. Hill

Flipside Vox Pop is pretty notorious for live shows.

Jeff: We always get a strong reaction. People either love us or hate us. Some people completely hate our guts...

Flipside There's also a lot of nudity and outrageous costumes.

Jeff: Nothings planned though, we just get together before a gig, get as much alcohol and other substances as possible and then what happens, happens. Nothing is done consciously.

Flipside Vox Pop isn't the only notorious band you've been in.

Jeff: I joined the Angry Samoans as lead singer, but we were banned from just about every club. I think the Samoans are basically one of the best rock and roll bands around, they're just misunderstood. Like the Rodney deal, that just started out as a joke, but it got us banned from every club. We had to go to New York or San Francisco to play.

Flipside Why did you leave the band?

Jeff: It was kind of mutual, the Samoans just kept doing the same songs and I wanted to move on. After that I played bass in the Mentors, I never really joined, I just filled in.

Flipside That brings us to Powertrip.

Jeff: We have a pretty arrogant attitude, we have no desire to play little shit clubs that don't pay and treat you like shit. We want to deal with professionals. Jan Ballard is going to set up a showcase for us. Most of our current plans center around recording. It's not like we have a lot of money or anything, we just have people who believe in us, like Mystic Sound Studios, that give us free recording time because they think we've got something. We have commercial potential. I hate to put it that way, but I guess that's what it comes down to. I'm totally into heavy metal, the band influences are mainly Stooges, Dead Boys, MC5, Blue Cheer, definitely a big dose of Blue Cheer, Motorhead as well.

Flipside What are your lyrics about?

Jeff: I don't consciously do this but a lot of my lyrics are filled with innuendos, double meanings, and things besides the obvious. Most of my other lyrics are psychotic shit, like "Permanent Damage" was the only song of mine the Angry Samoans would do, it's just psychotic ramblings about damaging yourself, like cutting yourself up with razorblades and cigarette burns.

Flipside Is this band a result of your solo stuff?

Jeff: I put out a solo single in 1976 (on White Boys label), and I was on the "Best of Washington DC" punk compilation album in 1978/79. We're not doing any of that material now, but I can see a relationship.

Flipside What did you do before moving to L.A.?

Jeff: I got kicked out of the house when I was 15, lived on the beach in Hawaii while I finished High School, joined the Army and was in Vietnam before the clamity, and was stationed at the Pentagon Heliport as an air traffic controller for three years (doing the solo single at this time), got out of the Army, went

back to Hawaii and then moved to L.A...

Flipside Have you thought about doing a Vox Pop tour?

Jeff: With Vox Pop we've rehearsed maybe twice in our 3 1/2 years of existence. We can't get ourselves to agree on anything, can't motivate ourselves to do anything. It's the epitomy of anarchy. Like Alister Crowly "Do what thou wilt". All these drugged out scatterbrained people running amok. Like the Throbbing Show was a total joke. A certain individual showed up having just done a massive dose of very naughty drugs and was vomiting on stage. Throbbing Gristle loved us. Genesis P-Orridge runs up and grabbed me while we were playing and tried to french me. I pushed him away so he went over to Don and stuck his tongue down Don's throat, just after Don had been vomiting on stage. I never do those things, of course.

Flipside Oh, of course not.

Jeff: Yeah, I'm a professional. Fuck it all. The only thing I'm into is speed, beer, rock n' roll and young girls. As far as I'm concerned those are the only 4 things worth anything. Fuck everything else.

BATTALION OF SAINTS

BOS were interviewed by Al, Hud and Helen on June 11 at Contempo Hall. This

Battalion of Saints - photo Al

was their first gig in L.A.

History: George and Chris were originally in a San Diego punk band called the Neutrons. The played many gigs and acquired a small following, including Mark Rude, future manager. After some time they went through a personal and attitude change, and changed their name to one that they found in the Readers Digest - Battalion of Saints. They released an ep in early 1982 that Mark did the art work for, and have songs on the BYO compilation. The band is Ted on drums, Dennis on bass, George on vocals and Chris on guitar.

Helen: Do you have an image that you as Battalion of Saints want to convey?

Dennis: Speaking for everybody, for all the punks, for all the hardcore people, we're all the Battalion of Saints and we're speaking for a whole mass of people, in a way inter-relating with the culture...

George: We're not trying to copy anybody else in music, lyrics or songs.

Al: You deal with a lot of anti-war subjects on

the EP...

Chris: When you look at it with Reagan and all this war bullshit going on, everybody is war hungry.

George: Like the Middle East countries have nothing else to do. They grow up and go "Well, you're a teenager now, let's kill somebody, let's fight some holy war." We're concerned about tomorrow, we're not laid back saying live day by day, we are worried about the future and want to make a change.

Ted: We're totally committed, we did all of the work on our record, did all of the promo and everything. We all have jobs...

Jordan: Why did you put the poster in with the record, why so glamorous?

Mark: The poster is free so you shouldn't bitch about it.

Chris: We give people a nice package, we don't want to rip anyone off with just a white sleeve.

Al: Chris, you've been playing a long time with some heavy metal influences...

Chris: I'll admit that I have a heavy metal feel, but I don't think I dwell on it, I just us it as a little flavoring added in with the music. A lot of things get monotonous, it's nice to have some ear piercing notes that make your ears bleed stuck in there. I'm not talking 15 minute solos.

Helen: What about your logo?

George: It's an offshoot from some, we got it from some Christian book of signs that should be banned. Mark reworked the sign into, like Battalion of Saints, the Bat. We like it. The skeletons and the skulls are on the EP because if there's a war, that's what we'd be.

Chris: We like to complain. Complain for the sake of change, for the sake of waking people up going "Look, things are fucked". Get people aware of what's wrong.

Ted: Our songs are also about, like the glorification of killers thru the media not only war..

Helen: Can you feel how conservative it is down in San Diego?

George: Yes. Oh yeah. I walk out of work and people shit their pants.

Dennis: There are so many cowboys down there.

JOHANNA WENT

Interview with the Johanna Went by by Peggy Photo June 21, 1982 in Hollywood. The band consists of Mark Wheaton-

Battalion of Saints – photo Al

keyboards, **Brock Wheaton– drums and Johanna Went– voice and visual art. Hans Reumschuessel, recently added on bass, was also here for the interview.**

Peggy: How long has this group been together?

Johanna: I met Mark and Brock here in L.A. when they were playing with Chinas Comidas. I had Zev play drums for me then. In Summer 1980 Zev had gone off to Europe, so I talked to Mark about it and he and Brock decided to start playing with me.

Peggy: Did you start playing music young?

Mark: Actually Brock started at a very young age. He was in a little kid punk band called the Sound Barriers when he was 10 years old, when their equipment broke he did 1/2 hour drum solos.

Peggy: Did you take piano lessons then?

Mark: No, as a matter of fact I didn't. I was not a musician at all, just an intellectual.

Peggy: What's the purpose of your music?

Johanna: What's the purpose of any music? I don't need a purpose to do what I do. I need to do it. I don't have a philosophy behind it. I'm not trying to put ideas across on other people. I'm a performer, an entertainer. I want to do shows and get paid for it.

Peggy: How is the record related to live shows?

Johanna: It's not. It's a seperate project. I don't understand why you go and buy and record and then go to a concert and see the band doing the same songs.

Mark: Well I think that it is related because of Johanna's style. She has the ability to respond to something immediately and come up with something interesting, funny, creative, whatever. It's what makes her live shows and the record interesting.

Brock: We are an improv band and we're proud of that because there's a real art to being an improv band. The record was kind of an extention to show that there's much more there than just jamming. The record is much more in depth.

Johanna: I like that they're interested in doing unstructured music. That's really important to me because I don't want to be a band that does songs. I think eventually there will be more bands doing less structured songs. I think that is a possibility for the future.

Peggy: Is you music an expression of rebellion?

Johanna: Not necessarily. Everytime I do a show I'm in a different mood. If I'm pissed off about something it will probably come out in

my show.

Brock: It's kind of a rebellion against a lot of the music scene just because we don't work on our show. Hans never even met the people in the band until the night at the Whisky.

Hans: I met them onstage.

Peggy: So were you pleased with the result.

Brock: I love it. The majority of the time we haven't had a bass player. Now me and Hans are kinda jamming on different grooves, doing different patterns, and Greg and Mark are sound effecting on top, and it's added a whole new dimension to it for me.

Mark: Greg Burke has been playing

Johanna Went – photo Peggy Photo

Mark: Brock and Hans are also in the Ju Ju Hounds.

Johanna: Music's not my main occupation, and it never will be. I'm a visual artist. I think visually. When I hear music sometimes the sounds stimulate my brain and it makes me see things and when that happends I really like it.

Peggy: Is you performance sometimes acting out those visions from music?

Johanna: My performance is not as pointed as that. I feel like I'm involved in the process of a vision. I don't do little skits. I think it is real important to give your audience something that is not calculated, it's better to give them a looser situation, that they can look at and interpret for themselves. I don't think people are stupid. Since all visual images that are being given to us through advertising, TV, movies are really pointed with messages telling us to buy something or believe something, to do something, to behave a certain way - you want to understand every kind of image. You become mistrustful of somebody who's giving you visual images because you gotta say: "Ok, what does it mean?". If the person who's giving you the images says: "I don't know what it means, it's just something I dreamed up." Then sometimes people find that is beyond what they want to believe. I don't even care if people think about what I do or not. But people are used to being pushed in their face all the time.

FLIPSIDE NUMBER 33

"One man in the city of L.A. everyone seems to fear
The Hillside Strangler, a dual personality monster that drove the streets
Looking for girls that he and his cousin Bono could rape and kill
No deep remorse for the most violent man of our time
I wanna make you scream
With my hands around your neck
I wanna make you scream
    It's a better world that you're... dead,
    Kenneth Bianchi whose killer other
    side was a madman named Steve
    Steve was the strangler and Ken was
    to be a loving father

The 10 women that died in a 121 reign of terror
From ages 12 to 28 the lives he did take he thought of as no great loss at all
On to Washington he goes leaving the clueless cops behind
Ken gets a job as a private security cop being an idol
But Steve didn't like being such a sap and having no fun
So he strangled two coed girls,
But something went wrong, he got caught
As dirt settled on early graves not too far away

LOOK WHO'S BACK!

WHITE FLAG
'WILD KINGDOM' LP *

+ 7" INCLUDES NON-LP B-SIDE / ●
SCREAMING BROCCOLI

JUSTICE LEAGUE
'REACH OUT' 12" EP ■

BEDLAM HOUR
'ROCK THE CRADLE' LP *

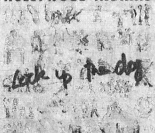

SCREAMING BROCCOLI
LP *

HOLLYWOOD INDIANS
'LOCK UP THE DOG' LP *

WEENIE ROAST
7" EP ●

mailorder
PRICES
* $6
■ $5
● $3
canadians add $1
euro add $5 air

STILL AVAILABLE:
PAGAN BABIES 'IMMACULATE CONCEPTION' 7" E.P.
TOKEN ENTRY 'FROM BENEATH THE STREETS' LP
7 SECONDS 'PRAISE' 12" E.P.
'ANOTHER SHOT FOR BRACKEN' COMPILATION LP
PLUS LOTS MORE !!!

COMING:
7 SECONDS LIVE LP
WAR ON THE SAINTS 12"
D-VISION 12"
MEAN OLD TOWN 12"

POSITIVE FORCE RECORDS

P.O. BOX 9184
RENO, NV. 89507
(702) 348-7838

SEND S.A.S.E. FOR CATALOG AND 7 SECONDS FRIEND CLUB INFO.

US!

marketed and distributed by
Dutch East India Trading
P.O. Box 570, Rockville Centre, N.Y. 11571-0570

ISSUE #: 33
DATE: July 1982
FORMAT: 8 1/2x11, rotary web offset with 2 color cover
PAGES: 48
PRICE: $1.00
PRESS RUN: 3000
STAFF: Al, Hud and Gus

This issue was another bit of a departure from the standard Flipside format. This being the "comic relief" issue that featured nothing but punk rock art and cartoonists. Check this list of featured superstar doodlers: Dennis Worden, Bob Ray, Raymond Pettibon, Pushead, Bob Moore, John Crawford, Fred Tomaselli, Mark Rude, Shawn Kerri and Lee Ellingston! Not to mention single contributions by the likes of Bill Bartell, Gary Panter and Matt Groening! Yes, this was brilliant and successful, the intentions were to do another one, but someone said there were plans for a big artist/ cartoonist comp zine being put together on the east coast so we slacked up. Anyway, this inspired a lot of would be artists to send their stuff to Flipside (people like Brain Walsby!) and kept us in comics for years to come.

FLIPSIDE POLL RESULTS

	1981	1982	1983	1984	1985	1986
Best band:	Circle Jerks	Minor Threat	Suicidal Tendencies	7 Seconds	7 Seconds	Minor Threat
	Black Flag	Bad Religion	Minor Threat	Husker Du	Minor Threat	7 Seconds
	Germs	Black Flag/TSOL	Social Distortion	MIA/Decry	Doggy Style	Naked Raygun
Best New Band:	Wasted Youth	MDC	Suicidal Tendencies	Decry	na	Dag Nasty
	45 Grave	Vandals/Dream Synd.	Suicidal Tendencies	Samhain	na	Cro Mags
	Agent Orange/ Salvation Army/ Symbol Six/ Bad Religion	Negative Approach	Decry/ Decry Neighborhood Watch	COC	na	Final Conflict
Best Record Of The Year:	Black Flag– "Damaged"	Descendents– "Milo... College"	Social Distortion– "Mommys... Monster"	Husker Du– "Zen Arcade"	Dead Kennedys– "Frankenchrist"	Dag Nasty– "Can I Say"
	V/A– "Decline of Western Civilization"	X– "Under the Big Black Sun"	Suicidal Tendencies– "Suicidal Tendencies"	7 Seconds– "The Crew"	Doggy Style– "Side By Side" / 7 Seconds– "Walk Together"	Descendents– "Enjoy"/ Conflict– "Ungovernable..."
	Wasted Youth– "Reagans In"/ TSOL– "Dance With Me"	V/A– "Not So Quiet On The Western Front"	Minor Threat– "Out Of Step"	Decry– "Falling"/ V/A– "Welcome to 1984"	Rites of Spring– "Rites of Spring"	7 Seconds– "New Wind"
Best Record Of All Time:	na	Sex Pistols– "Never Mind..."/ Black Flag– "Damaged"	Sex Pistols– "Never Mind..."	Black Flag– "Damaged"	na	na
	na	DOA– "Hardcore '81"	Minor Threat– "Out Of Step"/ Germs– "G.I."	Germs– "G.I."/ Sex Pistols– "Never Mind..."	na	na
	na	Dead Kennedys– "Fresh Fruit"	Black Flag– "Damaged"	Minor Threat "Minor Threat" EP/ Adolescents– "Adolescents"	na	na
Worst New Band:	Wasted Youth	Suicidal Tendencies	White Flag	na	na	na
Asshole:	Jerry Roach	Ronald Reagan	Wattie	na	Henry Rollins	Skins
Best label:	na	Dischord	Dischord	na	Dischord	Dischord
	na	Alternative Ten.	T&G / BYO	na	BYO	Combat Core
	na	SST / Slash	SST	na	Alternative Ten.	BYO
Straight Edge?	na	Mostly No	64% No, 36% Yes	60% No, 40% Yes	59% No, 41% Yes	61% No, 39% Yes
In A Band?	na	55% No, 45% Yes	57% No, 43% Yes	na	na	na
Ultimate band:						
--guitar--	Greg Ginn– Black Flag	Greg Ginn– Black Flag	Greg Ginn– Black Flag	Greg Ginn– Black Flag	Lyle Preslar– Minor Threat/ Rikk Agnew– DI & Adolescents	Jock– GBH
	Billy Zoom– X	Mike Ness– Social Distortion	Mike Ness– Social Distortion	Bob Mould– Husker Du.	Greg Ginn– Black Flag	Greg Ginn– Black Flag
	Pat Smear– Germs/45 Grave	Ron Emory– TSOL	East Bay Ray– Dead Kennedys	Al Barile– SS Decontrol/ Chris Smith– Battalion of Saints	Bones– Discharge	Brian Baker– Dag Nasty
--bass--	Chuck Dukowski– Black Flag/ Jeff Long– Wasted Youth	Chuck Dukowski– Black Flag	Chuck Dukowski– Black Flag/Wurm	Mike Watt– Minutemen	Steve Youth– 7 Seconds/ Klaus Flouride– Dead Kennedys	Steve Youth– 7 Seconds
	Roger Rogerson– Circle Jerks	Sid Vicious– Sex Pistols	Sid Vicious– Sex Pistols	Brian Baker– Minor Threat	Flea– Red Hot Chile Peppers	Klaus Flouride– Dead Kennedys
	Jay Bentley– Bad Religion	Kendra– Dream Syndicate	Mike Watt– Minutemen	Flea– Red Hot Chili Peppers	Mike Dean– COC	Mike Watt– Minutemen
--drums--	Lucky– Circle Jerks	Robo– Black Flag	Chuck Biscuits– Circle Jerks	Chuck Biscuits– Brown Sound	Chuck Biscuits– ?	Troy– 7 Seconds
	Don Bolles– 45 Grave	Lucky– Circle Jerks	Derek– Social Distortion	Wilf– GBH	Bill Stevenson– Descendents	Reed– COC
	Robo– Black Flag	Chuck Biscuits– Black Flag/ Don Bolles– 45 Grave	Jeff Nelson– Minor Threat	Mitch– TSOL/ Bill Stevenson– Black Flag/ DJ Bonebrake– X	Reed– COC/ Darren Pelegro– Dead Kennedys/ DJ Bonebrake– X	Bill Stevenson– Descendents
--vocals--	Jack– TSOL	Ian MacKaye– Minor Threat	Ian MacKaye– Minor Threat	Henry Rollins– Black Flag	Ian MacKaye– Minor Threat	Jello Biafra– Dead Kennedys/ Ian Mackaye– Embrace
	Keith Morris– Circle Jerks/ John Macias– Circle One	Henry Rollins– Black Flag/ Jello Biafra– Dead Kennedys	Mike Ness– Social Distortion	Ian Mackaye– Minor Threat	Jello Biafra– Dead Kennedys	H.R.– Bad Brains
	Darby– Germs/ Lee Ving– Fear/ Dez– Black Flag/ Henry– Black Flag	Milo– Descendents	Jello– Dead Kennedys	Jello– Dead Kennedys	Kevin Seconds– 7 Seconds	Colin– GBH

FLIPSIDE NUMBER 34

"I'm a person just like you
But I've got better things to do
Than sit around and fuck my head
Hang out with the living dead
Snort white shit up my nose
Pass out at the shows
I don't even think about speed
That's something I just don't need
– I've got the straight edge
I'm a person just like you
But I've got better things to do
Than sit around and smoke dope
Cause I know that I can cope
Laugh at the thought of eating 'ludes
Laugh at the thought of sniffing glue
Always gonna keep in touch
Never want to use a crutch
– I've got the straight edge."
"Straight Edge" - Minor Threat

ISSUE #: 34
DATE: August 1982
FORMAT: 8 1/2x11, rotary web offset with 2 color glossy cover
PAGES: 52
PRICE: $1.00
PRESS RUN: 4000
STAFF: Al, Hud, Pete, Pooch, Helen, Michele, Shredder, Carol and Kori

With this issue there are no physical changes, just more distribution and stuff like that. The scene is happening but spread out: remember the Galaxy in Fullerton? This place had a ten foot high stage! No shit. How about Dancing Waters in 'Pedro? This place had a real flowing water fall behind the stage!! What about Mercury Art Center in the Super Market? And best yet, the Olympic Auditorium, punk gigs in a wrestling/ roller derby palace! Yep, these were the happening places at this time. Actually the Olympic had started with Pil a few issues back, but this was the first punk rock marathon show! Could this be the start of something big???

5 Year Anniversary...

Yeah that's right, 5 years doing this fanzine – and now we're gonna look at where we (L.A. the oldest H.C. scene) are. In a short answer I'll say – practically nowhere! When you stop and think about what goes on now in L.A., it's seems really stupid. Ok, this scene started

with pretty low goals. Bands would form and be glad just to play, let alone get paid, or put records out. We were lucky to have gigs to go to, there was a unity in survival. And we survived. But where has it go us? who (bands) care about door prices anymore? You bigger bands have gone from being lucky to get gigs to demanding that you get paid or you won't play. What is selling out anyway? Sure, I think you should get what money you deserve, but what about these large guarantees I've heard you bragging about? What about these great managers and booking agents YOU PAY to get the clubs to give you MORE money. The the clubs want more money. It's a vicious circle and it never ends. If you want to demand something, demand a door percentage and refuse to play those clubs that don't pay fair: where is your integrity? So now there is almost no place to play in L.A. – that's true for you bands whose heads are so swollen that you'll only play the Whisky or for that matter the Olympic. What happened to putting on your own hall gigs? Our scouting out new clubs? They're out there you just gotta look. That might be a lot to ask of you big bands signed to Faulty or Posh Boy or... but shit, that ain't nothing! Selling 10 thousand records is shit. You still aren't doing anything but preaching to the converted. I mean get yourself in the right perspective, you might be at the top of the heap in this scene but you ain't no household word so get it out of your head. Come back to earth and play for the fans, or don't you enjoy playing anymore? This really gives new bands a bad attitude, they're practically sending out demos of their first practices in hopes of getting 'signed'. There is still a lot of room for more independents. But then look at the independents who still demand too much for their product (I must congradulate people like Dischord, Posh Boy, BYO etc for keeping their record prices low.) We're playing rock star/ record business on a small scale and it's getting us nowhere, except closer to the things we wanted to "destroy" in the first place. So right now, Boston, New York, DC are happening places with people with good attitudes, I say give them time, but I also say use US as an example! Learn from history, don't follow in it's steps. All I can say about L.A. is too look at what's going wrong now. If you band can demand $1000 and get it, that's fine, but don't expect me to be your loyal fan while you play those stupid "punkstocks", that bores me shitless, bring "punk" back to the clubs. And when we get a club, go easy on it, I'd like to see the scene go underground but I don't want to see it buried.

Joe Nolte - photo Al

JOE NOLTE, THE LAST

by James Moreland

Joe Nolte (vocals and guitar) and Vitus Matare (keyboards, vocals, guitar) have been in various bands together ever since they met at Loyola High School in the mid-70's. One of these bands evolved into the Last, who have been around in one form or another since the earliest days of the Masque. You can still buy some of their older recordings, such as the "L.A. Explosion" album and the relatively more recent "Fade To Black" ep (both on Bomp Records) at local record stores, though the band members will be the first to admit that none of these have come close to capturing The Last's live sound.

Flipside: You weren't really considered a punk band in the Hollywood scene, and you definitely weren't a pop band. Did you feel you should go one way or the other?
Joe: We were real tempted to go one way or the other. You see, the thing is, we were a hardcore band in '77.
Flipside: What about the south bay scene now?
Joe: When I was living at the Church, there was only a handful. I knew everybody who was into hardcore then: there were maybe 20 of them at the most, and there were 20 million long haired surfers who would constantly give us shit. We'd get death threats all the time. I would walk down Pier Ave. looking basically as I do now, as recently as '79, and they were very anti-punk.
Flipside: Are those the same people that are punks now?
Joe: Yes, you can really tell in retrospect, as the years go by, who the real poseurs were. Cause anybody who really liked punk is still into it.
Flipside: But you guys aren't a punk band anymore.
Joe: That's ok, we still like the stuff.
Flipside: Then why arne't you doing it?
Joe: There's no way you can be a punk band for ten years. Not punk in its purest form. It's a roots thing. Each band has to progress beyond it, but there's got to be new bands to take their places. It's not as shocking as it was in '77 when everybody was listening to Peter Frampton and disco. Punk is in the process of getting assimilated and becoming socially acceptable... it's not like deciding to get into punk rock in '77 and being the only kid in your High School who's into it.
Flipside: Don't we need something else now? Punk is almost the same boring thing that it replaced.
Joe: The basic worth of rock and roll is that in every generation you need something to play real loud when you're pissed off. What the Last is is a tie in between the hardcore level of I hate everything, I need music that makes windows break, that makes my parents get real pissed off. A combination of music that makes you feel justified in rebelling, and something like the pop angle of it, the thing that makes you feel good.... You're blowing off steam at the same time with a whole bunch of other people and it makes you more determined to be rebellious because you realize there are all those other people that are. When something you like gets popular you realize you are not alone... If Black Flag can get big, which they are, that means that there are a lot of other people who are feeling what you're feeling, and it leads to a sense of camaraderie, and maybe you're less scared to

DICKIES!

still had a following in the States and to tell everyone that, they weren't from England. That brings us to now. The Dickies present line-up includes: Stan Lee on guitar, and Leonard on voice, the only two original members. Steve Hufsteter (ex-Quick/Falcons) was also added on guitar. Steve has been long time friends with the Dickies and had a lot to do with forming the original band. On bass is Lori Burhe from Wet Picnic and on drums is Jerry Angel veteran of the local circuit. Although I can't say the new members have as strong as chracter as the old members, they certainly are good with their instruments. (More on where Billy and Carlos are next time). I'm sure as time goes on they will develop into characters we all know and love - just like before. The Dickies are definitly going for the big comeback. The tour was very successful with sold old clubs and halls all over the States. They found they had more

THE DICKIES!!!! Yeah, the Dickies!!! One of my favorite bands of the "good old days" and this my friends is sort of a preview of an interview that will hopefully be in the next issue. You all know who the Dickies are - but do you know where they are or what they have been doing? Well here it is in a nutshell. The Dickies formed in the Valley (yes - thee Valley) in 1977 and gained a large following playing some great gigs at the Masque, Whisky and Starwood. They got a lot of attention and were soon signed by A&M records in London. Since the label was in London, they had to do a lot of touring there (not that stuff wasn't eventually released in the States). They did a few big tours over there (here too) and became quite popular. Their popularity was biggest, however, in England, where the band had a few minor hit singles. Nothing really took over here, where they practically stopped playing.

They probably played four gigs in L.A. in 1979/1980. The group seemed to go into hiding - there were rumors of band members quitting and drug addiction. But finally they surfaced again. They had quite a bit of material under their belt - a ten inch single, a whole bunch of singles, and two albums: "Incredible Shrinking Dickies" & "Dawn of the Dickies". Then in the summer of 1981 keyboard player Chuck Wagon took his life with a gun. We all thought that would be the final kick that would break them apart for sure. But no. By Xmas they had a new band going - and they started to tour again. A&M had dropped them from the label in both England and the U.S. but the Dickies set out on a tour of the States called "We're not from England" tour. They financed the effort themselves to see if they

fans than they had imagined. So the next step is to get some vinyl out. Right now they are looking at a possible new deal with A&M in England and I.R.S. here in the States for release of an ep. Stan says they have over 20 songs right now that they always play that arn't recorded. The selection's for the ep will come from tunes like: "Stukas Over Disneyland", "Hunchback", "Communication Breakdown", "Rosemary" or even "Gigantor" and "Bananna Splits" that havent been released here. They are even talking to wizard produced Mike Chapman to have the honors (not that they need any help -"Dawn of" sounded perfect!). Others songs in the Dickies current set include "If Stewart Could Talk" about Leonards penis, like in the picture Leonard brings out a penis puppet to help him sing, "Pretty Please Me" an old song Hufsteter used to do in the Quick, and other songs with new props like a "Rawhide" song with cactuses! They will also be playing a lot more in the near future -so keep a look out for the Dickies, and if you think they've wimped out, listen to some of their old singles - then see them do it even better live! - - Al

The Hated

tell somebody to fuck off, or throw a brick into a nearby shop window... That's like the purpose of Flipside and fanzines everywhere: to get people in contact with one another, and to make people realize they are not alone.

THE HATED

The Hated were interviewed by Michele at their studio on July 20, 1982.
Chalmer farts......
Michele: Where are you all from?
Steve: I'm from HB, Chalmers from Newport, Gary and Bob are from Cerritos.
Michele: Why do you call yourselves "Hated"?
Gary: Because of Steve!! He's always been hated and thought up the name.
Steve: No way!!!
Michele: Why? Don't you have any friends?
Steve: No, I got lots of friends. You should have seen that chick I was with last night! It just seemed appropriate at the time, 3 years ago.
Chalmer farts again...
Michele: Are you famous for those?
Chalmer: Yes I am.
Michele: How do you catagorize your music?
Steve: Hard-on!!
Chalmer: Heavy metal.
Gary: No Michele, we are punk rock.
Bob: Now listen, this is our own style, there's a lot of bands that play real fast and the same three chords.
Gary: We've been together 3 years and when we started out we played the same thing, it gets boring.
Steve: Sorry! We can't be like everyone else.
Gary: Can I say something? This is serious for people trying to read it. Our songs have a lot of meaning. They have deep meaning. They're about life.
Chalmer: And about bugs...
Gary: And anarchy, hating your mom, killing cats...
Michele: How's your sex lives?
Steve: My dicks bigger than these guys!
Michele: Do you have girlfriends now or...
Band: WE DUMPED THEM FOR THE SUMMER! (band goes hysterical!)
Steve: Every summer.
Michele: Or did you guys get dumped!
Steve: Us get burnt! Come on. You should

have seen me at that party last night! Here's the Hated philosophy on girls: Get 'em in the winter and dump 'em in the summer. (Laughter). In the summer you've got to grab the best babe you can because summer is open season, get your gun, whew!
Gary: 1982 party naked, shots are free.
Steve: Yeah, Free Clinics like a block and 1/2 from my house, I've got my name on a parking spot right up front.
Michele: Don't you want to be famous and make lots of money?
Steve: The farther you go up, you gotta come down!
Gary: We'll stay at the bottom all our life.
Michele: So you just want to be unknown all your lives?
Gary: We don't worry about it.
Band: Party naked at Max's house!!!!!

THE BLASTERS

You're probably thinking "Why the Blasters' guitarist Dave Alvin and bassist John Bazz in Flipside?" and I Shredder am thinking "Why not?" They're just as aspiring bunch of nice guys with some inspiring boogie woogie and I know I've seen punk hordes at their shows. Too hardcore for you? Harr harr...
Shredder: I noticed there are quite a few punks from the Downey area. What did you do for fun as a kid down there?
Dave: When I was a kid, from like 3 to 6, there were all these surf bands in Orange County and Downey had a good share of them. Every block had one, so for awhile I was real fascinated with Fender guitars. What I would do for kicks when I was growing up was like pimping wine and beer and going down into the San Gabriel river bed and drinking. As I got older I got into vandalism and stuff like that.
Shredder: I know you were raised off the music you play but most of the people into rock-a-billy and rhythm and blues have picked it up from English bands. What do you think of that?
Dave: I think it's alright. I used to be real bitter against people like that. The main thing, and what I think is the main problem, is fashion. A lot of bands are sincere and some of their

following are, but the majority — or what I THINK are the majority, don't feel for the music. They just have their records of, you know Hepcats, Straycats, Johnnycats, Polecats, thiscats, thatcats and I try to tell myself that it's ok because I will always love the music and it's ok wherever it gets over. Be it American or English or African bands, it would be better than nothing. But people get hooked on the fashion and that's bad because fashion is a temporary thing.
Shredder: Do you think all this boogie woogie rock-a-billy can perpetuate itself in popularity?
Dave: I think it can if it's taken a certain way. If you put anything in any sort of faddish sense it becomes a fad. When you look at the so-called rock-a-billy revival, which has been happening ever since the Sex Pistols but hadn't picked up until now, you see that time and time again a big break is predicted. Like when Levi Dexter first came to America everyone said: "Oh now this stuff is going to be big big big" Then a week after the Specials and Madness came over everyone said: "Now it's ska mod music" and so on and so forth. With all this running around the only way our kind of music is going to survive is with bands- not to blow our horn or anything, but like us who don't play for the girls or for the look. It'll survive on it's own.
Shredder: But is the audience as sincere as you are?
Dave: Well it seem to me that the ones that are really excited about the music arne't trendy or fashion oriented. You know anything can become fashionable, even the Rhythm Pigs. Everyone will put on weight and get a pair of lardass jeans and throw up drunk everynight.
Shredder: What are some of the drawbacks to your success?
John: Things aren't as successful as they seem. Our hit record was just a crazy fluke.
Dave: But it's nice to go into a laundromat and some cute straight girl comes up and says "Aren't you in the Blisters? No, the Blusterers, no..." It can also be a pain. People are more scrutinizing of you and you can't get drunk at a club without someone thinking "What an asshole!" Before no one gave a shit.
Shredder: Is there still a thrill to play to as little as 100 people?
Dave: Hell yeah! Are you kidding, we shit in our pants before every show!

PHRANC

Being able to do an interview with Phranc was a dream come true... mainly because she had been around so long and has such a flexible attitude towards the scene. We met at Phillipe's for lunch and I hoped she would have a lot to say. She did!
Helen: You have a background in art...
Phranc: I never went to art school. I've always done a lot of art. Took art lessons as a kid. My grandmother is a painter. I was always encouraged.
Helen: I always think of you as a major part of the L.A. scene. Do you like L.A.? Do you ever feel like going away?
Phranc: Yeah I like it a lot. I want to go someplace else because I want to hear other peoples reactions to my music. I would be very difficult, I'd love to go and play all over the country, just take my guitar and go,.. but I don't think that I'm such a free spirit anymore. I think I'm more conservative.

DAG NASTY

Phranc with Nervous Gender — the first performance at Club 88 - photo Al

Helen: What do you think of some of the changes in the L.A. music scene?

Phranc: I think it's really great how OFTEN it changes. How new people come in. When a lot of new people were coming in they had read articles and the media was hyping it to death. I think it drew a lot of people in for the wrong reasons. Now it's back to people that are young and have the energy and are inspired. People that have done it (the scene) before have a choice: they can sit it or they can sit back. It's always going to change. It has evolved it's own kind of history. I really like talking to the new people on the scene because their perspective is so different. It's a different world. Different kinds of comraderie and rivalry. There are small gangs and bigger gangs. It's very exciting to me.

Helen: About the past... there was Nervous Gender, what do you think of them now?

Phranc: I haven't seen anything that they are doing. All I know is that they put out a little booklet that said nasty things about me... creative things, I should say. I happen to like Gerardo a lot. It was very interesting for me. I had never been in a band before. I came from a radical lesbian feminist background and all of a sudden I was in a group with three misogynists! Looking back at it now, I can't see how I could be politically so strong and working with something so opposite. I can not explain it, but I think it was a good experience. I had a lot of fun with them. I can't believe a lot of the things I sang, that I ever got up and sang: "Jesus was a cocksucking Jew from Galilee". I don't think I was concerned or thought about what I was saying.

Helen: How is it different now?

Phranc: In terms of music, I think a lot more of what I am projecting and what I am trying to say. With Nervous Gender it was more having a good time and did the most outrageous things we could do. The noise started driving me nuts. I have such synthesizer damage...

Helen: Catholic Discipline didn't last very long, did it?

Phranc: Catholic Discipline was never a real 'band' situation. Everyone was in at least one or two other bands. Some of it was conflict of interest or conflict of personality but it was perfect the way it started and ended.

Helen: Why did you choose to do acoustic music?

Phranc: Because you can hear the words better. I like that other bands are starting to play acoustic, just from time to time, to take a break. That was the point of the folk shows.

Helen: In you music, your politics is mostly local and temporary.

Phranc: Its become a problem. With the song about Nougucci– thank God they reopened the case! People don't read the newspaper, it's too depressing.

Helen: Do you think you are the voice of L.A.? Since so many songs are about this area.

Phranc: No I just wanted to play acoustic because it was the only way I knew to get a message across. The original message was that I was mad because people were wearing all these swasticas... I'm a little tired of being known as the angry young dyke. I'm not as angry as I used to be. I still get pretty mad - sure, life makes everybody pissed. It is what keeps you alive.

BANGS

We (Al, Pete, Pooch and James Moreland) got some beer and started to interview the Bangs at Sloans but several of the girls could not get in. So we went over to Barneys Beanery, had a few beers and decided it wouldn't work either. We ended up calling up Rodney, grabbed a few more beers and other refreshments and settled down in Rodney's living room/museum. Rodney had just gotten back from Hawaii with the Gogos...

Rodney: I walked into this party with the Gogos and everyone got mobbed. Belinda had to leave....

Bangs: Wow!!!

Al: What do you think of the Gogos?

Sue: We knew you'd ask.

Pooch: It just came up in conversation!!

Vickey: We like the Gogos but were not the Gogos, we'd like people to remember that please!! We think we're good and we've been doing this for quite awhile. It's a whole different thing. People think we like started singing and playing guitars three years ago when we saw them, I like them, I like their songs, but we didn't start playing in this band because of them. We are doing something that   is   our   own.

Pooch: When did you get together?

Debbie: Last January.

Vickey: We've been together a year and a half. The reason there are only three of us on the record ("Getting Out Of Hand" single) is because we did that last summer and Annette wasn't with us. So we just put it out basically to secure the name because we like our name and we wanna keep it.

Sue: We didn't expect to get any attention really.

Debbie: And it got #5 on the L.A. Weekly chart this week!

James: It's pretty obvious that you are influenced by 60's bands but are there any 70's or early 80's bands that your are influenced by?

Vickey: Eddie Money!

Sue: I don't remember the 70's.

Rodney: The Partridge Family!

Sue: Yeah!! I liked the Partridge Family, they were very good. I like some early Jackson Five, well I lied, a lot of the stuff that came out of the late 70.

James: Sex Pistols, Blondie, Ramones, I liked Patty Smith a lot...

Vickey: And heavily influenced by J.F.K.

James: Are you influenced by male groups more than female groups?

Sue: It's true a lot of people think we are influenced by groups like the Ronettes and all that and I think it's more guy groups like the Yardbirds, Beatles etc...

Al: Why do you think people like No Mag would be interested in you?

Sue: We have been wondering that. Like the first show we did was the No MAG show with hardcore punk bands, CH3 and the Descendents. The Descendents always ask us to go out on dates! We're going to the mountains with Salvation Army and Dream Syndicate on Labor Day.

James: Has it occured to you that the attention you're getting is because you are an all girl band?

Vickey: Of course, that's the only reason why we are up there! Anybody can get attention for anything, for being cute, for being young, for being this or that. I think that Rodney playing our record has helped us out a lot because people notice. We often dedicate songs at shows to you Rodney.

Rodney: Really!

Pooch: It's not weird to be an all male band, or have one or two females, but all females is kind of weird...

Rodney: It's a novelty. Every girl should be in a band.

James: Why are you an all girl band?

Vickey: Debbie and I have played with male guitarists...

Sue: I was always in bands with guys before.

Pooch: Do you do your own booking?

Annette: Yes we do.

James: Do you find yourselves getting shafted? (No one thought that was funny!)

Pooch: can a girl get away with playing more pop than a guy can?

Annette: I don't really know, I don't care.

Pete: Would you play with the Gogos?

Annette: I don't know.

Vickey: I don't think that I would. We wouldn't feel weird playing with another group that had a girl singer in it, like Bow Wow Wow or something, that would be terrific!

Al: Well, you're opening now, wait till you're headlining, that's another story.

Vickey: I don't think so, because that's saying that the only value in our group is the gender.

Bangs/Bangles - photo Pete L.

We've got to watch it, we are up against this exploitation thing all the time. Which is hard to handle.

Rodney: Do you date your fans?

Sue: Some of our fans are also in bands, so they have to hate the band in order to go out with us.

Al: Aren't there unique girl problems...

Vickey: Yeah yeah our periods happen right before a show! It's really tough.

Al: Do they ever all coincide?

Sue: Yeah they do!!! Ha ha ha. We get them on the same day a lot of times...

Vickey: Well it's like tuning into someone like when you're living with someone or you're best friends you start saying things the same time, you start thinking things the same...

Sue: James wants to know what our ultimate goal is. To be happy!

Vickey: Revolutionizing the radio.

Al: What will you put on the cover of your very first album?

Sue: A picture of us with perfect Rodney type bangs! 1960's hair!

Al: If you were on the cover of Rolling Stone, would you be in your underwear?

Sue: No.

Vickey: Of course.

Annette: Only if I had a bra on!

Sue: We'd be totally naked! Just kidding. Anyways, James wants to know what our ultimate musical goals are.

James: I didn't say musical goals, I just said goals!!

Vickey: We want to get AM airplay, we want to be a radio band, we want to get AM radio back! There's something so important about the stress you go through in life, you connect events in your life with what you hear on the radio.

(In a short time Annette left the band and joined Blood On The Saddle, the Bangs changed their name to the Bangles and became the best selling all girl group in history. Yes they did get a lot of radio airplay.)

MINOR THREAT

Minor Threat were interviewed on July 8 by Al... It's really hard to print an interview with these guys because they have so much to say - about everything. The are on of the few bands I've interviewed that really know what they are doing and all four members can tell you what the band is about. They also have their own opinions on just about any subject and each individuals character is expressed: "I tend to be overly optimistic" Ian will tell you, "Lyle is a bit pessimistic, Brian is open and loose about things, and Jeff likes to question, and we all clash!". This band is full of philosophy and ideas and that seems to be hard for them at times, as Jeff puts it "We are really idealistic and that makes it hard to do the things that you normally need to do" They manage to gain the respect of many people in a particular way that makes a relationship with the band more than just 'fan' and 'band'. They are themselves living examples of what they talk about in their songs.

Minor Threat originally formed in Washington D.C. in November of 1980 and played and recorded until September of 1981. At that time they broke up because of general band depression (their west coast tour being cancelled) and because Lyle choose to go to college. During that time they recorded and released records on their own Dischord Records. Ian and Jeff tried to form a band but it just didn't work out right. Finally after much discussion and putting off, they reformed when Lyle decided college in Michigan wasn't for him. One of the biggest deciding factors Ian told me, was when H.R. of the Bad Brains told him that he hadn't finished what he set out to do in Minor Threat – so with renewed enthusiasm Minor Threat got back together. With only two show in DC under their belt, they set off to complete the cross country tour that had ended their existence last time. "Washington was giving me bad feelings" says Ian "So we wanted to tour as quick as possible".

After a long talk and doing part of the interview on a broken tape recorder, we ended up talking about "straight edge" - a name of a song on their first ep and what seems to becoming a movement, especially back east...

Brain: Straight edge is not letting anyone interfere with doing what you want to do...

Lyle: Like not becoming obsessed with things like drugs sex, religion or violence...

Ian: To do things and be alert and benefit form it, to be a punk or whatever and benifit from it.

Lyle: In other words, going to a show and getting energy from the bands you see rather than getting fucked up or going out just to get some girl...

Jeff: So you don't follow your dick around or let anything lead you around.

Ian: Controlling things and not letting them control you and that's basically what straight edge is. And it works.

Lyle: On the other hand we're not like militant about it. We don't regard it as a club to be in to talk to us...

Ian: There's no rules or requirements.

Lyle: In this society it's not really normal not to drink or take drugs...

Jeff: All this stuff is not just aimed at punks.

Ian: It's aimed at everyone, all people. Part of the reason I align myself with punk is because to me it is a certain form of music where you really express something.

Jeff: ...a thinking kids music...

Ian: It's more than entertainment, it's beneficial, it's doing something, it says something.

Lyle: Sometimes......

Jeff: There's a lot of punk music that is bullshit... totally...

Ian: Detrimental...

Jeff: You hope people are level headed enough to pick out the good from the bad. A lot of people are spouting this anti-government stuff and they have no idea of what they are talking about...

Brian: I live 5 miles from where it all

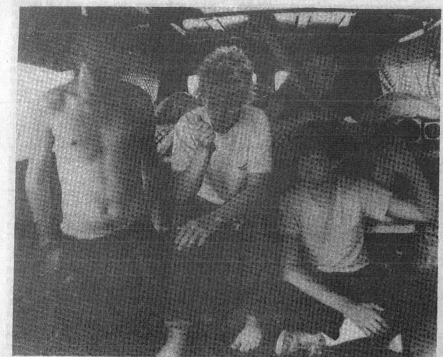

Ian: Charity starts at home...

Lyle: It's great that people have political consciousness, and everyone in the band has some sort of political consciousness, it just happends that we choose no to sing about it.

Ian: Same with religion, it's more a personal thing. If people would start with themselves, to make themselves better, then thats a step in the right direction.

Lyle: And things will get better. Right now all the kids in America are eventually gonna grow up and many of them will be in a position of influence. The whole point is if you deal with yourself and people you can exert influence upon, then maybe you can put those people in a mentality that will be beneficial to everybody else later on. And that's the only hope that you can possibly have.

Ian: We don't tell people what to do and we don't want people to look at our songs and go this is the way it is. We want people to take what the song says and apply it to themselves and see how it fits. Like a mirror, see themselves and think about it. If it changes them for the better then that's good.

Jeff: We don't offer solutions to anything, just alternatives.

Merril: When I met Ian I thought I was gonna get the rap cause I do drugs and I'm into the sex thing so heavily, I felt threatened and I took it out on Ian before he even said anything.

Ian: We get so much shit from people who take drugs, we get attacked!

Lyle: Because they're scared.

Ian: The fact that WE ARE able to deny it bugs them. A lot of people won't drink in front of me or hide it when I come into the room, that's stupid!!! ...about fucking, we should clairify this, as far as "Out Of Step" the line says "Don't fuck", basically that's not so much

happends, and I don't deal with shit, Ronald Reagan has no effect, its...

Ian: No DC bands are overtly political at all.

Jeff: We're not apathetic but we realize,... I hate politics but you can change stuff if you get involved but you have to base your whole life around it and then maybe change a little bit in politics or government. It's pretty much

hopeless, and there's a lot wrong, but it is great the way it is. The government is so free it's incredible – I control myself and take care of stuff that effects me more directly.

Lyle: Everybody should exert influence on things they have control over. In other words if you see John Doe walking down the street, you deal with John Doe...

Minor Threat - photos Al

Killing Joke at Whisky – photo Al

sexual intercourse because I'm not and none of us are asexual. It's more an approach to sex. I don't believe in fucking, it's more liberal out here but that fucks with peoples heads...

Jeff: We're not loose!

Ian: They take the like "Don't fuck" as a total literal thing – I personally don't fuck but it's more the idea behind it, I have sex, but I don't fuck, it's a term........

Lyle: We're really proud that in Washington, which is not an entertainment town, not a music or club town, we put together a band and got records out and financed it all.

Ian: We are one of the first legitimate scenes out of Washington DC, I'm proud to be a part of a scene that has a good, big, reputation. And it's true.... There's so many fucking kids here! It's like a family oriented place, beaches, the whole thing. DC is like single, professional people and you've got to realize that DC is 85% Black. It's not like Blacks can't be punks but they have a huge funk scene going, probably the biggest in the country and they have teenage bands. So it's really an accomplishment that we do have such a scene.

Lyle: It has it's advantages, because it isn't an entertainment town, we don't have the exploitation that goes on here. It's all PR out here.

Ian: When we are out here I hear "record label" and "getting signed" and you don't hear that in Washington. Bands just want to play, getting signed is like dream world. When we first started, getting a record out was a total dream to us – that the Teen Idles would ever put a record out. Out here it's a big market. People form a band which he intention to make it and put out records and be popular. We formed Teen Idles out of boredom and Minor Threat as a vehical to express what we were thinking about. And we put our own records out. It's better the whole way we go about it, it's in a testing stage but we don't promote ourselves like most bands do. And it's working real well. We don't make press packs..

Jeff: They're corny.

Ian: It's too masterbatory... If we make ourselves interesting enough, then people will come up to us and want to hear about what we have to say.

KILLING JOKE

Killing Joke were interviewed by Al and Pete in July 1982. This was our second confrontation with this controversal band, last year we did a short introduction interview and this year we got a lot deeper into their ideas. Killing Joke are not the life of the party - quite the contrary, they are very realistic and serious - to the point of being Stoic. Some people are put off by their apparent preoccupation with doom and the decline of this civilization, this is however, a very realistic point of view. America and especially Southern California are important to their scheme of things because the plastic culture here has a lot to say about the future of our species. You can deny the obvious and live each day as a party, but Killing Joke choose to very seriously observe and learn, and apply that to the future.

After a brief warm up talking about Disneyland, both the place and the attitude, we quite easily slipped into the way America reacts to Killing Joke...

Jaz: We're really out of order here, if I compare this to Europe it's unbelievable. All over Europe there's this feeling, before we go on it's acknowledged. Over here it's so relaxed and they can't understand the intensity of the music. There's no feedback, when we're on stage we have to feed off of each other, there's no tension to feed off of.

Geordie: We come from England where we play in front of 5 1/2 thousand live and we play here to this...

Jaz: They're not programmed to understand any other rhythm except the really accessible a) punk or b) disco. They are musically conditioned so anything out of the ordinary they stand and watch when they come to a show. I hate this whole culture, it's dispicable! ...I saw Black Flag the other night and I watched those punks and they weren't dancing to any music, just moving, you might as well have a saw mill going. It's inconcievable to compare it to the tension in Europe. It's like souless here. The whole fucking country – nothing. No foundation. A huge gap... We're not far away from the biggest bloodbath in the history of our species... I'm not worried about it, I'm banking on it. It doesn't matter where you live. It's your

free will to live anywhere as long as you fullfill the demand you need for yourself as far as being biologically and spiritually required. That's how I see it. It may mean you live 5 to 10 years more but that doesn't make that much difference in the long run. As long as you fullfill what you have to do.

Al: What do you have to do? Will it be done as Killing Joke?

Jaz: Sure. Leave a mark. I hate the attitude that young people take. They only see the period of time, now up until the intuitive feeling of a great big change like a nuclear war or something. They only see this time, not beyond that. I consider what comes after that more important. The furthur evolution or our species basically.

Al: If there's anything left.

Jaz: Of course there will be. There's no way the species will be extinct. I consider that nature only creates that which it can cope with - like from oil to a nuclear bomb. Ultimately in nature there's a synthesized product it can cope with - ultimately. Everythings a mutation. We are a mutation in our present form and I see evolution changing with the changes that will happen. And I consider preparation should be made for that.

Al: What kind of preparation can you make?

Jaz: An irrational view of existance I think is necessary, as opposed to the methods of reason that we are conditioned to.

Al: We read about your move to Iceland, is that part of the preparation?

Jaz: What do you think?

Al: Sounds like it to me...

Jaz: Of course, there's a motivation behind every holiday.

Al: Is Iceland a holiday for you?

Jaz: It's all a holiday isn't it?

Al: Well, a holiday to the nuclear missile bases of Iceland...

Jaz: It's one target as opposed to 20 in England. Taking a nuclear view is taking a short sighted view. That's only one aspect of the events taking place. I see natural changes in every aspect... Iceland is at sea level, you see a lot of water and maybe these icecaps will get exposed to the suns rays, maybe? Maybe the majority of the western world and some of the eastern is below sea level, maybe this might have something to do... in the Koran and in the Bible they say it will be fire followed by water, who knows? They say biologically all life stems from water so it makes sense to me.

Al: Do you keep up with what it says in Revelations or...

Jaz: I don't read the Bible, I read it once, it's the biggest sin of the last day and it's wicked, wicked, you know why? Because basically it's a doctorine that neither spiritually or biologically goes with nature. It's a doctorine that goes by restriction which is a doctorine that goes against the nature of our species.

Al: Do any of those books, you mentioned the Koran...

Jaz: No. None of them. They're all opposed to it. It's crazy.

Al: But the quote "fire followed by water"...

Jaz: Right, then it follows into a promotion of the individual religion after that. It's wank.

Al: The press seem to link your moves with the occult?

Jaz: That's a word that has no great level but we do take an irrational view and irrational methods to the necessary ends or beginnings required.

Al: What might these methods be?

Paul: Looking for as many things as you can

Looking to the source.

Jaz: As long as you're successful that's all that matters. We shouldn't question how it works or why it works as long as it works... In America it's futile to make an effort to change anything because you'll be continuing at the mercy of the mass consciousness. Therefore why make an effort except in personal development. It's a common feeling, were demanding words again, the words just mean Killing Joke if you need words. In one sense it can mean you the individual is in control or his or her self, will, or destiny – or you are at the mercy of that which will control you. I consider the future holds a heirarchy where there are basically those who are kings and those who are slaves. The King masters himself and the slave doesn't know his own will. You master what is your own individual will. I consider those necessary values for the future – inequality should be increased as opposed to supressed. Those people who have not found themselves individually should not be with those who have.

Al: What about people at the mercy of alcohol, sex or drugs?

Jaz: Slaves, slaves to themselves. Drugs are fucking important, if you know how to use them to can benefit 1000 percent. If you become a slave to the drug that's good to because you eventually die. You have a hand on it or you don't. And I consider that the law of nature – survival of the fittest. What determines it? Time can only tell.

Geordie: We like finding strategic locations.

Jaz: We're interested in geography., certain things about the earth basically – again in an irrational view. Icelands got some interesting qualities... I consider 500 years of dark ages, of barbaric times, all present morals/values shattered, all religions destroyed.

Pete: It's like that now almost...

Jaz: It's well on the way, but there's gonna be a big crunch...

Al: How does living in Iceland help you come to grips with this?

Jaz: Nothing. Exactly that. 150,000 people, underpopulation, a place where nature dominates the senses. Which is fine because in one sense Killing Joke has always used fear of the elements, fear of that which is beyond and taken that orally more than any other unit.

Al: Will you visit other places?

Jaz: Sure. Totally. Soviet Union, Peru, lots of other places.

Al: Energy centers of past civilizations or like there are great magnetic forces in Iceland...

Jaz: Iceland has particular qualities but that's our business. This place, the west coast is of particular interest to me because it is cursed by the Indians. They absolutely cursed it. There used to be sacred places between San Francisco and Los Angeles of the old Indians... it doesn't have too much of a future. I consider culture a vile thing taken literally, I think just the individual potential is important, whether you're born in the U.S. or the Soviet Union has no importance at all. All it is is the capacity of the individual to master himself in his own environment. Patriotism is a vile thing, a low trick designed for low mentality.

Al: A lot of that in England with the Faulklands.

Jaz: Excellent in one sense. I'm concerned with segregation of capable and incapable or mindless like the patriotic. They will be amongst themselves. People who have the ability to control themselves will find the people who it's best to be with. Birds of a feather flock together. That's the kind of segregation I intend to perpetuate.

FLIPSIDE NUMBER 35

"I'm a clean cut American kid
My mama raised right I ain't no skid
I've got job I pull my own
I've got a place I can call home
I don't smoke and I don't drink
I use deodorant so I don't stink
I wear a white t-shirt under my clothes
I don't fart or pick my nose
I'm a nice guy I'm so polite
I turn the other cheek, I never fight
I take a bath everyday
And you can hear all the people say
I go fishing with my dad
You know I'm always such a happy lad
I go to bed everynight at ten
I brush my teeth with a wide white grin"
"Clean Cut American Kid" – Ill Repute

ISSUE #: 35
DATE: November 1982
FORMAT: 8 1/2x11, rotary web offset.
PAGES: 24
PRICE: Free with ROTR Vol. 3
PRESS RUN: ?
STAFF: Al and Hud

- -

Again, this is a free insert that comes with the Rodney On The Roq Vol. 3 compilation album.

FLIPSIDE NUMBER 36

"Anarchy, kill a cat,
Shoot James Brady in the back
Raise an army of rabid rats
Beat your neighbor with a bat
Anarchy burger, hold the government...
Anarchy, go eat shit
Let them know you're sick of it
Write your congressman, tell me he sucks
He's only in it for the bucks
Anarchy burger, hold the government...
You're all potential anarchy burgers
If you want to be free
Order yourself an anarchy burger
Hold the government please...
America stands for freedom
But if you think you're free
Try walking into a deli
and urinating on the cheese
Say fuck in front of you mom,
go to school naked
Anarchy burger, hold the government"
"Anarchy Burger" – The Vandals

ISSUE #: 36
DATE: December 1982
FORMAT: 8 1/2x11, rotary web offset with 3 color glossy cover.
PAGES: 68
PRICE: $1.00
PRESS RUN: 5000
STAFF: Al, Hud, Gus, Helen, Pooch, Shredder, Michele, Pete, Paul, Kori, Carol, Gus, Maw, Robert Hill, Monk etc...

- -

This issue was different and historical in only two respects: first it was our only issue ever to use three colors (black, red, and green) on the cover, and it had the most pages ever (but what the heck it was Christmas.). The punk scene still plods away with no place to call it's own. This quarter saw the opening of the T-Bird Roller Rink (the closet place to Whittier yet). The place was run by a BYO sort of group called Punx, who tried to keep the scene in the hands of the kids. This place happened for awhile along with some other temporary halls like Comtempo in L.A. (check Necros interview).

ONE HUNDRED FLOWERS

Back by popular demand- 100 Flowers! Back? If you didn't know, a few years back when this band was called the Urinals we ran a big feature interview and stuck their mugs on our cover – now they have changed their name and to some extent changed their music and are interviewed here by two of their biggest fans: Maw and D.T.

These three, collectively known as 100 Flowers have been fusing and bending contemporary music styles since 1978 with their inception as the Urinals. The band has been busy with their own label Happy Squid. This interview took place in Kevin's apartment on November 7, 1982.

FS: Why the name "100 Flowers"?

Kjehl: The name "Urinals" didn't reflect what we were doing, it didn't match our change.

Kevin: Mao said: "Let 100 flowers blossom & let 100 schools of thought contend", which was one of the slogans of the cultural revolution in '49. It's about old vs. new ideas.

Kjehl: We don't have a real consensus among the band. We are all very different.

100 Flower: Kevin, Kjehl, John at Al's Bar (notice the hand) - photo Al

John: Kevin is the most politically aware, Kjehl is somewhere in the middle and I'm the least.
FS: So do you have a lot of political songs?
Kevin: All of them are political in one way because they espouse some way of looking at the world.
Kjehl: This band is real schizophrenic. Everyones got their own approach to things and quite frequently we don't see eye to eye on things. Interesting and frustrating.
FS: How do you feel about no having places to play?
Kjehl: We like playing the Whisky and going there, it's a focal point, it's history, seems like a loss. It's strange, there was a lot of excitement there, and at the Starwood - which seems to be missing at a lot of other places now. Better money deals too.
John: We feel personally responsible...
Kjehl: NO! Don't go on.
Kevin: For the killer nature of our band!
John: We closed the Starwood and the Whisky. Chuck Wagon blew his brains out the night we opened for the Dickies.
Kevin: And the club we played at closed.
John: We played with the Bags their last two shows, we closed Blackies with Black Flag - the night they got arrested.
Kjehl: We went to San Francisco with Middle Class for their farewell. We did the Human Hands last show at the Whisky.
John: We killed Slash, in the last issue they had an interview and a review of us. We feel responsible for a lot of misery.
Kevin: Al's bar, we played there the weekend before it closed.
Kjehl: We worked real hard trying to get into these places.
Kevin: When we were the Urinals, we were banned from places. We were just those dumb kids from UCLA. Blackies said our fans trashed their bathrooms.
Kjehl: All six of them!
John: UCLA said we pissed on stage.........

MILLIONS OF DEAD COPS

Singer Dave was interviewed on the phone by Al in late October 1982.

As you know, MDC are a hardcore punk band who were originally from Texas. They moved to San Francisco about the same time as they changed their name from Stains to MDC. They have been around for quite some time and originally caught my attention with the release of "John Wayne Was A Nazi". This single could have been just some stupid songs judging from the title - but after listening to the lyrics you could tell this band was really thinking about things.
FS: Do you guys have many problems with your name?
Dave: Well yeah. It does weird them out. We played Baltimore with Minor Threat and like 8 police came and helicopters came and a paddy wagon and they busted four punks, one had a "Millions of Dead Cops" shirt on. I couldn't help but think that the cop had leaned on him and his group because he had the shirt on. I made me nervous in some respects, not just for myself but for people who are into us. People who are digging the message. In weird places we came in as "MDC", Calgary Canada I wasn't gonna come in as "Millions of Dead Cops", but a lot of places like Chicago and New York, the Mafia is so big that they are putting on all the shows so they already paid all the cops off. So the cops don't care.
FS: Why did you pick that name? You had to change from the Stains...
Dave: Right. We were gonna be the Fatal Stains, we were just thinking of things. After we played at the Cuckoos Nest with the L.A. Stains we were driving home and we were thinking that they were such a great band and had a jump on the name by a year - we never knew there was an L.A. Stains... I mean we always thought small, the "John Wayne Was A Nazi" single we made 300 of them, that's how naive we were, ya know. That's how Texas was... We were hanging out with Buxf Parrot of the Dicks and he said "Millions of Dead Cops, now that would be a great name for a group". Then it was an inside joke - the MDC Stains, Millions of Dead Cop Stains. We didn't really change it until the day we were leaving

with the Dicks and the Big Boys.
Al: The name really says a lot, just how anticop are you guys?
Dave: I don't tell people to go shoot a policeman, but I don't tell them not to. Do what you want to. I'm not throwing bombs, I'm just throwing words and to me Millions of Dead Cops is like a mental image, political poetry. We're not being to facetious saying that. I think there's something real wrong with the police state that we have... I mean, I don't mind having a radical name like MDC, if it's used in the right way. I don't want to turn it into like an Oi thing where you go "Yeah kill a cop ahh ahh ahh" We want to appeal to people on a rational basis.
FS: Do you see a need for cops in America?
Dave: Well you know I think there needs to be what you call peace officers, ya know, I really believe that. Some kind of health safety thing available to society. I think how it's gone about is real wrong.
FS: Are you guys vegetarians?
Dave: Yeah, everyone in the band is vegetarian. Our roadie and our drummer eat meat if they need it on occassion. The whole idea isn't anyone ever eating a piece of meat again in their life, it's just that the abuse is real sickening.
FS: How do you feel about drugs and stuff like that?
Dave: We, ahhh, we're not ummm, we do them ha haaa... but we don't like them to mess around with our trip or our act which means like on the road, going across borders, even up until right after the show, that our policy. After the show relaxing is relaxing, ya know. Not into the needle thing at all, I mean we've seen it, we've been there. In Texas it's tempting because we were real bored and we experimented with drugs - out of boredom almost and then the priority became the group - then we couldn't afford them - straight edge came out of economics.,
FS: But you can relate to those straight edge people?
Dave: Oh yeah, real well because they are putting energy straight and forward into the scene...

SUICIDAL TENDENCIES

Mike Muir, lead singer fro Suicidal Tendencies was interviewed by Al on Nov. 18, 1982.
Suicidal Tendencies are a very notorious and very popular band - but they've had a lot of bad shit happen to them. The Penthouse article is the big one, but it seems like everytime something happends the name "Suicidal Tendencies" comes up. Here's what Mike has to say about that stuff...
Al: How long has ST been together?
Mike: I guess about 2 years, but it's been in different stages with a lot of different people. A lot of times we weren't playing because like one time our bass player got his finger cut and had his finger in a cast so we couldn't play for a month or so, our old guitar player got in a fight and got hit with a bat and got a concussion - his head was all split open and his wrist was messed up so we couldn't play for a couple of more months and then we would switch people, so there were like 6 months and we played like twice.
Al: Who named your band?
Mike: I did. A couple of people used to think was pretty crazy and they'd say "Yeah, you're gonna get killed, you're killing yourself", so

NEW FROM
SST

BRIAN RITCHIE

MEAT PUPPETS

ANGST

The Blend. Giving up the bass he played with the Violent Femmes for guitar, conch shell, banjo, jaw harp and elephant tusk, Brian Ritchie achieves "The Blend" on his solo album for SST. Combining influences as diverse as Sun Ra, Son House and Sonny Bono, he has concocted the perfect blend for the global village. From the untraditionally traditional version of John The Revelator to the hard funk of Alphabet, these eleven songs are THE blend for the eighties. SST 141 (LP/CA $7.50 CD $15.00)

Huevos. Hot on the heels of their amazing Mirage album, the Meat Puppets have done it again with a brand spanking new album on SST. Closer in sound to their legendary live shows, this record has balls. Starting off with the kick in the head double blast of Paradise and Look At The Rain and ending with the brain-crushing I Cant Be Counted On, this record reaffirms the Meat Puppets' status as one of the coolest bands on the face of the planet. SST 150 (LP/CA $7.50 CD $15.00)

Mystery Spot. Like never before, the songs of Angst are suffused with a shimmering glow. On Mystery Spot, the remarkable interplay between brothers Joe and Jon is fully realized with their best-sounding record ever. With a bow to country and folk, Angst take off on a hell bent for leather electric train ride on Outside My Window, Colors Of The Day, Mind Average and nine more songs. SST 111 (LP/CA $7.50)

THE LEAVING TRAINS Always August

NEGATIVLAND

F***. The second album from the Leaving Trains on SST finds them claiming the throne of true rock! From the "Exile On Main Street" punch of the guitars to the personal words of Falling James Moreland, this record is the one to play for people who ask "whatever happened to great rock and roll?" Hear for yourself what F*** is all about. SST 114 (LP/CA $7.50 CD $15.00)

Largeness With (W)holes. A cryptic title gives you the listeners the cipher with which to break the mysterious code that is Always August. Backwards, forwards and inside out, the lifecodes that Always August reveal on this album are the keys to a healthy psychic glow. From the stone groove of About Time to the triple-deadbolt lock of Rahsaan Rollin' Cat, the new album from Always August paints a startlingly whole picture of your life. SST 135 (LP/CA $7.50 CD $15.00)

Escape From Noise. Jello and Jerry on the same record? When the inspired genius of Negativland calls, everyone comes running. Starting with a cut and paste audio view of the world, Negativland creates some of the most disorientatingly normal slices of real life ever to grace vinyl. As a concept album about one man's escape from noise, the five inhabitants of Negativland have painted a picture that everyone can relate to. SST 133 (LP/CA $7.50)

Make check or money order payable in U.S. funds to SST Records P.O. Box 1, Lawndale, CA 90260

Visa, Mastercard, & C.O.D. can call SST mail order (213) 835-5810. Call the SST Hotline (213) 835-4955 for gen. info.

SST

MDC: Franco, Ron, Dave, Al at Flipside - photo Al

Mike Muir - photo Glen Friedman

NECROS

You all should know about the Necros by now, so for all the new comers they are: Barry on vocals, Todd on bass, Andy on guitar and Corey on bass.
Time: Necros first tour of the U.S.
Place: Some big house owned by Daphna of Unicorn Records in the Hollywood Hills.
Present: The Necros, the Misfits, various roadies, hangers on and people who lived there.
Needless to say the interview got really loud and Barry was bummed because Glen Danzig kept razzing him and in the end we decided to scrap this interview...

well, Suicidal Tendencies man.

Al: What about all the shit that goes around about the "Suicidal Tendencies Gang"?

Mike: I don't know anything about no gang, you would have to sight instances...

Al: You have quite a few fans in the Santa Monica, West L.A. area...

Mike: Yeah we play a lot around here and the family names known pretty good so people know about us - when people know the band is local they are more likely to give it a chance.

Al: What did you think about the Penthouse article?

Mike: It was pretty good from a fictional point of view, it was interesting but it was all lies. The magazine isn't out there for articles, so the articles they have they have to make interesting. The stuff I supposedly said I didn't even say, it goes right back to like the National Enquirer... a lot of stuff he had other people saying, I said. It was pretty funny. This guy came up to me and I agreed to do it but I didn't get paid or anything, nothing I could appreciate. When it came out it did make me look pretty bad. It was a farce. That guy went to one show and tried to be an authority. If I was reading it I'd be scared and make my kids stay at home. That was my first experience with the press, otherwise I wouldn't have done it...

Al: How do the ST rumors get started?

Mike: Like we played this one party and these guys got drunk and offended some people, so they chased them down the alley and I guess the guy got beat up pretty bad or something and the rumors started how he died, then it was in the papers and stuff. You know how it starts off "someone got killed" then it's "three

people got killed" then it's "the gang fight where 7 people got killed" – they have some really weird stories going. I've died like three times now. The only problems we have up here is people think it's a gang and stuff but that's pretty funny.

Al: What are some of your songs about?

Mike: Well I used to work at the Times delivering the papers in the morning, so I used to get up at 2am in the morning and you had to do something to keep your sanity. So I'd get these weird ideas in my head, our first songs were like, uh, "Incinerate Me, I'm A Jew", "Parents For Adoption" and all these things like that which had no meaning, just weird stuff. Now they're more political I guess, just saying how I feel. Not preaching in the sense of the Dead Kennedys because I don't appreciate when people exploit the fact that they're in a band, people like the music and they get up there and tell you you're stupid and stuff. My songs express, like we have this song "Two Sided Politics" and it deals with the hypocrisys of the world; if you kill someone in war you're a hero, but like if something happens, like right now I have these charges against me for fighting with these Iranians cause they were fucking with my friend... We have this other song that goes "I'm not anti-society, society is anti-me", they are the ones that are predjudiced against me. They're the ones that think I should be locked up because they can't understand the way I look. I just take the attitude on the world that I just laugh at everything - people don't like it when you're happy. When people call me up and tell me I'm gonna die, I just go: "Yeah, and you have a nice day too."

Andy: I like this house, it's got pool in the back. All the Necros are eating, Corey broke his ankle and foot skating a pool in Denver. Necros first gig of this tour was September 23 in Akron, first gig in our home state.

Glen Danzig : Ask Barry about "Rear Deliveries"...

Barry: Look I needed the money, so what, I got my dick sucked in a movie...

Corey: Ah, Barry, you got fucked up the ass!

Barry: Listen, I got a cameo appearance, it was cool, with big Johnie Holmes.....

Time: Next day.

Place: Kenter School in Beverly Hills, skate spot.

Glen Friedman: What do you think of the kids out here compared to Ohio?

Barry: I like the skate kids alright.

Andy: I don't like the limey punks.

Barry: I don't like those guys at all, those guys are sheep...

Al: What the big deal with people who want to look that way?

Andy: It's America remember.

Al: But it's also their own choice.

Barry: There's nothing wrong with it but they really do all look the same, even more so than the skinheads... it's a reflection of their mentality, it's sheep mentality and I don't like that.

Andy: All they think about is getting their daily

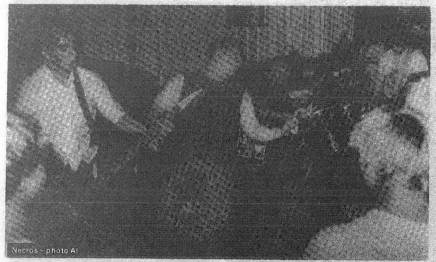

Necros - photo Al

water and walking around in a grassy field. That's all sheep think about!!

Al: Are there any spike head bands you...

Barry: I like Discharge, GBH are good. The point is they're the bands that inovated that look, they were the first people I saw with that look anyway...

Corey: How can these American "English" punks relate to so much of the Oi think that is going on over there? How can they relate to the National Front or the Dole?

Al: I don't think they try to relate, they just like the bands and put them on their jacket...

Glen: A lot of bands are into politics or totally against politics, are you guys...

Andy: Just against fake politics.

Barry: The whole point about what I write is, I'm not going to limit myself to things I cannot write about. The only limit I have is that I can't see myself doing certain things, like writing a song about being happy...

Andy: Or hating Reagan...

Barry: That's not as important as saying, ok, I have these emotions, these negative emotions and here's the situation where these emotions came out –here's a song about it.

Corey: We're not political for the sake of being political "I hate Reagan, fuck reagan", I hate bands like that.

Barry: Crass are fucking beating their heads against the wall, I used to love them, I'll admit, but how many times can you say "Fuck the system" when you're just singing about it? So what! Anarchy now and peace. Who cares?!?!

Corey: How many kids are going to go home from their show and do something about it? With stuff we sing about maybe they will go home and say "Hey maybe I can do something about the way I'm living." I don't think kids are that radical to hear a band singing about anarchy and want to go home and fuck the system.

Todd: Just so people have fun.

Barry: Right, I want them to have fun, but I want them to think.

Corey: I want them to feel the way I do, and I want them to feel something when they leave the shows too.

Andy: Like "God I had fun!"

Barry: But I don't want it to be some fucking little beach party where they're all jumping around going "Ohhhh!!! Everythings really groovy" scratch that. I'd like them to think, I'd like them to be aware of a lot of things.

Andy: Like we all want to get laid after!

Barry: We have songs about living for yourself and not worrying about other thoughts condemning you. I'm into that, we have a song called "Satisfyed" about everything I do is to satisfy someone else and how fucked up that is.

Corey: When we're done playing I feel something I don't feel any other time from doing anything else. Like I almost get sick sometimes. I don't feel bad. I feel like I've accomplished something and I feel relaxed – something I can only feel after we play.

Andy: I feel like I've taken a shit, seriously!!! Like all fresh and ready to go!

Corey: Like after you've been driving and you have to take a shit, and you feel really good afterwords.

Al: How do you compare the gigs here with the ones back home?

Corey: The Freezer is in a bad neighborhood, but nobody lives there anymore, it's like 100% black but they are a lot more mellow, they're mostly older but there's no problems with the younger kids. Bob's Place (Contempo Hall, Watts) was a Freezerish show but...

(Andy goes into details about problems with locals stealing cars, beating people, stealing equipment...)

Andy: We had to call the cops to break everything up so we could even get out the door with our money.

Al: You can't be totally anti-police if you end up using them.

Barry: We're anti- asshole police.

Corey: Being anti-police is as racist as being anti-black...

Al: Who were causing trouble at Bob's Place?

Corey: It was an all black neighborhood and it was all black people who were starting the fights, they were being racist, I heard "white" being screamed quite a bit.

Barry: It was like they took it as an invasion.

Corey: Yeah, but I didn't hear anybody yelling "nigger".

(Andy relates how the locals in Detroit don't act the same way as locals here).

Al: Where have you been skating?

All: Here!!

Barry: Santa Monica ramp. We got to meet a lot of people who we've always wanted to meet like Jay Adams and Jay Smith, and a lot of other people like Merril...

Al: How far and serious are you gonna take the band – will you do this as your living or what?

Corey: As long as it still means something, if I still feel they way I do after we play then I know it still has meaning for me. Whatever it means to anybody...

Barry: It's one thing I like to dedicate most of my time to.

Corey: If it gets to be a hassel and we're not having any fun doing it, then we'll stop, but right now it's cool.

NO CRISIS

No Crisis we interviewed in November by Al and Hud at their practice place in H.B.

Hud: I always thought you were a Hollywood band, but here we are in Huntington Beach?

Kurt: Well we used to live in Hollywood, when I lived at the Pondo, well when I first lived in Hollywood I met the Sterns and lived at Skinhead manor. I just kicked somebody out of a room there and moved my shit in. So after Eugene burned it down (laughs) I moved in with Dave. We had this dive over off Normandie called the Pondo. So I just got sick of it and moved down here and found people that could play better. Mark already lived down here.

Al: Why did you move down here?

Kurt: My dad lives down here. I'm one of the original people from down here. Me and Bob Swan were the first people to move from down here to up there. When we met the Sterns they had that big giant house and

No Crisis - photo Al

Harvey Kubernik and Henry Rollins

said "Yeah, that's our kind of trip".
Al: What are you guys trying to sound like, I mean you use harmonizing vocals and...
Kurt: I don't know..
Mark: It's just playing our stuff...
Kurt: My main influence is like Jake from Stiff Little Fingers and the singer from the Del Vikings...
Mark: We like the melodies but it's pretty much just what happends. We get an idea and we play it.
Kurt: And if it's shitty, we dump it.
Vid: We don't use pedals and shit like that, it's just us on the guitars. There are melodies you can hear so when you walk away you can hum it or something.
Kurt: It gets boring going blam blam blam all the time, we used to play that. When I first started singing I didn't have the slightest idea of what I was doing but it just came to me from singing to records. Ian gave me singing lessons in the shower. I used to be the Youth Brigade and Shawn Stern taught me a lot about singing and stuff. That was the first band I ever sang with... Like when we play the funnest thing about it is really getting a chance to cut loose and get it all out of your system for another week, ya know? That's all I look forward to is cutting loose. I figure 3 years from now we'll all be eating Tylenol on the West band anyway.
Al: So what are you guys singing about?
Kurt: Oh I sing about everything: chicks, politics, beer, speed...
Al: What are you gonna do with No Crisis?
Kurt: It's a vehical for my political movement, I'm going to be a senator, I'm majoring in Political Science at Golden West! I'm in the chorus there too... oh I have this recital coming up (laughs). I've learned a lot of things there though, I've learned how to sing right, from the gut, so I can do a couple of sets.
Al: Where did you get the name No Crisis?
Kurt: Well, our old bass player.
Vid: Johnny Snot thought up the name. So why release a record and not back it up, he left the band but we're keeping the name. "No Crisis" lets have a party!
Al: So a fun band...
Kurt: We don't want to be all rough and tough and hard to bluff. We want to have fun. We're not all bummed out, I think it's pretty good living in Southern California! I'm not anti-

this or anti-that, I hate everything! I used to be but, uh.....
Al: What happened?
Kurt: Ummmmm, girls..........

HARVEY KUBERNIK

Harvey (the "K") Kubernik really needs no introduction. Throughout his varied career he has covered the music biz from every angle: as a journalist in Melody Maker, LA Times, Bam etc., Corporate dog (A&M at MCA), promoter of local talent shows (like shows at places like Whisky, Improv. and Al's Bar), producer, song-writer, publisher and much more. Now he has formed his own label, Freeway Records, to present a different often overlooked view of Los Angeles.

His recorded output thus far has been small but selective, releasing a double-spoken work epic ("Voices of the Angels"), a Black Flag- Frazier Smith interview disc ("for radio and retail outlets) and a very limited pressing entitled "LA Radio". He has in the works, a live Alan Ginsberg/ Harold Norse poetry album (slated for "Pieces release") another spoken word album with some electric-acoustic accompaniment (" English as a Second Language") ' Voice Over Neighborhood Rhythem" (featuring several Beyond Baroque poets, with extended performances by Wanda Coleman, Dennis Cooper and Ivan E. Roth) and maybe a revised edition of the ill fated "LA Radio" (About time Harve!)

In typical Fairfax High fashion (he's a very proud alumnus), this interview took place at Canters.

Pooch: What makes you want to put all your money and effort into spoken word albums?
Harvey: Because I do these things, ultimately for my self first. if other people want to check it out, they're doing themselves a favor.
Pooch: Is there any profit to be made?
Harvey: The things I'm involved with have longevity, sales will always increase.
Pooch: You've been behind the scene & seem to have been boxed out on many occasions, what keeps you going, vengence?
Harvey: No, not revenge- karma and destiny

and the fact that I'm really talented.
Pooch: Why do you feel that alot of the LA critics have failed to get behind your projects?
Harvey: There's been some rejection, you know, if I was in any other community (NYC or UK) what I am doing would be embraced and I would be respected a lot more. We're just talking about a handfull of print outlets here and I don't have to mention them, but I'm only talking about it cause I was asked. It's fine, because since I use my own money I can take bating practice whenever I want, except I remember, as a journalist that has not come out of the closet to support the "Voices of the Angels" album, which is a cohesive statement about OUR community, should resign!! This is not out of scorn and anger, but while someone shows up to bring it all together and parts the seas for the underdog, don't ridicule and neglect him, acknowledge it and get on with the show already. I am not threatened by talent, I embrace it and support it.
Pooch: Why don't you move elsewhere to work on your project?
Harvey: I wanted to make it in my own backyard first, but if you really want to know the real reason why I never have move out of LA. it'S because where else can I see Twilight Zone episodes twice a day? Hey, c'mon man, Twilight Zone is #1. I regret the fact that I never got to meet or record Rod Serling. I'm learning to rely a lot more on my instincts and my belief in people. After dealing with enough idiots, grabbers, talkers and phonies in the Karma Bank you're also going to meet real people, the guides and thinkers...
Pooch: Any final advice you'd like to pass along?
Harvey: If I could say anything to Flipside readers it would be - 'Get out there and kick ass!" dilute your pleasure center and comfort zone, if it means getting the art produced out. Put our your own stuff independently and don't wait to be accepted. Don't be apprehensive about whatever it takes to get it out, tell all the people. Give a lot, you will get a lot back, more than you realize. Stay awake, keep pushing, be free think and work hard.
Harvey: Yeah, man?
Pooch: Thanks for the meal!!

THE VANDALS

The Vandals were cornered after their gig at the Galaxy on Nov. 5th. Interviewing were Al. Pete and Paul. The Vandals are Stevo on vocals, Human on the bass, Joey on drums and Jan on lead guitar. Needless to say, everyone was drunk.
Al: This isn't the original band right?
Jan: I'm the only original member. We started in um, we were trying to figure out who we'd get as a singer and we finally got Stevo. We had a different drummer and bass player and that was two years ago the first time we played
Al: Who wrote "Anarchy Burger" ?
Joey: I did!!! I wrote the music and the idea for the words and he...
Human: He stole the music from "La Bamba" he did!
Joey: It's an old Nordic Conquest song.
Stevo: We weren't gonna record that song but we were at Prospective sound and it needed words so I wrote the words, they made me, I'm just a puppet!
Human: He wrote the words in a half an hour, we said they suck but we used them anyway.

Al: What does it say, except " Anarchy burger—hold the Government"? That's a great song.
Stevo: America stands for freedom, so if you think it's free, try walking into a deli and urinating on the cheese."

"Anarchy kill a cat, shoot James Brady in the back, raise an army of rabid rats, beat your neighbor with a bat, write your congressman, tell him he sucks, he's only in it for the bucks" All kinds of shit you know, anti-government.
Al: So you call yourselves Vandals?
ALL: RIGHT %&#$"&'"#%!!!
Al: Is that a name or a theme or...
Joey: It's the closest thing to calling ourselves "the punkers" as you could.
Human: We do Vandalize?
Al: What do you vandalize?
Human: Anything and everything (and a lot of things we can7t mention...)and I drew all over it and I....
Stevo: Also we are the Party Vikings.
Joey: Me and him go to UCLA.
Al: Huh, what do you study?
Joey: He studies politics and I study old Norse and mid-evil Germanic Viking Civilizations!
Al: Why?
Joey: It's punk.
Stevo: I live in the 405 freeway off ramp on Seal beach Blvd.
Al: You guys must surf?
All: I do, he does, I don't, we do, they do..
Joey: I do, we must have surfed maybe only 15 times this summer..
Stevo: I surf... Lake Street dude.. can you smell that fart I just let? I really liked playing tonight because people threw stuff and it hit me in the face and it was really nice. They spit on us and threw stuff and dove off stage and they danced to our music and he hit in the face with his bass in my eye..
Al: Yeah, I saw you hit yourself with the microphone stand!!
Stevo: That'S different, my eye is still pretty swollen— and that's hip!
Al: What bands do you like?
Joey: Vibrators, Sex Pistols, Bowowwow, Sin 34, The Hated..
Stevo: I have no musical taste!
Human: Wire, Metal Urbain, Saints, Anti Nowhere League...

Vandals at Shamus O'briens – photo Al

Jan: Gang of Four, Bauhaus and art bands.
Al: Is it hard to get gigs named Vandals?
Joey: It's hard to convince someone we are not gonna mess anything up...
Stevo: Especially since we fucked up the KNAC building...
Joey: No, no we didn't....

Human: Yes we did and we're proud of it ha ha ha ha ha ha ha ha haaaaaa........
Stevo: No we didn't , we don't admit it...
Human: I do–I broke the ash tray and i threw the records out the windows and I pissed all over the walls.....
Stevo: That's an assumption, we were there, we did do an interview, there was some damage done...
Human: And I did it.!!
Stevo: And we don't know who did it! Our band is called the Vandals but some people sneaked in and the bald headed homos broke all the ash trays off the walls that were bolted on, shot off the fire extinguishers and peed in the electrical sockets and shorted the building.
Al: WHY?
Human: Because were punkers damn it were the Vandals!!!!!!

LEGAL WEAPON

Legal Weapon were interviewed by Shredder and Kori at two different times. Somehow Legal Weapon didn't notice that they had set up two different interviews Kori and Shredder both blame it on LW's. So anyway, here is the interviews combined for your reading pleasures.
Shred: There's a million bands in LA.. what do Legal Weapon offer that's different?
Kat: What's never been offered before!
Shred: That's vague...
Kat: It isn't vague. it's to the point. No one

Vandals: Human, Jan, Joey, Stevo; a day at the Museum– photo Ed Colver

Legal Weapon at PAL - photo R. Hill

plays real rock and roll anymore.
Adam: We're a rock and roll unit.
Shred: What do you think r & r is?
Kat: Having a party every time you play!
Shred: Where do you see yourself in 5 years?
Kat: Oh god, who knows, hopefully our of California.
Adam: On a farm in New Zealand.
Shred: Kat, dod you think it's tough being a female in a band?
Kat: Definitely. It's really fucked- guys resent it because they're not in a band, and they look upon stage and resent and hate it.
Shred: How do they hate it?
Kat: Well look,everyone looks at it in two ways-either they look at you sexually or they like the music. How many bands have girl singers in LA that are punk? The only one that comes even close is Red Scare. There are very few women that attempt to play like- party music. But there are so few bands out there with girls who aren't just coping. Like us, we don't try even attempt to be a punk band. We're just rock and roll.
Sred: Like Heavy Metal... like Joan Jett heavy metal rock and roll.
Kat: Well I like Joan Jet. One thing you can say for her is that she does do it all balls out-pardon the expression!
Kori: So you don't want Legal Weapon to be classified?
Kat: Right, they call us rock band, a rock punk band, all this weird stuff. and that's what is is to some people but it's Legal Weapon to us. I don't think we sound like other bands. We can play gutless music.
Kori: What are your favorite bands?
Kat: Carpenters!! Well I kinda like the Pazz band, it's like there are so many of them, Social Distortion, party bands I like a lot, the chick from X-Ray Spex, Vice Squad. I don't see a lot of chicks that sing at all our with their hearts, it's like they wimp out, they just scream or yell. They should be trying to sing. I don't see a lot of the women in the scene, everything is predominatly skinhead boys. it gets kind of depressing. they get all the glory and they're just a adequit and I see a lot of bands with women and they don't get publicity.
Shred: What are your hobbies?
Kat: Chasing little boys.
Adam: I like to make houses out of toothpicks! Not really I'm into chicks...

Shred: What kind of girls?
Adam: Oh. I'm not to choosy.
Kat: Whew!
Kori: What do you think of the scene?
Kat: It's gotten bigger. Brain and I have been into the punk scene for the last 4 years, we're old timers from the old masque. We watched the whole scene arise, watched it from viewers point. I remember when there was a handful of people and you could go out on the scene and know everyone- and how all these kids. I think it's better in a lot of ways. It's good there's a lot more competition, the bands have gotten better, I look at all the old bands- the bands now days don't compare with them. The music is faster too.

ALLEN GINSBERG

"Interview" with Allen Ginsberg. by roving reporter Helen. Last Feb. I saw and reviewed a poetry reading by Allen G. In Flipside Issue #30. Ginsberg refused to do any interviews... but I decided to push my luck by giving him a questionaire of sorts. Months later, I got the answers. Here is what he had to say...

Helen: Through the years you have experienced the world on both a spiritual and political level. Which has played as the greater force in your writing?
Allen: Spiritual vision of eternity Spiritual means (inspiration) breathing, literally. Open space spans paranoia, building glittering in the smokeless air.
Helen: You helped establish the Jack Kerouac School of Disembodied Poets in Colorado. Do you feel it has been successful and approached the ideals you had in mind when forming the school?
Allen: Ideal was to introduce poets to meditation practice and introduce meditators to golden-mouth poetic practice: show similarity between western open form & eastern open mind through of meditation or breath of poetic speech.
Helen: As most of the readers of this magazine are young punks, they would be interested to know what you think of the punk movement?
Allen: It's a new breakthrough of confusion & question & thus can lead to enlightenment; the energy's healthy, the wisdom is to come; punk shows suffering, so it acknowledges the real.
Helen: Many of our readers are unfamiliar with your personal history-- how you made a choice to quit the advertizing "straight" world to embrace the creative underground of the 1950's. Do you have any advice for others who are not quite sure how far to go?
Allen: Look in the heart, check out your visions with your friends; be bold and careful at the same time; Mind includes both sides of any argument; balance body feelings, reason and imagination. ALL 4 working together make whole man: read William Blake & Dostoyevski; listen to old Blues (Leadbelly Ma Rainy & Skip James); learn classical Buddhist style meditation practice; try everything; "If you see Horrible, don't cling to it." sez Tibetan Lma Dudjon Rinpoche. See Charlie Chaplin, Marx Brothers & WC Fields. Read Plato's Symposium. Tell your friends everything. Give away all your secrets. "Be wise as serpents and gentle as Doves." Feed everybody, Remember life includes suffering complete change and no ultimate personal identity, neither permanent self or permanent God. Cheerfull!! Help everyone!
Helen: How was it to work with Joe Strummer

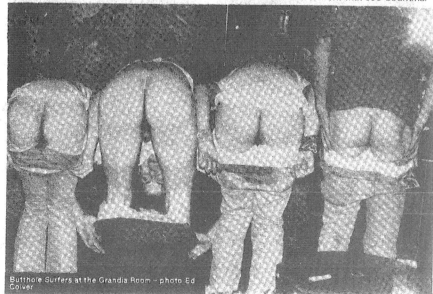

Butthole Surfers at the Grandia Room - photo Ed Colver

of the Clash (on last C. album)?

Allen: He's open minded, adventurous, no prejudice against old amateurs like me, I felt happy, inventing something new & learning from watching him sing & experiment & check me out for how I could be helpful.

FLIPSIDE NUMBER 37

"Running out of time again
Where did you go wrong this time?
When your problems overwhelm you
Go get drunk it's party time
Take a qualude, relax your mind
Relax your body too....
Run from your problems but you'll never get away
No one loves you and you wonder why?
Sitting there with your mouth full of beer
Your eyes are glazed your face is red
Who's gonna pick you up and use you for tonight?
When you're on the streets with a needle in your arm
Selling your body for another fix
Who's gonna pick you up
and take you home with them tonight? No me!
Old maid but you're only 15
You're losing your little girls charm
Cry all night but you'll never get it back

Don't be afraid it's not to late
Save yourself I need you here
Wearing off, wearing out
I can't think about this cause it makes me sick"
"Bikeage" – The Descendents

ISSUE #: 37
DATE: February 1983
FORMAT: 8 1/2x11, rotary web offset with 2 color glossy cover.
PAGES: 68
PRICE: $1.00
PRESS RUN: 5500
STAFF: Al, Hud, Pete, Helen, Pooch, Michele, Gus and Robert Hill.

DESCENDENTS

Anybody that is the least bit familiar with the L.A. underground music scene has heard about the Descendents. They have been around for quite some time, in various incarnations, always growing and changing, but somehow staying out f the spotlight. True, in their earlier days they didn't play much, but now they have a lot of gigs under their belt - and of course they are no longer an opening act. More importantly - they have an album out, a very good album to say the least. But they have problems: mainly the loss of their singer Milo, and Bill has joined Black Flag. Also with this transition of personnel, comes a change in music. In the next few months we will see if the Descendents can pull all of this off, I hope so. But let's back up and hear what the band has to say about where they've been and what they're into.(Interviewed Jan 18th at the Cathay De Grande by Al and Pete)

Al: Who were original Descendents? How did it all start?
Tony: Frank Naveta started the Descendents, it was his name, he had a couple of people before us...
Bill: There's no original Descendents that played anywhere besides pot filled bedrooms somewhere, the only Descendents that ever

recorded or played together live was Frank on guitar, me on drums and Tony on bass. The other Descendents was a concept that Frank had - but the people smoked too much pot and couldn't do it. We finally got it happening and put out a single "Ride The Wild" / "Hectic World". That was a three piece with Frank and Tony singing. We played like that for a long time and then got a female singer Cecilia and played with her for about a half a year and then fired her because we're prejudiced against girls I guess. Then we got Milo. When we got Milo we recorded the "Fat" ep and started playing a lot more and then recorded the album. Then Milo went to school, now we got ray. And Ray was our singer, but he's not gonna be our singer because he's a better guitar player. And that's where we stand right now.
Al: You put out "Ride The Wild" yourselves?
Bill: That was me, that was Orca Productions. That's the name of my boat, Orca.
Al: Just like the boat in Jaws, Orca?
Bill: I named my boat after the boat in Jaws cause I was real into that movie.
Al: How many of you fish?
Bill: Just me and Frank.
Tony: I never fished in my life.
Al: Who writes your songs?
Bill: We all write some songs.
Al: Who wrote "Myage"?
Bill: Me.
Al: What's it about?
Bill: Some girl. But I can't tell you who... you know her, she works on Flipside.
Al: We know... Michele, right? She told us all about it.
Bill: No. Noooo!!!! Oh, I've been burned! No way! I'm embarrased! Ahhgggh!
Al: What's the thing with "-age"?
Tony: It's just something that caught on.
Bill: When I was in 10th grade in my trigonometry class we used to call stuff, like notebook-age, pencil-age, homework-age, and we got into it and I started naming my songs. Like that was my first song - "Myage" so I called it "My-age".
Al: What about Milo?
Bill: Milo is a permanent egghead.
Tony: I wish he was our singer but he's a full time student (majoring in Bio-chemistry in San Diego).
Bill: Milo really isn't in the band anymore. Milo is good but we got this new thing going with all these new songs, if he was still in the band we'd work it out for him but he really wouldn't be right for it. We got a whole new thing.
Al: What kind of new thing?
Bill: We're playing a lot harder than we did on the album, a lot deeper, ore of the low end...
Tony: You can sink your teeth into it.
Bill: It hits you somewhere down here (stomach/groin area) rather than up here in the ears. It's something we've never played before because we've always sped it out real fast, like fast speedy punk rock type stuff. We're getting out of the coffee thing... I used to drink an awful lot of coffee when I played, so did Frank.
(Talk goes on to the audience)
Bill: We're pretty much anti any group or clique, and the same people that used to give me shit that had their alligator shirts on in high school are the same punkers that are giving me shit now because we don't have skinheads. It's all the same and we're against all of it. We're into playing what we play, if they are into see us that's good, if they don't they can go be punks somewhere else. I like punkers, most of my friends are punkers but a

Descendents at the T-Bird - photo Al

Merrill, Henry and Ian go skating! – photo Al

Exploited at the Cathay (actually this is during the second tour!) – photo Al

sounding pop, I'm real into the Beatles and the Last, I like playing a lot of pop songs. Punkers, this is really important. I really like when we play and everybody is getting into it and dancing and going crazy, getting on the stage and stuff, but I don't like when they break our equipment because we can't play. Everybody can have a good time

Al: Do you actually escape to Catalina?

Bill: Oh yeah!

Al: How big is your boat?

Bill: 16 feet!

Al: Isn't that a bit small to go to Catalina?

Bill: Well that's what makes it so fun, you get wet, you run the boat right up on the beach and you get on the island and you find some lobsters and cook them over a fire and eat them and there's nobody there to bother you except buffalo shits on the ground...

Al: How long does it take?

Bill: About 2 1/2 3 hours. It breaks sometimes, in fact it always breaks. Ya fix it if you can or else get a tow or call the Coast Guard - I have a radio and I call the Coast Guard. - or you just stay longer. Like the end of the verse says "My motors broken so it looks like I'm stuck here". Frank's been over there a couple of times, he's into fishing. He's got his own scams, he's working on Swordfishing boats. I was into that a lot too.

THE EXPLOITED

Wattie and Gary were interviewed by Al and Hud (and Dennis, Monk, Dream etc) at Dreams house...

The Exploited stopped off in L.A. at he very end of their first American tour, they seemed pleased at how they went over in this country. This interview was a bit rushed (done during what turned into a party of sorts) but talking to Wattie on 3 different occasions gave me the impression that the band were a lot like L.A. (west coast) punks. The entire band were very accessible to the audience at gigs, and in fact enjoyed getting drunk with their fans and showed a good bit of interest in local punk girls. Here's some of the stuff that we talked about:

Al: Have you gotten any shit playing in America?

Wattie: No, it's all been pretty good, in Chicago - it wasn't like punks, it was trendy people, I had to smash them with the mic stand. It was a really good gig but they started shouting really stupid things like "Do you wash?" and things like that. Like in San Francisco some guy, some trendy guy comes up and goes "You suck!" so I smashed him with the mic, fucking wanker you!! Back in the UK the only people we get at concerts is like mohicans and skinheads - punks ya know? We're not used to straight people coming to gigs, it's really strange for us. I've had a really good time over here. There were a few gigs, like Chicago, that people slagged us off and then we slag them off just as much and the whole think turns into a real shitty atmosphere.

Al: I know you get slagged off by a lot of people like Jello Biafra who calls you "Las Vegas punk", what do you think of that?

Wattie: I haven't heard that, but like anytime that guy wants to have a square go at it - I'll fight him anytime cause he's a wanker. A total wanker. So are Black Flag, they're the biggest bunch of piss going! Shit! There are a lot of American bands, but the only ones you hear in Britian is like Black Flag and the Dead Kennedys...

Al: Well is there any truth that you guys are like sympathetic to the National Front or

people like that?

Wattie: That's shit! I mean, I hate Packistanis right? But I like a lot of blacks and I'm on to the National Front and that's a load of shit. (something about some guy who write a weekly collumn in a British paper who says lies about the Exploited is an asshole) Some of these stories we hear come right from Jello Biafra, I mean there are a lot of blacks that are really great guys, but I hate Pakis, they're probably like Mexicans in this country, it's like you go into their shops and they charge much more than a normal shop, say a beer in a normal shop would be 50 pence or like 50 cents right, in a Paki shop the same beer would cost like a dollar. So that's why I hate fuckin' Pakis.

Gary: I like all colors!

Wattie: I hate white people as well, Jello Biafra is a fucking wanker!

Hud: Why are you guys into punk?

Wattie: To us it's like a living and it's our life, it's an alternative to living like normal people do. Like we just live day to day just the way we are now. It's an alternative to the system. Like when people give us shit we stand up for ourselves, like with Crass it's totally different, the peace thing, who cares? You have to stand up and fight for what you believe in.

Al: Having an attitude like that, do you get a lot of violence at your gigs?

Wattie: No. Not at gigs, no. The only time we get violence is like between us and the police.

Gary: Or like we get trouble when we walk down the street.

Wattie: That's why punks and skins got to stick together to fight everybody else.

Hud: What do you think of religion?

Wattie: It's like shit. It's bullshit that people die for religion...

Monk: What's your religion?

Wattie: I'm a Roman Catholic... I mean I don't

Joneses – photo Ed Colver

go to church... I believe there is a God and that's that. Something must have happened to make us here so there must be a God and that's as far as it goes. You should believe they way you want. Life is just to get drunk and get fucked and that's that. That's life.

Al: How long do you think you can do that as a band?

Wattie: Oh 50 years!!

THE JONESES

The Joneses (Steve, Steve Olson, Mitch and J.D.) were interviewed by Karl Markz and Craig Doucette.

Craig: Oh yeah, the name, how did you get "The Joneses"?

Mitch: Just because... it was like, you know, the Smiths, the Joneses, just a real common name to use to get us gigs.

Karl: Where did you guys meet?

Steve: From this one skateboard guy..

Craig: Scott Hosert?

Steve: We all know Mr. Hosert (Scotts father)... Mr. Hosert you can suck my balls!

Craig: What's with the dice on your shirts?

Steve: I'd just gotten back from Las Vegas. Lucky 7 appealed to me.

Karl: Who's the old man in the picture (in the BYO comp LP) with you guys?

Steve: Some drunk who smoked a big stogie and we were out front of some nudie place and we yelled "Hey old man, come and get your picture taken"

Craig: Let's talk about the record.

Steve: It's an ep so we can get some exposure. "Criminals" we be on it but a redone version, "Jonestown" will be on it...

Karl: Nobody knows about your single.

Mitch: Some station in N.J. do.

Steve: Now we're getting sued. We're gonna be on peoples court, each person gets like $250 if you win.

Craig: Who's suing you?

Steve: Chateau East. We had investors who backed out during the pressing of our single. Then we got stuck with all these singles with the labels on backwards (laughter).

Karl: Any bands you dislike?

Steve: The Dragsters... The Dolls inspired us – they had just a basic rock and roll feel. We're just like basic rock and roll.

Karl: Meat and potatoes rock and roll?

Steve: No, more like beer and drugs rock and roll.

Craig: Did you ever like the Beatles?

Steve: I like the Beatles in leather..

Karl: That's a great album "Beatles in Leather". (laughter). Very important question. Where's the head?

Steve: Down the hall to your left.......

THE U.K. SUBS

Nick Garret of the U.K. Subs was interviewed at Mendiolas ballroom by Pete and Al plus a couple of visitors.....

Flipside: Out of all the bands that started off a long time ago, the UK Subs are still pulling it off...

Nick: Probably because we've been unseccessful, cause we haven't made much money so we haven't been tired.

Flipside: Does that say a lot for your determination of what?

Nick: Another thing that you've got to look at is that it's better than working in a super market or something.

Flipside: Yeah, I guess so if you're breaking even. A lot of people put down bands for being not accessible, but I never hear anyone say that about the Subs...

Nick: It's not like we're making it accessible, that's the way it's always been, the nature of the band, you know we don't have to think about it, it's something that's happened. I think Charlie is that sort of person.

Flipside: He's so accessible that we can't get to him tonight.

Nick: Well he's there, he's surrounded by people, I mean sometimes I must admit that I like to tuck myself away and stay put.

Flipside: From listening to the records, basically you're doing the same stuff, it's different but you're still banging out the tunes.

Nick: The last album was more experimental, on one side of "Endangered Species".

Flipside: What bands were you influenced by?

Nick: Me persoanlly in the last 5 years I'd say Wire.

Flipside: what do you think of the old American sub culture bands before punk?

Nick: I prefer that stuff to the more modern day thrash bands... to be honest, although e are some thrash bands that I like, like

the Effigies, Battalion of Saints and also Toxic Reasons. I don't like they way it's happening in England and in the States, thousands of bands playing like this (points up to Husker Du) they all sound the same. I don't like it and I don't see the point in it.

Flipside: You think it dilutes the message of the whole thing?

Nick: I don't think there's any individuality and I think punk means individuality more than anything else.. or it should be.

Flipside: Do you consider yourselves a punk band?

Nick: Well no matter what we say or do musically we will always be a punk band, that's where we came from. We were all punks in '76, we all came together as a punk band and no matter what music we play whether it sells good or not, its always gonna be punk.

Flipside: Where are you gonna take your music, like the second side of "Endangered Species"?

Nick: Yeah, I think so. When you stop taking chances as a band you're finished, but if we turned out every album like the first album it would be pointless.

Flipside: But the new stuffs ok.

Nick: Yeah but I prefer doing the new stuff, because it's more of a challenge.

Flipside: Lyrically, what will the new stuff cover?

Nick: Depends what songs. Charlie writes different than the way I do.

Flipside: How much of the stuff do you write?

Nick: Right since the band started about 70 to 80% of the stuff is written by me and Charlie together and another 10% is written by Charlie alone.

Flipside: Is there a reason you don't have a leather jacket and a mohawk?

Nick: I have a leather jacket, I'm just not wearing it, I wore it on the whole tour apart from tonight, and I did have a mohawk, I just got rid of it...........

BEASTIE BOYS

Soho, home of more than a million pretentious New Yorkers, most of whom profess to be "artists". Situated amongst all of these struggling art cows is the Kitchen, an "experimental" video/performance space. The trouble with art cows is that they think too much, react to little, they are what they've been conditioned into being, passive spectators (on the other hand the trouble with hardbores is that they don't think and act uniformly) as was evidenced when Beastie Boys open a bill with, among others, ex-members of DNA playing. Then again, I've always thought the best gigs were the ones where pure contempt exists between audience and band. Anyway:

Kate: (Drums) Well, ask a question?

Larry: (reading questions out of the Face) You sound very sensible to me, how old are you?

Kate: I'm going to be 17 in a week.

Adam: (bass) I'm 18!

Michael: (vox) I'm 17 as of last month.

John: (guitar) I forgot.

Adam: I have an id that says I'm 21

Michael: John's 18.

Larry: What did you think of the audience there (gestures toward stage)?

Michael: They were gems, I loved them, they were dolls.

UK Subs Charlie and Nick at Mendiolas - photo Al

Adam: They suck moose pride.
Larry: What do you hope to accomplish with this band?
Michael: Not much. I hope to graduate from High School and then leave the band.
Adam: I hope to get a donut factory in Amsterdam and make donuts for the rest of my life.

Beastie Boys

Michael: Come on, there must be more questions?
Larry: ...all questions are stupid...
Kate: (reading from the Face) What kind of things annoy you?

Michael: The music that is playing right now, this band, David Silken (everyone applauds) the ignorance of the audience tonight, Adam?
Adam: (bewildered) uh well yeah...
Larry: Why do you say the audience was ignorant tonight?
Michael: Basically because they all had beards and it seemed like they didn't know how to shave.. other than that they seemed to be completely apathetic to everything that was going on.
Larry: So do you think that physical appearance constitutes ignorance?
Michael: I don't know, but they were visibly apathetic to everything that was going on around them, and the only reaction we got was that someone threw a bottle and another woman said "I hate all of these kinds of kids". But actually I liked doing this show because it gets pretty boring playing for hardcore audiences constantly.
Larry: What constitutes "hardcore"?
Michael: A bunch of people with mohicians and shaved heads dancing around and moshing on each other. Actually playing for a hardcore punk audience can be fun because they know all the lyrics to our songs. But on the other hand they might be just as apathetic and ignorant as this audience. Is that profound or what?
Larry: That's pretty fucking profound.
Kate: But they dance anyway.
Larry: Do you play your music primarily for people to dance to?
Kate: To have a good time and throw beach balls.
Michael: You know the overriding paradoxical thing about this show is the irony in that the seemingly "art" audience rejects the Beastie Boys whereas the seemingly "hardcore"

audience seems to equally reject the "art-homosexual" band. I find that to be the over ridding paradox... how about you Kate?
Kate: I think we should become the darlings of the Village Voice.
Larry: Do you think you reached the audience?
Michael: I don't know how we reached them. I had a lot of 20 year old women came afterwards and seemingly shoved their breasts in my face and told me how much they loved the set.... Yes I do look like Eddie Munster with my widows peak hairline. Wait, since this is our first interview in awhile, I'd like to clear something up. One: some people have termed us racist and I said I hate Rastafarians when such rumors are not true at all. I really despise all sorts of dogmas and various..... racist and sexist leanings.
Adam: I would like to clear something else up. We got really screwed over on that "NY Thrash" tape. Tim Sommers wrote cold things about us because we didn't thank him on the record. Dave Hahn didn't pay us because he doesn't like us that much, they wrote the name of our song wrong, it's not "Beastie" it's "Beastie Boys".
Kate: And they didn't give us any liner notes.
Adam: And he shook Haile Sellases hand.
Michael: It's true Neil Cooper did shake Haile Sellases hand.
Adam: Imagine touching Jah!
Kate: Oh, I want to say that I've always been in the Beastie Boys, I'm not "the new girl drummer", so there!
Michael: It's true, Jack Rabid take note.
Adam: The new girl drummer is someone else!...... Uh, well this is great, let's say something?
Larry: Say something....
Kate: Something....

7 SECONDS

7 Seconds were interviewed in December right after their first L.A. appearance by Al, Hud and Gus.
Kevin sings and plays guitar, Steve sings and plays bass and Troy drums.
Al: Fist off, what is "Skeeno"?
Steve: We were just kidding around how the big chic thing to do in Reno is ski, so then...
Kevin: Ski?, No!!
Steve: So everybody else started calling it that and it kinda stuck like a nick name. Skeeno is like the underground of Reno, Sparks and Tahoe. Within like 60 miles it's all one scene.
Al: Yeah like L.A. is gigantic.
Kevin: Yeah, and the kids are really great down here, we got all of these stories thrown at us like the violence and we're gonna get beat up, the cops are crazy and stuff and we get down here and everybody we've met is fucking great. We had a great time.
Al: How big is the scene in Reno?
Kevin: 200 max, about 150 punks, it's small but there's a lot of dedication. The kids don't say "Fuck the opening band", if it's a good hardcore band then they are hungry for it. We have a small organization, originally it was called Rockers Active, that started about 2 years ago and it kinda busted up for awhile. Then we heard about the BYO thing and thought it was good so we got the organization back together and it's called United Front. It's worked so far, there's like 6 people so far and we're trying to work a deal to take bands up to Reno and take care of

7 Seconds: Steve, Kevin, Troy - photo Al

them; make sure they get payed good, a place to stay and just open up communications with other places.

Al: And you guys do your own fanzines and Vicious Scam cassettes too.

Kevin: Yeah, goo I can get this out. Vicious Scam started out with a bunch of people and it was working, then in the middle a couple of people moved away, we were really busy with the band and then we found there were like back orders for a year ago. We're trying to get everybody paid off.

Al: (After getting a bottle of Bud from Mark Stern) Do you guys drink?

Kevin: No.

Al: Straight edge?

Kevin: Well not straight edge, just straight – that's got'en so out of hand.

Steve: It's not like we're against any of that, we're just straight, we've been straight for a long time. We don't put people down for drinking cause that sucks, cause it would be like putting us down for not drinking. As long as people don't force it upon us. Like we got to a party and the three of us will be drinking cokes and people think it's being defiant, like a slap in the face to the drinkers.

Kevin: We just don't want to get labeled DC clones like we did in the past, that sucks. We were straight even before we heard of DC. We have his song called "Drug Control" and it's like one minute somebody is your best friend and then they get fucked up and they're telling that you fucked their girlfriend.

Steve: Or you talk shit behind my back...

Kevin: And of course we're perfect targets because we're the biggest band there and when they decide to start rumors, it's always 7 Seconds.

Gus: What does 7 Seconds mean?

Kevin: Oh no, one more time.

Steve: Actually about 5 years ago we had a band called the Misfits!

Kevin: But the name 7 Seconds, this is a dumb story, I was ordering the Dils single "198 Seconds of the Dils" from Bomp and I wrote it on a desk and in the ink it said like instead of 198 it said 97 seconds. And then we saw this movie "Day Of The Jackel" or something and all through it were references to 7 seconds, and the Dils were like our idols... So we were looking for a name and we were looking at this racing book and it said 7 seconds and we said fuck it, must be an omen, so we picked t. It's a short intense name....

Hud: Do you guys really hate sports?

Kevin: I hate the mentality, I like soccer and hockey.

Hud: Are you guys on speed because you're so hyperactive and talking so fast?

Kevin: No, we're always like this, people tell me to take speed to slow down.

Al: How old are you guys?

Kevin: I'm 21, Troy is 19 and Steve is 16. I'm the old man of the group.

Al: What does 21 mean if you don't drink?

Kevin: You can get into strip joints. I don't know why but I collect pornography.

Steve: It makes me sick!!

Kevin: I don't know, I'm really lucky, I'll be walking down the street and I'll find torn out pages of porn books. I used to pick them up and save them but now I've got like thousands...

Al: Who's on the cover of your single?

Kevin: That's Dim from Section 8. Clenched fists, black eyes, that's like the motto for Reno, what it means is like we've always done the black eyes thing. A lot of kids come to the

shows and they put the black under their eyes. It's, uh, people call it trendy or fucking lame or uniformity but it's just like we did it as a joke at first, like we'd have ski masks on and black under our eyes, and pretty soon kids started doing it.

HUSKER DU

Husker Du were interviewed at SST in early January 1983 by Al, Mike, Gus and Pete.
Husker Du were down in L.A. for a week on their last American tour where they managed to record their new album for Reflex Records (their own label) and do a couple of gigs that were nothing less than great.

We start off by talking about their recording and Bob tells us about this new material. It's real different, it's sort of like "In A Free Land" but more realized. "In A Free Land" is what we wanted to sound like but we didn't know what we were doing with it, some of the new stuff is in that vein - but we know what we're doing now. There's still thrasers, but not as many." Greg adds "Our new record "Everything Falls Apart" is pretty balanced out with things like on "Land Speed Record" to slower things, when we first put out "Land Speed Record" it mainly sold up and down the west coast, but just with the pre-orders of "Everything Falls Apart" its gotten pretty balanced out, the whole country is into it".

Husker's new sound is also reflected in a little different approach in the lyrics, as Bob relates: "The lyrics are more personal, no "Reagans fucked", none of that, it's all personal stuff. It's pretty much a self analysis thing, people can look into the lyrics for what they want, it's a personal thing this time – how we're fucked or you're fucked or everybodys a little fucked at one time or another. Politics will come and go but we're still people, that will never change and that's what we're gonna sing about. That is just what I've got in my head. We're not worried if Reagan gets re-elected that much anymore. Ya know? I'll still be here, you'll still be here."

Husker Du in San Diego - photo Al

In Husker Du all members take an active part in writing the songs, and singing them. And this band has a great amount of material. We were just fooling around the other day between songs when we were recording and we had riffs from at least another dozen songs that we haven't recorded – we have at least 100 songs and probably a lot more than that by now... It's easier for me to translate through music, I can relate to that better than words sometimes. I'm not real good with words in songs because they're such a cut and dried thing. It's like once you write a song and you put the words on a lyric sheet, that's it. You've got to have guts to do that. It's hard to say something you really feel – then have it printed for everybody to read. Kids think about stuff and we try to get them to think about stuff, that's what we should be doing at least."

Husker Du doing feel like the old cliche "just one more band" applies to them: "It's like overpopulation, but I guess if you're real good it stands out. It's like the concept of evolution, this guy followed this lead and this guy followed this lead – and I don't think we did. Real good bands can get their message across. There's a wide variety of bands out there, different styles, people of different persuasions of "hardcore", some that I agree with and some that I don't. I have a hard time handleing a lot of ultra political bands... it seems like such a timely thing to do, such an easy subject, such a safe thing. There's no relevance to anybodys life, no substance. I just like bands where you put the record on and it blows you away no matter what, and when you see them it's some religious thing."

When we asked for any closing comments they added their "don't get discouraged" line which is almost like a slogan for them, it's a good bit of preaching that they certainly practice. Bob: "We're just trying to make people think, we used to make up a lot of reasons of how we could make people think, like breaking down peoples defenses thru repetition, that's always a good one. We're just trying to make people think and have a good time. It's alright to rag on things but you still gotta be able to rock, that's what it all comes down to, it's gotta have a beat...."

WHITE FLAG

White Flag were interviewed by Al and Pete at the Troubador right after White Flags first gig there. As you know White Flag is the notorious heavy metal punk fusion band that is made up of Riverside fanatics and Fountain Valley surfers... who are: Pat Fear on guitar, Tracey Element on drums, Doug Graves on bass and the almost legendary Al Bum on vocals. Also in the band sometimes is guitarist Al Fee and bassist Jello B. Afro.

Al: What is the song "Mirror Mirror" about?
Al Bum: Oh that, I ad-lib the whole song. "I look at the wall and what do I see, reflections of you, reflections of me, wherever I look you're all the same..."
Pat: It's normally about punk violence, but we have a better song called "A Question Of Intelligence"....
Pete: What kind of band are you?
Pat: We try not to fit into any catagories, so we made up our own...
Doug: We're a rubber band. Baid-aid...
Pat: People give us shit for being called White Flag and that we're ripping off Black Flag and all the Black Flag bros in Long Beach want to kill us – but the truth is Black Flag are our friends, our friends, Henry is like our biggest fan. So why are these Black Flag people trying to kick our asses???
Al: Why did you name the band that then?
Pat: The whole reason for the name is to reintroduce anarchy back into the musical aspect of punk, because when it started out it wasn't political and it was not violent. When Johnny Rotten was singing about anarchy he wanted musical anarchy. Not social or government anarchy or violence and people blew it out of proportion. Mainly the media blew it out of proportion. So we're trying to get back into an anarchistic state of music, which we are. We have a different band everytime we play, I don't think we've played twice with the same line-up.
Al: I think you rehearse that speech more than the band rehearses!
Pat: Yeah! You said we were so preconceived but we are the least preconceived band in the world!

Al: Al Bum, who is your idol? Ozz....
Al Bum: No. Probably Marty Smith or Roger Decoster. They used to go WFO but now they're retired. My real idols are probably Iggy Pop and Bowie.
Al: So what are you trying to do....
Pat: I think a quote from Greg Ginn is in order "We want people to start re-evaluating what they believe in"...
Al Bum: Punk started with no rules and no there's all these rules, you HAVE to have short hair...
Pat: We're breaking all the rules...
Al: But is that worth being a band for?
Pat: Sure it is, it's fun. If they come and laugh at us, good, if they come and enjoy us, it's good. we want to reinstate the pogo – these people have missed the pogo and missed all of the fun.
Al Bum: We try to appeal to the older crowd as opposed to the younger skinhead who just bought a Black Flag record last week.
Pat: But if they want to be open minded they're welcome to come to our shows. Like when we played with 45 Grave these skinheads were spitting on us....
Al Bum: Just cause we have long hair!
Al: I don't think it's the hair that matters, it's his (Pat's) moustache!! You look like a cop! (Hysterics!!)
Doug: Oh never say that, you blew it!
Pat: Yeah, lets talk about cops, there's some cops that are dicks but that's because punks set a bad example. Hating all cops because they wear a uniform is just as bad as them hating us, that's lousy, they're just people.

FLIPSIDE NUMBER 38

"John Wayne was a nazi, who liked to play SS
Had a picture of Adolph, tucked in his cowboy vest
Well he'd sting up your mama, sure he'd torture your pa
Sure he'd march you up to a wall
Sure he'd hang you by your last ball
He was a Nazi, not any more
He was a Nazi, life evens the score
John Wayne Slaughtered our indian brothers
Burned their villages and raped their mothers
Now he has given them the white mans lord
Live by this or die by the sword
John Wayne killed a lot of gooks in the war
We don't give a fuck about John Wayne anymore
We know your story of blood and gore
Just another pawn for the capitalist whore

White Flag: Jello, Al, Pat, Doug   photo Al

MDC: Dave and Franco

John Wayne wore an army uniform
Don't like us reds and fags that didn't conform
Well John we have no regrets
As long as you died a long and painful death"
"John Wayne Was A Nazi" – MDC

ISSUE #: 38
DATE: May 1983
FORMAT: 8 1/2x11, rotary web offset with 2
color glossy cover.
PAGES: 68
PRICE: $1.00
PRESS RUN: 6000

Flipside continues to expand it's distribution, and improve it appearance (this time with a new typewriter). But the big revolution at Flipside this issue was the move into video. With the price of home video equipment coming down drastically at this time, we found ourselves with access to equipment and quickly jumped into capturing the local punk rock action on tape. This of course was a lot of fun, and added another dimension to the scene for us, an alternative activity that actually got some new enthusiasm happening with some staff members. We video taped shows and put them out in a "video fanzine" concept. A show where about half of the tape was interviews. As it turns out, people want entertainment when they watch TV, whereas you won't play an interview twice, if the band is good and the footage strong, it will get watched. So by the third version of Video fanzine number one, the interviews were shorter (transcripts of DI and MDC in this issue), and the music selection were longer. And this is how it's been ever since.

As for the scene in general, well it's well into the Cathay era. Being that this is a fairly consistent place to play, has no objections to rowdy punk rock, and will book out-of-towners in advance - the scene explodes with millions of bands coming out of the woodwork from all the local suburbs, and we get to see lots of lesser name touring bands. Along with the Cathay, the Anti-Club and Roxannes are hot punk hangouts.

MILLIONS OF DEAD COPS

M.D.C. were interviewed in March by Al and Pete at Flipside headquarters in Whittier. Their first L.A. gig in some time had just gotten cancelled at the T-Bird and they were on their way home to San Francisco. M.D.C. have come into a lot of criticism lately for being such a political band and having such a popular first album. It's easy to slag them off as a bunch of left wing politics shooting their mouths off and being violent in their lyrics to the point of being sensationalistic, and this could be true. Everybody is judging them by their first album, and they will admit that it is pretty much a gut level album, but if you look closer you will see a band that is actually thinking about, and doing something about, the problems they sing about.

Al Flip: Tonight, the cops at the T-Bird were aware that you were Millions of Dead Cops?
Dave: He was telling us how we were lucky it was him down there because he understands, he likes heavy metal...
Ron: He was trying to relate, he wanted an album and a t-shirt, but you never can trust...
Franco: It's like "We're closing your show down but we like you anyway!"
Dave: He says "Millions of Dead Cops" and Ron was telling him what it really means is just no more cops, and he goes "Great, no more cops, I hope it happens during my retirement so I can just sit back..." He was kinda sarcastic.
Al: He had the assumption that we think all cops are assholes, which is not true. When they're beating in your girlfriend's head, now that might be an asshole...
Franco: The guy over there seemed relatively cool. In that situation he wasn't being a total asshole like a lot of cops usually are.
Pete: Why do you think they are?
Franco: In a lot of cases I think it's just a job that they've accepted that they feel has a place in society, like it's a dirty job and somebody's got to do it, and I've been hired for the job and I'm gonna do it the best I can.
Al: They took the job because they liked it. They liked shoving authority down people's throats.

Ron: It's pretty much a secure job where, if you want t force your ego, your prejudices on people in a violent way , you can do it and get away with it without any problems. It's pretty sad.
Al Flip You were saying you wanted to de-emphasize the name as "Millions of Dead Cops"...
Al: It's a problem of people who can't see the concept, they take it as a violent action of saying what to do. What we're saying is that it's a concept. It's hard for the police state to be dead, especially where it's the most violent, which isn't necessarily in the United States. The front force military against the citizenery in any given country are the cops.
Ron: Also the reason we want to take the emphasis of just "dead cops" is because if that's your focus point then people discard everything else and they say, "Well, this is what the title of your band is" and they don't want to hear anything else after that.
Franco: It's like "Millions of Dead Cops" as a concept is like the writing on the wall. It's what's been going on all through history. The consciousness hasn't been raised and people's human rights haven't been considered, and that's where you have a transition in the government leading to a better state of affairs. There is public outcry from the third world about human rights and rather than us promoting the idea of "yeah, let's go out and kill a bunch of cops" what we're saying is "Hey, this is the current state of affairs and it needs to be dealt with." People need to read and see the writing on the wall and know "Millions of Dead Cops" isn't the solution but it sure is pointing at the problem.
Al: One of the many, many problems.
Dave: The conformity bullshit that's in our society, fuck it! I felt it my whole life. It stank. All the sexism, the social orders, all the religious crap my parents were brainwashed to where "You've gotta be a professional in society to stay alive. And stay alive to the point where they didn't want me to tell people what religion I came from or what ethnic origins I came from because they were so uptight about how are you gonna fit into this grand master plan. The rebellion is "fuck that plan", "fuck trying to be white". Izod shirt, new American car with a $10,000 -plus salary, with a nice house , with life insurance, a family dentist, for a smooth ride to pick up your little dumpling at the elementary school. You know, it's like fuck it! And that's what we're feeling, and we combine this with the frustration we're feeling for other people who don't even have a voice. It's not like I'm a completely wet blanket. Like we're politico heavies that every moment are wrapped up in our serious heartfelt feeling for the neglected Third World. I'm not a missionary but I can't help but reflect it in my message in my art, in my political thought. And the people that are trying to make us feel like "Oh, boo-hoo-hoo, aren't there a million people starving a minute?" Where they're coming from is apathy- they can't fix nothing so just forget it. To me that deep cynicism where people have got to pick on you is like... "I've got a quick bit of thrills to be had and that's as conscious as I'm going to make what I'm doing."
Franco: As long as you sort of dance along with what's going on it's real easy for the system to just go ahead and do whatever they had planned, regardless of the consequences to you or the mass population. And until people stand up and say "Hey, we're not going to stand for this anymore", then things

just don't change.

Ron: When we say "Fuck the system", or "Fuck that shit" people say "Oh, what can you do?". What you can do is think about what you can do. You gotta realize that this whole system is based on money, so one way to start is who are you gonna support with the money you work for or who are you going to give your money to? And by channeling how you're going to spend your money and who you hand it too you indirectly influence what is the outcome of how these corporations are going to use these profits. Like if you buy Coca Cola or you buy products that you know the indirect effect is exploiting Third World countries. If you realize that and say "No, I'm not going to buy these products, or I'm not going to support them with these dollars" then that challenges their existence. The only way they exist is on money. If you keep feeding it, you feed the system and they get bigger off you.

Franco: First you have to recognize that there is a problem and the thing with American society is that the media I'm trying to convince people that there is no problem; "if there is an emergency you will be directed where to tune in and you'll be told exactly what you'll need to do". So, don't worry, you don't have to think, and until then just go out . It's another day, another dollar.

Ron: We had to say "We're an American, anti-American band" just to clarify the fact. Hey, we're not all Richie Cunninghams.

Franco: We slept on every floor from here to Berlin, in the U.S., in Canada, and Europe and the people know that if you're the type of band that like "We can come and visit you in your hotel room, but you can't come and visit us in our squat, and you can't share the little bit of beans and rice with us because you've got your wine and nine course meal waiting at the hotel. People want somebody they can relate with, and relate to. That's where you seperate entertainment from politics. Entertainment is a big show but if your politics are right there and you're living with the people, and you're breaking bread with them, then they know you're a brother.

Franco: Some of the strongest criticisms we took as a band was from Crass. They sat us down and said "Hey, what is this about?". We had to stop and say "Yeah, there is a very good possibility that people are going to misinterpret what we're saying". We had to think how can we more clarify our message so it hits the point without distracting from the point. That's why our name, rather than being "Millions of Dead Cops" is going to be M.D.C. because we can expand that. Our next album will probably be Multi-Death Corporations, which is also M.D.C. It expands it. M.D.C. is more like the block and that block stands for a number of different things like A. Millions of Dead Cops plus Multi-Death Corporations equals Millions of Dead Children. We're trying to get to a point where we can legitimately affect society without just saying "Fuck, fuck, fuck, kill,kill,kill".

Ron: Misguided Devout Christians, Male Dominated Culture.......

(Technically the interview was all over but we did talk about lots more after. We urge everyone to talk to M.D.C. themselves- then decide!).

SOCIAL DISTORTION

Nobody should need an introduction to Social Distortion. They have been one of Southern California's most popular bands for some time now. In that 5 year history they have gone through quite a few personnel changes. Our first Flipside interview appeared in issue #20, when they were still a 3 piece, and we felt we were overdue for a follow up interview, and we did this one a little differently – interviewing each band member seperately.

-- Brent --

Al: You are into SD's sound, but you're not into thrash bands, right?

Brent: Well, I don't like many thrash bands, no. I love punk, I used to love all the old punk bands. Thrash doesn't appeal to me that much, but there are a few exceptions that we'll play with that are really good. It's just lost the attitude towards punk in my opinion. I consider us to be a punk band. I have a wide range of musical tastes, like Generation X or the UK Subs, that's my kind of music. A lot of the thrash bands don't like us, but that's ok, we want to get shows with the Blasters and stuff, not just the same old stuff.

Al: What do you want to do with SD?

Brent: Put out 100 albums, make a million dollars! We really are trying to get more progressive, but not sell out, we just want o always progress. Our newer songs are even danceable, but we have some new harder ones too. Playing hall shows are ok, but we would like to play the Roxy or bigger shows with the Clash, or the US Festival, ha ha. We want to get as big as we can without losing the side we're playing for...

Hud: Your roots...

Brent: Yeah, our roots, we pride ourselves in that. We feel we have better roots than a lot of other bands, we have the same roots but we branch out in musical style. We all add our own style to SD.

-- Derrick --

Al: How did you join SD?

Derrick: My cousin told me about Social Distortion, I've heard of them so I jammed with them and practiced a few times and started playing gigs with them a week later.

Al: We you into that music?

Derrick: Yeah...

Julie: (Derrick's girlfriend) No!

Derrick: Well, I was into all kinds of weird shit. When I was in high school I was in marching bands, jazz bands and orchestra and at night I'd play in these weird art bands – so I figured "A punk rock band?". It sounded cool, why not.

Al: Do you like the SD sound?

Derrick: Yeah I like it, it's like a punk pop sound, it's not thrash, I'm not into thrash, I've seen too many thrash bands that sound all alike! We don't sport the forbidden beat either!

Al: The forbidden beat?

Derrick: 1234 1234 bop bop bop! There's too many bands that sound like that.

Al: Is it tough being in both Social Distortion and in DI at the same time?

Derrick: It's like having two girlfriends – that know about each other. Every once in awhile you have to shine one to do something with the other, but so far it hasn't been much of a problem. I'm also going to do a recording project with Jack and Greg from TSOL.

Al: What do you want out of SD?

Derrick: Fame and fortune!! Ha ha as I laugh. I'd like us to get kinda popular, sell some records, play some better gigs.

-- Mike Ness --

Hud: Do you write the bands lyrics?

Mike: Yeah, I write most of them, Dennis wrote a couple.

Al: What inspires you to write?

Mike: I don't know. Sometimes when I'm really high at night I get a brainstorm. I just write it down and look at it the next day and add stuff. Just social issues and I like to write about events that have happened to me.

Al: You're the only original member, right?

Mike: Yeaha, me and Casey. We started in his bedroom and for that whole summer we just learned how to play our instruments and just wrote songs. We wrote "Moral Threat" then, that was our first song. The we got some beatnik bass player and some singer. I was still in high school then and I used to get a lot of shit. I was just really angry. When I was first

Social Distortion: Brent, Mike, Derek and Dennis – photo Al

getting into punk I was just grrrr!!! Angry animal, I got into fights every weekend, plus I had a big mouth too.

Al: Why didn't you want to sing at first?

Mike: I couldn't! I tried. I had no voice or I couldn't get enough nerve to or something. I was just shy, at least then I was... A lot of our songs reflect us, "Mommys Little Monster" kinda reflects me a lot, it's like a book, maybe you don't do it on purpose but you see parts of yourself in that character. Just waking up wondering what you're gonna do that night, never a dull moment or something like that.

Hud: Is that how your life is?

Mike: Pretty much right now, I don't have a job or anything.

Al: A lot of people criticize you saying you glorify taking drugs or hanging out.

Mike: We don't really glorify it or anything. Maybe they misinterpreted a couple of our songs. "Mainliner" doesn't say it's cool to shoot up or anything, it's up to the individual. "Playpen" was about the Black Hole, my apartment, and I just wrote about what it was like living there, I don't want to preach or anything, like straight edge, it's up to the individual what he does, it doesn't matter either way.

Al: Where did the SD sound evolve from?

Mike: We used to watch the Mechanics a lot, I'd watch them play a lot of guitar progressions and I liked their style a lot. Metal guitars but not rock metal, more power chords constructed in a way that's it's not too trashy, but it's not too heavy metalish either.

Al: Some Stones influence?

Mike: Yeah, heavy Stones, heavy Bowie, Lou Reed, then everything form the Clash to X-Ray Spex, Pistols, Generation X...

-- Dennis --

Dennis: Hi, I'm Dennis, I play guitar in SD, I'm 21 years old, I'm watching Flipside Video right now, I'm extremely happy at the moment...

Al: Or is that drunk???

Dennis: Well, I just got a new amp 5 minutes ago, and we're getting ready to go see the Cramps.

Al: Ok, how did you get involved?

Dennis: I knew Mike since 6th grade, I lived on one side of Chapman Park and he lived on the other...

Al: Why weren't you in the band sooner?

Dennis: Cause I didn't play an instrument... I was just their main... I instigated them! I was the driving force behind them. They had problems with their first bass player so Mike said he could teach me bass in two weeks. I never played a instrument in my life before Social Distortion.

Al: What do you think of that name?

Dennis: Pretty fuckin' bitchen. You gotta think about what it means, everybody can think of it a different way but social distortion is definitely a problem... I make my living playing electric guitar, we're a fucking punk band. I wrote "I Just Wanna Give You The Creeps". I wrote the title to "It Wasn't A Pretty Picture". Mike and I always write songs. Writing just comes to you, ya know? You can't force it, I go through moods and stages, sometimes I can write some cool shit, sometimes fuck all. But I play my guitar everyday.

Al: People call you a lazy musician because of the way you play.

Dennis: Well when I'm playing my guitar I like to relax and sometimes I'm pretty high. Straight Edge is cool, I can't deal with it, it's healthy and there's nothing wrong with that — Straight Edge IS another state of mind, that is my answer to that.

DI: Casey, Tim, Derek, Fred - Video photography Hudley

DI

DI were interviewed by Al and Hud at Sherpa Studios. We also did a video taping this afternoon. If you know anybody in DI, especially Casey, you will know that they are a fairly intelligent and interesting band however their sense of humor never ends (especially Casey's) and it makes getting serious answers difficult.

Derrick: We're in "Suburbia"?

Al: Why?

Casey: Because Penelope called us up, she saw us play at the Anti-Club and she liked us so we did "Richard Hung Himself"... "Suburbia" is 100% Hollywood with a bullshit story to it.

Al: What other bands have you been in?

Tim: We've all been in Social Distortion at one time or another.

Fred: He (Casey) was in the Adolescnets, and he (Derrick) is in SD right now.

Casey: Let's talk about something serious like foreign policy, buy less foreign goods!

Derrick: Get Castro out of Cuba!

Casey: I'll do the interview, do you feel Fullerton has been a good mold to grow up in?

Derrick: It's a mouldy place.

Tim: It's going down hill but it's the only good place in North Orange County.

Casey: Just pray for peace in our barrios!

Tim: Cops are too busy fooling around with punk rockers and drugs and the crime rate is outrageous! Police spend their emotion on us when they should be spending their work energy on things that are a problem...

Derrick: The Galaxy is a good example of that, all it took was 100 neighbors to sign a piece of paper that says "We don't want punk rock in this town."

Tim: Without even a specific complaint... We feel good at what we do, we'd like to put out a lot of records, if people like them that would be cool.

Casey: People get off on he energy levels we have, I've been told, but I think we're shit... We're more informative live, just like on world topics and what pisses us off – what exploited angles are coming in on us we hit on it pretty much.

Tim: We're just into really playing shows, we like to play.

Al: Casey do you write the lyrics?

Casey: Yeah, pretty much. Fred writes some lyrics and the music and every once in awhile we get some gigs and eat some food, but we're all on perpetual diets...

Al: What about the other DI?

Casey: We, DI, played with the Gears, I played bass and we had another guitar player, but it was still going on and we were talking to the Gears, we were all bros and now they have our name!!

Tim: We like DI, it's just a stupid thing you can say anything about.

PETER IVERS

By John Bryant
As everyone knows by now, Peter Ivers, host of the TV Show "New Wave Theatre"

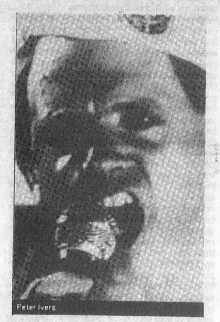

Peter Ivers

was beaten to death by a burglar at his loft downtown. Ivers was one of the most electric people in the new counter culture and one of the most misunderstood. First, he was not gay, he just had a high voice. Second, he was not a wimp but a strong bodied karate expert. Also, he did all kind of things in show business besides New Wave Theatre.

Not many people knew how much fun the tapings of New Wave Theatre were. The marathon 10 hour sessions gave you a chance to check out at least 10 or 15 bands for $1. Band members and Ivers and his crew (including Tuxedo bandit Zachary and talent coordinator Tequila Mockingbird) mixed normally with the punks and others who just

Crucifix - photo Al

been on this show: Black Flag, X, Fear, Circle jerks, Bad Religion, Angry Samoans as well as some of the newer wave of HC bands like Social Distortion, 45 Grave have been on 3 times. The first thing we asked Ivers was how he feels when punk bands make fun of him:

Ivers: Well, first of all part of my job is to be an object of scorn, to be a foil for their creativity. So it's just a collaboration.

Bryant: How about when the Angry Samoans did some song about "fucking queers, fucking fags", would you let someone do a song about "fucking niggers"?

Ivers: I wouldn't, no. But I don't decide who performs or what they do. I think people recognize that it's a performance. The idea is that the artist acts out stuff from his fantasy life that the normal person doesn't act out, and therefore he allows a release. I'm cool enough to allow them the freedom.

Bryant: Lets talk about your monologues.

Ivers: David Jove writes them.

Bryant: I really believe them! My friends say they are a bunch of babble.

Ivers: They're not taking the time or don't have the attention span – or maybe they aren't interested in finding out who they are to listen more closely. Yeah, it's difficult to interpret, but part of David Jove's trip is not to make it easy. He wants the people to have enough interest to peer into it and find the meaning.

Bryant: Some HC bands have a violent sound and image. What do you see in their eyes?

Ivers: I've asked the audience that very question. I see... wet soul, trying to get out. There's a lot of anger, but it's a way of... it's multiple artistic impulses simultaneously happening. Let's just say it's an intense energy that they have, which you could look at as anger or just energy.

Bryant: So what's the meaning of life?

Ivers: I don't have a glib answer for that.

Bryant: No, I really want to know, the readers what to know.

Ivers: The meaning of life is to take every moment to it's ultimate max, in all realms, emotional, physical, spiritual, astral – simultaneously – and to embrace the universe in perfect harmony while being imperfect and not caring.

CRUCIFIX

Crucifix were interviewed by Al and Hud in March at Roxannes Bar in Arcadia, just prior to their first U.S. tour.

Hud: We've heard that you've changed since our last interview, you're vegetarians now...

Chris: We don't believe in killing animals for food, it's not necessary.

Matt: We've learned more, last time we came down was about a year ago and we were just getting to the point of knowing how to be in a band. we had our ideas down as far as what we thought inside but not as far as what we put out as lyrics or as a band. As we progressed we got to be able to say what we wanted to say more clearly. Like last interview we said we don't talk about our politics in our music, that it was just personal, well now it is more public because we want to get our message across to people. We want to say something. We did before too, we just didn't know how to do it.

Sothira: This is our 4th time down to L.A. and each time has been a progression, a change.

Matt: The vegetarian thing is hard to talk about, because a lot of people say "You're vegetarians but you still wear leather?" and it's just the clothes that we have, we're not going to buy any more. Why store it in the closet, you still have it. The basic reasoning is what any vegetarian would say, like if all the grain wasn't used to feed cows to feed fat Americans, then there would be more grain to feed Third World countries that are starving. It takes like 28 pounds of grain to go into a cow to get one pound of protein.

Jake: We are also progressing towards wanting to live collectively and collectiveize all of our resources. It's cheaper and more economical and it puts our politics into action. That is a big part of being an anarchist.

Sothira: We think that what we're doing is positive and hope that people will pick up on what we are doing, we're trying to see ourselves as examples.

Al: Do you get much shit from people saying you look too English?

Sothira: Yeah all the time.

Hud: Who inspired this look?

Chris: Nobody inspired it, we just want to look this way.

Sothira: The spikey hair punk think was started a long time ago in the American scene with the Avengers, the Pistols now the English have got it longer, it's no different.

Matt: The music that we play is definitely not English and the ideas we have go far beyond being English or American, they're universal.

Sothira: It's good to look this way because a lot of people still haven't seen punk and the first impression still counts.

Matt: When people see us, they see that we are different and they want to know what we are about.

Jake: Punk redefines the standards of beauty that were imposed upon us by society, and it's a grey picture.

Hud: It's like deprogramming society.

Jake: Right, when people see you they feel threatened and there's a reason because the way you're supposed to look is a really heavy program in this society. But the punk look has really infiltrated the whole media, new wave fashions are now what people would have considered punk 5 years ago, they're so behind, but that's the way media is.

Crucifix: Jake, Chris, Matt, Sothira – photo Al

ANTI

Anti were interviewed by Al in March at Gary's house.

Anti are: Gary on guitar (he also plays bass in Mood of Defiance and tapes in Zurich 1916 with Don Bolles or whoever), Danny on bass (who also plays guitar in Mood Of Defiance), Burt on vocals and Steve on drums. Danny and Gary also run New Underground Records, the people who put out the "Life Is..." compilations. You may know Anti from their first album, which gained a lot of criticism for its lyrical content...

Gary: Those songs were written two years ago, they're old and that's where we were at the time. Our second album "Defy the System" the songs were written at the time of the first album, there's a big time lapse, we waited too long to put it out.

Al: You changed your sound too...

Burt: Yeah, you see with two guitars the thrash sound just seems so funny, because now we've got the possibilities and you can do different things.

Gary: There's only so long you can go on playing as fast as you can.

Danny: And also I started singing, Burt left so I started singing, we were a three piece, and now he's back.

Gary: Anti has very diverse influences. We are all completely different people. (Gary goes

through his massive collection of noise records) I like noise because how many times can you listen to rock in a day? Special music that doesn't have structure is better.

Danny: Me, I'm on the poppy side, I like Bad Religion, Agent Orange, Red Kross, Buzzcocks, Damned, Stranglers...

Burt: I like, um, seventies stuff, Jeff Beck, Eric Clapton, T Rex, that's what I like to listen to, but that's not what I like to see. I like to see stuff like the Vandals, I like to see anarchy and to see fun. I like to play punk rock.

Steve: I like playing and hearing a lot of fast stuff, I like the DK's and the Sex Pistols but I also like the Cramps style of playing.

Al: You always have these anti-war themes in your records, what inspires that?

Gary: Well we hear about these things that happen in war and see pictures like on the Crass albums. Like "I Don't Want To Die In Your War", that was inspired by the cover of Discharges "Why?". It was shocking, horrible that that stuff goes on, because it's totally useless... But most of my songs are like sociology or psychology. Danny's songs are descriptive, we all write different stuff.

Al: Do you have a specific Anti message?

Burt: Have fun, don't hurt people and don't start a war. And take it easy on the clubs, don't trash them or shit on people's lawns, because it all comes back.

FLIPSIDE NUMBER 39

"if your body's feeling bad, & it's the only one you had
if your mind is in a state, stainless steel penetrate
I can ease your pain away, just an hour everyday
Now relax have faith in me, and I'll start your therapy.
And I can help you
And you can help me
And together we'll find perfect harmony
I can make you understand, only gotta take my hand
Close your eyes lie down, I'll slip into my white gown
My needles are being sterilized,
the power of the pins are not recognized
Now relax have faith in me, and I'll start your therapy
Faith hope and charity, will set your tortured body free
The secret lies in your own mind,
I only seek payment of a kind
Your body sleeps while mine takes pleasure
Wake slowly at your own leisure

Anti

Now relax have faith in me, it's the end of your therapy"
"Needles and Pins" – GBH

ISSUE #: 39
DATE: August 1983
FORMAT: 8 1/2x11, rotary web offset with 2 color glossy cover.
PAGES: 76
PRICE: $1.00
PRESS RUN: 6500

Flipside and the scene chug on – six years after the fact. The weird thing happening in L.A. is the move away from the clubs (which at the time we had a few of: Shamus, Roxannes, Cathay, Vex, Sun Valley) to the big arenas. The clubs are having killer bills, with no attendance, while the arenas are packing them in. The newer punks are going for the "events" that make for big social affairs, rather than really experiencing the bands. A classic example is GBH and the Exploited both doing Olympic and Cathay shows on the same tour - with no crowd problems. Anyway, touring bands are plentiful this summer....

GBH

GBH were interviewed at the Tropicana Hotel in Hollywood by Al, Hud and Big Frank the night before their debut gig at the Santa Monica Civic Auditorium.

Al: Why did you pick a name like GBH, aren't here other GBH's in England?

Colin: We just thought of it, short and simple, three words: **Grevious Bodily Harm.**

Al: And then you added "Charged"?

Colin: Yeah, we used to play and people would say that there's another band in Glasglow or another part of England called GBH, so we just put the charged in front of it. People in Birmingham all know us as GBH so we just added the "Charged" to distinguish ourselves. That other band was a metal band and I don't think they're still around.

Al: Do you write most of the lyrics?

Colin: Yeah I do, they come up with the tunes and I write words to them.

Hud: How did you come up with "Alcohol"?

Colin: We just mad it up on the moment, we had about an hour of studio time left and we just made it up.

Al: Who came up with "Slut"?

Colin: I did.

Frank: And "Big Women"?

GBH at Perkins palace - photo Al

Colin: We all did.

Al: A lot of people would consider that sexist?

Ross: It's like a joke, that's all.

Hud: I thought it was more sarcastic.

Colin: It is, it's totally sarcastic, it's a piss take of heavy metal. You know how they go on and on about how beautiful women are, it's just a view from the other side.

Jock: It's just a joke and people take it so seriously.

Colin: In England we can't play in the Universities and Rough Trade won't stock any of our records because they think we're sexist. There's a song on the new album in the same vein... we have to back and record the album, it's called "City Baby's Revenge...."

Frank: Are any of you married?

Colin: I am. I am when I get back. No. I'm gonna... I don't know!!!!

Al: Then you'll write love songs....

Colin: Oh we do write love songs!!

Hud: Do any of you have kids?

Ross: Yeah, Jock and I have daughters. She's three, mines called Lisa and his is called Charlotte. She's a head case.

Hud: Why?

Ross: Well I like the Crass and when I put on their records she's jumping around to them, she likes Siouxsie and the Banshees as well. She'll point to the records she likes to play and it's either them two. She knows. "Securicor" by Crass is one of her favorites.

Al: What about GBH records?

Ross: I don't play them. I don't know I don't like them very much. The production stinks...

Al: Do you get shit over here for having leather and bristles?

Jock: I think the way you look should reflect s the way you think. If you think vicious, you look vicious, ha ha ha..

Mick (sound man): Are they gonna have skateboards at the gig tomorrow?

Frank: They won't bring them in.

Al: There's skate parks in England?

Colin: Yeaha but not for punks, the only people who skateboard are kids like 12 or 14 years old...

Al: Yeah, those are the kids coming to the gig tomorrow! Your fans. Do you like to play in bigger or smaller places?

Colin: Smaller.

Ross: It depends on the audience.

Colin: As long as you're dripping in sweat. We like just enough room, if there's a good atmosphere it doesn't matter where you are.

Al: You've been accused of having "rock star attitudes".

Ross: I don't know, why?

Colin: ...the other night in Denver we were doing our sound check and we're not perfectionists but we like a good sound. We had about 5 minutes and we hadn't sorted out the problems so the next band comes up and says "move your equipment, our sound check is at 5 oclock". And I said, move our equipment? Our sound check was at 3 and we just got started!! It wasn't our fault.

Ross: I've had loads of people stay at my flat in Birmingham, people that weren't from Birmingham, how could they fucking call you a rockstar?

Jock: Maybe because they call our music heavy metal, like we're trying to get into the heavy metal market.

Frank: Do you think you're a cross over?

Jock: No. What it is is the music we listen to. I listen to a bit of Motorhead and listen to a lot of punk. He listens to rhythm and blues and it all comes together.

Wllf: We just play what we want to play, we don't play music to come under any particular category.

Frank: But do you consider yourselves a punk band?

Ross: Yeah we're a punk band!

Jock: We just do what comes naturally to us.

Frank: What inspired you to form the band?

Jock: Nobody formed the band, it was just there!

Colin: Boredom. There was just fuck all to do. We had a club called "Barbarellas" in Birmingham, the best punk club in England, and all the bands would play there. When that closed down we started a band.

Frank: Are you still close with your fans in Birmingham?

Ross: Yeah! They're all our mates. We grew up with them. All the punks in Birmingham are our mates.

Al: Are you a political band?

Ross: No. You're never gonna change anything, you might as well go our and enjoy yourselves, just fuck everybody else.

Colin: Just tell me on band that has changed a world view or anything?

Frank: Crass have at lease made a few more people aware of things.

Ross: It's not worth flogging your guts on a political point of view if you're only gonna change a handfull of people. Just go out and enjoy yourself.

Wllf: that's what punk is about, enjoying yourself.

Jock: There are heavy political bands about, and that's good. But there are enough of them.

Al: You have you songs that lean in that direction?

Wllf: But it's not political, it's personal statements.

GBH on tour

Al: A lot of people see "GBH" on the back of all the leather jackets and start a backlash...

Ross: We were told we were popular here, but it's one thing to be told and another to find out.

Wilf: What happened in England with the Exploited, they were real popular, top 20 in the national charts, and most punks had Exploited on their backs, then the backlash started and they're not so popular now. We got a call in our hotel asking us to do a gig in England when we get back, with the Exploited supporting us, and that seems really funny. When we first started they were already popular. Since we started, everything that happends to us really surprizes us. We can't believe it. When we first started we thought we'd just be doing it for a laugh.

Hud: Just go "Wow, this is great!"

Wilf: But that gets into the rockstar thing.

Hud: You just have a lot of fans, you guys are really friendly...

Wilf: We get on with fanzines better than people from proper papers, fanzines print the truth, the music papers blow everything up.

Al: You've been touring in a van rather than flying.

Wilf: Oh it's much better, you get to see some of the country.

Ross: It's brilliant, but the most boring thing that I've ever seen in my life is Nebraska!

Al: What do you think of "our" missiles all over Europe?

Wilf: Well before we came over I thought American's were right bastards cause they put their nose in everybody elses wars, argue with Russia, they're pig headed, and all you hear in the papers in England is the bad things, but then you come over here and meet the real people and the real people are brilliant!

Ross: And the real people of Russia, they're just the same as us.

Wilf: All the people are the same, it's just the people that run the world that are bastards. You don't really realize that until you go to the country and meet the people.......

II always love GBH– hudley :])

NO TREND
----
o Trend were interviewed at Roxannes ar on June 21st. by Al.

Al: Is there a reason why you're putting out your records yourselves, instead of say, Dischord?

Jeff: We don't affiliate ourselves with anything, we are No Trend. We don't conform to any trend at all. We are all our own. independant.

Jim: We're not a DC hardcore band. We're not straight edge either.

Jeff: We play hardcore shows because a lot of the people that are into the hardcore scene are supposedly openminded and we thought that they might open their mind to a new music. That's why we like to play punk shows.

Jim: But all kinds of people like us, not just hardcores.

Al: How do you describe your sound?

Jim: The best way I've heard of describing it is "unbearable". That's sums it up. It's kind of like torture. Audience torture.

Al: What kind of influences do you have? Like I hear a lot of Velvet Underground in "Teen Love".

Jim: No. That song is based on pop music of the 70's, kinds distorted. I'm influenced by all sorts of music.

Jeff: We have songs like "Mass Sterilization" that is just raw noise and then there's "Teen Love" that is almost a pop song, Jim listen to surf music, so we have that style...

Jim: I play all kinds of different styles. We all listen to hardcore and other types of music.

Jeff: I like a lot of noise like Non, SPK, of course all Throbbing Gristle is great.

Chris: I like hardcore but I like a lot of classical music too.

Jeff: I like Muzak too. It kind of controls peoples bodies.

Jim: People seem to deserve muzak, they seem to like it.

Al: How long have you been a band?

Jim: Since September.

Al: What is No Trend trying to get across?

Jim: Humans are basically just mindless sheep, waiting to be lead in one direction or the other, and most hardcore are no better.

Al: How are you any different?

Jim: We are playing the music we want to instead of trying to please every crowd. A lot of hardcore bands have childish, lame lyrics. If you're gonna call yourselves rebellious, you lyrics should be saying something. Punk rock isn't as threatening as it used to be because people just laugh at it these days. A housewife sees some kid with a mohawk on the street and she just laughs at it because she saw it on Square Pegs or Quincy.

Al: What are you lyrics about?

Jim: The thing I'm against is conformity to any group, there are just too many people. The planet can't support this many people. A couple should have at the most 2 kids if that. We have a song called "Too Many Fucking Humans" and that pretty much tells the whole story. We try to put things as simply as possible so people get the message. Most people take it for granted that the world

No Trend at Roxannes – photo Al

Kraut at Cathay – photo Al

should be over run with humans, I think it is unnatural and perverted for there to be this many of any one species controlling the whole thing, polluting it and fucking it up. I'm against the way ecology is now and people make fun of it. We're against any kind of governmental control, we are not necessarily anarchists. Anytime people live together, there will be a system that arrises. I think democracy is pretty much the best thing they've come up with.

Chris; I think the old American Indian tribes had the best thing. I wish things WOULD get messed up so we could go back to that. I like their religious outlook.

Jim: I really respect a lot of the Indian culture because they had respect for nature.

FAITH / ALEC MACKAY

Alec was interviewed at the Vex on June 18 by Al

Al: Is Faith still together?

Alec: Yep.

Al: With no personnel changes lately?

Alec: We we have two guitarists, but that was awhile ago. Other than that, no.

Al: I've always wondered about the name of your band, "Faith", that's pretty powerful.

Alec: We all named it. We had a few names kicking around but that's the one we wanted. It's not having anything to do with religion or anything like that. The fact is it's just a word – "Faith"... what you believe in is... faith... that's what drives you. That's why we thought it was a proper name.

Al: Is there a general thing driving you?

Alec: Well not like each one thing, we're a band, so we're a unit, but it's not like we have one driving thing that we're all into. Not like one goal, except for the fact that we all want people to think about everything and be true to themselves, have faith in themselves. To make sure that what they are doing is what they want.

Al: Do you have any problems being that Ian (Minor Threat) is your brother?

Alec: Well, not really problems. There's the comparisons between the two bands, no problem except when they say were trying to be like Minor Threat. I can't help be like my brother, that's not my fault. I didn't plan it that way but I'm not ashamed of it either, it helps

me out personally in some ways just because people say "Oh, You're Ian's little brother!" Riding on someones coat tails, I don't know if it's helping our or whatever.

Al: Do people expect a DC sound or attitude from you?

Alec: I imagine so. Like one of my songs I mention "Straight edge" and that makes people click – Oh, DC straight edge. I guess we got it if there is one.

Al: What influences you?

Alec: Just the whole fucking, do what you want and not having anybody hold you back and you have to really believe in what you want if you want to get it. There's a lot of things, not one thing in particular.

Al: Well, were did you and Ian grow up?

Alec: In DC, my parents met in grade school in DC, my grandfather came from Ireland.

Al: It's strange how some families have openminded kids...

Alec: Well there's 5 kids in our family. I have 3 sisters, one is into punk and all that. She was the one that showed me and Ian the first Damned and Gen X albums. My parents think it's all the greatest thing, they support us all the way. I can't tell if it's my parents being particularly cool or if it's just the way we treat them. If you're assholes to your parents because punk is supposed to be assholes to your parents, that causes a lot of troubles. But I love my parents all the way.

KRAUT

Kraut were interviewed on July 21st at Perkins Palace by Al. I was drunk and tired but...

Al: How come everybody used to say New York sucks so bad?

Doug: Cause they don't know about it.

Don: Cause they're not from New York.

Johnny: We had a bad reputation at first being trendy and all that shit, but it has changed and no one has said anything about it being changed.

Al: What did it change to?

Doug: It's been about the same as this whole fucking tour we've been on, except like here there's a lot more people.

Dave: New York seems a little more united, less seperation of people that are out there,

everybody is there to enjoy it.

Al: Why did you name it Kraut?

Don: Just cabbage.

Johnny: It makes people think, you might think German Nazi bullshit, like that but it's not..

Dave: Kraut is like an insult to a German.

Doug: Ok. The first band I ever was in, when we first formed we had other names, when I quit that band I knew the next band I was in would call it that cause it would piss them off, and it was Kraut.

Al: What influences YOUR musical style?

Doug: Pink Floyd, Mountain...

Al: Yeah, yeah, I can hear it...

Doug: Jeff Beck, Alice Cooper.... The song "Onward" is like, I got into a spat with a bunch of skinhead kids, and I was talking about some music and they go "Oh that sucks". But there's a background to rock and roll, what we play is rock and roll...

Al: Are you a punk band?

Doug: We call call ourselves a punk rock hardcore rock and roll band, if you want to label it like that.

Dave: When we started there was no such thing as the hardcore scene. All we knew is went went out one night and there were all these kids and we were suddenly labeled...

Doug: So I was getting fed up with kids coming down on music I used to listen to, I'm 21, my past was like Alice Cooper, Mountain... I was always sort of into the heavy metal underground like Iggy Pop and stuff like that. That's why I wrote "Onward", the music to it is basic rock and roll played really fast. "You've got to go backwards to go onwards". We're a rock and roll band, we're just a new generation.

Al: You all work, but would you like the band to be your job?

Don: We haven't taken it that seriously because obviously it doesn't pay. If we were in it for the money we wouldn't be here.

Dave: We're in it to have fun and that's what we do.

GOVERNMENT ISSUE

GI were interviewed at Shamus O'brians on Aug 10 by Al and Pete.

Al: This isn't the original GI line-up, give us a brief history.

Tom: It started off with John Barry and Brian Gay being the original bass player and guitarist. John Stabb and Mark Alberstadt are still the singer and drummer.

Mark: We're the core, the nucleus of the band.

Tom: I've been in the band for 2 years, starting off on bass and switching to guitar. Rob Mos has replaces Mitch Parker, who is on "Boycott Stabb".

Al: Why is the record called "Boycott Stabb"?

Tom: There was some graffitti that some unknown artist put on a construction site across from the record store where John Stabb works. John took a picture of it and we all liked it sooo much we put it on an album cover.

Al: Why would they want to boycott him?

Mark: If you knew him with any intimacy that would explain it right there. He's an excentric lad.

Al: Who came up with the name GI?

Tom: It's in an old Black Market Baby song, says "You're just a bunch of GI's" a song called "World At War". At first it was "GIs", the we just used "GI" then "Government Issue

A
GIANT
RECORD
FROM
A
GIANT
LABEL

GOVERNMENT
ISSUE
YOU

HH 6100-1 (LP) $8.98 list
HH 6100-2 (CD) $12.98 list
HH 6100-4 (CS) $8.98 list

All titles available:
Dutch East India Trading
P.O. Box 570
Rockville Centre, NY 11571-0570

GIANT
records

manufactured and distributed by:
Dutch East India Trading

Government Issue at Shamus – photo Al

They're all interchangaeble really.

Al: What kind of message do you have?

Tom: Well we don't like Journey and we don't like what people have listened to in the past so we're just giving people music.

Mark: An alternative music?

Al: Well, do you have the attitude where you're pissed off at society?

Tom: No. We're all from rich homes.

Mark: We're from suburban castles so what do we have to complain about. Well, not castles, but we're middle class.

Tom: That's what the whole DC scene is about. I mean we're not poor or struggling or on the dole or anything like that. We're bored like anyone else.

Al: I thought if you live in DC and pass the Washington Monument everyday...

Tom: No. Do you write about the ocean in L.A.? Or surfing?

Al: Just skating. (John Stabb arrives). What do you write your songs about?

John: Personal politics, I don't write about political things that go on, just feelings. Things that go on around me. I don't write about things that are over my head, I don't write about El Salvador or things like that. More on a gut level. In the vein of Black Flag and bands like that. I try to put more of a positive attitude into it and not be negative like too many bands are. I think politics should be in newspapers and not preached on stage.

Al: You have a bad reputation, people always say "John Stabb is an asshole".

John: That's cool. I don't know, whatever people wanna say. I can't go up to everybody on the street and go "What's new?". I mean some people rag on me, some people rag on everybody. Like some people rag on Henry. It's funny. I don't know what to say, I don't go around fucking people up.

Tom: Yes you do!

Al: Well at least you cause a reaction.

John: That's all we're in it for, we're not there for people to worship us or to love us to death or hate us, just so long as there's a reaction. Everything is a reaction whether it's good or bad. That's all I play shows for, the reaction....

ANTI-NOWHERE LEAGUE

ANWL were interviewed at Perkins Palace in July after their sound check by Frank H.

Frank: What type of band would you consider yourselves, a lot of people consider you a punk band, but I don't think you agree with that label.

Winston: No. I never really put ourselves in any category. Just the Anti-nowhere League. It's what we started as and what we consider ourselves now.

Animal: When we started out to be the League we wanted to be totally different. Right from the start everyone hated our guts. We could have played it safe but we were committed to not giving in.

Frank: What was your inspiration?

Winston: We done loads of other things on the streets, been in gangs altogether. It was one thing we had never done, be in the music scene. The music scene in England was getting really boring. The punk thing had died in 77-78 and we thought it was time we did something and we did.

Animal: When we started we never thought we'd get to tour America - twice! Our beginning was a total piss take. We never even intended to be successful. I think we can all say we were inspired by the Sex Pistols and about the time they ended we started up.

Frank: What do you see in the future?

Animal: We look forward to our next record and that's it for now.

Frank: What bands do you all enjoy?

Animal: We really all get off on our individual tastes.

Winston: You could ask any of us and get totally different things. For me, from the Police to Peter Tosh... we like everything, not just punk or hardcore.

Frank: Is there any place you'd like to play or anyone you'd like to play with?

Animal: Japan, that's the place for us.

Winston: I don't think there's anybody we'd like to play with, we have no heroes.

Frank: Do you mind discussing the carrot incident in the Damned dressing room. I have always heard about it...

Winston: It was on the tour with the Damned. It was a dare really between Rat and myself to see who could disgust the other one. So anyway I took the carrot and dipped it in cream cheese, Sensible kicked it up my ass. And I pulled it out and ate it. Scabies went to the toilet and threw up. Sensible was rolling on the floor, didn't know what to do.

Animal: I mean no one on the tour knew who we were and everybody was drunk, and when he did it all these girls just freaked out and ran.

Frank: You don't like to put any politics into your songs.

Winston: We never liked politics, you can say what ever you like and it isn't going to make any difference.

Frank: You don't think that a band like the Clash have opened peoples eyes a little?

Winston: The Clash have their ideas and that's all well and good, but we don't give a toss about politics at all. Five people in a band are not going to make a difference.

Frank: Anything else you want to say?

Winston: Have a nice day.

Decry

Decry were interviewed in early August by Al.

Al: When did Decry start?

Farrell: December of last year. We got Matt in December and that's when we got serious. We were the first punk band to play

Anti-Nowhere League – photo Al

Decry: Todd, Farell, Rod, Andrew – photo Al

Roxannes, Roxannes is the home of Decry.
Al: How many times have you played there?
All: Too many!!!
Todd: Seriously about 15 times.
Al: What is some of your new material about?
Farrell: "Symptoms of Hate" is about dumb things like, um, the Mod scene where people just repeat other people, they want to be like someone, and then just break away and say "No more am I going to be like you, I've got a mind of my own". Our songs are like, think for yourself.
Todd: Breaking out of stereotypes.
Farrell: If you believe in something, stick with it – no matter if the odds are for or against you. Stick with what you believe in. "Fight To Survive" is like what "Warlords" is about, actually it's about a movie called "Warlords", like the hero is always the clean guy with the gun, all in white, it's about a Vietnam Vet, it's about "Just out of school, go to war to be a man like so many fools, drafted and you don't understand, killing for causes you don't even know, come back home and you're no hero". There's no coming home parades for Vietnam Vets. They got shafted.
Al: What's "Falling" about?
Farrell: It's about the party scene and everyone going "It's cool, it's cool, these drugs are cool, cocaine is great" but if you tell your friend you just shot up heroin, what does he say? Gee, that's not partying. You find out and go, "nobody told me it would feel like this."
Rodney: When you first did it you go, "Oh, I'm cool, I'm doing it", but then you finally realize you are fucked up.
Al: What did you mean when you said you were serious now?
Farrell: At first we didn't know what we...
Andrew: Just the attitude towards the crowd, sometimes you just laugh, like "Wow, we're playing again" and just go through the set.
Farrell: But now we take it song by song and think about every song.
Todd: And no fucking around between songs, we used to drink beer and laugh, now we're trying to make a real fast, tight set.
Al: What does Decry mean as a band name?
Rodney: Openly speak against, condemn.
Farrell: It's like a message, don't be fooled, don't be pushed around. If you believe in something, stick up for it, that's what Decry

really means.
Rodney: De Cry, like a prefix, instead of sitting down crying, you're de-crying.
Farrell: They spell it wrong all the time.

PUSHEAD

Pushead was interviewed June 18th at the Vex by Al and Hud.
Hud: I thought you were a short, 17 year old kid with a skinhead...
Pushead: What made you think that?
Hud: I don't know, just from that picture of the back of your head with pus coming out.
Pushead: Oh no. I'm 24. A lot of people think I am younger.
Al: Why do you think so?
Pushead: I don't know if it's because of my artwork, but when people meet me they try to guess my age. It's funny because Mark Rude is older and a lot of other artists are older.
Hud: Why do you always draw dicks?
Pushead: Dicks! I've only drawn, what, three.
Hud: But it's always masculine men, why not more women?
Pushead: Uh I don't know, I'm trying to get

Septic Death – photo Al

away from the male figure. When I first started drawing I did draw girls, girls are very critical of what they look like. So I stayed away from it and drew a cartoon and it didn't have to be masculine or feminine. I'm trying to get into other things besides that so I don't make a generalization. To me if you draw a girl, you should draw her the right way, not as naked, or a sex object but as a feminine figure.
Al: What kind of feedback do you get from your drawings, like the on for the "Blood Saussage" Meatmen record?
Pushead: That was probably one of my most popular drawings. I don't know if people like it because of what it is, I don't think they know what it represents, they just like it. They say "How can you draw that?", "That hurts me just to look at it". So I fullfill a point just by that.
Al: What does it represent?
Pushead: Like the knife represents disease and how people take advantage of their sexual prowess and what not. And it's like they're ruining it because they just like fucking around, sorry I don't like to say that word, but they mess around a lot and they get disease. Once you get a disease you're ruined for life, just like if you cut off the limb, just like if I took a knife... I'm not into that. I think if you love someone, that is the person you should love and that's the person you should be with.
Al: Some people think you're burning out your skull character?
Pushead: I don't know if I'm burning it out, people out there who write to me, that's the character that they want. I'm doing new characters and changing different things because I've been in this space. But the way I draw skulls appeals to them, and they want THAT skull. I've got to find a way to change the skull around if I'm gonna continue doing skulls. I'm getting to a thing where people say I'm going to get burnt out or people will get tired of me, so I'm trying to involve myself in other things.... I write to everybody, and I write to new people. I like to write articles and I'm going into writing and stuff. I like what's going on in this hardcore thing and I like to support everybody...
Al: You're doing Thrasher.
Pushead: Yeah, I'm doing Thrasher, I'm doing stuff for **Maximum Rock N' Roll** & I'm doing stuff for Forced Exposure and Straight Edge. Annie's involved in writing articles too. Thrasher I do a lot with, I do "Puszone"...

Stretch Marks: Sick and Dick - photo Al

one "Foreign Policy" that basically deals with how we're just letting the American government come up and test off their cruise missiles.

Kel: There's all kinds of things that we feel the effects of...

Hud: Like acid rain!

Kel: Yeah. We're like Sweden of North America. It all ends up over us.

Bill: You've heard that Canada's got a lot of natural resources, well the US owns about 99% of them!

Hud: What's the name of your record label: "Dick and Butt"?

Bill: No! "Head Butt". We're big wrestling fans. Instead of a skate punk band, were a wrestling punk band. It's not mindless. It's totally wrestling inspired.

Dick: We're trying to have a really good time. If people don't listen to he message, fine. The music's still there...

Bill: We're live entertainment...

Al: What about that song "Professional Punk"?

Sick: These guys in Winnipeg, they were always hanging us behind our backs and they were studio musicians and stuff and all of a sudden they came out and they were this punk band!!!

DIE KREUZEN

Interviewed at Shamus O'Briens on June 23 by Al and Hud in their tour van....

Present were Herman (guitar), Danny (vocals), Keith (bass) and later Eric (drums) found us.

Al: So, you guys used to be called the Stellas?

Herman: Well first of all Danny and I moved up from Roxville, Illinois, 90 miles from Chicago to Milwaukee... three of us came up and we spent 9 months looking for a drummer.

Danny: We had a number of different drummers, including a girl who was pretty good. Then we came across Eric. How did we get Keith?

Keith: I was the one who gave you Eric's phone number!

Herman: The Stellas were just like get drunk and go play "Ya hooo" and bash the joint around...

Al: Do you skate a lot?

Pushead: Yeaha, I skate all the time. I'm into vertical and I've had pictures in magazines. I've been skating for years, I used to be a local at Del Mar Skatepark. I designed their logo. I've also designed a skateboard wheel and a deck. There's a lot more when you're an artist - you have a level of design. I like to design things. I'm really into creativity and imagination and being able to use that. I you want to be like all these people out here and you want to get attention then you have to do it in a way that you're different. If you want to be different, then you've got to be creative.

Al: You're in a band too, Septic Death?

Pushead: Yeah. That's something that we've had for about a year and a half. We've played a few gigs, we're playing in Portland next friday with Poison Idea.

Al: And you call yourself straight edge.

Pushead: Very.

Al: You don't mind the label?

Pushead: Straight edge is fine. I've been what's called straight edge for 8 or 9 years now, I've always called it anti-poison or device.

STRETCH MARKS

The Stretch Marks were interviewed in June by Al and Hud at Sun Valley Sportsmans Hall.

Al: What kind of name is "Stretch Marks"?

Dick: Dick: A disgusting name!

Kel: It's a name we thought would stick in peoples minds. It has different connotations, like for one thing we are pissed off at how the government stretches things out of proportion - always stretching the truth, so we are stretch marks of society. That's one connotation, it's not the sexual one. But then again that's one for sure, that is one reason you may not want to have kids...

Dick: Or from drinking too much beer.

Kel: Dicks pretty big and he's usually bigger nd he's got stretch marks on him so...

Al: In Canada the government is pretty different than here in the States...

Bill: It's different...

Sick: But it's better in a lot of ways, there's Medicare. Free medicine, like you never have to pay for a doctor, you just go into a hospital and show them your medical number.

Dick: Canada is actually a really good country. Our lyrics don't gripe about Canada because it's hard to gripe about it.

Bill: We get no police harrassment in Winnipeg. It's not a huge scene but...

Kel: We get a little, but they don't actually attack the scene. We haven't hardly seen any Smokies yet.

Al: What do you sing about?

Dick: Everything... Everybody is singing about this and that so we try to write about a lot of stuff that people don't cover. We sing about a lot of social issues: rape, child abuse, stuff that goes on everyday but it doesn't seem to bother a lot of people. They're big problems but they just get shoved to the side. We have songs about the government, like our new

Die Kreuzen ready to tour - photo Al

Keith: It's indicated a change of attitude more than anything.

Danny: We decided we were gonna change to do something instead of just wasting our time.

Hud: How do you pronounce your name?

Danny: Die Kreuzen (D Kreut Zen). Michael from JFA, his girlfriend is German and she told us it means "the crossing"..

Keith: Nobody would know what it means, we weren't looking for anything with deep meaning. It's just something to call us rather than something that would have obvious conotations, just something different.

Al: Why did you leave Wisconsin?

Keith: Just looking for a wider variety of experiences...

Danny: At first it was just gonna be a tour and we were gonna go back but then we decided, well, there's a bigger audience out there, let's stay out there awhile.

Keith: It's like none of us would have jobs if we went back or places to live or anything, so we can stop anywhere really.

Al: You're pretty much dedicated.

Danny: Oh yeah, the band is all that matters, it always was though too.

Herman: We felt we hit our peak back there. There's really no places to play there or to make any money.

Al: You were saying that you weren't a political band?

Keith: Strictly on a personal level.

Danny: It's just stuff that's happened to me, or us, problems like just being in school or "On The Street" is just about hanging out on the street corner. I quit high school to be in the band.

Al: What happends if the band doesn't make it?

Danny: Then I'll probably go back home and have my dad get me a job as a janitor, I don't know.

Keith: That's not one of our main big things to think about. But it depends on your definition of "making it".

Herman: This is more than we expected.

Keith: We're making enough money right now to pay for gas and eat and... it's great. That's all we need. we're seeing a lot of new places and a lot of good bands. (Talk about seeing the Exploited) That was just a joke, I'm sorry. We played with the Exploited in Chicago and it was just the most pathetic thing. I don't like to slag bands but that is just the ultimate.

Danny: If that is what punk rock is all about I don't want to have anything to do with it.

Keith: Wattie was like kicking people in the face, being obnoxious, he was drunk and falling all over. For me it was an example of all the bad things that people think about punk rock, all the cartoonish, jokey things, ya know. People were lapping it up, begging for more. The thing we're trying to get across is if you like the music, try to get involved in any way you possibly can, no matter how old you are.

Eric: Or how you look.

Keith: Just try to get involved or it's never gonna grow. Especially the kids, because they're the future.

Eric: People have to get away from the fashion end of it and just listen to he music.

Keith: If that's people's main criteria then fuck it, it's not even worth my time.

Eric: Hair grows, we all HAD short hair.......

TWISTED SISTER

Twisted Sister is one of the few heavy metal acts to date to have an appeal that

Dee Snider - photo Bill

spans the average metal and punk rock consciousness and finds some middle ground that attracts the more open minded fans from both genres. Along with the likes of Motorhead and a few others, Twisted Sister puts forth the raw energy of heavy metal without turning off your average Black Flag fan in the process. Their lack of pretense is the key here, something many bands of both types might benefit from in these days of superstars amongst both the metal gods and the punk warlords. The following is an excerpt from a lengthy interview conducted with guitarist Jay Jay French and lead vocalist Dee Snider, who can only be described as a cross between the Tubes' Quay Lude and Bette Midler on dust, a true showman and a heck of a nice guy. Ex-Dictator Mark Mendoza is the bassist, A.J. Pero handles the drum kit and Eddie Ojeda traded the lead spot with Jay.

Bill Bartell: So this is your first trip to L.A., have you been out to see any bands or anything?

Jay: We haven't even seen the sky!!

Dee: No, really we've been busy with the tour and doing a lot of this sort of thing. It's hard for me to go down to the metal clubs, I don't want to walk around like I'm some sort of important person, and I don't like the attitude in the clubs. So I figure why go to a club where I'm gonna start hasseling people and calling them assholes so I just sit in the hotel rooms and watch David Letterman.

Bill: So you broke big in England with the first LP, what happened when you came back to NY?

Dee: Well we lost some people, purely due to the fact that we're no longer their local club band, like they want to see us make it but they don't want to have to see us in bigger places, but it's gotta happen.

Bill: What about the new album?

Dee: Some people think it's more commercial, but how much more commerical is it than "Bad Boys" or "I'll Never Grow Up"? I've always written power pop now and then, it's just that the SOUND is more commercial, more studio and there's a reason for that. There's a ton of heavy metal bands out there, and hardcore, all uncompromising and the fans love 'em. But they go out to make it and maybe put out one album and break up because they have no money and can't survive. So now their big fans have one record and a band that doesn't exist. I don't

want to be a legend to 20 people. Our live sound is almost punk, so fast and furious, so hardcore, so we gave up on trying to get that in the studio. Maybe clean up the sound here so Twisted Sister sells albums, tours and we can keep on putting out records. So we've compromised the desperation and flat out assault we had when we were hardcore, but since we did we're here talking to you and you don't have to fly to NY to see us again.

Jay: The essence of the band is still the same, live we're still the same.

Dee: So we'll keep doing it and we'll be around, not a legend.

Bill: There's a lot of punks out here into you, how do you feel about that?

Dee: In England too!

Jay: It's the attitude we bring to the stage, a heavy aggressive performance, we cross over like Motorhead, the speed and reved up action.

Dee: I've always liked the Sex Pistols, if they were out with no catagory they would have just been a weirdo heavy metal band.

Bill: Anything else you want to add?

Dee: Why does every band that makes it have to be an asshole and go "Ha ha, it's my turn now, no sound check". It takes a big man to say "Fuck it, I'm putting a stop to this" and that's what were going to make sure happens when we're in the headlining position.

Jay: If you're a confident band you can be nice and not worry about it.

Dee: Look like women, talk like men, and play like **motherfuckers!!!**

Bill: I know, I know!!!!

ARTICLES OF FAITH

Interviewed by Al in June just prior to their debut gig in Los Angeles at Shamus O'Briens.

Al: What is "Buy This War" about?

Vic: Salesmanship. I was watching Reagan on TV one night and it just seemed like he was a used car salesman, it's like "Hey man, what's good for Exxon is what's good for you". He seemed to me like a real glorified salesperson, so I wrote the song. The song isn't about him parse, but the whole attitude that national security and national interests are your personal interests or the interests of Exxon or IBM are your interests too.

Al: You guys have a reputation as a "political band".

Vic: I think that is the most political song that I've even done.

Bill: Bill, you wrote in a letter saying that you were a communist.

Bill: Right, that was me, but there are different view points in this band. There are certain things that we agree and disagree on, it's inevitable when you get 4 different people. In some ways I consider us a political band, especially the way it gets used where it's a band that writes about Reagan, War and issues and so on. Any band is really gonna be political, it depends what their politics are cause they are gonna have some kind of viewpoint that emerges. To me the songs we sing like "My Fathers Dream", you could say there's politics to that and a viewpoint, and "Buy This War" and we're dealing with two different subjects. To me to say your band is political sort of narrows the focus of what you should about.

Vic: We would never be the cliches in a million years. "Buy This War" is far

Articles of Faith - photo AI

FLIPSIDE NUMBER 40

"Hatred and destruction, it seems so cool.
I don't want to be a part of it and be like you.
You wear a swastica, to shock and offend
It's become so passive, it's only a trend
But why do you do it
Why do you try
You've got no reasons
Just your instincts in life
Boredom is the reason....."
"Boredom Is The Reason" ~ MIA

ISSUE #:40
DATE:November 1983
FORMAT: 8 1/2x11, rotary web offset with 2 color glossy cover.
PAGES: 68
PRICE: $1.00
PRESS RUN: 7500

This issue is pretty much the same as the last one, so is the scene. The Cathey De Grande has turned into THEE punk rock hang out. Bands from all over the local scene: Grim, Americans Hardcore, Basic Math from the Valley, MIA and the Vandals from the beaches, Aggression and III Repute from

sophisticated, it's not sloaganeering, we'd never do that.
Dave: We're pretty much about the politics of feeling, the politics of being beaten down and the politics of rising up. It's not so much a definite stance on anything, it's more like we're painting a picture. Then letting the listener decide what his political feeling about what this or that is.
Dave: And at the same time our feelings definitely come through in the songs.
Vic: Like if you take a good photograph, it's worth a thousand words... It's real important that you learn history, and music sure isn't a good vehicle to learn history from. I think there's a problem with dealing with politics, rhetorical and dialectic issues in music get reduced to a real pat slogan or a real simplification of the way things are. Politics is a real complicated affair, you really need a lot more time to sit down and reflect on what politically is happening and stuff. I support bands that are real political because I feel there's a need for that and I'm kinda hopeful that they can educate people in certain ways. But we operate from a real emotional stand point, and that's probably where we differ from a lot of other bands.
Dave: It's not any better, just different.
Al: Getting back to being a communist...
Bill: Yeah, we don't hide any of our viewpoints.
Al: You sympathize with those people?
Bill: The RCP yeah, I do really. I've read a lot of the stuff and my feelings about what they have to say and their analysis on conditions going on and the practicing that they've done, I think is pretty on the mark.
Dave: I'm not an anarchist, not a communist, not a republican... I have my feelings on a lot of issues. I don't go by any subscribed field or anything, I just try to decide on each issue.
Al: Where did you get the name "Articles of Faith"?
Vic: I wrote a song called "Articles of Faith" which was about religion, an anti-religion song. We were talking about songs and Dave's girlfriend said "I think 'Articles of Faith' is a good name for a band" and when you think about it, it is because having faith in things is worth while, and I think it is a positive name and we're trying to do something a little positive.

Oxnard, Top Jimmy, Detox etc from Hollywood as well as bands from all over the country are playing here every week. The place sucked, but the place was there.

MIA

MIA were interviewed by Al and Pete on November 3 at Pulsar Sound Lab in Fullerton. The whole band was present and they are:
Mike: Vocals
Nick: Guitar
Paul: Bass
Larry: Drums
Pete: What does MIA mean?
Nick: It is a symbol more or less I'd say...
Mike: It stands for us. It's the name of our band. (Mike later told us it did originally stand for Missing in Action, and idea he got because at the time one of his relatives were MIA. Mike and their manager also worked out that it was a symbol for a feeling of uncertainty, as if waiting for news about a MIA).
Nick: It really means Minority In America or Masterbating in Allies, Mike in Action.
Mike: It's kinda like MDC. It stands for a lot of things basically.
Nick: It's not like MDC at all, it doesn't stand for anything at all...
Paul: We never really sat sown and thought about it, we just picked the letters...
Nick: We're from Las Vegas originally (from here we went into a long band history, which like usual, I will try to summarize: Mike is the only original member, started the band in 1979 in Las Vegas. Paul and Nick joined they played Vegas for awhile and decided to move to greener fields and ended up in Newport Beach, Mike feels LA is where it is if you're a musician. So here they are. But here they played practically exclusively at the Cuckoos Nest, couldn't quite gain a following although they did have some fans, and called the quits. At this time a demo tape that was never intended for release appeared as one side of an album on Smoke 7, a cut on the 'All's Quiet On the Western Front' comp. and on the 'American Youth Report' comp. Mike went to jail, Nick and Paul joined other bands, and eventually formed the Panty Shields. Eventually MIA reformed first with Chris from Shattered Faith and now with Larry (who has done one gig do far), and here they are...
Al: So what do you do at the beach, do you surf or skate?
Mike: I surf once in awhile, surfing is a good sport...
Larry: I surf... maybe once a week, at 55th street in Newport.
Nick: I tried surfing once but got too much water in my nose.
Mike: Once in awhile if it's really good I'll go out and surf with my friends. It keeps myself in shape both physically and mentally... we don't live to surf. But I've been skating since the beginning days. All the punk rock scene in Vegas evolved from the skaters. We had cadillacs, we came in around the cadillac (one of the first urethane wheels) era. There was like 10 of us that lived to skate. Tony Alva and all those guys were in the mags with their long hair, we had long hair too. All of a sudden Steve Olsen come out in this new mag and he has his hair cut... Jay Adams, all those guys, we saw Devo on their shirts and we said "What is this stuff?". Then a friend of mine turned me onto the Pistols and from then on it was history. I was a radical little guy, pumping

MIA: Mike, Larry, Nick jumping at the Nest. – photo Al

pools into hotel rooms, stuff like that.

Nick: But now we are drawing on a lot more influences than the punk rock scene.

Mike: Trying to evolve into MIA, you know. We have to refine ourselves and I don't think we've done it yet. Soon as we do, I'll call ya!

Al: What is involved in the lyrics?

Paul: Well we pick on politics a lot. We dwell politically as far as lyrics are concerned. Like US foreign policy, our new hit single is "Murder In A Foreign Place" which Nick wrote.

Nick: Basically I wrote that song after all of the problems the US foreign policy was having with some of the nations around the world. I guess El Salvador inspired it, but it doesn't necessarily have to be about El Salvador. It describes how we fight for our money and how that's the most important thing. All through history we've had people that we've used, and it's the same now.

Mike: We also talk 'bout situations that we see. Like I'm always aware, when I'm driving in the car I'm not listening to the radio or searching on the floor for roaches, I'm looking around trying to see things. Trying to pick up things off of society. We have a song called "Help Me Out" which is about a lonely person in the city, they just have no home. People go "Well that's their own fault", but sometimes it's not. Without my family I'd be there, I feel my mother has helped me a lot. They helped me out when times were rough. But some people just have nobody. The songs just not about bums in the city, I'm sure everyone in the world has had a time when they go "Fuck, I'm fucked". Nobody can help you. But it always seems to work out where you get back on

your feet again, keep the PMA ya know?

Al: How big a place do you think you can play in and still come across?

Mike: I could play a big place. Let me loose in that Olympic Auditorium and you're gonna see a crazy fucker, you watch. I love crowds, you get such energy off it. You know, I just want to say that people should be more into the

music, instead of the social scene so much. I mean, we are all there to be social, meeting people, making connections but...

Nick: They forgot that the music is the reason...

ANGST

Angst were interviewed at the Lhasha Club by Al, Hud, and Gus on a nice summer night...

Al: How did you get your name?

Jon: Well we were looking in magazine and we saw a picture of an old building in Germany with "Angst" over it.

Joseph: Angst is like general uncertainty. It's like what's apprehensive in the suburbs, it's not like there's not future, it's just that they don't know what it is.

Michael: It's like people with fashion, it changes so much that they don't know what the new fashion will be tomorrow and they're full of angst.

Jon: We're just 3 normal guys out to have a good time and play, and have people like us.

Al: When you call clubs, what type of music do you tell them you play?

Joseph: Well a sort of countrified punk that defines the punk barrier with elements of funk and surf garage 80's and 90's...

Jon: We've been described as everything. If I had to I would call it beat music, but we don't describe our music.

Michael: Like if we said we were gonna play this or that, then we couldn't play something else.

Al: Well you are on three punk album ("All's Quiet On The Western Front" comp.).

Joseph: Yeah, hardcore.

Jon: 46 punk bands and Angst!!

Joseph: It's like Jon said, we don't care, we don't define ourselves, so it wasn't like we wanted a certain song or anything, it's all us, you know?

Al: You have this song "Neil Armstrong", who wrote that?

Joseph: Uh, I put the John Glenn part... We got it off my moon, I have a box set "Journey To The Moon", it starts off with Gemini One and everything, goes through the whole trip, it

Angst: Jon, Joseph, Michael

BLACK FLAG

SST 081 BLACK FLAG: Annihilate This Week (12" 45 $6.50). The ultimate party anthem of all time is backed with Best One Yet and Sinking on this smoking 12" by Black Flag. Culled from "Who's got the 10½?" these three are available only on this disc and the cassette (SST 060).

SST 060 BLACK FLAG: Who's Got The 10 ½? (LP, CASS $7.50, CD $15.00). From the old classics Gimmie, Gimmie, Gimmie, My War, Wasted, and Louie, Louie, to the newest masterpieces In My Head, Loose Nut, Slip It In, and Drinking And Driving. This release catches the Flag unfurled one night in Portland, Oregon. LP 40 minutes, cassette 70 minutes. Either version has enough Flag fury to raise the dead.

SST 045 BLACK FLAG: In My Head (LP, CASS $7.50, CD $15.00). Nine new Flag songs produced by Greg Ginn on this 1985 release of crunching rock tunes like Drinking and Driving. Retired At 21 Cassette features three bonus tracks.

SST 045 BLACK FLAG: The Process Of Weeding Out (12" 45, CASS $7.00). Greg, Kira and Bill combine on this 1985 recording of four instrumental cuts of pure Flag fever. Screw The Law, The Last Affront, Southern Rise, and the title track.

SST 035 BLACK FLAG: Loose Nut (LP, CASS $7.50, CD $15.00). 1985 saw this release of nine slabs of Flag's potent blend of metal and madness. Greg, Kira, Henry and Bill combine to create classics like Bastard in Love, Annihilate This Week, plus seven more.

SST 029 BLACK FLAG: Slip It In (LP, CASS $7.50, CD $15.00). Also released in 1984, this Flag album has Kira, Bill, Henry and Greg working thru eight pile-driving songs like Slip It In, Black Coffee, My Ghetto, and You're Not Evil.

SST 023 BLACK FLAG: My War (LP, CASS, $7.50 CD $15.00). This pivotal 1984 release features nine blasts of primal power. Henry and Greg are joined by Dale Nixon (Greg Ginn) on bass and Bill Stevenson on drums for My War, Nothing Left Inside, I Love You and six more.

SST 001 BLACK FLAG: Nervous Breakdown (7" 45 $3.00)
SST 003 BLACK FLAG: Jealous Again (12" 45 $5.00)
SST 005 BLACK FLAG: Six Pack (7" 45 $3.00)
SST 012 BLACK FLAG: T.V. Party (7" 45 $3.00)

SST 015 BLACK FLAG: Everything Went Black (2xLP $9.00, CD $15.00). A compilation released in 1983. This record examines the era of Flag before Henry: Johnny Bob, Chavo, and Dez plus outrageous radio ads. Songs include Gimmie (three versions), My Rules, and Louie Louie.

MAIL ORDER
MAKE CHECK OR MONEYORDER PAYABLE IN U.S. FUNDS TO
SST RECORDS, P.O. BOX 1, LAWNDALE, CA 90260
CALL THE SST HOTLINE (213) 835-6955 FOR GEN. INFO.

SST 007 BLACK FLAG: Damaged (LP, CASS, $7.50). Recorded in 1981, the songs on this LP defined an era. Dez Cadena has moved to guitar, and Henry Rollins takes over as vocalist. Stunning dual guitar Flag on: Rise Above, Damaged I & II, and 15 others.
SST 007/3 BLACK FLAG: Damaged/Jealous Again (CD $15.00)

SST 021 BLACK FLAG: The First Four Years (CASS only $7.50)
SST 026 BLACK FLAG: Family Man (LP, CASS $7.50)
SST 030 BLACK FLAG: Live '84 (CASS only $7.50)

SST

has a book with Neil Armstrong on it. It's cool, ya know, he was the first guy to walk on the moon!

Al: That seems a little different from your other songs.

Joseph: It's faster than most, I guess.

Jon: You know it's old, it just started with "Na na na na whatever" and I think we used to say "white linoleum". But after awhile you think about it and you find something that is a little bit more relavent or you feel better about saying and you just put it in.

Al: Who came up with that poster, it's almost like your logo now, you know the one with the nude girl on the cross with the gas mask?

Joseph: I found that in a book and it just seemed appropriate for Angst. We stand against oppression of any sort, governmental, peer, anybody telling anybody else what to do, that's not good. It just seemed anti-repression, it's the epitomy of repression: somebody on a cross with a gas mask...

Jon: Crucifixtion of youth, of beauty and the prostitution and use of it for war – the gas mask. We got a lot of slack for that because it's a woman, she's nailed to the cross, it's sexual.

Joseph: And that's everything it stands against. I mean if anybody is sexually stimulated by that they are pretty highly disturbed.

AGGRESSION

Aggression were finally interviewed by Al the the Cathay De Grande in October. Aggression are a very intense band who live in Oxnard (about 60 miles north of L.A.). They have been around for quite awhile and are quickly becoming quite popular.
Bob– bass
Mark H.– vocals
Henry– guitar
Mark A– drums

Al: Why is there punk rock in Oxnard?

Mark: It started about 3 1/2 years ago with all of us getting into it, then it really caught on. At first a lot of our friends wouldn't even talk to us just because we started a band and cut

Sado Nation at the Cathay – photo Al

our hair. But our real friends took us for what it is. The cops really haven't caught on to it yet. We've worked in a lot of different clubs, all of us have, and we know it's the cops that are what fucks it up. They get bummed and THEY decide to close it down. They haven't even been to the places where we're having gigs yet.(Mark is smoking some pot).

Al: Well you obviously aren't straight edge!

Bob: I only smoke pot, no alcohol or drugs or anything like that. I used to but I can't handle it. I don't like waking up in the morning going "Argh" with my head pounding from side to side. I just smoke pot and not worry about it. Plus drugs have a bad effect on your body.

Mark H: Reverend Bob, the rest of us use drugs! You have to have something to pass the time in Oxnard. There's a heavy scene in Oxnard, the only mellow place is the beach, the rest is full of mexican gangs and stuff.

Mark A: It makes it a kind of interesting place to have a band, it's a weird atmosphere.

Al: What are you writing your new material about?

Mark H: We have a new song called "Salty Leather" it's supposed to be a little suggestive.

It goes "the smell of salty leather is starting to smell better than I ever thought it could". It's all about a gig and everyones smelly leather that comes off of a gig. The whole trip, how it becomes self appealing. It's all about having a good time at a gig. We have another one about how we've always been weird, afraid of normality. We figured it was good to be different from the rest but as life goes on you find that square pegs don't fit into round holes. So people say change your shape or hit the road, but I want to be an average citizen, above suspicion... We're into being aggressive in our creativity – but controlled to the amount that you don't fuck people up.

Al: What inspires you to write?

Mark H: Well it's like with "Money Machine" I just can't stand the hassle that people get into where they go to school and college all their lives, so they can get a job, and then they work all their lives, every day, just to fucking live. You get nowhere at all. I just can't see doing that, I'd rather go out and have a good time and do whatever I can but productively make something out of my life but not work for somebody else.

Al: So you'd like to make the band your livilyhood?

Mark H: Yeah. That's the big dream. That's all we want to do is live semi-comfortably off the music. We don't want to be big stars, that would be nice! But we just want the music to take care of it. I think that is the ultimate as far as musicians are concerned.

SADO NATION

Were interviewed at the Cathay De Grande by Al and Hud.

Steve: This band started in late 1978...

Dave: I was the original guy with a guy named John Shirley, who was a science fiction writer. He wrote "Dracula In Love" and shit like that. I named the band and he came up with all of the songs. Sado Nation, it's all the bullshit we as a country go through but we don't realize we're being this sadistic sort of country. Like we watch all these bizarre commercials and we do all of this weird political shit with other countries, and it's like we just sit here and take it all in.

Mish: No questioning. They just say "Do this" and everyone does it.

Dave: Picture this: you're watching TV – Ban

Another Cathay night with Aggression – photo Al

Roll On comes on, it's a big fucking dildo right, and they're rubbing it all over...

Chuck: Or Maxi-Pads "Oh in our dance class, we even have the Maxi-Pad dance..."

Dave: And we sit there and take it in, everyday all this subconscious imagery comes into our mind and they're manipulating us. These big corporations with a lot of bucks are doing everything they can to control the masses. So it's like a masochistic thing really, as a nation we're flagellated and all kinds of other weird shit.

Mich: Flagellated!!!

Dave: Yeah. By all these corporations. I thought that's what we are as a country. Some of our songs, like "Fight Back" is what to do when all this shit comes into your mind. How are you gonna deal with it? You've got to have you're own ideals about freedom and shit. But our freedom is being taken away everyday and still we don't know about it. So time out, let's go back. John Shirley was the singer, I played guitar, Mark Sten played drums. The whole thing was only supposed to be a two show gig. Shirley thought it was pretty decent, so we made a real band out of it. After a real weird friction thing developed between me and Shirley, he quit... So Mish gets in the band and she's working out great, really, but we didn't know what to do with her.

Mich: They always tell me I have too much energy that I don't know what to do with... I wrote a song called "Military Whore". It's basically another Reagan song. I'm on food stamps, I'm unemployed, I'm living on the street and this guy sends me a letter putting down liberal subversive groups and people living on welfare - he wants donations, he wants money. From me!!! And he's putting me down. So I wrote a song which is about his 3 different salaries from his 3 different jobs, Presidential job, California Governor... Another song is called "Verbiage" which is about all of the shit I get everyday, mostly from guys, all of the stupid lines they're feeding me. They never have anything to say. I'm not a typical meek female, I'm pretty scary I guess. I don't come off as "oh the little female in the mini-dress" I'm not real girly. I get called all sorts of things like "fucking bitch dyke". Guys come up and say "Hey baby, wanna go out?" and I say "No, leave me alone" and they go "Oh, you don't like guys!", "No, I like guys, I don't like you, get out of my face!", "Oh you dyke, I'm gonna kick your ass!". Gimmie a break, just leave me alone. I just let go on stage. I have a lot of energy and built up frustration and anger. It's out of frustration that I write those lyrics and I get up there and just sweat! And stink!

Dave: At first I thought Mish was interfereing with the band when she told club owners to fuck off and stuff like that, now I think it is a perfectly legitimate political thing for us to do.

JOHN CRAWFORD

Here is a short interview we did with that legendary cartoonist Mr. John Crawford. Most people will remember him (I hope) from before the days of his "war" with Maximum Rock N'roll, when he became very popular in the fanzine network by having his cartoons published in just about every fanzine there was.

Flipside: What compels you to be in touch with fanzines all across America.

John: People seem to like the strip, I mean they print them and I'm getting requests for

them from new fanzines all the time, both from North America and Europe. It's great fun having a mailing list, you always get back more than you send out. I don't send my stuff out to punkzines exclusively. I like to take in all the independent and self published zine community. People who are limiting themselves to punk alone are really missing out on a lot. But I like to think the reason I get so much print is because the cartoons are good and have become popular because people like them.

Flipside: What do you think punk rock is about?

John: I think anyone who tries to tell you what punk rock is, is probably trying to sell you something, be it a political philosophy, a haircut, or a pair of leather pants. The last thing anyone needs is some clown laying down laws and regulations. Society has a million laws, isn't there one place you can get away from them? Ever notice that when certain people talk about freedom, in the next breath they're making up rules that take freedom away? Rules are for people too weak or scared to deal with life in the raw, therefore they create these arbitrary barriers to keep out a world that intimidates and confused them. Ever notice the rule makers are usually some old geeks from the past? I think they do it because they are afraid of punks. It's up to the musicians and the fans to decide what punk is. The day the music doesn't attract an audience, it's over. All this blabber about what punk is ain't exactly filling the clubs now is it?

Flipside: How long have you been doing "Baboon Dooley"?

John: I've been doing Dooley since I was 23. Which is almost 5 years ago now. All told there are 198 cartoons, plus a couple of other strips with other characters, which might make a nice book someday. Dooley is anybody I know, though he is a known advocate of the "NY Rocker Aesthetic" as it is called in Hoboken. The reason why Baboon doesn't have any eyes is because he never really sees the point in things. He believes in every fad, every piece of propaganda played before those holes, and he never questions the intentions of the people who created those things. He's a slave of the media, out of touch with the human race and only judges others, and then only by the standards of fashion.

Flipside: What type of formal training have you had?

John: None.

Flipside: Would you recommend others taking stabs at issues thru comics or printing their own fanzines?

John: Yeah. I think the fanzine underground or whatever you choose to call it is the greatest thing going. Everybody gets an opportunity to say and do what they want. It's STILL incredibly democratic, you can go as far as your talents will allow. There's nothing like it anywhere else. It's rarer than a Moscow scene report. If you're part of the scene and you are not participating in fanzines you are really missing out.

SUICIDAL TENDENCIES

Mike Muir was interviewed by Al and Pete on November 14, 1983. As you probably know, Suicidal Tendencies have quickly gone form an unknown garage band to one of L.A.'s most popular live bands, not to mention being a very popular request on daytime KROQ. Without trying for this kind

of commercial success, Suicidal Tendencies are finding that they have more followers than they had ever known. We started off by talking about this subject:

Mike: We never expected to get played on KROQ or anything like that. It's nice turning on the radio and hearing it. The best part about it is all of the people writing letters and everything. When we were live at the station, people called me up, and they weren't punks or anything but they liked it. Just normal people. They said they had never been associated with the music before but when they heard it they like it. It's like we can do something that other people like, like with punk rock there's not really a lot you can accomplish, but it shows that we are accomplishing something while we're keeping our integrity. A lot of people try to say that we've sold out, which is ridiculous , the record is the first thing we ever did. We were basically nobody. We did the record and that song fits right into our set. It's not like we did that one for KROQ.

Al: Who makes all the shirts, like the one on the album cover?

Mike: Originally it was Jay Adams and Rick Clayton who does a lot of our artwork. Rick did a lot of the ones on the album, but most of the individuals did their own.

Al: A lot of people use satanic imagery on their shirts, does that represent the band in any way?

Mike: No. It's just when you have something like "Suicidal Tendencies" you know, it's very easy to go over the line. It's basically art work, and we all can appreciate art work.

Al: How did you end up on Frontier?

Mike: Glenn Friedman was our first really big supporter, we had a demo tape we made with the old band and he gave it to Lisa. She said it sucked, which it did with the old band. So we did a new one with Amory and she said she liked it. She took a chance because when you say the name "Suicidal" it's "Oh no" you know? She took a risk. She has an established label and as soon as people found out people would call her up "I don't know. You sure you want to do them?". But that's been everything we've done.

Al: Is that because of your reputation?

Mike: Yeah, but what have we done though?

Al: I remember seeing you fight at Godzillas.

Mike: But how many years ago was that?

Al: Things like that carry on...

Mike: Well I know that there's at least 5 Mike Muirs, because I'm only 20 years old and I couldn't have done all the things people have said. It's impossible.

Al: Are you think about more recording?

Mike: We're writing new material, the lyrics are all personal stuff. I'm not into politics and stuff. You can only say Reagan sucks so many ways. It gets really tedious. We're in it for the music, we got in it because we feel it's the most powerful music there is, and there's a lot of good things involved. It's that power and energy, that's what we're into.

Pete: How do flys land on the ceiling?

Mike: With a fly swatter!

Al: That's a suicidal naswer!

Pete: What do you mean by "suicidal"?

Mike: It doesn't mean you want to kill yourself. There's meaning in the name, it like a rally cry around here, in "Suicidal Failure" it says: "I'm a punk, don't want to die, it's a rally cry". If you look at the news people are getting killed everywhere, most Americans stay home and sit in front of their TV. And they call that living! If you're gonna go outside of your house you're gonna take your life into you hands. But to live your life you have to go out and not necessarily act stupid or crazy, but if you're gonna do something ya gotta do it and do it with full force. You gotta go for it whether it's right or wrong, you'll find out. It's kinda like "got for it", it's "suicidal". If you're gonna live your life you're gonna have to take chances. It's not saying you wanna die, I don't wanna die. It's just saying I want to live my life to the fullest.

Al: Do you want to make the band your living?

Mike: It's punk rock you know, you're not going to make any money. It would be nice to live off of it, but I don't think I'd feel right that way. The band, I'm doing it because I like to do it. I don't know. It seems like a conflict of interest there somewhere.

Al: Ok, anything that we missed that you want to add?

Mike: I just want to emphasize the way we dress, people don't have to dress that way at all. And anybody can be in a band and they don't have to dress anyway. People just assume that if you dress that way, you're from Venice. But I've met people from all over that dress that way. I dressed that way ever since I was a little kid. If I wore a leather jacket, for me that would be a pose.

Al: What did you think of people voting you "worst band" and "biggest assholes" of last year?

Mike: Well we only played 2 shows in all of 1982, so that shows it was rumors and stuff...

FLIPSIDE NUMBER 41

"You got money? Well then you're living the good life
You got a big fat daddy at home, writin' checks tonight
You got nothing? Well then you're living a bad life
You got a big fine car,
And you eye me while you pass me by
A rich daddy? No! I never had one!
A rich daddy? No! No! I never had one!
You got money? Well then you're living the good life
It seems like everything you touch wants to turn to gold
You got nothing? Well then you're living the sad life
And I guess I won't have nothing when I'm sick and old
A rich daddy? No! I never had one!
A rich daddy? No! No! I never had one!"
"Rich Daddy" - the Dicks

ISSUE #: 41
DATE: February 1983

Suicidal Tendencies at Perkins – photo Al

FORMAT: 8 1/2x11, rotary web offset with 2 color glossy cover.
PAGES: 68
PRICE: $1.00
PRESS RUN: 7500

The scene continues very strong with lots of places for big and small touring bands to play. Out of town (ie English) bands play at either Perkins Palace or the Olympic, while domestic groups opt for opening the big concerts and picking up gigs at Roxannes or Cathay. Never the less the band traffic is heavy with a good interchange of ideas.

For the first time L.A. is experiencing a political "peace" punk movement. Where bands in the past were happy to just sing about atrocities, the new attitude is one of interest in practical alternatives and setting examples for the rest of the scene. L.A. has never had the equivilent of the Dead Kennedys, MDC or Crucifix. Perhaps their recent tours brought inspiration to bands like The Iconoclast, Body Count and Armistice. In any case, at about this time the Iconoclast were probably the most popular of the new breed, their influence was felt strongly for a band that played few gigs and had little recorded output. They and their friends promoted a healthy ideology that included playing shows at just about any venue with any bands. Unfortunately things quickly changed as the peace punks choose to segregrate themselves, and play for and with their friends, rather than try to open new eyes to what good ideas they sang about.

THE DICKS

The Dicks finally got to play L.A. and we finally got to interview them. This is a whole new band of Dicks from the one on the album, they are: Gary (singer and original member), Lynn (Drums and former member of the Wrecks), Sebastian (bass and former member of DRI) and Tim (guitar and former member of the 12 Year Olds).
Al: You are the original Dick?

Gary: The original, but not the best. The old band is doing some things in Texas, we're still friends. I just came out to San Francisco and found a new band. We play some of the old Dicks things that I had a big hand in writing, plus we have a lot of new things that the new band has done together. We're playing some stuff from "Kill From The Heart", yeah, um political things in the band change from time to time, it's like shifting gears from being such a... which I don't think we ever were, but we had a reputation for being a dogmatic marxist band or something which we never really were. It's like we're playing music and having fun doing that and certain things come out in our songs. So we're tired of the whole run down. It's a really bad time to be dogmatic – to be thought of as dogmatic, so the whole emphasis has sort of.... The world is about to blow up and it's a good time to unite people together no matter what their political views are, and stop nit picking about what sign somebody has hung over their neck. Our new songs are more topical instead of dogmatic, if you listen to the music and go by what the lyrics are saying you are dealing with individual situations: "Rick Daddy", "Anti Klan", it's really spelled out. The lyrics are really clear. The Dicks never really changed that much musically so to speak, different people, but the main objective is to like have a good time while not being apolitical.

Tim: Our dogmas and our personal political things are our personal political things and we are allowed to have them and they may come out in interviews, and people can agree or disagree. It's nice to argue face to face and discuss things, but the songs themselves are topical. We are pointing out a situation and discussing it.... Musically, we're not a thrash band spacifically, there are a couple of different genres we address.

Gary: The less titles we have the better, so many people get hung up on titles that it becomes a fad.

Debbie: (Dicks manager) Anarchists, Communists, Marxists, we all basically agree and hate what is going on right now. We don't need to fight each other.

Dicks: Lynn, Gary, Sebastian, Tim relaxing at the Cathay - photo Al

Al: What do you call yourself?

Gary: I'm a marxist, and it's not like something I got into a year ago. I've studied it a long time. Most of the people that oppose it are the ones who have never studied it at all. I think it's a good form to live by basically because it believes in sharing...

Al: What does it mean to be a Marxist?

Gary: Well right now in 1984 what does it mean to be an Anarchist? Or a Communist? Or a Marxist? All these definitions. I think what it means to me is I'd like to get all these people together and share what they have with me and then I'd share what I have with them and then that would mean something. A ruling body of bourgeois people dictating what I'm gonna do, I don't want that. Actually now that I look at it, I'm more of an anti-fascist, yeah I would rather be identified as an anti-fascist.

ICONOCLAST

Interviewed in January by Al and Hud.

Hud: What inspired you to become anarchists?

Rene: (bass) Well, we're like, um, personal anarchists, we're not gonna go out like, circle 'A', that's just part of the scene, it's just...

Greg: (vocals) You just associate punks with the circled 'A' now, it's just on their jacket or on their arm, we're more personal, we don't stress it on anybody. In our own conversations we talk about it, that's about it.

Rene: We don't go flaunting "Anarchy"...

Al: How did this come about?

Greg: At first, close to two years, we were just excited to get a band together. This was my first band. We wrote nowhere lyrics and it just has no effect, you can't get into the lyrics or anything. When people ask you about your lyrics, you don't really wanna say because they're so ridiculous . There were a lot of joke bands around so we thought we'd be serious.

Brendan: (guitar) Just by expressing ourselves through the band.

Nick: (drums) We all had these feelings so we just decided to put it into our music.

Rene: It's funny because we've heard people say we were copying Crucifix. We went up to

San Francisco and stayed with Crucifix you know.

Nick: People say we jumped on the 'peace' bandwagon.

Greg: It's so ridiculous to say there are too many peace bands, I wish there were a million peace bands. As long as all of their beliefs were true and honest and they're not trying to bullshit you and jumping on the bandwagon. If that's what they feel I wish there were more peace bands, then maybe some things would change. I don't mean preachy, I mean personal beliefs, I wish more people were that way.

Nick: If more bands were like that, then when they mention punk they wouldn't right away think of violence.

Hud: You might get labeled a hippie band?

Greg: I wouldn't care.

Rene: I saw this program the other day and they were interviewing some old hippie and he was saying how he was against capitalism and things that have to do with nuclear war. And he's standing in front of this big corporation he owns that makes something that has to do with nuclear arms. The hippies had some good ideas but they conformed. I

got this tattoo to remind me to never conform because it is reality that we're into. It's not a phase or some stage, it is reality.

Greg: A lot of people put us down or this kind of band down are people that are afraid to do something hard. It's so easy to go be a punk, go out to a gig, get drunk, hang out, be cool, spike your hair, this and that. It so much harder to get really involved and try to learn other things, and to carry on intelligent conversations rather than "Where are you gonna hang out?". They want punk to be a big joke, and I don't believe that. That's so stupid. Back in their mind they're know we're right and it disturbes them.

CHEETAH CHROME AND THE MOTHERFUCKERS

CCM are one of Italy's oldest and best known punk bands, this December Antonio their bass player was in California and we got a chance to talk to him about this band and the scene in Italy....

In my town there are about 12 punks, and when the most famous punk band in all of Italy has a gig there there are more than 300 people there. My band is the oldest band in Italy, we started back in 1978 and we have the same line-up today. There are about 1500 punks in all of Italy, not any more than that. To move from place to place is very expensive so the punks usually don't travel so much. The most famous band is probably mine, then I Refuse It from Florence.

Cheetah Chrome was a hero, he was also the guitarist of the Dead Boys, but we have nothing in common with him. He was the hero of some comic strip back in Italy and he was so cool he almost killed all of his enemies. Sid choose that name and then I put "the motherfuckers" because I want to shock people, right, and the only way to shock people is to say something that they don't want to hear. Even in Italy, where English isn't he best language, if you have "I'm a motherfucker" on your leather jacket, it really shocks people. That's why I choose the name.

Here's a story about one of our songs "Our Best Party Ever". We had a gig at this place by the seaside called Lerici. In the summer the rich people go there so the punks wanted to play shock the rich people and all the rednecks. We got onstage and about 200 punks were there. We played 3 songs before

Iconoclast: Rene, Greg, Brendan, Nick - photo Al

Cheetah Chrome and the Motherfuckers

the pigs got there. One pig took the microphone from Sid. We kept playing and people kept slamming. So the cop took out his gun and shot it twice in the air. People were astonished and Sid grabbed him and he shot in the air, he wouldn't stop shooting so Sid hit him in the neck and the cop fell down. The other cop took out his gun and pointed it right at Sid and shot at him but luckily missed. A lot of people were rioting and we really beat the cops black and blue. 5 minutes later there were about 100 cops there picking people from everywhere to arrest. They grabbed me by my leather jacket but I punched the cop and ran. Two people in my band got arrested and were in jail 10 days and are still on trial, the law says that Sid tried to shoot down the cop. They showed a video tape of that show on TV (the local news was there) and all they showed was Sid punching down the cop. Nothing that the cops said or did before or after. Now the cops always come by about 100 and they try to provoke you. They called you asshole and faggot. That's how it goes in Italy. They see you walking down the street and they stop you to waste your time. They know you well because there's only 12 punks in my city, but every night they have to stop you and try to provoke you till you burst. If you even say "take your dirty hands off of me" that's a crime and you can be in jail for 3 years. Then they are sure you are junkies, they stop me all the time "Let me look at your arm!" I tell them, you know me well, you know that I am straight edge. I never even smoked marijuana ever. "Shut up, let me look at your arms!". Once the day before Christmas in the central square where my parents could have been passing by, they made me strip naked to see if I had heroin in my asshole!!

(Referring to Discharge show at Perkins Palace) I used to really look up to Discharge but now I won't go see them again because of what they've become. Those kids don't give a fuck who's on stage. What's worse is the people on stage like Dave MDC, were saying such wonderful things, he was trying to let them know what the problem is. It isn't that we are just playing music, we do have a message. But they don't give a wank, so I have this impression that you have the same problems that we have in Italy. we got 12 punks down here and maybe every three of them, one is a shit. We call this place the hardcore paradise back in Italy, but it's not true. I had more fun back in Italy because I saw people more interested. I see so many people into hardcore for fun, or as a joke.

THE TOY DOLLS

Interviewed in January by Al and Frank at Media Blitz TV studios during their taping...
Al: This is your first timeover here?
Olga: Yes!!!
Al: And you just played your biggest show ever, right here in L.A.?
Bonnie: Yep, Perkins Palace.
Frank: What was your influence to start a band?
Olga: It's the same influence that makes people from all other groups really. I formed it because I used to get picked on and things in school and I wanted to show that I could actually do something. I think that was the main thing, plus I just love music. I love touring different places.
Bonnie: Me too.
Frank: What kind of music do you like and listen to?
Olga: We're all different, I like Rezillos, Dickies, Damned, Anti Nowhere League, things like that, Peter and the Test...
Bonnie: I like fast guitar music with a bit of melody. Like the Buzzcocks, Slaughter and the Dogs, Lurkers, Sex Pistols. I also like Status Quo but don't hold it against me.
Dicky: I used to be into heavy metal, man!
Bonnie: Everybody's been a heavy metal man! Like Motorhead!
Olga: We're a very visual band.. so we like a big stage with as much room as possible to play.
Bonnie: It's ok now and again, but not that many people at a time, Olga got his lip busted last night when someone smashed the microphone into his face.
Al: On the album, it says you want to bring back people singing and laughing with the band..
Olga: yeah, but we do get serious sometimes. We're not like Splodgeness Abounds where they're idiots all the time. We've got political views and all that which we don't talk about. When you come to a show you want to be entertained, you get politics and world views rammed down your throat by the media, you go to a club to enjoy yourself. You go out to avoid that.
Bonnie: But there are some good groups doing that.
Frank: Because of your English pub sound, do you get a lot of skinheads?
Bonnie: We don't get many, we check on places to see how many skinheads go to these places but some of my best friends are skinheads, there's good ones and bad ones. But there happens to be more band ones!!
Olga: We've done good gigs in places with the stage the size of a matchbox, with sweat running off the walls, the atmosphere is

Toy Dolls at Media Blitz – photo Al

tremendous. It was a privilege and a pleasure
to play Perkins Palace because that's such a
nice place, big stage, big crowd...
Frank: How long have you been going?
Olga: 4 1/2 years!! Altogether the Toy Dolls
have done about 500 or 600 gigs!
Al: What do you think about being on "Oi"
records? (Compilations)
Olga: We got an offer to do another one but
we turned it down, just because the violence
the second Oi album created, it might have all
come out of nothing, but still people connect
Oi with violence. Whether they're wrong or not
makes no difference... We don't regret being
on the record, because we didn't know what it
meant in any case but we wouldn't go on
another one.
Bonnie: People would think we were a Nazi
band! It's the association, so it's best to stay
on the safe side.

Toxic reasons – photo Al

TOXIC REASONS

Interviewed by Gary Indiana
Tufty - bass
Bruce - lead guitar
Rob - guitar
Jimmy Joe - drums
Gary: What are the origins of Toxic Reasons?
Bruce: In 1979 me, Ed Pittman, Joel Agne
and Mark Patterson. Joel quit and Greg Stout
joined. We came out to the show with the
Dead Kennedys and DOA in Vancouver, then
Mark quit and JJ joined. Rob came with us as
a roadie, coz he had money. We fucked up
and stuck out 6 months before heading back
home, playing little gigs, no money. We got
back and Greg quit - various tours and
personnel changes, then we picked up Tufty.
Then Ed quit, we did another tour, nobody
quit and then we got the next album done.
And I'm eating burritos and working in a
marketing research place.
Gary: Why don't you ever play in L.A.?
Tufty: We have and it's been horrendous
every time.
Gary: You played the SIR riot.
Bruce: THAT was a fun show. And a show at
the Cathay, on the way back the van blew up
and we got stuck in San Luis Obispo.
Gary: What about the show I got for you at
the Mexican Bar in N. Hollywood?
Tufty: Oh yeah, we went down there on your
advice and wild mexicans with baseball bats
came after us! And then we came down here
recently to do a show at the Cathay and 15
people showed up. I hope I can pay them
Circle Jerks back because they were of no
help. We asked them to help us get some gas
money and they wouldn't. When we play up
here with DOA or the DK's or any of those
bands, they always help and make sure that
bands at least get gas money.
Bruce: We do to. But the guy that was
managing us at the time was so drunk he
couldn't talk to the club owners, so Tufty
bashed him one in the head. The guy is laying
on the sidewalk going "gaaaargh!"
Rob: Dripping blood.
Tufty: He was so drunk that when he woke
up we told him that bouncers had beat him
up. So he went all over San Francisco saying
"L.A. bouncers are fucking awful".
Gary: You are starting a European tour,
where are you going on the continent?
Tufty: We're gonna sell all of our gear and fly
to England. Then Rome, Hanover, Hamburg,
Milan etc. We'll spend like a month in each
country. We haven't got the big help over

there like the DK's and Black Flag get but
we're gonna give it a go anyway. We're a
band that's really out there. We've given up
our families, our love lives (some of it) to travel
about and promote the music. We'd just like
to see more unity and less close mindedness,
the fighting and all....
Gary: Who's the big sex symbol of the band?
JJ?
Tufty: Me. Naw, we don't have one.

JOHN DOE, X

**X is a band that came out of the original
L.A. punk scene going on to bigger and
better things and attracting a lot of
attention in the process. Although they can
be found in almost any rock mag on the
stands, have been raved about by God
knows how many critics and were #1 in the
L.A. Times critics poll and #2 in BAM even,
constipated commercial radio programmers
continue to give them little if any airplay. X
was last interviewed in Flipside #10. We
thought it would be interesting to do it
again now that they're 'famous'. We
managed to get part of the band, namely
John Doe. He was plied with several beers
in the plaza off Olvera St. in downtown L.A.
on 12-29-83. Interview by Helen and Gary
Indiana.**
Helen: Do you think that your success was a
matter of lucky breaks, timing, being in the
right place...
John: Yes, the right place at the right time,
and having the creativity to back it up. I think
that our musical range has helped us,
whereas maybe, the Bags, didn't have that. I
think we were good but if we came out now
we'd have so much of a harder time. If people
won't listen to new music they'll listen to
something that's more tried and true, and they
won't go out on a limb. I'm talking about, not
the public, the underground, y'know, the
lesser underground public.
Gary: And all the critics are on your side.
John: Well I think that helped then, I think it
hurts now.
Helen: Do you get tired of being the critics
choice, like in the L.A. Times records of the
year you were tops.
John: It does give something for people to
talk about in the industry, which I hate. I HATE
the music industry.
Helen: Do you feel like you're being the

token...
John: Sometimes, yeah. Like Electra using us
to say "Hey look, we're cool!" But I actually
know that the president of the company really
likes us, and likes the band and stuff. But I
think it's really hard, a lot harder for groups
now because music doesn't mean as much
now as it ment in 1977 and 1978. It's more
just, music, and it doesn't have that much
social impact. I think the hardcore groups do
with the people that come see them but
sometimes they just get to be background
too. It pisses me off, that fact that now it's just
music again. Occasionally you'll have a gig
where people really understand what's going
on and they understand the reason why we're
on stage, and whether it's because they can't
sing or play an instrument, which I don't
believe, I think if you have the desire you can
learn... they understand that it means
something to their life. It's rare now, it really is.

John Doe and Helen – photo Gary Indiana

Helen: The whole analogy between you and the Doors, do you think that has been over emphasized quite a bit?

John: We were convicted on circumstantial evidence, which is that we're from Los Angeles, we played at the Whisky and those kinds of places, we have kind of, if you want to call them "poetic" lyrics. And, we were part of like, an underground thing. To me they were like a blues synthesis band. Y'know, Ray Manzarek grew up in Chicago and went to see Muddy Waters and all the blues musicians and that's where they got their sound from. Let me put it this way, I'd rather have people draw a comparison between us and the Doors, than us and the Mamas and the Papas or the Jefferson Airplane, or the Doobie Brothers. They come up with some pretty insane ones, the best one was Bachman-Turner Overdrive and Michael Nesmith.

Helen: Since you guys are photogenic, have you been approached for films?

John: No. Not really. I read a part of 'Diner'. They flew me to New York and everything.

Gary: Wow, but you guys would be so great in movies, I mean can't Lee Ving get you a part?

John: Ha ha. Lee Ving's looking out for his own ass, are you kidding me? He's no dummy.

Helen: So you're perhaps the big L.A. band, but most of your songs slag L.A. or at least show the underbelly of society. Do you think that's unusual, or would you be doing the same thing in New York?

John: Probably would.

Helen: Is it supposed to be Any City USA?

John: Yeah. A lot of people don't pick up on that, but it is. That's the thing I like about L.A. is that it is screwed up, and it is "the heart of the beast" or whatever.

Helen: You've always had a point like, "Don't call me a poet, call me a writer", what's that about?

John: Well I think it's because poetry has such a bad name. But if you think of the definition of a poet, like Hank Williams or Chuck Berry or Iggy Pop are poets. Hank Williams said that he was a poet. I'd say that I'm a poet. I really wish that I could write songs that were just songs.

Helen: Does the intense fandom impress you?

John: Well there comes a point where someone comes up to you and they say "I really like your band". Then either they go on to something else, or they keep repeating that in different forms. Then they become a sucker. They want to be around you to draw from your creativity, or personality or whatever, you know? It becomes like a negative draw on your thing. That sounds real hippie and cosmic and stuff like that but it's true. They keep telling you that you're great, but actually what they're saying is that "I want something from you and I'm sucking away and I don't really even care about you, I care about me". But then the cool thing is that somebody that you've never met before comes up to say "You were really good tonight" and then they say "You know what happened to me yesterday, it was really weird" bla bla bla. And they go into a completely different subject. And then pretty soon, and we have friends all over the country now because of that, and that's really neat. That's fun.

(Talk goes on to "selling out" and "they're not hardcore anymore" criticisms...)

John: Basically, we were never hardcore, it's like the same kind of think that perpetuates bands like the Who, or Led Zeppelin is that somebody doesn't say "well you're not the same as me, so I'm gonna find something new." I like that. I think that's one thing that I like about hardcore. I think that's good. I think you're supposed to say that: "I don't care".

JELLO BIAFRA

Interviewed by Al in January

Al: I guess we can start out by talking about the recent show here at the Starlight Roller Rink on New Years 1984.

Jello: Well they wanted us to play the Olympic, which seemed to me to be way the hell to big for our kind of band. We generally try to put a ceiling of about 2000 people. We feel at a quandry at this point, in a way it would cheapen the thing in a different way if we did two set a night at some place like the Whisky every night for 2 weeks! A tour of small places is not that bad of an idea, but we've had a problem with that with clubs closing. We were getting a list of all the places we had lined up in L.A. that fell through, places like Dancing Waters, the Galaxy, talk of the Palladium and several others that we actually booked. The worst was Devonshire Downs where we found out the night before that it was cancelled... the New Years show was a fiasco of a different sort, we put a lot of time into the art work and promoting the show because it was New Years Eve of 1984 – then I walked into the place, ha ha, I can't think of anyone who would neglect to measure the height difference between a low ceiling and a high stage! There was only five feet of room, and everyone except Klaus and Frank Discussion wound up doing Billy Zoom imitations to be seen! And to top it off I discovered all my personal belongings gone before I went on stage.....

Al: Where do you come up with the information that you let out in interviews and in lyrics, it seems like it's stuff that some people would want to hide, but you come up with it.

Jello: Sometimes magazines, occasional books. Some stuff that seems real outlandish I've gotten to the point where I figure I better toss it around and ask people who know the subject and double check it. Some of the songs are composites of different songs thrown into one, like "Police Truck" or "Bleed For Me". A lot of that stuff I get because I know a lot of people who are really into researching forbidden information and into sinister trivia and 1984isms and have a kinda bank of information stored up in their heads. People like Winston Smith who does our art work, Vale, Frank Discussion, Jeff Bale is real knowledgable about these kinds of things. Jeff and Vale probably being the most well read of the people I know real well and we talk about his kind of thing. Winston's partner in Fallout Magazine, Jay, really knows his stuff. I pick up bits and pieces from different people wherever I go, it's not like people sitting down in a cell and grimly discussing the oppression of the proletariat or anything like that. We think it's interesting.

Al: Do you ever dig up good things?

Jello: Oh yeah. I just think at this time it's more emotionally fullfilling to accentuate the negative. There's a certain joy in complaining that many people miss.

Al: Since it is now 1984, what do you think about that?

Jello: Well there's an old quote of Black Randys that is real appropriate: "1984 happened in 1930 and we're just now finding out about it", meaning a lot of the surveillance and state control has been going on for years as if it was never there before.

Al: Getting back to shows, you guys are getting bigger all the time, and it's gonna get to the point where, where are you gonna play?

Jello: Oh, there's ways around that, just look at the second Bad Religion album! (laughter) We're in a unique position in charting new ground, we'll have to just take things as they come and keep the lid on it at the same time. On one hand I'd like to at least give everybody the option of knowing we exist, on the other hand I wouldn't want to end up in a Clash or Motley Crue situation where the only

Dead Kennedys pre-Wilmington riot - photo Katz

people you ever play to are mindless geeks. Mindless starworshippers or whatever. I have experienced a little too well the feeling of being isolated as a zoo animal and dehumanized by people who just don't treat you as equal because they think you are some kind of powerful star or kingpin whatever.

Al: Are you a vegetarian?

Jello: No.

Al: I was wondering why you've never picked up on that or vivisection...

Jello: Vivisection might turn up sooner or later, but in a different form than bands are doing it now, something unique a la "Kill The Poor" is a rather unique anti-nuclear bomb song I would say. I haven't figured out an angle on vivisection yet. One thing I am kinda moving into is environmentalist songs, trying to communicate songs about that without sounding like a "save the whales" type of person that people write off without actually listening to what they have to say. It amazes me how few people in the hardcore scene have any kind of feeling for the earth at all.

Al: Why haven't you ever become a vegetarian? I'm sure the MDC guys have made their points clear...

Jello: Oh yeah, they talk to me about it a lot too believe me, uh, I don't really have a good answer for that. When I was really young I was the classic little boy who wouldn't eat his vegetables, and I still really don't like the taste of them although I eat a lot more of them than I used to. By choice this time.

CODE OF HONOR

Code of Honor were interviewed in their van by Al, present were:

Johnithin Christ: Vocals
Michael: Guitar
Dave: Bass
Sal: Drums

Al: Ok, I've read interviews with you guys and I know you came from different bands, refresh my memory.

Michael: Ok, Johnithin was in Society Dog and us three were in Sick Pleasure. And I want to dedicate this interview to my dead girlfriend Brenda...

Al: Brenda got murdered by drug dealers, and they caught him.

Johnithin: Did you hear about the two barrels that were found in Golden Gate park in San Francisco?

Al: With chopped up bodies in them.

Johnithin: Mike's girlfriend was one of them, sealed in a oil drum.

Dave: That's kind of why we're where we are now compared to where we would be. We would have played LA like 15 times or more.

Johnithin: But we've had a lot of personal problems. Mike's girlfriend was just one of them, some of us had drug problems that we have just recently got over.

Sal: Totally.

Johnithin: Thanks to the support of us pulling together and getting us out of the bad drug habits we were in.

Michael: This band means everything to me.

Sal: To us to all of us.

Michael: This band, well me and Johnithin got together after his band broke when he moved into this house where I was staying....

Johnithin: And took it over compleatly!

Michael: We were talking about putting something positive together, to put out a message that we really believed in and get

people supporting each other. Something that was going on several years ago back in San Francisco when it was political and people were going for a message...

Johnithin: Because we would see cops come in and brutalize people and kids fighting amongst themselves and we were going: "My God, how can kids be into punk rock and do these things". Punk rock is supposed to be social consciousness...

Michael: The Vat bands that were going on then, when we started, weren't the Dils and the Avengers, back then it was a close knit scene. So that's what we wanted to do and how we put our band together.

Michael: It's like morals kind of our own morals....

Dave: But we're not preaching to people, we are not saying like "you should follow us", while we sing it, we sing it to ourselves, we're saying we're not perfect and we know it but you have to have something. You have to have your own code of honor for yourself. Just to keep your shit together and not fuck up. This world wouldn't be like it is if people would accept other people and things around them for what it really is.

color glossy cover.
PAGES: 68
PRICE: $1.00

Code of Honor – photo Al

FLIPSIDE NUMBER 42

"Silence – is no reaction
'Violence' – that one word caption
Can you – say it in just one word?
Unspoken – the sins that go unheard
Government..... bullshit
Black and white.... fight
Look through – this broken window
From normality – into the ghetto
Broken – through madness, hate and boredom
U.K. – a disunited Kingdom
Enquiries – but no solutions
Faceless – empty illusions
Reasons – are always pushed aside
Remember – the day the counry died"
"Black and White" – UK Subhumans

ISSUE #: 42
DATE: April 1984
FORMAT: 8 1/2x11, rotary web offset with 2

PRESS RUN: 8000

Big shows are the order of the day, with some bands playing both Olympic and Perkins on consecutive weekends. With consistant shows at these two place, AND at the Cathay, people again take the scene for granted and the scene again gets over run with violence (the old punk gang syndrome). For us at Flipside, this is almost as depressing as the Fleetwood era, but the violence nevers gets that bad. There are alternatives, and some bands choose to find other venues, including clubs at the beaches (like Safari Sams) and Hollywood clubs like the Anti, Lingerie or Lhasha.

Flipside's format has pretty much remained unchanged for the past few issues. Notable content differences include: Hud's Alternatives section, an ever expanding classifieds section (the biggest anywhere), more letters and extra heavy duty publications listings.

WHIPPING BOY

Whipping Boy became a band in mid-1981, Interviewed by Al in March 1984. I left all of the questions out because it was long enough as it is, We started off talking about them all going to Stanford University....

Eugene: The school trip is a one way thing. They give to me. I take from them. They are a major resource. I find that people who allow school to use them are people who would be used regardless of who was doing the using. These are the same people who don't know why they are where they are, no matter where that is.... There are a few punks at Stanford of the assholeish kind. There are a few cool ones, but for the most part the others are afraid of us, mostly because they don't understand our 'concept'. I don't know if punks can use school or not... There are just as many sheep in the 'punk rock movement' as there are anywhere else. Some could, some couldn't. We have. We've never paid for shit like rehearsal space, so I guess it's been to our benefit... One of the biggest mistakes we made when we first began was to decide to play 'punk'. We should have just gotten together and jammed and whatever type of music would have emerged from that we could have called punk or whatever. I avoid catagories. Since I am determinant of my own reality, whatever I should define punk as, would be what it was... People who catagorize music are killing creativity.

Steve: We have progressed quite a bit. Mostly because we changed from being a band, a business organization, to a concept. Not that we reject business, we just reject the nickel and dime aspect of it. Our minds shape what we do and that is more than play music.

We are about fucking eternity.

Eugene: We have been all over and everywhere and when we detected this pregnancy in the air... people are waiting for something to happen, but no one is taking he chance to make it happen, hence the generic thrash or mindless leap upon the heavy metal band wagon. We are different because we have finally reached the stage where we really and truely don't give a fuck about what happens to us on a business level and that has allowed us to free ourselves from the tyranny of the masses. The larger bands that could do a lot to open up the movement haven't done that. Black Flag is the only band that's taken a balls out leap into something different. There are bands that start out different and bands that become different, the braver of the two is the second type.

Dave: Just think about it. People who call themselves punks have been doing the same dance for 7 years now. The swivel was a decent attempt at something new, but it has gone the way of all flesh.

Steve: Whipping Boy's preeminent desire is to communicate. We have found that the best way to do this is to widen our base. Call it a band, a family, whatever, we are more than just people who play instruments. Whipping Boy is more than just the 4 of us. We have widened our base to the point where we have become, I hate to say this, like a commune or cult. We are more interested in living in the best of all possible worlds and that is what we are in the process of creating for ourselves and everyone involved with us. Come the summer, we, well the rest of them, I can't because I am married, will move into a house.

Eugene: We have got truth by the fucking tits, man! Yeehaw!!!... We have shoved lies under the rug to the asshole of the world. I had been living in a tree and it was there I started having these visions, see...

Steve: Not again...

Eugene: Shut up. I have these visions and that's where we're going. I'm going to run for president someday.

Steve: Tits and ass. Dripping vaginal...

Eugene: No, not like that... Nothing is representative of Whipping Boy. Our trademark is that we try not to do things twice.... When most people think about mysticism, they thnk about hippie bullshit or nonsensical garbage. That is because they don't understand it or it is hippie bullshit or nonsensical garbage, what I'm dealing with is a different approach to the same problem that we are all trying to puzzle out. Why and how? Are they questions and the answers, in my opinion, though I try not to give my opinion because I don't believe that I could ever accomplish anything with words except to furthur the confusion. Words are too easy to misunderstand. So I end up using words to destroy words and hope that people will understand on some other level. Words are symbols for what is and what is not and they must be forgotten because their meaning is already understood and you only need to be told something once. Words are finite and we are infinite, therefore how could they ever suffice? I'm busting a motherfucking nut. I've said it so many times, we are dealing with eternity, with the one and it's relation to sex and it's relation to the common market and it's relation to itself. I am you and you are me and we are all is us together or something like that. It's confusing but I'll be glad to explain any and all of his to anyone. If you want the easy answer to life, contact me.

Subhumans – photo Al

THE SUBHUMANZ

Interviewed at the Olympic Auditorium by Al and Gus: In April of 1984. ...I'll admit I knew little about this band besides what I heard on their records. I wasn't surprized to see them all eagerly downing the brewski, but I was surprised to see most of them smoking heavily.

Al: On your first LP you have this song Ashtray Dirt...

Dick: Oh yeah. This is a weak excuse, but the song wasn't written by any of us. It was written by the singer of the band Bruce was previously in. Secondly, we did it because it was part of our set then, and we carried it on the feeling that we wouldn't persuade anybody else to start smoking. We all smoke because we like the taste, and then we got addicted.

Al: You guys just got here yesterday, you first time in America...

Dick: You realize that all the roads are very straight and parallel with each other. There's no old churches and there's quite a lack of civilized presence before the year 1500. There seems to be a lot of consumerist things about—the grossness and extremeness and the size of everything—all based around bigness.

Al: Including the gig tonight?

Dick: In a way. Theoretically, we shouldn't be doing this gig because I think $7.50 is too much, but we might as well not have come because, if we didn't do this gig, we couldn't have gotten over here in the first place.

Gus: It's really not a bad price for L.A. Plus, you have six bands on the bill too.

Dick: I think there's no excuse based around words like typical, the kids are used to it and they'll pay. It's a weak excuse because you can do it for less because the rest of our gigs are only around four or five dollars.

Al: You have a new album out. Is there anything you're trying to do with your music from album to album?

Dick: Everyone is getting more complicated. We're trying to keep the same energy that's in the earlier songs, but with more into it—make it more interesting to listen to musically. A lot of the old songs, you can listen to a few times and then they get really boring. We want to make it so that it stays fresh longer. Lyrically much the same, but I'm writing less non serious songs, and try to make it more poetic. So, you'll have to think about it a bit more and so I can say more in less words. Get more intensity in there, instead of just saying I hate fucking war.

Al: You sing songs to change attitudes, but do you go further than that...

Dick: If everybody that came in tonight, if I could change their attitude towards the authorities, government, war, religion, and sexuality, then the process would just carry on from there. The whole of them would start thinking and doing the same as I was doing to them. If I can convince someone else that what I think is wrong is right, then he goes off and tells someone else. It does work because it has happened to me. I wouldn't know about

bombs if I hadn't heard records about it and read lyrics. Since we're in a band, we put the information down on vinyl and I think we get through to a lot more people than going on a march. People can participate in a march, but a record can get through to ten thousand people...

Al: Your songs seem to complain a lot, but what alternatives can you offer?

Dick: I think that politics is the big basis for the whole trouble anyway, so the alternative is to be self sufficient. We are, but only because we're in a band telling everybody to be self sufficient. It's ironic that that's so. You can tell people not to go to work and work for someone else, to work for themselves and be self sufficient and all this, but for most people it is just totally impossible. They can't do something that they can make a business out of or they don't have the money to exploit what they can do in the first place. So, we're lucky. The only answer is to build yourself your own existence with as little contact as possible with the system outside you. It's just like autonomy—when you've managed to tell enough people around you to do the same and they've agreed, then that becomes anarchy. That's rather difficult. Spreading it all around is just dreaming at the moment. The more people that think like we do in this generation, and they have kids and they bring them up as they think, then surely it will get bigger through time. It's gonna take years, but sooner or later, there's gonna be a majority of people who don't vote and wouldn't fight war...

CHARLIE HARPER

Of the U.K. SUBS was interviewed at the Cathay in March by Al.

Al: Charlie, how long have you been doing this?

Charlie: For seven years now.

Al: But, you were in bands before the U.K. Subs?

Charlie: Yeah, I was in bands in the seventies. 1970 Charlie Harper's Free Press.

Al: And you're still doing the U.K. Subs. How have you managed to do that so long?

Charlie: It's just that we enjoy what we're doing. Luckily we have just about the best audience in the world. That's what keeps us going.

Al: What do you think of the spirit of the kids now as compared to '77?

Charlie: It's better now. The Cathay is like a Roxy (London) but ten times as good. You don't realize how bad the Roxy was. It was the first club, and maybe the only club ever to have punk every night. There were only a few people around on any night to see any bands. Then, when there were bands that people knew about it was packed solid. It only holds about 200 people. It's probably the same now for any small band, but we were in that position then. Now, it's better because we're sort of a big band. We can draw crowd now—but only 'cause we kept going. We're no better now than we were then.

Al: How do you like it now when kids climb all over the stage?

Charlie: Oh, we don't mind. It's always happened. What sometimes ruins our shows is over zealous security who know of our reputation. We don't mind people on stage as long as they don't wreck our guitars.

Al: The new song, "This Man's Private Army", what's it about?

Charlie: It's about the Russian mobilization in Afghanistan and the mountain people, who are fighting against them led by one man, Amar Shaw Masu. He's got all these rebels and they're beating the Russians. Where there is a will, there is a way. People should stay independent and not be taken over that way.
Al: How long has this tour been going?
Charlie: Only about two weeks. This is supposed to be an all ages tour. Out of the forty gigs about five aren't. It's the same thing in England. We have a completely new audience; they are very young. I really relate to that because I've never gone further. I've never had a decent job. I never had to pay taxes. As soon as the Subs got successful, we had to pay tax insurance and stuff like that. The Subs have always been an outlaw, a radical band. Now, we've come sort of respectable--a contradiction in terms, isn't it?
Al: You played over in Poland, didn't you?
Charlie: We played to ten and twenty thousand people. We couldn't believe it. Their radio staions make the best American ones sound like bullshit. They play punk and tasteful new wave stuff. There is a really good music scene over there. They've got it to fight against, so they believe in it. They're not into it for the money. They know, they really know.
Al: What keeps happening to the musicians in the U.K. Subs?
Charlie: They keeps thinking they're big stars, and keep getting these ideas, like Flock of Seagulls and Heaven 17. They're all big over here, so, since they're all ace musicians, they say, We can do that. We'll make a lot of money over there. I have to play what comes to me. I leave them or they leave me. The Subs have always been true spirit. We always play from our hearts.

DR. KNOW

Dr. Know have been around for a few years and haven't gotten much publicity. I had the opportunity to interview them at Mystic sound on April 14, 1984. by Mouse
Dr. Know are:
Kyle Toucher: vocals, guitar, and self proclaimed sexual dynamo of the eighties.
Ismael Hernandez: bass
Rik Heller: drums
Mouse: Where are you guys actually from?
Ismael: Oxnard California!
Mouse: Do you skate?
Rik: Ismael used to skate for Pepsi, Kyle used to skate for Sims. I didn't skate, I used to surf for Spendrick.
Mouse: How did the band start?
Kyle: Well, I put gas in (ha ha). It started three years ago. Ismael and myself are the only original members. This is the only line up that matters. We won't delve into the past.
Rik: Please don't ask us where we got our name from.
Mouse: Better yet, what does it mean?
Kyle: Absolutely nothing...so people can't call us those guys.
Mouse: Do you consider yourselves more of a metal band?
Kyle: Absolutely not.
Mouse: The reason I ask such a stupid question is that after listening to your record, it seems to have a metal edge to it.
Ismael: Why? Because we have leads in our songs and know more than two chords?
Mouse: No, because I can't play your songs on my touch tone phone. Seriously, what's the lyrical content of your songs?

Kyle - photo Mouse

Kyle: Uh, usually English. I write about God a lot, I guess. I had it shoved down my throat and now I'm throwing it all up. I had a strict Catholic dad that would yell at us all the way to church. It was fucked for the whole week and the next Sunday we'd repeat the whole process. Once you go to Catholic school and have God shoved down your throat twenty-four hours a day, you've gotta barf sometimes.
Mouse: Do you work?
Ismael: We have this tendency to loose jobs after the first week.
Kyle: We've all been fired from the same store for theft.
Mouse: What does the name of your album (Plug in Jesus) mean?
Kyle: It's a night light, but you can take that one a step farther and say, Oh, it's commercialization of religion. But, that's not it. If you really want to know, we took the Dr. Know logo, turned it upside down, and it looks like a cross plugged into a wall.
Mouse: What label?
Kyle: Ghettoway, a subsidiary of Mystic. Due out soon I hope. It's a mini album, a virtual bonanza of hits (laughter).
Mouse: Any tour plans?
Kyle: Yeah, but our van got repossessed.
Rik: We were out on a P.E.A.C.E. (Punk Exploration and Anarchy Corp Elite) mission at a haunted dairy and when we came back, it was gone.
Kyle: It's a burnt out dairy in Camarillo that's supposed to be haunted. We go out and explore abandoned buildings.
Mouse: What prompted you to put "Fist Fuck" on your record?
Rik: Because we never get laid. There are no girls in Oxnard.
Mouse: Do you have a common idea that holds the band together?
Ismael: We don't take anything seriously except our music.
Kyle: We try to laugh at everything. One of the funniest things to do is be completely absurd. We often succeed.

THE GRIM

The Grim were interviewed at the Cathay in March 1984 by Al. The Grim are:

Bob: guitar
Jordan: drums
Shawn: bass
Tim: vocals
Al: Why did you call the band Grim?
Bob: It was our drummer's idea. All of our songs are kinda related to that...
Shawn: "A Dark Outlook On Life"
Bob: That's our 45 that's gonna be out. We have songs like "Sipan Death March", back in World War II where they marched all the soldiers to death. We have "Gumby Grave" which is an anti Gumby song. We don't have any fuck society songs.
Al: Why not?
Shawn: We live in Woodland Hills!!! It's not real. We just write about things that happen to us everyday.
Al: Then, you would be happy, not Grim?
Bob: It's an ugly world, but things never happen to me; only to my friends--even at the Cathay... Ok, Mystic, they've gotten a lot of bad shit lately, but, they've been very cool to us. They're giving us our first 45 and we don't have to pay any money. We're on two compilations. They're going out of their way to help us out.
Al: So, how long...
Shawn: We've been together a year. Jordan's been in the band three months. We started out last March at a high school and kept going...
Bob: Mostly parties. Killroy got us our first gig. Now we're getting gig after gig and we have to turn down a lot of them. We will be on

Grim - photo Al

M.T.V.!
Shawn: They're playing that Kraut video everyday, so we want to make a video. I wrote the script at school. It has sexy models and stuff like that...
Al: What makes you so different M.T.V. would even want to show you?
Shawn: Style and power.
Bob: Personality. We're fun loving friendly people...
Al: With a name like Grim?
Tim: It's a good name 'cause it's just four letters and easy to remember.
Bob: It says everything about our songs. "Old Town Mall" is about getting trapped inside & being tortured by harmonica music. "Son Of Sam Over" is about a guy who strangled this

little girl...

Shawn: He was in my class. He was a normal guy, but tried to kill this girl because she laughed at him.

Al: Do you live at home?

Bob: Yeah, I'm happy as hell at home. We practice in Tim's garage. His dad wants us to make a lot of money so he won't have to work. The Sheriffs showed up with helicopters just because we were practicing. They were trying to pull the garage door open, and it has an electric opener (laughter)! Hey, I'm not anti-Reagan. I'll vote for him in 1984; not for that astronaut...

Shawn: He's had his head in zero gravity. I wonder what that does to you?

Bob: My dad builds bombs for Hughes. I go to school, he paid for my guitar.

Al: Hmmmm, most bands are against all that.

Tim: We have no comments about other bands...

HEART ATTACK

HEART ATTACK were interviewed by Al and Hud at Perkins Palace in Pasadena on March 10, 1984.

Al: How about a little background.

Jessie: I started the band about four or five years ago and since then the members have changed a lot. I got together with Javier, our drummer, about two to three years ago. We were playing steady and then we got Paul, who's been with us about two years. We started playing around New York and we released a single in 1981. Last year we released another record, a 12 inch, "Keep Your Distance". We have another record coming out in April called "Subliminal Seduction". It's a four song twelve inch. Basically, we've been playing around the New York area, up and down the East Coast, Mexico City, and we decided to come out here.

Al and Hud: Mexico City?!?

Jessie: Javier is from there. Basically, when we play we want to communicate. Most bands just want to use it as an escape form, just fun and rock and roll. We try to make it where you can have a lot of energy and fun, but still really look at things. We try to raise questions to the audience and not play up to them.

Hud: Do you think people understand what you're doing?

Jessie: No, it's really hard. We try to give out lyric sheets and I try to talk between songs. But, we don't want to make it like we're an encyclopedia. We just want to use art and creativity as a form of communication.

Hud: I noticed that Paul had Pledge Allegiance to Love written on his pants when you played the Olympic.

Jessie: We're not into countries or any separation like that. It all brings war and feuding. You should really just pledge allegiance to yourself, not to some flag of a country run by people who are into business and power.

Hud: What about the song "God Is Dead"?

Jessie: People always used God when when they didn't have an answer. Now it's become where people use God to control you. God has become a tool of supression. I don't believe there is a God. I believe there is some sort of intelligent force that made us because we're all so well designed. I don't need an answer to fill my head and then let it run me... I don't think people question enough. People keep taking punk so much it will become a big comodity--another product, a fashion. Bands should be questioned to the maximum. I love people to criticize everything I've done. We're not trying to be purists, but you can only do by trying. Bands that don't try just keep feeding the machine. It's just another lazy attitude--giving in to the mainstream. We make songs as clear as possible, but not put ourselves in that rockstar position. I always thought punk was all about if you had something to say, get up there and do it.

Al: Do you consider yourselves anarchists?

Paul: I don't like to have to live up to anything. Anarchism was created before I was born and I'm not at a point now in my life where I can say I'm anything. I have similar beliefs as them, but there are so many different factions.

Jessie: It's just labels. I wouldn't call myself an anarchist or I wouldn't call ourselves a punk band just because of what punk has become. The majority of people see punk as just chaos and fashion. It's just a trend to dress up. But, I got into it for different reasons and I saw it in a different light. The main definition of punk is not my definition.

PLAIN WRAP

Plain Wrap were interviewed in April by Al and Hudley.
Present were:
Don Wrap-vocals, guitar
Bob-bass
Dave-drums

(Plain Wrap started when Don and the drummer for Mox Nix quit and started the new band. He quit and Don went through a few more drummers and bass players until it became what it is now.)

Al: Why did you quit Mox Nix?

Don: Personal reasons plus I was only playing guitar and I wanted to sing also. I felt I was being held back.

Al: What's your excuse Dave?

Dave: I got a hold of Don at a party. I was just asking a lot of people if they needed a drummer.

Don: That was the night we did the air band at the party. We all played air instruments, making the sounds with our mouths. I guess he was really impressed by that. Then, we found out he could really play drums.

Al: You guys really have a nice printed out lyric sheet.

Don: Plain Wrap is about genericising. Society is trying to push everybody into a mold and we're Plain Wrap. We're trying to awaken people to the mold--to the fact that we're becoming domesticated. "Look Out" gets that point across to a certain extent. It's all about people who are into getting a good job and making a lot of money, thinking only of being materialistic, and closing their eyes to thinking.

Bob: We have songs with humor in them too, like "She's So Ugly".

Don: Everybody can relate to that song and it's not just physical ugliness, inside ugliness too. It was not meant to be taken seriously. "Meat Between The Treads" is a short song, about three seconds, five seconds if we do it slow. It's a fictional story. It goes: "I ran over a dog today / I tried to stop but it got in the way / And now it's just meat between the treads." Pretty rank.

Al: What about your song "Punk Rock"?

Don: That's a very serious song about how much I love punk rock. It's such a sincere form of music. It comes straight from my heart.

Hud: What about There is no God?

Don: That's just about certain atheistic views, but I do condone religion. A lot of the ideas and the beliefs of religion are good, but people take it to extremes. They should believe in themselves and not rely on something else for strength.

Hud: Where do you guys work?

Don: I work at a car stereo shop. I install sounds into rich peoples' cars and test them with Plan Wrap tapes.

Bob: I just got an office and a desk. A cable manufacturer; were doing all the cable for ABC TV. Since I've been working, time has been going by faster than anything. It doesn't matter what I'm doing as long as I'm having a good time. Money is important, but I just like fuckin' living.

Don: We always get the Plain Wrap jokes. People say we should paint our amps with a blue stripe that say Amp on them. But, I don't want people to get the impression that we're a complete joke band. But, then there're bands on the other side of the spectrum--all their songs are serious. I really like Discharge and what they say is definitely something to think

Heart Attack at the Olympic - photo Katz

Plain Wrap: Mike, Don, Bobby – photo Al

about, but every song?!?

Al: What inspires you to write songs?

Don: Right now I'm in a humorous phase and I write about everyday things. Sometimes I write songs about just how I feel. I write songs about everything--politics, driving, women... We're really concerned with our music and we really try to go for our own sound. There's so many billions of songs in music. It has to be real original.

Al: What are the goals of Plain Wrap?

Don: We're gonna make it bigger than Billy Idol ever dreamed of!!! I love to play and I love to entertain people, to say what's on my mind, and to let people know what I'm thinking about. Hopefully by having words that people can think about people can better shape their lives as an alternative.

TRUE SOUNDS OF LIBERTY

TSOL were interviewed by Al and Frank in April at Ron's house in Anaheim.

Al: Since our last interview you guys had a different singer and drummer and you had keyboards so briefly...

Mike: It wasn't Todd so much as Jack. Jack drifted away from our original ideas a lot and it called the break up of the band. Actually, Ron and I never broke up the band...

Ron: I just said that I would never play with Jack...

Mike: So, Ron and I kept playing and we never thought it was a new TSOL reforming, but people kept calling it that, so why not. Todd got into a car crash and the law caught up with him, so he didn't want to do it.

Al: How do you think the band is different from the old one?

Mike: In the beginning, the old band was a lot similar to this band. Everyone contributed.

Ron: At the end, Jack wouldn't accept any words that we would write. He would say, I'm the singer, everything I write gets played. If you guys want to write a song, you can sing it.

Mike: That wasn't True Sounds of Liberty at all. At one point, he was talking about changing the name of the band to The Voice.

The band is always changing. We felt that keyboards weren't a cop out because there's a million different flavors to music and we didn't want to feel tied down to one thing. This band is back to the original ideal of being able to do anything musically we want. We're strongly into a really rocky kind of thing right now, rootsy...

Ron: But, it's not all one style. We have a set of about twenty songs already.

Mike: Now, were used to each other too. Joe will throw a melody line in a song and we'll come up with the music... We have to slow down. We already have twelve songs recorded besides what's on the new album.

Frank: Did you find a hard time at first getting accepted as the new lead singer?

Joe: Yeah, it was tough, but I was always into this band. The kids never went to my face, but I heard all the crap. They want to have fun and if we sound good and play hard and sweat, then, weather they like us or not, they will respect us for trying.

Al: What are some of the new songs about?

Mike: All the songs deal with personal liberty and things that enter your life everyday. Different points of view and things that strike us--nothing fictitious or ridiculous. I can't be up there playing a song if it's about something that doesn't have to do with anything. This band is really new and we're having fun. We've done thirty or forty shows already. Some bands will play the same songs through ten different line ups. The only old songs we do play either Ron or I wrote. Maybe later down the road we'll do some old ones. I think the people like the new material. Now that the record's out, only time will tell. We're all going to tour together. Everyone gets the same pay every night. No one is pulling in more than another. It's a real productive healthy thing. It's the best working situation we've had yet

Ron: A lot of bands ask us how we get on shows and how we tour. You just do it. Don't sit there and wonder why you can't do it. People aren't coming to you; you have to go out and do it. And the whole scene is cool and it's getting bigger all the time. There's places all over the country. There will always be a need for entertainment and to get out aggression.

Mike: We have a lot of freedom. We've still retained creative freedom. Everything we want is honest...

SUBTERFUGE

SUBTERFUGE were interviewed at Ichabods in Fullerton by Al, Hud, and **Gus:** in February of 1984...

Al: You guys are the big Las Vegas band, I've heard your name associated with that scene for a long time...

Mark: Yeah, the Las Vegas scene never had the get up and go to get out of town you know. We were always just happy to mess around town and play gigs and parties there. But now it has grown so much.

Gig: We were one of the first bands in Las Vegas. We formed about two years ago and it seems like a lot of bands are forming there now.

John: As far as Subterfuge goes this is the second generation. We have gone though personal changes and don't have the original drummer or rhythm guitarist.

TSOL: Ron, Mike, Mitch, Joe – photo Al

Gig: Plus the whole L.V. scene has become different since the beginning. It's a really tight scene. Like tonight (Suicidal Tendencies were headlining), there were a bunch of fights--you never see that in L.V. We take care of each other. The police are even cool.

Mark: At the last gig that Guy Smiley did, the police came and he was ready to go to jail. He was putting his jacket on and the police go,"No, man we're not gonna take you in, and if you're looking for a new place for gigs try North Las Vegas." So, we don't have any anti-police songs.

Gig: We don't write a lot songs about the international things except,"Irish Eyes," but we try to write songs about stereotyping.

John: We're more socially aware then we're a political activist band.

Al: How does coming from L.V. effect your lyrics?

Mark: We write songs that are about the things happening in the society around us. Macho Man is about guys who go to bars and drink a lot--and this happens a lot in Vegas. These cowboy types who are always trying to pick up on chicks and stuff... Last night we played at the Cathay and eleven bands played.

Gig: No, only ten, and we were number ten! All the bands before us were like bzzzzzzzzzzzzzzzzzzzzzzzz!!!!!!!

John: It really knocked me for a loop. I didn't realized that thrash was so predominant. I figured there was a variation.

Gig: Well, we were looking forward to playing because we're a little choppier and slower and you can hear more of what we're trying to say.

Al: How did you come up with your sound?

Rob: We go a little bananas when we play, but I think we're tying for a little more professionalism--not Discharge professionalism--but were trying to get it together. I work on my drum sound all the time at home. When I go on stage I want to put out at least six or seven hundred percent. I want to get off stage and shake for a half an hour and not be able to talk, just use up all my energy.

Al: You didn't always live in L.V.?

Mark: I moved over here from England three years ago. I got in trouble with the law, so my dad sent me over here. He said there were no punks in Las Vegas, but I ended up getting in a band and having more fun here than in England.

FLIPSIDE NUMBER 43

Too much too soon too little too late
Can't feel no love can't even hate
Caught in a limbo in a barren land
People don't know me I'm a Marginal Man
Eyes straight ahead, I got my feet on the ground
Noise all around me, I can't hear a sound
Viewing life from a window pane, I'm outside looking in
My luck ran out a short time ago
I've lost myself and there's nowhere to go
So I've curled up in the corner of my room
Like a rat in a cage
People speak but it makes no sense
They give me strange looks – what's going on?
Allergic to the outside world – outside looking in
Out of the picture – I can't cry
Out of the picture – Don't know why
Out in the cold, ain't life grand?
Out in the cold...

Subterfuge, their last show – photo Al

Now I know who is who, but I still can't talk to you
I'm standing here in despair,
I'm all alone and I don't care"
"Marginal Man" – Marginal Man

ISSUE #: 43
DATE: August 1984
FORMAT: 8 1/2x11, rotary web offset with 2 color glossy cover.
PAGES: 68
PRICE: $1.00
PRESS RUN: 8500

It finally happened, the Cathay closed for good. For those of you who never had the pleasure to go to this fine establishment, let me describe it briefly: no air-conditioning in this low ceiling basement (although in later days the stage was moved upstairs), no stage lights to speak of (ok 5 light bulbs), the ceiling so low that it actually got in the way, a shitty sound system that probably would be ok except there was no sound man that knew how to run it (except Don Bolles). Gigs were mostly over priced (except for dollar night, and that was over priced some nights as well), and bands were always under paid. The cops were very aggressive, conducting many raids and often employing undercover "Quincy punks" to check things out. The gangs were also aggressive, but by now they had their targets picked out, and for the most part if you didn't participate in their activities, you were left alone. The best bands in the world played their worst gigs here, and the worst bands in the world played with them. A lot of bands got their start here, not many lasted, and a lot of touring bands played their only L.A. gig here, but no one saw them. All in all the Cathay was a fucking great place, there were plenty of good streets (like Hollywood Blvd. on the next corner) to hang out at and plenty of good alleys to drink and socialize in. I really miss the Cathay now that it is gone, it is something L.A. sorely needs right now. Roxannes, a bar/club in the suburbs and Shamus Obriens, also closed about this time, although they had been fizzleing out for some months.

The only thing new in this Flipside is the "fanzine of the month" section, this issue featuring **Ink Disease.** This was part of our idea to expand the format beyond: bands, records and letters.

LOVE CANAL

Love Canal were interviewed by Al and Hudley one fine summer evening in August at Dead Zone studios in Santa Ana. Present were Arab - guitar, Kerry - vocals, Louie - bass and Eric - drums (filling in for Bobby).

Al: So, Love Canal has two meanings....

Arab: Being that I'm a gynecologist and a proctologist...

Kerry: And an asshole..

Arab: And an asshole, right, well actually Kerry kind of came up with the name...

Louie: My mom gave it to me.

Al: What about the political...

Louie: The toxic waste dump...

Kerry: It was also one of our old girlfriends.

Louie: Mine! Love Canal is my old girlfriend, her name is Tricia.

Kerry: Actually, I played my last show with the Skoundrelz and I told them just to spite them, because they kicked me out, that I had another band called Love Canal. They all laughed, so I thought it was appropriate.

Al: We've noticed that in this political day and age, you choose to put the fun back in.

Kerry: Yep. Put it this way, we're old enough

SUMMER THRASH BASH

Debut live album from L.A.'s
JANE'S ADDICTION

51004-1 album   51004-4 cassette.

"...Some of the best psychotic rock I've encountered for years." **John Wilde MELODY MAKER**

"...A thundering wall of sound that walks strictly on rock's wildside." **John Matsumoto RIP MAGAZINE**

"Freewheeling, unclassifiable metal/funk hybrid." **BILLBOARD**

"The bottom line is that Jane's Addiction rocks hard." **CMJ**

D.I.
"Team Goon"
XXX1002 album XXXC1002 cassette. Features "Richard Hung Himself," "The Saint" and "Nuclear Funeral."

D.I.
"Horse Bites, Dog Cries"
51007-1 album. 51007-4 cassette. Includes the favorites "Johnny's Got A Problem," "Pervert Nurse," "Living In The U.S.A." and "Obnoxious."

D.I.
"Ancient Artifacts"
51006-1 album. 51006-4 cassette. D.I.'s first album with the hits "O.C. Life," "(I Hate) Surfin' in H.B." and "Hang Ten in East Berlin."

RHINO 39
"Rhino 39"
XXX1001 Album XXXC1001 Cassette Hardcore from Long Beach! This long awaited album rocks with such tunes as "Bars and Bricks," "Take Your Medicine" and "Hurry Up and Wait."

THE DILS
"Live 1977/1980"
51003-1 album 51003-4 cassette. Features 14 live classic tunes from one of the originators of the West Coast punk scene--includes "Tell Her You Love Her," "It's Not Worth It," "You're Not Blank," "Mr. Big," "Class War" and more!

Coming in September: Debut album from Orange County's MIND OVER 4 and D.I. "Witch In The Canyon" (all new material produced by RANDY BURNS). All albums are available from TRIPLE X—send money order or check for $8.00 per album or cassette ordered (includes postage and handling), to: TRIPLE X RECORDS, 6715 Hollywood Blvd. Suite 282, Hollywood, Ca 90028. Distributed by IMPORTANT.

YOUR EXCUSE TO GO OFF

Love Canal dressing for photos – photo Hud

to know about politics. But there are more bands out there that are saying the right thing, like MDC or whomever. They really know what they're talking about.

Arab: Wait!! I've got a quote here (pulls out a BAM) "They're turned being ugly into a business". My point of view is, punk rock, music, rock and roll is all about having fun, and I like to have fun.

Louie: Plus, when he drinks beer before we play he comes up with some real imaginative lyrics...

Kerry: I change the lyrics everytime we play anyhow, spontaneous...

Hud: Are you guys as sexist as everyone says you are?

Arab: Oh well.. can we go off the record?

Louie: Larry Flint for president!

Arab: What? Fornicate more in 84!

Kerry: Try to survive till '85.

Arab: There you go. There is our sexual political views.

Louie: Larry would run for president, but since he's in a wheelchair he has to roll for president!

Arab: We're just looking to have some fun, playing a lot and skateboarding.

Kerry: Arab is the real skateboarder of the band. I've just been around them so long.

Al: But you hate them?

Kerry: Yeah. No. That is just a joke song because I was in a skate band and got kicked out...

Arab: Skating is fun, I've been around it all of my life. I was on the Pepsi Team, we skated on the Mike Douglas show...

Al: Where does your unique guitar style come from?

Arab: Crazy guitar players like Kerry Martinez from Shattered Faith, what's his name from the Ramones, Ronny Emory, Human of Detox, Greg Ginn for his abstract leads, just about anybody who lets loose. Who influences your singing?

Kerry: Biscuits from the Big Boys. Not the way I sing obviously, but he's just a good guy and he told me just get out there and play

our ass off if there's 2 people or 2000 and I think that's good. He likes to have fun.

FANG

So anyway Fang were on their way to L.A. to play the Cathay but the gig got cancelled so I agreed to interview them.......

Al: When you drive around and play all these places, what do you want to get across?

Chris: We're your basic entertainment.

Sam: Uh, anarchy, communism, socialism and respectability and the moral majority. Usually, depending on the night.... It's not, not trying to insult people, it's expressing a way of life, of what I see in the world today.

Chris: Some things are funny, but they're serious too, ya know?

Sam: Like I could look at what I write about

and become depressed about it. Because some of it is pretty ugly, pretty sleazy, some of it is sickening, makes me want to puke, I hate it, BUT, I can also look at it and laugh. What's the point of looking at things and getting depressed and going "Hmmmm, bummer deal"? Or you can sit around and go "Ha ha that's funny!!". Like when you see a whore walking down the street, you can go: "Wow, at one point she was a nice girl, and here she is now selling her ass on the street, hmmmm bummer deal". Or you can go "Hey, check it out, a hooker! Hey, do you take credit cards?!"

Chris: Yeah, yeah. That's really clear now! You have to look at the whole thing to get a clear picture. And laugh at the things you do too. It's just part of being a person.

Al: Do people ever get upset with you guys when you're playing?

Sam: The only time was when we played the Cathay and there were 6 undercover cops there and they told us to stop playing and one guy was yelling to Chris to keep playing or there would be a riot. He didn't know how to mow his yard. Oh it was it Flipside too, I accidentally hit someone too and they wrote a letter, but I apologized. I'm out there to have a good time and I hope everybody else is too. I don't like when people make dancing into a battlefield, people shouldn't be out there to hurt each other. Sometimes people take the wrong attitude, and I don't want to lend to that attitude by accidentally hitting someone.

Al: Well you're starting a new tour and have a new LP, you must be serious about the band.

Sam: I'm as serious as hell, Helen Ready. Hell and ready to go!!!

Tom: After a US tour I'm gonna try to set up a UK tour.

Chris: And we're preparing for that by going to Canada... Our direction is more light hearted than the political bands, but there is thought promoted, there's entertainment basically, we want to play music and go places and have a good time. It's not a real serious thing, we don't have a spacific cause or thing we want to stand behind........

Sam: You know, we were in Hollywood and I had my horn up and this old man came up to me carrying a bible and he said "That's a devil lock, you should cut it off." and I told him that

Fang at the Cathay – photo Al

I've been trying to, but it keeps growing back. And he goes "Oh no" and ran down the street clutching his bible.....

F

Interview by Bill Bartell
F is probably the most popular Florida punk rock band, with the likes of Sector 4, Gay Cowboys In Bondage running a close second and third. Their 77 style hardcore is powerful and their lyrics harsh and meaningful, even though they may seem tongue in cheek at times. This interview is with guitarist Ugly Stupid Ken Decter and vocalist John Galt, who is also known as Phil.

Ken Decter of F

Bill: Well, aren't the members of F gay?
Ken: Well, Eddie isn't and we don't have a drummer right now so I can't speak for him. It's really just Phil and I.
Bill: Do you ever get hasseled for being openly gay in a band?
Phil: It's funny, we don't have sex at all. It's like we know we don't like girls and we're

The FU's

quite fond of each other but we've never kissed or anything. I guess we're not ready for it, neuter, we have no sex at all.
Phil: I'm saving myself for marriage!
Bill: You're pro-Reagan aren't you?
Phil: Yes and anti-drugs. Reagan is cool, in our record we have a list of hysterical things he does in public, like falling asleep during the Pope's speech - how can you help but love the guy?
Bill: If punk sucks and you hate punks, why are you in a punk band getting popular?
Ken: Well I'm a fool I guess, I guess slamming is in our blood, kind of like salmon going up stream to spawn.
Phil: Punk is a cult where even losers like us can be cool. If you're proud of being a derelict drunk scum you've really got something wrong with you.
Bill: Any last words?
Phil: Let's say if you have any of the major punk records of the early eighties or late seventies, you own a record made by a queer!

FU'S

Boston's FU's have to be one of the most misunderstood punk bands in America. In their 3 years together they've put out 2 albums, toured the country and raised a lot of questions about what exactly the 'rules' about being a punk are. Drummer/ song writer Bob Furapples was spoken to by Bill Bartell as the band prepared to leave for a 2 month US tour.
Bill: You got bored with politics?
Bob: Yeah, we got bored. We still have our same beliefs, we still like this country and that stuff, but we figure we've made our point. Everyone knows by now, an apparently a lot of people aren't gonna let us forget it! This is the best country that you can possibly live in and people are always complaining how terrible it is...
Bill: Do you think that's slowed down your popularity being almost 'too radical' for punks?
Bob: There are a lot of people who have just gone along to be punk, too afraid to say what they mean, but there's a lot of bands, not just us, that see things almost the same way. They're not all these 'anarchy/peace' bands, that won't ever work.

Bill: Has MRR's negative press effected record sales?
Bob: I think it has. Especially foreign sales, people see the mag before they hear the record and get a distorted impression of the message. Our message is that you should be proud of your country, no matter where you're from, if you're not proud, leave. It has to do with being proud of yourself. Every country has good things about them, including Russia and other communist countries, not that I'd want to go there. Like that fans that we get letters from that live behind the Iron Curtain, they're still proud of home, because they have to be, without that pride, what else have you got? So we're playing no matter what almighty Tim says...
Bill: Wasn't punk a rebellion from that, an escape from pressures and control and someone telling you how to play music, how to dress, what politics to believe in, and that kind of stuff, parental rebellion?
Bob: That's what I thought but the longer you're in the scene the more crap you see. I'm not gonna run around in leather and spike my hair to prove how punk I am. We've been together 3 years. Punk is an attitude. I just do what I feel like, you don't need punk as a label, punk as a word is pretty derogatory.
Bill: What are you going to do with your life?
Bob: I plan on becoming a state cop, Wayne's going back to school, Steve wants to be a helicopter pilot, and John's gonna get a real job.
Bill: But you're not planning to break up?
Bob: Well as time goes by you think about it more and more, but no time soon. We want to accomplish everything we can. Like if 3 years ago you told us we'd have our own album out and have toured the country I'd have laughed. But now we're on our second tour and 3rd lp. People write to us and buy our records. It's like a real dream come true but you have to put everything into it. Make it the first thing in your life, loose friends and family, the band comes first. When I'm sixty I can pull out the FU's lp's and smile and say "This is something not everyone can do" but then if we could learn to play - anyone could. I quit school, lost 2 jobs and it's worth it. When people have fun, it makes it all worthwhile.

FACTION

Interviewed by Al, Hud and Gus at the Fab Stardust Ballroom on Skateboard night.
The Faction are:
Gavin Obrien - vocals
Adam Bomb - guitar
Keith Rendon - drums
Steve Caballero - bass
Al: So I hear there's this real long history behind your name?
Gavin: Peter Gifford, who is a very old skateboard pro, he and Craig Ramsey made up a skate team that had divisions in Sacramento, San Francisco and San Jose. This was three years ago and I was in the San Jose division. But it never really came around. Then we got the band and the name was cool so we just took it.
Al: Are you all skaters?
Faction: Yep. yeah. What?
Hud: How long have you been skating?
Steve: Around 6 1/2 years, I ride for Powell/Peralta.
Gavin: I've been riding for 6 1/2 years too.

Faction: Keith, Gavin, Steve, Adam at the Stardust - photo Al

Hud: What did you start on?

Gavin: Just on my front driveway, just fucking around.

Al: Do you have your own ramps now?

Gavin: Steve has a ramp that my brother and I helped build.

Steve: 9 feet high, 12 feet wide, a foot of vertical and 6 foot of flat.

Al: Are you a skate band then?

Adam: No. Not really. We're just a band that happens to skate.

Keith: People start to get it confused, because of Steve mainly (who is a world famous pro) but just because we all skate.

Gavin: We never really went around saying "Yeah, we're a skate band". All we do is skate.

Adam: We have a skateboard on our emblem, but that's about it, we're not gonna use that anymore. People like to say "Oh Faction, that's Steve Cabellero's band, he's a pro skateboarder". We want people to know the Faction because they've heard our records and they were stoked.

Hud: Why do you have skulls on the badges and on the records?

Steve: Why? We want to be scary. We want to be a scary skate band, um, band that skates.

Adam: Somebody has to be scary now that the Misfits broke up.

Al: No drugs right?

Gavin: No, no drugs, no beers, cigarettes that's it.

Al: Why don't you like L.S.D.?

Gavin: Because, because, because, because, becahhhhhhhhzzzee (Wizard of Oz, alright), I don't like drugs.

Steve: I used to smoke but I don't anymore because I found out ti's bad for your health, no good for my sport. It gets me tired.

Al: Does it ruin Gavins voice?

Gavin: Well I don't care because the more they lean towards heavy metal the more I'm gonna lean towards punk screaming.

Adam: We have a major heavy metal influence, but I think we are a punk band. Heavy metal punk. HM is cool because it has so much power, which is cool because punk is so fast sometimes you loose your power. So if you slow down and rock out a little you get your power back and people get stoked.

Gavin: I don't like heavy metal at all.

INK DISEASE

Interview done in a car headed towards San Diego with Thomas, Steve and Rachel.

Al: What do each of you do?

Steve: Uh uh (with finger up his nose) I'm it all, I am the magazine, it's me, I'm publisher, editor, financer, the whole works. It's my brain child.

Al: What do you do Rachel?

Rachel: Not much. Just sit around, I do layouts, take some pictures, write some articles, some artwork, get some ads.

Thomas: I'm mediator between these guys because they argue a lot. I try to keep them from fighting.

Al: Is there anyone else on the staff?

Rachel: Brady! And Joe who I argue with most. They cause arguements.

Steve: And emulate us.

Thomas, Joe and Steve Ink Disease somewhere in New York - photo Al

Al: What makes a man start a fanzine?

Steve: Well there's the will to change, when a person has a vision, like I do...

Rachel: He didn't even start it, it was me, Thomas, Antonio and Ivan Armistice.

Al: Ok, so what makes a woman start a fanzine?

Rachel: Boredom.

Thomas: Antonio started it, I stole it. Me and Steve bought it.

Al: What do you want to accomplish?

Thomas: I don't know. Well, it's nice to start it and then get to the end of it. It's not like work where you have to go everyday. You can finish it and see it, and show it to people and they can say things about it "You're a dick" or whatever....

Al: What's the press run?

Steve: 2500, we get rid of most of them. I don't know how but we do. We work hard to sell them and to get advertisments. My mom might advertise in the next one. Thomas's dad will put an ad in for computers.

Al: Who named the zine?

Thomas: Our next door neighbor's dad.

Al: What's the significance of it?

Thomas: Oh, it sort of sounds like it's spreading.

Steve: And everytime you read the magazine it gets all over your hands and you have 'Ink disease'.

Rachel: Well we were always reading Flipside and we said this magazine sucks so we made up our own.

Steve: A week before a new Flipside would come out I would get an erection. But there was a time when I stopped getting that erection so I knew I had to do something. Ink Disease is a form of masterbation for me. It gives me an erection to write and have other people read it.

Thomas: It gives me a pain in the butt.....

MARGINAL MAN

Interviewed at the Cathay on June 28 by Al, Pete, Hud and John Crawford. The entire bands were present:

Pete - guitar
Mike - drums
Kenny - guitar
Steve - vocals
Andre - bass

Al: Ok, you guys are from DC?

Mike: Maryland, it's just a hair above DC.. We

Marginal Man - photo Joe Henderson St.

formed in December of 1982. Me, Steve and Pete used to be in Artificial Peace, and Kenny and Andre were in a band called Toaster Head Our roadie, Monelo was also in the band.

Kenny: Nothing really happened with the band, but it was something to do, an experimental project.

Al: Who wrote "Marginal man"?

Pete: Kenny wrote the lyrics and I wrote the music.

Al: What is "Marginal Man" about?

Kenny: Well first I'll start off by defining the name "Marginal Man". It's a term sociologists use to describe a person who is on the fringe of two or more cultures which may or may not be conflicting. To put it simpler, he's partially assimilated into each culture but fully assimilimated into none of them. So as a result he doesn't belong to any of them.

Mike: Ok, for example the Marginal Man would have friends in certain peer groups, like say the preppies or the jocks or the freaks, and the punks. But he's not really fully accepted into any of those groups.

Kenny: When I wrote the song I wrote it basically about feeling isolated and not really getting into the mainstream of things as they were, and it just ended up that way I guess.

Al: Did you write the song before the band got the name or after?

Kenny: I wrote that about a week and a half after the band got the name. I named it.

Al: Did you hear that in class?

Kenny: Yeah. It caught my ear in a sociology class. The professor said: "Now we will discuss the Marginal Man, who is always on the outside looking in" So I woke up and went "Ohhh". It just sounded interesting so I brought it to the guys. They thought it sounded ok too.

Al: You all go to school, right?

Steve: Except for me.

Al: If you all go to school, that must be your outlook for the future, what about the future of the band?

Mike: We've already done more than we expected to do originally. We're just taking it as it comes. We haven't compromised either band or school, yet.

Andre: A lot can happen in just two weeks, right now we're just touring and whatever happens happens.

Al: Getting back to the lyrics, you seem to take a more inner, personal outlook when writing.

Mike: Being real general and talking about the record, most of the lyrics are from Steve, and most of the music is mine, now we all pitch in...

Steve: As far as general theme whatever, that just happened. We're lucky it did turn out that way instead of conflicting. Artificial Peace was real superficial, just like scraping on a piece of chicken but this is... just total emotion now, it is pure heart felt stuff.

Kenny: If you write about these situations in a very direct way then it wouldn't have as much meaning to me, nor as much impact than if it was written a little more ambiguously. Then people can put a little bit more of themselves into it, so they can relate to it. If you get too specific then the scope becomes too narrow and very few people can truely relate to what you're saying.

Mike: This band has become so involved now that we all act as one unit. The way I look at it, if any member of this line-up changed, we just couldn't do it. It's more than just a band, it's all emotion, this band, these people are my crowd. I talk with these people, with my band and Menolo more than I do with my girlfriend, it's true.

Steve: We'll do this band until it loses meaning, then you're just clutching at straws, soon as the songs no longer have meaning, or we just don't feel the same way we'll get out. That's when we call it quits.......

EXPLOITED

Interviewed by Al, Frank, Harvey (among others) at their Tropicana Hotel room. All the band was present but Wattie did all of the talking.

No matter how you feel about it you have to admit that the Exploited, or should I say their singer/songwriter Wattie in particular, is one of the most controversal and popular punk bands in the world today. It is obvious that a lot of people must like this band, but there are also a significant amount of people who are very outspoken that hate this band. It's pretty clear that

most people dislike them because of their lyrics, their actions or what they say in print. Well I can't say I agree with everything that this band says or does but I do know that I have a different opinion of the band, especially Wattie, now that I know them a little better.

Frank: What is your favorite place to play?

Wattie: I like California. I like L.A. and I like Canada. I like the people in L.A. and San Diego, the best places we played were in Washington and Canada. I liked New York for the night life but over here you have the sunshine, ha ha. My favorite country is Finland. Finland is brilliant. The punk scene is flourishing everywhere but England. In England it's dead, it's true. We really like the USA. The song "Fuck the USA" is not about the people in America, it's about the rich and the government.

Frank: A lot of kids don't hear that, they just hear "Fuck the USA".

Wattie - photo Al

Wattie: (here's the complete lyrics): There is nothing really nice about the USA/ You go to the hospital, you have to pay/ the dollar is the language that they all speak/ they don't really bother about the radiation leak./ They keep their secrets undercover/ the rich don't bother about those that suffer/ this ain't the land of milk and honey/ cause all they want is money money money./ Nuclear bombs are fuck all new/ You'd better start running when they drop on you/ run into a shelter, play hide and seek/ cause when you die your body reeks/ fuck the USA... That song is about the American system, not they people who matter. In other words, the working class.

Frank: You played with Crass awhile back, why did you do that?

Wattie: For years us and Crass had been slagging each other off, right, we have different beliefs and we just kept slogging each other. So we got quite friendly with this girl Annie Anxiety, and she's ok but she tries to get your body, but she's ok to talk to. So we needed a couple of support bands and we asked her if she wanted to do a couple of songs, she said ok. Later she came back and said Crass would want to do a couple of songs so we said ok. So that way we could stop the rivalry between Exploited punks and Crass punks, they don't like us because I think we slag them off a little more.

Al: Why didn't you like them?

Wattie: I did like them, I liked some of their stuff, but they started slagging us and we started slagging them. Since then I think it has started all over again, ha ha. I still don't agree with what Crass say, but there's no harrasment. If they asked us to play with them again we would.

Frank: So what does punk mean to you?

Wattie: Enjoying yourself. Drinking Schnapps! Ha ha. You go for the music, if you like the music you feel happy, that's what it is to me. Doing what you want, you don't have to conform to what other people want you to be, everybody has their own ideas. I always write songs about everyday life. If something bugs me I write a song about it, what effects the punks.

Frank: So can the Exploited last another 5 years?

Wattie: I hope to, I'm only in it to tour abroad, there's not much money to be made, money is no object. Just touring abroad and meeting people and having a good time. If you're an established band you can do that. If you work hard and believe in what you're doing. So we'll stick together.

Al: How many brothers and sisters do you have?

Wattie: 2 brothers, one sister. My mum and dad are divorced, my mum stays in London, my dad in Scotland – he's a nutter as well. He always writes songs for me. He comes up: "I've got a great tune for ya" and it's shit. Ha ha. He drives me crazy!

Harvey: Anything you like besides punk?

Wattie: Sure, the Cure, I like "The Wall" Pink Floyd, I saw the movie 4 times on acid, sheee, great. I like a lot of different music. I think Elvis Presley is shit! He was alright before he got fat!

Harvey: Lots of people say the Exploited have a reputation for being really violent and causing fights and having fights at shows, how do you feel about that?

Wattie: If people have a go at us then we'll stick up for ourselves. I don't want people to come to a gig to get their face kicked in. I don't want that. In older days we used to be more crazy and get into fights, we used to get into causing a lot of damage, but now we realize that you can't go around causing damage.

Harvey: Do you think you're a different person on stage?

Wattie: I just go crazy. I don't know, I can't explain it. It's just different.

Harvey: Are you always fucked up?

Wattie: Oh always..

Harvey: How do you feel about playing sober?

Wattie: I don't know, it's been a long time. Ha ha, no never.

Harvey: Did you first get a mohawk because you saw someone else with one...

Wattie: We were the first ones with mohawks, first ones in Scotland and there couldn't have been 20 in all of Britain.

Harvey: Do you think that look is important?

Wattie: To me it is. I have no respect for people who have been into it for years and dress like hippies. I'll go talk to somebody dressed like me first before I'll go talk to somebody with long hair. I respect people like myself who dress hardcore. I don't like to talk to assholes!

Al: You're one of those kind of guys that

people either like or hate, why do you suppose that's true?

Wattie: I like to say what I believe in, it's always been like that. If people like what I say or what I believe in that ok, if they don't like me, that's ok too. I think that there are more people that like us because we are one of the biggest punk bands in the world.

ISSUE #: 44
DATE: November 1984
FORMAT: 8 1/2x11, rotary web offset with 2 color glossy cover.
PAGES: 68
PRICE: $1.00
PRESS RUN: 8000

COC: Reed, Mike, Eric, Woody – photo Al

CORROSION OF CONFORMITY

COC are **Eric** - vocals, **Woody** - guitar, **Mike** - bass and vocals, **Reed** - drums

This is not exactly an interview but a compilation of facts and trivia: Philadelphia is **Mike** and **Reed's** favorite place to play.- North Carolina (Raleigh, where they're from) is boring.- Red Necks are more of a problem than police there. This is also know as the 'Bible belt' where all the big money preachers are based. Religion is good for America because "It's keeps 'em happy". "I can go to Church and get something out of it, but I don't want anybody telling me to go to Church." **Mike** is the only vegitarian in the band. It took a long time and we fucking worked for out shit" (talking about equipment)- Their parents support them, **"Mike's** parents bought us a van". Influenced by Black Sabbath and Black Flag but all are self taught musicians. **Eric** got arrested for 3 assaults on a police officer, **Mike's** mom got charged with assault for slapping the sound man at the same gig. Only 1/2 of COC skate. COC are not 'straight edge' **Reed** named the band so "no motherfucking band from Pomona California would have the same name!" **Mike:** "We would like to see Corrosion on all levels of society... just yer basic punk rock non-conformity trip".

FLIPSIDE NUMBER 44

"Here comes Nick wearing a skirt
Here comes Jane you know she's sporting a chain
Same hair of revolution
Same build, evolution
Tomorrows, who's gonna fuss
And they love each other so, androgynous
Closer than you know, love each other so,
androgynous.
"Androgynous" – Replacements

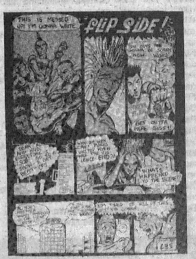

REPLACEMENTS

At first the idea to interview the Replacements seemed to be easy, but over the period of several days it got harder and harder. So what I ended up doing was talking to Paul Westerburg and Tommy Stintson first outside the Lingerie and second with Paul outside of Al's Bar. Bob Stintson didn't really care if anybody talked to him, only if it included mind altering substances and Chris Mars I didn't even get a chance to get to. So after some nagging I got something, here goes...

Outside Lingerie, FS is Pete and Thomas Ink Disease):

Flipside: So you are...

Paul: Drunk Paul.

Tommy: I'm Tommy the louse, I mean a brat. He's a louse (points to Paul), he's a louse, he's drunk.

Flipside: So are you satisfied with the way things are going?

Paul: I'd say yes.

Flipside: Do you like L.A.? Is it cool?

Paul: You know, a couple of days it's ok. I mean I wouldn't want to live here or nothing. It's too warm.

Tommy: I second that emotion!

Paul: Yeah, where's the snow? That's how we make our living, shoveling snow in the winter.

Flipside: Is all that cold and snow an inspiration?

Paul: That's how you learn how to rock. You gotta keep warm.

Flipside: Yeah, you go into the basement and party till it hurts.

Paul: That's right.

Flipside: So tell me about the band....

Tommy: Can I give you the bio. Let me tell you brother like it started back when me, Chris and my brother Bobby started playing. So my brother showed me how to play bass when I was 11, we started jamming...

Paul: They had a band that played covers and had long hair and played really fast and I was walking by one day and I heard them cause they were so loud. I told them I was a singer but I had never sung before...

Tommy: We kicked out every other member we had. He fit in like a glove on a tombstone.

Paul: We were doing Johnny Winter, Aerosmith...

Flipside: So then you joined the band.

Paul: Yeah in 1980, 1979. We started writing songs, you know started rehearsing for 2 months and then got our first gig. The guy who got us the gig worked on Twin Tone records - he liked us and got us into the studio.

Flipside: And you made the demo which is on "Sorry Ma"...

Paul: Two songs are, actually not the tape we gave him but the initial demos.

Flipside: Are there any filler songs on "Let It Be"?

Paul: Sure, you got "Tommy Tonsils".

Flipside: That's filler huh?

Tommy: Well it wasn't ment to be filler, like we say filler, like if Michael Jackson puts out a record that's half filler and he calls it filler, but no he doesn't, he calls it "Thriller".

(Talk about them playing still playing clubs back in Minneapolis)

Tommy: They can't possible take it seriously because after 5 years, seeing us both ways,

they couldn't possibly think I just paid 5 bucks "We'll just wait and see what happens"..

Flipside: In other words you want to go one step furthur into a major.

Paul: Hell, we don't want to go backwards, but we don't want to change and be slick.

Flipside: Is that selling out, maybe?

Tommy: You know what selling out is? It just happens, it's not like some guys says "I've got some good songs and I'm gonna sell out."

Flipside: You're looking for a life where you can be in a band and make money off of it.

Tommy: We're looking for it to be fun. I don't want vengence against him if and when we break up. We just do it as fun and what comes natural. You figure if you're gonna be unhappy playing we might as well make some money. I mean that's the rule that we're going by, sometimes it gets like that - "what the hell are we doing here?"

Flipside: Are you happy with what your doing?

Paul: You can't put a big thing on it, some nights it's great, it can vary from song to song. Some songs are fun to play, others a fucking drag.

Flipside: Musically you've changed, more production, fancier things, slower songs...

Paul: We're getting a little tired, I'll be the first to admit that. I don't like screaming all night. I do that for a week.

Tommy: I like playing all night.

Paul: We're old men.

Tommy: Our thing is we like to play the music we wanna play, be comfortable with it, it's not a matter of making tons of money or this or that and doing the things you do....

Paul: You figure you can always go back and sweep the floors or something, you know, it's probably where we're all headed.

(Now over to Al's bar a week later. FS is Pete and Stan Lee.)

Stan: Right now we're observing the singer of the Replacements, he's snorting coke waiting to give us this interview, he's been hounding us for awhile, I've agreed to help Pete...)

Flipside: How ready are you to talk now?

Paul: Fuck.. fuck, I'm ready as I'll ever be.

Flipside: Do you alter your brain with any stimulants?

Paul: Sometimes I take something to help me sleep.

Flipside: Medicine for old age?

Paul: It's foolish for idiots, what the hell is that stuff (to Stan).

Flipside: Water, want some? How come you

called your album "Let It Be"?

Paul: Why not? If someone complains about that then they're old and can't take a joke.

Flipside: Has anybody complained about it?

Paul: My older brother thought it was a really dumb idea. He said "Somebody did that before, you can't do it".

Flipside: I have a good source that says you might be signed to Warner Brothers?

Paul: Um, I'm not sure...

Flipside: Would you if you had the chance?

Paul: I mean it depends, I don't think we can change a whole lot. If they take us the way we are I'd jump at anything.

Flipside: If they offered you $100,000?

Paul: I'd do it for a carton of smokes.

Flipside: As far as the Replacements go, there are no rules.

Paul: Ah fuck no.

Flipside: Is that punk rock?

Paul: We have no musical guide lines to got by, so we figured, well, we can't really do what we're doing, so let's try something else we can't do.

MAD PARADE

Interviewed by Al and Pete in October.

Bill: There aren't enough bands around these days that are doing what we think is important. Doing stuff that makes you feel motivated, that makes you think. There's a lot of bands, but how many good ones? So instead of waiting, we decided to do it ourselves.

Joey: It seems like everybody is influenced by the same thing. A lot of people are afraid to have their ideas out. Like if people form a punk band, the sound like the Circle Jerks, not putting down the Circle Jerks but why sound like something we already have?

Ron: A lot of bands don't go back far enough to sound like the bands we like - their roots go back as far as the Circle Jerks.

Al: What are you guys doing that makes people think?

Bill: I think that a lot of punk rock groups tend to dictate to people and tell them "this is like this", "don't do this", but if you listen to any of the lyrics to our songs it's more or less ideas set up so people can make choices for themselves. I don't like to be told what to do, nobody really does. Instead of 'gang' mentality, it's 'individual' mentality. It seems to me when punk started off it was all about being individual, apart from the norm - these gangs and stuff, the fights, it's stupid. Put it this way, maybe those kids are getting into it now and they think that's what it's all about. Hardcore, punk whatever is here in L.A., but there is a lot more out there, so much older punk. BUT there aren't a lot of new groups today doing that kind of stuff with that kind of emotion and body. And that's what we're trying to do.

Joey: It's not like we're trying to bring up the past because a lot of our stuff is influenced by L.A. hardcore, it's faster, no band in '77 had a song as fast as "Frightened Again".

Al: Do you have problems because you are a "punk" band which is sort of inbetween a thrash/hardcore band or a pop/rock band?

Bill: Yeah, it's harder to get gigs because we are doing something that isn't done much now, but I believe if you stand by what you believe in and stick with it, and if it's good then people will eventually come around to it.

Mike: If we kick up enough ruckus people will listen.

Replacements – photo Pete L.

Mad Parade - photo Al

Al: What do you write about?

Mike: Show people how they're settleing for mediocrity.

Bill: Basically everyday life things, like thoughts about sticking up for yourself, not telling your parents to fuck off, but learning to stand up on your own two feet. What we say is important and we don't just rumble through it. I have my idea what the song is about but I'm more interested in what you think it's about. You may get something out of it that I never did and if you do then I succeeded because that's what I'm trying to do. I want you to think.

Al: Ok, you do a cover of "One Tin Soldier", how do you interpret that?

Mike: Early punks used to care...

Bill: It's a battle between good and evil, the law as we know it and everything else. We're down here and they're up there and all we want is what is naturally ours.

Al: You got your name from the Sex Pistols song...

Bill: Yeah, we thought it sounded good.

Joey: It's a world gone insane, people are crazy, they're greedy and stuff, it's like saying to them "You're a mad parade!".

Bill: No, I think Mad Parade is just a name, no real meaning, just a name. The Sex Pistols song he says something about "God save her mad parade", so her whole thing, the way it's all set up over there. So mad parade like insanity, like he says, ok...

Joey: Thank you..........

DECRY

Interviewed in early November by Al on the eve of their first major US tour. We did an interview with these guys about a year and a half ago, since then they've had personnel changes, have a single out, an LP out and are on many compilation LP's.

Al: So, what new?

Todd: We're slowing down a little bit and trying to put a little more intricacy into our music. I know how to play bass now!!

Pat: A lot of bands say they're going heavy metal but they're not, they're just progressing with their music. They are just progressing towards stuff they always wanted to do. Now they can pull it off. For us, now we're really

not heavy metal, but rocking out a little bit more. Kicking it out a little more.

Farrell: I think we are putting more energy into it. I don't think we're slowing down, there's more energy. Like the old saying, speed kills, you can go thrash out 90 miles per hour playing punk thrash or you can slow it down a little and put some real feeling into it –and the music can have a lot of feeling in it and be more powerful.

Pat: We still have real fast songs but when you hear them it's not like "da da da da da", it's fast but you can understand what's going on. It's not speed metal. It's just us.

Al: What do you think of the gig situation right now in L.A.?

Todd: Sucks.

Pat: People put down Goldenvoice but I think they are doing a really good job - they give a band a chance to play on a really fucking great sound system on a god like stage and they treat the bands real good. They pay bands and do good things for bands so I don't see why people cut them down.

Al: Do you think they spoil a band, I mean why play a club when you can wait and play a big Goldenvoice show?

Pat: What clubs are left? Music Machine, that's it. Roxannes is going way down. Cathay is gone. That was one of the worst places when it was open, it was a joke...

Al: What are your new songs about?

Farrell: We have a song on Flipside Vinyl Fanzine 2 called "Island Paradise".

Pat: Taz and I wrote that song two years ago, it was an Atoms song.

Farrell: But we all wrote the lyrics, it's about escapism - about escaping to your own, not going somewhere, just inside yourself. You want to get away from something so you go escape in your mind you can escape by thinking of your own place to go. It can be with drugs or it can be in your mind, ya know? Just slip away. "Nothing Sacred" is brand spanking new, it's a religious song, it's not against religion or against the devil, it's just opening your eyes to both sides. You worst enemy in either case is a closed mind....

NONE OF THE ABOVE

Interviewed by Al and Gus right after their big gig at the world famous Cathay de Grande.

Al: It seems you gained most of your notoriety with your "Live At The Crystal Pistol" tape.

Jeff: Right, that turned out to be a great thing for us for some reason. That was recorded on a 4 track, on mic was a clip on lapel mic, it worked fine. That's where we fucked up on the ep, we used real mics!

Al: How many copies did you sell?

Jeff: We sold about 20, but I gave out about 300. I still get requests for it. That was all on the strength of fanzine reviews - we never advertised for it. I made them one at a time on my stereo at home.

Bruce: "Propaganda Control" the cut on the MRR compilation is from that tape.

Al: Why do you suppose the choose you to represent that part of the world on an international compilation record?

Jeff: I think there were two reasons really, one was that they wanted bands that didn't have vinyl, although some of the Europeans did, and second they wanted obscure bands or bands from weird places. Like Oklahoma. I think they wanted to demonstrate that hardcore is an international or worldwide movement. And it is everywhere. Well people

Decry - photo Joe

NOTA - photo Al

don't realize that Oklahoma... the Sex Pistols played here, the Ramones played here before they were big and just about all the early punk bands did play Oklahoma. It's not like punk rock is a really new thing to anybody out there. There has been a scene for a long time.

Al: Being from Oklahoma, what inspired you to form a punk band?

Jeff: Boredom, I guess. Bruce and I were sitting around a couple of years ago and going "fuck, rocks dead". We'll have to start a band or something. So we started it for fun because we always wanted to be in a band. And we decided to go for it and take it as far as we could. Here we are, I guess this is as far as we can go!

Al: The west coast. What about lyrics?

Jeff: We don't consider ourselves a "political" band, although if you look at our lyrics it's right in there in the quagmire. We do try to write our songs honestly about shit that goes down around us. In that sense perhaps we exist in a real political environment, Oklahoma is a real Nazi place. A real redneck place. But we have songs like "Dumbshit", "Drugs and Sex" that aren't political. We want people to have fun at shows, we don't want to preach but then we are not totally apathetic slobs. we try to give people enough credit to think for themselves. I mean, how much is there to lyrics? If 90% of these bands were truthful they would say it's just shit they threw in there to fill it up.

Bruce: I think if we didn't have any lyrics the music would get the point across. You could take the Discharge approach and just have three lines that sum it up...

Jeff: The latest song that I've written is called "Identity Crisis" about how some people seem to be looking for heroes and some sense of identity out of the punk movement, rather than relying on their own smarts to get them through. People look to bands to be rock stars...

Al: Who came up with your name?

Jeff: Well Bob did and then when we decided to go with it he said "No way!"

Bob: No other name suited us so well.

Jeff: Plus we'd get real shitty billing in Tulsa like with all the new wave poseur bands so when they put us on the bill it was like "none of the above", so fuck these guys. That worked out cool. Plus we don't look like other punk bands, we don't sound like other punk bands, it's a real fitting name.

RASZEBRAE

Deborah Patino - vocals
Ingrid Baumgart - guitar/vocals
Janet Housden - drums
Katie Childe - bass
Perfect setting: the five of us are sitting in someones toolshed with Black Flag in the living room. There's still beer left in the plastic baby swimming pool. Is this Manhattan Beach? RZ have been together for 2 years and are all original members except for Janet who used to be in Red Cross and the Disposals. Interview by Mawshein.

Maw: What the hell is a Raszebrae?

Debbie: I thought of Zebrae and she thought of Ras. We went to college together and had a Music of India course and learned about the Rasa (the inner beam?).

Maw: Are you Ratt groupies?

All: A couple of us take care of their fan mail. Secretary stuff.

Maw: Some people say they can't hear or figure out the lyrics to your songs.

Katie: We don't really have any lyrics.

Maw: Tell me about one of your songs?

Ingrid: I wrote "Hit Or Miss". It's about Jimi Hendrix in a way after I read that dumb book "Hit Or Miss". I kind of got inspired. Stole the title right off.

Debbie: She gave the poem to me to read. We took it to rehearsal and wrote a song.

Katie: Then Ingrid does all this mock Jimi Hendrix stuff.

Debbie: Most of our songs you can guess what they're about by the title, but some are hard like "Rangeriders" which is about riding on life.

Janet: That's not what you told me!

Debbie: It's about literature, drugs and society all mished into one. The inward struggle. Used to be very angry.

Maw: Were you guys angry in the beginning?

Ingrid: I have nothing to be angry about.

Debbie: Our songs can be about anything, the feelings are more important than the subject. Something that just makes you feel where you have to write about it.

Maw: Do you write about your experiences?

Debbie: We change them into universal experiences.

Maw: The inevitable question: what are the advantages and disadvantages of being an all female band?

Janet: On one hand it's kind of a gimmick, people notice you more. But then people can be quick to dismiss you because a lot of gimmick bands can suck. People sometimes assume you're like that. Other people just think that girls are so lame, or really great, some expect less.

Debbie: Then there's the physical thing.

Ingrid: You don't have to worry about dressing in front of each other, you don't have to hide anything.

Katie: We all get on our periods at the same time.

Ingrid: I like playing with both guys and girls. Basically being in a band is just being who you are as a musician.

Raszebrae

Katie: I know a disadvantage: Lesbians! I wore a Castration Squad t-shirt once, it was all over for me man!

Ingrid: We're not going to talk about sex.

Maw: This is a somewhat permanent marriage?

Janet: Yes, we want to stay together and we want to be good. I want to do something with it. I don't want to be a secretary or a housewife. We'd like to be big and make a lot of money and be on the cover of BAM!

Maw: Do you want to play the Forum?

Katie: Yes, I want to be as big as Queen!

Maw: Where do you like playing?

All: Anti Club, On Club was good. Music Machine sucks, Madame Wongs is a brain fry. You get these poor guys with long hair in polyester.

Maw: How would you describe your music?

Ingrid: Zone rock and roll.

CIRCLE ONE

John Macias was Interviewed in late October. For those of you who don't know John is the lead singer/songwriter for L.A. based Circle One, is the main organizer of PUNX (loc___g promoters) and a member of the 'fam__'. He has been around for quite awhile and is quite a visible person in the scene...

Flipside: In the face of public criticism in Flipside (and other places) why has it taken you so long to grant us an interview or somehow answer to the public?

John: It has taken so long because I've felt in the past that we, as in PUNX, have a lot to accomplish and it would do more harm to talk about them instead of doing them.... When I first started going to shows, my hair was quite normal you could say, and it made no difference. Until I made friends with some skinheads and other punx who were later on showing up to gigs with black eyes and other injuries. I felt hurt that people would treat these kids like this for being different or dedicated as we say. So that's when I became Mr. Clean (aka skinhead). Then I found out what they were talking about and I lost friends who I thought were my friends (superficial jerks), and got teased, snubbed, harrassed, discriminated against – hey, you name it. I got it and as big as I am I didn't like it and stopped taking it. C'mon, when you start poking a dog with a stick, sooner or later it's gonna bite you. You gotta remember that back then we were a super duper minority 2 – 3 punx per school and sometimes not even that. So when we (dedicated patriots) went to gigs and consumed limited amounts of courage (black beauties and alcohol) we would go out onto the dance floor and have one great time (aka slam dance to nerds) and the only thing that ruined our night was seeing the type of people who were regularly harassing us (aka hippycrits). I can honestly say most of them were jerks getting what they came for: TROUBLE. Because of this (I also admit), innocent people got chased out because of the strong hatred and resentment towards them. Yes, back then a gig was our only escape from this ever condemning world. So we decided that the only way to spare the innocent was to tell all of them (hippycrits) to get their butts in the back and we'll pretend they're not their. Yes it seemed stupid but could you think of a better alternative and do it? I have to say it was a good move we made because what once was chaotic started to gradually disappear (not the longhairs, but the violence). You may be thinking, how does this answer the question of criticism. Well this is the flipside of the story: all those nasty, ridiculous letters were written by hippycrits who got offended because they didn't have the balls to change their appearance to take part in a growing movement and wanted to be accepted by a world who they say they hated so much for being so sheep like. And counted all of us dedicated patriots as fashion plates and trendies. Yes, so I let all of their half truth letters pile up knowing one day they'll all be answered and the truth will stand like it's done, like it's doing and like it always will. Amen.

Flipside: Are you still involved with Christians to the point that you were in the movie "Another State of Mind"?

John: I've always believed in Jesus Christ, but lived the Christian way for 8 months and slipped because of all the burdens and idiots I encountered in that time. So I was crawling with the rest for awhile. But I can honestly walk and see and hear and feel right now and I'm marching on that narrow path and all praises to the King for not forgetting about this soldier John or the very few in the scene for that matter.

Flipside: What is your relationship with Richard Bolton or the Wig Factory?

John: I first met Rich when he was doing shows at Bards Apollo, we played out second and third shows there. After that we went up north and did some promotion with Paul the Rat. By the time we came back we had done three shows at the T-Bird and were barely staying alive. So Rich booked our next two shows and saved PUNX from financial ruin by getting rid of guarantees and working on a percentage basis (getting paid what you're worth). As for the Wig, it was the headquarters for PUNX. One day we were working out front on some landscaping and some punk rock kids (runaway) started helping us. When we found out their predictament we decided to give them food and shelter. Eventually the word spred and within a month we were supporting 25 runaways. About 1/2 were addicted to various kinds of drugs and came from broken homes. Our bills were tremendous, but all of the people who attended our concerts (T-Bird, Cathay) were actually helping us pay for necessities, in other words, we couldn't have done it without you.

Flipside: What is the "Family"?

John: The Family is a name that started surfacing about the time PUNX started surfacing. At the time we had multiplied through different areas, so everybody didn't quite know everybody and sometimes a standoff would appear. The older brothers would get between them and tell them to cool it and that we're brothers and brothers don't fight, but protect each other from bouncers and big jarheads out to hurt people in the pit. So the name Family was born. And out of all the partiers, musicians and peace keeping soldiers came bands who were shouting for what they believed in. Some people call it a gang because there are (very) few idiots around, 3 or 4, who have to use a name to back up their big mouth, please ignore them and confront me personally, not in front of the idiot, and I'll give them a verbal lashing or worse.

Flipside: On to Circle One, when did the band actually start? I saw an early gig you Circle One and Suicidal Tendencies and there seemed to be no animosity then, is there now?

John: Circle One formed in November of 1980. As for ST, we've been friends since before that show, during and forever after. It seems ST has the same target problem as us. People seem to point at people that everyone can recognize and the more lies and exaggerations the jucier the story.

Flipside: What does the name Circle One mean?

John: Circle One was named by the founder of the band Michael Vallejo and it stands for: Circle - a group of people bound together by a common interest. One - Undivided, forming a whole. United.

Circle One - photo Al

Flipside: What are some bands that have influenced Circle One?

John: Musical influences include: hard rock bands, 60's bands, thrash and heavy metal bands. Favorite bands include: Kenny Rogers, Frank Zappa, Jethro Tull, Beatles, Frank Sinatra, Tito Puente, Jimi Hendrix, Cream, Doors and Aerosmith.

FLIPSIDE NUMBER 45

DETOX·DOGGY STYLE·C2D
SAMHAIN·JUSTICE LEAGUE
AGNOSTIC FRONT·A.O.D.
INCEST CATTLE·STEPS·SNFU
UNIFORM CHOICE·CORPSE
CHUMBAWAMBA

"Woooooooooooo wooo woooo wooo
Came out here in '33
Just an old jalopy and me
We left the east to come out west
This is the town I love the best
I love you town, I love you town.....
Came out here in '44
She couldn't get a job so became a whore
We left the east to come out west
This the town I love the best
I love you town, I love this town
Came out here in '55
I was so jacked up, barely alive
We left the east to come out west
This is the the town I love the est
I bet you I bet you I bet you I bet
I bet you I bet you I bet you I bet..."
"ick the Emm" – DETOX

ISSUE #: 45
DATE: February 1985
FORMAT: 8 1/2x11, rotary web offset with 2 color glossy cover.
PAGES: 76
PRICE: $1.00
PRESS RUN: 9000

With this issue Flipside tried an experiment and used a higher grade of inside paper, which worked real nice but was quickly abandoned because of the cost. Otherwise, were cranking them out and distribution is bigger than ever. We started an exclusive distribution arrangement with WOT in London, and since our overseas sales have gone way up! And we even break even on it.

The real big news is the re-formation of Flipside Records. After a few years, we decided to try our hand at a record label again. Last year we started with the release of Vinyl Fanzine Vol. 1, a compilation put out by Gasatanka/Enigma, of which we compiled.

This time it's Vinyl Fanzine Vol. 2 on Flipside/Gasatanka. The next two releases are the debut from Detox and an Iconoclast ep, which are on 'Flipside Records'. At this point L.A.'s bigger independent labels were not paying attention to what was going on in the local punk scene, so we decided that we'd try to get some vinyl out by deserving, but ignored bands.

As for the scene, Orange Country is on the rise again, with a scene focused on a small by very exciting club called the Flash Dance, many new bands quickly gain a local following. Bands like Doggy Style, Uniform Choice, HVY DRT, Large Hardware etc are making a name for themselves without even playing a gig in L.A.

DETOX

Interviewed at Control in February by Al and Frank.
Detox started in 80/81 with a line-up that consisted of Shirley on vocals, Weeny on bass, tony on guitar and eventually Dan on drums. After many personnel and instrument changes, Krantz joined in 1983 and Human in 1984. This is the 'matured' line-up. Detox have a very unique, driving, punk rock sound, this is probably due to Tony's infamous unique guitar style.....

Tony: I don't play regular guitar, I don't know how. People go "Can I play your guitar?" I go sure, "Oh my God"...

Human: Being the bass player its extremely difficult to keep up with him, everything is a different tuning.

Tony: It's a set thing I learned when I was 13, it's... it's....

Human: It's completely wrong, the first guitar he picked up was tuned wrong and he always tunes to that wrong tuning. He has all new chords that correspond to the right chords and new ones that don't correspond to

anything. He always breaks strings because half of his strings are 8 notes above where they should be the other half are 8 notes below. We have a song called "The String Breaking Song" to cover these long gaps....... (Detox, as a name sounded good but was never a serious statement until recently when both Krantz and Human quit their drug habit the hard way.)

Human: Yeah, we are really in Detox now, real detox....

Krantz: My girlfriend told me they had a deathbed priest there ready to read me my last rites... It was just dirt, they found five different kinds of drugs...

Human: I thought I WAS gonna die. I had a fucking tube that was threaded right through my heart and came out on top – for three days. Kidney AND liver failure are instigated by R.I.P. drug abuse.

Krantz: I had a thermometer up my ass, a tube up my dick, a thing through my chest, five hoses coming out of my arms... but now we are detox...

Human: I thought I could fucking skate on anything, and I ended up there........

Al: So, what are some of your songs and what are they about?

Dan: "Linoleum", you know when you get aluminum pans and you put it on linoleum and it scratches it real weird?

Al: Uh...

Dan: Linoleum, aluminum, when you crash it on there, I sing about that stuff. Nothing political, just everyday stuff, human things.

Tony: "Placidol Polka", I wrote that one when I was indulging in these little man made wonders, but it's about misfortune and discouraging aspects of drug...

Krantz: Like when you wake up and you don't know where you are and feel like an idiot.

Dan: See, we're not a drug band, I don't sing about drugs anymore at all.

Tony: "Child Of One" is about at time where

Detox bring the ceiling down at the Cathay – photo Al

Justice League - photo O

there were all these girls about 13 or 14 losing their virginity behind Oki Dogs and Godzillas and I thought it was really a joke, because they wouldn't use any kind of contraceptives, so I wrote "Child Of One" because they kinda deserved it.

Dan: I change the lyrics every show pretty much except for the standards like "Submerge" or "No Reggae In Russia", Human and Tony write the music...

Krantz: I try to figure out a beat!

Human: Tony write these rockin' songs and my songs are just fucked beats... Real repetitive, real droney...

Tony: I couldn't play heavy metal if I wanted to. That's bullshit music, those big leads are bullshit. Even if I could I don't think I would and I can play bullshit leads!!

Al: I noticed that you like to play sober.

Tony: What's the best way to relate to people you're with except being like them? It a coincidental thing that our audience is drunk, and it makes it a lot of fun.

JUSTICE LEAGUE

Interviewed at the Flashdance by Al and Kerry Love in February.
Justice League are: John Roa - vocals, Ted Edison - lead guitar, Skip Turner - drums, Brian Hoffman - guitar, Shawn Godfrey - bass.

Al: So what is Justice League all about?

John: The name came for a bunch of different sources and means, I guess you could say, justice for all, like we're colored blind, we don't see colors, we only see people. Straight or not straight, black or white...

Al: You mean you're not a straight edge band?

John: Uh, no. We're just punk rockers. Me and Brian are the only ones that don't do anything, don't drink or smoke.

Ted: The band is mainly based upon unity and peace, bringing people together, everybody having a good time.

Brian: Where's 'musical influences'?

Al: Ok....

Ted: Ranges from Neos to Metalica...

John: The three people who have influenced my singing are Henry Rollins, Leonard Graves, and Ian MacKay. Those are my three favorite singers of all time.

Shawn: I would say Broken Bones, Varukers, Partisans and Fallout...

Brian: He likes all the English stuff, I like metal stuff: Anthrax, Metalica...

Skip: I like everything from weird stuff to hardcore...

Ted: I like MDC, Queen, Kansas, Phil Collins, anybody who has any degree of talent.

Al: Who writes the lyrics?

John: Me.

Brian: We try to get together and we try to think up something positive.

John: It's weird because people condemn us for flocking with the sheep for writing about unity and stuff, but why don't people say that about Die Kreuzen when they write about their scene? We write about what we see around our scene - and that is total chaos, nobody ever wants to get together so we write about unity. If we lived in South Carolina I'm sure we'd write about hicks or cows and beer, but we live in Chino and Pomona where it's really violent.

Brian: We have cows, but no beer, ha ha...

Ted: A lot of our songs are really self explanatory, like "Be Yourself" and "Use Your Own Head". It's just think about what you're doing before you do it.

Brian: Those are some of the older songs, we're getting more into personal dealings.

Ted: The new stuff is dealing with how our minds work, why we wonder about certain things that we don't understand. You have to sing about what you feel, that's what this band is all about, expressing yourself. It's preaching but I'd like to be like Dave MDC and take a half an hour before each song and tell people what you really feel. Sometimes words just can't say enough.

Skip: It's hard to grasp the meaning when he's singing the words out so fast.

Shawn: Right now we're trying to get away from the basic 4 chord progression, and sometimes it sounds metalish or rock, but hey that's ok, we're trying to get more perspective in our sound.

Ted: We're getting slower, but it's still powerful, a powerful clear sound is what we're trying to get.

Brian: As long as it ends up through Marshalls.

CONDEMNED TO DEATH

Interviewed in Pasadena by Al and Gus.
C2D are: Scott - vocals, Tim - guitar, Keith - bass and Mike - drums.

Al: So where were we, talking about your drug habit...

Tim: What have you got? (ha ha ha)

Al: Does this influence your songwriting?

Keith: Oh yeah "Stoned to Death"...

Tim: No, it's not really about that at all.

Scott: As far as habit go, I think drinking is probably our main and worst habit.

Keith: This band is spilt up, those two (Scott and Mike) are alkies and we (Tim and Keith) smoke pot. That's how we get a balance.

Mike: They're like two Hunter Thompsons and we're like two Ed McManns.

Scott: Dean Martins, yeah....

Al: What about your name?

Tim: We got that name on Easter Sunday two years ago.

Keith: It's a conversion for LSD to C2D.

Tim: It was a choice between "Hand Full of Flowers" or "Satans Penis"... we got this letter from a guy in prison and he asked if we knew that C2D was the real abbreviation for Condemned to Death behind bars. He was on death row, but he wanted an album, we sent him one and he grooved on it.

Al: What a fan! What do you want to get across on tour?

Scott: Craziness, chaos, I'm into chaos, that's my main thing. The more chaos the better the show. I don't like people just standing around ya know?

Al: What do you think of the term 'horror band' being applied to you guys?

Scott: We don't like it but Tim does. (Tim being the big horror flick fan of the band).

Tim: I think it's part of the whole picture.

Scott: A horror band to me is like Specimen or Bauhaus.

Al: What would you call yourselves?

Mike: Just heavy, heavy...

Scott: Heavy with power. Just put heavy in front of everything: heavy punk rock, heavy metal, heavy horror rock...

Al: What about the Satanic stuff...

Tim: We've read Alister Crowley but we're not satanists or anything."

Kieth: We've read the Satanic Bible and have been informed of all the ways but we don't let it get to us.

Al: I noticed you don't use pentagrams...

Scott: Naw naw...

Tim: It's a gimmick for these heavy metal bands but we don't need that. There was a time when we would anoint ourselves with success oils before we played but...

Keith: We've been exorcised!

Al: Have you ever been called a 'peace band'? You're on the International Peace compilation.

Tim: A lot of bands are tied in with the political bands, I mean we're all underground and anti-authority.

Keith: Everyone has their own personal politics and we all don't agree on it.

Tim: We have the feelings, we're just not writing blatently political songs anymore. It's just getting to be the same sort of thing over and over, we didn't feel like we had anything new to say....

Keith: And we couldn't say it any better than anyone else anyway.

Al: Do you think it inspired you to write more politically when you lived at the Vats?

Keith: We were more influenced by the things around us, it was a communal living situation with all the street types.

Tim: You come home every night and DRI is doing their same set, echoing thru the building...

Keith: Or "John Wayne Was A Nazi" 8 million

Adrenalin OD – photo Joe

times, we pick up on that stuff.
Tim: But we did humorous songs right from the start.

ADRENALIN O.D.

Interviewed by Donny the Punk outside of CBGB's in New York Dec. 2 1984
Donny: How did the band come together and evolve?
Paul: I met up with them around 5 years ago maybe, Me and Dave started, he was a friend of their too, and Jack..
Donny: You're all from NE New Jersey?
Dave: Pretty much, Paul lives about a 1/2 hour away, and we all live a couple of minutes away from each other.
Donny: How do you songs get written?
Jack: We listen to a lot of radio and steal everyone else's ideas..
AOD: We sit around and talk and come up with ridiculous ideas.
Donny: On the album, y'all seem to be making a lot of observations of people as a typical style.
Bruce: A lot of the stuff is what we grew up around, like jocks that just aspire to be on a football team, that's New Jersey high school. Get sent to the pros, get dumped. That's a true story, "Clean And Jerk", and they're stuck in a gas station because they're too stupid to take advantage of schooling or anything.
AOD: What?
Bruce: I don't know, but it sounded intelligent didn't it?
Paul: They're about things that happen to us everyday, not like any ideals.
Dave: We use our gift of sarcasm to try to approach it.
Donny: Who wrote the song "White Hassle"?
Paul: I wrote that.
Donny: Could you compare that to "Corporate Death Burger" by MDC?
Paul: "White Hassle" is just about like nasty people that work at White Castles. You go in there and they're all nasty with you.
Jack: MDC are taking it on a corporate, more widespread thing, like anti-corporation. We're just anti-hassle.
Donny: It's from a more personal perspective, right?

Jack: That's what most of our stuff is, personal experience.
Bruce: It's just a ritual in New Jersey.
Donny: How about "Corporate Disneyland"?
Bruce: Just drive through Jersey, that's what it is. So much space, the real estate is really high, everywhere you look there's corporate parks and office buildings. It's like Disneyland.
AOD: If there's an empty lot, 2 months later there's an office building. They're not even filling them up, just building them. Beauty has left. Any trees, they're just choppin' em all down.
Bruce: It's like the Garden State is gonna be the Cement State pretty soon.
Donny: That seems to be your comment on the corporate level.
AOD: (Loud mock anguish) Oh God no! (laughter)........

AGNOSTIC FRONT

In sociobiolgy, "leadership" is defined by who gets attention from whom. By this standard Agnostic Front is without a doubt the band which "leads" the New York City hardcore scene. Often at the center of controversy, the band is deliberately hard to define ("agnostics" is philosophy deny the possibility of knowing Absolute Truth). With their first lp "Victim In Pain" now out on Ratcage Records, people can evaluate their lyrics and music for themselves. More difficult is the question of how well the members of the band practice what they proclaim, and how they have handled their position of leadership. But nothing about Agnostic Front is easy.
The band was interviewed by Donny the Punk at CBGB's on November 4: Vinnie Stigma, the bands founder on guitar; Roger the singer; and Rob Kabula bass player. A new drummer, Jimmy was added in January.
Donny: Since there are a lot of Flipside readers who haven't heard a great deal about Agnostic Front, let's start off with a little history about the band.
Vinnie: We started out with a bunch of guys, that were just regular guys, that came to the shows, all friends; Agnostic Front was always at every show, supporting the scene in every way, and those are the guys that are in the band, all my friends, and that's what it's all about. Basically a lot of them weren't musicians when we first started... That was about 2 1/2 years ago.
Rob: I was in the band for awhile, then quit, then rejoined them. They begged me to come back.
Donny: (To Roger) You been in the band since the beginning?
Rob: (prompting): Since I got out of jail in Cuba.
Roger: Since I got out of jail in Cuba.
Donny: When was that?
Roger: (embarrassed, declines invitations from bandmates to pursue that one any further) I wasn't the original singer tho, there was about 3 singers before me.
Donny: How long have you been singing?
Roger: Me? Oh wow, a year and 1/2, 2 years.
Vinnie: 2 years, I've been trying to play guitar, I always make mistakes but then again we're not Van Halen. We're a hardcore band, no rockstars.
Donny: How much have you evolved

Agnostic Front at 12XU – photo Thomas Ink Disease

musically in the past year or so?

Vinnie: We have evolved a real lot, a real. In the beginning we started out with just regular crazy skinhead kids...

Roger: Not musician kids...

Vinnie: Dancing to the band. It was a good unity thing, a bunch of guys having a good time. It wound up evolving into better music.

Roger: Musically, they couldn't play and shit, it took Vinnie up til now to play, he's doing better tho! (laughs). We're basically a hardcore band. That's what we'll always be into. We have a little metal lick here and there, we have a little bit of everything. You got old punk in it and stuff like that.

Donny: Y'all have been in some ways, according to some people, "spiritual leaders" of the skinhead group and to a large extent the New York hardcore scene itself, that is my own perception. How does this effect the way the band works?

Roger: Well, the reason why a lot of kids like us- not just skins, not just punks, hardcore, we get every type of crowd, is because we're at every show and we always support. We don't sing any anti- a lot of bands sing anti-peace songs, even tho we don't believe in world peace, we're not gonna sing about what we don't believe in, we wanna sing about what we believe in and what we could do about it. We believe in peace within the scene, but not world peace.

Donny: Do you feel like your lyrics are really getting across to your audience?

Rob: Yeah, people dance to them and read them and understand them.

Roger: That's one main reason why we did this record with the open up cover and lyrics and everything.

Vinnie: We try to pull the scene together, like when we started the New York BYO chapter and we did a lot of good stuff like that. We put on shows, we started bands, we got bands minimum wages in clubs, we try to make union style, you know. We never really did no wrong, like Maximum Rock N'Roll used to say, there's no National Front movement in New York, that doesn't exist.

Donny: The NY hardcore scene has a very strange reputation on the West coast.

Vinnie: Yeah!

Donny: And Agnostic Front is part of that strange reputation.

Roger: Just because we're skinheads, right, and the majority of the kids, it's just peer pressure - you get a haircut and all of your friends get a haircut. The majority of the kids got haircuts, that's not our fault. We didn't tell them to shave their heads.

Vinnie: We're proud Americans, my uncle died for this country and I'm not gonna see my uncles death go in vain.

Roger: We love our country, not necessairly how our government works... We love our country, if they're coming in here, we're gonna do something about it, but we're not going to fight in some other country while the US and USSR leaders sit back... We're not a preaching band. We'll tell you what's wrong and what's right, what we think is wrong and right, and that may not be what you think - everybody has got different beliefs.

Donny: How do you reconcile the rejection of the system?

Roger: We do things opposite, first of all. We try to keep away from any big systematic thing. Most of us, we don't vote, we're anti-ar, we don't do a lot of things.

Donny: In one song you say the system is essentially anti-social and is gonna fall. Is that

a wish or do you see that happening?

Vinnie: Yeah, it's like a dream, sooner or later all of them fall. Rome fell, it might take a little bit longer for this one. Destroy power not people.

Donny: What is the "hardcore handbook" in the song "Hiding Inside"?

Roger: People - - you're hiding your feelings and trying to be something when you're just not. You're afraid to express yourself and lose your pride. People trying to be real macho and trying to be like... a comic book on "How To Be A Skinhead" or "How To Be A Hardcore".

Vinnie: Textbook skin, something like this: he wears these boots, gonna kick ass...

Roger: I'm just saying; try to be yourself. It's just a book that I saw in my mind.

Donny: Do you think it's widespread here, people trying to live up to an image?

Roger: I tried to live up to an image! I was young and I figured, wow, I'll be the hardest skinhead or something like that, bullshit! Why can't I just be myself?

Donny: Is that why you grew your hair long?

Roger: My hair has nothing to do with it. I can have hair down to my fucking asshole, and I'm still, and I'm still an asshole! (Laughter) I don't care what the fuck you want to call me. The punk style is really exploited right now, and we want to try to stay away from it. We want to stay away from being exploited.

SNFU

Interviewed by Al, Hud and Joy at the Flashdance.

Al: Ok, what are some of the song titles off the album you've been recording?

Mark: "Broken Toy", "Bodies On The Wall", "Cannibal Cafe"...

Al: Is that about junk food.

Chi: No. Actually I was in this restaurant and I was eating this really bad hamburger and I was thinking, how do I know this isn't another human being? So I thought about this cafe where all they serve is humans. It's just a joke song, a lot of songs are funny in that sort of way.

Al: That didn't turn you into a vegetarian or anything?

Chi: No way, I'm a carnivore! "To the max" as they say here in California. What I heard most was "Got any free stickers dude, DUDE!!"

Al: It's cool, ehhh, EHHHH!!! (laughter!) Who writes your lyrics?

Chi: It just turns out that I have more time to write lyrics because I don't play an instrument, so I write a lot. Everybody does contribute and are capable of writing lyrics, I'm not like the only one that is allowed.

Evan: I write lots of songs but I can never think of them the next day, but I wrote one "Money Matters", I just wrote the music.

Chi: I wrote the lyrics, it's about how sort of depressing it is that life has to revolve around a little piece of paper, money. But you need money to see yourself on to the next day. I write whatever pops into my head and I write it down then like a week later I look at it and if I get a kick out of it we'll use it. We try to to just dwell on just one subject matter, we like to go on to a lot of different things. We have 14 songs on the album and they're about 14 different things. We want a variety and we don't want to stagnate.

Al: The you couldn't lump SNFU into a "political band" or a "funny band"...

Jimmy: We try to avoid that, we try to avoid the labels.

Chi: As a band we don't have a message like some big political thing, but we all have our personal things.

Mark: Everybody in the band is different, we are individuals, we don't think like a band or have a band stand.

Al: What does SNFU stand for?

Chi: It's a military term that they used to do a long time ago, it's called Snafu. Let's say a plane is crashing, the guy would say "snafu snafu" meaning he's in trouble. Situation Normal All Fucked Up, or something like that. It has an "A" in it but a lot of people were drawing a circle around it, ha ha, so we left the "A" out. We used "Societies No Fuckin' Use" for awhile but our ideals have been changing and stuff. How many times can you say these words, so we just say SNFU. Just make something up.

Al: It seems a lot of people run into that problem with initial names. Jimmy, since you write the music, what do you draw your influences from?

Jimmy: I try to listen to any kind of music, I don't hate any kind of music. I do have favorite bands. Two of them are Personality Crisis from Canada and Minor Threat. But everything I see influences me either positively or negativily. I can see bands that I wouldn't want to sound like as much as ones I like.

Al: Being Canadian, what do you think of the United States?

Mark: I don't think it's that much different than

SNFU with Joy at Carl's Jr. - photo Hud

Uniform Choice: Pat, Pat2, Dave, Vic - photo Al

Canada, you can't really even tell!

Jimmy: I don't think there's anything wrong with the American people, they're just like everyone else, but the American government is a bit aggressive at times. I've noticed that the police are a bit more assertive and aggressive.

UNIFORM CHOICE

Interviewed by Al and Kerry Love Canal at the Flashdance.

Al: Why did you pick a name like 'Uniform Choice' and what does it mean to you?

Pat: Yeah, some people don't really understand the meaning, it's really our ideas about the scene. Everyone is going in so many different ways these days and nobody wants to work for the best. And what we think is the best, not necessarily everybody fitting into one mold but everyone seeing that the best thing to do is to make a positive scene. So when everyone has that choice in mind, for a positive scene, then it would be a uniform choice. That's when we feel the scene will be the best.

Al: What are some aspects that would make it a positive scene?

Pat: Just kids going to shows realizing that there is a time to drink and a time not to, not to make the clubs social hangouts where you just come to hang out in front, and cause fights. Fights are the worst. When people get drunk it causes a lot of stupidity. And when they hang out in the parking lots it causes the police to come by. It only takes a few people to mess it up for everyone else. we just think that when people just really use their heads and think and honestly see what punk rock is not. It is being yourself, but not going out of

your way to be an asshole. There are rights of others and you shouldn't infringe on their rights.

Al: Are you guys straight edge?

Pat: Yeah.

Dave: Yeah.

Al: I noticed you make the point "straight and alert" on your shirts.

Pat: That's just one of our songs, straight and alert is just how we feel... who farted man!!?

Pat 2: O farted shit......

Pat: Straight and alert means we feel the best time people can think and have a clean head is when they're straight. Not fucked up or anything.

Al: It seems that you guys have gotten established really fast and are now a big draw out here in Orange County.

Pat: Well see, we really don't sing about social matters like political matters. We sing about stuff that kids can relate to. They see that we are really trying to make an effort. Our message is serious but when we get out there on stage we're out to have fun. We do everything to support the scene and keep it going....

Al: Where do you go to school Pat?

Pat: At Pepperdine.

Pat 2: He's a baseball player dude. A pitcher.

Pat: Yeah, I'm on a scholarship. I've always been you know, I don't have the jock attitude so I don't talk about it. We have a song about those kinds of people. I've been around them all my life and I know exactly how they are - so when people see me they can't believe I'm a jock, but I am. It's just something I'm good at and I don't see why I should waste it. Plus I've got to get an education somewhere, and it's a good school so I'm taking advantage of it.

Al: Let's talk about your musical influences.

I'm sure you've heard you sound like Minor Threat.

Pat: Minor Threat, 7 Seconds, MIA, but it's mainly Minor Threat. What happends is I have some basic morals and we all basically support the same ideas. We don't have a big set but what we have is good and we've taken time to write it and yeah, we are all influenced by Minor Threat... We'll never change, like bands going heavy metal and stuff. That's great for them. We know what we like and we like this. When people say we sound like Minor Threat we think we don't sound like anybody but I can take that as a complement because I think Minor Threat were the best punk band that were ever around. So for us to come along and keep up that image, that's fine with me.

Victor: We might try experimenting in the future.

Dave: But right now we are happy and we're gonna stick with what we have.

Pat 2: Fast pace, high energy.

DOGGY STYLE

Interviewed at the Flashdance by Al, Kerry and Thomas Ink Disease.

Al: Explain "Doggy Style".

Brad: Doggy Style is an expression of freedom. If you want to get into sexual origins, um, you have to look at one thing - you have the option of any position, we choose Doggy Style because you don't have to hold back, you can go all out.

Al: Do you all prefer Doggy Style?

Dan: Ed: Definitely!!

Lou: Yeah!

Brad: We wouldn't have it any other way.

Lou: When the name Doggy Style is presented to someone the first reaction is maybe a chuckle, a deep laugh or maybe a calm one, all in all it's a humorous thing. I guess what the band tries to touch on is the positive, happier, humorous side of things, rather than the dark, gloom, negative side of things. We see the scene or the music as two different worlds; you have the negative and the positive world. Humor is the positive thing, the term "Doggy Style" is a humorous thing plus positive is what the band is all about.

Thomas: How about an example of that in one of your songs?

Brad: A lot of our songs are serious with positive messages and a lot are humorous, it's a blend.

Lou: You have to grab someones attention first, that's the catch. We'll make you chuckle with the names of some of our songs like "Nymphomaniac" or "Rookie Cop". They're humourous and if you blend humor with a serious positive message we think we're accomplishing something.

Brad: It's a new way of breaking through to the scene.

Al: What is the serious side?

Brad: Well we're not a straight edge band, but I'm straight edge, so is Lou and Dan, Ed pounds brews with the best of them. I don't think there will ever be a total scene unity, but as long as you give the message to everybody, or at least think, and come to the clubs and help shows go on, and not just come to fight... They have to have their gangs but they have to do that some place other than a club. I don't associate gang mentality with punk rock. Everyone is going to different no matter where you are in the world, you can't start putting people down for dressing

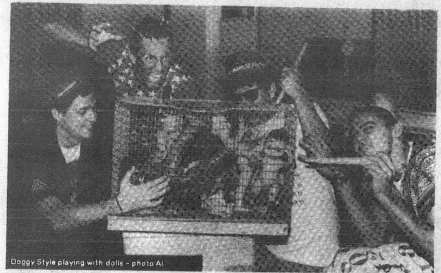

Doggy Style playing with dolls – photo Al

certain way...

Dan: Or dressing at all...

Brad: Right, nudity is the answer if you ask me.

Dan: Right, Brad was probably the most open minded in there (he just got finished with a nude performance), can you express yourself that easily? Most people have sexual holdbacks, you starting breaking those barriers when you start letting loose. The kids at first, when the pants come off, they're all like "what the hell is he doing??" Then they're over looking and they're having even more fun. Now they can jump in and do it Doggy Style with their pants on and it's alright...

Lou: Let's not misinterpret what the "Doggy Style Hop" is all about. In the 50's our parents did the bunny hop, back then it was considered disgusting and risque. Well, we're right in the middle of the sexual revolution, Boy George leading the way, and it's time for a new and innovative dance. "Doggy Style" is not a gross or perverted gesture, it's a statement of unity, it's working as one. But it's also a way for kids to have some fun, that's what our shows are all about.

SAMHAIN

Samhain may be a new band to some, but the characters in this band have achieved legend status to others. First and most noteworthy is lead singer, song writer, guitarist Glenn Danzig. A former founding member of the infamous Misfits, and head of Plan 9 Records (Misfits and Samhain label). Glenn is a mastermind at transforming the suspense and terror like found in the best horror films, from splatter to a foggy crypt, into a personal, musical and lyrical experience. Sure he carries a lot from the Misfits tradition, but that parting was more because of personal than musical reasons.

On bass we have Eerie Von, who was best know for his drumming in Rosemary's Babies, on drums Steve Zing from Mourning Noise and Damian on guitar.

Al: Where did you dig up the name Samhain?

Glenn: Samhain is the real Halloween – the season of the dead. It sort of signified the death of the Misfits and the rise of Samhain. Samhain is something I personally was into and still am.

Al: As far as lyrics go, I didn't notice a big

change between Samhain over the Misfits.

Glenn: Lyrically things have changed far more drastically than you've noticed. The lyrics are more challenging and severe than they've ever been.

Al: How important do you think your stage look is in the overall picture?

Eerie: At least 50%.

Steve: As much as the music.

Glenn: At least as important as the music in our band.

Al: With the subject matter that Samhain deals with, it seems like it would be easy for

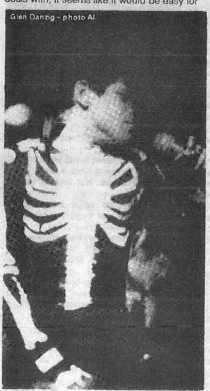

Glen Danzig – photo Al

you guys to slip a few pentagrams into the art work.

Glenn: Al, you asshole, why tag a Satanic tag on us if you don't know what you're talking about.

Al: I'm just asking why not.

Glenn: I do lots of research into my subjects and many things people think are Satanic are

not.

Eerie: Rather than have to think about our stuff it's easy to just lump it in with all the other crap.

Al: Ok, then what do you think of bands like Motley Crue who do play up the Satanic imagery stuff?

Glenn: The music is ok except for the vocals, but their fake image has been done to death. Regardless of your image of us, we do not play up a satanic imagery thing and do not use pentagrams.

Al: I don't think of you that way at all, I guess the difference is between real and staged horror?

Glenn: Yes, that's as far as it goes.

Al: No devil worshippers.

Glenn: No devil worshippers.

Al: What do you think of God worshippers, religion?

Glenn: I hate organized religion.

Steve: I don't care, to each his own.

Eerie: Organized religion has too many rules.

Al: What are some recent things that have inspired songs?

Glenn: Good and evil and the constant struggle between them. Peoples unwillingness to accept life and death.

Al: What do you want to do with Samhain?

Steve: I'd like to be the first band to make it and not sell out.

Eerie: I want to get on Carson.

Glenn: I want to do what I want musically, lyrically – make a living and not prostitute my music.

Al: Samhain is really into audience participation when you play, do you ever feel you sacrifice performance for that contact?

Glenn: No. It's part of the live thing, but sometimes it gets a little bit hectic on stage (especially in L.A.).

Al: Do you write songs with catchy choruses for the sing along thing?

Glenn: No, none of our songs are written purposely like that. For example in "He Who Cannot Be Named" everyone sings the backup melody at our shows. You never know what people will pick up on.

CHUMBWAMBA

Chumbawamba are obviously a band most people have heard of. Their individuality in their songs, both music wise and lyrically show their intelligence, and the theatre work that they do at their gigs, proving how important those lyrics really are, make Chumbawamba stand out amongst the hundreds of bands with the same feelings. They are a band that are not interested in listing their line-up, giving out photos or logos and their music is very appealing. It's not three chord thrash, more slower, more melodic, and the lyrics are very very easy to make out through all the varying speeds/styles in their songs. In fact, I should think that people from all ages and walks of life could easily listen to them and everyone can learn something. I cannot think of a word to sum up how excellent this band are, they are the most inspiring band I have come across and liable to come across. Extremely thought provoking. All I can say is go see them if you get the chance.

Interview done by Mick of Obituary fanzine on Nov. 21 1984

Mick: Where did you get the idea to do theatre work along with your songs at gigs?

Chumba: The idea to mix theatre and song isn't new, there's a long tradition of this sort of thing amongst other types of music. Unfortunately, the rock and roll traditions have instead used swivelling hips, sneers, guitar-phallus posing etc as substitutes for theatre. The way we use it helps a lot, it is an aid to make what we are saying/singing about so much clearer. The clarity is very important to us. We've been in different bands before, but we've used theatre before in a different way. The problem may be where as you can see a band and get something out of it quite a lot of times, you get bored if you watch a film more than twice. It's a challenge to have to change the theatre parts, it's much harder than changing the music or so it seems. We'll carry on using theatre as long as it's interesting and useful.

Mick: Do you think that the visuals have the effect that you want? Do people like it?

Chumba: The effect is that a certain visual image fixes in someones mind longer than a tune or a sentence. I think most people like it. Maybe because we live in a TV society where we've been brought up to be able to concentrate on visuals.

Mick: Do any foreign bands interest you? What do you think of the European/US scenes?

Chumba: Personally, I think it's important that we learn something from each other and not just trade different cultures. I think some foreign music can be really interesting, from Crucifucks to kuci. What can U.S. thrash bands tell me baout America, McDonalds, cruise missles. I'm literally asking for that information, it's important in terms of how we can get rid of all the plastic crap the U.S. imports. What can we learn from European music? Well, what about squatting, about organizing resistance etc. We must communicate our ideas. The "scenes" are catalysts for real action, hopefully music should give it that push into movement.

Mick: What U.K. bands do you like? Do you still think there's a big gap between different types of bands?

Chumba: I like ome defunct bands that inspired me to do something more than just play rock and roll; like ATV, Fall etc. And bands sin the UK now who are inspiring me to think about things; like Crass, Flux, No Defenses etc. Actually I like people in bands more more than the bands themselves in most cases.

Mick: Although you obviously wouldn't sell out, would you ever go out to get a wider audience? As the different styles of you music could easily appeal to more people.

Chumba: Yes we would, we do have to compromise in some ways in order to avoid getting boxed in and useless. But we do have to draw the line somewhere. We've seen bands who want a wider audience, their door prices go up, their records get dearer, their principles fall and their audience gets less and less militant in their attitudes. You can't sell the non-violent revolution on Top Of The Pops! You can sell the slogans, but you always loose the heart, the inspiration.... Dance music is for feet, not heads and radio music is for wall paper so.......

Mick: How long have you held the views that you have? What do you think started your thinking the way you do?

Chumba: Personally I started thinking about things for myself whilst in school but it wasn't until about 4 years ago that I really sorted out

C2D: Scott, Keith, Tim and Mike - photo O

what was going on in the world. And it's only in the last 3 years that I've been working towards solutions to these problems. Punk has a lot to do with it, later, Crass, and people of course who bothered to question things with me.

Mick: Did any of you have morals thrusted upon you at an early age? (With the track 'The First 7 Years" in mind.)

Chumba: We all did to a certain extent. I was brought up in a strictly Christian environment, which I did rebel against, but parts of which I've kept with me as useful. Morals which say sex is bad, masturbation is dirty, wars are ok, government/bosses are acceptable. We all live with these morals, and it's up to all of us to help disseminate information which helps prove otherwise. "The First 7 Years" was written by Dan and is his personal view of what affected him as he grew... but it applies to most people.

Mick: How did the ten of you come to meet?

Chumba: We met gradually for different reasons and under different circumstances and we've lived together about 2 years. Though some have lived together up to 5 years. Being together creats a lot of love and strong sense of being close, but it also brings us awareness of each other... we know each others faults as well as each others good points and living together can vary between a wonderful experience to being a struggle. Communication is sometimes easy and sometimes difficult. There is always a sense of working towards similar aims, helping each other. It isn't always easy, but it is so worth it.

FLIPSIDE NUMBER 46

"The state, the church, the plans, the vote,
What's the verb behind it all!
The how, the why, the where, the when, the who,
can these words find the truth?"
'According to Nouns'- Minutemen"

ISSUE #: 46
DATE: June 1985
FORMAT: 8 1/2x11, rotary web offset with 2 color glossy cover.
PAGES: 68
PRICE: $1.00
PRESS RUN: 10,000

PAINTED WILLY

Were interviewed at Spinhead Studios in

This band originally started out as a four piece with another guitarist named Willy. Vic quit because he couldn't stand him, but soon Dave and Phil couldn't either and threw him out; then Vic came back. The first 7 was with Nick. The second vinyl offering, the 12 EP My Fellow Americans, Dave and Phil experimentally wrote on the spot in their studio.

Dave: My Fellow Americans came out of a rap. We had all these people over in the studio and we had this concept of left and right. If you listen carefully, the left wing stuff (the guys from BGK) is on the left channel while the right wing stuff in on the other. No one told anyone what to say; it just happened. ...Painted Willy has made their new debut, but we've only played a few select shows. I don't know why people expect us to sound like the other two bands (Phil and Dave were in Sin 34, while Vic was the original front man for SVDB.). They were fun--they were learning experiences. This is a new band--a new thing.

Phil: A problem we had in Sin 34 that we don't have in Painted Willy is that we had three music and lyric writers and competition would arise. In Painted Willy, we still have three writers, but it flows a lot better.

Dave: And we have more money to divide up at the end of a gig!

Vic: I just write whatever I feel. I can't say, I'm gonna write a hardcore song. What comes out is just mood oriented.

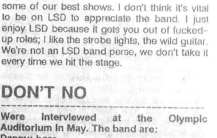

Painted Willy: Phil, Vic, Dave – photo Al

Phil: It's all emotions. I think my song writing has been a little more confined because everytime I get inspired to write, it's about a personal conflict with the member of the opposite sex. We spent too many years all caught up in the hate thing. We don't want to keep on writing about what we've written about. The music too; eventually, we will have complete sets of songs that we can play depending on the mood we are feeling that night. It's nice having that variety. We don't want to be known as any one kind of band. We want to keep ourselves happy before anything else.

Dave: It's sad to see bands stuck in their own little cliques just because they've met with some success at it. It's OK to stick to things, but they lock off any other possibilities. It's like being in jail.

Dave: I'm heavily into film making. I made my biggest feature last year, Desperate Teenage Runaways or Love Dolls as it later became. I'm working on the sequel called Love Dolls Superstar and it's going along very well.

Phil: Naming a band is really hard, but we decided it should be something sexual. So, we looked under the sexual heading in Roget's International Thesaurus. Under the homosexual subheading Painted Willy appeared. Maybe Painted Willy because the penis takes on a different sort of hue after homosexual activity.

Vic: One of my teachers was really curious when I wrote Painted Willy on my desk. To this day, I'm still worried about it.

BUTTHOLE SURFERS

Were interviewed by Donny the Punk around 5 A.M. (9-22-84) in a Second Ave. eaterie after they had been in Gotham for six weeks and played nine shows.

Donny: How did the band get started?
Gibby: Myself and Paul are the original members. We started in San Antonio about four years ago. The EP was recorded two years ago, the live EP was released yesterday
Donny: How did the two drummers come about?
King: Me and Teresa are brother and sister and we started playing in various Texas high school marching bands. I joined the band and

it was natural that Teresa should try it eventually.
Donny: You've played as so many different clubs in New York, each with their own crowd.
King: I don't want to get just the hardcores. I want to get anybody that can get into the band, that feels like seeing the Butthole Surfers.
Donny: Do you get a lot of flak on account of you name?
King: Only from people in fanzines asking us, Wherever did you get that name? Our parents give us more harassment about the name than people in clubs. Nobody else really cares.
Donny: You've been around New York long enough to make some observations.
Gibby: New York has too much pizza; everyone I know eats only pizza; it brings me down. The cross-section of people is cool. You can't go down the streets in San Antonio and see all the Rastafarians.
Donny: Do you try to be deliberately outrageous on stage?
King: I think the word is literally outrageous; we're a reflection of a deliberately outrageous society.
Donny: Do you feel that the hardcore dominance is now receding?
King: It seems that there's a growing skinhead/Nazi punk/right-wing punk thing going on nationwide. I don't think it will ever become a major issue. It's the "we're not punks, we're skins" mentality. I think it's great to see bands like Sonic Youth and Husker D, who are playing from the heart and doing what they want to do. That's what punk was about from the beginning, anyway.
Donny: How does a song come about?
Gibby: Usually someone gets either a bass rhythm or guitar melody. It evolves into a structure and then lyrics are added later.
Teresa: In New York, we recorded two songs we'd been been playing as instrumentals, and Gibby added vocals in the studio. They'd never had any before then.
Donny: What role does psychedelics play in the band?
King: I think psychedelics might be the best drug. You see and experience different things every time.
Donny: How does it affect your playing?
King: Sometimes we do acid on stage and do

some of our best shows. I don't think it's vital to be on LSD to appreciate the band. I just enjoy LSD because it gets you out of fucked-up roles; I like the strobe lights, the wild guitar. We're not an LSD band perse, we don't take it every time we hit the stage.

DON'T NO

Were interviewed at the Olympic Auditorium in May. The band are:
Danny: bass
Alby: vocals
Warren: lead guitar
Skid: guitar
Danny: We're hardcore. Our following is mostly from Huntington Beach. We're a beach band. All of our cities have beach in their names. That doesn't mean that we surf or anything.
Al: This isn't the original line up, is it?
Danny: Matt is the only original member! For awhile we didn't even have him. Our EP has no original members on it. He and a guy from Malibu, who is now a Hari Krishna, started and then a pot head named Stuart played guitar. Then, they got Alby and me and it went downhill from there.
Al: What makes you guys different from the other hardcore bands?
Skid: I think the attitude of just going out there and playing good fast, tight hardcore.
Alby: We are a personal band. It's hard for us to write lyrics that don't personally relate to us. This is what we feel. When we play, it's more like an expression.
Matt: Everyone writes the music and has been trained in harmony and structural stuff. We've had classical and jazz training. We go for a lot of the odd times like 7/8 and 5/8, which you don't find too often, and we go for double time on the guitars and bass.
Warren: We enjoy ourselves and have a good time, but the band isn't for fun. We want to accomplish something. Musically, I have a lot of jazz study. I want to catch people's ears.
Danny: If you notice, he's not just playing as fast as he can in the right key. We sit down and work out harmonies, so the lead does sound good.
Al: What's your vocal style Alby?
Alby: Henry, from Black Flag, impressed me when he started with them, but now I think it's just an act. Ian, from Minor Threat, really impressed me. I'm not thinking about style so much as just screaming and yelling and saying what I have to say.
Al: What about the name Don't No?
Alby: In the beginning, the bass player just thought it up. Then it evolved. A Don't No state of mind is like ignorance is bliss--it's an easy way out for people.
Al: But, you spell it No not Know.
Alby: We changed it because of Dr. Know. People still fuck it up all over the place. They mix it up.
Al: What do your parents think of this?
Warren: My parents are extremely supportive of what I do. They came here tonight and they bought tickets. They wore our t-shirts and are very supportive. They're not extremely liberal, but they support it as long as it's not anti-me or anti-anyone else.
Alby: I went back to Boston recently and my father said, It's not a fad, is it? But, he did like the fact that I had hair!
Matt: My parents are in their 70's and my mom wanted me to play in an orchestra. She's just glad I did something with my music.

Don't No - photo Al

JOEY RAMONES

Was interviewed at the Ritz in New York City on December 29th 1984 by Donny the Punk.

Donny: How do you feel about the directions the Ramones are going in now with the new album Too Tough To Die?

Joey: I think this is our best album yet and I'm real happy. I feel like a proud father. This album is maybe a little more serious, a little more reflective of now. It's sort of looking within ourselves. I think it's a very diverse album. We wanted to make a real Ramones record and say, Fuck everything! We're gonna do exactly what we wanna do this time.

Donny: When you're singing songs that were written by other members of the band, does that imply that you agree with the sentiments expressed there?

Joey: On this album I do. I feel like my best vocal efforts are on this album. I enjoy Danger Zone. It's sort of a challenge to sing something a different style, it was exciting. It's not exactly what I'm really into, but I like the outcome of it.

Donny: How do you relate to the punk scene today?

Joey: All the hardcore bands are saying that the Ramones are the originators. I feel like we finally have gotten our just due. For years, a lot of people wouldn't admit to the fact that it was us who kicked it off; I guess because of rivalries or whatever. Now people, like Joe Strummer and John Lydon, are finally opening up; and that makes me happy. I feel we're the last genuine rock and roll band left, whereas a lot of people have made it, but there really isn't anything left that's genuine. Most bands make one or two great albums and it's downhill from there. Eight albums later people are saying it's our best album; that says a lot. We've got our self-respect and integrity and I feel we're up there with the best of 'em. We revolutionized rock and roll in '74; we put excitement and fun back into what wasn't there. We kicked off something that changed the course of rock history.

Donny: Today, you seem to be re-emphasizing your punk identity. Do you keep in touch?

Joey: Yeah, we do. One thing about us: we're not saying, Yeah, we're great, and we're living in a bubble. Dee Dee's really into hardcore. He even says that hardcore has reinspired his own creativity as far as songwriting.

Donny: When did people start calling your music punk rock?

Joey: I guess right from the time we used to play CBGB's in the early years when there were not that many people. We had the song, Judy is a Punk and everybody started calling us punks. (laughs)

Donny: How did you come to use that term in the song?

Joey: I was walking down the street and it popped into my mind, but, it's a true story about her. She's a wild, wild thing.

NAKED RAYGUN

Were interviewed on 2/4/85 somewhere between Los Angeles and New York. This was a mall interview since the band found they had some serious and mysterious

The Ramones - photo Joe

date changes when they reached L.A. This brings us to the first question:

FS: On your recent West Coast tour, you were supposed to play the Cathay a couple of times. Your dates were all changed, what happened?

NR: The Cathay originally booked us on two different occasions which we canceled both with phone calls and confirmation letters. The day we showed up, Mike B. said he knew nothing of it. Being the nice guy that he is, he let us play anyways. That night we played for nothing--zero dollars--thanks a lot Sin 34. Actually, Mike got real blasted and fell off his chair. When he woke up, he was quite dizzy and marked us down on his calendar three times. So, we went to the beach, got really drunk and picked up girls. It was sort of a contest to see who could pick up the most butch looking girl; John won.

FS: What are you trying to do musically?

NR: We are trying to write the ultimate song, the grande sonata, the pupa de la pupa, the penultimate riff, the blast crunch dropper pseudo heart gorger.

FS: What about the style of music you play? Do you call it punk?

NR: Blast furnace monomania. Punk is prefered to hardcore, but we hate being pigeon holed. It's as bad as being corn holed. We play aggressive, melodic, intense, chanty music... To get with our music as opposed to our lyrics, we'd like to get across that you can be aggressive and good without being repetitious of other bands and other widely known styles of music.

FS: I noticed you lightly touch on political subjects. Is there any reason why you don't go deeper?

NR: Politics suck. Even writing this much about it is a waste of time. Congress will meet every year to pass laws, regurgitate age old puny puny issues, and hash out cigar stoking world reflecting garbage until the end of time.

FS: Are lyrics a big part of NR?

NR: Lyrics are not a big part of Naked Raygun, case in point I Lie. They are, of course, a necessary ingredient.

FS: What's the story behind your old name Negro Commando?

NR: We just liked the sound of it. It wasn't meant to be racist. We only had the name for one show, we didn't have a drummer then.

FS: What about the name Naked Raygun, why not Naked Reagan?

FINALLY!

WHITE FLAG
Wild Kingdom

OUT NOW ON

Send SASE to Positive Force
for lyric sheet!

18 SONG LP
AND
LIMITED 4 COLOR
'UICIDE KING' 7"
w/ non lp b-side

POSITIVE FORCE RECORDS

P.O. BOX 9184
RENO, NV. 89507

PRICES:

LPs $6
7" $3

postpaid in U.S.,
CANADIAN add $1,
Overseas add $2

Naked Raygun – drawing by Joy

NR: The name was chosen before Ron's time, the loser had to win, oh well. Naked Reagan-- there you go again with that political stuff.

FS: What would you like to accomplish as a band?

NR: Mostly, become as well know all over the U.S. and eventually everywhere as we are in Chicago. We'd like to cause some person to look at us and say, Yeah, that's it! and run out and buy a guitar and start creating his own music.

FS: Where does NR fit into the U.S. music scene?

NR: We're the band your brother sings to in the shower. Clever enough to be the next Beatles, original enough to never be signed to any major or large independent.

FS: How have you change since you have started?

NR: We can stay in tune for sometimes two songs in a row.

FS: Naked Raygun has had a few personal changes, why don't people like to play with Jeff?

NR: Everyone has their own reasons for quitting Naked Raygun, some to find fame and fortune--we don't know.

THE FALL

The Fall have been a personal obsession for this writer ever since I first stumbled under their image of influence at a show they gave at the Anti Club in 1979. During their return visit in 1981, I was one of an intrepid trio that set out to conduct and interview with singer Mark E. Smith for that unique but short lived fanzine Night Voices. This time around the band has become even more famous, and an interview was not confirmed until the last minute with Mark's wife, guitarist and vehement Fall supporter Brix Smith - originally from, of all places, Pacific Palisades. By a srtoke of bad timing I had not slept at all and Mike Sheppard of Iridescence Records and I barely barely had time to prepare ourselves beforehand. My first question about Brix's local background was swept away in the cross currents of her energy - after that I just hung on for the ride.
Interview by Rose O'Meara and Mike Sheppard

Mike: Well I hear that the single has charted in England really well.

Brix: Yeah, and the album, the albums charted quite high for us... (The singles) were quite poppish, and what we were doing was stabbing at the general market, just trying to um... the Fall was always put in this catagory in England, and so we wanted to do something SO different that they would feel shocked.

Mart: It's really structured there, more so than here.

Mike: You're predefined as to what you are.

Brix: Yeah. And so we did those two singles, which are really weird and then we came back to the hard sound. Two singles and we'll probably never do anything like that again, but they were successful, we think they're good and the lyrics... the music is like very sweet but the lyrics are like the nastiest sentiments that you could ever imagine to hear, which I think is a really interesting combination for a pop song. So I think a lot of fans, when they hear those new ones, they go "Oh my God, what's happened to the Fall? They've changed so much" and stuff. But now they've all come back, after that, I mean they never left, they just questioned. But now the new album blew everything away, and anyways, the new albums coming out on Jem today in America.

Mike: How do other band members feel about Mark - Marks the writer so I guess he gets all of the attention. Is that ok?

Brix: Yeah. Of course, we share the tasks out, you know what I mean, like he writes the words and I write most of the music, like for the last album. Sometimes someone else will write the music and we all work on it together really. We're all happy that he's the front man, because personally I don't want the pressure of it. He's a genius and he should be. I not going to say that he's the most pleasurable person to work with night and day....

Mike: But you're proud to.

Brix: Yeah, right. It's the best band in the world to me. We all respect each other, but we all play a part in it... Well a lot of people think, there's a lot of misconceptions, they think like Mark's a maniac or something, he's very feared and everything, and he probably IS to some people, if that's what he wants to get out of it, then that's good. That's the thing about Mark's lyrics too. I mean he may be saying one thing, but you may be hearing a completely different thing, or hearing it but thinking a different meaning and that's the beauty of a good writer. That's the beauty of a band like the Fall, that every one can get something out of it and it doesn't matter if that's what they think. I don't care.

Mike: Right, at least no one is unaffected by it.

Brix: THAT is the MAIN thing, either they love it or they hate it, do you know what I mean? When people hate the Fall they hate it with such a passion, that it makes them really like sick to listen to it, and I think that's really good.

Mart: I don't know anybody like that!

Mike: Um, it's one of the groups that my mom didn't like when I lived at home.

MINUTEMEN

Musically the Minutemen have little in common with most hardcore bands or any other rock bands for that matter. An electic mix of jazz, funk and punk, the mini songs of the San Pedro group blazes a unique and challenging trial in the ostracized sphere of X's "Unheard Music". But if the qualities of individualism and risk taking mean anything in hardcore circles (and I think they mean quite a bit) the Minutemen may be THE model punk band of the 80's. I talked to Minutemen bassist Mike Watt back on March 2, just after the bands late afternoon soundcheck at UCLA's Ackerman Ballroom. Mike proved to be as nice a guy as you'd ever want to meet. Even though he was frantically trying to repair D's failed guitar pickup in time to "save the show", the fleetfingered bassist was courteous and cordial....
Interview by Jon Matsumoto

Jon: The sound you guys get is incredible. It's a real mixture of different musical styles. You have the jazz improvisational element, the funky bass sound and all of it is thrown together with punk rock intensity.

Mike: Our roots are actually early 70's, Alice Cooper, BOC... We're 27 now, so we grew up in the 70's, unfortunately, Creedence too...

Jon: I noticed you covered a Creedence tune on the last lp.

Mike: Actually we did a couple of them, we also used to do a funky version of "Fortunate Son". We learned off of records how to play. It wasn't like punk rock where you learn your own songs. You copied people, which I didn't like. But in our town Pedro, that was the only way you did it.

Jon: So you guys played covers?

Mike: Never wrote a song until we heard punk rock. It was the mentality of the times. That's why I say you're never just an individual. You're also part of a culture.

Jon: What made you decide to write short songs in the first place?

Mike: It was rebellion. But it was also making the most of what we had. We heard Wire too and they influenced us. You don't have to have the old format.

Jon: You must have been influenced by some jazz artists as well?

Mike: Not when we were young. When we got into our 20's that when we started listening to jazz. Yeah I appreciate it a lot, especially Ornette Coleman's stuff.

Jon: I guess you were also influenced by Steely Dan and Van Halen. On "Double Nickels" you play "Katy Lied" and "Ain't Talking About Love" back to back!

Mike: Steely Dan was my 70's pet band. It was the intellectual band for me. I just wanted to pay tribute to them.

Jon: Do you guys like travelling?

Mike: Not for 2 months. We did a 2 month tour last summer and that's too long.

Jon: Did you go by bus or car?

Mike: We have a van. we don't sleep at hotels, we sleep at peoples houses. Our tours make money because we live very cheap. Econo we call it. We do the most with what we got. That goes for everything. We did "Buzz or Howl" for $150. We did the double album for about $1200. But it doesn't matter, that's how much we got so we go for it.

Jon: Whose idea was it to have pictures of each of you in a car on "Double Nickels"?

Mike: We had an album recorded already. This was November of last year and then we heard the Huskers had a double record... so we said "What?" So we recorded a whole record worth of songs, but we and no concept to link the two. So we made up one – our cars, it's kind of a joke.

Jon: So each one of those is your individual car?

Mike: Right, you hear the sounds. That's as far as the concept goes. We didn't have a unifying theme. It's strange. I think one of our problems with radio is that we don't write songs, we write rivers. We're more of an instrumental band. We play against each other, guitar and bass, we don't set up a background for our narrative. The words are almost like our lead guitar.

Jon: That's why I think of the band in a lot of terms as jazz. I've read articles that refer to you as "the thinking mans band". There's a strong message in a lot of your songs. Do you like being thought of in that way?

Mike: Yeah, I hope think about it. That's why we're saying what we're saying. But it's weird about words, it's weird how words can mean different things to different people. But that's also the magic of it too. Things can keep loose enough that nobody really knows but they get something out of it, a feeling that trancends and strict definition.

Jon: Do you get a sense that the kids are taking what you're saying and digesting it in a serious matter?

Mike: I don't.

Jon: Does it bother you?

Mike: No. Because when I was that age I didn't. Some of them do. Some of them are a lot brighter than I was at that age. We hope to shake up the young guys because punk rock doesn't have to mean hardcore or one style of music or just singing the same lyrics. I can mean freedom and going crazy and being personal with your art.

Jon: Would you say you make records for the average guy?

Mike: We are playing for the average guy. We play for the hardcore too because that's what the kids who are old enough to come to our shows. It really hasn't gotten to colleges yet. Most of the colleges I've been on, the trend is right wing preppy, young republican thing. Our audience is mainly college but right now all we got is high school and a couple of colleges.

Jon: Do you feel you fit into the hardcore movement in any way?

Mike: We were liberated by punk rock. But hardcore is more like middle class rebellion. Like hippies. Middle class kids who don't like their parents values. Me, D. Boon, George, we come from working class backgrounds. My dad was a sailor. D's dad is a mechanic, George's dad's a machinist. we never wrote anti-parent songs. I don't reject their values. ve lived in an apartment all of my life. I've never had a house or a swimming pool. I

don't plan on getting one but I don't have any rebellion against that. I'm not damning it. I think it's a natural cycle.

Jon: You guys really seem to like San Pedro.

Mike: Yeah. I was born in Virginia and I moved here when I was 9. I like it because the airs clean. It's kind of a nice because it keeps you insulated so you don't become fashion conscious. But we're still close enough to play gigs in Hollywood.

FLIPSIDE NUMBER 47

"Drink deep, its just a taste,
and it might not come this way again,
I believe in moments, transparent moments
Moments in grace, when you've got to stake your faith
(but why do I confine when all I want is release?)
It moves inside you, it stays outside you
And it's not something that I could prove,
Or could choose to be moved,
It's a promise and it's a threat
And it's not something that I'll let you forget
Not just yet, not just yet
(but why do I chase when all I want is near?)
If it's not the rule then it's always the case
Good intentions get fractured,
Good intentions get replaced
So close to reach but so hard to hold
The only chance you get is past your control
It's so hard, it's so hard
Drink deep, it's just a taste
And it might not come this way again
Time to surrender, sweet surrender of all things in time
All things one place, one place."
"Drink Deep" – Rites of Spring

ISSUE #:47
DATE: September 1985
FORMAT: 8 1/2x11, rotary web offset with 2 color glossy cover.
PAGES: 68
PRICE: $1.00
PRESS RUN: 10000

This was a special issue because it contained the interviews and articles (DC family tree etc) from our 'vacation' to the east coast. A very influential trip indeed.

Other than summer vacations, the big happening thing for us is the record label. With this issue we release the debut LP from Orange County's Doggy Style and a split LP featuring Vicious Circle and Perdition from Australia. The label is proving to be a very popular project for us.

On the video front, we are still doing Media Blitz (local cable program where we "review" records), which we actually started some time ago. And we are still doing the 'Video Fanzine' concept, releasing volumes 8, 9 and 10 at this time. We are also starting to dabble in networking re-edited shows to other cable outlets.

The scene has arrived in it's Fenders/ Olympic mode, a time when touring bands pay little attention to playing local clubs and local bands might as well tour to get gigs. Unless, of course, it is to open for big touring bands. It really doesn't have to be this way, since there are still some clubs that are available if you do it right (Central Services, Anti, Rajis, Lengerie, Music Machine, Safari Sams, Meadowlark, Bogarts etc...) but then again that takes some work.....

CONFLICT

Interviewed at Fenders in Long Beach by Al, Big Frank and Gary Tovar (Goldenvoice), Ivan (Iconoclast) and Gus.

Al: Why don't you start off by commenting on tonights gig. (A bit of trouble caused by "skinheads" and the band reacted to that while on stage).

Colin: In England it's about the same but it varies. We used to have really bad trouble in about '82. On gig we had about 50 skins outside, once they got inside altogether there were about 120 and they completely trashed the gig, wrecked our equipment, put me and John in the hospital... We had decided we were a peaceful band, we wouldn't get involved in fighting back but after that gig we said stuff this. We are peaceful people but we weren't going to let people trash us like that. After that gig we took on our own ways to sort it out. We're not saying that violence is the answer to everything, what we're saying is that in some circumstances it is the only language that some people know.

Al: So it's working out better this way?

Colin: I think so... a lot of bands have come to England to realize that, especially at demonstrations, that we get a thick line of police resistance and it's no good. When policemen come and band to no good and turn around and say we believe in peace, then smash you in the face. We have to get in first and then run. I think that's where Crass and Flux actually learned that resistance is the only way, cause those people won't listen to you.

Al: Um, it seems that you are more of a gigging band than either Crass or Flux...

Colin: I like to play live. I think it's important to play live because all along the line there's been so many bands like your GBH's or Exploited's which just like rip the piss out of punk and like use it to their own extreme to make as much money as possible, and fuck up as many people along the way. Whether the bands actually ment to or not, I don't know because a lot of bands don't look deep enough to understand it before they start. They get controlled by managers and agents and stuff like that... They just don't know what's really going on. Which is why I like to play live all the time. I feel it's really important to communicate. It's no good just releasing vinyl. That is just a quick way to make money.

Al: Well do you think that that has helped the evolution of your band, lets say faster than Crass or Flux because you are out in front of more people...

Conflict at Olympic - photo Al

Colin: I am really glad that we came, I mean the main reason is because we have been asked for two years from various people...

Gray: I've been trying to get them for a year.

Colin: We agreed to come and I'm really pleased that we did. We came through Goldenvoice, there are a lot of people who think good or bad about Goldenvoice, and one think I want to say to Flipside is that I am glad we did come over with Goldenvoice. The main reason is that we wouldn't have been able to afford it otherwise. You know there's a lot of people that would probably like to know that there was even a member of our band slagging the band off for coming over here. But you know that's the only way we could have got here and you know I don't think it has been that bad.

Gray: The first time these bands come over here they're looking for something fucked and then they don't find it. The second time the band gets out here they cruise. They have gotten over the culture shock of the first time, they're much more relaxed.

Ivan: I am really interested in the Anarchist movement over in England. Is it unified or is it something that is split up like here?

Colin: Right, um no. I used to be split up about two years ago. There used to be a thing with the pacifist movement which involved at the time; us, Flux, Crass and stuff like that which was banded together and the other movements like the hippies, the Stonehenge people. There was a lot of friction on which way to go. The turning point was when everybody realized that the CND (Campaign For Nuclear Disarmament) was fucking us over. That's when the pacifists and the people who believed in resistance turned against the CND. The CND was being infiltrated by the left wing of the labor party, it got really controlled. Even though the pacifists didn't join the resistance. I got fucked off of them and that's when people got talking, that's when the idea "Stop The City" and stuff like that came about.

Ivan: So maybe it's good it happened.

Colin: Yeah, it's great that it happened, the main thing is that everybody started together on "Stop The City", because it was the resistance side that went down and started fighting with the police when the Pacifist side were going to demonstrate. Then the pacifist side got so much shit from the police that they said fuck this and fought back. Since then everybody's kept a certain amount of pacifism, but now it's not "pacifism" as a label, but it's like peaceful people that will fight back if they need to. It's gotten past labels, it used to be struggling to achieve a name that was anarchy. Now it's struggling to stay in existance because it's getting that bad. The police are smashing up everything that's got to do with anarchy over in England... I know everyone must think that that symbol means "CND" but it was never intended that way. It means anarchy and autonomy. If you look at the "N" you have Anarchy on the bottom and Autonomy on the top. The "N" in the middle also stood for nihilism. The three don't mix but you can take your pick. They will all roughly come out the same in the end. Nihilism is the negative way of looking at things. Whereas anarchy and autonomy are not. The badge does look like CND which is great with us, we still respect the Campaign for Nuclear Disarmament. But it's very important for us to get rid of all weapons all over the world, not just nuclear.

Al: Have you been bothered in your homes by the police because of your records or the band?

Colin: Not in our homes. We've been stopped in our cars and had our record covers taken away. A few months ago the police smashed up a gig we were playing at. The last three London gigs we played at were the worst. They've lined the streets with police. We choose to play in the suburbs in a place called Serpent, which is a royalist type area. That's where they arrested me and about 40 others and some got 3 months in detention centers. They charge people with conspiracy to riot. No one was starting anything but the police coming in arresting people and we just chased them out. Our police don't have guns so we chased them out and that's when they called for the heavy brigade and everyone got arrested. We get a lot of stick at gigs.

DETONATORS

Interviewed in September by Al and Danny Phillips. Present were Bruce (guitar and vocals) and Juan (rhythum guitar).

Al: I was just wondering why you would want to be interviewed by Flipside?

Bruce: To be realistic, it helps.

Al: Well, I've read more than one fanzine interview with you guys and you didn't seem to like Flipside much...

Bruce: Well that stems from frustration. We didn't know what to do to get a mention and it was a weird time for us. We read a review of one of our shows where the guy didn't see us play but he heard that we sucked.

Juan: It was a hard time for us then, all the work we put in and we weren't getting noticed, we put the LP out ourselves, we tried to book stuff ourselves and we found we weren't getting anywhere.

Bruce: We've done like 4 or 5 tours now. We've been to Canada twice. But we come here and it's kinda depressing. We're on a waiting list to play some of the shows here, but that's why we tour, it beats hanging out here. The promoters tell us, yeah next week, call me tomorrow... And we're not worried about the money either, if we could get like 50 bucks from the club, we could make like another 50 selling shirts if we have to. Or play in somebody's garage the next day, we don't care. We are leaving for another tour, and we're gonna try to get to Europe this time... The main thing for me is to play, because we work like dogs at our regular jobs. Fuck that!

Joe: Isn't that running away from the situation, leaving town because you can't seem to break in.

Bruce: Well we're always waiting on somebody and this is more like taking matters into your own hands.

Juan: Just like our LP, we had it recorded and our ex-singer got all frustrated because he couldn't get anybody to sign us. So he gave up. We decided if we didn't do it ourselves, it was never gonna come out. So we did it ourselves. Just like playing, we could rot away here waiting to play, so we decided let's get out of here.

Al: What about the things you guys write about?

Bruce: Well, we don't want to tell anybody how to vote, think for yourself. It's more situations. The single is about a friend of mine who killed himself in my backyard.

Juan: He didn't have the balls to live.

Bruce: "Your Childs War" was about these kids they were kicking out of school because they had mohawks and stuff. They had these two psychiatrists duel it out. "Cause of Desperation" on our new lp is, why does someone snap? Why?

Juan: Like the guy at McDonalds, people look at him and they don't know, they think he's so normal looking why would he blow up? They don't know it could be the smallest things in the world. There are pressures that people don't question and they are shocked when it happens. The talk about violence in punk rock, but they don't even understand it – violence is in football, sports, they pay for it – but the don't discuss that yet. Like our name, Detonators, people might think that's new wavey but we like what it means – the pressure point.

Bruce: You can push a man so far, then he's gone, he can't be held for his actions.

Juan: A man, a woman, a child, it can be anybody. Why do people join gangs, Why do they join Mexican gangs? They don't want to wear Op shorts, there's pressure right there. They go to school with Joe Arian as class president, there's pressure.......

RITES OF SPRING

Al: Let's talk about "Rites of Spring", why di you pick that name?

Guy: I guess it happened in my room. I ha the record "Rites of Spring" by Stravinsky an

Rites of Spring, 9:30 Club, WDC – photo Joe

I thought it was cool because I had read the back cover which said the first time it was performed the audience beat each other on the heads with canes and stuff and they stormed the stage. Stravinsky, who wrote the opera, had to jump out of the window and run down the street to escape all the angry fans – cause it was such a daring piece of music, it just fucked with everybody and I thought that was kinda cool. The name fit real well with what was going on at the time because Minor Threat, Faith, Insurrection – all the bands I cared about, had broken up. Nothing else was really going on. So when we formed we hoped it would all come together again, so "spring" was a cool theme because of the re-birth idea. And it seemed to happen because after us there was Beefeater, Lunchmeat, now Embrace. To the point now where it's as good as anything that came before.

Al: The whole Revolution Summer...

Brendan: Exactly! Mission Impossible, Lunchmeat, all those bands...

Guy: And not just the bands, it's a total vehicle for creation, everybody is getting immerse in it again.

Mike: All it took was someone to "bang! Oh look what they're doing!" and they feel they can do it too. And that's what we're trying to do, is to just get people to do their own thing.

Al: It seems to me that you guys and at least Embrace are on this full sincerity and big emotional experience thing...

Brendan: That is where it all happens when we play, the climax...

Guy: It's always been there for me.

Mike: Even when we practice it's there, I don't know why.

Brendan: It was like the first time seeing Faith live, it was a constant chill the whole time, it was at that level.

Guy: When I was in Insurrection we were writing things and having fun but it wasn't – it didn't seem really serious. So I thought if I ever started a band again I would want it to be. If I was gonna put a lot of energy into it, it was going to be meaningful to me and a lot of other people. I had to do it full on seriously. The only think you have to put into it is yourself, so whether it's words or we are playing live, it's that moment in it's total and I

give everything I have and I'm not thinking about anything else I'm just concentrating directly on what I'm doing.

Al: You guys get to the point where you look like you're in pain on stage and the audience is out there crying..

Guy: But it's not like it's depressing or cynical, some people think the songs are sad and stuff, but were dealing with emotions that sometimes seem to be sad but at the same time I don't think we treat them cynically or like these gloom doom bands. I am serious and I deal with realistic things but at the same time it not dispairing. It's realistic but it's – it's sad, but this is sad, life is sad. Songs like "Drink Deep", I'm saying this is it, let's do it, and stake your faith and have a commitment. People react to it positively cause we are not saying "fuck this"... It's frustrating times for people in general and it's a constant friction between what you see and what you want to achieve and things that you know are right. It's the same politically and personally – to me it's all one issue because the same problems keep coming up over and over again – lack of commitment, lack of caring...

Al: Do you think that the audience that comes to see you guys is any different than say... well first off, do you consider yourselves a punk band?

Mike: I don't call it punk because of the people around here, we don't really play for them.

Guy: At one point in my life I would have said "Yeah, we're a punk band and proud of it!". And I don't think I feel any differently now than I did then, things have changed around me so for me to say that would imply something that isn't true anymore.

DISCHORD HOUSE RESIDENTS

For those of you who don't know, Dischord House is an old two story house in Arlington, Virginia (just a mile from Washington D.C.) where a small, but very active and influential group of people live. By the name you have probably guessed that this is home of Dischord Records, but that is only one room. In the other rooms

are: Eddie Jenny (guitar for Rites of Spring), Tomas Squip (vocalist for Beefeater), Mark Sullivan (aka Garlic man singer for DC's first thrashers the Slinkies and now with Kingface), and of course Jeff Nelson and Ian Mackaye the Minor Threat guys who need no introduction. This interview was compleated by Joe and Al with Tomas, Ian and Mark. We started off talking about what they call "Revolution Summer"....

Tomas: Revolution Summer is a movement that isn't concrete of anything, it's a mutually agreed upon, sort of subliminal, a very airy thing but it's heavy at the same time. It takes the commitment and energy that was in the original punk movement. This is a movement where the whole emotional aspect is brought in, which I don't think punk ever really had – the Heart felt emotion. It used to be an aggressive emotion so the difference between the old punk movement and what is happening in Revolution Summer is that it is a heart felt thing.

Ian: Everybody is making a conscious effort to re-establish our feeling back into a music situation but not just going to the punk thing. We all consider ourselves "punks" basically, although we have a great distaste for the punk scene here. The punk scene everywhere for that matter. We don't really feel akin to the more fashion, or angry type trip, that "punk" type thing – we feel a little alienated by that. The whole drug trip, alcohol and the party thing – the common American teenager trip, we are not akin to. So basically what we have done was to open a whole new thing, all of us, and there are people all over Washington that are into it. If anything, we are not trying to "fix" the punk scene, or change it, we're just opening up a sub division of it.

Mark: Revolution Summer is a celebration of doing things because you can.

Ian: The name means nothing – it's just this is the summer we plan to re-attack, or at least re-establish ourselves. We feel our own responsibility to play.

Tomas: The drive!... The original punk philosophy for us was first of all "fight bullshit" and second of all to do something real, the individuality thing. And the punk scene was

Dischord House party with Rites of Spring (Brendan, Mike, Eddie, Guy), Tomas Beefeater, Jane and Ian Embrace. - photo Al

getting into the alcohol thing, smoking, being the tough guy, or being a lawyer and that is exactly the bullshit that punk was originally supposed to defy...

Ian: Our punk, for us this was true.

Tomas: Revolution Summer is getting back into fighting bullshit again; don't let it pass you by, don't let yourself grow up. It was putting the protest back into it and fighting bullshit again because it has snuck up on us.

Ian: This is our lives, this isn't just something we're doing like a hobby – this has been six years of my life and everyday I put everything I got into it. I am what I am. The punk thing from morning to night, the band, the label, this is my life. So of course I'm bitter, all of us are bitter when we see things we've worked on so hard become petty and negative... I think personal purifying is the beginning of everything. Once you get your own shit together, once you get your own mind together it makes life for you and the people around you so much more agreeable and understandable as opposed to constant fucking problems. The same petty shit that goes on between you and me is the same shit that goes on in the world, it's just on a smaller scale.

Al: Something that surprised me a lot was the Punk Percussion P, in general it seemed that DC bands didn't lean towards the political side, even Marginal Man are endorsing it from stage...

Mark: Action speak louder than words.

Ian: Of course all of us have always been against this stuff because basically we think that politics are shit. People can say "Oh, Ian's into politics" whatever, fine, but in the end it's just a humanitarian thing for me. Just like the Civil Rights movement in the 60's this is a chance for us all to ban together, and even though we might not agree with all the other people in the Anti-Apartheid thing, we ARE anti-Apartheid. Whether it's political or not I don't know. It's an emotional issue, just like the Civil Rights thing was.

Joe: More of a statement against Apartheid than encouraging a certain policy.

Ian: Just stopping the abuse of humans.

Tomas: The people that are protesting everyday are pro-divestment so in that sense we are automatically pro-divestment, but at the same time we are against apartheid and

violation of human rights everywhere. The first day of Summer we has the first PPP and the next one will be at the end of summer. So we will kick off the rest of our lives with the next one.

Ian: In think that in our house, our own family of people, we are trying to adopt a healthier attitude about the world, we don't think that anyone of us are going to change the world but we at least want to live our lives into the healthiest manner we can with as much care and consideration and love for the people around us. We're still gonna be human beings and get angry at each other but if we can at least put aside some of the pettiness and not be concerned about our money, or image or "how proud we are to be Americans", then we feel we are moving in the right direction.

Al: Taken literally, is that where your vegetarianism come in?

Tomas: It's getting back to applying wisdom to punk, when I say "fight bullshit". Vegetarianism is something I've spoken to so many thousands of people about over the

years, and they all agree that meat eating is bad or that killing animals is wrong, but yet they eat meat. And there are all kinds of wishy washy excuses for it. If you see something wrong in your life, change it. I saw that meat eating was wrong, so I changed, so simple.

Ian: My final thing was that out of all animals, humans are the only ones that can make the choice. And we should use it. To me it makes total sense. It's something I've thought about for years. Certainly the MDC guys had an influence, and suddenly I realized that the only reason why I rejected the vegetarian thing was out of convenience. Because everywhere you go they serve meat. I stayed with the Crass people when I was in England and other people and I just said, what the fuck am I doing. It is just so simple. I was the same thing as alcohol I realized, and it's such a logical step for straight edge – it's such a logical step for my thing.

Mark: Something that is important for me is the political thing. The way that things are right now, I think that anyone that runs for office couldn't possible represent my interests. Too much is implied, and too much money and too much power for them to be concerned with doing something "good". There are exceptions. In the end I don't think my vote counts for very much, and I do vote, I don't do it with very much relish. What I think is more important is the way we spend our money. People should vote with their money. And my big vote man, is against mechanized death. It is ridiculous.

Ian: I think the gist of all this is you have a group of people in their 20's now who want to continue to do socially relevant things...

Mark: Rebellion is a life style....

ASEXUALS

Interviewed at the Olympic Auditorium in August right after their performance...

Al: You have the name Asexuals...

Joy: Could you demonstrate for us.

John: Ha ha, well at the time we named the band we didn't have girlfriends and we thought it was a very appropriate name. And that's how it went. We wrote the song

Asexuals - photo Joe

"Asexuals" at that time.

Al: Well a name says a lot, have you ever thought of changing it?

John: No, we think it's a fine name, we like it a lot we we know nobody else would ever try to pick it up.

Al: Is there anything in particular that you write about?

John: We've been writing stuff on tour plus when I was in Europe I saw all the "Stop The City" stuff and I was really shocked. I didn't know too much about it but it was amazing.

Al: Does that influence a more political approach for you?

John: No. Maybe a couple of songs. It's just things we see and things that shock us. We want to write about things that haven't been written about before.

Sean: Song wise I like to keep away from sounding "generic thrash". We keep it mixed up, I hate bands that only talk about politics: "i hate cops", "Fuck the system", it's all been said before. I like to write about stuff I've seen.

Al: What about "Contra Rebel"?

John: "Contra Rebel" is like, what can I say, it's a old song.

Al: You circle your "A" in the name.

TJ: No! No meaning at all. The guy that made the shirts made them that way.

Al: Well you're on the bill tonight with "anarchy" bands (Conflict etc...).

John: If the circled "A" helped us out then we might as well quit now.

Danny: (Don't No) Ask them to speak French?

John: 80% of the people in Montreal are French.

Al: You guys all speak French?

John: Yeah.

Al: Do you ever sing in French for the French section of Montreal?

Sean: No, but the French punk bands sing in English.

John: It's hard to tell who is a "French punk" because all the punks are bilingual.

Al: What kind of bands influence your sound?

TJ: Subs and Clash.

Sean: I know every single Suns song they ever wrote.

John: And the Misfits.

Al: Will you continue in your present direction or go metal or...

John: No. We're happy with our sound. Metal is the worst. I don't agree with the sound and I don't agree with the attitude.

DI

Interviewed 10/28/85 at Lampost Pizza in Fullerton by Al and O (who appears invisible on tape). There was plenty of noise and distractions in the Pizza place that was crowded with local color, but we started.

Al: Where's Rikk?

John: He doesn't like interviews because we're never serious about what we're doing. So he bums out and doesn't want to be around.

Al: Why can't you get serious?

Bosco: Because we're rediculous!

Casey: Rikk gets into his own syndrome and just can't make interviews.

Jack: (DI manager) Alfie made it though.

Bosco: Alfie is straight edge.

Alfie: (smiles)........

Casey: There is some sort of unity with DI, we all flow with the same punches, but we all have added advantages that pull us all together. Alfie helps out because he's straight

Casey Royer - photo O

edge, Rikk is stressed but art, and Alfie is a good guitar player, and Bosco is like, drinks and so does John and so do I – so do we all, well almost we all.

Al: What happened to the "Drug Ideology" band?

Casey: Concepts like that never stop.

Bosco: It's the idea as saying "Drunk Idiots" or "Dumb Idea" or...

John: Drug Ideology died with the drug addictions in our band that died.

Casey: Drugs are really bad, stay away from drugs. You can smoke some pot, drink some beer – but like hard drugs, stay away from them, you don't need them.

Al: So there's one original DI person in this band but two Adolescents...

Casey: Ok, here's what's going on. While the early Adolescents were going on there was an underground DI with Rikk on drums, I played bass and Steve Roberts played guitar and a guy named Darrel sang. Then it was a power trio for awhile... Like me and Rikk were also in

early Adolescents, and this new DI, these young guys were like totally wheened on the Adolescents. They like idolized us. So we felt they'd be good in the band. They thrived on being the band.

John: I didn't cum in my jeans or anything. I don't treat him like a big God but it was a big deal, ya know. It really felt good to be asked in this band.

Al: You guys are reviving those old Adolescents songs like "Amoeba"...

Casey: We've only played a couple of songs like we did "Kids of the Black Hole" and "No Way" and um, "Word Attack" for like 2 shows. Oh yeah, we did "Amoeba" at the Olympic. It went really well, it was like 4 years since we had played that and the pit just exploded, it went really good.

Al: The are billing you as the ex-Adolescents all over the place.

Casey: Well we sound a lot like the Adolescents because of these schleppy guys that we picked up, Rikk and I wrote a lot of those songs and promoters find it a good ploy to use because we are pretty much established as having that same type of sound. It doesn't really bug me because they are into that sound.

John: Like the kids in this band get mad when Gary Tovar puts "former Adolescents" in the ads but only for the fact that we weren't in the band. What it boils down to is DI is DI. Because we work as DI and play Adolescents songs because people can relate to what's going on. When I first started listening to music Social Distortion and the Adolescents were like God to me. But I want DI to be know as DI.

Al: But Casey, you've been around long enough to see bands around you go to shit, heavy metal whatever...

John: Because Casey has a virtue, Casey has patience and it's starting to pay off.

Casey: It's kinda a combination of the Royer/Agnew energy with the Golobule /Knight intensity.

John: The Golobule/Knight rhythem section with the Agnew guitars blasting and the Royer master vocals.

Bosco: It's chaotic surge rock.

SCREAM

DI: Alfie, Bosco, John, Casey, Rikk

The Washington DC based band Scream was interviewed by Donny the Punk over several days while on tour in February. The band is: Pete Stahl- vox, Franz Stahl- guitar, Skeeter Thompson- bass, Kent Stax- drums, Robert Lee ("Harley") Davidson guitar and with them were Joey- manager/ soundman and Dave- roadie.

Donny: How did Scream start?

Skeeter: I was taking lessons from Franz, playing guitar and we started jamming together, then Pete came into the act after we found a drummer and he had a lot more control over the whole action. We all wanted to jam.

Pete: I kinda knew what I wanted to do... Scream actually came together in spring of 1979. We originally had a different drummer, Steve Alton. We used to do a lot of Sham, Buzzcocks, and we were influenced to start the band by local DC bands like Razz and the Bad Brains.

Skeeter: It was a small community from a high school. Bailey's Crossroads in Fairfax Co. Virginia, a Washington suburb. We just wanted to play for our friends and have a good time. We were in our late teens.

Pete: We were the first band to start in our area.

Donny: What happened between '79 and your first LP in '82?

Pete: After playing parties, the Bad Brains gave us a chance to play at the Wilson Center, I guess in the summer of '80, we played here and there. The '81 the Bad Brains got us our first show in New York at CBGB's. In summer of '82 we did our first tour. When we got back Dischord (Ian and Jeff) offered us a chance to record an album, so we did and it was released.

Donny: How has the bands sound evolved and changed since 1979?

Franz: Actually it's stayed the same.

Pete: It's just gotten better, we play our instruments better. We've found some new musical styles, like reggae, but we haven't thrown any away, it just becomes part of our music.

Donny: To what do you attribute the stability of the membership of Scream?

Scream: We get along with each other, and we're all into doing the same thing.

Skeeter: With a lot of bands they don't know each other that well. They're fair weather friends, they only see each other when they practice. A lot of competition, who's in charge etc... It still happends with Scream but we're able to talk it out. We yell at each other but we still pat each other on the back. We have weeks when nothing seems to go right, but we still practice, when some other bands would start to crumble, stabbing each other in the back and a lot of hatred builds up. It happens in most bands after awhile.

Franz: We definitely argue a lot. If we keep it bottled up, then we wouldn't stay together. There's a lot of compromise involved, when you band people together like that. Decisions, it mainly comes down to Pete.

Skeeter: Pete is like a leader, but he's not like a leader that would send you into battle when you'd rather retreat. He motivates me.

Pete: I feel like we're brothers and I'm mainly like an older brother.

Donny: What qualities are most important in providing leadership for a band?

Pete: Probably thinking that you know what's right... You got 4 or 5 energy sources in the band, I try to pull it all together, instead of going in all different directions; sometimes you

Scream

gotta take it by the throat, make that first step and just go for it.

Donny: How do you all earn a living and how do you work out conflicts between your income producing and the band?

Pete: The pressure is always on you to make a career for yourself. If you've been in a band in a few years and you haven't made any moves to do something else with your life, you start worrying about it. A regular person, you get out of high school, you start working towards your retirement. I don't really want to be part of that type of system. I just want to do what I want to do right now, play rock and roll, sing. If you get yourself a career in the long run it's kind of a slow suicide because you loose your identity as a person and right now I'm staking out my own identity that's something a lot of people can't say.

Skeeter: It's terrible when you think about all the people

Skeeter: It's terrible when you think about all the people that wake up every morning with the sole purpose of going to work, really got their whole life set on working hard: their deal is to do that. The Establishment tries to mold you from a child going to school. The hours are almost the same.The teacher is your boss, telling you what to do... You got your upper class, the really rich people, they keep the other people oppressed and it's an oppressed system, Oh on down the line. Do what you want if it makes you happy, but the system doesn't make me happy at all, because for our people the system is just a lot of shit.

Donny: What musical influences have had effect on your own music?

Franz: All 60's music, southern rock, jazz classic punk. I didn't start getting into reggae 'til a little after I started getting into the punk music, more like ska like the Specials. At the beginning there may have been one force that drove us to write a certain type music, but now our influences are really coming out. Before it was the fastest and the loudest.

Skeeter: My 'Idol'if I can use that word was wilder-type soul, later on mellow or soft rock, Cat Stevens... I think we're a band that could mesh between a lot of scenes: our main scene is music.

Kent: Bands from the 60's: Beatles, Rolling Stones, Doors, Bob Marley. When the punk

thing came out I was really interested in it: I heard a lot of stuff. In my drum playing, my god is definitely John from Led Zeppelin. I really liked led Zeppelin a lot, still do.

Donny: What does it feel like to be up on stage and performing?

Skeeter: A long time ago I used to be really paranoid, very unsure of myself, very tense: and I think Franz and everybody else was: but we have more confidence now when we go up on stage. When we play, the concentration is very intense, even though it seems like we're doing' it pretty easy. I can't see after ten feet.

Harley: To me it's like a dog. It's like adrenalin starts flowing: I swear to God it's like a drug. After the show you walk off stage it's like withdrawals, you start coming down. It happens in a flesh: an hour-and-a-half set seems like ten minutes.

Kent: You can have 15 hours of sleep, go up there and play for 15 minutes and you're exhausted.

Donny: Do you think someone who could only make out the words of the chorus would get a very different impression of the song than someone who knows the whole lyrics?

Pete: Yeah might.

Donny: Does that concern you?

Pete: Yeah, not worried about that. What can you do? It's like putting a bag over your head and suffocating your brains.."Still Screaming": the lyrics are old. That song really exemplifies alot of my feelings about fans. I've been singing those lyrics to different songs since we started.

Donny: It relates to the name of the band?

Pete: I guess so.

Donny: Where does the name come from?

Pete: I thought it was a good name for a rock n' roll band. You can take it alot of different ways, but it's to be heard above everything else...

Donny: Where do you see the punk scene going now?

Kent: I think it's growing! The music is definitely going towards a heavy metal/hardcore type of sound. I don't think it'll ever die.

Franz: I see a cycle, returning back to the early type of punk, more melodic, less generic thrash, it seems to me more emphasis is

being put on playing of the instruments. As far as the direction of Scream, our influences are coming our real strong right now. We're really not satisfied sticking to one type of sound.
Donny: Do you feel you have a purpose in life?
Skeeter: Society has covered up alot of powers that I think I have. Just recently I've discovered more of them, like being able to sense when something is gonna happen; just trying to get more aware of that, use the other parts of the brain.
Pete: No, I don't think so. Or I haven't figured it out yet.
Franz: I really don't know. I wasn't put on this earth to my asking.
Harley: Playing my guitar. That's a hard question!
Kent: Yes, to be alive I guess.
Donny: And now we'll turn over a card and see what our audience said....
Donny: Is there any significant areas in the life of the band we haven't covered yet?
Skeeter: On thing about the band, it's an obsession almost like a drug. It's more like a habit.

FLIPSIDE NUMBER 48

"Riding on the rocket, I wanna go to Pluto
Space foods are marshmallow, aspara and ice cream
Blue eyed cat said, 'Let me go with you'
Let's go, Let's go, Let's go with me
Mercury, Venus, Earth, Mars, Jupiter,
Saturn, Uranus, Neptune and Pluto
Be in radio communication with you Hello Hello...
Earth became a star Hello Hello...
Blue eyed cat is dancing the manbo shaking hip
Floating, floating, floating in the air
Space walk dance party, Bottoms up,
drink to space walk."
'Riding on the Rocket'- Shonen Knife

ISSUE #: 48
DATE: February 1986
FORMAT: 8 1/2x11, rotary web offset with 2 color glossy cover.
PAGES: 68
PRICE: $1.50
PRESS RUN: 10,000

The only big change in this issue is the cover price. Yes, after five years we booted up the charge to $1.50. Paper, printing, shipping etc costs went up in the last five years, not to mention we've added more pages along the line, so the price just had to go up a little. So

there.

The scene continues "healthy" with some new bands sporting some great ideas. One of those bands is Final Conflict, who seem to be the strongest carries of "political" punk that L.A. has ever scene, and their attitude about it is well thought out. It's 1986 and this seems to be punk rocks ten year anniversary, but no big deal, life goes on....

WHATS CHANGED IN TEN YEARS

A lot of people are calling 1986 the ten year anniversary of punk rock. This is probably the case if you must date such things so accurately - and without getting into definitions or debating "who was first", I'd just like to comment on what point we seem to have gotten to in the "first" ten years.

Nowhere. Yes, on one hand I see that we have come full circle in the last decade. Everything that so called "punk rock" set out to destroy has crept back into our scene and and in some cases has taken over. Most obvious is the recent embrace by a lot of punks of "heavy metal". Now I'm not talking about the music, which in some cases is very similar. But what about those egotistical solos? They can keep it. It's the attitude that is the problem. I've been to the shows, I've talked to the people and this is indeed the completion of the circle. Everybody's fave metal band Motorhead are the classic example: they demand a very high door price - only so they could spend the money on their limo, full meals (that were left backstage for food fights) an overkill pa that sounded like shit anyway, etc... I could go on about the inept sexism of Slayer or the absurd "satanism" of the rest of them, but what's the use. In my eyes that will be "punk rocks" coffin. But I have faith that, like all the rest of the trends, heavy metal is just the latest dying fad.

But what about the attitude of the members of our own scene? Yeah, the heavy door prices are with us too, the bands wanting a guarantee over a percentage, big time management and lawyers and the ever popular squabble over billing. Those things have always been there, whether on not people wanted to acknowledge it. They are worse these days with some bands, but others are still trying to carry the punk flag. Basically I think it is the problem of bands getting out of touch with their own business - bands that are letting others do too much for them. A few years ago a band would have been excited to get a gig - then go out of their way to make and distribute a creative flyer. Now it seems that bands don't want to play the small shows, and would rather sit around and wait for their big "arena concert". And of course went that comes up they do no promotion of their own, but simply sit back and let the promoter do it. I think the old way built more character. It's the same with records - most bands that sign up with label have no idea whatsoever of where their records go, what fanzines review them, what radio stations play them, or what stores are selling them. "It's the labels job!". Well remember the DIY (Do It Yourself) attitude? It's really dying.

I think the simple answer is that it is ten years later. You can't blame people for getting tired of doing things the hard way. We are not as young as we used to be - and at some point your energies get directed in some

other direction. It's easy to get bored with the same old thing and you have to move on. That isn't bad - but there is a certain element that creeps in to manipulate people at this stage, and fuck them over for whatever amount of money. If that doesn't happen then some of those old punks just get co-opted into the system that doesn't look so different anymore. In fact it may be quite appealing. If you look at most punk bands of days gone by, you'll know what I mean. After all, they aren't punks anymore, right?

So who are the punks? The press always refers to "punks" like it's the same group people who have been around for a long time and never change, never get any older. No. All of those people that I condemned above, they "were" the punks, they served their time. In their day and age they served with as much dedication and energy as any new kids serving today. I'm not saying that their day is over either, they can still contribute if they want to, maybe not directly in the "punk scene" anymore, but, but hopefully by spreading the values to the outside world. Punk is an attitude that should only change its mode of expression with time. The punk scene is a dynamic movement of people that will exist as long as there are youth out there to keep it happening, to be rebellious, energetic and outrageous. I don't necessarily mean politically rebellious - I'm talking about kids who reach the age where something clicks inside them and they feel they want to do things themselves. Kids that are fed up with conditions around them - be it socially, musically or whatever. I think that as long as these kids are attracted to the punk scene as an openminded place where "new" ideas can be shared, then the punk scene will keep regenerating itself, and will survive another ten years. If not, it will die like the first metal wave did in the seventies - as something that everyone just got bored with.

FINAL CONFLICT

Interview by Joy Aoki.
Ron- vocals, **Jeff-** guitar, **Warren-** bass and **Dave-** drums.
Joy: Do you get classified as a "peace punk" band or an "anarchist" band?
All: We're a punk band!!
Warren: We're punks and we have anti-nuke views. But...
Ron: We're not going to label ourselves.
Jeff: Anarchy can only be a personal thing - as long as you have to pay taxes in this world. But when it comes to getting booked for a show...
Dave: It's like "Well, we'll put you on THIS bill..."
Ron: Cause there's another peace band playing.
Jeff: Yeah the guy goes, "We'll put you on another bill that you fit". Like who would want to go to a show with 5 bands all into the same thing. Let's see some variation.
Dave: That's kind of silly in the punk scene. We'll play peace bills but we don't want to do nothing but those.
Jeff: "We'll play nothing but 2 dollar gig with nothing but vegetarians". It's that old thing, tell me something I don't already know. They've heard it all a million times. We want to play in front of people who have never heard what we've got to say.
Ron: We might get ragged on behind our backs by people for playing Goldenvoice

Final Conflict - photo Joy

shows, but we will play any Goldenvoice show and take the money he'll give us because he reaches a wide audience.
Jeff: He (Gary Tovar) is a nice guy also, I mean he's making a living just like I do when I go to work everyday.
Joy: Do you all have jobs?
All: Yup!
Jeff: Ron and I are printers.
Ron: That's how we get our flyers printed.
Dave: People see our flyers, posters and people might think "Oh, who's making these for them?"
Ron: Like we're rockstars or something.
Jeff: Ron does them at his work, on his own time, and I do them at my work on my own time.
Ron: And we usually do it for free. So we're not paying for the leaflets we hand out. I do it myself at work. The posters that we have to sell, we sell them cheap. we're jeopardizing our jobs for this but it means a lot to us.
Dave: But don't write us off as "political". I got asked by some guy one night "what's politics?" We're into survival.
Ron: I don't think that people have to know every fucking thing that goes on in the world everyday but maybe they should at least be aware of things going down so when something bad happens, they just won't say "well, that's the way it is..."
Jeff: "There's nothing I can do".
Ron: That's how Hitler took over Germany so easily. People bitch about how bad the cops are, but they don't do anything about it. We tell them: call the ACLU, call the Press, do something. They'll say "Ok" but when I ask them about it a week later they'll just say "It was nothing".
Jeff: If you've got the right representatives and the constitution behind you, pick it apart. Spell it out for them that you're right and they're wrong.
Ron: Actually, sometimes it is futile, you just can't do anything. But if more people would at least try to do something, the cops will think "these guys won't take the shit" and maybe be more conscious of their actions.
Joy: What do you like on your pizza?
Dave: Aw? Gee, that's good...
Ron: Olives, mushrooms, but I heard

mushrooms aren't all that good for you, high in carcinogens... Bell peppers...
Warren: I like meat on mine.
Dave: You can eat pizza without meat and not know the difference.
Warren: Are you kidding, DUDE!?
Dave: Well you have the vegetarian people who are respectful for animals and everything, but I see them turn around and be disrespectful of people. That's a contradiction. Why are they disrespectful to me?
(Talk goes into anarchism)
Warren: If you talk about how perfectly anarchy could work, by the same token perfect democracy can work, perfect communism can work...
Dave: While people are saying "think for yourself", a lot of people are actually saying "think like me". I have a friend like that, and sometimes that's coming across as really insulting. It's a contradiction to disrespect people, insult them and tell them they're wrong.
Ron: Don't make your lifetime judgement on

us just by what we've said in this interview, it's hard to do but don't pass judgement until you meet or know us.
Jeff: People write and ask us "Well, what could we do?" Well, we're doing our flyers and our main goal is to make people aware as far as Nuclear disarmament is concerned...
Ron: Maybe we won't change the world but at least we're trying...

FISHBONE

This interview was done in the darkest corners of the Olympic Auditorium before and after Fishbone opened for the Dead Kennedys.
Joy: Why did you name your band Fishbone?
Fish: A Fishbone can represent many things. It represents a fish, which is the only animal that is submerged in a sinking situation that survives. Also, the bone itself is what holds us all together. Without your bones you'd be only loose skin with some eyes and teeth, no you wouldn't have your teeth, all gums.
Hudley: You all grew up together?
Fish: Yes. We all met in Jr. High. we went from the bedroom to the club circuit to be signed to the biggest record label there is.
Joy: How are you guys staying away from the rock star image?
Special K: Well, by not doing a lot of drugs, or stepping on people, and hanging out in the crowd. It shows. I'll probably slam to the D.K.'s like anyone else here tonight.
Pooch: I've seen you play with so many different types of bands.
Special K: That's what it's all about. It doesn't matter because we dig all kinds of music. It's all about getting your message across and breaking down barriers.
Pooch: You reacted very well with the kids tonight. They were jumping all over you.
Special K: That's happens anyway. It gets pretty radical at Fishbone shows, even with thee band itself. You get people stage diving, slamming, skanking or whatever. It's not that, but it's fucking ignorance. Even though our bass player got stabbed, he didn't what the show to be stopped. After all the time we've been playing, we have never been spat upon. You know it's something you live with because I've been

Fishbone - photo Joe

to a hardcore show. It wasn't so much that. It was the fact that people came up on stage and it was their first hardcore show. They were going "Fuck you" flexing their muscles and impressing their friends. People were here tonight simply to fight. I said "If you want to fight, come up here on stage, we'll take you on!".

Angelo: Once we get enough power we want to convert the whole world. What I'm really obsessed with is that Fishbone feeling. It's the feeling that you get when you listen to a certain type of music, the feeling that will make you go insane, the feeling that will make you dance, the feeling that unlocks the deep emotions of all people. It's really hard for me to control and I want other people to share it. Norwood had that feeling and someone tried to fuck it up for him by stabbing him in the armpit.

Pooch: You guys were more topical tonight as opposed to your record which is a lot more fun. For example you dedicated "Ugly" to Reagan.

Angelo: We have always been politically oriented. The government mainly wants to control the whole world. If someone doesn't do something they are going to destroy the whole human race and there will be no more nothing nowhere!! We're really concerned about the whole thing and we gotta say something. Most of the top 40 radio stations put on these sissy new wave bands who sing about "fucking my baby in the back seat of the car". All it is is subliminal fascism.

Special K: If you read through all the bullshit and find out what we're talking about, we're not all that motherfucking funny. The whole thing is people dance to forget. You ask somebody right in the middle of the slam pit "What did that group say tonight?" He'll say "I don't give a fuck!" and they don't. People come to shows for their emotions and dance to forget. It is sad if punk rock is the positive movement it professes to be. It's really fucked because these same people are going to join the Army, Air Force or Marines because they happened to see it on TV.

Joy: Do you believe television warps peoples minds?

Fish: When I was young, my mind was warped by cartoons. I plan on sueing the government because of those damn cartoons. You can't escape form 'em. Now I have a cartoon mind. Everything I do seems sort of animated. That goes for the whole damn band.

Angelo: I've been brainwashed by cartoons. Look at me man! I look like a fucking cartoon!! The majority of people out there grew up watching Yosemite Sam getting blown up and coming back to life. That's what Viet Nam was all about. As weird as it seems fascism is taking over. It's not open in the United States, it's subliminal. It's a world wide thing. We can't say that just the U.S. is fucked, USSR is fucked, England is fucked... everybody is so goddamn stingy! Everybody has got to have a fucking chair up their ass!

Joy: So, what's the solution?

Angelo: The solution is peace, which I think will never happen because man isn't perfect.

Special K: If you want to take a microcosm of society, look at this show tonight. How many FFF's and Suicidal boys will beat their heads together tonight?

Angelo: The only way peace is going to happen is with a miracle. It's time we stopped and everyone started over again, it could

happen. It's because people are so pigheaded today, it pisses me off. However, if things weren't so fucked up, I'd be a boring person because I wouldn't have anything to get mad about.

Special K: everyone in the world should bone. Maybe if we fucked each other, we wouldn't fight each other.

NECROS

Interviewed at the Olympic Auditorium sometime in December by Al, Joe and Bill.

Al: What direction are the Necros headed musically, band wise, spiritually...?

Barry: Musically we're going in our own direction. That's all I can say, it's the Necros direction. We've had various record company problems. After Corey left the Necros we thought we were still on Touch and Go, but we were always waiting to record, he never had the money. So we were being blown off without being told.

Andy: After January there will be a flood of records...

Barry: We'd like to have a record out every six months now.

Al: Last time you were out here most of you had shorter hair.

Barry: It grew, that's all there is to it.

Al: I was going to say that people might lump you into the blossoming new metal thing...

Andy: "Blossoming new!"

Barry: Our attitude on this thing is that we have nothing to do with it, our attitudes are completely different. We are a brotherhood of one- there is no brotherhood in what we do, we have no brother bands... I think punk rock covers any form of hard raunchy music, fast music that is based more on aggression, more on getting aggressions out rather than showing how pretty you are on stage like a band like Yes or something. Bands like the Stooges or MC5 can be considered punk rock and I think even Aerosmith can be considered punk rock. Maybe not today, but in 1974 when they were as punk rock as GBH.

Andy: In Detroit people don't think we're a hardcore band, maybe the kids do, but half of the crowd is just other kinds of people.

Barry: What we've achieved in Detroit is what

we want to achieve nationally and that is to be taken on our own, regardless of what's going on around. I'd like to develop to a point where we're putting records out that you can put on ten years from now and still like, that you wouldn't say: "Wow, this is dated and terrible". I put on a Stooges or New York Dolls record and I think it sounds great – they were way ahead of their time.

Al: Barry, you are writing the lyrics, what's on your mind for lyrics these days?

Barry: It's less anthemic. It's more personal. "Tangled Up" is about frustration, not knowing where you're going, worrying about the future – but I doubt if you could descern that from the lyrics. It's not straight forward, it's not like out in your face.

Bill: What do you think of the new kids bringing up straight edge and...

Barry: Straight edge is ok...

Al: I was shocked, I saw you pounding the brews Barry!

Barry: I had some beers, yeah, I don't smoke pot, rarely do drugs.

Bill: As your hair gets longer.... no, you drink with a mature attitude?

Barry: No. I drink with a completely spastic adolescent attitude.

Andy: Otherwise it's no fun.

Barry: I don't go out and get into a car and drive, and I don't pick fights. The straight edge thing is fine but it's weird to see west coast bands being influenced by east coast bands.

DESCENDENTS

Interviewed at their headquarters in December by Al.

Al: What is the "Bonus Cup" story?

Bill: It's just a cup, more a novelty type item than any part of the bands roots – in a sense it is the bands roots because a lot of the "food" type songs would have never come about if I wasn't into my caffeine problem. I would have never wrote something like that. It's like when I used to commercial fish, my partner was a real speed guy – he took lots of pills. And I've never taken a drug before, never. Just caffeine. I'm not saying I'm Jesus Christ or anything.. so he taught me like "let's

Necros – photo O

Descendents intermediate stage with Frank, Bill, Milo, Tony and Ray – photo Al

go fishing tonight, and let's go fishing tomorrow night too and the next night..." I was into it and he would have these pills and I didn't have anything so I would make these bonus cups, where I'd put a real lot of instant coffee in, if you look at the cup there's lines... I mean everybody has shirts and stickers and we have cups.

Al: It seems to me that the Descendents have gone thru a few stages of development.

Bill: I'd say there were 5 stages, obviously each day is a new stage, but there were 5 stages the way I look at it. The first was the trio, the "Ride the Wild" trio: me, Frank and Tony. It was more of a heavy power pop thing, it's wasn't quite a distorted guitar thing, more like the Last...

Milo: Or surf music...

Bill: More "let's have fun" with a little harmonies and singing, more acoustic based songs. Then there was the blurry period where we had various singers. Milo surfaces as our actual singer at that point.

Al: At that time you had trouble getting gigs.

Bill: Oh yeah. "Weinerschnitzel" broke us in that sense, because that even got airplay on comersh stations because it's so fucking funny. That was the last thing I expected. But once we got Milo and got started we had a good thing going. Then was like our "Fat" period. we released the "Fat" ep, we were all fat, we were huge boys, except Milo and Tony, me and Frank were huge. We were into just songs about fishing and food. that was our total "punk" thing if you're gonna call it that. Then came the point where we decided to start practicing a real real lot and record an album, it will be hot. And it will be the last record with Milo, it will be the document of our 4th stage – with Milo, the Milo stage. "Milo Goes To College" got released late 82. Then there was the dormant stage when I was in Flag, I did that and Milo went to college. Now I quit Flag, we're back together and we put out "I Don't Want To Grow Up".

Al: So you went form singing about "fishing and food" to on "Grow Up" there's a lot of songs about girls.

Bill: Well, Milo's got more songs on "Grow Up" about girls, every song is about girls.

Milo: We sang about girls on both records, it's just that on "Milo Goes To College" I didn't express the kind of stuff I wanted to express the way it should have been expressed. I was basically screaming the whole way through. Which is cool, but when you talk about "this girl left me" it's a bummer, and maybe it's not

a good thing to scream about because you're not feeling that way. On "Grow Up" is was more melancholy, we're singing about the same things, just approaching it a different way.

Al: Do people ever comment that songs like "No Fat Bever" might sound sexist?

Milo: In Lincoln Nebraska a girl came up to me and she said she was real happy to meet me and everything but she said she almost had to cry when she listened to our album because of those two songs: "No Fat Bever" and "Pervert". I spend half an hour explaining to her that when you write a song it's like a flash or something. I wrote "No Fat Bever" is was like "stay away from me", which is what I felt about this one girl.. I may have only felt that way for two minutes, then two minutes later I might have felt "well she's not that bad looking" or whatever. In those two minutes I wrote that song. She was bummed because I was making this big sexist statement. Like I was putting the whole feminist movement back 100 years or something.

Al: People write Flipside letters and tell us that the Descendents were here "and boy were they aggressive girl hunters!"

Bill: Oh. (Laughter) Sometimes, if I don't have a steady girlfriend for any reason, yeah, then I go on a little rampage there. But it's just to maintain my physical thing. I have a real high hormone level or something. I need a lot of sex. I just do, it's not something I can help. I'm not a womanizer, none of us are....

(Talk goes on to farting etc...)

Bill: I do see a definite place in this culture for the kind of shock prevented by several band members whipping out parts of their bodies or pretending like they're doing gross things or laying down a nice bare ass fart right next to someone. I don't think that is rude or crude, but I think that it is good for society to be exposed to that sort of thing. If more of that went on there wouldn't be things like cops or insurance, or nuclear reactors... Someone has to make those go away but I don't think it's by playing songs about getting drunk or something – you have to stir people up by offending them. I played guitar in the Nig Heist, that was fucking culture shock at it's most. I thrived on that. I felt like I was doing my duty to this world by being in that band. Mugger is like a saint for that.

Al: What going on in college Milo, did you graduate?

Milo: I don't know, It's like... I have a problem. I like to immerse myself in things. I'm obsessed

with music and I'm obsessed with biology – so what can I do? You can't have more than one obsession, you dilute the other out. At this point I'm obsessed with music, with the Descendents, with going somewhere and making music. In 5 months I may be totally obsessed with biology, with finding the cure for cancer. Then I'd have to change all my energies to that.

Bill: I'm totally immersed in music.

MICRONOTZ

This interview was done by mail Nov/Dec 1985 after I had the pleasure of seeing the Micronotz play live, only the third gig I've gotten to see inside Leavenworth Prison. The Micronotz are Jay– guitar/vocals, John– guitar, David– bass and Steve– drums. The are the best band to ever come out of Kansas. Interview by Shane Williams.

Shane: What is the names orgin?

David: We got the name from the little robot toys we used to have, based on the comic book "Micronauts". The "mortal" was added because that's what we are and the spelling was changed so we weren't ripping off the comic book people. We dropped the "mortal" because the name was too long, and everyone else was dropping it too.

Shane: When you guys sing "Proud To Be A Farmer", it's easy to think that you're entirely facetious, but the chorus "you don't know nothing so don't put me down" belies that. Do any of you come from farm families?

Steve: The song is serious and isn't supposed to be a putdown on farmers. Actually Jay has a shirt that says that and he was wearing it when we were working on the song so that's what it was called, and then we wrote the words. Being from Kansas there are lots of farmers around, but we're not farmers. John's parents have a farm and we've all been on farms, for sure we hope the farmers situation improves.

Shane: From what I understand, you guys are going to be a touring band, always on the move. Do you think that you miss out on anything being on the road? What do your folks or girlfriends think of this dedication?

John: If we're going to miss out on anything by being a touring band, it's going to be a bunch of bullshit. Commitments I personally don't want.

David: Of course we'll miss out a lot, but we'll gain more by being on the road. The problems are more involved. You can't be on the road all of the time, you have to have some other type of life or you'll go crazy. The hard part is keep it all together financially and mentally. I think everybody is pretty much all for it. Everybody knows how long we've been doing this and we'll do it till we can't take it anymore.

Steve: Off and on it's a real problem with girlfriends and parents who don't always understand the devotion, but they're gonna get on your case no matter what you do.

Shane: Let me preface this question by saying that I despise the attitude of a lot of older, established punks that they are the only decent bands around. When I saw you your equipment was covered with stickers of various bands. Do you enjoy listening to lots of bands?

Steve: Sometimes if bands say they're great then people will believe it and so they are. We've played with all sorts of cool bands of all types and styles. It's alright to have favorite bands that you listen to, but hopefully we've all chosen our favorites from as wide a selection as possible.

John: There are lots, tons of decent bands in the US and the world, the problem is that many of them are still doing the same thing, no excuses, so are we, but it seems pretty futile to try and be the best at something that's been worked into the ground. It's almost as boring as seeing a band do covers of Stones or Beatles, or try to see a band outdo those bands in the same vein. Hardcore, as far as I'm concerned has peaked. It may not decline for awhile but it's not growing.

Shane: On an earlier album you had lyrics by William Burroughs...

David: Good, we always get a Burroughs question, glad to have Bill answer it.

Bill: (Bill Rich, Fresh Sounds Records) The Micronotz relationship with Burroughs came about because I was working with James Burroughs manager, in the studio on some jects. The band was ready to record and had one song without words and William had a pop song that he gave us. I've been working and helping since then. Through some other business associates I started distributing some unique videos and the new releases with the cut ups fit in well so we're doing it.

Shane: You guys are pretty handsome, what's the groupie scene like if any?

Steve: You meet lots of different types of people under lots of different circumstances playing on the road. People come to see us for different reasons. If they come to mingle, we're background music, if they come for sex, well... There are lots of different ways to communicate and relate to other people. There's nothing wrong with sex, but we try to be fairly selective.

SHONEN KNIFE

Interviewed through the mail by Hudley:.
Hud: How long has Shonen Knife been together?
Naoko: We formed on December 29th, 1981. We have been playing with the same members since then.
Hud: What does your name mean?
Naoko: Shonen = boy. "Shonen Knife" is the brand name of a pocket knife for children.
Hud: Who influences you musically·
Naoko: I'm influenced by all of my favorite

music, before and after 80's punk, southeast Asian pops, Mowtown sounds rock and roll and etc... Especially the Ramones, XTC, the Jam, Nick Lowe, Style Council, the Beatles and Marvin Gaye. Lyrically... I'm influenced by books, by experiences and by other informations. I made many lyrics about foods. I make lyrics with comical essences.

Hud: Who writes the music and lyrics?
Naoko: Michie (bass) and I (guitar) write pieces together, for example from the last tape "Burning Farm" Michie wrote "Watching Girl", "Miracles", "Animal Song" and "Banana Fish". I wrote the other songs "Parallel Women", "Twist Birbie" and "Elephant Pao Pao" etc.

Hud: Do you play a lot of gigs?
Naoko: Yes we do. We play one or two times a month in Osaka or Kyoto, and we play in Tokoyo occasionally.

Hud: What are your audiences like?
Naoko: High school and college students or ordinary twenties people. Male to female ratio is 6 to 1.

Hud: What are the bands that you play with?
Naoko: With Japanese new wave bands, for example: Rosaluxembury, Vchotan and etc. And lots of kids dance in various styles.

---**Introduction to members:**
Naoko Yamano - vocals/guitar
Hobbies- Playing tennis, watching comedies of Osaka, reading, watching Sumo on TV (Sumo is a Japanese sport), playing in Shonen Knife.
Favorite food- Ice cream, noodles, choco-bars, mints, hot taste foods.
Hope- Live in UK and USA.
Michie Nakatani - vocals/bass
Hobbies- Watching movies, drawing pictures, cycling, swimming.
Favorite writers- Boris Vian, Jean Austin.
Favorite foods- Sashimi, curry rice, ice cream with carmel.
Favorite fruit- Japanese pears
Happy time- When eating delicious foods.
Atsuko Yamano - drums/side vocals
Hobbies- Dress making, playing in the band, watching Sumo in breathless suspense, watching comic back chat.
Favorite foods- Ice cream, chocolate, potato chips, shabu-shabu, tempura.
Favorite fruit- Banana, melon
Hope- Go to UK again and live there, row a boat at a pond in Hyde Park.

FLIPSIDE NUMBER 49

Shonen Knife

"What's this world coming to
No one ever cares
People so worried about their looks their hair
Everything is twisted, minds are on rewind
Are we still looking
But no one seems to find
Freedom is a word
That no one ever knows
Money is their greed
Money they can have
Look and you shall find
It's not true anymore
This world we will never be
How I want it to be
Faces, faces, faces
All I see are faces
Burning holes right through my back
Trying to hold on
But still trying to withdraw
Holding to the rail
I think I'm going to fall."
'In My Heart'- ASF

ISSUE #:49
DATE: June 1986
FORMAT: 8 1/2x11, rotary web offset with 2 color glossy cover.
PAGES: 68
PRICE: $1.50
PRESS RUN: 10,000

This is a pretty standard Flipside, on the outside, but underneath it all this is the firs issue produced with the help of a computer! A one hundred dollar investment got us the basics, and introduced us to what we would need. A lot of inspiration from Maximum Rock N' Roll helped as well. So there it is computerized mailing lists, fanzines lists and radio station lists in this issue. Soon to come would be the records reviews and letters section. Now, this entire issue was done on our computer, an upgraded version of tha first machine of course.

In Tune
Hudley's Editorial

Did you know that Coffee Shops are becoming obsolete? Do you care? How about clubs, did you know they've become obsolete too!

Both are important places, special places, magical places, because they bring people together in a rather quaint way. And here is where people get in tune with each other!

Near my house (in the middle of the block) in the town of Whittier, I often go to a near by Coffee Shop. The place is called 'Jacks Salad Bowl', it's about as tacky as it sounds but it's cool. Lots of elders hang-out there since their teens and maybe even longer. I go there to listen mostly, but I often share in a conversation or two. I talk to all sorts of people such as the local Preacher or a nice lady Child Psychologist. And maybe a smile from a waitress might take my blues away, usually does.... a historical situation!!

Going to 'Jacks Salad Bowl' helps me get in touch with where people are at, and it's better than sitting at home watching T.V. or listening to the same records on the stereo.

Clubs are the same as Coffee Shops because they also bring people together though, the club have mostly the youthful. But that's becoming obsolete no-thanks to over 21 clubs.! I've met quite a lot of interesting people at clubs, there's nothing like the experience of a small show at a club were everyone's into the bands. People are in tune at these types of shows, and just being there one can communicate so much to an individual, even if not to many words are shared.

The tunes of the past are changing. The clubs that brought individuals together in the past have metamorphosized into Hall shows and Olympic concerts! The individual people type of scene is now a group or gang scene. The punk social happening really has materialized into a pattern of violence and conformity. The stereotyped punks of yesterday, have become the punks of today, no-thanks to the media and films.

What tune can be tuned into now? There is like this crazy distortion between the individual tuning forks. The shining moments of the scene have become dull and void.

This brings me to some words by an interesting person named Geza X (aka: Dead Beats, Geza X and The Mommymen). He was around at the beginning of the LA Punk scene and is still around!? He once described the scene as having a kind of mass telepathy power. Something that brought the kids together. And he said more of that power is needed for what he called an 'Evolutionary Leap'! And he states that in the song he called,

'We Need More Power' :

"We need more power, Civilization is in pretty deep, We all want to win, but the price is too steep. Our backs are in the corner, we're gonna die like sheep. Our backs are in the corner, we've got to make an evolutionary leap.
But there's a problem, we need more power...
Extra, extra read it and weap, the futures getting grim and life is getting cheap, our ethics are a shambles, Our history is a heap, we've got to make a evolutionary leap.
We need more power, form a human winch, let's grab reality, and move it over about an inch. If the river is there, then the river is crossable, We've got to concentrate on doing the impossible,
But there is a problem, we need more power."
I'd have to say: Where is the power now? And where is the human winch? Maybe the scene is dying out.

Maybe 'Hands Across America' could be used as an example of the type of power we need!!! The Saturday evening before 'Hands Across America', I had a strong pull to listen to music from the original soundtrack of 'Woodstock' and to listen to some music by 'The Who' and 'Janis Joplin'. The 60's had a power going and it died? Maybe some of the old hippies helped create the whole 'Hands Arcoss America'?

Almost two decades ago the hippie/flower children movement was alive, but it died, is the punk scene also dying or is it already dead?

Personally I feel torn between bands, people in the scene and lyrics. What I tuned into has faded because of so many reasons. Maybe I'm growing up, maybe others are? The bands and the lyrics I believed in are not relative anymore. They have all moved far apart from each other. The magnifing glass no longer has the sun shining through it's lens. The suns rays no longer are burning it's focal point and a dark shadow has blocked the source of power. of the light!!

I'll end this little editorial by sharing a 'tuning in' moment.

After 'Hands Across America', we all let go of our hands and we said goodbye to people we'd probably never see again. We crossed the street and while walking to our car (In Jacks Salad Bowl parking lot), I happened to catch a biker kind of guy walking near me, and he was saying.... "From 'Woodstock' to 'Hands Across America' I made it, I'll have something to tell my grandchildren". (This guy was beaming) Of course I was drawn to him like a warp in spacetime and said, "You were at Woodstock?!!!" (Remembering my last nights evening musical entertainment!!) He told me he had been there and I politely asked if I could shake his hand, and we did shake hands!!! And at that moment I felt a reality move through me because of that touch, that tuning in!!! At that moment two youth rebellions were brought together and were united, '66 to 86', two decades, brought to a timeless now!!! I also remembered his remark, "I'll have something to tell my Grandchildren!"

His grandchildren maybe part of a future rebellion, which the two of us may never visit, maybe not even in our dreams. And if I ever have children, I'll have something to tell them... and of course my grandchildren.....

THE PAST
The Who 'Tune In On You'

"I'm singing this note, cause it fits in well with the chords I'm playing.
I can't pretend there's meaning here in the things I'm saying.
But I'm in tune, right in tune, I'm in tune, and I'm going to tune right in on you (repeat chorus)
I got a little tired having to say do you come here often.
But when I look in your eyes, I can see the harmonies, and the heart ache softens.
I'm getting in tune, right in tune (Repeat chorus)
I got it all here in my head, there is nothing more needs to be said.
I just banging on my own piano, I'm getting in tune to the straight and narrow.
I'm singing this note cause it fits in will with the way I'm feeling.
There's a symphony that I here in your heart sets my heart a reeling.
But I'm in tune."

NEAR PRESENT
Marginal Man 'Fallen Pieces'
"As they fall by the way side, who's there to pick them up?
People who were once just on the same level, are now just weeds by the highway.
They used to be friends and they used to be enemies.
Dropping like flies with no cries of distress."

PRESENT
ASF "In My Heart"
(Same song, see above #49)

RANK AND FILE

Chip and Tony Kinman first made themselves known to inquiring ears as the Dils, pioneers of revolutionary music and one of the most political, controversial, irritating, and ultimately influential bands to emerge from the early punk ear. Eventually, fed up with the West Coast scene and seeking a new sound with which to offend audiences, they fled for Austin and found Rank and File. In doing so, laid down the groundwork for the legions of new country bands that exist today.

The interview was done at Cantor's Deli in Hollywood by Martha Rose O'Meara.

Martha: You were talking about country music being a fad in England...

Chip: Yeah, they have been listening to country for a long time--they're not rock 'n' rollers. They're people that rock 'n' rollers hate.

Tony: When you find trendy English people going, I love country music, they don't know what they're talking about. They'll have listened to Hank Williams or another fairly established legend, but they won't listen to what's happened for the last twenty years.

Chip: It's a hip thing, but, it might not be by the time this interview comes off. We were in England two years ago and I was walking down King's Road. I had cowboy boots, a fringed jacket, a cowboy hat, 501's, and a plaid shirt. People were looking at me like I was from Mars. And these were people with purple mohawks and shit. Now they're all wearing cowboy gear. I think the Long Ryders had a lot to do with popularizing that 'cause they were in the right place at the right time.

Martha: So, do you have a lot of friends from the real old days?

Tony: We don't do too much socializing, I suppose--different circles. You know, everyone's got their own lives except us.

Martha: Some people have really glorified that period. Other's turn their backs on punk completely.

Tony: It's mostly those old punks, who glorify that peak in their lives, who never did anything after that. It's like being a big athlete in high school and you're managing a gas station at 22.

Martha: What happened the last time you were interviewed in Flipside?

Chip: We just called a lot of people boring. In those days, you could say what was on your mind, or so I thought. That was part of punk rock--honesty and breaking down old

Rank and File - photo O

barriers. Everyone hated us after that. Magazines would watch our every move to see if we would fuck up. Then, they'd write editorials about how the horrible the Dils were and how they're selling out the revolution and they're trying to destroy the scene.

Martha: Then, when you started changing your music, did it get worse?

Tony: No, people didn't care any more. People who wanted to hear Class War came around for one or two shows. After they understood that we weren't going to be playing that, they stopped coming around.

Martha: You still get some Dils fans...

Tony: A lot of the people that sit around and talk about the Dils now didn't go see us back then. The Weirdos drew five more times as many people than we did. We were an unpopular band.

Martha: But a lot of people claim to be influenced by the Dils.

Tony: Our influence might have been bigger than the actual impact at the time because we were right on. Especially now, when you don't see those Flipside articles and stuff. We were the enemy!

Martha: I was surprised to find out that Sound of the Rain was a Dils song.

Chip: Sound of Rain was written right after that Flipside interview and all that stuff came out. Our drummer came over to my house and he was going, Oh God, why'd you say that stuff, everyone's mad at us. It really made me angry, and I said, That's punk rock. When he left I wrote Sound of Rain as one of those Fuck You songs--say what you want and believe in it. It doesn't matter what else happens as long as you do what you think's right.

Martha: Do you think the reasons that Rank 'n File are influential are similar to the reasons that the Dils were influential?

Tony: We're never afraid to do anything different. Besides, what we do is pretty good.

It usually creates something that's better, or at least just as interesting, than what was before. Most people will wait for a band like the Dils or Rank 'n File to do it first, and then they'll follow it. Back before hardcore happened, you had people saying the Dils suck because they're political. It took a band like the Dils to say, Yeah, what we sing about we take seriously. When country music was the last thing to like, we decided to say, Yeah, we play country music. KUSF Wave did the first live review Rank 'n File ever got. They said, What are these guys trying to do, start a trend? Well, that's the way it worked out because we were brave and smart enough to do it first. That's how you get to be influencial.

Otherwise, you're just another dumb ass band.

MIA

Two of Orange County's biggest bands, Shattered Faith and M.I.A., recently broke up. Members of each went their seperate ways, but fate found a particularly strong fusion between the two bands--forming the basis for a new M.I.A. This interview took place at London Exchange in Newport Beach April 26, 1986.

Al: Since Shattered Faith broke up, you guys started this new band...

Chris: I left Shattered Faith to go back to Las Vegas. My mind was on a few different places and I wanted to get away. So, when we got done with that red album I left.

Denny: We kept it going with a couple of other drummers, but it was a burn out. Spencer and the bass player got married--it was like watching Ozzie and Harriet at practice. Kids all over and wives. It just wasn't going anywhere.

Al: When that fell apart, did you and Chris try to get anything happening?

Denny: Chris was gonna start a band with his roommate, and Mike started to jam with them on bass. Chris called me to play guitar, just to screw around.

Chris: Then, when everyone quit on Mike I said, Let's do it.

Mike: I kinda gave up on M.I.A. for awhile too. Larry and I were gonna keep it going, but I set up a few rehearsals and he didn't show. It was discouraging. It was tough emotionally too--the trauma of breaking up after all that time.

Denny: It's just like a relationship; you figure how hard it is to just keep going with one girl. Just imagine having four girlfriends! You've got the same head trips and hassles.

Al: Didn't it start peaking when you were recording Notes from the Underground?

Mike: There were some conflicts going on in that session. I didn't like Write Myself a Letter and Nick didn't like Shadows of my Life. It went back and forth.

Al: How has the critiques of Notes... affected what you're going to go for now?

MIA: Denny, Chris, Frank, Mike - photo O

Denny: I think some people will hate the new one. I don't mind that, as long as they don't say, Eeeehhh, it's ok.

Mike: I don't want to be middle of the road. I don't mind if ten people hate me, just so a few really like us.

Denny: Too many bands are lost in the same little area in the middle of punk. Everyone is trying to build a blue box. You can't build it any better or worse, it's still a blue box.

Mike: Nick and I talked about that a lot. We could write stuff like on the first record, but we felt that we would be selling out--to ourselves.

Al: How did you get Frank, your bass player?

Mike: When M.I.A. broke up he called me and said if I ever wanted to start a band, call him. Well, I took about six weeks off. Then, we tried three different bass players, but Frank knew the stuff and was into it. He fits in with our ideas. He's a little young. I mean, he's eighteen and we're all twenty-five.

Denny: But, we need a young guy we can all load on!

Al: What's the direction of the new M.I.A.?

Mike: The last record was over produced. When we play live, we don't sound anything like that. Writing is a real scary thing to me...

Denny: It's like pulling down your pants and saying Look at me, what do you think? (laughs)

Mike: The minute I stop producing material is the day I have to hang it up. So, it's a battle with myself.

Chris: Personally, I like everything Mike writes. I can't write, so when Mike comes up with a song I think it's great.

Mike: Me and Denny work well together as far as our styles. He's really good and I'm not that good yet.

Al: Plus you have to jump around.

Mike: Yeah, but that's gonna end I think.

Denny: Either that or stay in tune!

SCREAMIN' SIRENS

By Gary Indiana

This is an interview with L.A.'s notorious Screamin' Sirens. These sultry Amazons roam the clubs and gutters of L.A., creating havoc and a lotta noise. When things get too hot, they career across America, breaking hearts and causing terminal wet dreams for thousands of simple country boys. Many of these shattered youth, hoping for one more glimpse of those buckskinned thighs, one more note from those heavenly voices, leave their nests and head for Hollywood. Their nights are spent at the seedy dives where the Sirens play, their days scrounging a living as male prostitutes or movie extras. Youth of America, beware!!

Rosie Flores-lead guitar, vocals
Marsky Rein-fiddle, rhythm guitar, vocals
Pleasant Gehman-vocals
Boom Boom Lafoon-drums, vocals
Laura Bandit-bass

Gary: How did the band start?

Pleasant: I just wanted to have a really wild all-girl band that was like a gang or something. Boom Boom was the only drummer I could think of, so even though we hated each other, I wound up calling her. We had all the same ideas about bands, life, and drinking.

Boom Boom: And liking the same kind of guy. Fuck you, I saw him first!

Gary: Was that a big problem?

Rosie: Yeah, Laura joined the band and says,

Screamin' Sirens - photo Al

Kick me out now! It's not gonna work, we like the same guys! But, we've learned to share.

Boom Boom: I got married so they don't have to worry about ME no more.

Gary: What bands were you in before?

Laura: My first band was Doesn't Swallow and then Hard As Nails, Cheap As Dirt.

Pleasant: Just from hearing the names of the first two bands, I knew she was the perfect Siren.

Rosie: We've been through nine bass players 'till we found Laura.

Pleasant: We were both seeing the same guy...

Laura: We 86'ed him and she asked me to join the band.

Boom Boom: I was in Keith Joe Dick and the Goners for three years. We had Rosie come on stage at Berkeley Square and sing a song with us. One time Pleasant did the same song with us in L.A. None of us knew each other.

Pleasant: Jefferey Lee Pierce forced me to be in a band for two gigs, and he forced Tex to be in a band. he's responsible for us being in music, and I'm sure he regrets it.

Gary: What kind of response do you get from men at gigs?

Pleasant: These guys in Sacramento were all dressed up like Mexican bandits and Indians and they were skateboarding around. One time, we played and the only other girl was the cocktail waitress. There's a whole country full of men that are complete love slaves.

Gary: Do you ever find that men are intimidated by you?

Pleasant: Some think we're really horrifying, but most of 'em love us. Lots of women come up and say we inspired them or they ask how we got started, but a lot of girls really can't stand us, especially girlfriends of bands we've played with.

Gary: Do people take you seriously?

Pleasant: A lot of people thought that we were just a novelty, that it was never going to go anywhere. They might have seen us three years ago and though we sucked, but they'll see us now and say, God, I can't believe you guys kick ass! A lot of people tell us we've got more balls than any girl band, they've seen because we get real wild onstage. We're not into wimpiness at all.

(Pleasant is one of the early punks. Thanx to X-8 communication w/her and Flip has never been good?)

THE BRIGADE

Interviewed April 25 at the Alexandria Hotel in L.A. by Hud, Al, Joy, and Steve and Thomas Ink Disease.

Al: You changed your name, or at least shortened from "Youth" Brigade.

Mark: We figured that the bands changed, the musics changed.

Shawn: It hasn't changed that much, it's just kind of a new stage for us.

Al: I'm sure people remind you: "How long can you be 'Youth' Brigade?"

Shawn: And it was a good time to do it. With the new record coming out...

Al: Is this the first 'Brigade' interview?

Shawn: Yeah. You got it.

Mark: Basically we got old - we just got done carrying our equipment up one flight of stairs! Let's go have our nap now! (Laughter)

Shawn: Some guy actually called us the Geriatric Brigade after the 'What Price' ep came out.

Al: I've heard all these comparisons of your new material to Duran Duran or U2.

Shawn: I like Duran Duran and U2!!

Al: Do you see your direction going that way?

Mark: I don't really see it sounding like anybody really, that's the good thing about it.

Shawn: What seperates the good bands from he great bands, and there are a lot of good bands around, is when they take all of their influences and make a unique sound out of it. Their sound. We have a lot of diversity as well. If you listen to 'Sound and Fury' you have everything from the rap part in "Men in Blue" to a song like "Jump Back" to a cover of a Do Wop song like "Duke Of Earl", then on to "Sink With California". We don't play in any set catagory. Catagories are so stupid but I understand the need for them because we, as human beings, want to simplify things to get a better grasp on them. But I don't think it's necessairly right. That's what punk rock is all about - being individuals and not setting yourself into any catagories. Doing what you feel, what you believe in.

Al: If this band is your vision lyrically, Shawn, what is the basis of what you want to get across?

Shawn: Well, just like what we were talking about earlier, sort of the existential, we have the responsibility to act the way we would

Brigade: Mark, Bob, Shawn – photo Al

I'm bargaining with life to be as just.
Let me alone,and stop hurting me,
disappointing me, humbling me.
Please let me live one month in peace
With no disasters to make me bleed"
"I Don't Want To Be Alone' - Frightwig

want to see other act. If everybody would have that attitude, and act accordingly, then this world would be a better place. What I'm trying to get across is that we can, as a human race, live together in peace and harmony and survive, and still enjoy ourselves. I'm not trying to preach to anybody, just to put out my philosophy to others. If you go back to the spiritual thing, our whole purpose for being here is that we are here to learn, and repay karmic debts, and that's what it's all about. I'm trying to learn as much as I can and put that back out to everybody. Hopefully that will help people.

Al: Do you guys feel the same way?

Mark: Yeah, I pretty much feel the same way. There are none of Shawn's lyrics that I disagree with, otherwise I don't think we'd be doing them. I mean, I don't write lyrics because Shawn is good enough to write all of them. I believe in what he says!

Bob: And I agree.. For my attitude I write a lot of songs for my fool around band: Bob Gnarly and the Failures, and we do a lot of humorous things like Plain Wrap used to.

Al: You still have a lot of humor live with the rapping and break dancing.

Shawn: Yeah, we'd never take ourselves too seriously that we couldn't enjoy it. If we didn't enjoy it we wouldn't do it. There's humor on this record. I mean we are serious about what we do, but we still enjoy ourselves... Since day one BYO and Youth Brigade have been about promoting the positive aspects of punk rock - promoting kids who are rebelling but have something to say. We (punks) are the only ones in our generation right now who are trying to change anything - at least predominently. There are other people but it's a pretty big - I don't want to call it a movement, but a scene or something.... But I don't know, I don't know if I want to do this for much longer. I want to make films. BYO will always be around. It's all forms of communication. Music is a way to get our message across now but there are other means, one is film. My dad makes films, he's a director and a writer, my uncle is a director, my step mother is a set designer/art director- so we have a lot of connections.

Al: What do you think of metal bands?

Shawn: I don't care for it. I can respect the bands for their musical ability, but I don't like the music. It's bombastic, it's boring, it's pretentious. Some of it is alright, but I wouldn't buy those records, I wouldn't play them. I'd rather listen to love songs. Love is something that is gonna make the world a lot better, not singing about the devil or some pseudo Christian band. I don't believe in all the organized religion, so to me Jerry Falwell is just as evil as Ozzy Osborne. It's the same thing. If you don't adhere to their ideals and their philosophies "you're nothing but heathen and you'll go to hell". Same if you worship the devil. Our culture has been dominated by religion up until this century. Now you've got science taking over, especially in this century. You have a big reactionary backlash against it, because it is too hard for people to deal with. Like I said, they want to simplify life - you're good, you go to heaven, you're bad, you go to hell. It's just not that way...

Al: What do you want to achieve as a band before you go into films?

Shawn: I didn't set any time. This album is done and there is the next one that I want to do... I have all these ideas, and I want to help these other bands, and I want to keep the organization and the record company going - but unfortunately I spread myself too thin and we don't get everything done. It's taken us three years to get another album out for our band, it's ridiculous.

Mark: The last year hasn't been so good for the independent market, so it's good anyways...

FLIPSIDE NUMBER 50

"I'm here all alone, just flesh and bones.
The things I've seen have been pretty amazing.
I'm cynical sometimes or just angry,
dancing trible dances,
offering sacrifices.
'cause I don't want to be alone,
I'm only flesh and bones,
I don't want to be alone,
But here I am alone.

ISSUE #: 50
DATE: July 1986
FORMAT: 8 1/2x11, rotary web offset with 2 color glossy cover.
PAGES: 68
PRICE: $1.50
PRESS RUN: 10,000

GBH

Interviewed in July at various L.A. locations during their 4th US tour. GBH were interviewed during their first tour 4 years ago. They have a new drummer Kye, who replaced Wilf who is now married and living in Texas.

Al: I've noticed that you guys are playing a lot faster on this tour than last time.

Ross: Yeah, we're tighter, it's more energy, it's better.

Al: Do you think you loose the melody?

Ross: No. It's there, just more energy. We have a different drummer, we can go faster.

Al: I guess we'll hear faster stuff on the new LP?

Jock: More concentrated energy. We're into the faster stuff because you have less time to think about what's going on around you on stage, you just play.

Kye: I did play fast in Napalm. We had songs that were real short, 2 or 3 chords up and down that's it, that's what I like. GBH are much more experienced and more exciting to play with. When they asked me to play drums there was no question for me....

Al: What about the new metal bands?

Jock: I like Metalica the best. Venom are like so over the top it's funny.

Al: Would you mind playing with those bands?

Jock: Yeah... I'd try it just to see what happends.

Ross: I wouldn't... I wouldn't want to.

Al: I read lots of magazines that lump GBH in with the speed metal bands...

Jock: Energy wise maybe.

Al: What do you think when you read things like that you only play large halls and won't

Jock

Kye photos O

talk to people.

Jock: We're just people, we don't walk around going "who the fuck should we talk to now?".

Al: You guys are a bit shy.

Jock: And people take that the wrong way!

Ross: If you're not in a band, it's ok to have any mood, but if you're in a bad mood and you're in a band then people take it as like you're having a "rockstar" attitude. I'm not usually in a bad mood, but I'm usually not in a mood to socialize.

Al: But you've been answering all the bands mail now?

Ross: Yeah, I do that.

Al: Don't you like to answer mail Jock?

Jock: Right now I've been sorting my own life out, for about the last year, seeing where my wife and I fit in... The whole movement,

punk, the whole thing has gotten older and changed,. It's stretched really far, it's taken 10 years but it's stretched from 10 year old kids going to gigs to about to about 40 years old. We're about 24, so we're right in the middle. The range encompasses everything. I could see it including entire families. In Denver there were about 10 kids at the show between 8 and 13 and they were dancing with older kids and were knocking the shit out of each other. No fighting. Just having a good time. The older people were in the there but mostly around the sides and in the back. It was a whole community there, it was a really good scene... The main thing is sorting yourself out - before worrying about world problems.

Al: This is your first tour Kye, and you're in America?

Kye: Actually when I was here before I was

drumming around with Condemned to Death a few years ago at the Vats in San Francisco. I was there for about 5 months.

Al: Colin, you changed the lyrics in "Drugs Party" tonight.

Colin: Yeah, "Wilf's living in Texas and he's getting fat!" He just lost interest. He was getting lazier on stage.

Al: Are there any messages you want to put across lyrically?

Colin: I like them to make sense, either as a story, like tales of yesterday, or as comments. All of my lyrics have meaning, but then there's songs like "Bellend Bop" which is a fun song, but still is a story. A lot of people who know the band know exactly what the songs are about, but other people who are into us or know us, read between the lines and find the truth. Someone who is not into the band might not understand the lyrics fully. Like "Gimmie Fire" could be about pyromania, but it's a Rasta term about someone who smokes pot.

Al: What about "Needles and Pins"...

Colin: That has two meanings as well, to me it's like stay away from drugs, heavy drugs that you inject. The lyrics paint a picture of an acupuncturist who's like perverted. You can create a spark in peoples minds just by a few lyrics - then it gets them thinking.

Al: You touch on a lot of "political" subjects.

Colin: But their disguised political subjects, it's how we feel, and our ideas about it; like "Diplomatic Immunity", "Children of the Dust"...

Al: What is your connection with the punk scene in England, do you still play at punk venues?

Colin: Oh yeah, we're still a punk band, we play with punk bands and listen to punk music. The hardcore scene, to us it's all punk.

INSTIGATORS

Interviewed at Fender's Ballroom in Long Beach in August 1986 by Al and Dave Dissident.

Al: Where do you guys fit into he English rock scene?

Andy: Well we try to play with a lot of cross-over bands, we don't try just for one scene. We try to be as diverse as possible. So we play with a hell of a lot of different bands. A lot of people have this preconceived idea that England is the punk mecca of the world, but it's not. I hate to disappoint anybody, but the scene is a lot smaller there than elsewhere.

(Nick Toczek walks up, an English "poet" who is on tour with the Instigators)

Al: Nick, what is it that you are up there talking about?

Nick: Politics. America is really good to perform in because they go really big on sex. But you add "ism" on the end of it and most of them couldn't fucking spell it, let alone understand it. The American conception of sexism is so minimal. I mean even to the point of the Circle Jerks wanting the girl to come up on stage and dance. That's fucking pathetic. That's not slagging the Circle Jerks, that's slagging off American attitudes on sex. America still sees women as sex objects and really can't understand that. Of all countries America should know. The atrocities perpetuated against people because o America are just unbelievable. In England they are finally beginning to get a grasp things like sexism, racism, victimization of a kinds. America has a good grasp of racism they do. I really dislike the band attitudes i

Colin

Ross

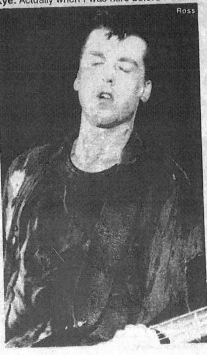

Six Easy Ways To . . .
Make Your Parents Hate You

1) Grow your hair really really long
2) Drink a lot, even if you're twelve
3) Buy the Necros' new album "Tangled Up"
4) Play it backwards to get the real meaning
5) Turn it up so loud it blows your speakers *
6) See the Necros with the Circle Jerks when they play near you

*You can simulate this step by plugging speaker wire directly into an electrical outlet!

Instigators at Fenders - photo Al

America., where they all go: "Lets get laid". They go up on stage and come out with good solid politics and go back stage and all they're after are tits and getting their pricks inside someone. That sickens me up something terrible. You go around America doing gigs and it's a really big groupie scene.

Al: Well so far with what English bands have come over here, I don't see any different attitude.

Nick: Well they have the attitude "America is where you get laid". Well fuck that. I hate that.

Dave: What were some of your ideas of America before you came over here?

Andy: Just from what we'd seen on TV. And there actually is a lot that lives up to that stereotype. Like the people with the fuckin' hats and the truck drivers and all. But I expected a lot more violence and guns and stuff.

Cuzzy: We get a lot of programs like Chips and shit like that, and they portray America as really violent. We haven't come across any violent people since we've been here. Oh, the other night we were down on the beach drinking beer, which to my astonishment is illegal, and we were walking back and a cop came. He said "Freeze, stay where you are, I want to see some ID". Nick had his arms in his pockets and the cop told him to take his arms out. Nick explained that he is an English tourist and isn't used to be treated this way. The cop said "Look I don't know who you are, but you might have a gun in your pocket." He went for his gun and said "If you don't take your hands out of your pocket I'm going to shoot you."To me it was like "Are you for real". If it were a cop in England we would have walked up to him and started talking, the cops aren't armed in England. And if he would have given us shit he'd have got the shit kicked out of him. Although the Italian cops were worse.

Dave: How well did you expect people to know the Instigators in America?

Cuzzy: I came here with no expectations what so ever of being like a "rock star" band. Like in England when you first form a band you have to get yourself known, and when we first come here I expect it to be that way. But it's

turned our really well.

Al: How do you feel you complement what Nick is saying, since he opens for you guys?

Cuzzy: It 's a contrast. He attracts peoples attention. There are people shocked by what he is saying. But when we go on stage there are some people who know our songs and things are more at ease. We try to make people think our songs and things are more at ease. We try to make people think ourselves. It's really trendy to be political in England right now, and to shout a lot of bullshit about neo-nazis and shit like that. We try to meet people as much as possible and break into different scene, I mean if a band like Screwdriver needed a support band we'd do it, because that is a chance to get across to a different scene, a different crowd. Not that we are fascists or anything like that, it's just a chance to play to a different crowd.

Al: A lot of people would take that the wrong, no matter what you say..

Cuzzy: I know what you mean, but you have to be openminded. A band like Conflict go on stage and they pretty much preach to the converted. We are trying to get across to all areas. Our foremost reason for being in the band is playing music, mine is. Andy is up there singing his head off, and I hope the crowd listen to him..

ASF

Anti Scrunti Faction were interviewed at Flipside in June 1986 by Al, Hud and Gus. Present were Tracy (bass and vocals) and Leslie (guitar and vocals), also present was Jason (Non-roadie) and Jill (den mother, shitworker)

Al: Ok, at one point you were an "all-girl " band...

Leslie: A long time ago in a galaxy far away..

Al: Wait. Let's continue from where we left off in our last interview (issue # 41- Jan. 1984).

Leslie: We were 4 little girls and we drank 3.2 beer...

Al: What do you think of being labeled" a all girl band" when you are not?

Tracie: Well it's just a thing that you can't get

away from. When we played in San Francisco, after the show somebody said "As an all feamale band do you think this...?" Wait, you just saw us play, ya know?! I mean Eric is in back but you can see him.

Al: Do you guys fit in with the whole "peace punk" thing?

Leslie: No.

Tracie: I mean they have really good ideas and everything, but I don't really believe in everything they believe.

Leslie: We like pizza and they don't, well maybe they do but it's the cheese or something.

Al: You two are vegitarians aren't you?

Leslie: uh huh.

Tracie: I stopped eating meat when I got food poisoning at McDonalds. That was about the time we were recording our album.

Leslie: I've been a vegitarian for almost 7 years.

Hud: Would you ever write songs about that subject?

Tracie: No way. I feel there are more important things, or just as important things like women rights or animal rights. It's been over used, it's already a subject that every fuckin' band writes about, other things are more immediatley important to me.

Leslie: Tracie is a vegitarian because it's trendy.

Tracie: Oh fuck you!! I live with Leslie and we didn't cook meat and we don't eat meat. I ate it when I lived at home because my mom cooked it. But when I started to live on my own I was aware of the choice. I never bought meat at all, even when I ate it. then I got food poisoning..

Al: You have sort of picked up on "Women's Rights" to sing about..

Tracie: Well we sing about things that we have to deal with everyday, that, and the police, Frat Houses in Boulder- we have to deal with everyday. And we write some cheap songs about our friends bother us...

Al: Well, you have enough songs in your set that alot of people look at you as "feminists"...

Leslie: I don't know, it's hard for me to see what other people perceive us as. It does come up a few times. I've only seen one review of our record that was written by a women, Barbara from Truely Needy. I like her review a lot, it was accurate. One of the things that punk or hardcore has always been one of the issues in hardcore-the fuck authority type attitude. And with women there is one more aspect, not that we always say this but alot of times we feel that men are oppressing us. And that is another issue for us. a lot of people don't see it but it goes along with "hardcore" thinking.

Tracie: So many women bands get shit when they do try to speak out in that area. When we first started we got so much shit. When Frightwig came through Denver they got shit from a lot of guys. These people were saying Frightwig were anti-men. I don't see where they get that if they listen to any of their lyrics. But starting bands get so much shit for speaking out that it seems that they want to give it up, quit or just not sing about those things. We went through it but we didn't give it up. That is probably why there are so few women bands. You get so much shit from like skinheads and the audience is just cutting you down. You don't even get a change. It just bums you out. You feel it's just not worth it. and the girls, it seems that they just don't have any opinion at all. It seems that would rather have their boyfriend doing things, than for

ASF: Tracie and Leslie - photo Al

them to do it.

Tracie: But it's not just women in the scene that are like that, it's everywhere.
I mean, every single day I see things, even if it's just like a billboard or something, a book, a magazine, or television I see all these things that where you get real depressed about it.

Al: Well I'm sure all women see that kind of stuff, but it doesn't seem to bother them...

Leslie: Well they are just brough up to think that , that is just how it is. I mean kids are brought up on television and that is one of the most sexist and racist tools that there is. you are just taught to look at these billboards and say: "That's the kind of make-up I should have". or you see a magazine and say: "Wow, that is the body that I should have."Or you see a magazine and say "That's the kind of make-up I should get", Instead of thinking that it isn't for real, that's it's not a real person - the photographs are all touched up and stuff...

Tracie: The women put themselves in that situation too - the pose for the ads and stuff, they have the choice to say "no".

Al: Ok, this interview wouldn't be complete without us asking about your name.

Tracie: A "scrunti" is a slut. But we did change it since we've been out here to "scrotum". Because the name is versatile, it's just made up so...

Leslie: Besides we are so "anti-men" that we had to change it.

Tracie: We can change it to anything, just like MDC, we were "A Sure Fuck" for awhile. "Scrunti" is a word that a couple of friends that I had kind of made up for young, pretty "things", ha ha. Young pretty sluts.

Hud: Males and females?

Tracie: Well that was a controversy in Boulder for awhile... Everybody asks us "What is a Scrunti?".

MAD PARADE

Interviewed by Al, Gus, Joy, Dave Dissident 7/10/86.

Made Parade are: Bill- vocals, Joey- guitar, Mike L.- bass, Mike S.- drums.

Joy: So what are the major changes since the last interview?

Mike I: Right here (raises his hand).

Bill: Our new bass player.

Al: What happened to Ron?

Joey: He grew up.

Bill: Ron?

Gus: I saw him right after your tour and he was really bummed out because he thought the tour was awful.

Joey: No way! The tour went great. Oh, the first one, that was mediocre.

Bill: The reason it was mediocre is because the guy who booked it couldn't tell his ass from a hole in the ground!

Joey: But Toxic Shock did the booking for the other one and we got some really good shows. He (Bill Toxic) did a good job.

Dave: What sort of things go through your mind before you go on a tour?

Bill: How we're gonna eat...

Joey: We ate really good this time, we didn't have to steal this time.

Bill: This time we don't have to go to a grocery store, put bread and lunchmeat down our pants.

Al: So is there a message you've always tried to come across with in your lyrics? Subconsciously or otherwise?

Bill: It's boring, it's kinda corny, the simplist message is "imagine all the people living in harmony". Imagine. That's the greatest lyrics in world. It may be stupid to THINK people in the world can all get along... but we're all in this together... There are so many little things we are trying to get across. But those things can be interpreted in many different ways for the individual. We don't try to tell people what to do, we set up songs where there's ideas. It's pretty ambiguous. One person might get something different out of it than I would. So... our songs are about surfing and eating popsicles!!

Joey: Ya know, so people think we're turning glam. How can you just "turn glam"?

Bill: We wear what we want to wear, whatever's comfortable.

Joey: Music comes first, image is secondary.

Bill: If the majority of people who listen to music cared as much for music as image and fashion, then bands like Mad Parade, MIA, Social Distortion, those bands would be top 40 radio, but it's not. When we first started off, we never tried to pretend we were a hardcore band, I don't know how to sing that! We play what we know how and that is what it is, what we've done all along.

Joey: If you become a better musician, you're going to change your music style.

Bill: As long as the energy and the excitement is there. We're doing what we feel is us.

Joey: In the pop business, especially in this punk rock business, either you gotta have a gimmick or nostalgia. Vandals, Doggy Style, they've got a gimmick.

Bill: But if you've got a gimmick you've got to be able to crawl out from under them or they start becoming stupid. Like Devo - what are they going to do for an encore? If you're bigger than your gimmick, that's cool, but if you're not, you're stuck. So I always wonder when people look at us, what are they thinking, how are they feeling......

HUSKER DU

Husker Du is extraordinary because the Minneapolis trio has expanded musically without sacrificing its incredible, electric intensity. A lot of bands develop into other areas, but usually this also means the tempo is slowed down to a semi-crawl or the heavy guitars are held back. Not with this new and improving Husker Du. While the Huskers have gotten more melodic and engagingly folksy, it still resounds with the energy and volume of the best hardcore bands.
Interview by Jon Matsumoto at Warner Bros. in early May

Jon: How did the signing with Warner Bros. come about? Did you approach them or did they approach you?

Greg: We weren't actively seeking out any kind of deal. They contacted us and we were flattered. This was awhile ago. We didn't see any reason for leaving SST at the time and we put out "Flip Your Wig". We kept in touch and it started to sell really well and started to get more "straight press" from Cream and Spin and stuff like that. Pretty much the decision was made for distribution purposes. Now all these kids that walk into their local drug store to buy their favorite teen magazine can also buy our record at the drug store.

Jon: Did you get offers from other labels?

Bob: Everybody.

Jon: How did you decide on Warners?

Bob: Warners was the most reasonable of the labels about listening to our concerns about not wanting to be packaged or marketed. Don't make a big stir, just let us put out records. Don't try to make us something we're not.

Greg: There were real sincere.

Bob: Yeah, you have to grill them about why they're interested in you. "You've got Van Halen, Dire Straits and ZZ Top. What do you want us for?" Warners was interested in us when "Zen Arcade" came out, we kept turning them down. But when we finally sat down to talk to them, they had some good reasons... We said we didn't want to be the next whoever, and they said "We don't want you to be anything else, we like the way you sound."

Jon: Has there been a back-lash by die hard fans because you're now on a big label? I remember X got some flack when they signed to Electra.

Greg: There hasn't really been a back-lash I'm sure there were a lot of people who were anxious about the release of the album. They might have worried about a major label sell-out. But once the album came out and they heard "Crystal" they probably said "That's the right band!". It's kind of interesting, I've met people who have "Candy Apple Grey" and they thought it was an SST record. They went "Oh, you're on Warner Brothers now?"... Bob writes a lot of his songs on acoustic guitar, "Flip Your Wig" was more of an up record, "Candy Apple Grey" is darker and a bit more down. The way I've seen it is that it's all a maturing process. When we first started in 1979 we all sort of knew how to play but we didn't really know how to "play". We just played as often as we could and in the span of 7 years we've matured as musicians, song writers and producers. It's kind of a natural kind of thing. You would hope that the more you did something, the better you'd get at it.

Jon: Do you see Husker Du going in a certain direction artistically?

Bob: Each record, we work on the blueprint and then take it to the studio. If we haven't been doing it live then we have a little bit of work to do. If we have been doing it live then it stays the way it is. As far as the direction of each album., basically is just the mood of where we were at the time. As far as conscious change, we're changing all the time. It's hard to say if there's a direction we're headed for. There's sort of this road but there are a lot of detours that you can take. There are a lot of different gas stations out there.

Jon: Was there a hardcore scene in Minnesota that you identified with or belonged to? I was sort of surprised when I saw you a few years ago because I didn't see a big punk contingent there.

Greg: When we started, I guess for lack of better term, we were a punk band. I guess hardcore didn't get going till 1981. And in 1981 it was our first time on the west coast. We didn't know what hardcore was. We just got up there and played real fast and loud. We were real abrasive and we jumped around a lot and people said: "Wow, what a great hardcore band!" And people started writing that. We never really considered ourselves hardcore.

SWA

Interviewed after their ragin' set one hot summer night outside the Music Machine. Present were Al and Joe as well as Chuck Dukowski (bass), Merrill Ward (vocals) and Sylvia: Juncosa (guitar).

Al: The first time I saw SWA was in Culver City with Throbbing Gristle, but it doesn't look like this band?

Merrill: It had a much bigger guest list.

Chuck: It's an extrapolation on the same concept. Instead of approaching it on a verbal level, we're approaching it on a physical emotional level. We would make music and were able to totally express ourselves without having to think about it because it would flow together well. We said "Check it out. Let's do it again" So we did and decided that was the thing to be - a band and make records. The whole trip. We were truely SWA (laughter).

Al: For me, I had the hardest time thinking of SWA because I considered it a joke band.

Merrill: A joke band? Is the end of the world a joke band?

Chuck: We're trying to save the world.

Merrill: Get the fuck out of the pit and get the fuck back into your fuckin' mind. Look into yourself. Look at what the fuck is going on with you because you are the only one that matters.

Chuck: What about me?

Merrill: Fuck you!

Al: It seems that you started up SWA and it got put on the back burner.

Chuck: That was a different thing. There was an idea and I named the band after it.

Al: What is the idea?

Chuck: It's an emotional idea. If I were to describe it, it would do it a disservice. Everytime I think about putting it to words, I decide not to. It's like I say. when we hit it, we're on it, we got the SWA thing, it's happening.

Al: Do the letters "SWA" mean anything?

Chuck: Sure they do. I'm not into this verbal linear approach. I think the real truths in people are in their hearts. Words are only an expression of those things and capable of being inaccurate. Thoughts that come by you verbally tend to lead you astray from what you are truely doing and wanting. Therefore, I'm not into that whole thing.

Al: Unfortunately we are a printed publication.

Chuck: It's in the music. You can't really describe it. We can only talk about the music in a certain way. If you can see through to

what you really feel, then you can avoid being used. Linear ideas serve for lies, people hide behind them and create whole lives of lies. So, I prefer not to give people linear ideas.

Al: Do you think people will judge records and bands by their record album cover?

Chuck: Although this is true to a certain extent, it is not the point. The cover is part of the art. It all fits together.

Sylvia:: The cover is also prophetic because after I joined SWA I was in a car accident. I had to see my doctor and he jumped on me.

Joe: Do you already have the concept down for your next album? (Evolution)

Chuck: It's a metaphor for mankind- the evils which go along with his strengths and the challenges that are his on this earth in regard to his eternity. It's all put in a simple SWA acronym.

Al: Is SWA going to be touring band?

Chuck: Probably not because we don't make money. We can play here and, as long as we can live, we don't have to worry about making money off playing. We can take it easy and just play gigs here for what we can get.

Joe: But, on the other hand, doesn't having a job tap your creative energies?

Chuck: It's totally a release. I like to do something which gets my emotional thing happening. After I quit Black Flag, I used to take long five mile walks to try to work it off. I tried drinking, but I didn't sleep well and I woke up gross. The jamming thing lets me feel good.

Al: How do you communicate with these guys Sylvia ?

Sylvia:: Through my guitar- it just flows. Jamming is like sex, each person expresses themself with their own energy. It's the most passionate experience intertwined with being artful.

VICIOUS CIRCLE

Interviewed at Flipside in June 1986.

Al: What kind of guitar sound were you looking for Les, I know you like a lot of metal bands?

Les: Well, we thought we could add another guitar and get a fuller sound, plus making it easier for me to do more... But I'm influenced by a lot of things not just metal, there is an influence there, but every song we have in an entirely different direction.

Alby: We are at the stage where we listen to all kinds of music, and some of it we can't play, some of it we could, but Vicious Circle is not just Vicious Circle music, all of our musical influences put together.

Dave: On the new LP, every song is just totally incomparable to the next song, they are all a different mode, it keeps it interesting with variety.

Paul: Different moods and ideas are expressed in every song. I like to write about moods or the things I see around me in my environment, I've written about being supressed by governments or Christian fanatics to songs about people just wanting to live there lives free.

Al: A lot of your songs lean towards the political side of things, is that a big concern?

Alby: You could call it that, but we are not preaching to people.

paul: We offer our opinions and people can take what they want from what we say.

Alby: It's something to think about, people can make their own decisions. We don't have all of the answers, no one has......

SWA: Sylvia and Merill - photo Joe

Vicious Circle – photo Al

Paul: It's amazing just coming into this country and see all of the patriotism being pushed.

Alby: I can understand why these people follow the patriotism, most people, have got things pretty comfortable here, and they want to protect what they've got, and they think the government will do that.

Dave: Those are the people that will supposedly look after them for the rest of their lives, so there is "no" need to speak out against that.

Al: Well, is it much different in Australia? You guys don't have it so bad.

Alby: No we don't, but we still don't push all the patriotism.

Al: We get tons of ads in newspapers and on TV trying to push Australia.

Alby: Ahhh, that just tourism, they're trying to push Australia over on you, not us!

Les: They're doing a good job! There's tons of American tourists in Melbourne.

Dave: I've got this impression for Americans that I've met in Australia that Australians are well respected.

Alby: Over here people really seem to like Australians, they hear our accent and go "Oh, Australia!" and they want to give you their phone number! (Laughter)... American companies want the American dream to be the Australian dream.

Dave: It's scary to think that some people in America get elected because of what they represented on the screen. It's really scary to think about, like if Stallone ran for office, what he represents... The government in Australia now were voted in on the promise of stopping uranium mining, soon as they got in they scrapped that idea. Australia has got the largest uranium mine in the world.

Les: And American companies come in and run them.

Alby: It's not just uranium either, all kinds of products and consumer items.

Dave: Now we have McDonalds and 7-11's all over just like America. Some of our lyrics hint at these things, the frustration...

Alby: Vicious Circle is a series of messages, it's not just the message that's in the vocals, it's the whole live thing. The lyrics are pretty serious, but altogether when we play we have fun...

Paul: Kids come to our shows to have a good time – and to release energy, but fighting, things like that that build ignorance, we don't want that. That's one of the major things we are against. When we're playing and people start fighting, you just think to yourself: "What am I doing here?" The whole mentality of being tough and thinking that you are accomplishing something by beating someones head in – that's not accomplishing anything.

Al: Do you see a lot of similarities between the scenes here and in Australia?

Paul: Yeah. Like I said there are the trouble makers, the drug users... We've met a lot of people who have a lot to offer, as in thinking, generosity and feeling.

Dave: That's the great thing about the punk scene, you can go anywhere in the world and you can find people with the same attitudes, that you can talk to on the same level – it really helps to break down barriers.

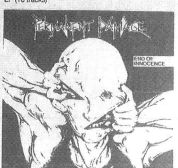

FLIPSIDE FANZINE
P.O. Box 363
Whittier CA 90608

SUBSCRIPTIONS
-All subs are for 4 issues.
-Please list the issue you want your sub to start with.
-Remember, we come out bi-monthly, so you will get a new issue every two months or so - not every month!
-An alternative source for distributors or for single recent copies or back issues is:

ALL THE MADMEN
Box 396
Hackney, London
E8 4PL England

BACK ISSUES
#42 – Agent Orange cover with UK Subs, Dr. Know, Plain Wrap, TSOL, Subhumans, Grim...
#46 – Farrell cover with Don't Know, Ramones, Minutemen, Butthole Surfers, Painted Willy, Vicious Circle, Positive Force...
#47 – Casey cover with DI, Conflict, Rites of Spring, Scream, Dischord, Asexuals, Detonators, Punktography ...
#49 – Collage cover with Rank and File, Screamin' Sirens, Brigade, Germany, Canada, Punktography 2...
#50 – Firehose cover with ASF, Husker Du, Instigators, GBH, Vicious Vircle, Mad Parade...
#51 – Bulimia Banquet cover with Saints, Beat Happening, GASH/ Depression, Negazione, Attitude Adjustment, Dag Nasty, Wasted Youth, Bad Opera etc...
#52 – Pencil drawing cover with Half Off, Janes Addiction, Agent Orange, Short Dogs Grow, Bulimia Banquet, Scratch Acid...
#53 – DOA cover with DOA, Visions of Change, Stupids, No Ones Allie, Pillsbury Hardcore, Hangmen, Fact Sheet Five...

AD RATES
Full page	(7 1/4" x 10")	$125.00
Half page	(7 1/4" x 5")	$65.00
Quarter page	(3 5/8" x 5")	$35.00
One sixth page	(2 1/2" x 5")	$20.00
Business card	(3 1/2" x 2")	$10.00
Classifieds	per 40 words	$2.00

-Note: All sizes measured width x height, and thats how we print them.
-These prices are for camera ready art.
-10% discount with cash!
-NO CREDIT - Payment due with ad.

AD DEADLINE
January 15 will be the deadline for issue #55.

CATALOG
Details of all our shit is in our Winter 87 catalog available for just a 22 cent stamp.

RECORDS
#002 – Detox "Start... Finish" LP
#003 – "Flipside Vinyl Fanzine V2" A 20 band compilation LP with lots of big names and good sounds.
#004 – Iconoclast "In These Times" 4 song 7"
#005 – Doggy Style "Side By Side" debut LP
#006 – "Australia Part 1" A Vicious Circle / Perdition split LP, two of Australias best.
#007 – ASF "Damsels In Distress" debut LP
#008 – Out of print.
#009 – "Uboats Attack America" – All German band compilation LP.
#010 – "Australia Part 2" A GASH / Depression split LP, two more hard hitting Australian bands on this 60 minute LP.
#011 – MIA "After the Fact" MIA redefine hard powerful rock without compromising integrity and power on this 12 song LP.
#012 – Doggy Style "Doggy Style II" New, stronger vocalist and 19 songs on this full length LP with the controversial cover.
#013 – Flipside Vinyl Fanzine Volume 3! Yep

it's our 21 band compilation. Check elsewhere for details.

VIDEO
#1 – S.D., Vandals, Sin 34, B.F., RF7, MDC, TSOL, Descendents, DI, Circle Jerks, Husker Du, Youth Brigade.
#2 – White Flag, GBH, 7 Sec., Minor Threat, Big Boys, Stretch Marks, BOS, 100 Flowers, BF, Minutemen, Angst, Dickies.
#3 – Agent Orange, Big Boys, AHC, MIA, Subterfuge, Darby Crash, Suicidal T., Killroy, Toy Dolls, Mad Parade, Eddie Subtitle, Iconoclast and No Trend.
#4 – GBH live, interviews and etc. Pure GBH on 83 and 84 tours.
#5 – Decry, Heart Attack, Red Cross, UK Subs, Basic Math, Conflict USA, Iconoclast, TSOL, Justice Leaague, Bad Religion, Vagina Dentata, Pariah, Subhumans.
#6 – DOA, Sonic Youth, TOD, Love Canal, Oilsbury HC, C2D, Exploited, Toxic Reasons, Stretch Marks, Kraut, Detox, DI.
#7 – Stukas Over Bedrock, GI, Ads, Big Boys, Plain Wrap, Armed Citizens, 76% Uncertain, Dandelion Abortions, CCM, I Refuse It, Skate Death, Psychedelic Skeletons, Clyng Onz, Gay Cowboys, Bastards, Riistetyt, Rappio, Musta Parraati, Lama.
#8 – Doggy Style, Plain Wrap, Circle Jerks, Agression, Asexuals, Entropy, Marginal Man, Detonators, Agnostic Front.
#9 – MDC, Dicks, Perdition, BGK, Conflict, DK's, Final Conflict, Subhumans, Reagan Youth, Vicious Circle, Scream and Iconoclast.
#10 – GI, Radwaste, COC, Raszebrae, 7 Sec., Sin 34, Necros, Frightwig, Big Stick, Grim.
#11 – "A Hard Dogs Night" featuring Doggy Style in a full on zany crazy hectic and fun normal day, with live footage.
#12 – "Exploited Live At The Palm Cover"A full hour of Wattie! This Jettisoundz tape is now available in NTSC.

FLIPSIDE BBS

"The future is alternative communication, freedom through technology..."

Yes, Flipside has it's very own Electronic Bulletin Board System up and running. This is a computerized information system, which consists of a central message and electronic mail base that can be accessed with a computer and modem (via telephone line). Our BBS has three sub-boards that are ment for: general messages and classifieds (just like in Flipside!), a bands news and reviews board, and Hudleys own poetry, alternative, weirdness subboard. There are already hundreds of messages on these boards. There are also plenty of bulletins (like the complete Flipside catalog, and cable show directory and calendar), as well as downloadable files from our users. In the future we plan to have our letters section on line for all the users to answer! As well as a way for people to review records for direct inclusion into the printed fanzine. So all of you people out there with computers, give us a call. The board is open from 12 midnight to 10 am Pacific Time. The number is 213-693-6971. 300 / 1200 baud. Communicate!

IT'S FINALLY OUT!!!
FLIPSIDE VINYL FANZINE
VOLUME THREE

Adolescents "The Liar"
76% Uncertain "Critic"
Slapshot "Straight Edge In Your Face"
The Brigade "Living With The Bomb"
Mad Parade "Second Chances"
Bulimia Banquet "Calloused"
Shonen Knife "Cycling is Fun"
7 Seconds "A Place"
Copulation "First Recidue"
**Tesco Vee and White Flag
  "Hot Rails To Hell"**
COC "Intervention"
Lemonheads "Hate Your Friends"
Circle Jerks "Fortunate Son"
Problem Children "Energy"
Vatican Commandos "Last Wish"
MIA "California Dreamin"
**Little Gentlemen
  "Just Waiting (for the Civil War)"**
SNFU "Heavy Menu"
Doggy Style "Pre-Teens"

VINYL FANZINE 3 DISTRIBUTED BY DUTCH EAST INDIA, NY

Made in the USA
Middletown, DE
30 November 2021

53858219R00126